FLAVIUS JOSEPHUS
ON THE PHARISEES

STUDIA POST-BIBLICA

INSTITUTA A P.A.H. DE BOER

ADIUVANTIBUS

L.R.A. VAN ROMPAY ET J. SMIT SIBINGA

EDIDIT

J.C.H LEBRAM

VOLUMEN TRICESIMUM NONUM

FLAVIUS JOSEPHUS ON THE PHARISEES

A Composition-Critical Study

BY

STEVE MASON

E.J. BRILL

LEIDEN · NEW YORK · KØBENHAVN · KÖLN

1991

The paper in this book meets the guidelines for permanence and durability of the Committee on Production Guidelines for Book Longevity of the Council on Library Resources.

Library of Congress Cataloging-in-Publication Data

Mason, Steve.
    Flavius Josephus on the Pharisees: a composition-critical study / by Steve Mason.
        p.   cm.—(Studia post-Biblica, ISSN 0169-9717; v. 39)
    Includes bibliographical references and index.
    ISBN 90-04-09181-5
    1. Josephus, Flavius—Views on Pharisees. 2. Pharisees—Historiography. I. Title. II. Series.
    DS115.9.J6M37   1990
    296.8'12—dc20   90-19845
                                                          CIP

ISSN   0169-9717
ISBN   90 04 09181 5

PRINTED IN THE NETHERLANDS

For my parents,
Terry and Grace Mason

CONTENTS

PART III

THE PHARISEES IN THE *JEWISH ANTIQUITIES*

PART IV

THE PHARISEES IN THE *LIFE*

PREFACE AND ACKNOWLEDGEMENTS

No one can write and publish a scholarly monograph without massive assistance from various quarters. This is especially true when the manuscript in question begins its life, as this one did, "in fulfillment of the requirements for the degree, Doctor of Philosophy". All sorts of people and institutions helped pilot this project through the perilous waters of the doctoral programme; many others have helped me to recommission it as a book. I am delighted here to record my gratitude.

In the first place, my entire career as a doctoral student would have been impossible without the financial support that I received from the Social Sciences and Humanities Research Council of Canada, which granted me a four-year doctoral fellowship. It was this funding that made possible my two years of research abroad, in Jerusalem and Tübingen. The SSHRCC has made Canada a most congenial environment for humanistic scholarship; may it always be so.

An equally indispensible condition of this project was the intellectual stimulation and encouragement that I received from my teachers at McMaster University: Professors B.F. Meyer, A.I. Baumgarten, and E.P. Sanders. These scholars showed me, among other things, that first-century Judaism was a rich and exciting world, and not merely the "background" to nascent Christianity.

When I was at the Hebrew University of Jerusalem, for the first phase of the project (1983-84), Prof. Daniel R. Schwartz always lent a willing ear to my developing thesis and offered much helpful advice, in spite of his very busy schedule. I also benefited from conversations with Professors D. Flusser, I. Gafni, and L.I. Levine. And my research was greatly assisted by the generous privileges offered to me by the École Biblique et Archaeologique in Jerusalem, which privileges included a personal work area in their outstanding library.

When I was at Eberhard-Karls Universität in Tübingen (1984-85), Prof. Dr. Otto Betz and Prof. Dr. Martin Hengel both listened patiently to my sundry hypotheses and offered sage counsel from their treasuries of knowledge and insight. On a practical note, the Institut zur Erforschung des Urchristentums (on Wilhelmstrasse), then directed by Drs. Burton and Bonnie Thurston, graciously made me a "fellow" and afforded me a secure work space.

Back in Canada, Prof. Richard N. Longenecker willingly sacrificed himself the the thankless task, as my advisor, of reading an unwieldy (700-page!) manuscript and making editorial suggestions. Everyone who has worked with Prof. Longenecker will testify to his warmth and fatherly care; we have all benefited from his remarkable foresight and his ability to shepherd the anxious doctoral candidate over (sometimes around) the institutional hurdles that beset our paths.

A glance ahead at the text of this work will give the reader some appreciation of the pain that my wife Glenna was willing to endure on my account, for she typed out the entire manuscript, including the ubiquitous Greek (which she does not read), and that in the age of the typewriter. For the final (dissertation) draft, she was joined by my sister Kathy, who made a special trip from England for the purpose. And since I had no access to a computer in those days, the entire manuscript had to be keyed in again (on disk) before I could revise it for publication. This final task was undertaken by the General Services support staff at the Memorial University of Newfoundland, where I taught from 1987 to 1989.

It remains to thank the staff of E.J. Brill for their professional handling of a difficult manuscript. Dr. F.Th. Dijkema first agreed to take on the project and has been unfailingly helpful since. Prof. Dr. Peter van der Horst, of the University of Utrecht, read the entire script for Brill and saved me from some embarrassing errors. Hans van der Meij and Gerard Huying have done a superb job as editors of this book.

None of the academics mentioned above, as far as I know, would want to have his name tied to the hypotheses that I advocate in the present work. Nor can any of them be blamed for defects of either style or substance that may appear. But all of them, along with the non-academics mentioned, have contributed enormously to the emergence of this book. If it has been a worthwhile project, they all deserve credit.

The substance of chapter 10 first appeared in an article entitled "Josephus on the Pharisees Reconsidered: A Critique of Smith/Neusner", in *Studies in Religion/Sciences Religieuses* 17:4 (1988), 455-469. It is reproduced here by permission of the journal editor, Dr. T. Sinclair-Faulkner.

The substance of chapter 15 first appeared as the article "Was Josephus a Pharisee? A Re-examination of *Life* 10-12", in the *Journal of Jewish Studies* 40:1 (1989), 32-45, and is reproduced by permission of the journal editor, Dr. G. Vermes.

In the following exploration of Josephus's Pharisee passages, I offer thorough analyses and new translations of key phrases and sentences. For bulk narrative quotations and incidental references, however, I follow the Loeb Classical Library translation unless modifications seem necessary. Where the Loeb text is cited, the translator's name is included either in parentheses after the citation or in a footnote. The Loeb text is reprinted by permission of the publishers and the Loeb Classical Library from *Josephus*, in ten volumes, translated by H.St.J. Thackeray, R. Marcus, A. Wikgren, and L.H. Feldman, Cambridge, Mass.: Harvard University Press, 1981.

Steve Mason
Toronto, 1990

ABBREVIATIONS

Ag.Ap.	*Against Apion*, by Flavius Josephus
Ant.	*The Jewish Antiquities*, by Flavius Josephus
ARW	*Archiv für Religionswissenschaft*
ATR	*Anglican Theological Review*
BJRL	*Bulletin of the John Rylands University Library in Manchester*
CCARJ	*Central Conference of American Rabbis Journal*
CQ	*Classical Quarterly*
EJ	*Encyclopaedia Judaica*
ERE	*Encyclopaedia of Religion and Ethics*, ed. J. Hastings. Edinburgh: T. & T. Clark.
HR	*History of Religion*
HTR	*Harvard Theological Review*
HUCA	*Hebrew Union College Annual*
HZ	*Historische Zeitschrift*
IDB	*The Interpreter's Dictionary of the Bible*
IDBS	*IDB, Supplementary Volume* (1976)
JBL	*Journal of Biblical Literature*
JE	*Jewish Encyclopaedia*
JES	*Journal of Ecumenical Studies*
JJS	*Journal of Jewish Studies*
JQR	*Jewish Quarterly Review*
JR	*Journal of Religion*
JSJ	*Journal for the Study of Judaism in the Persian, Hellenistic and Roman Period*
JSNT	*Journal for the Study of the New Testament*
JTS	*Journal of Theological Studies*
LCL	"Loeb Classical Library"
LSJ	*A Greek-English Lexicon*, edd. H. G. Liddell, R. Scott, H. S. Jones
MGWJ	*Monatsschrift für Geschichte und Wissenschaft des Judentums*
NovT	*Novum Testamentum*
NTS	*New Testament Studies*
PWRE	*Paulys Realencylopädie der classischen Altertumswissenschaft*, revised by G. Wissowa
RevQ	*Revue de Qumran*
Stobaeus	J. Stobaeus, *Anthologium*, 5 vols., edd. C. Wachsmuth and O. Hense (1957)
SVF	*Stoicorum Veterum Fragmenta*, 4 vols., ed. A. von Arnim (1903).
TDNT	*Theological Dictionary of the New Testament*, edd. G. Kittel and G. Friedrich, trans. G. W. Bromiley.
TLZ	*Theologische Literarzeitung*
TSK	*Theologische Studien und Kritiken*
TWNT	*Theologisches Wörterbuch zum Neuen Testament*
War	*The Jewish War*, by Flavius Josephus
ZAW	*Zeitschrift für die alttestamentliche Wissenschaft*
ZNW	*Zeitschrift für die neutestamentliche Wissenschaft*
ZRGG	*Zeitschrift für Religions- und Geistesgeschichte*
ZTK	*Zeitschrift für Theologie und Kirche*

PART ONE

INTRODUCTION

CHAPTER ONE

METHOD IN THE STUDY OF PHARISAIC HISTORY

Until recent times, scholarship on the Pharisees has been in complete disarray. A major problem has been the lack of commonly accepted criteria for deciding questions of Pharisaic history: scholars coming from different religious backgrounds and with different purposes, using different sources in different ways, have necessarily come to different, often incompatible, results.[1] How and when did the Pharisees appear in history?[2] From what sectors of society did they originate?[3] What was the significance of their name?[4] What were their central, constitutive tenets?[5]

---

[1] Programmatic in many ways was the debate between Abraham Geiger (*Das Judenthum und seine Geschichte* [2. edn.; Breslau: Schletter, 1865], 102-151) and Julius Wellhausen (*Die Pharisäer und die Sadducäer* [2. edn.; Hannover: H. Lafaire, 1924], 8-25, 76-123). These scholars agreed, however, on the details of Pharisaic origins; they were preoccupied with the evaluative question, as to whether Pharisaism represented a development or decline in post-exilic Judaism.

[2] Cf., e.g., I. Lévy, *La Legende de Pythagore de Grèce en Palestine* (Paris: Honore Champion, 1927), 235-250; O. Holtzmann, "Der Prophet Malachi und der Ursprung des Pharisäerbundes", *ARW* 19 (1931), 1-21; W. Foerster, "Der Ursprung des Pharisäismus", *ZNW* 24 (1935), 35-51; W. Beilner, "Der Ursprung des Pharisäismus", *BZ* n.F. 3 (1959); S. Zeitlin, *The Rise and Fall of the Judean State* (Philadelphia: Jewish Publication Society of America, 1962-1978), I, 176; L. Finkelstein, "The Origin of the Pharisees", *Conservative Judaism* 23 (1969), 25-36; H. Burgmann, "'The Wicked Woman': der Makkabäer Simon?", *RevQ* 8 (1972), 323-259; idem., "Der Gründer der Pharisäergenossenschaft: der Makkabäer Simon", *JSJ* 9 (1978), 153-191.

[3] The Pharisees' predecessors are variously described as: priests (R. Meyer, "Φαρισαῖος", *TDNT* IX, 15f.); lay scribes (E. Rivkin, "Pharisees", *IDBS*, 659f.); the prophets (J. Z. Lauterbach, "The Pharisees and their Teachings", *HUCA* 6 [1929], 77-91); Jerusalem's "plebeians" (L. Finkelstein, *The Pharisees: The Sociological Background of their Faith* [2 vols.; Philadelphia: Jewish Publication Society of America, 1938], I, 74); and the *hasidim*, whether these last are understood to have been religious quietists (Wellhausen) or zealous nationalists (Geiger).

[4] Cf., e.g., M. D. Hussey, "The Origin of the Name Pharisee", *JBL* 39 (1920), 66-69; T. W. Manson, "Sadducee and Pharisee: the Origin and Significance of their Names", *BJRL* 21 (1938), 144-159; J. Bowker, *Jesus and the Pharisees* (Cambridge: University Press, 1973), 4; and A. I. Baumgarten, "The Name of the Pharisees", *JBL* 102 (1983), 411-428.

[5] Was their core motivation: zeal for their oral tradition (so G. F. Moore, *Judaism in the First Centuries of the Christian Era, the Age of the Tannaim* [3 vols.; Cambridge, Mass.: Harvard University Press, 1927-1930], I, 66, and E. Rivkin, *A Hidden Revolution* [Nashville: Abingdon, 1978], 71); the promulgation of liberal democracy (so Lauterbach, "Pharisees", *HUCA*, 69, 119, 133); the practice of tithing and levitical purity (so R. T. Herford, *The Pharisees* [New York: Macmillan, 1924], 29-35); an insistence on separation from the heathen (so I. Elbogen, *Die Religionsanschauungen der Pharisäer* [Berlin: H. Itzkowski, 1904); a messianic hope (so K. Kohler, "Pharisees", *JE* IX, 664); belief

Were they inclined toward apocalyptic views?[6] Were they involved in political life?[7] If so, what political principles did they espouse?[8] How great was their influence in Palestinian Judaism before AD 70?[9] How

---

in resurrection and angels (so Manson, "Sadducee and Pharisee", 154); or the repudiation of apocalyptic (so K. Schubert, "Jewish Religious Parties and Sects", in *The Crucible of Christianity*, ed. A. Toynbee [London: Thames and Hudson, 1969], 89)?

[6] For a negative answer, see: Geiger, *Geschichte*, 93f.; B. Jacob, *Im Namen Gottes* (Berlin: S. Calvary, 1903), 65f.; Elbogen, *Religionsanschauungen*, 8; Moore, *Judaism*, I, 127f.; Herford, *Pharisees*, 185; Lauterbach, "Pharisees", *HUCA*, 136; J. Klausner, *The Messianic Idea in Israel* (London: George Allen and Unwin, 1956), 393; and Schubert, "Parties and Sects", 89. For an affirmative answer, see: Wellhausen, *Pharisäer*, 22-24; W. Bousset, *Die Religion des Judentums im späthellenistischen Zeitalter* HNT 21 (4. edn., ed. H. Gressmann; Tübingen: Mohr-Siebeck, 1966 [1926]), 204f.; R. H. Charles, *Religious Development Between the Old and New Testaments* (London: Oxford, 1914), 33f.; idem., *Eschatology: The Doctrine of a Future Life in Israel, Judaism and Christianity* (New York: Schocken, 1963 [1899]), 171-195; C. C. Torrey, "Apocalypse", *JE*, I, 673b; W. D. Davies, "Apocalyptic and Pharisaism", in his *Christian Origins and Judaism* (London: Darton, Longman & Todd, 1962), 19-30; and P. D. Hanson, "Apocalypticism", *IDBS*, 33.

[7] Affirmatively: Geiger, *Urschrift*, 150; Elbogen, "Einige neuere Theorien über den Ursprung der Pharisäer und Sadduzäer", in *Jewish Studies in Memory of I. Abrahams* (New York: Jewish Institute of Religion, 1927), 145-147; G. Alon, *Jews, Judaism and the Classical World* (Jerusalem: Magnes, 1977), esp. 1-47; and W. Farmer, *Maccabees, Zealots, and Josephus* (New York: Columbia University Press, 1956), 189f. Negatively: Wellhausen, *Pharisäer*, 22, 100-102; E. Schürer, *Geschichte des jüdischen Volkes im Zeitalter Jesu Christi* (3./4. edn., 3 vols.; Leipzig: J. C. Hinrichs, 1901), II, 463; Herford, *Pharisees*, 45-52; E. Meyer, *Ursprung und Anfänge des Christentums* (3 vols.; Stuttgart-Berlin: J. G. Cotta, 1921-1923), II, 286; Moore, *Judaism*, II, 113; C. Steuernagel, "Pharisäer", *PWRE* XXXVIII, 1828; Lauterbach, "Pharisees", *HUCA*, 70; and D. Polish, "Pharisaism and Political Sovereignty", *Judaism* 19 (1970), 415-418. Between these two extremes, various mediating positions have emerged, the most popular of which holds that the Pharisees' interests shifted at some point from politics to religious matters; cf. V. Tcherikover, *Hellenistic Civilization and the Jews* (Philadelphia: Jewish Publication Society of America; Jerusalem: Magnes, 1959), 253f.; M. Black, "Pharisees", *IDB*, III, 777-780; and J. Neusner, *From Politics to Piety: The Emergence of Pharisaic Judaism* (Englewood Cliffs NJ: Prentice-Hall, 1973).

[8] Wellhausen (*Pharisäer*, 90) held that the Pharisees broke with Judah Maccabee and were thereafter in perpetual conflict with the Hasmoneans. Others think that the Pharisees accepted Hasmonean rule until the break with John Hyrcanus (Lauterbach, "Pharisees", *HUCA*, 77-80; Herford, *Pharisees*, 29-31). Others, rejecting the historicity of a split with Hyrcanus, find the Pharisees supporting the Hasmoneans until their struggle with Alexander Janneus (I. Friedlander, "The Rupture Between Alexander Jannai and the Pharisees", *JQR* n.s. 4 [1913-1914], 443-448; Alon, *Jews*, 7-17; M.J. Geller, "Alexander Janneus and the Pharisees' Rift", *JJS* 30 [1979], 203-210). Still others deny that the Pharisees ever opposed Janneus (C. Rabin, "Alexander Janneus and the Pharisees", *JJS* 7 [1956], 5-10). On the vexed question of the Pharisees' relations with the Hasmoneans, see also P. Kieval, "The Talmudic View of the Hasmonean and Herodian Periods in Jewish History" (dissertation, Brandeis, 1970), whose conclusions have an indirect bearing on the problem.

[9] On the basis of such evidence as is cited by J. Jeremias (*Jerusalem zur Zeit Jesu* [Göttingen: Vandenhoeck & Ruprecht, 1958], 134-138), most scholars have believed that the Pharisees exercised the dominant religious influence in pre-70 Palestine, even if they

did they relate to the rest of their society?[10] All of these issues, which would seem elementary for understanding the Pharisees, are not only unresolved; they are still vigorously debated.[11]

The diversity of competent opinion on these matters is so profound that it seems hazardous to say anything significant about the Pharisees, except for the vague propositions that (a) they especially valued a body of extrabiblical tradition and (b) they contributed significantly to the formation of rabbinic Judaism.[12]

In response to the perceived bankruptcy of previous research on the Pharisees, a new scholarly effort has emerged within the last two decades. Represented principally by J. Neusner and E. Rivkin, this endeavour is characterized by the willingness to pose anew the basic and (in that sense) radical question: How can we know anything about the Pharisees? Neusner opens his study as follows:

> While every history of ancient Judaism and Christianity gives a detailed picture of the Pharisees, none systematically and critically analyzes the traits and tendencies of the sources combined to form such an account. Consequently we have many theories, but few facts, sophisticated theologies but uncritical, naive histories of Pharisaism which yield heated arguments unillumined by disciplined, reasoned understanding. Progress in the study of the growth of Pharisaic Judaism before 70 A.D. will depend upon accumulation of detailed knowledge and a determined effort to cease theorizing about the age. We must honestly attempt to understand not only what was going on in the first century, but also—and most crucially— *how* and *whether* we know anything at all about what was going on.[13]

---

have differed over the size of the group. It is now fashionable, however, to emphasize the plurality of pre-bellum Judaism and to characterize the Pharisees as but one of many small sects, with correspondingly limited influence; cf. R. Meyer, "Φαρισαῖος", *TDNT* IX, 31; M. Smith, "Palestinian Judaism in the First Century", in *Israel: Its Role in Civilization*, ed. M. Davis (New York: Harper and Brothers, 1956), 67-81; and J. Neusner, *Politics*, 8-11.

[10] In the literature cited in the notes above, the Pharisees appear variously as a large nationalistic movement and a tiny sect of pietists, enlightened progressives and narrow-minded legalists, an esteemed scholar class and an irrelevant sect.

[11] Useful synopses of some aspects of the scholarly debate are given by R. Marcus, "The Pharisees in the Light of Modern Scholarship", *JR* 32 (1952), 153-163, and H.D. Mantel, "The Sadducees and the Pharisees", in *The World History of the Jewish People*, first series, VIII: *Society and Religion in the Second Temple Period*, edd. M. Avi-Yonah and Z. Baros (Jerusalem: Massada, 1977), 99-123.

[12] Even Neusner, who may be considered one of the more cautious historians of Pharisaism, allows these two points. On (a), see his *The Rabbinic Traditions About the Pharisees Before 70* (3 vols.; Leiden: E.J. Brill, 1971), III, 304. On (b), see his "Pharisaic-Rabbinic Judaism: A Clarification", *HR* 12 (1973), 68

[13] *Politics*, xix.

Rivkin likewise proposes a thorough re-examination of the sources for
Pharisaic history.[14] Although these two critics arrive at very different interpretations of the group, they agree in calling for a return to first principles. E. P. Sanders comments:

> The question of who the Pharisees were and of how they saw themselves
> *vis-à-vis* the rest of Judaism appears quite wide open. One must welcome
> the attempts of Rivkin and Neusner to pursue the question *de novo* and to
> try to establish rigorous academic standards for answering it.[15]

The present study is intended as a contribution to this *de novo* question-
ing about the Pharisees. It will examine in detail the evidence of a key
witness, Flavius Josephus, concerning Pharisaic history. What principles
ought to guide such an analysis? How will this study of one source serve
the larger effort to understand the Pharisees? Rivkin and Neusner provide some initial guidance, both in their explicit reflections and, implicitly, in their own procedures; nevertheless, they give detailed
methodological proposals only for the rabbinic literature.[16] In this
chapter I shall attempt to fill out their preliminary insights—i.e., those
that are applicable to all sources—by considering also (a) the problems
that have hampered previous research on the Pharisees and (b) some
results of contemporary historiography.

Once the methodological requirements for a study of Josephus's
Pharisees have become clear, I shall survey previous treatments of the
topic, in order to show that those requirements have not yet been met
or even, in most cases, intended. That deficiency will provide the rationale for the study that follows.

We turn, then, to examine the goal, the sources, and the procedure
for research on the Pharisees, as a means of determining the desired
characteristics of a study of Josephus's Pharisees.

I. *The Goal of Research on the Pharisees*

One reason for the ''heated arguments'' referred to by Neusner is that
scholars have come to study the Pharisees with different aims and interests. Now it would be naive to disallow any motives other than the
''purely historical'' as reasons for studying the Pharisees; to indulge

---

[14] *Revolution*, 31f.

[15] E. P. Sanders, *Paul and Palestinian Judaism* (Philadelphia: Fortress, 1977), 62.

[16] Cf. E. Rivkin, ''Defining the Pharisees: the Tannaitic Sources'', *HUCA* 40 (1969),
205-249; J. Neusner, *Form-Analysis and Exegesis: A Fresh Approach to the Redaction of the
Mishnah* (Minneapolis: University of Minnesota Press, 1980); idem., *Method and Meaning
in Ancient Judaism* (Chico CA: Scholars Press, 1981), 36-50; idem., *Judaism: The Evidence
of the Mishnah* (Chicago-London: University of Chicago Press, 1981), 48-72.

such personal interests, however, would be to deny the *wissenschaftlich* character of history. One must distinguish, then, between the private factors that motivate one to study Pharisaism and the shared, professional goal of the enterprise.

One of the obvious motives behind the study of the Pharisees is to shed light on the formative years of one's own tradition, Jewish or Christian. On the one hand, Judaism tends to see itself as the descendant of ancient Pharisaism. K. Kohler writes, "Pharisaism shaped the character of Judaism and the life and thought of the Jew for all the future."[17] So also R. L. Rubenstein: "All contemporary branches of Judaism—Reform, Conservative and Orthodox—are the spiritual heirs of the tradition of the Pharisees."[18] So the Jew might understandably have a historical interest in the Pharisees.

On the other hand, the classical Christian texts appear to define the aims of Jesus and Paul over against those of the Pharisees.[19] This circumstance attracts the attention of Christian theologians and biblical scholars to the problem of the Pharisees. In the past, as is well known, such investigators were predisposed to regard Pharisaism as a foil for emerging Christianity. This tendency was not limited to those with a "high christology"[20] but showed up even in the classic liberalism of A. Harnack.[21]

Religious tradition and other factors must be acknowledged as the source of much interest in the Pharisees. Nevertheless, if historical research means something more than the reinforcement of tradition and private intuition, the critic's own motives and interests must submit themselves to norms and controls that are recognized across the discipline of history. We must posit a goal for research on the Pharisees that derives from general principles of historiography and can therefore be pursued by the community of scholars. Ultimate judgements of value remain the prerogative of the individual historian as a moral being; since, however, the criteria for these judgements arise from sources other than the discipline of history itself and are not subject to its controls, they can form no part of the common agenda.

---

[17] Kohler, "Pharisees", *JE*, 666. Cf. also Elbogen, *Religionsanschauungen*, 3.

[18] R. L. Rubenstein, "Scribes, Pharisees and Hypocrites: A Study in Rabbinic Psychology", *Judaism* 12 (1963), 456.

[19] For Jesus, cf. Mk 7:1-23; Mt 23 and *passim*. For Paul, cf. Phil 3:5-9.

[20] The implications of a high christology for one's assessment of the Pharisees were forthrightly stated by one L. Williams, *Talmudic Judaism and Christianity* (1933), 63, cited by H. Loewe, "Pharisaism", in *Judaism and Christianity*, edd. W. O. E. Oesterley, H. Loewe, and E. I. J. Rosenthal (3 vols.; New York: Ktav, 1969 [1937-38]), I, 158:

> If Jesus, who was the Incarnation of God, and therefore the personification of perfect knowledge and truth, thus depicts the Pharisees, thus they must have been and not otherwise; no more is to be said.

[21] *Das Wesen des Christentums* (Stuttgart: Ehrenfried Klotz, 1950 [1900]), 43, 62f.

Modern historiography is pre-eminently concerned with the aims, intentions, or thoughts of those who acted in the past to effect the events known collectively as history. R. G. Collingwood calls this thought-determined aspect the "inside" of an event.[22] The outside of an event, he says, is "everything belonging to it which can be described in terms of bodies and their movements", for example, that Caesar crossed the Rubicon on a particular date. Collingwood unites the outside and inside of an event as the dual object to be known:

> The historian is never concerned with either of these to the exclusion of the other. He is investigating not mere events. . . but actions, and an action is the unity of the outside and inside of an event. . . . He must always remember that the event was an action, and that his main task is to think himself into this action, to discern the thought of its agent.[23]

This emphasis on apprehending the intentions of historical actors provides the goal for modern research on the Pharisees. Our purpose is to go beyond the events in which the Pharisees were involved to try to grasp their motives, their intentions, and their thoughts.

It may not always be possible, given the state of the sources, to get behind the events to the Pharisees' intentions. Although, then, the apprehension of Pharisaic thought must be the final goal of research, we shall have to consider many events from the "outside" on the way to that goal. Because of the subsequent impact of Pharisaism on Western Civilization,[24] those events are already important in their own right[25] and the reconstruction of them can be considered an end in itself. As E. Meyer long ago pointed out, "Die erste und fundamentale Aufgabe des Historikers ist also die *Ermittelung von Tatsachen*, die einmal real gewesen sind."[26] But of the sum total of reconstructed events, it is to be hoped, some insight will be gained into the Pharisees' aims and intentions.

---

[22] R. G. Collingwood, *The Idea of History* (Oxford: Clarendon, 1948), 213.

[23] Ibid.

[24] The *Wirkungsgeschichte* of Pharisaism is no less impressive for its having occasionally been exaggerated or misunderstood, as in Finkelstein's remark that "Fully half the world adheres to Pharisaic faiths" (*Pharisees*, I, ix).

[25] This position is in contrast to Collingwood's extreme view that the historian "is only concerned with those events which are the outward expression of thoughts, and is only concerned with these in so far as they express thoughts" (*Idea*, 217). Such a view would seem to exclude Jesus' crucifixion, the fall of the Temple, and the Balfour Declaration as proper objects of historical study; they are important events because of their impact and not because the various actors' intentions are recoverable. On *Wirkungsgeschichte* as a criterion for the selection of historical topics, see E. Meyer, "Zur Theorie und Methodik der Geschichte", in his *Kleine Schriften* (Halle: Max Niemeyer, 1910), 42-48.

[26] *Kleine Schriften*, 42.

II. *The Sources for Research on the Pharisees*

Where is the critic to begin in his or her quest to understand the Pharisees by reconstructing their past? A basic task is the delimitation of admissible evidence. Differences on this score will necessarily promote diverse conclusions.

A large group of scholars, for example, has considered the apocalyptic literature indicative of Pharisaic ideas; yet many others deny the association.[27] Some interpreters use the DSS for (indirect) information about the Pharisees:[28] it is in a Qumran document that H. Burgmann grounds his theory that Simon the Hasmonean founded the Pharisees[29] and W. Grundmann draws his portrait of the Pharisees largely on the basis of the Scrolls.[30] Others find the Pharisees alluded to already in the Hebrew Bible—in Ezra, Nehemiah,[31] or Malachi.[32] Finally, 1 and 2 Maccabees, with their references to the *hasidim*, have frequently been pressed into service on the question of Pharisaic origins.[33]

None of these sources, however, mentions the Pharisees by name. How, then, can their purported allusions to the Pharisees be identified? Clearly, the criteria for this judgement must issue from some previously acquired knowledge of the Pharisees. It is precisely on this point of prior knowledge that vagueness envelops the research: few scholars take the trouble to demonstrate the high quality of prior knowledge that is an indispensable condition of such attributions. As Neusner insists: "Secure attribution of a work can only be made when an absolutely peculiar characteristic of the possible author [in our case, a Pharisee] can be shown to be an essential element in the structure of the whole work."[34]

When the grounds for the attribution of some works to the Pharisees are disclosed, they are often dubious. For example, G. B. Gray (in the Charles volumes) identifies *Psalms of Solomon* as Pharisaic on the basis of: (a) its opponents, whom he judges to be the Hasmoneans; (b) the beliefs reflected in it, such as a messianic hope, political quietism, and the com-

---

[27] See n. 6 above.
[28] Cf. D. Flusser, "Pharisäer, Sadduzäer und Essener im Pescher Nahum", in *Qumran*, edd. K. E. Krozinger *et al.* (Darmstadt: Wissenschaftliche Buchgesellschaft, 1981), 121-166, and A. I. Baumgarten, "Name", 421 and n. 42.
[29] See n. 2 above.
[30] J. Leipoldt and W. Grundmann, *Umwelt des Urchristentums* (2 vols.; Berlin: Evangelische Verlagsanstalt, 1965-66), I, 269-278.
[31] Geiger, *Geschichte*, 87ff.; *Urschrift*, 103.
[32] Holtzmann, "Malachi".
[33] Wellhausen, *Pharisäer*, 79ff.; Foerster, "Ursprung", 35ff.; and Beilner, "Ursprung", 245f.
[34] Neusner, *Politics*, 4.

bination of fate and free will; and (c) its date (mid-first century BC).[35] The *Psalms* have often been considered Pharisaic, presumably on the basis of such evidence.[36] Yet the assumptions involved are clearly debatable: (a) presupposes that the Pharisees (i) were indeed opposed to the Hasmoneans and (ii) were the only ones so opposed; (b) assumes that the messianic hope was peculiar to the Pharisees, that they were political quietists, and that Josephus was correct in his claim that the combination of fate and free will was a Pharisaic distinctive. Every one of these tacit assumptions is now vigorously contested in the scholarly literature,[37] yet such assumptions have been common. Wellhausen openly confessed his belief that the only significant *Gegensatz* in first-century BC Palestine was that between Pharisees and Sadducees; hence, opposition to the Jerusalem authorities automatically identifies *Pss. Sol.* as Pharisaic.[38]

In view of the vaporous criteria used to establish Pharisaic authorship for *Pss. Sol.*, it can be startling to realize the amount of weight that is placed on this identification. M. Black writes:

> Fortunately there is no doubt about the Pharisaic authorship of the Psalms of Solomon (ca. 60 B.C.), *doctrinally one of the most important of the Pharisaic and anti-Sadducean documents* of this century, since it supplies our main evidence for the Pharisaic messianic hope.[39]

Unfortunately, there is doubt. K. Schubert, with a very different pre-understanding of Pharisaism, claims that *Pss. Sol.* is anti-Pharisaic.[40] This sort of dispute is legion with regard to literature that does not mention the Pharisees by name. So, Schürer thinks *Assumption of Moses* to be Pharisaic;[41] Grundmann calls it anti-Pharisaic.[42] Schürer believes, *ohne*

---

[35] Charles, *Apocrypha and Pseudepigrapha*, II, 628ff.

[36] Cf. Wellhausen, *Pharisäer*, 111; E. Kautzch, *Die Apokryphen und Pseudepigraphen des Alten Testaments* (2 vols.; Tübingen: Mohr-Siebeck, 1900), II, 128; Moore, *Judaism*, I, 182; Black, "Pharisees", *IDB*, 777, 781; D. S. Russell, *The Jews from Alexander to Herod* (Oxford: Clarendon, 1967), 164; Grundmann, *Umwelt*, I, 278; A. Finkel, *The Pharisees and the Teacher of Nazareth* (Leiden: E. J. Brill, 1964), 7f.

[37] See nn. 6-8 above. It is a further question whether the exegesis of *Pss. Sol.* has not itself been tailored to fit a presumed Pharisaic provenance. One wonders about this with respect to Gray's reading of a fate/free will combination in *Pss. Sol.* 5:4; 9:6. Would anyone have found such a combination in *Pss. Sol.* if Josephus had not claimed that the Pharisees combined fate and free will (*Ant.* 13:172; 18:13)?

[38] Wellhausen, *Pharisäer*, 111.

[39] Black, "Pharisees", *IDB*, 777, emphasis added.

[40] Schubert, "Parties and Sects", 89.

[41] Schürer, *Geschichte*, III, 375.

[42] Grundmann, *Umwelt*, I , 286.

Zweifel, that *Jubilees* is Pharisaic;[43] H. D. Mantel considers it non-Pharisaic[44] and A. Jellinek, anti-Pharisaic.[45]

A sobering example of the precariousness of attributing a source to the Pharisees without rigorous criteria presents itself in the Damascus Document (CD). J. Jeremias felt able to write in 1923 that:

> es darf heute als erwiesen gelten, dass die Lehrer der Damaskussekte auf der älteren pharisäischen Halakha und Glaubenslehre beruht und dass wir in Gestalt der Damaskusgemeinde eine Jerusalemer pharisäische Gemeinschaft des ersten vorchristlichen Jahrhunderts kennen lernen.[46]

By the second edition of his book (1955), Jeremias was able to cite H. Gressman, L. Ginzberg, G. F. Moore, A. Schlatter, and G. Kittel in support of his claim that CD was a Pharisaic production.[47] Since, however, fragments of the work were found in Cave 4 at Qumran, and since the document seems to correspond well to the Manual of Discipline (1QS),[48] the theory of Pharisaic authorship is no longer tenable, unless one is willing to believe that the Qumran community as a whole was Pharisaic—a proposal that has not received wide support.[49] The impressive array of scholars who were proven incorrect in their claim of Pharisaic authorship for CD stands as a reminder of the multiplicity of religious groups in ancient Palestine and of the consequent danger of prematurely assigning a given document to a particular group.

In the work of Neusner and Rivkin, only those sources that (a) unmistakably mention the Pharisees by name and (b) seem to have independent access to pre-70 realities are admitted as evidence. Rivkin insists:

> Josephus, the New Testament, and the Tannaitic Literature are the only sources that can be legitimately drawn upon for the construction of an objective definition of the Pharisees. They are the only sources using the term *Pharisees* that derive from a time when the Pharisees flourished. *No other sources qualify.*[50]

Neusner is more cautious: "But for now, the only reliable information derives from Josephus, the Gospels, and rabbinical literature, beginning

---

[43] Schürer, *Geschichte*, III, 375.
[44] Mantel, "Sadducees and Pharisees", 99.
[45] Cited in Schürer, *Geschichte*, III, 375.
[46] Jeremias, *Jerusalem*, 131.
[47] Ibid.
[48] Cf. T.H. Gaster, *The Scriptures of the Dead Sea Sect* (London: Seeker & Warburg, 1957), 43.
[49] M. Mansoor (*The Dead Sea Scrolls* [Leiden: E.J. Brill, 1964], 145, 149) cites this as the view of "a few scholars" but confirms the virtual consensus that identifies the Qumraners with the Essenes.
[50] Rivkin, *Revolution*, 31.

with the Mishnah."[51] The qualification "for now" is important because a permanent exclusion of all other sources would be premature. Because sectarian, pseudonymous, and especially apocalyptic literature rarely mentions the actual names of its characters, preferring codes or ciphers, the absence of the Pharisees' name from these texts might be expected even if they were being referred to. Nevertheless, a decision on this point will presuppose a prior body of "control" information on the Pharisees, which can only be safely acquired by historical analysis of the three first-order witnesses: Josephus, the tannaitic literature, and certain works in the NT corpus. If a control body of information can be securely established on the basis of these witnesses, then and only then shall we possess sure criteria for determining which, if any, other sources contain allusions to the Pharisees. For now, however, these three source collections can be the only admissible ones.

III. *The Procedure of Research on the Pharisees*

Narrowing the field of admissible evidence goes some way toward providing a common base for discussion, but not all the way; for the three sources agreed upon are still vastly different from one another in motivation, religious outlook, genre, and even language of composition. Josephus, the Jewish historian under Roman auspices, who may have been connected with the Pharisees at some point, stands over against the rabbinic heirs of the Pharisees on the one hand and their Christian adversaries on the other. Whereas Josephus's narrative speaks mainly about the Pharisees' public activities and "philosophical" beliefs, one might infer from the tannaitic writings that their sole concerns were religious-halakhic. It is not even clear that the rabbinic פרושים can be simply identified with the Φαρισαῖοι of Josephus and the NT.[52] Neusner's judgement meets the point:

> Almost nothing in Josephus's picture of the Pharisees seems closely related to much, if anything, in the rabbis' portrait of the Pharisees, except the rather general allegation that the Pharisees had 'traditions from the fathers', a point made also by the Synoptic story-tellers.[53]

---

[51] Neusner, *Politics*, 4.

[52] Cf. R. Meyer, "Φαρισαῖος", *TDNT*, 12f. A similar difficulty in reconciling the Greek and Hebrew sources presents itself in the study of the Sanhedrin; cf. H. D. Mantel, *Studies in the History of the Sanhedrin* (Cambridge, Mass: Harvard University Press, 1965), 54ff., and S. B. Hoenig, *The Great Sanhedrin* (Philadelphia: Dropsie College, 1953), xiiif.

[53] Neusner, *Rabbinic Traditions*, III, 304.

The obvious and trenchant incongruities between the sources have evoked at least three responses.

The traditional response was to select one source as preferable to the others, whether on a criterion of religious authority or of supposed historical objectivity, and to give that source pride of place as the "base text". All three of our witnesses have enjoyed the prestige of such a position. Thus R. T. Herford called rabbinic literature "the real and only true source of information as to the Pharisees".[54] And L. Finkelstein opted for "the objective, almost scientific, approach of the Talmud, and its kindred writings" for his analysis.[55] W. Bousset considered the NT to be the best source on the Pharisees and disparaged the meagre (in his judgement) evidence of the rabbis.[56] Josephus has usually been adopted as a more "neutral" supplement to either the NT[57] or the rabbis,[58] but he also finds his own partisans.[59]

A second way of handling the disparity between the sources is more sophisticated inasmuch as it recognizes that no document is free of bias. It sets out, therefore, to consider the three source collections synoptically, in order to isolate their common testimony concerning the Pharisees. A. I. Baumgarten, for example, finds the idea of "precision" or "specification" behind both the ἀκρίβεια-forms used of the Pharisees in Josephus and the NT and in the rabbinic פרוש.[60] A. Guttmann and J. Bowker attempt to fit all the sources together with their theories of the history of the Pharisees' name.[61] The virtue of this synoptic approach is that it represents the overthrow of parochialism in dealing with the problem of the Pharisees.

It still falls short, however, in one crucial respect, namely: it continues to reflect an old but false assumption that the statements of the sources are so many raw data that can be selected and combined at will, without full regard to their meanings in their original frameworks. Thus a large

---

[54] Herford, *Pharisees*, 14.

[55] Finkelstein, *Pharisees*, I, xxiii; cf. Elbogen, *Religionsanschauungen*, pp. IV, 2-4, and Kohler, "Pharisees", *JE*, 661.

[56] Bousset, *Religion*, 187; cf. Wellhausen, *Pharisäer*, 21, 33f. For the documented accusation that Christian scholars have often relied too heavily on the NT for their understanding of Pharisaism or Judaism in general, cf. Herford, *Pharisees*, 11f.; Moore, *Judaism*, I, 13f.; J.F. Parkes, *The Foundations of Judaism and Christianity* (London: Vallentine - Mitchell, 1960), 134f.; and Sanders, *Paul*, 33f.

[57] Wellhausen, *Pharisäer*, 33f.

[58] R. Marcus, "Pharisees", 156; A. Guttmann, *Rabbinic Judaism in the Making* (Detroit: Wayne State University Press, 1970), 124f.

[59] W. W. Buehler, *The Pre-Herodian Civil War and Social Debate* (Basel: Friedrich Reinhart, 1974), 5 *et passim*; O. Holtzmann, *Neutestamentliche Zeitgeschichte* (Freiburg: J. C. B. Mohr, 1895), 158-162.

[60] Baumgarten, "Name", 413-420.

[61] Bowker, *Jesus*, 36; Guttmann, *Rabbinic Judaism*, 162ff.

part of Bowker's book is an anthology of Pharisee passages from the various sources; the supposition appears to be that these are the colours, as it were, with which one may paint one's portrait of Pharisaism.[62] This approach was taken already by Schürer, who began his chapter on the Pharisees and Sadducees by citing relevant portions of Josephus and the Mishnah. The whole conception, now often labelled the "scissors and paste" method, stemmed from a positivistic concern for objective facts, which were considered to be embodied in documentary sources.

The third response to the disparities among the three sources is that taken by Neusner and Rivkin. Neusner prefaces his work with the judgement that "all previous studies of the Pharisees are inadequate because, in general, the historical question has been asked too quickly and answered uncritically".[63] What does he mean by saying that "the historical question has been asked too quickly"? We can only surmise from his own approach. Before posing any questions about who the Pharisees really were (*wie es eigentlich gewesen ist*), Neusner proceeds to devote whole chapters to the examination of how each source presents the Pharisees. His brief chapter, "The Pharisees in History", comes only at the end of this single-source analysis. Thus we find in Neusner a two-stage historical inquiry which involves, first, listening to each source's presentation and only afterward asking historical questions. Similarly, Rivkin sets out his procedural intentions:

> Each of these sources will be cited, for the most part, in full and thoroughly analyzed, source by source, in successive chapters. . . . Only after we have constructed three definitions, independently drawn from Josephus, the New Testament, and the Tannaitic Literature, will we then compare each of the definitions with the others.[64]

We are confronted, then, with a purely exegetical phase of historical research. This phase is called for by the realization that every written source is limited by its author's perspective; it is not, therefore, a collection of bare facts but is already an interpretation and formulation of events that needs to be understood in its own right. As A. Momigliano observes, "Between us (as historians) and the facts stands the evidence".[65] The source conveys only δόξα, opinion. It is conditioned

---

[62] Bowker concedes, vii, that "the passages necessarily occur out of context, and may require the context for their full understanding". This does not yet meet the criticism, however, for the question is whether any particular statement of a source can be understood at all, or be directly usable, without reference to its context in the author's thought and purpose.

[63] Neusner, *Politics*, 6.

[64] Rivkin, *Revolution*, 31f.

[65] A. Momigliano, "Historicism Revisited", in his *Essays in Ancient and Modern Historiography* (Oxford: Basil Blackwell, 1977), 368f.

negatively by the author's imperfect perception of events[66] and, positively, by his conscious purposes in writing and by his own style.

How accurately an author perceived events is not a question that exegesis can answer. The author's style and intentions can, however, be uncovered, for literary analysis seeks to answer the question: What does the author mean to convey?[67] In exegesis, the author's motives and purposes, the genre and structure of his work, his emphases, key terms, and characteristic vocabulary all come under scrutiny. The interpreter considers, as a stimulus to grasping the author's intention, how the original readership would plausibly have understood the document. All of this is familiar to the biblical exegete. But it is a necessary first step in the probing of any historical problem; to bypass the literary analysis, as Neusner says, is to ask the historical question too quickly.

Applied to the problem of the Pharisees, these considerations will require that the passages bearing on the Pharisees in each of the relevant sources cannot be seconded as data for any historical reconstruction until they have first been understood within their original frameworks. Documentary references to the Pharisees may serve as ingredients of larger narratives, as with Josephus and the Gospels, or they may appear within an ordered collection of traditional sayings, as with the rabbinic literature. Either way, they owe their existence to the design of an author or editor and possess little immediate meaning outside of that design. Therefore, the historian is only entitled to make use of documentary statements about the Pharisees when he has first understood the literary meaning and function of those statements.

We are now in a position to specify the desiderata of an analysis of Josephus's Pharisee passages. Before doing so, however, we must complete the picture begun above by giving a proleptic answer to the question: How does the historian convert the several δόξαι of his sources into ἐπιστήμη, knowledge?[68] Having listened to the claims of each source, how can the critic discern what really happened?

Rivkin's own procedure becomes inadequate at this point In the end, he expects simply to compare the resulting presentations of the Pharisees in the hope of finding agreement among them:

[66] Cf. M. Bloch, *Apologie der Geschichte oder der Beruf des Historikers* (2d. edn.; E. Klett - J .G. Cotta, 1974), 65, who points out the limitations of eyewitness evidence, even under the most favourable circumstances. See now G. L. Wells and E. F. Loftus (edd.), *Eyewitness Testimony: Psychological Perspectives* (Cambridge: University Press, 1984).

[67] Cf. B. F. Meyer, *Aims of Jesus* (London: SCM, 1979), 89f.

[68] Cf. Collingwood (*Idea*, 20-30) on ancient attempts to grapple with both the philosophical and historical aspects of this problem.

Should it turn out that these definitions are congruent with one another, then shall we not have cogent grounds for postulating that such a definition is truly viable and as objective as the nature of our sources will allow?[69]

Despite his clear perception of the two-tiered nature of historical research, therefore, Rivkin ultimately falls back into positivistic assumptions about how the second phase of the programme is to be carried out, namely, by a simple comparison of the different portraits. He can only expect such a result because his proposed "thorough analysis" of each source[70] turns out to be less than thorough. He still regards the statements of the sources as "raw material for a definition of the Pharisees".[71] In principle, however, it is futile to hope that the sources will yield "congruent" presentations, since each source has its own aims and interests, as different from those of the other sources as they are from those of the historian.[72] Any points of intersection will, of course, be welcome. One must, however, anticipate divergences and be prepared somehow to exploit those also in one's search for the truth.

Nor is it enough to hope that, once each author's aims and proclivities have been identified, they might simply be evaporated off to leave a residue of bare fact. To hope for such a result would be, first, to underestimate the complexity and pervasiveness of an author's *Tendenz*. For that bias is not restricted to some obvious themes overlaid on the material; it comprises rather the whole network of processes by which the author has (a) imperfectly perceived events, (b) found the motivation to record them, (c) exercised his will in selecting, omitting, and shaping the material to serve his ends, and (d) imparted his style, both conscious and unconscious, to the whole production. The author's viewpoint cannot be excised from the facts because the facts are only available through that viewpoint.[73]

Second, the attempt to strip off the author's concerns in order to expose the facts assumes, gratuitously, that those concerns necessarily contradict the reality of the past and were not themselves shaped by the facts as the author perceived them. This fallacy is well known in historical-Jesus research.[74] In the study of Josephus, critics from R. Laqueur to S. J. D. Cohen have displayed a marked tendency to dispute one or another of Josephus's claims on the simple ground that Josephus wanted

---

[69] Rivkin, *Revolution*, 32.
[70] Ibid., 31.
[71] Rivkin, *Revolution*, 54.
[72] Cf. B.F. Meyer, *Aims*, 89f.; M. Bloch, *Apologie*, 125f.
[73] Cf. M. Bloch, *Apologie*, 65, 76f.
[74] I refer to the logic of the "criterion of discontinuity", a trenchant critique of which is offered by B. F. Meyer, *Aims*, 84ff.

his readers to believe it.[75] It is enough for these historians to connect a particular claim with one of Josephus's discernible motifs in order to cast doubt on its validity. The doubtful assumption here is that an author's intentions always, or regularly, arise from somewhere other than his own experience of the "facts".[76]

For these two reasons, it would be naive to hope that we might discover facts about the Pharisees by taking each source, filtering out its "tendentious" elements, and accepting the residue.

How, then, to convert the "potential data"[77] offered by the sources into historically probable information about the Pharisees? An adequate approach must certainly take into account the tendencies of the sources (Laqueur, Cohen) and any coincidence of detail that might emerge between them (Rivkin), but it cannot enlarge either of these factors into a complete system for reconstructing the past. Such a system requires a method and this can only be imparted by the historian as a thinking subject.[78] What is required is that the critic, having now listened to each of the sources' presentations of the Pharisees, step forward to pose his own

---

[75] R. Laqueur (*Der jüdische Historiker Flavius Josephus* [Darmstadt: Wissenschaftliche Buchgesellschaft, 1970 (1920)], 246) claims that Josephus's autobiographical statements in *Life* 1-12, because they serve an apologetic purpose, are of dubious worth (*allerunsicherste und unzuverlässigste*): "wo Josephus eine Tendenz hat, da pflegt er es mit der Wahrheit nicht genau zu nehmen". Similarly, S. J. D. Cohen (*Josephus in Galilee and Rome* [Leiden: E. J. Brill, 1979], 107, 144) views Josephus's claim to Pharisaic allegiance as spurious because (allegedly) apologetic. M. Smith ("Palestinian Judaism", 77) is more cautious. Arguing that Josephus's statements in *Ant.* about Pharisaic influence are apologetically motivated, he remarks: "Such motivation does not, of course, prove that Josephus' statements are false, but it would explain their falsity if that were otherwise demonstrated."

[76] Cohen himself unwittingly proves the fallaciousness of this assumption in two cases, by ultimately accepting data that he first disputes because of their apologetic character. (a) He argues (p. 197) that Josephus's account of the selection of generals for the revolt (*War* 2:562-568) is "suspect" because "motivated by apologetic considerations": it assumes that all of the generals were chosen at one time. On the same page, however, one reads: "Nevertheless, even if Josephus has exaggerated and simplified, we have some reason to follow his account. It is inherently plausible." And finally (p. 198): "In the following discussion I assume that all the generals were chosen at one time although I admit that it is uncertain." (b) A more fundamental contradiction lurks in Cohen's accusation that Josephus is guilty of reductionism in portraying the Jerusalemites as divided into a "war party" and a "peace party". Says Cohen: "There must have been a wide variety between the two extremes, the desire to surrender to the Romans as soon as possible and the readiness to die in a blaze of glory" (p. 183). But Cohen employs the very same reductionism as a major criterion of his study, for he refuses to countenance Josephus's claim that he and other aristocrats wanted peace, on the ground that Josephus was a general in the rebel army and therefore could not have wanted peace (pp. 152ff.). Cohen himself thus excludes any possibility of ambivalent loyalties.

[77] The phrase is from B. F. Meyer, *Aims*, 90.

[78] Cf. M. Bloch, *Apologie*, 79f.

questions and develop his own reconstruction of events.[79] Thus B. F.
Meyer proposes, "The technique of history is the hypothesis."[80] The
critic seeks to formulate a hypothesis as to what really happened that will
account for all of the relevant presentations in the sources. As
Momigliano puts it, the historian "has to assess the value of his evidence
not in terms of simple reliability, but of relevance to the problems he
wants to solve".[81]

This formulation and demonstration of hypotheses requires of the interpreter a fundamental shift in perspective from the exegetical phase of
the investigation. Then, he was concerned with grasping the author's
meaning; now, he will present his own account. Then, he was looking
for the witness's intentional statements; now, he seeks the unintentional
evidence that will expose the witness's biases and limitations.[82] Thus,
historical analysis has often been compared to a courtroom cross-
examination.[83] Once the witnesses have all been heard on their own
terms and have given their own interpretations (the exegetical phase),
the investigator steps forward to pose his questions, in order to
rediscover the events that stood behind all of the accounts.

Summary and Conclusion

A new blueprint for research on the Pharisees, informed by the mistakes
of earlier scholarship, by the experiments of Neusner and Rivkin, and
by general insights from contemporary historiography, will seek to
recover both the external or physical history of this group and, so far as
possible, their intentions and their thought. This goal can best be
reached by an initial limitation of the admissible evidence to Josephus,
the pertinent NT documents, and the rabbinic corpus. The procedure
will fall into two broad phases: first, the analysis of each source's presentation of the Pharisees, by means of exegesis, and, second, the
hypothetical reconstruction of events and intentions.

Although the proposed programme embodies certain controls, it by no
means excludes subjectivity. On the contrary, it acknowledges both the
private interests that may motivate scholars to study Pharisaism and also
the individual's right of ultimate (and private) moral judgement on his

---

[79] Cf. Collingwood, *Idea*, 218f.
[80] B. F. Meyer, *Aims*, 88.
[81] Momigliano, *Essays*, 368f.
[82] On the value of unintentional evidence, see M. Bloch, *Apologie*, 76-84.
[83] So already Polybius 4.2.4; cf. Collingwood, *Idea*, 26, 281ff.; A. W. Mosley,
"Historical Reporting in the Ancient World", *NTS* 12 (1965), 11-15; and Momigliano,
Essays, 162f.

subject. Further, it calls for the interpreter's complete involvement and imagination, both in exegesis and in historical reconstruction. Thus our two chief examples of the *de novo* quest, Neusner and Rivkin, have produced flatly contradictory results. Nevertheless, their work raises the possibility of a new consensus on method, on the "standards" of which Sanders speaks. That achievement is far more important than any particular set of conclusions. If scholarship on the Pharisees takes up this new agenda, which offers some semblance of a language for common discourse, then proposed hypotheses should encounter clearer discussion and critique than had been possible before the new beginning of Rivkin and Neusner. To the degree that arbitrariness can be contained and public accountability enhanced by commonly accepted criteria, the discussion will become more "objective".

If the foregoing proposal for research on the Pharisees has any merit, one can envision the role that a study of Josephus's testimony about the Pharisees ought to play in the larger endeavour. Of our three primary sources, Josephus is the most self-consciously historical: as we shall see, he sets out to write history pure and simple. Moreover, unlike the authors of the other sources, he unquestionably had direct, intimate contact with Pharisaism before 70.[84] His portrayals of the Pharisees, therefore, are of paramount importance.

Josephus refers to the Pharisees in three of his four extant works, viz., *The Jewish War*, *Jewish Antiquities*, and the *Life*. Analysis of his accounts falls within the first, exegetical, phase of the endeavour described above. One must, therefore, determine his purposes in writing and then ask how his discussions of the Pharisees serve those purposes. What is the role of the Pharisees in any given narrative? To what extent do they illustrate any of Josephus's overriding themes? Why does he discuss them at all? Does he describe them with significant, "charged" vocabulary? In short: How do the Pharisees function within his vision of things?

It is necessary now to survey the previous interpretations of Josephus on the Pharisees in order to test the adequacy of those interpretations, by the criteria formulated above. I shall argue that we do not yet possess the kind of comprehensive analysis that could serve as a suitable basis for historical reconstruction. Nevertheless, the previous scholarship raises many issues that will serve to clarify our own aims and procedures.

---

[84] On these points, cf. Rivkin, *Revolution*, 32f.

CHAPTER TWO

SCHOLARLY INTERPRETATIONS
OF JOSEPHUS'S PHARISEES

A discussion of previous interpretations of Josephus on the Pharisees will
demonstrate the need for a new attempt, for none of them yet satisfies,
and most do not claim to satisfy, the requirements set forth in Chapter
1. Nevertheless, the previous research is extremely valuable. First, it
points up some of the factors that complicate any literary study of
Josephus. Second, it highlights the particular problems that must be addressed in a comprehensive study of Josephus's Pharisees. The resolution of these particular problems will become part of the larger task of
the following study.

Since almost every writer on the Pharisees includes some discussion
of Josephus's testimony, and since most authors on Josephus have cause
to mention his connections with and information about the Pharisees,
the number of scholarly references to Josephus's portrayal of the
Pharisees is very large indeed.[1] It is neither practical nor desirable to
review each instance here. The following survey describes rather the
most complete and most programmatic discussions of Josephus on the
Pharisees that have appeared since the mid-nineteenth century.

One word of explanation: the two matters of Josephus's descriptions
of the Pharisees and of his own relationship to the group are often discussed together in the scholarly literature, and both will be important in
the present study. Nevertheless, the determination of Josephus's relationship to the Pharisees involves many factors other than his actual
descriptions of the group—such as his views of the Law, of fate and free
will, and of immortality. To raise those issues in this survey would require many deviations from the main point, which is to assess the
previous analyses of Josephus's portrayals of the Pharisees. The question
of his own relationship to the Pharisees will suggest itself naturally in Part
IV, with reference to a particular passage in his autobiography (*Life* 10-
12). I propose, therefore, to leave until then a discussion of the various
ancillary factors that bear on the question. For the present, our concern
is with scholarly treatments of Josephus's descriptions of the Pharisees.

---

[1] One can gain some impression of the number of potential references to Josephus's
Pharisees by perusing H. Schreckenberg, *Bibliographie zu Flavius Josephus* (Leiden: E. J.
Brill, 1968), the *Supplementband* thereto (1979), and L. H. Feldman, *Josephus and Modern
Scholarship (1937-1980)*, ed. W. Haase (Berlin: W. de Gruyter, 1983).

Two Early Views: H. Paret and E. Gerlach

It was in an 1856 article that the twin issues of Josephus's descriptions of, and relationship to, the Pharisees were first broached seriously. H. Paret wrote his "Über den Pharisäismus des Josephus" in order to show that Josephus was a Pharisee; this identification, he hoped, would enhance the value of Josephus's works for the historical background of Christianity.[2] Paret advanced many arguments, but we are concerned here with his treatment of Josephus's descriptions of the Pharisees (and the other sects), which he takes up first.[3]

Remarkably, Paret did not think that Josephus's explicit comments on the Pharisees, taken by themselves, implied the author's Pharisaic allegiance: "Diese, rein für sich genommen, lässt freilich nicht vermuthen, dass ihr Schreiber ein Pharisäer, sondern weit eher, dass er ein Essener gewesen sei."[4] He conceded that Josephus's main passage on the sects (*War* 2:119-166), to which Josephus later refers as his definitive statement (*Ant.* 13:173, 298; 18:11), portrays the Essenes with obvious *Vorliebe*. Paret also allowed that Josephus's depiction of the Pharisees, by contrast, was at times unfavourable and even censorious (*Ant.* 17:41-45).[5]

In spite of these difficulties, Paret maintained that Josephus was a Pharisee, by arguing (a) that a Pharisee could have expressed such admiration for the Essenes because the two groups were so similar and (b) that the negative portrayal of the Pharisees in *Ant.* 17:41-45 is outweighed by the good things said about them elsewhere—such as their concern for the exact interpretation of the Law (cf. *War* 2:166) and their close communion with God (*Ant.* 17:41-42).[6] Paret further proposed that Josephus had been compelled to sacrifice some of his fellow-Pharisees in *Ant.* because of criticisms that had arisen over his attempt in *War* to present his party as a *harmlose Philosophenschule*. But these concessions are not to be taken as indications of Josephus's own antipathy toward the Pharisees.[7]

Josephus most clearly revealed his Pharisaic viewpoint, according to Paret, in his consistently negative attitude toward the Sadducees.[8] A

---

[2] H. Paret, "Über den Pharisäismus des Josephus", *TSK* 29 (1856), 309-844, esp. 809-811.

[3] Ibid., 816-823. The other arguments, as indicated above, will be considered in Part IV of this study.

[4] Ibid., 816.

[5] Ibid., 816-818.

[6] Ibid., 819-820.

[7] Ibid., 818.

[8] Ibid., 820-823.

Pharisee could admire the Essenes, Paret suggested, but the Sadducees must have appeared to him as infidels. So Josephus presents them (probably falsely) as denying Providence altogether (*Ant.* 13:173), as always unkind toward one another (*War* 2:166; *Ant.* 18:6), and as inhumane in punishment (*Ant.* 13:294). Josephus's use of the Bible and his own theological emphases, Paret claimed, were calculated to challenge Sadducean views.

Soon after Paret's article came E. Gerlach's attempt (1863) to demonstrate the inauthenticity of the *testimonium flavianum.*[9] By Gerlach's time, the literary and textual arguments concerning the *testimonium* were already well known.[10] Gerlach wanted to press another line of argument, namely, that with such views of prophecy and the messianic hope as he held, Josephus could not have penned the *testimonium.*[11] As a preface to this study, Gerlach considered Josephus's religious ties and concluded that he was not a Pharisee but an Essene—a judgement based chiefly on Josephus's portrayals of the Jewish religious parties.[12]

Gerlach began by calling into question the usual interpretation of *Life* 12, to the effect that Josephus ended his religious quest by opting for membership with the Pharisees. Gerlach contended that this interpretation is contradicted by (a) Josephus's conspicuous fondness for the Essenes and (b) the fact that Josephus's own outlook corresponds to that of the Essenes.

Like Paret, Gerlach noted the pro-Essene slant of *War* 2:119-166, which includes the comment that the Essenes "irresistibly attract all who have once tasted their philosophy".[13] He allowed that a Pharisee might have expressed some acknowledgement of Essene piety, but he denied (against Paret) that a Pharisee could have presented such a detailed and admiring portrayal of the Essenes while at the same time giving the Pharisees short shrift. He doubted, for example, that a Pharisee would have implicitly shamed his own party before Roman readers by mentioning the Essene oath to obey all earthly rulers.[14] Indeed, Josephus's own religious beliefs seemed to Gerlach to correspond

---

[9] E. Gerlach, *Die Weissagungen des Alten Testaments in den Schriften des Flavius Josephus* (Berlin: Hertz, 1863). The *testimonium* is the paragraph *Ant.* 18:63-64, which speaks of Jesus as "the Messiah".

[10] Ibid., 5.

[11] Ibid., 6, 85. Gerlach argues that Josephus's treatment of Daniel in *Ant.* reveals his expectation of an earthly, political Messiah, not of a quasi-divine figure.

[12] Ibid., 6-19.

[13] Ibid., 8.

[14] Cf. *War* 2:140.

closely to those that he attributes to the Essenes—for example, that the soul is alien to the body[15] and that fate is supreme.[16]

On the other side, Gerlach was at a loss to find a single passage in Josephus in which the Pharisees were described favourably, without reservation.[17] Against Paret, he denied that Josephus's references to the Pharisees' kindness to one another, love for the Law, and gifts of prophecy were indications of the historian's favour, for in all of these qualities the Pharisees appear to be matched, if not surpassed, by the Essenes. The brief notice about the Pharisees' concern for one another (*War* 2:166), said Gerlach, is contradicted by the many unfavourable references to the group. *War* 1:110-114, he believed, presents their corruptibility, vindictiveness, and hunger for power. In *Ant.* 13:288-298, 398-407, he found their contempt for rulers and their provocation of the people to rebellion. Above all, Gerlach suggested, *Ant.* 17:41-45 openly attacks the Pharisees' pretensions to superior piety.[18]

What, then, is to be made of Josephus's self-described religious quest, which ends with the notice: ἠρξάμην πολιτεύεσθαι τῇ Φαρισαίων αἱρέσει κατακολουθῶν? This signifies nothing more, Gerlach suggested, than that Josephus followed the Pharisees in the political sphere; for such an accommodation is set down by Josephus as a condition of success in public life (cf. *Ant.* 18:15, 17).[19] For Gerlach, therefore, Josephus was not a Pharisee and never claimed to be one. He was an Essene.

Source Criticism of Josephus: G. Hölscher

A major assumption underlying the work of both Paret and Gerlach was the literary unity of Josephus's writings: Josephus was assumed to have one more or less consistent view of the Pharisees. This assumption, however, received a devastating blow in the researches of H. Bloch (1879), J. von Destinon (1881), F. Schemann (1887), W. Otto (1913), and G. Hölscher (1916).[20] Although most of these authors expressed no particular interest in the Pharisee passages of Josephus, their source analy-

---

[15] Cf. *War* 2:154; 7:344; *Ag.Ap.* 2:203.
[16] Gerlach, *Weissagungen*, 13-16.
[17] Ibid., 11 and n.
[18] Ibid., 10.
[19] Ibid., 18f.
[20] H. Bloch, *Die Quellen des Flavius Josephus in seiner Archäologie* (Leipzig: B. G. Teubner, 1879); J. von Destinon, *Die Quellen des Flavius Josephus I: die Quellen der Archäologie Buch XII-XVIII + Jüd. Krieg Buch I* (Keil: Lipsius & Tischer, 1882); F. Schemann, *Die Quellen des Flavius Josephus in der Jüd. Arch. XVIII-XX + Polemos II, 7-14* (Marburg, 1887); W. Otto, "Herodes", *PWRESup*, II, 1-15; G. Hölscher, "Josephus", *PWRE*, XVIII, 1934-2000.

ses harboured serious implications for that material. Only Hölscher, whose article for the *Realencyclopädie* marked the peak of the movement, spelled out those implications; we may thus focus our attention on his study.

Of Hölscher's sixty-three column article on Josephus, about fifty-four columns are given over to a source analysis of Josephus's writings.[21] This proportion reflects the degree to which, by Hölscher's time, an understanding of Josephus had come to be identified with an understanding of his sources. Destinon had long since concluded that *Ant.* 12-17 was little more than a compilation of Josephus's major, intermediate sources—the Anonymous and Nicolaus of Damascus—and that Josephus's own input here was minimal:

> Seine Quelle also hat Jos. das Material gegeben, hat ihm die Disposition desselben übermittelt und schliesslich sogar ihn so zu bestricken gewusst, dass er sein selbständiges Urteil drangab.[22]

Following Destinon's lead, Hölscher denied to Josephus any substantial role in providing the content or even collecting the sources for the twenty volumes of his *Ant.*.

Hölscher's first observation on the Pharisee passages in Josephus is programmatic for his analysis:

> Sein pharisäischer (und damit antisadduzäischer) Standpunkt verrät sich mehrfach in seinen Schriften, obwohl seine Urteile über die drei jüdischen Schulen, je nach den von ihm ausgeschriebenen Quellen, vielfach verschieden auffallen.[23]

On Hölscher's view, although Josephus was a Pharisee,[24] he simply failed to alter the judgements of his sources, even when those judgements contradicted his own Pharisaic sentiments. Of the Pharisee passages, he believed, *War* 1:110-114 is "recht unfreundlich" toward the group. *Ant.* as a whole is "teils unfreundlich" and "teils ziemlich neutral"; only 18:11f. is "anerkennend".[25] Like Paret and Gerlach, then, Hölscher did not find any strong Pharisaic perspective in Josephus's Pharisee passages. His argument, however, was that these passages, like most of *Ant.* and a good piece of *War*, tell more about Josephus's sources than they do about Josephus himself.

---

[21] The article comprises cols. 1934-2000, the last four of which are devoted to bibliography. The source analysis extends from cols. 1943 to 1996.

[22] Destinon, *Quellen*, 101. Similarly, Bloch (*Quellen*, 157-159) found Josephus guilty of *sklavische Abhängigkeit*.

[23] Hölscher, "Josephus", 1936.

[24] Ibid., 1945.

[25] Ibid., 1936 and n. + + . Hölscher also suggests that Josephus's own Pharisaic standpoint comes through in *Ant.* 13:297f.

Hölscher discerned two main sources for *War*, the first reflected in 1:31-2:116, the second in 2:117-283. After that, in discussing the actual events of the war against Rome, Josephus was presumably relying on his own memory, his notes, Vespasian's official report, eyewitness testimony, and other aids.[26] Hölscher's criteria for identifying the two sources in books 1 and 2 included the presence of doublets, differences in style, and distinct preferences for certain terms.[27] He attributed 2:117-161, with its detailed description of the Essenes, to a Jewish written source[28] and the brief remarks on the Pharisees and Sadducees (2:162-166) to Josephus himself. That 1:31-2:116 comes from Nicolaus of Damascus, Herod's court historian, Hölscher argued chiefly on the basis of a comparison of the style in that section with extant fragments of Nicolaus in F. Jacoby's collection.[29] Other considerations were: (a) that the material is pro-Herodian; (b) that it seems to be a condensation of a much more detailed source; and (c) that it is the work of a non-Jew.[30] In support of this last proposition, significantly, Hölscher pointed to the negative presentation of the Pharisees in *War* 1:110-114.

For *Ant.* the picture is more complex. Whereas, according to Hölscher, Josephus had provided much of the content of *War* (books 3-7) himself, in *Ant.* he confined himself almost exclusively to passing on literary traditions.[31] In *Ant.* 1:27-13:212, for example, Hölscher identified large blocks of material from the teaching notes (*Lehrvortrag*) of the Alexandrian Jewish schools.[32] It was in these schools that the Hebrew Bible, the LXX, pagan traditions, and Jewish apocrypha and legends were synthesized; Josephus himself probably never saw any of this material first hand. His contribution at most consisted of copying, excerpting, and combining large blocks of material—all of which implies, "dass man sich die eigene selbständige Arbeit des J. so gering wie möglich vorzustellen hat".[33]

On the content of *Ant.* 13:212-17:355, Hölscher observed that, although it parallels the account from Nicolaus in *War* 1, it sometimes corrects Nicolaus, is often anti-Herodian, and distinctly favours the

---

[26] Ibid., 1939, 1942, 1949.
[27] Ibid., 1944.
[28] Ibid., 1949 and n. + .
[29] Ibid., 1946f.
[30] Ibid., 1944-1948.
[31] Ibid., 1951.
[32] Ibid., 1956-1966. Hölscher argues that, since Josephus's biblical paraphrase sometimes departs from both the LXX and the Hebrew Bible, he must have used these sources only at second hand, already in processed form.
[33] Ibid., 1962.

Hasmoneans.[34] These observations led Hölscher to propose that Josephus is here using a tendentious reworking of Nicolaus by a pro-Hasmonean Jewish polemicist. This polemicist was able to critique Nicolaus by consulting also a biography of Herod, which became the main source for *Ant.* 15-17.[35] In addition to these two main sources, Nicolaus's *Verfälscher* used local Jewish legends, a high priest list, collections of official documents, and various pagan writings.[36] The polemicist was even responsible, Hölscher thought, for the asides and reflections that appear in *Ant.* 13-17.

Hölscher also attributed *Ant.* 18-20 largely to the Jewish polemicist.[37] Here, however, the polemicist has outrun his two *Hauptquellen*—Nicolaus and Herod's biography—and so the narrative becomes more disjointed.

In essence, then, Hölscher thought that some unnamed polemicist was responsible for the whole of *Ant.* 13:212-20:455 and, therefore, for all of the Pharisee passages in *Ant.*[38] But since he conceived of the polemicist as only an intermediate source, Hölscher could also trace the Pharisee passages back to earlier origins: some he regarded as elements of Jewish tradition or legend,[39] another as the contribution of Nicolaus,[40] and another as a story from the biography of Herod.[41] All were reworked by the polemicist before coming into Josephus's hands. To Josephus's own pen Hölscher attributed only (a) the brief description of the Pharisee-Sadducee dispute that follows the story of John Hyrcanus (*Ant.* 13:297-298) and (b) an anti-Herodian notice connected with the Pharisee Pollion (*Ant.* 15:4).[42] Finally, Hölscher attributed the description of the schools in *Ant.* 18:11-25 mainly to the polemicist, on the ground that Josephus the Pharisee could hardly have named a Pharisee as a co-founder of the zealot faction.[43]

---

[34] Ibid., 1970-1973.

[35] Ibid., 1977f.

[36] Ibid., 1973f.

[37] Ibid., 1992. Among the alleged proofs that Josephus did not write this section himself (1986-1992) are: (a) its unfulfilled cross-references; (b) Josephus's purported inability to read the Latin sources that appear therein; and (c) the polemic of *Ant.* 20:154-157, which reminded Hölscher of *Ant.* 16:187, which he had already attributed to the polemicist.

[38] *Ant.* 13:171-173 falls outside this block; nevertheless, Hölscher (1973) attributed it also to the polemicist.

[39] Ibid., 1973f. He included *Ant.* 13:171-173; 15:3, 370-372 in this category.

[40] Ibid., 1973, 1975 (and n.), on *Ant.* 13:400-432.

[41] Ibid., 1979, on *Ant.* 17:41-45.

[42] Ibid., 1973f.

[43] Ibid., 1991; cf. *Ant.* 18:4.

How are we to imagine the Jewish polemicist who wrote most of *Ant.* 13-20? He was, according to Hölscher, a compiler and not a historian, who allowed tensions and doublets to stand unresolved in his presentation.[44] He was a conservative, priestly, pro-Hasmonean aristocrat, who had no sympathy for the rebels and little respect for either the masses or the popular Pharisees.[45]

Important for Hölscher was the belief, based on *Life* 10-12, that Josephus was a devoted Pharisee. This belief implied that Josephus could not have written derogatory accounts of the Pharisees, so someone else must have written them—whether a non-Jew or an anti-Pharisaic aristocrat.[46] Josephus's own Pharisaic allegiance remains, as we shall see, an important criterion for the source-critical analysis of his Pharisee passages.

Reactions to Source Criticism: B. Brüne, R. Laqueur, H Rasp

During the forty years from Bloch to Hölscher, source criticism was the common way, but not the only way, of explaining Josephus's writings. An important dissenter was B. Brüne (1913), who, while acknowledging Josephus's use of sources, continued to look on him as both a genuine historian and a full-fledged writer, whose purposes and interests coloured the whole of his work.[47] Of *Ant.*, Brüne wrote:

> Den Zweck seiner Archäologie hat Jos a [*Ant.*] I, 14 klar ausgesprochen, und auf denselben sind alle eingestreuten Erzählungen, auch die nichtbiblischen, offensichtlich zugeschnitten.[48]

This classic redaction-critical proposal is characteristic of Brüne's entire study, most of which is devoted to an examination of key themes and verbal expressions that recur throughout Josephus's four writings.

Brüne found no warrant for the kind of assumptions made by Hölscher. For example, whereas Hölscher had supposed that a Pharisaic education would preclude Josephus's serious familiarity with Greek language and literature, Brüne thought it self-evident that Josephus belonged to circles in which the knowledge of Greek culture would have been compulsory, if only as a means of defending the tradition against

---

[44] Ibid., 1981f.

[45] Ibid., 1974f., 1982, 1983.

[46] Ibid., 1936. Hölscher also appealed to Josephus's Pharisaic education as proof that he could not have known well the Greek authors cited throughout *Ant.*, so that someone else must have provided those references (1956).

[47] B. Brüne, *Flavius Josephus und seine Schriften in ihrem Verhältnis zum Judentume, zur griechisch-römischen Welt und zum Christentum* (Gütersloh: G. Mohn, 1969 [1913]).

[48] Ibid., 20.

that culture.[49] Brüne finds many changes of expression throughout
Josephus's works, but he attributes them to the author's desire for
elegance and the avoidance of monotony, rather than to new sources.
The crucial point for Brüne is that one can discover throughout
Josephus's works clear and consistent themes; and it is those themes that
evidence Josephus's overall control of his material.[50]

A more self-conscious reaction to the source critics came with R. Laqueur's *Der jüdische Historiker Flavius Josephus*, which appeared in 1920,
soon after Hölscher's article. Laqueur questioned the credibility of a
source criticism that had turned Josephus into a "stumpfen
Abschreiber".[51] The mischievous claim that Josephus had mechanically
copied his sources, Laqueur believed, was but one manifestation of a
conceptual error that was leading astray the whole field of classical
studies in his day.[52] That error was the refusal to recognize the one
legitimate and indispensable presupposition of historical research,
namely, "dass der Verfasser eines Textes ein vernunftbegabtes Wesen
gleich uns selbst ist".[53]

To illustrate the deficiencies of the prevailing source-critical approach,
Laqueur examined *Ant.* 16:183ff., where Nicolaus's partisanship is attacked and the author cites his priestly credentials and Hasmonean
heritage as guarantors of his own historical accuracy. Whereas Hölscher
had attributed this critique of Nicolaus to a priestly, pro-Hasmonean
polemicist, a hypothetical intermediate source, Laqueur asked whether
it would not be more reasonable to identify the author with Josephus
himself, who elsewhere claims both priestly and Hasmonean roots.[54] Laqueur, then, wanted to allow Josephus responsibility for his own
writings.

---

[49] Brüne (13-16) pointed to the rhetorical skill evident in Josephus's speeches as
evidence of his facility in Greek style. Brüne's assumption that educated Palestinian Jews
of the first century would have been familiar with Greek has been more than vindicated
since his time; cf., among others, S. Lieberman, *Greek in Jewish Palestine* (New York:
Jewish Theological Seminary of America, 1942); idem., *Hellenism in Jewish Palestine* (New
York: Jewish Theological Seminary of America, 1950); M. Smith, "Palestinian
Judaism"; M. Hengel, *Judentum und Hellenismus* (Tübingen: J. C. B. Mohr-P. Siebeck,
1969), 108ff.; and T. Rajak, *Josephus: The Historian and his Society* (London: Duckworth,
1983), 47-51.

[50] Brüne does not deal specifically with the Pharisee passages. His section, "Der
Pharisäismus bei Josephus", 150-157, attempts to show (as Paret had done) that
Pharisaic themes, such as reward and punishment, are common in Josephus. This argu-
ment will be considered in Part IV.

[51] Laqueur, *Historiker*, VIIf.; cf. 128-132 and 230-245 ("Eine methodische
Grundfrage").

[52] Ibid., 129.

[53] Ibid., 231.

[54] Ibid., 130-131; cf. *Life* 2.

If that view is correct, how can one explain the differences in Josephus's writings, for example between *War* and *Ant.* in their attitudes toward Herod? Hölscher had posited two sources, one friendly toward Herod (Nicolaus, in *War*) and the other opposed to him (the Jewish polemicist, in *Ant.*). Laqueur, however, extrapolated an answer to this question from his explanation of the differences between *War* and *Life* in their parallel material, concerning Josephus's activities during the revolt against Rome.[55] On that issue there was no possibility of invoking source hypotheses to explain the divergences, since Josephus was recalling his own career. Laqueur posited, therefore, an actual change in Josephus's thinking: whereas *War* had been tailored to please Agrippa II, the *Life* has lost this interest completely, because the king has died.[56] Similarly, Laqueur argued, Josephus underwent some development in his estimation of Herod between *War* and *Ant.* Whereas *War* had been a Roman propaganda piece, *Ant.* reflects Josephus's more natural sympathies.

Although Laqueur made no attempt to deal specifically with the Pharisee passages in Josephus, his work is important because of its major methodological contribution. Source criticism had been carried to the point where its results implied "dass Josephus überhaupt nicht existiert hat, sondern nur seine Quelle", as Laqueur sarcastically put it.[57] Over against such a view, Laqueur insisted that Josephus truly was an author, "dass Josephus mit seiner Person die Richtung seines Werkes deckt".[58] Out of this fundamental proposition grew Laqueur's distinctive contribution. He argued that Josephus was subject to change and development in his outlook and that this capacity for change accounts most adequately for the incongruities in his writings.[59]

Laqueur's analysis of Josephus was to have considerable impact on both German and English-speaking scholarship, the latter through the mediation of H. St. John Thackeray (1929).[60] After Laqueur, the ambitions of Josephan source criticism adjusted themselves radically downward. Most significant for our topic, Laqueur's emphasis on the vicissitudes of Josephus's life as the key to understanding his writings paved the way for two important studies of Josephus on the Pharisees.

---

[55] This question occupied the first half of Laqueur's study, pp. 6-128.

[56] Ibid., 132.

[57] Ibid., 131.

[58] Ibid., 132.

[59] Ibid., 131ff., 246.

[60] H. St. John Thackeray, *Josephus: the Man and the Historian* (New York: Jewish Institute of Religion, 1929). Thackeray modified but accepted Laqueur's theory of the origin of the *Life* (18f.) and built on Laqueur's theory of the purpose of *War* (27, 30). He also agreed in general with Laqueur's discovery of a stronger religious apologetic in *Ant.* (52).

The first of these was H. Rasp's article, "Flavius Josephus und die jüdischen Religionsparteien" (1924).[61] Rasp began with the proposition that the different sequences in which Josephus orders the Jewish schools in his various descriptions of them indicate his changing relationships toward each group.[62] In particular, Rasp saw *Ant.* 18:11-25 as an intended correction of *War* 2:119-166[63] and he tried to interpret that correction by examining the individual changes.

The principal changes discovered by Rasp were: (a) a drastic reduction in the amount of space and degree of enthusiasm devoted to the Essenes; (b) a notable increase in precision with respect to Pharisaic beliefs; and (c) new material on the relations between Sadducees and Pharisees.[64] Rasp approached these changes with an unmistakably Laqueurian judgement:

> Der Gegensatz zwischen den Schilderungen im *Bell.* und in der *Arch.* ist und bleibt auffallend. Will man nicht die eine verschlimmbessern nach der anderen oder gar als Fälschung streichen, dann muss man eben annehmen, dass der Schreiber Josephus in der Zwischenzeit sich gewandelt hat.[65]

What were the circumstances of Josephus's life that caused him to write so differently? Rasp began with the proposition that Josephus's priestly lineage (*Life* 2) must have entailed Saducean allegiance and, as a consequence, hatred of Rome.[66] Thus when Josephus embarked on his mission to Rome to free some priests imprisoned there (*Life* 13ff.), he went full of contempt. Once in Rome, however, he had a change of heart: first, because he saw the awesome power of Rome; second, because of the friendliness of Nero's consort Poppea, whose gifts "brachen wohl den letzten inneren Widerstand".

So Josephus returned home with a new political outlook, of which the key ingredient was submission to Rome. He decided that the best way to promote his new faith would be to acquire a position of influence, which meant joining the Pharisees.[67] For the Pharisees had by now lost touch with the yearnings of the people and were counselling submission

---

[61] *ZNW* 23 (1924), 27-47.

[62] Ibid., 29. In *War* 2:119-166, the Essenes are discussed first and at length; in *Ant.* 13:171-173 the order is Pharisees, Sadducees, Essenes; in *Ant.* 18:11-25 the Pharisees are discussed first and the Essenes last.

[63] Ibid., 31. He reasoned that, since Josephus in *Ant.* 18:11 refers the reader back to the account in *War* 2, but nevertheless proceeds to give a new and somewhat different account, he must be intending to modify the earlier portrait.

[64] Ibid., 32f.

[65] Ibid., 33f.

[66] Ibid., 32-35. Rasp rejects as "nur Spiegelfechterei" Josephus's claim (*Life* 10-12) that he sampled all three Jewish schools and ended up following the Pharisees.

[67] Ibid., Rasp, 36f.

to Rome. Installed as a Rome-friendly Pharisee, Josephus was entrusted with the administration of the Galilee, with a mandate to quell the rebellious activities there. But he was not up to this *Charakterprobe*. Once in Galilee he capitulated to his pre-Pharisaic impulses. The delighted rebels made him their general. And Josephus continued to relish the role of rebel strongman until the Romans took him captive. When captured by the Romans, however, he revised his allegiances yet again and became a Roman favourite.[68]

It was under Roman patronage that Josephus undertook to write *War*, with its major passage on the Jewish schools (2:119-166). Since Josephus could not present himself to Roman readers as a rebel leader, he chose to dissociate himself from any political stance. To that end he passed himself off as an Essene. Hence his long and admiring portrait of this group, which includes the notice that they swear an oath to honour all authority as from God (2:139f.). The Pharisees and Sadducees, however, receive little attention. In Josephus's remark about the Sadducees' rudeness "even to one another" Rasp found the veiled reminiscence of a former member who had since felt the sting of their wrath. The things that Greeks despised in the Jews, Rasp suggested, Josephus ascribed to the Sadducees; what the Greeks admired, he attributed to the Essenes.[69]

Rasp proposed that by the time Josephus came to write *Ant.* he had rethought his priorities and wanted to repair his reputation with his people.[70] Josephus's literary peace offering was his attempt to rewrite the history of the Pharisees. This party had since won Roman support for its religious authority in Palestine and so Josephus intended "die an der Herrschaft mitbeteiligten Pharisäer reinzuwaschen von jeder Schuld".[71] This accounts, according to Rasp, for the revised portrait of the Pharisees in *Ant.* 18. Josephus now rated their political influence very high (18:15, 17) and accurately reported their beliefs, hoping thereby to make amends for the disappointing treatment that he had given them in *War* 2. Rasp comments:

> Ja, er scheint überzeugt zu sein, dass er mit diesem anerkennenden Zeugnis alles wieder gutmachen werde, denn gleichzeitig hat er die Dreistigkeit sich vor aller Welt als allezeit treuer Pharisäer hinzustellen (Vita 12).[72]

---

[68] Ibid., 36-43.
[69] Ibid., 44-46. Cf. *Ag.Ap.* 1:182 // *War* 2:120, 133, and *Ag.Ap.* 1:19_ // *War* 2:152.
[70] Ibid., 46-47.
[71] Ibid., 46.
[72] Ibid., 47

The influence of Laqueur on Rasp's analysis is clear.[73] That the alleged differences in Josephus's portrayals of the Pharisees can be explained largely on the basis of changes in his circumstances and attitudes is an idea that continues to attract scholars. Before discussing its more recent representatives, however, we must give some attention to the work of A. Schlatter on Josephus.

A. Schlatter: The Pharisees as Rabbis/Sages in Politics

In 1856 Paret had argued that the identification of Josephus as a Pharisee would enhance the usefulness of his writings for *Religionsgeschichte*. Some seventy-five years later, A. Schlatter exploited that identification. For him, Josephus was a Pharisee and, as such:

> zeigt uns in griechisches Denken und griechische Rede gefassten Pharisäismus und führt uns damit zu derjenigen Bewegung im Judentum, die die Herrschaft über ganze Judenschaft. . . erlangt hat.[74]

By and large, Schlatter's *Theologie des Judentums* (1932) presupposed Josephus's Pharisaic allegiance;[75] that allegiance was what bestowed special importance on Josephus for Schlatter. In discussing Josephus's portrayal of the Pharisees, Schlatter wanted, first, to show how the Pharisee Josephus could have written the material as it stands and, second, to discover what that material teaches about the Pharisees.

On the former point, Schlatter proposed that Josephus's Pharisees were early representatives of rabbinic religion.[76] That was clear to him because various persons identified as Pharisees by Josephus—such as those who came to power under Queen Alexandra, the teachers Pollion and Samaias, and Simeon ben Gamaliel[77]—are known from the Talmud. Yet, Schlatter noted, Josephus displays a strong antipathy ("eine kräftige Abneigung") toward most of these figures. How can this be explained, given that Josephus was a Pharisee?

Schlatter answered on three levels. First, Josephus's coolness toward the Pharisees is due in part to his objectivity as a historian. This accounts, Schlatter believed, for his detached portrayal of the Pharisees as

---

[73] Rasp acknowledged it (34, 36).

[74] A. Schlatter, *Die Theologie des Judentums nach dem Bericht des Josefus* (Gütersloh: C. Bertelsmann, 1932), V. Cf. also his *Der Bericht über das Ende Jerusalems: ein Dialog mit Wilhelm Weber* (Gütersloh: C. Bertelsmann, 1923), 38.

[75] Schlatter occasionally points out ideas of Josephus that seem to him Pharisaic (cf. pp. 62, 210f.) but he offers no systematic treatment of the question; nor does he explain how he knows such ideas to be distinctively Pharisaic.

[76] Ibid., 198-199.

[77] Cf. *War* 1:110f.; *Ant.* 15:3; *Life* 191.

but one αἵρεσις among many.[78] Second, Schlatter held that much of
Josephus's Pharisee material came from the pagan Nicolaus of
Damascus, whom Josephus allowed to determine not only the content
(*Begrenzung*) but also the nuance (*Färbung*) of his presentation.[79] Nevertheless, according to Schlatter, Josephus himself snubs the *Rabbinat* by
(a) failing to name his own teacher, in violation of rabbinic protocol, (b)
failing to mention the "rabbinic" leaders in the Galilee during the
period of his administration there, although they must have played an
important role, and (c) undertaking a full defence of Judaism, in *Ag.Ap.*,
without once mentioning the rabbinic leaders who controlled Judaism at
the end of the first century.[80] Josephus's own anti-rabbinic attitude,
therefore, calls for an explanation.

Schlatter suggested that Josephus's use of the name "Pharisees" for
the rabbis, rather than "sages/σοφισταί", indicated that his dispute with
them was political and not religious.[81] That is, Josephus revered the
rabbis as such, in their religious and teaching functions, and commended their exegesis of the laws.[82] Their (alleged) hostility toward
Rome, however, was a frustration to Josephus's own efforts at *rapproche-
ment*: "Sein eigenes politisches Ziel machte ihn zum Gegner der Rab-
binen; denn diese lehnten die von J. gewünschte Versöhnung mit Rom
ab."[83] Thus Josephus was committed to Pharisaic-rabbinic religion; he
portrayed his fellow-Pharisees in a negative light only because of their
troublesome political stance.

Having explained Josephus's unfavourable presentation of the
Pharisees by these means, Schlatter asked what could be learned objectively about the Pharisees from Josephus's narative, which is after all the
account of an insider. He discovered:[84] (a) that the Pharisees' goal
always appears as ἀκρίβεια, exactitude or precision in the laws; (b) that
this striving after the laws included adherence to the "traditions of the
fathers"; (c) that, in order to keep the tradition alive, the Pharisees
sponsored a vigorous programme of education;[35] (d) that their teachers
occurred in pairs, which reflects their self-understanding as tradents

---

[78] Schlatter, *Theologie*, 196.
[79] Ibid., 201f.
[80] Ibid., 202.
[81] Ibid., 203-204.
[82] Cf. *War* 1:110, 649; *Ant.* 17:149, 216.
[83] Ibid., 203.
[84] Ibid., 205-208.
[85] Cf. the references to "disciples" or "students" at *War* 1:649; *Ant.* 13:289; 15:3; 17:149.

rather than as individual innovators;[86] (e) that the Pharisees relied on
proselytism, as well as natural reproduction, for their constituency;[87] (f)
that the Pharisees combined divine providence and human responsibility; and (g) that the popular influence of the Pharisees grew in the
early part of the first century.

Like those who went before him, Schlatter both recognized the
negative tone of Josephus's portrayal of the Pharisees and sought to explain how Josephus, as a Pharisee himself, could have written it. One
can discern in his treatment the combined influence of source criticism
and Laqueur's emphasis on Josephus's circumstances as decisive.
Nevertheless, Schlatter's work is a strange combination of literary and
historical analysis. He went far beyond Josephus's intentional, explicit
remarks about the Pharisees, supposing that virtually any religious
teacher who had an interest in the Law was a Pharisee/Sage and using
that identification to shed light on the Pharisees. But this procedure
bypasses the question of Josephus's literary purpose. Further, Schlatter
invoked external criteria, such as his belief that the Pharisees/Sages were
unwilling to co-operate with Rome, to interpret Josephus's account.
These factors make it difficult to compare Schlatter's work directly with
simple analyses of Josephus's Pharisee passages.

M. Smith and J. Neusner: Anglophone Heirs of Laqueur

After a hiatus of some three decades, Rasp's approach to Josephus's
Pharisee passages, based on Laqueur's insights, was introduced to the
English-speaking world by M. Smith. Smith's essay, "Palestinian
Judaism in the First Century", set out to demonstrate both the pervasive
Hellenization and the plurality of pre-70 Judaism. It drew together
evidence from the NT, Josephus, the Talmud, and elsewhere to show
that many different religious groups operated in pre-war Palestine.[88] In
view of this well-attested variety of religious outlook, Smith asked how
the notion could have arisen that first-century Jews embraced a "normative", essentially Pharisaic, Judaism.

Much of the blame for this distortion he laid at the feet of Josephus,
because of the latter's frequent statements in *Ant.* about the Pharisees'
great influence over the people (cf. 13:298, 400-402; 18:15).[89] If these

---

[86] Cf. Pollion and Samaias and the two scholars who urged the removal of the eagle
from Herod's Temple, Judas and Mattathias (*War* 1:648).

[87] Cf. Josephus's own "conversion" to Pharisaism, *Life* 10-12.

[88] Smith, "Palestinian Judaism", 71-73. He cites, for example, various baptist
groups, the Essenes, and the many practitioners of magic.

[89] Ibid., 74-79.

statements are not simple reflections of fact, how are they to be explained? Smith found the key in *Ant.* 13:400ff., the story of Alexander Janneus's deathbed recommendation to his wife Alexandra that, on her accession to the throne, she yield some administrative power to the Pharisees. For Janneus points out to his wife that the Pharisees have enough influence with the people both to injure their enemies and to assist their friends (13:401); he allows that his own rule has been embattled because of his harsh treatment of the Pharisees (13:402). Since these observations on Pharisaic influence are absent from the parallel account in *War* (1:106f.), written some twenty years earlier, Smith discovered a new theme in *Ant.*, to the effect that Palestine cannot be ruled without Pharisaic support.

In the Laqueur/Rasp tradition, Smith sought to explain this new promotion of the Pharisees on the basis of Josephus's circumstances in the last decade of the first century, when *Ant.* was written. Smith's proposal:

> It is almost impossible not to see in such a rewriting of history a bid to the Roman government. That government must have been faced with the problem: Which group of Jews shall we support? . . . To this question Josephus is volunteering an answer: the Pharisees, he says again and again, have by far the greatest influence with the people. Any government which secures their support is accepted; any government which alienates them has trouble.[90]

According to Smith, then, Josephus wanted to throw in his lot with the rising fortunes of the Pharisees after 70 by commending them to the Romans as the group which they should support in Palestine. To accomplish this goal—a service to both Romans and Pharisees[91]—Josephus rewrote history in *Ant.* so as to give the Pharisees enormous popular influence.

In Smith's view, the truth about the Pharisees is more accurately reflected in the school passages of *War* and *Ant.*: they were only one among many philosophical schools that flourished in Palestine before 70.[92] For him, the presentation of the Pharisees in *Ant.* arose from Josephus's political interests and is therefore unreliable as history.

In many respects, Smith's theory echoes Rasp's earlier proposal: Josephus's perspective on the Pharisees changed between *War* and *Ant.* and this changed perspective accounts for *Ant.*'s (alleged) promotion of the Pharisee. Smith's position, however, differs from Rasp's in two

---

[90] Ibid., 72.

[91] Smith believed (p. 77) that the Pharisees were negotiating for Roman support when Josephus wrote *Ant.*.

[92] Ibid., 79f. Smith also adduces parallels between the Pharisees and the Greek philosophical schools.

significant respects. First, whereas Rasp had viewed *Ant.* as a peace-offering to the Pharisees, Smith claimed that Josephus wrote to help the Romans, who were still in a quandary about whom they should support in Palestine. Second, whereas Rasp had viewed *Ant.* as more accurate than *War*—in *War* Josephus deliberately obscured the political facts, Smith took the opposite view.

Smith's theory went virtually unnoticed for some fifteen years—that is, until his student J. Neusner publicized it in a 1972 essay.[93] Referring to the five relevant pages of Smith's essay as a ''landmark study of Josephus's pictures of the Pharisees'', Neusner lamented the lack of interaction it had thus far elicited. His own article, therefore, was intended to publicize and further substantiate Smith's view:

> Here I wish to review the several references to Pharisees in Josephus's writings and to spell out the sources in such a way that Smith's study will both receive the attention it deserves and be shown to be wholly correct, therefore, to necessitate the revision of our picture of pre-70 Pharisaism.[94]

To achieve this goal, Neusner begins with the references to the Pharisees in *Life*, in which he finds Josephus eager to claim Pharisaic credentials (10-12) but silent about the implications of this affiliation. In *Life* 189-198 Neusner finds the Pharisees presented as important politicians during the revolt.[95]

In *War* Neusner finds two distinct emphases with respect to the Pharisees. First, in 1:107-114 they appear as a powerful political group under Alexandra Salome. In 2:162-166, however, they appear simply as the opponents of the Sadducees, both groups being portrayed as philosophical schools who differed only on theoretical issues. Neusner notes that the Pharisees of *War* are not prominent in the narrative.[96]

Following Smith, Neusner argues that the key to understanding the Pharisees in *Ant.* is Josephus's new advocacy of the group: Josephus has now taken the side of the Pharisees and is lobbying for Roman recognition of them as the new leaders in Palestine. Neusner summarizes:

> The Essenes of *War* are cut down to size; the Pharisees of *Antiquities* predominate. And what Josephus now says about them is that the country cannot be governed without their cooperation, and he himself is one of them.[97]

---

[93] J. Neusner, ''Josephus's Pharisees'', *Ex Orbe Religionum*, 224-253.
[94] Ibid., 225.
[95] Ibid., 226-227.
[96] Ibid., 227-230.
[97] Ibid., 238.

Like Smith, Neusner considers the story of Alexandra's admission of the Pharisees to power (*Ant.* 13:400ff.), in comparison to the *War* parallel (1:106ff.), to have been "strikingly revised in favor of the Pharisees".[98] The new story of John Hyrcanus's break with the Pharisees ends with a comment on the people's support for the Pharisees (13:297f.). These and other additions lead Neusner to fall in with Smith's conclusion, which he cites at length, that *War* more accurately reflects the true state of affairs; *Ant.*, he claims, represents a tendentious reworking of the facts.[99]

Neusner did, however, add something to Smith's conclusion. That was the observation that in *War*, the Pharisees appear not only as a religious-philosophical group in the early part of the first Christian century (so *War* 2:162-166), but also as a powerful political organization in the first century BC, under Alexandra Salome (*War* 1:110-114). This qualification allowed Neusner to absorb Smith's theory into his own reconstruction of pre-70 Judaism, which he outlined in *From Politics to Piety: The Emergence of Pharisaic Judaism* (1973). Neusner argues there that the Pharisees moved from active political involvement, in Hasmonean times, to solely religious concerns, under Hillel's leadership, then back to political involvement after 70.[100] His chapter on Josephus's Pharisees is essentially his earlier essay in defence of Smith.

Smith's theory gave Neusner justification for rejecting *Ant.*'s portrait of the Pharisees in favour of the account in *War*, which account well suited his politics-to-piety scenario. In return, Smith's theory won a major supporting role in a famous study of Pharisaism. Under Neusner's sponsorship, it is winning broad support.[101]

---

[98] Ibid.

[99] Ibid., 238-243.

[100] Neusner, *Politics*, 146.

[101] Cf. J. Blenkinsopp, "Prophecy and Priesthood in Josephus", *JJS* 25 (1974), 256 n.80; D. Goodblatt, "The Origins of Roman Recognition of the Palestinian Patriarchate", *Studies in the History of the Jewish People in the Land of Israel* 4 (1978), 99 [Hebrew]; I. L. Levine, "On the Political Involvement of the Pharisees under Herod and the Procurators", *Cathedra* 8 (1978), 12-28 [Hebrew]; S. J. D. Cohen, *Josephus in Galilee and Rome*, 237f.; H. W. Attridge, in M. E. Stone, ed., *Jewish Writings of the Second Temple Period* ("Compendia Rerum Iudaicarum ad Novum Testamentum", 2:3; Assen: Van Gorcum; Philadelphia: Fortress, 1984), 186; R. A. Wild, "The Encounter Between Pharisaic and Christian Judaism: Some Early Gospel Evidence", *NovT* 27 (1985), 110f. The editors of the new Schürer indicate their agreement with Smith (G. Vermes, F. Millar, M. Black, edd., *The History of the Jewish People in the Age of Jesus Christ*, by E. Schürer [3 vols.; Edinburgh: T. & T. Clark, 1979], II, 389 n.20), but they cite him in support of the position that he explicitly rejects, viz., that the Pharisees "represented not a sectarian viewpoint but the main outlook of Judaism" (389).

E. Rivkin: Return to a Univocal Interpretation

A challenge to Smith/Neusner came with E. Rivkin's *A Hidden Revolution*
(1978). Rivkin's total isolation from the Laqueurian stream of interpretation can be seen in his initial proposition that "parallel passages in
War and in *Antiquities* will be treated side by side", in order to analyze
Pharisaic history "chronologically".[102] Thus he begins with *Ant.* 13:171-
173, which introduces the sects at the time of Jonathan the Hasmonean,
and then passes quickly to *Ant.* 13:288-298, the story of the rupture between John Hyrcanus and the Pharisees.[103] The latter passage is important for Rivkin because it lays out the basic features of his "definition"
of the Pharisees: they were a "scholar class" that had developed an entire legal system for the people. This system was based on the Unwritten
Law, Rivkin holds, which had its roots in the "fathers".[104] Rivkin
thinks that throughout Josephus's writings the Pharisees appear as aggressive ("goal-oriented"!) power-seekers and not as irenic con-
templatives:

> The Pharisees in the time of John Hyrcanus, Alexander Janneus, and
> Salome Alexandra were a law-making scholar class capable of stirring up
> and abetting rebellion against king and High Priest, sanctioning the use of
> violence to attain power and authority.[105]

In contrast to Smith/Neusner, then, Rivkin insists on the dominance of
the Pharisees and Pharisaic law in pre-70 Palestine. Even Herod, he
argues, had to "bend before" Pharisaic power: the Pharisees were able
to refuse an oath of allegiance to Herod and not be punished (*Ant.*
15:3).[106] The Sadducees were compelled by popular opinion to follow
Pharisaic laws (*Ant.* 18:15, 17). In Josephus's own account of his decision to govern his life (πολιτεύεσθαι) in accord with the Pharisaic school
(*Life* 12), Rivkin finds further evidence that "in following the Pharisees
one does not join something, but one governs oneself by a system of
laws".[107] Thus the Pharisees were not at all a "sect" but a class of
scholars that, with their special laws, gave leadership to the people.[108]
Rivkin offers the following definition of the Pharisees as they appear in

---

[102] Rivkin, *Revolution*, 33.
[103] Ibid., 34-37.
[104] Ibid., 38-41.
[105] Ibid., 49; cf. 63.
[106] Ibid., 53.
[107] Ibid., 66f.
[108] Ibid., 70. Cf. 316 n. 1, where Rivkin insists that Josephus's term αἵρεσις be
disabused of the modern connotations to the word "sect". We shall discuss the question
of Josephus's meaning in chapter 6, below.

Josephus: "The Pharisees were the active protagonists of the Unwritten Law who enjoyed, except for a brief interval, the wholehearted confidence and support of the masses."[109] As Rivkin himself observes, his interpretation of Josephus's Pharisees is utterly incompatible with the Smith/Neusner theory.[110]

D. R. Schwartz: A Return to Source Criticism

A recent challenge to Smith/Neusner has come in an article by D. R. Schwartz, entitled "Josephus and Nicolaus on the Pharisees" (1983).[111] As the title suggests, Schwartz wants to contest the increasingly popular Smith/Neusner theory by reviving a source-critical explanation of Josephus's Pharisee passages:

> Moreover, the question [of sources] takes on special importance insofar as it has been ignored by several recent studies which have sought to explain some of Josephus's statements on the Pharisees, namely those which ascribe to them great influence and popularity, solely on the basis of his own needs and politics.[112]

Thus Schwartz sets out to determine which Pharisee passages can be attributed to Josephus himself and which ones were simply taken over by Josephus from Nicolaus.

Of special interest are Schwartz's criteria for deciding the source question. For each of the four passages that he attributes to Nicolaus,[113] he can cite various linguistic details, which we shall consider below in our analysis of the respective pericopae. When Schwartz comes, however, to summarize his reasons for attributing passages to Nicolaus, his main criterion is that they "express hostility toward the Pharisees".[114] Specifically, the Pharisees appear as "those who incite the masses against rulers".[115] Two other passages, by contrast, "present thoroughly positive accounts of the Pharisees", and "these improvements in the image of the Pharisees show that it is Josephus who is speaking".[116] For Schwartz, then, as for Hölscher long ago, the author's attitude toward the Pharisees is the crucial factor—though by no means the only factor—in deciding whether Josephus or someone else was the author.

---

[109] Ibid., 70.
[110] Ibid., 330.
[111] *JSJ* 14 (1983), 157-171.
[112] Ibid., 157.
[113] These are *Ant.* 13:171-173, 288, 401f.; 17:41-45.
[114] Ibid., 162.
[115] Ibid.
[116] Ibid., 163. The passages are *War* 2:162-163 and *Ant.* 18:12-15.

Josephus the Pharisee cannot be expected to have portrayed the
Pharisees in a negative light.

How does Schwartz's analysis confront the Smith/Neusner theory? In
the first place, of all the passages adduced by Neusner to demonstrate
Josephus's promotion of the Pharisees in *Ant.* (13:288, 401f.; 17:41-45;
18:15-17), Schwartz argues that only the last comes from Josephus
himself; the others mention Pharisaic power but "in a way which would
hardly commend them to the Romans, emphasizing their subversive
capabilities".[117] This shows that Josephus did not invent his statements
about Pharisaic power in order to appeal to the Romans; rather, most
come from Nicolaus. Second, Schwartz denies a major premise of
Smith's, namely, that the Pharisees at Yavneh were bidding for Roman
endorsement.[118] In place of the Smith/Neusner theory, therefore, he offers a reconstruction more along the lines of Rasp's.

In Schwartz's view, *War* reflects the most thorough and sustained
polemic of all Josephus's writings, for that work manages to obscure the
Pharisees' political activities.[119] For example, although *War* mentions Simeon ben Gamaliel as a leader in the revolutionary government (2:628;
4:159), it does not identify him as a Pharisee; only *Life* 191 does. In *War*
1:67, Schwartz argues, Josephus suppressed the fact, which he only
divulges in *Ant.* 13:288, that the Pharisees had headed the revolt against
John Hyrcanus. And *War* does not mention that the oath of allegiance
refused by the Pharisees named Augustus himself (but *Ant.* 17:42).
Finally, *War* 2:118 claims that the rebel sect of Judas had nothing in
common with the others; but *Ant.* 18:10, 23 links it closely with the
Pharisees. On all of these points, Schwartz contends, it is *War* that omits
the "damaging pieces of information which connect the Pharisees with
rebels".[120] In *Ant.* and *Life*, on the other hand, although these works are
still conditioned by Josephus's biases, "Josephus was less cautious and
therefore much source material, which indicated Pharisaic involvement
in politics and even in rebellion, found its way into these books.[121]

Thus Schwartz concludes against Neusner that it was Josephus's intention to confine the Pharisees to a harmless, purely religious domain
and that *War*, because it reflects this tendency most closely,[122] is not a
reliable guide as to what the Pharisees were really about. In *Ant.* and

---

[117] Ibid., 165f.
[118] Ibid., 167f.
[119] Ibid., 169.
[120] Ibid.
[121] Ibid.
[122] *War* 1:110-114, in which the Pharisees do appear in a political role, Schwartz
describes as the only passage in *War* that "got through" from Josephus's source, contrary to his own intention (170).

Life, on the other hand, Josephus was less cautious because the issue had lost some of its urgency. So he allowed his source (Nicolaus) to assert its claim that the Pharisees were inciters of the masses against the rulers. And these admissions of Pharisaic political power, because they contradict Josephus's own intentions, must be seen to carry considerable historical weight.

With Schwartz's article we bring to a close this survey of scholarly interpretations of Josephus on the Pharisees. Not only is his contribution recent, but it also draws together many threads of the previous discussions. Like the earlier source critics, Schwartz allows that Josephus could mechanically copy passages on the Pharisees that were inimical to his own interests as a Pharisee. Like Laqueur and Rasp, he looks to Josephus's circumstances to explain some of the Pharisee material (especially in *War*). And all of this is directed against another effort along that line, namely, the Smith/Neusner theory.

CONCLUSION TO PART I: TASK OF THE STUDY

It remains in this introductory section to specify the contribution that a new study of Josephus on the Pharisees might hope to make. On the basis of the insights gained thus far, I shall propose a justification, a set of goals, and a procedure for this new investigation.

I. *The Need for a New Study of Josephus's Pharisees*

It is not necessary here to give an extended critique of the previous analyses of Josephus's Pharisees that were surveyed in chapter 2. The weaknesses of any given approach have often been pointed out by successive critics. We shall also interact with specific hypotheses in the course of the following analysis. The only point that needs to be established here is that none of the studies considered above represents a complete literary analysis of Josephus's testimony about the Pharisees. Yet such completeness is a prerequisite to any historical investigation of the Pharisees.

Most of the studies considered do not claim to be comprehensive. Gerlach was interested only in the issue of whether Josephus was a Pharisee. Hölscher did not even try to interpret the Pharisee passages as Josephus's own compositions. Rasp focused on the differences between *War* 2 and *Ant.* 18 and largely ignored the other pericopae. Neusner, by his own admission, was concerned to substantiate Smith's theory, a preoccupation which precluded any serious attempt at interpretation.[1] Finally, Schwartz's purpose was only to decide who authored the various Pharisee passages in Josephus. None of these scholars has aimed at a complete analysis of the Pharisee passages in the context of our author's thought and literary purposes.[2]

---

[1] For example, Neusner's half-dozen sentences of comment on *War* 2:162-166 ("Josephus's Pharisees", 230f.), which is arguably the most important Pharisee passage in Josephus, are almost solely concerned with what the passage does not say about the Pharisees, *vis-à-vis Ant.*.

[2] Rivkin, it is true, does claim that "each of the sources will be thoroughly analyzed" (*Revolution*, 31). Yet, in spite of this promising proposal, he quickly lapses into the positivistic assumption that Josephus presents "raw material for a definition of the Pharisees" (54), an assumption that leads him to treat all of the sources as if they were of one piece. In practice, therefore, if not in theory, Rivkin ignores a fundamental principle of interpretation: he fails to recognize that what Josephus says about the Pharisees is not "raw material" but a formulation.

In chapter 1 we saw that historical investigation presupposes an understanding of the testimony of each witness. One cannot, therefore, use Josephus's evidence about the Pharisees until one knows what it means. Why does Josephus mention the Pharisees? What place do they occupy in his vision of things? What does he want to say about them? These questions all hinge on understanding Josephus as a writer, a task that has been all but ignored in the scholarly literature.

Not many years ago, W. C. van Unnik gave a lecture entitled "Josephus, the Neglected One". He surveyed the state of Josephan studies and remarked:

> Josephus ist und wird immer wieder benutzt und zitiert. . . . Und doch lässt sich fragen, ob der vielzitierte Historiker auch wirklich gekannt wird. Ist er nicht viel mehr Lieferant von Daten als verantwortungsvoller Autor? Hat man seine Schriften wirklich gelesen, exegesiert und in richtiger Weise ausgeschöpft?[3]

The deficiencies noted by van Unnik are nowhere more evident than in the scholarly use of Josephus for the study of the Pharisees. That is the justification for the present study.

A necessary tool for the exegesis of any prolific author is an accurate and exhaustive concordance. The absence of such a resource for Josephus in the past may partially explain the lack of scholarly interest in his thought. What makes a new study of Josephus's Pharisees especially timely now is the recent completion (1983) of the *Complete Concordance to Flavius Josephus*, edited by K. H. Rengstorf *et al.*[4] That work will doubtless revolutionize Josephan studies.[5]

II. *Aims of the Study*

Our goal, then, will be to interpret Josephus's descriptions of the Pharisees. Interpretation is necessary because his statements (like anyone's) are not autonomous, self-evident units of truth, but rather productions of his own thought. Josephus could conceivably have omitted any reference to the Pharisees. The interpreter must ask why he elected to mention them, what these accounts contribute to his narratives, and why he chose certain words and not others to describe the Pharisees. If Josephus claims, for example, that the Pharisees δοκοῦντες

---

[3] In W.C. van Unnik, *Flavius Josephus als historischer Schriftsteller* (Heidelberg: Lambert Schneider, 1978), 18. The lectures printed here were delivered in 1972.

[4] 4 vols.; Leiden: E.J. Brill, 1973-1983. *Supplement I: Namenwörterbuch zu Flavius Josephus*, ed. A. Schalit (1968).

[5] As van Unnik himself pointed out, in anticipation of the work's completion (*Schriftsteller*, 16, 21).

εὐσεβέστερον καὶ ἀκριβέστερον εἶναι τῶν ἄλλων (*War* 1:110), one must ask whether this particular choice of vocabulary and construction has any significance. If Josephus describes the Pharisees' activities under John Hyrcanus or Alexandra Salome, one must ask why he introduces them there, what he thinks of the Hasmoneans, and what role he gives the Pharisees in Jewish history. Although these basic kinds of questions have usually been ignored, they are indispensable for historical research: one cannot get behind Josephus's intention as a witness unless one knows what that intention is.

If this holistic approach is successful, it should also yield defensible conclusions on three specific issues that recur in the secondary literature. These are: (a) the problem of Josephus's own relationship to the Pharisees; (b) the question whether he deliberately changed his presentation of the group between *War* and *Ant./Life*; and (c) the problem of his use of sources for his descriptions of the Pharisees. The resolution of these particular issues will be a function of the overall interpretive process.

III. *Procedure of the Study*

Finally, it is necessary to explain the subtitle of this work, "a composition-critical study", and to indicate its significance for our procedure.

The literary analysis of ancient texts, the search for the author's vision of things, corresponds largely to the programme of "redaction criticism" in biblical studies. That movement is characterized, over against "form" and "source" criticism, by its concern to identify an author's thought and literary tendencies. Nevertheless, redaction criticism has come to mean different things to different critics. Some believe that only a comparison between an author's own production and his sources can properly be called "redactional"; others think it possible to understand the redactor even without sure knowledge of his sources, simply by an interpretation of the final work as it stands.[6]

Now the following study will contend that Josephus's descriptions of the Pharisees in the present tense (thus: "the Pharisees are a group that...") are his own and that where he describes their past actions, under Hasmonean or Herodian rule, the exact shape of his sources is usually irrecoverable. This study could only be called "redaction-

---

[6] Cf. W. G. Thompson, Review of J. Rohde, *Die redaktionsgeschichtliche Methode*, *Biblica* 50 (1969), 136-139; D. Juel, *Messiah and Temple* (Missoula: Scholars Press, 1977), 1-39, esp. 30; and F. G. Downing, "Redaction Criticism: Josephus' *Antiquities* and the Synoptic Gospels", *JSNT* 8 (1980), 46-65; 9 (1980), 29-48.

critical'', therefore, if the term were understood to signify ''vertical'' redaction criticism, which is the latter type mentioned above. To avoid both confusion and the appearance of making false promises, I have chosen the adjective ''composition-critical'' to describe the present study. Coined by the NT scholar E. Haenchen, it has come to be used of the effort to interpret an author's writings in and of themselves, as self-contained compositions.[7] The narrative is assumed to contain within itself the keys to its own meaning.

In keeping with this principle, our procedure will always be to look first within Josephus's writings for clues about the significance of his chosen words and phrases. His general usage and the immediate context will, so far as possible, be the arbiters of meaning. Only when these resources have been exploited shall we look to external parallels for further enlightenment.

The compositional thrust of the study also has important consequences for its emphasis. Josephus mentions the Pharisees in fourteen different passages. Of these, nine are deliberate, reflective discussions of the group.[8] In the other five cases, we have incidental references, which simply note that certain Pharisees were present somewhere or that someone was a Pharisee.[9] For a historical investigation, which seeks to circumvent the witness's intention, incidental notices are the most valuable because they are more likely to yield unintentional evidence. Since our purpose, however, is to *grasp* Josephus's intention, we must try to be sensitive to his own emphases; this will require that primary attention be given to his deliberate discussions of the Pharisees. It is in those discussions, if anywhere, that he spells out what he wants the reader to know about the group.

Finally, our procedure will be governed by the need to deal with the familiar circles of interpretation, especially that of the whole and the parts. For one cannot understand the whole without understanding the parts; yet one cannot understand the parts without understanding the whole. Josephus discusses the Pharisees in three of his four extant works, in *War*, *Ant.*, and the *Life*. These books will be considered in Parts II, III, and IV of the study, respectively. To break into the circle of the whole and the parts, we shall begin each part with an overview of the purpose and outlook of the work in question. To analyze an individual pericope, we shall examine first its immediate context (the ''whole'') and then its key terms (the ''parts''), before we attempt an interpretation

---

[7] Cf. Juel, *Messiah*, 30.

[8] *War* 1:110-114; 2:162-166; *Ant.* 13:171-173, 288-298, 400-431; 17:41-45; 18:12-15; *Life* 10-12, 191-198.

[9] *War* 1:571; 2:411; *Ant.* 15:3-4, 370; *Life* 21.

(the ''whole''). Each chapter will include source-critical observations on the passage under discussion.

To summarize: the investigation of Josephus's presentation of the Pharisees is not new. Nor is the study of ancient authors in terms of their compositional aims and interests. What is new in the following analysis is the application of this particular method to this particular problem. If successful, this inquiry will clarify several preliminary issues in the study of the Pharisees and will also yield some insight into the thought of Josephus.

A PRELIMINARY ASSESSMENT OF JOSEPHUS AS
AN AUTHOR

In the Introduction I have advocated a "composition-critical" approach to Josephus's descriptions of the Pharisees. Those descriptions
are to be interpreted in the light of the author's motives and outlook.
Such an approach, however, presupposes to some extent that Josephus
can justly be regarded as the author of the passages under discussion.
Is that assumption justified, at least as a working hypothesis? Three
factors might seem to militate against it and must be considered here.

I. *The Source Problem*

That Josephus used sources for his presentations of the Pharisees is
undeniable. We must ask, however, whether it would be legitimate, on
the basis of some assured results of scholarship, to begin this study by
designating certain passages as the work of Josephus's sources alone
and therefore as non-Josephan. The question arises with particular
poignancy in relation to *Ant.* 17:41-45, which we shall consider in Part
III. Our concern here is with general principles that obtain for
Josephus's writings as a whole.

The source-critical movement, it will be recalled, proposed various
evidences that Josephus was a rather dull copyist who failed to impart
any independent judgement or outlook to his material. These evidences
can be grouped under three rubrics:

A. Material inconsistencies, such as unfulfilled cross-references,
doublets, dissonant chronological systems, and conflicting high-priest
lists.
B. Stylistic variations, such as Hölscher observed between *War* 1:31-
2:116 and 2:117ff.
C. Circumstances that suggest Josephus's use of large, secondary or intermediate sources. Hölscher, for example, doubted that Josephus used
either the LXX or the Hebrew Bible directly, in *Ant.* 1-11, since he
departs from both.[1] Hölscher also supposed that Josephus's Pharisaic

---

[1] Hölscher, "Josephus", 1952-1955.

education would have prevented him knowing first-hand the many pagan authors that he cites.[2]

With respect to the Pharisee passages in particular: a major criterion of the source critics was that Josephus, being a Pharisee, could not have consistently disparaged his own party. We have seen the importance of this criterion for Hölscher and Schwartz. One of the more enduring proposals of source criticism, it turns up in G. F. Moore, W. Bousset, M. Waxman, and even M. Smith.[3] Although the source critics differed considerably on the actual sources behind the Pharisee passages, they agreed that many of them could not have been written by Josephus; he must have absent-mindedly copied them.

Contemporary scholarship, however, has progressed far beyond the heyday of source criticism. We may note the following insights that would seem to justify the *a priori* assumption of Josephus's authorship of the Pharisee passages.

A. Laqueur demonstrated that Josephus could present his own activities in various, not entirely harmonious, ways. Since there is no question of sources accounting for these differences, one has to reckon with Josephus's own initiative and purposes.

B. Many assumptions of the older source criticism are no longer considered valid. Such an assumption was Hölscher's belief that Josephus's Palestinian education would have precluded a serious knowledge of Greek language and literature on his part.[4] Further, Josephus's supposed allegiance to Pharisaism has been reduced by some scholars (Smith, Neusner, Cohen) to a spurious claim.

C. Hölscher's theory that Josephus used intermediate sources has not worn well.[5] But if intermediate sources are done away with, then Josephus himself was the one who artfully combined, and sometimes criticized,[6] his sources.

---

[2] Ibid., 1957.

[3] Moore, *Judaism*, I, 62 n. 4, 65 n. 3 (on *War* 1:110ff.), 66 n. 1 (on *War* 1:114 and *Ant.* 13:411-417); Bousset, *Religion des Judentums*, 187 (on *Ant.* 17:41ff.); M. Waxman, *A History of Jewish Literature from the Close of the Bible to our own Days* (1932), cited in Feldman, *Modern Scholarship*, 554; Smith, "Palestinian Judaism", 75 (on *War* 1:110-114).

[4] Cf. n. 49 of chapter 2 above.

[5] Cf. Thackeray, *Josephus*, 63, and Momigliano, "Josephus as a Source for the History of Judea", *Cambridge Ancient History*, X: *The Augustan Empire 44 BC - AD 70*, edd. S. A. Cook, F. E. Adcock, and M. P. Charlesworth (Cambridge: University Press, 1966), 885f.

[6] E.g., *Ant.* 16:183-187.

D. Many recent studies have discovered consistent motifs and redactional concerns in Josephus's writings. H. Lindner's study of *War*, for
example, reveals a clear view of history and of Israel in that work.[7]
Analyses of Josephus's biblical paraphrase (*Ant.* 1-11) have demonstrated marked editorial themes.[8] Thus H. W. Attridge discovers "an
important theological dimension in the work of Josephus. . . in its interpretative presentation of scriptural narratives".[9] In Josephus's use of
Aristeas, A. Pelletier likewise points out several discernable tendencies.[10]
H. R. Moehring's conclusion, with respect to the "novelistic elements"
in Josephus's narrative, anticipated the results of these recent studies:
"Josephus can justly be called the author, in the true sense of this term,
of the works attributed to him: even when he borrows . . . he impresses
his own personality upon his work."[11]
E. H. Schreckenberg's analysis of Josephus's style, for text-critical purposes, has also shed light on the fundamental integrity of Josephus's
works. As Schreckenberg notes: "Nicht das unwichtigste Ergebnis der
hier vorgelegten textkritischen Arbeit ist eine neue Einsicht in die
sprachlich-stilistische Einheit der Werke des Josephus, die
verschiedentlich bezweifelt wurde."[12]

The reaction, then, to a source criticism that denied Josephus the true
function of an author has been broadly based and forceful.

For Josephus's Pharisee passages, the following question suggests
itself: if Josephus was so obviously capable of shaping his work to reflect
his own agenda, interests, and style, is it reasonable to suppose that,
when he came to describe the Pharisees—a group of which he had personal knowledge (*Life* 191-198), he simply parroted some remarks from
his pagan sources, without regard for his own sentiments? L. H.
Feldman makes the point well. Noting that Josephus's sources for the
Pharisee passages are, in any case, unknown, he continues:

---

[7] H. Lindner, *Die Geschichtsauffassung des Flavius Josephus im Bellum Judaicum* (Leiden:
E. J. Brill, 1972), 40-45, 141-14.

[8] Cf. M. Braun, *Griechischer Roman und hellenistische Geschichtsschreibung* (Frankfurt: V.
Klostermann, 1934); B. Heller, "Grundzüge der Aggada des Flavius Josephus", *MGWJ*
80 (1936), 237-246; T. W. Franxman, *Genesis and the "Jewish Antiquities" of Flavius
Josephus* (Rome: Biblical Institute Press, 1979), 288f.

[9] H. W. Attridge, *The Interpretation of Biblical History in the Antiquitates Judaicae of Flavius
Josephus* (Missoula: Scholars Press, 1976), 17.

[10] A. Pelletier, *Flavius Josephe: adapteur de la lettre d'Aristée* (Paris: Klincksieck, 1962),
252ff.

[11] H. R. Moehring, "Novelistic Elements in the Writings of Flavius Josephus"
(dissertation, University of Chicago, 1957), 145.

[12] H. Schreckenberg, *Rezeptionsgeschichtliche und textkritische Untersuchungen zu Flavius
Josephus* (Leiden: E. J. Brill, 1977), 173.

> But when we definitely know Josephus' source, as in his restatement of the
> 'Letter of Aristeas', we see that he can rework his source with considerable
> thoroughness. It is hard to believe that in an issue as important as the
> Pharisees, where he had personal knowledge and experience, he chose
> slavishly to reproduce his sources.[13]

To summarize: it is clear that Josephus used sources, especially for events
beyond his own experience. That he used them as an anthologist and not
as an author, however, is a proposition made untenable by several major
studies. One cannot deny that a few clear material inconsistencies remain
in Josephus's works, but these tensions cannot overturn the overwhelming evidence of Josephus's control over his literary productions.[14]

II. *Josephus's Literary Assistants*

It was H. St. John Thackeray, in a 1926 lecture, who proposed that
Josephus had employed literary assistants for the writing of both *War*
and *Ant.* 15-19.[15] Thackeray drew on the following evidence.

A. Josephus's Palestinian background would have prevented him from
mastering Greek; he must have learned his Greek only in Rome. Yet the
style of *War* "is an excellent specimen of the Atticistic Greek of the first
century", and therefore unimaginable from a writer who had previously
written only in Aramaic.[16]

B. In *Ag.Ap.* 1:50, Josephus reports that in writing *War* he had benefited
from "certain collaborators for the sake of the Greek" (τισι πρὸς τὴν
Ἑλληνίδα φωνὴν συνεργοῖς). Although Thackeray had first thought of
these συνεργοί as nothing more than Josephus's "literary friends in
Rome", he came to regard them as slaves, retained by Josephus for their
literary skill.[17]

C. In *Ant.*, Thackeray finds evidence of Josephus's weariness at the end
of book 14, for the account in *War* is repeated almost verbatim. With
book 15, however, a new style and rearrangement of material *vis-à-vis*
War take over. Moreover, *Ant.* 15-16 and 17-19, seen as two blocks,
possess distinctive stylistic features that bear affinities to particular
classes of Greek literature.[18]

---

[13] Feldman, *Modern Scholarship*, 554.
[14] Such problems are common to all writers, especially those of long works—even
when remarkable technological resources are available for assistance!
[15] Thackeray, *Josephus*, 100-124.
[16] Ibid., 101f.
[17] Ibid., 105.
[18] Ibid., 107-115.

In *Ant.* 15-19, therefore, Thackeray discerns the work of two literary assistants, the one "Sophoclean" (books 15-16) and the other a "Thucydidean hack" (books 17-19).

How much leeway did Josephus grant these assistants? Thackeray is not absolutely clear, but he does indicate that after *Ant.* 14, "the work has been entrusted to other hands",[19] and that the Thucydidean was "responsible for writing practically the whole of Books xvii-xix . . .",[20] as well as various "purple patches" in the earlier narrative.[21] In general, the work of Josephus's assistants ranged from "polishing his periods" to "the composition of large portions of the narrative".[22]

For the Pharisee passages, Thackeray's analysis would seem to require that *Ant.* 15:1-4, 365-379 were written by the Sophoclean, *Ant.* 17:41-45 and 18:11-25 by the Thucydidean. (Recall that the source critics, by contrast, attribute *Ant.* 17:41-45 and 18:11-25 to different sources, because of their difference in tone toward the Pharisees.) His interpretation of the συνεργοί as full-fledged writers has not, however, proven durable.

In a 1939 article G. C. Richards showed, on the one hand, that certain characteristics of Josephan style appear in the books that Thackeray had attributed wholly to assistants and, on the other hand, that the imitation of Thucydides in *Ant.* 17-19 is too awkward to be the work of a skilled assistant.[23]

In a 1961 study, R. J. H. Shutt subjected Thackeray's proposal to careful scrutiny and also rejected it.[24] Shutt argued as follows.[25]

A. The break between *Ant.* 14 and 15 is a natural break in the story of Herod: book 14 closes with his entry into Jerusalem, whereas in book 15 he begins to consolidate his position in the city. Further, there are important narrative links between books 14 and 15.[26]
B. *Ant.* 15-16 contains reminiscences of Sophocles but, since Josephus claimed to have studied Greek in Rome (*Ant.* 20:263), that is not surprising. Such reminiscences also occur in *War.*[27]

---

[19] Ibid., 107.
[20] Ibid., 113.
[21] Ibid., 106.
[22] Ibid., 100.
[23] G. C. Richards, "The Composition of Josephus' *Antiquities*", *CQ* 33 (1939), 36-40.
[24] R. J. H. Shutt, *Studies in Josephus* (London: SPCK, 1961), 59-75.
[25] Several of Shutt's arguments were anticipated by H. Peterson, in an incisive footnote to his article, "Real and Alleged Literary Projects of Josephus", *American Journal of Philology* 79 (1958), 260f. n. 5.
[26] Schutt, *Studies*, 63.
[27] Ibid., 64-65.

C. Although Josephus's compositional (as distinct from conversational) Greek may have required assistance when he arrived in Rome and wrote *War*, an assistance that he acknowledges (*Ag.Ap.* 1:50), it seems unlikely that when he came to write *Ant.*, having lived in Rome and studied Greek for many years, he needed the same assistance; he does not acknowledge any.[28]

D. In a detailed examination of the Thucydidean expressions in *Ant.* 17-19, Shutt demonstrated that they are also present in *Ant.* 20 and *Life*, which Thackeray had attributed to the *ipsissima verba* of Josephus.[29] Shutt, therefore, found Thackeray's hypothesis "basically unsound" and "unnecessary". In its place he proposed that Josephus took up a striking phrase, "worked upon it, extended it, in a comparatively short space, and then discarded it", after the manner of Livy.[30]

T. Rajak's recent study of Josephus (1983) has confirmed and extended Shutt's critique of Thackeray.[31] Rajak identifies Josephus as a member of the "upper echelons of the Palestinian priesthood, an outward looking, flexible group", a status indicated by his selection as an emissary to Rome and as a commander in the revolt.[32] In this capacity, Rajak argues, Josephus must have possessed a basic facility in Greek, which could only have been enhanced during his eight years or so of Roman captivity before he wrote *War*.[33] Thus, the kind of linguistic deficiencies for which he required help in the writing of *War* were not basic but involved precision of idiom and style.[34] Rajak thus inclines toward the view discarded by Thackeray, that the συνεργοί of *Ag.Ap.* 1:50 were simply friends who were willing to edit *War* for style, as Agrippa II apparently had done for content (*Life* 364ff.). She remarks:

> It would be rash, therefore, to suppose that he [Josephus] would not be fit, when eventually he came to the Greek *War*, at the very least to collaborate fruitfully with his assistants, and to take the ultimate responsibility for substance and style alike.[35]

---

[28] Ibid., 66-68.

[29] Ibid., 68-74.

[30] Ibid., 74-75.

[31] Rajak, *Josephus*, 47-63, 233-236.

[32] Ibid., 8, 21, 42.

[33] Ibid., 47, 62. Cf. Hengel's comment on life in Palestine even before the Christian era (*Judentum*, 108), that Greek "war die Sprache der Diplomaten wie der Literaten, und wer gesellschaftliches Ansehen oder gar den Ruf ein gebildeter Mann zu sein, suchte, musste sie fehlerfrei beherrschen." Cf. also Laqueur, *Historiker*, 127, and Schreckenberg, *Untersuchungen*, 173.

[34] Ibid., 50.

[35] Ibid., 62-63.

Rajak is especially reluctant to allow the συνεργοί any significant role in *Ant.*, since, as Shutt had noted, Josephus does not acknowledge any assistance for that work.[36] Moreover, she points out, the Sophoclean and Thucydidean styles cannot be attributed to different writers because (a) Thucydideanisms occur throughout Josephus's writings and (b) the two styles are sometimes interwoven in a single passage (e.g. *Ant.* 4:89-95). Rajak's own explanation of these classical reminiscences is that Josephus, as he himself says (*Ant.* 20:263), had studied the classics; she notes that the masters were studied precisely for the purpose of imitation.[37] Other inconsistencies in his writings she attributes to (a) the influences of sources and (b) the occasion and purpose of the writing.

In sum: Richards, Shutt, and Rajak all support Thackeray's observation that Josephus's works exhibit an unevenness of style: they do not, however, endorse the other premises required for his inference that literary assistants actually composed large sections of the narrative. Since no defence of Thackeray's hypothesis has appeared, it would seem legitimate to take the position of the later scholars as the verdict of contemporary scholarship on the συνεργοί:

> It is quite safe to take Josephus's works, starting with the first, the *War*, as his own, and to treat him exactly in the same way as we do other ancient writers. It is as well to dispel all fantastic notions of ghost writers at this early stage.[38]

In this matter, as with the source question, the interpreter of Josephus's Pharisee passages cannot begin by separating some of them as the work of another author.

III. *Christian Influence on the Text*

A third possible reason for suspecting that Josephus was not responsible for all of the Pharisee passages in his works is that those works were preserved from antiquity by the Christian Church, whose anti-Pharisaic stance was already revealed in the Gospels and continued unabated. It is widely believed that the *testimonium flavianum* of Josephus has at least been glossed by a Christian hand.[39] Is it not conceivable, then, that the Church altered Josephus's accounts of the Pharisees, since this group was the object of its displeasure?

---

[36] Ibid., 233-236.
[37] Ibid.
[38] Ibid. 63.
[39] The literature on the *testimonium* is enormous. For a brief overview see the LCL edn. of Josephus, IX, 48ff. (by L. H. Feldman).

Although a logical possibility, the idea of Christian tampering with Josephus's Pharisee passages has hardly ever been put forward. I. Elbogen was one of its few advocates. Arguing that the rabbinic literature offers the only suitable entrée to Pharisaic thought, Elbogen suggested that the Christian copyists who handed down Josephus's writings suppressed (*unterdrückten*) everything in them that was inconvenient for Christian belief; the censored material allegedly contained favourable presentations of the Pharisees.[40] Elbogen pointed to Josephus's repeated claim in *Ant.* (13:173, 298; 18:11) that he had already given a full discussion of the Jewish schools in *War*; but *Ant.* expands considerably on the material that we now possess in *War*. Elbogen proposed that Christian copyists deleted from *War* those descriptions of the Pharisees that contradicted their impressions from the Gospels:

> Da die Pharisäer als die eigentlichen prinzipiellen Gegner des Christentums angesehen wurden, so glaubten man in der Charakteristik des Pharisäertums durch Josephus nicht mehr die Wahrheit zu finden und liesst nur stehen, was neben ihrem von den Evangelien entworfenen Bilde sich sehen lassen konnte.[41]

Elbogen did not actually suggest, then, that copyists altered the Pharisee passages that now stand, only that they deleted a more positive portrayal from *War*. (This theory, significantly, reveals Elbogen's judgement that the remaining Pharisee passages are unfavourable toward the group.)

Unfortunately, Elbogen's idea remained unsubstantiated by more precise indications of what the deleted material had contained, where it had stood, and when it was excised. Without these crucial supports, the hypothesis could not survive.

The other theoretical possibility, of Christian responsibility for the Pharisee passages that remain, runs aground on the circumstance that the passages most hostile toward the Pharisees come in pieces of historical narrative, concerning events under the Hasmoneans and Herod, which the Church can hardly have supplied. Christian influence would thus be limited to some sort of "colouring"; the problem would then be to separate this colouring from Josephus's own contribution.

No hypothesis of Christian tampering with Josephus's Pharisee passages is being proposed in this study and consequently no obligation is assumed to discover the hand of the copyist. For our purpose, it is sufficient to note that the Church's transmission of Josephus's writings has never been shown to have included any tampering with his descriptions of the Pharisees.

---

[40] Elbogen, *Religionsanschauungen*, 4.
[41] Ibid.

Summary

Three factors might seem to complicate any attempt to read Josephus's writings as his own compositions. They are: (a) his use of sources; (b) his use of literary assistants; and (c) the Church's transmission of his works. It is impossible to rule out any of these factors *a priori* as possible influences on the accounts of the Pharisees that appear in Josephus. Nevertheless, the results of recent scholarship establish a strong *prima facie* case for the presumption of Josephus's authorial responsibility. We have no basis in the results of contemporary research to claim that any single passage on the Pharisees must be separated at the outset, as the work of someone other than Josephus himself.

If striking inconsistencies should appear among Josephus's Pharisee passages, they will call for an explanation. In that case, one possibility would be difference of authorship, a theme that has three variations. Our first task, however, is to try to interpret Josephus's statements about the Pharisees within the context of his own thought and writing, as his own testimony.

PART TWO

THE PHARISEES IN THE *JEWISH WAR*

Between AD 75 and 79 Josephus completed his history of the "Jewish war" in Greek.[1] By that time he had been granted Roman citizenship and was lodged securely in the emperor's former residence.

So far as is known, Josephus's first published descriptions of the Pharisees are those contained in *War*.[2] To understand what Josephus wished to convey about the Pharisees to the readers of his first work is the purpose of Part II. We shall look first at the purpose and outlook of *War* and then at the relevant passages.

---

[1] The *terminus a quo* is the dedication of the Temple of Peace in AD 75 (Dio Cassius 66:15), which is mentioned by Josephus in *War* 7:158. The *terminus ad quem* is the death of Vespasian in AD 79, for Josephus would later claim (*Life* 359, 361) that he had presented a copy of *War* to Vespasian. It is possible, as S. J. D. Cohen (*Josephus*, 84-87) suggests, that the version presented to Vespasian was incomplete and that the later books were only completed after 79. For our purposes, a decision on this point is unnecessary; the Pharisee material of *War* falls exclusively in the first two books.

[2] This would be true even if Laqueur's theory were accepted. He argues that at the heart of Josephus's *Life* (issued after AD 100, he thinks) lies a much earlier document, a self-justifying presentation of his command in the Galilee, which he submitted to the Jerusalem authorities in AD 66/67 (Laqueur, *Historiker*, 121). Of the two Pharisee passages in *Life*, however, Laqueur attributes the first (*Life* 10-12) to the polemic of the final version (pp. 54f., 246) and therefore to a period after 100. The second passage (*Life* 189-198), it is true, occurs in a block that Laqueur attributes to the earlier *Rechenschaftsbericht* (p. 114). Since, however, the Pharisees are introduced there as if they were unknown to the reader, the passage could hardly have been written for the Jerusalem authorities, who were the intended recipients of the *Rechenschaftsbericht* (p. 121). I shall treat both passages in *Life*, therefore, as later discussions of the Pharisees than those found in *War*, without otherwise debating the merits of Laqueur's theory at this point.

CHAPTER THREE

PURPOSE AND OUTLOOK OF THE *JEWISH WAR*

Fortunately for the interpreter of *War*, Josephus takes some trouble to enunciate his goals and point of view, both in the proem to *War* itself and in later reflective comments on that work.[3] Among all of these elaborate statements of intention, however, one item has riveted the attention of much twentieth-century scholarship. It is Josephus's notice that in the Greek *War* he was providing for a Greek-speaking audience what he had already composed in his native language (τῇ πατρί) for the Parthians, Babylonians, and others (*War* 1:3, 6). This reference to an earlier, presumably Aramaic,[4] edition of *War* has for many scholars provided the key to the purpose of the extant Greek version.

I. *Historical Approaches*

R. Laqueur posed the inevitable question:

> was es besagen soll, wenn in der ersten Hälfte der siebzigen Jahre der vom Kaiser bezahlte und mit einer Villa beschenkte jüdische Schriftsteller in Rom in aramäischer Sprache ein Werk verfasste, welches für den fernen Orient bestimmt war.[5]

His now classic answer was that Josephus wrote *War* on behalf of the emperor Vespasian, to be a vehicle of imperial policy in the Orient. It was an official propaganda piece, calculated to deflate any ambitions the "oberen Barbaren" may have been nursing for a campaign against Rome. Laqueur's evidence was elaborated by H. St. John Thackeray and the results may be summarized as follows.[6]

A. That the Parthians and their neighbours constituted a threat to Rome Laqueur and Thackeray infer from various sources. In the mid-40's, according to Josephus (*Ant.* 20:69-74), the Parthian king Vardanes contemplated a war with Rome. In the preface to *War* (1:4) Josephus notes that the Jewish rebels hoped for assistance from their fellows beyond the Euphrates and that, with the revolt, the Eastern Empire was

---

[3] Cf., in particular, *Ant.* 1:1-4; *Life* 361-367; *Ag.Ap.* 1:47-56.

[4] So the common opinion, but cf. J.M. Grintz, "Hebrew as the Spoken and Written Language in the Last Days of the Second Temple", *JBL* 79 (1960), 32-47.

[5] Laqueur, *Historiker*, 126.

[6] Laqueur, *Historiker*, 126-127; Thackeray, *Josephus*, 27-28.

placed in jeopardy. Agrippa is made to ask the rebels, rhetorically, whether they are expecting help from the Jews of Adiabene (*War* 2:388); indeed, some proselytes from that country did join the revolt (*War* 5:474). Pliny (*Panegyric on Trajan* 14) reports that the Parthians came very close to war with Rome in AD 75. And finally, we know that the Jewish Diaspora in Mesopotamia did revolt under Trajan in 115-117.

B. The invincibility and fortune of Rome are recurring themes throughout *War*.[7] In his appeal to the rebels to quit their insurrection, Agrippa repeatedly cites Rome's δύναμις and τύχη (2:360, 373, 387). Josephus draws a compelling portrait of Roman military procedures (3:70-107), by which he intends to offer "consolation to those who have been conquered and *dissuasion to those contemplating revolt*" (3:108).

C. That *War* possessed some sort of official status is suggested by the circumstances in which it was written. The Aramaic version, which seems to have been Josephus's first literary project in Rome under Flavian sponsorship, was dispatched with notable speed. Upon completing the Greek edition, Josephus presented copies immediately to Vespasian and Titus (*Ag.Ap.* 1:51; *Life* 361); the latter, we are told, intended that Josephus's *War* should become the standard account of the conflict in Palestine and to that end ordered its publication (*Life* 363). Finally, Josephus's glorification of the future emperors, especially Titus, is so pronounced that W. Weber could posit as the principal source for *War* a Flavian work that recounted the rise of this dynasty to power.[8]

Taken together, these three groups of evidence seem to lend considerable support to the Laqueur/Thackeray interpretation of the motive behind *War*:

> Josephus was commissioned by the conquerors to write the official history of the war for propagandistic purposes. It was a manifesto, intended as a warning to the East of the futility of further opposition and to allay the after-war thirst for revenge which ultimately found vent in the fierce outbreaks under Trajan and Hadrian.[9]

This view of the Aramaic *War*'s purpose has become standard.[10] Most of its sponsors appear to believe that in uncovering the purpose of the

---

[7] Cf. now Lindner, *Geschichtsauffassung*, 42ff., 89ff.

[8] W. Weber, *Josephus und Vespasian* (Berlin-Stuttgart-Leipzig: W. Kohlhammer, 1921).

[9] Thackeray, *Josephus*, 27.

[10] Cf., e.g., Shutt, *Studies*, 26; M. Hengel, *Die Zeloten* (Leiden: E. J. Brill, 1961), 7, 10f., 11 n. 1; J. Goldin, "Josephus", *IDB*, II, 987; A. Momigliano, "Josephus as a Source", 884; S. Safrai and M. Stern, edd., *The Jewish People in the First Century* ("Compendia Rerum Iudaicarum ad Novum Testamentum", 1; Assen: Van Gorcum & Co., 1974), 24; Z. Yavetz, "Reflections on Titus and Josephus", *Greek, Roman, and Byzantine Studies* 16 (1975), 421; O. Michel and O. Bauernfeind, edd., *De Bello Judaico: Der jüdische*

lost Aramaic work they have also discovered the intention of the extant *War*; the latter is seen as but a Greek version of the former.[11]

A number of considerations, however, would seem to call for a reappraisal of Josephus's intention in the *Jewish War*.

A. In the first place, it is not clear that Parthia posed a serious threat to Rome in the early 70's, when Josephus wrote *War*.[12] In AD 63, the two powers had concluded a major peace treaty:[13] after that, the prevailing atmosphere seems to have been one of peace and cooperation, if only out of mutual self-interest.[14] The single known rupture during this period, noted by Laqueur, was an exception to the rule and, in any case, was resolved diplomatically.[15] Josephus alludes to the calm relations when he has Agrippa say that the rebels ought not to expect help from the Jews of Adiabene, for even if the latter wanted to intervene, their Parthian overlord would prevent it because of his truce with Rome (*War* 2:389).

B. Even if the Parthians had been of a mind to challenge Rome, as Rajak points out, it is doubtful whether they (a) could have distilled a clear propagandistic message from the lengthy narrative of *War*[16] or (b) would have been moved to reconsider their designs because of the fate of tiny Judea.[17]

C. Although it is clear from Josephus's own statements that *War* received some sort of official recognition subsequent to its publication (*Life* 361ff.), this does not imply that the work had its genesis in a "commission" from the emperor to write a propagandistic account of the revolt. Even Thackeray, who sponsored the propaganda theory, conceded that Josephus "was no mere hireling; his own deepest convictions told him that the only road to amelioration of his nation's unhappy lot lay in submission to the empire".[18] A perusal of the speeches in *War* (which are

---

Krieg (4 vols.; Darmstadt: Wissenschaftliche Buchgesellschaft, 1959), I, XXIf.; and the discussion in G. Hata, "Is the Greek Version of Josephus' *Jewish War* a Translation or a Rewriting of the First Version?" *JQR* 66 (1975), 106f.

[11] Of the scholars mentioned in the previous note, only the last two, so far as I can discern, make a clear conceptual distinction between the purpose of the Greek *War* and that of its Semitic predecessor.

[12] Cf. Rajak, *Josephus*, 182f.

[13] Cf. J. G. C. Anderson, "The Eastern Frontier from Tiberius to Nero", *Cambridge Ancient History*, X, 770f.

[14] Cf. the examples of Parthian cooperation with Rome given by R. Syme, "Flavian Wars and Frontiers", *Cambridge Ancient History*, XI, 139-144.

[15] Ibid., 143.

[16] Yavetz ("Reflections", 431), points out the limited value of historical narrative as "a major means of propaganda" in the Roman world.

[17] Rajak, *Josephus*, 180.

[18] Thackeray, *Josephus*, 29. Cf. B. Niese, "Josephus", *ERE*, VII, 571.

Josephan creations) confirms this assessment.[19] Lindner discovers in the
speeches a religiously based argument, not superficially overlaid, that
fortune (τύχη) has passed to the Romans.[20] Rajak is able to trace
Josephus's political sentiments to his upbringing and social position;
they are not the contrived slogans of propaganda.[21] Yavetz proposes that
even Josephus's flattery of Titus stemmed from genuine admiration and
gratitude.[22] In any case, the same attitude of submission to Rome that
we find in *War* appears also in *Life* (cf. 17ff.), which Josephus wrote
more than two decades after the revolt.

So the question urges itself: If Josephus's portrayal of the Romans'
might and divinely ordained rule springs from his own convictions, and
if this respectful portrayal explains the Flavian endorsement of *War*
subsequent to its publication (of which he speaks), where is the evidence
that *War* was conceived as a propaganda piece?

D. Most problematic of all, the Laqueur/Thackeray theory depends
for its viability on a close similarity between the extant Greek *War* and
the lost Aramaic version. This is clear in two connections. First, the contents of the Aramaic version are inferred from the Greek: scholars cite
the prologue, the speeches, and even the references to Roman τύχη as
evidence for the purpose of the original Aramaic edition. Then they co-
opt the intention of the Aramaic *War*, discovered in this manner, for the
Greek version.

Almost no one, however—least of all Laqueur and Thackeray, really
believes the Greek *War* to be a translation or even a close paraphrase of
the Aramaic. Even though the μεταβάλλω of *War* 1:3 is customarily
rendered "translate/übersetzen", the modern editors who use such
equivalents are quick to add that the Greek can be a translation only in
the very loosest sense. It shows no clear evidence of a Semitic
substratum.[23] Indeed, "The style of the whole work is an excellent
specimen of the Atticistic Greek fashionable in the first century", according to Thackeray.[24] This suggests to him that the Greek *War* has
been "practically rewritten" *vis-à-vis* the Aramaic.[25]

The indications that our Greek *War* is an original Greek production

---

[19] Cf. Lindner, *Geschichtsauffassung*, 21ff. and 41f. (in reaction to Thackeray's propaganda theory).
[20] Ibid., 92.
[21] Rajak, *Josephus*, 185.
[22] Yavetz, "Reflections", 424-426.
[23] Michel-Bauernfeind, *De Bello Judaico*, I, 403 n. 3.
[24] Thackeray, *Josephus*, 34; cf. LCL edn., II, ix.
[25] Ibid.

are numerous and obvious.[26] In addition to the absence of translation-Greek, noted above, the reader of *War* is confronted by several forms that are native to Greek literature.[27] They include the carefully formulated prologue,[28] the rhetorically honed speeches with their philosophical vocabulary,[29] the entertaining digressions, and the many dramatic-novelistic episodes.[30] These formal traits combine to locate the extant *War* squarely within the Hellenistic historical tradition.

Further, although Josephus mentions the Aramaic version in his prologue to *War*, his later discussions of *War* refer only to the final Greek version.[31] As G. Hata points out, the words used by Josephus to describe the writing of *War* (γράφω, συγγράφω, *Ant.* 1:5; 20:258) do not suggest translation.[32]

Finally, Hata also argues that the verb μεταβάλλω, which Josephus uses to describe the relationship between the Greek *War* and its Aramaic predecessor (*War* 1:3), rarely means "translate" outside of Josephus and, elsewhere in *War*, always means "to change something fundamentally". Therefore, he argues, it ought to be understood in *War* 1:3 in the sense "to rewrite".[33]

Although it cannot be denied, then, that Josephus's Greek *War* was preceded by an Aramaic account of the revolt, the relationship between the two works is a matter of conjecture. B. Niese long ago commented:

---

[26] Laqueur's reason for believing this was that the Greek *War* had made use of the Greek *Rechenschaftsbericht*, whereas the Aramaic had not (*Historiker*, 126, 128). Since, however, the very existence of the *Rechenschaftsbericht* is not at all secure (cf. Cohen, *Josephus*, 18), this argument cannot now be used with force.

[27] Cf. G. Hata, "Greek Version", 106f.

[28] Cf. H. Lieberich, *Studien zu Proömien in der griechischen und byzantinischen Geschichtschreibung*, I: *Die griechischen Geschichtschreiber* (Munich: J. G. Weiss, 1899), 34; D. Earl, "Prologue-form in Ancient Historiography", *Aufstieg und Niedergang der römischen Welt* (Berlin-New York: W. de Gruyter, 1972), I. 2, 842-856. Clearly, whatever prologue the Aramaic version had must have differed somewhat from the Greek, since the latter reflects on the earlier version.

[29] Cf. E. Norden, *Die antike Kunstprosa* (5th. edn.; Darmstadt: Wissenschaftliche Buchgesellschaft, 1958 [1898]), I, 89; H. J. Cadbury et al., "The Greek and Jewish Traditions of Writing History", in *The Beginnings of Christianity*, edd. F. J. Foakes Jackson, K. Lake, and H. J. Cadbury (London: Macmillan, 1922), II, esp. 12f.; G. Avenarius, *Lukians Schrift zur Geschichtsschreibung* (Meisenheim-Glan: A. Hain, 1956), 149-157; Lindner, *Geschichtsauffassung*, 21ff., 85ff.

[30] Cf. H. R. Moehring, "Novelistic Elements". On all of the enumerated points see Hata, "Greek Version", 96-106, and Rajak, *Josephus*, 176.

[31] Cf. *Ant.* 1:1-4; *Life* 361-367; *Ag.Ap.* 1:47-52. The passage in the *Life* appears to leave little room for an Aramaic *Vorlage*.

[32] Hata, 94f., seems to have overlooked the appearance of ἑρμηνεύω in the epilogue to *War* (7:455), which certainly can have the meaning "translate". In the context there, however, the word seems to refer to the stylistic formulation of the narrative in *War* (cf. *War* 1:16, 30), as Thackeray's translation indicates.

[33] Hata, "Greek Version", 90-95.

> No part of this Aramaic record has come down to us, and we are, therefore, not in a position to fix its relation to the extant Greek narrative. The latter was probably a complete recast, constructed on a more comprehensive plan.[34]

Our present *War* is an independent, self-contained Greek production. Fascinating as it may be to speculate about the lost Aramaic treatise, it would be vain either to infer the contents of that document out of the Greek version or, conversely, to transfer its alleged purpose to the Greek version. If one's goal is to interpret the extant work, then one ought to begin with that work itself and with its own statements of purpose.

The widespread scholarly neglect of Josephus's declared literary aims is particularly baffling in light of the rationale for the prologue in Hellenistic historiography. For the prologue was intended, first, to inform the potential reader of the content and perspective of the work and, second, to stimulate the reader's interest by indicating the significance or usefulness of the subject.[35] The potential reader should have been able, merely by unrolling the first few lines of the papyrus scroll in hand, to determine its subject, scope, and tone.[36] If he opted to read it, the prologue would serve as a guide, according to which the whole could be interpreted.[37] Since the proem to *War* seems intended to satisfy these ancient requirements, it would seem appropriate for the modern interpreter of *War* to begin with that opening statement, where Josephus intended his readers to begin.

II. *Exegesis of the Prologue to War*

The preface to *War* is at once thoroughly conventional and strikingly original. It is conventional inasmuch as it furnishes examples of most of the τόποι that had come to be associated with historical prefaces since the time of Thucydides.[38] In keeping with the dual purpose of the preface—to inform and to arouse interest—commonplace remarks on such themes as the following had become standard:[39] the subject and its importance

---

[34] B. Niese, "Josephus", *ERE*, VII, 571.

[35] Cf. Lucian, *How to Write History* 51-53; Lieberich, *Proömien*, 5, 12; Avenarius, *Lukians Schrift*, 115f.

[36] Earl, "Prologue-form", 856.

[37] Lieberich, *Proömien*, 47.

[38] A handy collection of Greek and Hellenistic historical prefaces is provided, in translation, by A. Toynbee, *Greek Historical Thought* (New York: New American Library, 1952 [1924]), 29-97.

[39] Cf. especially the prologues of Thucydides, Polybius, Diodorus Siculus, Dionysius of Halicarnassus, and Herodian; also Earl, "Prologue-form", 842-845. Lieberich, *Proö-*

(cf. *War* 1:1, 4-5); the author's credentials (1:3); reasons for and circumstances of writing (1:2, 6);[40] the inadequacy of previous treatments of the subject (1:2, 7-8);[41] the causes of the events in question (1:10); the author's strenuous efforts at accuracy (1:15-16);[42] his utter impartiality and concern for truth (1:2, 6, 9, 16, 30);[43] his historiographical outlook (1:13-16?);[44] and an outline of the work's contents (1:17-30). These conventional notices account for practically the whole of the preface to *War*.

Adherence to convention, however, does not automatically preclude significance. D. Earl aptly comments:

> Beginnings are a problem. The first paragraph is difficult; the first sentence frequently impossible. Tradition and style may help. To the Greeks, who tended to stylize everything, this appeared the solution.[45]

Just as the τόποι of the modern scholarly preface (e.g., circumstances of writing, acknowledgements) do not suggest a perfunctory attitude on the author's part, the standardization of the Greek historical prologue served not to stifle creativity but to facilitate the introduction of the subject. The challenge facing the historian was to preserve the conventions, which had been canonized by the masters and elaborated by rhetorical theory,[46] while at the same time fashioning a unique and compelling prologue, determined by the subject at hand.[47]

War 1:1-8

Judged by this standard, the prologue to *War* is a success: Josephus has crafted an engaging invitation to his subject. Within the first sentence he delivers the core of his argument, the conclusion of which is that he ought to write an account in Greek of the Jewish war against the Romans (1:3). This conclusion is supported by three premises and each of these is, in turn, the conclusion of a subordinate argument. The three premises are as follows.

---

mien, *passim*, discusses the development of the prologue-form through the Greco-Roman period.

[40] Cf. Dio Cassius 5.72.23.

[41] Cf. Dionysius 1:3-6; Herodian 1.1.1.

[42] Cf. Diodorus 1:4 and Dionysius, *Rom.Ant.* 1:8.

[43] Cf. Thucydides 1:21; Lucian, *History* 38-39.

[44] Cf. Polybius 9:2; Diodorus 1:4; Dionysius, *Rom.Ant.* 1:7-8; Arrian 1.1-3. I shall argue, however, that *War* 1:13-16 does not really reflect Josephus's historiography.

[45] Earl, "Prologue-form", 842.

[46] For the pervasiveness of rhetorical influence on Hellenistic historical writing, cf. Norden, *Kunstprosa*, I, 81; Lieberich, *Proömien*, 5, 17, 20; F. Halbfas, *Theorie und Praxis in der Geschichtsschreibung bei Dionysius von Halicarnassus* (Münster: Westfälische Vereinsdrückerei, 1910), 7-10; Avenarius, *Lukians Schrift*, 167.

[47] Lieberich, *Proömien*, 13.

1. The Jewish-Roman war is an important subject for Greek-speaking readers (1:1, 4-6, 8). It is important because: (a) it placed the eastern empire in jeopardy (1:4-5); (b) it required large numbers of forces on both sides, along with extreme effort and considerable time (1:8); and (c) it is unseemly that the remotest non-Hellenes should have been accurately (ἀκριβῶς) informed about the war, thanks to an earlier work by Josephus, while the Greeks remain in ignorance (1:6).

2. Previous accounts of the war are totally lacking in historical accuracy (τὸ ἀκριβὲς τῆς ἱστορίας, 1:2).[48] (a) Some were written by authors who lacked first-hand knowledge and had, therefore, to rely on poor sources and on their own rhetorical skills (1:1). (b) Other authors were indeed eyewitnesses, but they falsified (καταψεύδονται) their accounts, out of either flattery of the Romans or hatred of the Jews (1:2), which means that the Jews always appeared in a bad light (1:7-8). Josephus reprises this theme at the end of 1:6, where he allows that the Greeks and Romans should not be left with flattering (κολακείαις) or fictitious (πλάσμασι) accounts of such an important event.

3. Josephus is in a unique position to make good the deficiency, that is, to provide a complete and accurate (μετ' ἀκριβείας, 1:9) account of the war (1:6, 9). His credentials are: (a) that he is a Jerusalemite priest, a living specimen of the exotic nation in question; (b) that he personally fought against the Romans; and (c) that, by force of circumstance, he has been in a position to observe the Roman side as well (1:3).

From the first sentence of *War* (= 1:1-6), then, the reader learns that the subject is important, that previous treatments in Greek are misleading, and that Josephus will exploit his uniquely informed position to provide the requisite accuracy. Indeed, these arguments all appear within the first division of the sentence (1:1-3). §§ 4-5 is a parenthetical elaboration of the war's importance and § 6 summarizes the whole. §§ 7-8 elaborate on the ineptitude of the war's previous chroniclers.

War 1:9-12

With § 9 Josephus narrows the focus from a general conspectus of his subject and its importance to the specific purposes and themes of his work. Thus the paragraph §§ 9-12 constitutes something like a "thesis

---

[48] Even allowing for rhetorical exaggeration, Josephus's statements presuppose at least two previous accounts of the war. Like his Aramaic account, they must have appeared shortly after the war's end. This circumstance takes the force out of Thackeray's proposal that the speed with which the Aramaic version was dispatched reflected its urgent official purpose.

statement'' for *War*. In a smooth transition from §§ 7-8, he begins by
disavowing any intention to imitate the Roman chauvinist historians by
exaggerating the feats of his countrymen. Rather, his sole aim will be to
portray both sides with accuracy (μετ' ἀκριβείας, 1:9).

At this point, however, Josephus runs into some difficulty. He has set
for himself a high standard of ἀλήθεια and ἀκρίβεια, over against the
treatments of his Roman contemporaries. Yet he declares that he plans
to add his own commentary to the events (ἐπὶ τοῖς πράγμασι τοὺς λόγους
ἀνατίθημι) and to allow his own feelings rein to lament his country's
misfortune (τοῖς ἐμεαυτοῦ πάθεσι διδοὺς ἐπολοφύρεσθαι ταῖς τῆς πατρίδος συμ-
φοραῖς). His basis for lament—and this is the *Leitmotif* of *War*—is that it
was domestic troublemakers (οἱ 'Ιουδαίων τύραννοι) and no foreign army
that brought the downfall of Jerusalem (1:10-12). Josephus is aware that
the elaboration of strong personal feelings may be considered inappropriate to the ἀκρίβεια of history: he predicts that someone (τις) might
take him to task (συκοφαντοίη) and he even admits that such self-
expression contravenes the ''law of history'' (τὸν τῆς ἱστορίας νόμον,
1:11).

This law of history merits further attention. Cicero declares that the
first two laws (*leges*) of history are that one must dare to speak only the
truth (*ne quid falsi dicere audeat*) and one must dare to speak the whole
truth (*ne quid veri non audent*); there is to be no hint of partiality (*gratiae*)
or of malice (*simulatis*).[49] He allows that the *leges* of poetry and history
are different, since the latter is judged only by the standard of truth (*ad
veritatem*).[50] Some decades after Josephus, Lucian echoed these high standards: the historian must write as if he were a stranger to all countries,
without pity (ἐλεῶν), shame (αἰσχυνόμενος), or special pleading
(δυσωπούμενος). This principle of impassiveness, says Lucian,
Thucydides long ago enshrined as a law (ἐνομοθέτησεν).[51] Evidently,
then, the law of history was often considered to exclude any personal
feelings. As Avenarius remarks, ''Zu einer objektiven Wahrheitsfindung
gehört . . . die Ausschaltung persönlicher Gefühle.''[52]

---

[49] Cicero, *On the Orator* 1:62.
[50] Cicero, *Laws* 1:5.
[51] Lucian, *History* 41. The value of this treatise for understanding Hellenistic
historiography has been significantly increased by Avenarius's study of the work. He
shows (*Lukians Schrift*, 165-178) that practically every one of its assertions reflects a commonplace of that historical tradition. We may, therefore, view the work not as an
idiosyncratic production of the mid-second century but as a repository of Hellenistic insight into historical method, which had its roots in Thucydides and Polybius. Since Lucian's work is the only thing resembling a manual of historical method that has come
down from antiquity, the service that Avenarius has performed is immense.
[52] Avenarius, *Lukians Schrift*, 41.

Josephus reveals his familiarity with this ideal of objectivity both in
the prologue passage under discussion and again in 5:19-20. Having described there the desperate plight of Jerusalem under various rebel factions, and having addressed an impassioned lament to the city in the
second person (5:19), he immediately recants:

> By the law of history, however, one has to restrain even one's emotions
> (καθεκτέον γὰρ καὶ τὰ πάθη τῷ νόμῳ τῆς συγγραφῆς) as this is not the occasion
> for personal lamentations (ὀλοφυρῶν οἰκείων) but for a narrative of events.[53]

This apology is hardly convincing, since he has already declared (in the
preface) his intention to give his πάθη free rein; he will later indulge in
lament without regret. The confession does, however, confirm that he
was aware of a principle of objectivity that excluded personal feeling.

Josephus's difficulty, then, appears to be as follows. On the one hand,
he has justified his own work by asserting that all previous histories have
missed the standard of ἀλήθεια; they are strong on denunciation and encomium but nowhere exhibit τὸ ἀκριβὲς τῆς ἱστορίας (1:2). When, however, he comes to state that his own goal will be ἀκρίβεια pure and simple
(1:9), he must concede that he will not on that account exclude his own
opinions, especially his lament for his country's misfortunes (1:10). He
also makes clear at this early stage that he harbours no ill will toward
Titus and the Romans for the fall of his city; for them he has only esteem
(1:10). For these intrusions of πάθος, which violate the law of history, he
asks pardon (συγγνώμη, 1:11).

What are we to make of this pleading tone? Can it be that Josephus
is here, in his opening lines, confessing his failure to live up to the ideals
of history and breathing a hopeful prayer that, in spite of his failings,
someone might be willing to read further? Hardly. As we have seen, the
purpose of the preface was to excite interest and to stimulate the reader
to read further. From that perspective, one may note at least four ways
in which Josephus's professed violation of historical convention actually
serves his ends well and lends power to his preface.

1. First, as Lieberich points out, Josephus's intended Greco-Roman
readership (1:6, 16) might have been reluctant to pick up a book written
by a Jew, purporting to tell how his country was destroyed by the
Romans.[54] The potential reader might have balked at the prospect of a
new history that promised not to flatter the Romans (1:2, 7-8) but to tell
the truth about how they quelled the revolt (1:9). If Josephus desires a
wide readership, therefore, he must make it plain in his prologue that

---

[53] Josephus may be making a similar point in 7:274.
[54] Lieberich, *Proömien*, 33f.

he does not intend to heap guilt on the Romans. This goal he achieves by locating all responsibility for the revolt in the domestic strife (στάσις οἰκεία) engineered by a handful of Jewish power-mongers (οἱ Ἰουδαίων τύραννοι, 1:10). The reader is put at ease when Josephus confirms that the cause of the catastrophe was not any foreign nation (1:12). If Josephus is not out to encourage anti-Semitism (1:2), he nevertheless makes no *a priori* demand that the reader disavow entrenched prejudices and adopt a critical stance toward Rome. This book will be "safe" reading. Thus relieved, the reader can easily forgive Josephus's transgression of strict historical convention.

2. This attempt to set the reader at ease is not a mere invention for the prologue, however, but arises out of Josephus's deepest sentiments as these come into view throughout the book. In the prologue, he expresses his lament over Jerusalem with the words ἐπολοφύρομαι (1:9), ὀλοφύρσις, and ὀδυρμός (1:12). This theme of lament he will pick up quite early in the narrative (2:455; 4:128) and he will re-emphasize it as the catastrophe draws nearer.[55]

Lindner has pointed out striking parallels between Josephus's lament over the city and the lamentations of Jeremiah.[56] Josephus differs from Jeremiah, however, in his assigning of blame to a few tyrants only (rather than to all of Zion) and in his friendly portrayal of the occupying power (whereas Jeremiah had presented the Babylonians as the enemy).[57] And these two peculiar points coincide with the πάθη that Josephus introduces in §§ 9-12, namely, his disgust for the rebels and his esteem for Titus and the Romans. Each of these themes will be recalled frequently, justified by further information, and otherwise developed throughout the body of *War*. The reader is offered a taste of things to come in Josephus's outline of the book's contents (1:19-29), where he promises to describe the ironic savagery of the Jewish rebels toward their own (ὁμοφύλους) and the consideration shown by the Romans toward ἀλλοφύλους (1:27).

Thus the paragraph §§ 9-12 is the vehicle by which Josephus introduces the leading themes of his work. Since those themes contravene historical convention, because they express the historian's personal emotions, it is only by tampering with the convention that Josephus can find a place for them.

3. A third benefit that accrues to Josephus by his appearing to break with convention is the resulting sense of immediacy. Josephus shatters

[55] Cf. *War* 5:19-20; 6:7, 96-111, 267, 271-274.
[56] Lindner, *Geschichtsauffassung*, 133-140.
[57] Ibid., 139f.

any suspicion that he might be a perfunctory historian, dutifully and dispassionately recounting the events of a far-off war. On the contrary, he claims that the sheer weight of the catastrophe in his homeland compels him to transgress the pettiness of convention:

> For of all the cities under Roman rule it was the lot of ours to attain the highest felicity and to fall to the lowest depths of calamity. Indeed, in my opinion, the misfortunes of all nations since the world began fall short of those of the Jews. (1:11-12; Thackeray)

By appealing to the enormousness of the events as justification for breaking a rule of historical writing, Josephus meets the challenge of creativity. The reader is drawn by events so tragic that the author cannot recount them with the usual detached style. He comes to share Josephus's impatience with any critic who might be too harsh (σκληρότερος) for compassion (οἶκτος, 1:12).

4. Finally, Josephus's apparent disregard for historiographical norms actually enhances his credibility as a historian. He has only been driven to inject his emotions, he repeatedly says, because the country whose misfortunes are the subject of his work is *his* homeland (ἡ πατρίς, 1:9, 10; τὴν ἡμετέραν, 1:11). Josephus will not allow the reader to forget that this is the Jerusalemite priest writing, one who personally fought against the Romans and who possesses first-hand knowledge of the entire war from both sides (cf. 1:3). This αὐτοψία—the most prized possession of a historian[58]—is Josephus's single greatest asset and he cannot let it slip by the reader. He admits to strong emotions about his subject but he emphasizes that they arise precisely from his close involvement with the events, which is itself a virtue.[59] Indeed, it is probably to drive home this advantage that Josephus includes the following lengthy attack on certain Greek savants (1:13-16), to which we shall turn presently.

Before proceeding to that passage, however, we might ask how serious a violation of convention Josephus's introduction of evaluative judgements really was. It is true that the attack on encomium and invective in historical writing, which Josephus also wages (1:2), was widespread in his time.[60] Curiously, however, the most vociferous spokesman

---

[58] Cf. Thucydides 1:21; Polybius 4.2.1-4; Lucian, *History* 47f.; A. Momigliano, "Tradition and the Classical Historian", in his *Essays in Ancient and Modern Historiography* (Oxford: Basil Blackwell, 1977), 161f.

[59] H. W. Benario (*An Introduction to Tacitus* [Athens GA: University of Georgia Press, 1975], 148) remarks on Tacitus's notoriously exaggerated claim to write *sine ira et studio* (*Annals* 1:; *History* 1:1), "only men who believe deeply about their subject, whether with favor or disfavor, can write great history".

[60] Cf. Diodorus 21.17.4; Polybius 8.8.3-7; 8.11.12; Lucian, *History* 7-13; Herodian 1.1.2; Avenarius, *Lukians Schrift*, 13ff.

of the period for the exclusion of emotions from the "law of history" is
Josephus himself (1:11; 5:19; 7:274), who also turns out to be the most
self-conscious offender! This raises the question whether he really
believed that his expression of feeling would be a hindrance to the reception of his book or, conversely, whether he raised an extreme standard
in order deliberately to transgress it and thereby to achieve the results
that we have noted.

It seems that the latter was the case. For Hellenistic historiography
was open to censure and praise of historical actors, as long as these were
judiciously applied.[61] That is because, as Thucydides had already insisted (1.22.4), the purpose of studying history was to learn from the
mistakes and triumphs of the past. Although this guidance from the past
was at first thought of as primarily strategic and political, under
rhetorical influence it soon widened to include a general moralizing
sense.[62] Even Polybius, the great exemplar of critical historiography,
stressed the moral function of history. He believed that the distinctive
feature of history was its praise (ἔπαινος) for virtuous conduct and its
demonstration of the bases for negative moral judgements (2.61.5-6;
12.15.9). From Polybius onward, moral judgement on characters of the
past (ἔπαινοι καὶ ψόγοι) was an honourable component of historical
writing, provided that it was cautious and demonstrable.[63]

But Josephus attempts from the start to justify, with much evidence,
both his lament over Jerusalem and his strictures on the rebels. It seems,
therefore, that his unsolicited confessions of guilt are actually rhetorical
devices, contrived to show that the events of his narrative are of such import, and that he has been so closely involved in them, that he is pushing
the limits of historical custom simply to recount them.

War 1:13-16

The paragraph on the Hellenic savants (1:13-16) has vexed interpreters,
who generally believe that the recovery of its meaning depends on an
identification of the λόγιοι (1:13); these are usually considered to be a
party of Josephus's opponents. Suggestions for the identification have
ranged from the Roman author of a competing history of the war (so
Schlatter) to Nicolaus of Damascus—Josephus's chief source for the
early part of *War* (Hölscher)—to Josephus's literary assistants
(Thackeray).[64]

[61] Avenarius, *Lukians Schrift*, 25, 157-159.
[62] Ibid., 22f.
[63] Cf. Diodorus 15.1.1; Lucian, *History* 59.
[64] Schlatter, *Bericht*, 44, 67; Hölscher, 1948, Thackeray, *Josephus*, 195.

The purely speculative character of these proposals has been shown by
H. Lindner.[65] His own suggestion, more closely grounded in the text,
draws attention to the legal terminology employed by Josephus: the
learned Greeks "sit in judgement" (κάθηνται κριταί) on current events
(1:13) and where fees (λήμματα) or lawsuits (δίκαι) are concerned, their
oratorial prowess is quickly demonstrated (1:16). Lindner proposes,
then, that the appearance of *War* caused certain Greek historians in
Rome to bring lawsuits against Josephus, who then raised the matter in
his preface.[66] According to Lindner, Josephus polemicizes against his
opponents and their paid lawyers as follows: if they are concerned about
historical truthfulness, then they ought to present their own narratives
of events; the courtroom, in which they can display their oratorial training, is an improper forum for such matters and relieves them of the
labours that Josephus has had to endure.[67] Josephus's legal difficulties
irritate him so much, Lindner suggests, that he embarks on a campaign
against Greek historians generally (1:16), which he will continue in
Ag.Ap. (1:6-29).[68]

By focussing on the legal activity of the Greek λόγιοι, however, Lindner fails to explain the bulk of the paragraph (13-15), which criticizes
their preoccupation with ancient history to the exclusion of current affairs. On his reading, further, the paragraph becomes fundamentally
enigmatic, laced with veiled references to Josephus's present circumstances and including a gratuitous attack on Greek historians in
general. We have seen, however, that the purposes of the Hellenistic
historical preface were to attract, stimulate, and instruct the reader. As
Lieberich points out:

> Das Proömium ist in erster Linie dem Bedürfnis entsprungen, dem Leser
> im voraus eine kurze Aufklärung über das Werk zu bieten, ihm, wie
> Aristoteles treffend sagt, 'eine Handhabe zu geben', dass er sich daran
> halten und der Rede folgen kann.[69]

Until now (1:1-12), Josephus has displayed an acute sensitivity to these
tasks and has handled them deftly. In 1:17-30 he continues to demonstrate his mastery of the prologue form. Is it reasonable, then, to suppose
that Josephus has chosen the mid-point of an otherwise compelling preface to vent his emotions about some undisclosed personal difficulties,

[65] "Eine offene Frage zur Auslegung des Bellum-Proömiums", in *Josephus-Studien*,
edd. O. Betz, K. Haacker, and M. Hengel (Göttingen: Vandenhoeck & Ruprecht,
1974), 255-258.
[66] *Ibid.*, 257f.
[67] Lindner, "Frage", 257f.
[68] Ibid.
[69] Lieberich, *Proömien*, 47f.

thereby creating an obscure paragraph? One expects him, on the contrary, to provide enough information for the reader to follow at least the main lines of his argument, for only by such a course can he hope to fulfill the goal of the preface and to win a substantial readership.

Nearer to the mark is the recent analysis of H. W. Attridge. Attridge's point of departure is the well-known correspondence between Josephus's remarks in 1:13-16 and the historiographical principles of Polybius.[70] Namely: Josephus claims that certain learned men among the "Hellenes" (apparently shorthand for Greeks and Romans, cf. 1:16), although living in a time of stirring events, disparage current affairs as an object of historical research (1:13) and choose rather to write about ancient times, especially the Assyrian and Median empires. Josephus's critique of such a practice comes from many sides: (i) the ancient writers already covered this ground well (§ 13); (ii) their modern counterparts are inferior to them in both literary capacity (δυνάμεως ἐν τῷ γράφειν) and judgement (γνώμης, § 14)[71] and are thus reduced to futile rearrangements of the older accounts (§ 15); (iii) writing about contemporary events has the double advantage of providing the clarity that comes from an eye-witness's perception and of being subject to challenge from other living witnesses (§ 14); (iv) writing about one's own times is in fact the example set by the ancient masters; and (v) writing of contemporary events is the more virtuous enterprise because it requires a really industrious writer (φιλόπονος) who can produce an original historical contribution (§ 15).

All of these historical principles, Josephus charges, have eluded the natural heirs (γνήσιοι) of the Hellenic tradition, who put out their best efforts only in the courtrooms (§ 16). It has fallen to him, therefore, a foreigner (ἀλλόφυλος), to maintain the old virtues of painstaking effort in ascertaining facts and of truthful speaking in historical writing. Historical truthfulness is being slighted by the Hellenes but among the Jews (παρ' ἡμῖν) it is still held in honour (§ 16). Josephus, a prime example of Jewish historiographical prowess, has spared himself neither money (ἀναλώματα) nor labour (πόνος) in producing the present work.

In several places, Polybius defends his own choice of a modern starting point and his mistrust of ancient history (cf. especially 4.2.1-4). He points out, for example, that another historian's work covers the period immediately preceding the one he has chosen (4.2.1). Elsewhere he

---

[70] Attridge, *Interpretation*, 44f.; cf. already Lieberich, *Proömien*, 34, and Avenarius, *Lukians Schrift*, 81.

[71] Significantly, Lucian posits as the two supreme qualifications of the historian "political understanding" (σύνεσις πολιτική) and "power of expression" (δύναμις ἑρμηνευτική).

claims that the whole field of ancient history has been so often and variously worked over that any modern author on the subject faces the equally repugnant alternatives of plagiarism and futile rearrangement (9.2.1-2). Second, he explains that his chosen focal point coincides with his own and the preceding generations, which means that he can always consult living witnesses on his subject (4.2.2) and thereby control his material. To reach any further into the past, he says, would force him to write on the basis of hearsay (ὡς ἀκοὴν ἐξ ἀκοῆς γράφειν), which would preclude certainty (ἀσφαλεῖς) in judgement (4.2.3).[72] Finally, it is only with the events he has chosen to narrate that one can see the hand of Τύχη rebuilding the world (4.2.4). This theme was already sounded in his preface (1.4). Although, however, Polybius claims that it is Fortune's activity that makes contemporary history most compelling (4.2.4), in his polemic against the rhetorical historian Timaeus he draws mainly on the more concrete principles: (i) that what has been covered adequately by others needs no reiteration and (ii) that only what can be checked through living witnesses is secure. To these factors he adds the contrast between the comfortable circumstances in which one may write ancient history (by simply finding a good library!) and the severe hardships (κακοπάθειαι) or even danger (κίνδυνος) that await the personal investigator of events—hardships both physical and financial (12.27.4-6).

On these points (excluding the argument concerning Fortune), it is easy to see shades of Polybius in Josephus's argument in *War* 1:13-16.

The difficulty is to know what to make of the correspondence between the principles of Polybius and *War* 1:13-16. Attridge takes this passage to be Josephus's statement of historiographical principle for *War*, a statement that recognizes only recent events as the proper object of history. When Josephus comes to write *Ant.*, Attridge argues, he will have changed his principles; only his new devotion to the "rhetorical" school of historiography allows him there to write about ancient Jewish history.

A full discussion of the historiography of *War* and *Ant.* would be out of place here. In "Appendix A", at the end of the study, I shall offer some considerations along those lines, in response to Attridge's proposal. These may be summarized, together with our observations thus far, as follows. (a) *War* 1:13-16 contains a critique of those who deal exclusively with ancient history. (b) The arguments assembled to make this point are τόποι of Polybian ilk. (c) By the time of Josephus, however,

---

[72] Cf. the preface to Luke, where the author claims that he can prove τὴν ἀσφαλείαν of the events which he describes (1:4) because: (a) they were accomplished ἐν ἡμῖν— therefore, within living memory (1:1); (b) they were passed on by αὐτόπται (1:2); and (c) they have been followed with accuracy (ἀκριβῶς) from the beginning by the author himself (1:3).

these principles had lost much of their compelling justification; many, if not most historians, were electing to write about antiquity. (d) The polemic against ancient history is wholly unrelated to Josephus's actual views about writing ancient *Jewish* history. The paragraph does not, therefore, represent his statement of historiographical principle. It is unlikely that Josephus had any deep convictions about whether the Hellenes should have been writing ancient or modern history. His own task was Jewish history, which he evidently considered *sui generis* (*Ag.Ap.* 1:29-43).

Why, then, the harangue about the shoddiness and laziness of those Greeks who write ancient history? We have seen that the *mea culpa* in 9-12 achieves many things for Josephus; in particular it serves to remind the reader yet again of the author's privileged status as an eyewitness. This theme he introduces early and emphasizes repeatedly in the preface (1:1, 2, 3, 6, 9-12). He has been driven to contravene the norm of objectivity in historical reporting, he now claims, because the catastrophe happened in his land and he witnessed the patience of the Romans and the obstinacy of the tyrants. Although his confession serves him well, however, Josephus must pay a price for including it. That price is reflected in his final admission (1:12) that some critics (though pettifoggers, to be sure!) might still find fault with him. Although he has attempted to win the reader's support for his unorthodox approach, he cannot yet rest his case. He requires a more persuasive note on which to end.

In order, then, to extricate himself fully from any suspicion of malpractice, Josephus decides to shift attention away from his own possible deficiencies to the comparatively heinous sin of others. Hence the opening words of the paragraph (1:13): καίτοι γε ἐπιτιμήσαιμ᾽ ἂν αὐτὸς δικαίως τοῖς Ἑλλήνων λογίοις, rendered well by Thackeray: "Yet I, on my side, might justly censure those erudite Greeks". If Josephus might be censured (§ 11) for expressing πάθη that result from his proximity to the events, he will hasten to point out a much more serious failure on the part of his contemporaries: many of them do not even possess that treasured quality of first-hand knowledge. Under the *Pax Romana* it was rare that educated writers found themselves in the midst of momentous upheavals, of the sort that Thucydides had witnessed.[73] For this and other reasons historians had come, by the first century, to deal primarily with events of bygone ages (see Appendix A). But the great historians who had been able to write of current events retained their glory, as Momigliano remarks:

---

[73] Avenarius, *Lukians Schrift*, 83f.

In Late Antiquity antiquarians were in a mood of self-congratulation. Yet they never get the upper hand. The prestige of the interpreter of recent events—of Herodotus, Thucydides, Polybius . . . remained unshaken.[74]

It is this prestige that Josephus wants to share. He fully realizes his incredible good luck, from a historian's perspective, in having witnessed first-hand the events of a major war from both sides. His eyewitness status is therefore the theme of the whole preface to *War* (1:1-3). To reinforce his point now, Josephus reaches into the reservoir of Hellenistic historiography and draws out an appropriate and venerable weapon, the Polybian attack on ancient history.

The Polybian broadside, however, is only a tool in Josephus's hands. If, as seems probable, he had no stake whatsoever in the question whether Greeks should choose ancient or modern themes for their study, then the tirade may be read less as a heartfelt denunciation of his contemporaries than as an indirect means of praising his own work. Josephus (§ 13) accuses the λόγιοι of disparaging "great events of their own lifetime" (τηλικόotων κατ' αὐτοὺς πραγμάτων γεγενημένων) although these "by comparison reduce to insignificance the wars of antiquity" (ἃ κατὰ σύγκρισιν ἐλαχίστους ἀποδείκνυσι τοὺς πάλαι πολέμους).

This charge recalls Josephus's opening words (1:1) in which he opines that the Jewish war against the Romans was the greatest (μέγιστον) of practically all the wars of recorded history (cf. also 1:4). The correspondence between that early claim and the charge in § 13 suggests that the great events which the Hellenic savants ignore to their peril are not current affairs in general but precisely the events of the Judean revolt. The suggestion is confirmed by the recapitulation (16): what the Greeks neglect are called "the deeds of the rulers (τὰς πράξεις τῶν ἡγεμόνων)'': presumably, the deeds of Vespasian and Titus.[75] But the theatre in which these two cooperated so famously was the Judean revolt. Josephus is not, therefore, simply admonishing his Greek counterparts to abandon their vain enquiries and join the virtuous league of those who report current events. He is criticizing them because, in their dual preoccupation with ancient history and with the courtroom,[76] they have let the

---

[74] Momigliano, *Essays*, 164.

[75] *War* (or part of it) was published in the lifetime of Vespasian (*Life* 359-361) and authorized by Titus (*Life* 363).

[76] Writing history in the Hellenistic world was usually an avocation, not a profession, for the rhetorically trained. Dionysius suggests that Theopompus's full-time work on history was unusual (*Letter to Pomp.* 64.6; cf. Lieberich, *Proömien*, 20). By profession, many historians were lawyers (cf. Cicero, *Orator* 1:44, 234-250). This fact explains Josephus's references to the oratorical abilities of the Hellenic historians "in the courtroom" (1:16) more simply than does Lindner's proposal that some of the Greek hstorians were bringing a lawsuit against Josephus.

truth about the Judean revolt suffer at the hands of inferior and unin-formed writers.[77]

Does Josephus really believe that these Hellenic savants ought to have written about the Judean campaign, or indeed that they could have done so responsibly? Probably not. That is the point. His ostensible attack on Greek historians for writing ancient history is really nothing other than an oblique recitation of his own credentials. The self-commendation loses its obliqueness finally as Josephus spells out what he wants the reader to understand from all of this, namely he himself is the φιλόπονος mentioned earlier, whose work deserves praise and acclaim (§ 15), because he has spent tremendous sums and personal effort (ἀναλώμασι καὶ πόνοις μεγίστοις) to bring an accurate account of this great and recent war. It is Josephus, the foreigner, the Jew, who has fulfilled the require-ments of writing history—truthful speaking and painstaking collection of the facts—while the Hellenes have missed the mark.[78]

Thus the paragraph 1:13-16, like the one before it, accomplishes several things for Josephus. First, it shifts attention far away from his confessed violation of the "law of history". Second, the purpose of the attack on those who write ancient history, drawing as it does on Polybian commonplaces, is to emphasize Josephus's own virtues as the historian of the Jewish war. He has first-hand information, which he acquired through great effort and expense. Finally, Josephus anticipates his final work, *Ag.Ap.* (1:6-27), by casting the whole polemic in David/Goliath, Jew/Hellene, or ἀλλόφυλος/γνήσιος terms: Josephus the Jew is out to pro-tect τῆς ἱστορίας ἀληθές, for which the Hellenes have lost all concern.

Following this polemic, Josephus offers his justification for beginning where he does (17-18), discussed above, then an outline of the seven books of *War* (19-29), and a concluding word (30).

III. *Josephus and the* Ἀκρίβεια *of History*

Probably the clearest single impression left on the reader by the preface to *War* is Josephus's claim that he, as an eyewitness of a great war, will present an accurate account. We have noted that references to his privileged status as an eyewitness on both sides of the conflict recur throughout the preface (1:1, 2, 3, 6, 9-12, 13-16, 18, 22). The only theme more common is his resulting claims to ἀκρίβεια and ἀλήθεια (ἀκρίβεια: 1:2, 6, 9, 17, 22, 26; ἀλήθεια: 1:6, 16, 17, 30). Likewise, all

---

[77] Presumably, these are the writers already castigated in 1:1-2, 6-8.

[78] P. Collomp, *Technik*, 278ff., finds in Josephus's polemic against the Hellenic historians the claim that truthfulness in history lies with those called "barbarians" by the Greeks.

of Josephus's later reflections on *War* demonstrate that the goal of accuracy was for him the most prominent feature of the work's purpose. For example, the epilogue of *War* is essentially a reprise of this theme:

> Here we close the history, which we promised to relate with perfect accuracy (μετὰ πάσης ἀκριβείας) . . . . Of its style my readers must be left to judge; but, as concerning truth (περὶ τῆς ἀληθείας), I would not hesitate boldly to assert that, throughout the entire narrative, this has been my single aim. (7:454-5)

In *Ant.* and *Life* also the reader is referred back to *War* for a more accurate (ἀκριβέστερον) account of various topics (*Ant.* 13:173, 298; 20: 258; *Life* 412). Finally, *Ag.Ap.* 1:47-56 dwells on the ἀλήθεια and ἀκρίβεια of *War* (in response to the charges of Josephus's later opponents) and again bases the claim squarely on Josephus's privileged eyewitness status.

The difficulty before us is that the vehement claim to historical ἀκρίβεια was a commonplace of Hellenistic historiography. It was Thucydides who defined the principle of truthfulness (ἀλήθεια) in history by invoking the kindred concept of scrupulous, detailed accuracy (ἀκρίβεια). For him, ἀκρίβεια gives nuance to the bald principle of ἀλήθεια.[79]

Polybius's attack on Timaeus reveals his agreement with Thucydides that ἀκρίβεια is the standard by which historical writing must be judged.[80] In Timaeus he finds the claim to ἀκρίβεια but no evidence to support the claim.

Polybius might have had similar comments on Dionysius of Halicarnassus, who also speaks frequently of the standards of truth (ἀλήθεια) and just consideration (δίκαιος προνούμενος) as the basic credentials of all history (*Rom. Ant.* 1.1.2; 1.4.3; 1.6.5). Dionysius sets out to portray accurately (ἀκριβῶς) the early history of Rome (1.6.3) because no accurate (ἀκριβῆς) portrayal has yet appeared in Greek (1.5.4). The reader becomes suspicious, however, when Dionysius proposes that, in keeping with his goals of truth and justice, he intends to express his goodwill toward Rome and to repay her in some measure for the benefits that he has received at her hand (1.6.5). By the time of Dionysius (mid-first-century BC), the standard of ἀλήθεια in history had obviously become a standard rhetorical theme. He calls history "the priestess of truth" (*On Thuc.* 8). In practice, however, he is notoriously uncritical and, as his theoretical essays show, he is concerned solely with the formal and moral aspects of historical writing.[81]

---

[79] Cf. Thucydides, 1.20.3, 22.2, 97.2, 134.1; 5.20.2, 26.5, 68.2; 6.54.1, 55.1; 7.87.4.
[80] Cf. Polybius 12.4d.1-2, 10.4-5, 26d.3, 27.1; 29.5.1.
[81] Cf. Halbfas, *Theorie*, 19ff.

By the time of Josephus, then, claims to ἀλήθεια and ἀκρίβεια were commonplaces of the historical preface. F. Halbfas observes:

> Seit Thukydides gab es wohl keinen Geschichtsschreiber, der diese Eigenschaft nicht als die erste Bedingung für ein erspriessliches Wirken in seiner Wissenschaft bezeichnet hatte, ohne dass diese Ansicht in allen Fallen auf die praktische Gestaltung der Darstellung ernstlich eingewirkt hatte.[82]

Given the widespread indifference to the implications of ἀκρίβεια among Hellenistic authors, we must ask to what degree Josephus was conscious of those implications. Lieberich charges:

> überall führt er die Wahrheit im Mund; leider entsprechen aber seine Werke nicht immer seinen Worten und das Hervorkehren der Wahrheit erscheint somit mehr als ein Mittel der Rhetorik.[83]

We must ask then: To what extent is the conception of historical ἀκρίβεια, which Josephus has made into a major motif of *War*, a meaningful concept for him?

At least three factors indicate that Josephus cultivates the ἀλήθεια/ἀκρίβεια theme consciously and deliberately.

A. First, unlike Dionysius and Diodorus, among others, Josephus bases his claim to ἀκρίβεια on his indisputable first-hand knowledge of the revolt (*War* 1:3, 16; *Ant.* 1:3; *Ag.Ap.* 1:47f., 55f.). Although many of Josephus's claims are debated, no one seriously doubts that he was a Jerusalemite priest who fought in some capacity against the Romans, who became known to Vespasian and Titus, and who ended up in a privileged position in Rome. These credentials, unlike Diodorus's worldwide travels, are not invented. When, therefore, Josephus bases his claim to accurate information upon them, he is making a reasonable argument. He is aware that the remarkable historical accidents of his career have placed him in a unique position to write accurately about the Jewish war; that is why he parades this asset throughout the preface and elsewhere. Whether he *did* write accurately is another question. The point here is that his claim to accuracy is not an empty repetition of cliche but a conscious proposition, made in order to exploit fully his unique situation. He is aware of the conditions of accurate reporting and claims to have fulfilled them.

B. Further evidence of this is the consistency of the ἀλήθεια/ἀκρίβεια motif for *War*. It is not mentioned in any perfunctory way but appears throughout the preface in strategic places (1:2, 3, 6, 9, 12, 18, 30). The

---

[82] Cf. Halbfas, *Theorie*, 35f.
[83] Lieberich, *Proömien*, 35.

theme is recalled in the epilogue to *War* (7:454-5) and again several times in the later works, as we have seen above.

C. Finally, ἀκρίβεια and its cognates form part of Josephus's characteristic vocabulary.[84] He employs this word group 134 times. In his paraphrase of *Aristeas*, he inserts the word six times and takes it over once from the source. In the context of historical reporting, he employs the word group frequently—about 52 times. Equally as significant for our purposes, he uses it about 28 times in the context of religion. Indeed, the concept of ἀκρίβεια lies at the heart of his religious understanding, as we shall discover in the next chapter. Since, further, the boundaries between "religion" and "history" are extremely fluid for Josephus,[85] it is difficult to believe that he employed the ἀκρίβεια theme historiographically with little thought of its implications.

It must be emphasized that the question being pursued has to do only with Josephus's intention: Did he understand the concept of ἀκρίβεια and employ it seriously, or did he, like many of his contemporaries, take it over frivolously from the current world of ideas? The evidence cited indicates that Josephus consciously chose to assert the factuality of *War* on the basis of his eyewitness status, fully aware of the obligation to accuracy that the claim entailed.

This conclusion presents an entrée to the historical question: *Did Josephus write accurately about the Jewish revolt?* It is of great importance for that question that we have in Josephus a *bona fide* witness, with privileged access to both sides of the conflict, someone who seems able to control his material and who intends factuality. Nevertheless, the historical question cannot be answered by such *a priori* considerations. Josephus could not have observed all the simultaneous events of the conflict; he depended heavily on the reports of others. Those events that he did observe he can only have perceived and remembered imperfectly, as is true of any witness. Finally, that whole body of resulting information is only mediated to us *via* his own interests and *via* his intellectual and stylistic tendencies.

We have, then, a potential for reasonable accuracy in *War* but only if Josephus did as he claimed and exploited his uniquely knowledgeable situation to check his evidence rigorously and present what he genuinely believed to have been the course of events. Whether he lived up to his claims can only be determined by extensive historical reconstruction based on a comparison of (a) his other writings, (b) other, contem-

---

[84] With this point, I anticipate the investigation of the following chapter; full documentation will be given there.

[85] Cf. especially *Ag.Ap.* 2:144; also 1:32, 36.

porary literary sources and (c) non-literary, especially archaeological, evidence.

That historical question is still *sub judice*. One might summarize its present state by saying that point (a) above—especially the comparison of *War* and *Life*—continues to challenge those parts of *War* that deal with Josephus himself[86] but that points (b) and (c) increasingly vindicate his account with respect to places and events.[87] All we can say on the basis of a *literary* analysis is that Josephus intended accuracy, that he seems to have been conscious of the obligations thereby assumed, and that he was evidently in a position to satisfy them.

Summary

Before proceeding to consider the Pharisee passages in *War* it is necessary to summarize the argument and leading themes of the preface, since the preface is evidently intended as a key to the work as a whole.

In 1:1-8, we find the simple argument: (a) the Jewish war is of great importance; (b) previous accounts of it are hopelessly inadequate; and (c) Josephus is in an excellent position to render an accurate account.

In §§ 9-12, Josephus allays any potential reader's fears that he is going to offer an *exposé* of Roman wrongdoing. He accomplishes this by introducing the leading themes of the work, namely: lament for the "tyrants" who brought about the Temple's destruction, and praise for the Romans, especially Titus, who tried to save it. Since the introduction of these themes may be thought to contravene the "law of history", Josephus appeals once more to the enormousness of the events and his proximity to them as his justification for such strong emotions. He does not believe that the introduction of his own value judgements vitiates his claim to accuracy. If anything his strong emotions testify to the closeness of his personal involvement with events of great import.

In order to remove the slightest hint of malpractice on his part, Josephus turns in §§ 13-16 to accuse those who ignore current events (he is thinking of the Jewish war) as objects of historical study. Theirs is the greater failure, he claims. Framing the charge in general terms, he is

---

[86] Cf. Laqueur, *Historiker* and now Cohen, *Josephus*.

[87] Cf., e.g., Luther, *Josephus und Justus*, 81f., and the editors' preface to the O. Michel *Festschrift*, *Josephus-Studien*. One indication of the archaeologists' confidence in Josephus is the present search for Herod's tomb at Herodion, solely on the basis of Josephus's notice (*War* 1:673). His information has proved invaluable for the excavations of Jerusalem, Masada, Caesarea, Herodion, and other sites. Cf. the judgements of N. Avigad, B. Mazar, and G. Cornfeld in *Josephus: The Jewish War*; edd. G. Cornfeld, B. Mazar, and P. L. Maier (Grand Rapids: Zondervan, 1982), 6f. Rajak, *Josephus*, 106f. *et passim*, makes a sustained case for Josephus's accuracy.

able to invoke the venerable aid of Polybius. We soon see, however, that his real purpose is not an abstract critique of ancient history but a reiteration of his own historical prowess as chronicler of the Jewish War. He has laboured very hard to provide this account of the history of his own times (§ 16). This claim recalls once again the eyewitness theme which has already been well cultivated.

Among the various themes introduced by Josephus in the preface to *War* we may distinguish between those that he explicitly cites as his peculiar literary concerns, arising from the subject itself (lament for Jerusalem, disgust for the tyrants, praise for the Romans), and the more general historiographical themes or *topoi* that find a place also in his work. Both will need to be taken into account where relevant, in the interpretation of the Pharisee passages in *War*.

It is a commonplace in Josephan scholarship that *War* was the historian's apostate work and *Ant.* his apologetic effort. In the former, Josephus speaks as a *Römling* of the "Jewish campaign"—a title that signifies his distance from his own people and his Roman viewpoint. He speaks as the mouthpiece of Rome to his coreligionists. *Ant.* is held, to a greater or lesser degree, to be a work of repentance. Josephus has now matured and rediscovered the value of his roots; with *Ant.* and *Ag.Ap.* he chooses to publicize these insights.[88]

Our examination of *War*, however, points in a different direction. Josephus writes in order to capitalize on his own knowledge of the conflict. He writes, however, as an unabashed Jew.[89] From the very first sentence he declares his Jewish heritage, his priestly identity, his love for the Temple and his country (1:3). He presents the Jews as better historians than the Greeks (1:16). And whereas all previous accounts of the revolt had vilified the Jews, he intends to set the record straight, though without compensatory exaggeration (1:7-9). What he wants to present to his readers is a Jewish story (1:17, 18) and indeed, in the narrative itself he glides over the years of Roman prefecture in Judea until the revolt (though he does pause to elaborate on brief reign of Agrippa,

---

[88] Cf. Thackeray, Rasp, Weber, Laqueur, Smith/Neusner, and Cohen, who are discussed in chapter 7, below.

[89] Niese, *HZ*, 201, sees Josephus's inclusion of the whole pre-history of the revolt, from the Maccabean period on, as an attempt to acquaint the reader with Jewish history and to remove prejudice. He presents Josephus (p. 206) as a Jew who genuinely mourns the loss of Jerusalem and its Temple. Finally, Niese understands Josephus in *all* of his works as a Jewish apologist (p. 237):
Sein Zweck ist, die Griechen und Römer mit den Juden zu versöhnen und sie mit der wahren Gestalt der jüdischen Geschichte und Religion bekannt zu machen. Alle seine Schriften sind daher direkt oder indirekt apologetisch, und überall wird das Jüdische in hellenische Form gekleidet.

the Jewish king).[90] He believes that the Jewish δῆμος itself was guiltless in the conflict with Rome (1:10, 27). The Jewish context of the work is such that Josephus can refer to it decades later by the titles ἡ βίβλος τῆς Ἰουδαικῆς (*Ant.* 13:173) and simply ἡ τῶν Ἰουδαικῶν (*Ant.* 13:298).

In spite of Josephus's obvious flattery of Vespasian and Titus, therefore, and his admiration of Rome in general, he can hardly be called a Roman functionary.

---

[90] *War* 2:167-187, 220-276. This may be due (so Hölscher, "Josephus", 1944) to the sparseness of Josephus's sources for the period; on the other hand, however, it would also fit well with the overall Jewish theme of the work, established in the preface.

CHAPTER FOUR

WAR 1:107-114:
THE PHARISEES AND ALEXANDRA SALOME, I

Josephus introduces the Pharisees to his Greco-Roman readership in *War* 1:110, in the course of his narration of events under the Hasmoneans. Coming to speak of Alexandra Salome's reign, he offers a brief account of the distinctive characteristics of the Pharisees, as follows:
παραφύονται δὲ αὐτῆς εἰς τὴν ἐξουσίαν
Φαρισαῖοι σύνταγμά τι 'Ιουδαίων
  δοκοῦν
  (a) εὐσεβέστερον εἶναι τῶν ἄλλων καὶ
  (b) τοὺς νόμους ἀκριβέστερον ἀφηγεῖσθαι
This is the first piece of information about the Pharisees that Josephus saw fit to give his readers. It must, therefore, be significant for our purposes. Moreover, among all of the descriptions of the Pharisees in the Josephan corpus, something very close to the above occurs in two other places:
War 2:162: οἱ μετ' ἀκριβείας δοκοῦντες ἐξηγεῖσθαι τὰ νόμιμα καὶ τὴν πρώτην
            ἀπάγοντες αἵρεσιν
Life 191: οἳ περὶ τὰ πάτρια νόμιμα δοκοῦσιν τῶν ἄλλων ἀκριβείᾳ διαφέρειν
Nor can one ignore the *prima facie* similarity[1] between these statements and *Ant* 17:41:
μόριόν τι 'Ιουδαικῶν ἀνθρώπων ἐπ' ἐξακριβώσει μέγα φρονοῦν τοῦ πατρίου καὶ νόμων οἷς χαίρει τὸ θεῖον προσποιούμενον. . . .
Since these passages together constitute a large segment of what Josephus says about the Pharisees, from his first to his last remarks about the group, and since the key terms that they share (superlative ἀκρίβεια, νόμοι/νόμιμα/πάτρια, δοκέω/προσποιοῦμαι) go back to *War* 1:110, it is all the more important to strive for a thorough understanding of this first attempt at definition.

The "first impression" of the Pharisees that Josephus offers his reader will be interpreted here according to the following procedure: (1) consideration of the context; (2) analysis of the key terms; (3) narrowing the

---

[1] This passage is often treated as the product of one of Josephus's sources, which has been taken over by him uncritically, cf. Baumgarten, "Name", 14f. n. 15, and the literature cited there; also *Revolution*, 321-324. The source problem will be discussed at the end of the present chapter.

range of plausible meanings to the single most probable interpretation. We shall also need to consider (4) the implication of such an analysis for the source question.

I. Context

Josephus's first recorded reference to the Pharisees falls within his narration of Hasmonean history. His view of the Hasmoneans is basically positive: Mattathias and his sons rose up against the impious and brutal Antiochus IV and fought with courage (1:34-40). Simon's administration was excellent (γενναίως—1:50) as was that of John Hyrcanus, who ruled thirty-one years (1:68). After Hyrcanus, however, things turned sour. That ruler was permitted by the Deity to foresee that with his two older sons the government would falter (1:69). Josephus proceeds to describe the year-long καταστροφή (1:69) of Aristobulus's reign, which ended with the deaths of both Aristobulus and Antigonus. With the accession of Hyrcanus's third son, Alexander Janneus (1:85), the reader's question is: Will the downward trend continue or will Janneus be able to reverse it and recapture the lost good fortune of his father (1:69, τῆς πατρῴας εὐδαιμονίας)?

Alas, Josephus portrays Alexander Janneus as a warmonger who was consistently hated by the Jewish people. Josephus is always partial to moderates (μέτριοι)[2] but he characterizes Alexander as one who only seemed at first to be moderate (μετριότητι προύχειν δοκοῦντα— § 85). On coming to power, however, this ruler killed his brother (§ 85) and plunged the nation into continual wars (§§ 86f., 89, 90, 93ff., 99f., 103f), often unsuccessfully (§§ 90, 95, 100, 103). His own people wearied of him quickly and openly expressed their hostility (§§ 88, 91f., 94, 96, 98). Only with the help of his mercenaries was Alexander able to quell the revolts (§§ 88, 93), during the course of which he killed tens of thousands of Jews (§§ 89, 91, 96, 97).

Josephus describes the accession of Alexandra Salome, Janneus's widow, as a promising moment for the nation. Alexandra not only lacked her husband's brutality (τῆς ὠμότητος αὐτοῦ μακρὰν ἀποδέουσα); she opposed (ἀνθίστημαι) his crimes and was therefore loved by the people (§ 107). On account of her reputation for piety (διὰ δόξαν εὐσεβείας) she was able to take firm control of the government. Unlike her husband's case, however—the public δόξα about his moderation had quickly proved false (§§ 85ff.)—Alexandra's reputation for piety was

---

[2] *War* 2:275, 281, 306, 455, 649; 4:283; 5:391; 7:263. Josephus sides with the "moderate" position in the revolt.

well-founded: she really was scrupulous about the national traditions (ἠκρίβου γὰρ δὴ μάλιστα τοῦ ἔθνους τὰ πάτρια) and she used to dismiss offenders from positions of authority (§ 108). Appropriately, she gave the high-priesthood to her older son Hyrcanus, who was indifferent to public affairs, and thereby restricted the younger Aristobulus, a "hot-head", to private life.

Into this promising situation Josephus introduces the Pharisees, who are yet a third party with a reputation (110): "a body of Jews with the reputation of excelling the rest of their nation in the observances of religion, and as exact exponents of the laws" (Thackeray). Alexander's reputation (δοκοῦν) for mildness had been quickly debunked; his wife's renown (δόξα) for piety, on the other hand, was well founded. The reader is now ready to ask: Did the actions of the Pharisees support or undermine their reputation (δοκοῦν) for piety and observance of the laws?

II. *Key Terms*

A. Παραφύομαι, to "grow beside", occurs only here in Josephus. It may suggest the metaphor of "suckers around a tree"[3] and is in any case certainly pejorative: the Pharisees grew increasingly to assume the ἐξουσία that rightfully belonged to Alexandra.

B. Σύνταγμα, "something drawn up in order". As we shall see, Josephus uses various labels for the Jewish religious groups, such as: αἵρεσις, φιλοσοφία, τάγμα, and γένος;[4] σύνταγμα he uses only of the Pharisees and only here.

Altogether, Josephus employs the word some 16 times, 12 of these in *War*. He once reproduces Strabo's use of the word as meaning simply a group or "troop" (*Ant.* 14:116). In 13 out of 14 cases,[5] however, Josephus uses σύνταγμα in a distinctly pejorative sense: in the realm of ideas, it refers to something deceitfully arranged, a plot or fabrication (*War* 1:495; 2:107, 172, 290). When used of a group of people, the tone is always one of dislike or disgust. For example, Josephus speaks of a γυναικῶν σύνταγμα that collaborated with the wicked Antipater to cause trouble for Herod the Great (*War* 1:568). Most frequent is Josephus's use of the word to describe groups of rebels or "brigands", under one of the ἀρχιλῃσταί, thus: τὸ σύνταγμα τῶν λῃστῶν (*War* 4:135, 509, 513, 558; *Ant.* 20:161; *Life* 106). Outside of our passage, then, whenever

---

[3] Thackeray, n. *b.* to *War* 1:110, LCL edn.
[4] Cf. the convenient table in J. LeMoyne, *Les Sadducéens* (Paris: Lecoffre, 1972), 32.
[5] That is, excluding our passage and the Strabo citation.

Josephus himself uses the word σύνταγμα to describe a group of people, it always means "band" or "gang"; it is never honorific or even neutral. In our passage, as we shall see, the sequel appears to suggest the same negative sense. G. Cornfeld's rendering, "an important sector [of the Jewish community]",[6] is hardly appropriate.

C. Εὐσεβέστερον, "more pious". With the two comparative adjectives we reach the heart of Josephus's first definition of the Pharisees: σύνταγμά τι 'Ιουδαίων δοκοῦν:

(a) εὐσεβέστερον εἶναι τῶν ἄλλων καὶ
(b) τοὺς νόμους ἀκριβέστερον ἀφηγεῖσθαι

Both of these terms reflect Josephus's characteristic vocabulary in the field of religion.

Εὐσέβεια and its cognate verb and adjective occur 144 times in Josephus. Although he occasionally speaks of "filial" piety,[7] he uses the εὐσέβεια word-group almost always to denote piety toward God. Every nation has its own traditional form of εὐσέβεια[8] but Josephus wants to show (especially in Ant. and Ag.Ap.) that Jewish εὐσέβεια is particularly worthy:

> Could God be more worthily honoured than by such a scheme, under which religion is the end and aim of the training of the entire community (μὲν τοῦ πλήθους κατασκευασμένου πρὸς τὴν εὐσέβειαν), the priests are entrusted with the special charge of it, and the whole administration of the state resembles some sacred ceremony? (Ag.Ap. 2:188, Thackeray)

The Jewish νόμος, delivered by God through Moses, promotes a genuine piety (Ant. 1:6; 10:50; 14:65; Ag.Ap. 2:146, 291, 293). The customs (ἔθη) of the Jews, Josephus says, are all concerned with piety (εὐσέβεια) and justice (δικαιοσύνη, Ant. 16:42).

According to Josephus, this εὐσέβεια finds its centre in the Temple cult. It requires the offering of prescribed sacrifices and the celebration of feasts (Ant. 8:122-124). Menasseh began to show piety (εὐσεβεῖν), according to Josephus, when he sanctified the Temple and purified the city of Jerusalem (Ant. 10:45). The tenacity of Jewish εὐσέβεια is indicated by the firm resolve of the priests to continue with the prescribed daily sacrifice even when under attack from Pompey (Ant. 14:65). Indeed, Josephus views the high priest as the one who oversees the sacrifices and

---

[6] Cornfeld, Jewish War, 32.
[7] E.g., War 1:630, 633; Ant. 16:95, 112. These may be attributable to the influence of Nicolaus of Damascus.
[8] Of Pythagoras (Ag.Ap. 1:162); of Egypt (Ag.Ap. 1:224); of Claudius (Ant. 20:13); of the Romans (Ant. 14:315); of Ptolemy (Ant. 13:69); of Antipater the Idumean (Ant. 14:283); of the Athenians (Ag.Ap. 2:130); of others generally (Ag.Ap. 2:131). Note especially Life 113: everyone should worship God (τὸν θεὸν εὐσεβεῖν) as he sees fit.

thus presides (προεστάναι) over the εὐσέβεια of the nation (*Ant.* 4:31); for this reason, he can claim that when the Idumeans slaughtered the chief priests they effectively ended the possibility of εὐσέβεια (*War* 7:267).

If the Temple and priesthood constitute the focal point of εὐσέβεια, however, they by no means exhaust its significance. Josephus has Samuel declare that obedience toward God (ὑποτάσσεσθαι) is the condition of acceptable sacrifice and the sign of true piety (*Ant.* 6:148). This obedience extends to the laws in their entire scope, which is the whole of human life:

> Above all we pride ourselves on the education of our children and regard as the most essential task in life the observance of our laws and of the pious practices, based thereupon, which we have inherited (τὸ φυλάττειν τοὺς νόμους καὶ τὴν κατὰ τούτους παραδεδομένην εὐσέβειαν). (*Ag.Ap.* 2:184)

And again:

> For us, with our conviction that the original institution of the Law was in accordance with the will of God, it would be rank impiety (οὐδ' εὐσεβές) not to observe it. (*Ag.Ap.* 2:184)

Thus εὐσέβεια requires careful observance of food and purity laws (*Life* 14, 75). John of Gischala is castigated for lacking εὐσέβεια in both areas (*War* 7:264). As the story of King Izates tells us, εὐσέβεια amounts to doing what is commanded in the Law, in this case circumcision, without concern for the consequences (*Ant.* 20:44-48). Further examples of the same principle are Sabbath observance (*Ag.Ap.* 1:212) and the continuation of sacrifice (*Ant.* 14:65) in the midst of war, both of which Josephus considers impressive examples of εὐσέβεια.

For Josephus, then, εὐσέβεια is a one-word summary of the whole Jewish system of religion, instigated by God, articulated by Moses, administered by the priests, and shared by the whole nation. Moses' success, he allows, lay in his making all of the virtues elements of εὐσέβεια rather than making εὐσέβεια count for only one virtue among many (*Ag.Ap.* 2:170). "Εὐσέβεια", he says, "governs all our actions (πράξεις) and occupations (διατριβαί) and speech (λόγοι)" (*Ag.Ap.* 2:171).

It is no surprise, then, that Josephus sets up εὐσέβεια as the crucial test for the competence of Jewish (and other) public figures. He summarizes the activities of Abraham, Amram, Joshua, Boaz, David, and Solomon, for example, by commenting on their εὐσέβεια (*Ant.* 2:196, 212, 3:49; 5:327; 8:13, 196).

When speaking of public figures Josephus often juxtaposes the two characteristics of εὐσέβεια and δικαιοσύνη. Especially telling in this regard is his paraphrase of the *Letter of Aristeas* § 46, where he inserts this favourite pair of qualifications for a ruler. *Aristeas* has: καλῶς οὖν ποιήσεις, βασιλεῦ δίκαιε . . . . Josephus renders (Ant. 12:56): ἔσται δὲ τῆς σῆς εὐσεβείας καὶ δικαιοσύνης.

The significance of this double designation comes to light first in David's instructions to Solomon. Four times David admonishes Solomon to rule in a pious (εὐσεβῆ) and just (δίκαιον) manner (Ant. 7:338, 342, 356, 374). On the fifth occasion, as David is dying, he finally elaborates: Solomon's task is, "to be just toward your subjects and pious toward God" (δικαί μὲν εἶναι πρὸς τοὺς ἀρχομένους, εὐσεβεῖ δὲ πρὸς τὸν . . . θεόν, 7:384). This explanation of εὐσέβεια as describing the relationship toward God and δικαιοσύνη, the "horizontal" relationship to men, is confirmed several times. The righteous King Jotham, "εὐσεβῆς μὲν τὰ πρὸς τὸν θεόν, δίκαιος δὲ τὰ πρὸς ἀνθρώπους ὑπῆρχεν" (Ant. 9:236). John the Baptist, says Josephus, exhorted the Jews to act πρὸς ἀλλήλους δικαιοσύνῃ καὶ πρὸς τὸν θεὸν εὐσεβείᾳ (Ant. 18:117). Finally, according to Josephus the first two of the dozen oaths taken by the Essenes (War 2:139) were: πρῶτον μὲν εὐσεβήσειν τὸ θεῖον, ἔπειτα τὸ πρὸς ἀνθρώπους δίκαια φυλάξειν. Even when the man-ward qualification of δικαιοσύνη is lacking, we frequently find the qualifier πρὸς τὸν θεόν appended to εὐσέβεια.[9] There can remain little doubt that the almost formulaic εὐσέβεια καὶ δικαιοσύνη that Josephus employs in characterizing public figures is to be understood in terms of this vertical/horizontal distinction.[10]

In its earliest Greek usage, εὐσέβεια was usually qualified with respect to its object; one could speak of "reverence" toward one's parents, toward the dead, toward's one's homeland, and so forth, using the forms εὐσέβεια εἰς/ πρός/περί.[11] By the Hellenistic period, although all of these formulations remained current, εὐσέβεια had also come to be used without qualification for "reverence toward and worship of the Divine". W. Foerster suggests that the development was a natural progression from honouring the various constituent elements within the world order (parents, homeland, etc.) to honouring that order itself and the divine powers that guarded and protected it.[12] In all of its ramifications, εὐσέβεια was a virtue in Hellenistic thinking.[13]

[9] War 2:128; Ant. 9:2, 222, 236, 276, 10:45, 51, 51, 58; 12:43, 290; 13:242; 14:257; 16:172; 18:117; Life 113; Ag.Ap. 1:162; 2:171.

[10] As G. Schrenk ("δίκαιος", TDNT, II, 182) shows, this coupling of δίκαιος (re: obligations to men) with ὅσιος, εὐσέβεια or the like (re: obligations to God) was fairly common among Greek writers, e.g., Plato, Gorgias 507b; Polybius 22.10.8; Xenophon, Memorabilia 4.8.7.

[11] The word is analyzed by W. Foerster in both his TDNT article, "εὐσέβεια", VII, 168-196, and in his article "Εὐσέβεια in den Pastoralbriefen", NTS 5 (1959), 213-218.

[12] Foerster, TDNT, VII, 175ff.; "Pastoralbriefen", 214f.

[13] Foerster, TDNT, VII, 177f.

Εὐσέβεια, then, is fundamentally a Greek concept. So Foerster:

> Εὐσέβεια ist eine griechische Wortbildung, zu der das Hebräische kein sprachliches Äquivalent hat und die eine religiös-sittliche Tugend, deren Übung öffentliches Lob, deren Unterlassung moralische Abwertung erfährt.[14]

The word does occur a handful of times in the Septuagint, to render יְראַת יהוה,[15] and the adjective εὐσεβῆς occasionally renders נדיב, חסיד, and צדיק.[16] But the word-group does not render any particular Hebrew conception very well. C. H. Dodd summarizes:

> Thus these terms [the εὐσεβ-group] belong chiefly to the vocabulary of those books of the Bible which were composed as well as translated in the Hellenistic period, and whose Greek translation is comparatively late. It is clear that the words, and the idea they represent, are characteristically Greek, and in Hellenistic Judaism replace Hebrew terms of a different colour.[17]

Since it was only Greek-speaking Judaism that incorporated the concept of εὐσέβεια as a constituent feature of its self-understanding,[18] it would be futile in this case to press further the question of a "Semitic background" for Josephus's thought.

Josephus's concept of εὐσέβεια as a communal Jewish endeavour, as consisting in obedience to the divine Law, and as the special task and virtue of the priests, is most closely paralleled in 4 Maccabees. Within the short compass of the work, εὐσέβεια forms appear 64 times and have precisely the Josephan sense of "pleasing God by adhering faithfully to his Law". What makes this most interesting is that 4 Maccabees was traditionally thought, on the basis of testimony from Eusebius and Jerome, to have been written by Josephus under the title Περὶ Αὐτοκράτορος Λογισμοῦ.[19]

To summarize: the term εὐσέβεια is part of Josephus's characteristic vocabulary; it occurs most frequently throughout *Ant.* and *Ag.Ap.*, which both seek to explain and defend Judaism. It is less common, but still appears in characteristic form, in *War* and *Life*, which describe events connected with the revolt. Josephus often uses the word to summarize the whole end and means of Jewish life, centred in the Temple cult and

---

[14] Foerster, "Pastoralbriefen", 213.

[15] Only Prov. 1:7; 13:11; Isa. 11:2; 33:6.

[16] Judg. 8:31; Job 32:3; Prov. 12:12; 13:19; Eccl. 3:10; Isa. 24:16; 26:7; 32:8.

[17] C. H. Dodd, *The Bible and the Greeks* (London: Hodder & Stoughton, 1935), 174.

[18] The term occurs some 200 times in Philo, 64 times in 4 Maccabees, and, as noted, 144 times in Josephus.

[19] Eusebius *Eccl. Hist.*, 3.10.6; cf. W. H. Brownlee, "Maccabees, Books of", *IDB*, III, 212; Niese, *HZ*, 236f.

supervised by the priesthood. He can also restrict εὐσέβεια to action that is directed toward God, in which sense it is complemented by δικαιοσύνη, which refers to human relationships.

Most significant for our purpose is the simple observation that the concept εὐσέβεια does play a large role in Josephus's thinking. When, therefore, he describes the Pharisees as a group of Jews δοχοῦν εὐσεβέστερον εἶναι τῶν ἄλλων he is using terminology that is theologically charged for him: they have the reputation of being (or suppose themselves to be)[20] the most Jewish of the Jews, those who most perfectly fulfill the communal ideal.

D. 'Αχριβέστερον: "more precise, exact". For Josephus, the road to attaining εὐσέβεια is adherence to the laws, customs, or traditions of Judaism. It was the great lawgiver (νομοθέτης) who instructed the people in εὐσέβεια (Ant. 1:6). Since God has given the Law to mankind, piety consists in adherence to it (Ag.Ap. 2:184). Εὐσέβεια, in the Jewish context, is closely bound to observance of the divine commandments (cf. Ant. 7:338, 374, 9:2, 222; 14:65; 15:267; Ag.Ap. 2:146, 159). For the laws teach εὐσέβειαν καὶ ἀληθεστάτην (Ag.Ap. 2:291). King Josiah succeeded so well in εὐσέβεια precisely by following the laws (Ant. 10:50).

If the road to piety is observance of the laws given by God, then it follows that the most pious Jews will be those who follow the laws most scrupulously and accurately. The connection between εὐσέβεια and ἀχρίβεια is especially clear in the context of our passage, where it is said of Queen Alexandra that she was enabled to take control of the government:

διὰ δόξαν εὐσεβείας. ἠχρίβου γὰρ δὴ μάλιστα τοῦ ἔθνους τὰ πάτρια καὶ τοὺς πλημμελοῦντας εἰς τοὺς ἱεροὺς νόμους ἐξ ἀρχῆς προεβάλλετο (War 1:108.)

The substance of Alexandra's εὐσέβεια was her scrupulous adherence to the laws. When, therefore, Josephus describes the Pharisees as the group δοχοῦν εὐσεβέστερον εἶναι. . . καὶ τοὺς νόμους ἀχριβέστερον ἀφηγεῖσθαι, he is not really saying two different things about the Pharisees but is rather defining their reputation by means of synonymous parallelism: to be εὐσεβέστερον for him is to be ἀχριβέστερον with respect to the νόμοι. As he remarks in another context:

The Jews certify the wisdom only of those who know the laws exactly (τοῖς τὰ νόμιμα σαφῶς ἐπισταμένοις) and who are competent to interpret the meaning of the holy scriptures (τὴν τῶν ἱερῶν γραμμάτων δύναμιν ἑρμηνεῦσαι δυναμένοις). (Ant. 20:264)

---

[20] We shall consider the exact sense of δοχέω below.

Paret rightly comments: "Die Frömmigkeit ist ihm wesentlich Akribie".[21]

'Ακρίβεια and its cognate verb and adjective occur 134 times in Josephus. We have already noted the importance of the concept for his historiography: ἀκρίβεια is the goal of all his writing and he alludes to it frequently in his programmatic statements. In *War*, as we have seen, Josephus bases his claim to accuracy on his close involvement with events.

With Josephus, however, as with ancient Judaism generally, one cannot force a division between history and religion.[22] For the purpose of studying the past is to learn God's will. So Josephus writes of his *Ant.*:

> But, speaking generally, the main lesson to be learnt from this history (ταύτης τῆς ἱστορίας). . . is that men who conform to the will of God, and do not venture to transgress laws that have been excellently laid down, prosper in all things beyond belief. . .; whereas, in proportion as they depart from the strict observance of these laws (καθ' ὅσον δ' ἂν ἀποστῶσι τῆς τούτων ἀκριβοῦς ἐπιμελείας), . . . whatever imaginary good thing they strive to do ends in irretrievable disaster. (*Ant.* 1:14, Thackeray)

A passage in the first book of *Ag.Ap.* likewise blurs the distinction between history and religion, by positing that the records of Jewish history have been kept with ἀκρίβεια by the priests and prophets (1:29-36). Indeed, the records of the past are "sacred" records (1:54). And Josephus appeals to his own priestly lineage as support for his claims to have accurate information about Jewish history (*Ag.Ap.* 1:54). Most significant is his judgement on the anti-Semite Apion. Throughout his polemical work against this author, he repeatedly charges him with propagating ignorance and lies about Jewish history and customs. His final judgement on the propagandistic historian, however, is fundamentally religious (*Ag.Ap.* 2:144):

> The duty of wise men is to adhere scrupulously to their native laws concerning piety (τοὺς μὲν οἰκείοις νόμοις περὶ τὴν εὐσέβειαν ἀκριβῶς ἐμμένειν) and not to abuse those of others. Apion was delinquent with respect to his country's laws and told lies about ours.

Apion's historical inaccuracy is portrayed by Josephus as a religious deficiency. Josephus cannot separate the spheres of history and religion. For him, the concept of ἀκρίβεια moves freely between the two areas.

---

[21] Paret, "Pharisäismus", 826.

[22] Indeed, the ancient world as a whole viewed history as a study to be undertaken primarily for its present value; cf. Thucydides 1:22; Polybius 12:25b. 3; 1.35. 1-3, 7-10; Avenarius, *Lukians Schrift*, 22f., 166f. So history was not an autonomous discipline in the modern sense.

One way to observe Josephus's taste for the ἀκρίβεια word group is to examine his paraphrase of the pseudepigraphous *Letter of Aristeas*. That document, in the parts of it that Josephus uses, has the adjective ἀκριβῆς once (§ 32). Josephus takes it over (*Ant.* 12:39) along with the phrase in which it occurs. In six other places, however, he paraphrases *Aristeas* in such a way as to include an ἀκρίβεια-cognate where it was absent from his source. Since all of this happens within the space of *Ant.* 12:35-104, the incidence is noteworthy. The passages are as follows:

(1)   *Aristeas* 28b: διόπερ καὶ τὸ τῆς εἰσδόσεως καὶ τὸ τῶν ἐπιστολῶν ἀντίγραφα κατακεχώρικα καὶ τὸ τῶν ἀπεσταλμένων πλῆθος καὶ τὴν ἕκαστου κατασκευήν, διὰ τὸ μεγαλαμοιρία καὶ τέχνη διαφέρειν ἕκαστον αὐτῶν.

Ant. 12:35: διὸ καὶ τὸ τῆς εἰσδόσεως ἀντίγραφον καὶ τὸ τῶν ἐπιστολῶν κατατετάκται καὶ τὸ πλῆθος τῶν ἀπεσταλμένων ἀναθημάτων καὶ τὸ ἐφ' ἕκαστον κατασκευασθέν, ὡς ἀκριβεστάτην εἶναι τὴν τοῦ τεχνίτου τοῖς ὁρῶσι μεγαλουργίαν καὶ διὰ τὴν τῶν κατασκευασμάτων ἐξοχὴν τὸν ἑκάστου δημιουργὸν εὐθέως ποιῆσαι γνωρίμων.

(2)   *Aristeas* 39: καλῶς οὖν ποιήσης καὶ τῆς ἡμετερᾶς σπουδῆς ἄξιως ἐπιλεξάμενος ἄνδρας καλῶς βεβιωκότας πρεσβυτέρους, ἐμπειρίαν ἔχοντας τοῦ νομοῦ, καὶ δυνατοὺς ἑρμηνεῦσαι, ἀφ' ἑκάστης φύλης ἕξ, ὅπως ἐκ τῶν πλειονῶν τὸ σύμφωνον ἐνεργῇ, διὰ τὸ περὶ μειζόνων εἶναι τὴν σκέψιν.

Ant. 12:49: καλῶς οὖν ποιήσεις ἐπιλεξάμενος ἄνδρας ἀγαθοὺς ἓξ ἀφ' ἑκάστης φυλῆς ἤδη πρεσβυτέρους, οἳ καὶ διὰ τὸν χρόνον ἐμπείρως ἔχουσι τῶν νόμων καὶ δυνήσονται τὴν ἑρμηνείαν αὐτῶν ἀκριβῆ ποιήσασθαι.

(3)   *Aristeas* 56: ὅσα δ' ἂν ᾖ ἄγραφα, πρὸς καλλονὴν ἐκέλευσε ποιεῖν ὅσα δὲ διὰ γραπτῶν, μετρὰ αὐτοῖς κατακολουθῆσαι.

Ant. 12:63: καὶ ὅσα ἦν ἄγραφα ἐκέλευσε ταῦτα κατασκευάζεσθαι καὶ τὰ ἀναγεγραμμένα πρὸς τὴν ἀκρίβειαν αὐτῶν ἀποβλέποντας ὁμοίως ἐπιτελεῖν.

(4)   *Aristeas* 183: προσεχέστατος γὰρ ὢν ἄνθρωπος ὁ Δωρόθεος εἶχε τὴν τῶν τοιούτων προστασίαν. συνέστρωσε δὲ πάντα τὰ δι' αὐτοῦ χειριζόμενα, πρὸς τὰς τοιαύτας ὑποδοχὰς διαμεμερισμένα. διμερῆ τε ἐποίησε τὰ τῶν κλισιῶν.

Ant. 12:95: ὃ δὲ καὶ περὶ τούτους ἐγένετο, Δωροθέου διὰ τὴν περὶ τὸν βίον ἀκρίβειαν ἐπὶ τούτοις καθεστῶτος. συνέστρωσε δὲ πάντα δι' αὐτοῦ τὰ πρὸς τὰς τοιαύτας ὑποδοχάς, καὶ διμερῆ τὴν κλισίαν ἐποίησεν.

(5)   *Ant.* 12:99 is a summary statement of the tedious account in *Aristeas* 200-294, which tells of a seven-day banquet in which King Ptolemy asks

each of the seventy-two Jewish elders a question and receives a wise reply. Josephus's summary remark is that the elders, "after considering the questions, gave precise (ἀκριβῶς) explanations, a comment lacking in his source.

(6) *Aristeas* 302: οἱ δὲ ἐπετέλουν ἕκαστα σύμφωνα ποιοῦντες πρὸς ἑαυτοὺς τὰς ἀντιβολαῖς . . . καὶ μέχρι μὲν ὥρας ἐνάτης συνεδρείας ἐγίνετο μετὰ δὲ ταῦτα περὶ τὴν τοῦ σώματος θεραπείαν ἀπελύοντο γίνεσθαι.

Ant. 12:104: οἱ δ' ὡς ἔνι μάλιστα φιλοτίμως καὶ φιλοπόνως ἀκριβῆ τὴν ἑρμηνείαν ποιούμενοι μέχρι μὲν ὥρας ἐνάτης πρὸς τούτῳ διετέλουν ὄντες, ἔπειτ' ἐπὶ τὴν τοῦ σώματος ἀπηλλάττοντο θεραπείαν.

Particularly striking here are the parallels *Aristeas* 28b/*Ant.* 12:35; *Aristeas* 39/*Ant.* 12:49; and *Aristeas* 183/*Ant.* 12:95f., because of the exact verbal replication in the immediate vicinity of the ἀκρίβεια forms. The inescapable conclusion is that ἀκρίβεια represented a significant category in Josephus's thought.

Josephus presents the entire Jewish community as a group striving to observe the laws with ἀκρίβεια. Moses, he claims, called together the whole nation and extracted from them an oath, "to observe the laws, becoming strict stewards of the mind of God" (τῆς τοῦ θεοῦ διανοίας ἀκριβεῖς λογιστὰς γινομένους, *Ant.* 4:309). Indeed, Moses went so far as to require that every week the men should leave their occupations to hear the Law, in order "to obtain a thorough and accurate knowledge of it" (τοῦ νόμου συλλέγεσθαι καὶ τοῦτον ἀκριβῶς ἐκμανθάνειν, *Ag.Ap.* 2:175). Josephus can, therefore, propose that Plato follows Moses when he prescribes that all citizens have a basic duty to learn their laws ἀκριβῶς (*Ag.Ap.* 2:257). For it is the Jews who practice their laws punctiliously (πραττόμενα μετὰ πάσης ἀκριβείας ὑφ' ἡμῶν, *Ag.Ap.* 2:149).

Although ἀκρίβεια with respect to the laws is a communal goal, certain groups and individuals are commonly thought to excel in this regard, according to Josephus. That is the case with the scholars Judas and Mattathias, who advised their students pull down the golden eagle from Herod's temple (*War* 1:648), with a certain Eleazar, who insisted that King Izates of Adiabene undergo circumcision in his conversion to Judaism (*Ant.* 20:43), and with certain inhabitants of Jerusalem who objected to the stoning of James, the brother of Jesus (*Ant.* 20:201). In three places, including *War* 1:110, Josephus claims that the Pharisees have such a reputation (also *War* 2:162; *Life* 191). All of these parties seem to be, or are reputed to be (δοκοῦσιν),[23] accurate in their interpretation of the Law.

---

[23] We shall examine the sense of δοκέω below.

Josephus himself, however, is somewhat more sparing in his judgement. After asserting his own ἀκρίβεια, in rather strong terms, for the material that he presents in *Ant.* (20:260, 262), he allows:

> The Jews certify the wisdom only of those who know the laws exactly (σαφῶς) and who are competent to interpret the meaning of the holy scriptures. Thus, although many have laboured at this training (πολλῶν πονησάντων περὶ τὴν ἄσκησιν ταύτην), scarcely two or three have succeeded (μόλις δύο τινὲς ἢ τρεῖς κατώρθωσαν). (*Ant.* 20:265)

That Josephus considers himself to be among the few who have succeeded is confirmed by the contrived modesty of the sentence immediately following:

> Perhaps it will not arouse jealousy or strike ordinary folk as gauche if I also review briefly my own ancestry and the events of my life (καὶ περὶ γένους τοὐμοῦ καὶ περὶ τῶν κατὰ τὸν βίον πράξεων βραχέα διεξελθεῖν, 20:266).

This proposal is not fulfilled in *Ant.* itself but is probably intended to introduce Josephus's autobiography, the *Life* (᾿Ιωσήπου Βίος).[24] It is in that work that we should expect to find more information about Josephus's claim to ἀκρίβεια.

The opening words of the *Life* fit neatly with the epilogue to *Ant.* quoted above and make clear the reason for Josephus's pride: he is a priest.

> My ancestry is not undistinguished; indeed it has its origin among the priests. If each of the races has some sort of criterion for nobility, with us it is participation in the priesthood that is a sure sign of illustrious descent. (*Life* 1)

Josephus goes on to point out that he is not only a priest but a "priest's priest", for his ancestors belonged to the first of the twenty-four courses (1:2).

It is, then, to his priestly lineage that Josephus proudly points as the basis for his claim to ἀκρίβεια. He relates that as a child he made great progress in his education, becoming known for his excellent memory and understanding (§ 8). By the time he was fourteen years old:

> . . . the chief priests and leaders of the city were always coming by because with my help they could grasp more accurately some aspect of the laws (παρ᾽ ἐμοῦ περὶ τῶν νομίμων ἀκριβέστερόν τι γνῶναι). (*Life* 9)

---

[24] *Life* appears in all of the MSS as an appendix to *Ant.* Eusebius, *Eccl. Hist.* 3.10.8-9, cites it as if it were part of *Ant.* Laqueur's theory, adopted by Thackeray with qualifications, is that *Ant.* 20:259-266 was added to the second edition of *Ant.* (c. AD 100), to introduce the newly written *Life* (Laqueur, *Historiker*, 1-6; Thackeray, introduction to LCL edn., I, xiiif.).

It is important to understand Josephus' claim here without regard to its historical plausibility: it is solely on the basis of a priestly lineage and up-bringing that he claims to have achieved ἀκρίβεια with respect to the laws.

We have noted several other passages in which the priesthood is con-nected with ἀκρίβεια;[25] the clearest of these is *Ag.Ap.* 1:54, where Josephus bases the ἀλήθεια and ἀκρίβεια of *Ant.* on his priestly descent and training. We may now adduce further *Ag.Ap.* 2:184-187. He is there praising the theocratic constitution (πολίτευμα) of the Jews, which:

> sets God at the head of the universe, assigns the administration of its highest affairs (τὰ μέγιστα) to the whole body of priests (τοῖς ἱερεῦσι. . . κοινῇ), and entrusts to the supreme high-priest the direction of the other priests. (§ 185, Thackeray)

He claims that Moses entrusted to the priests τὴν περὶ τὸν θεὸν θεραπείαν (§ 186). But this charge to direct the nation's worship implied also strict attention to the Law and to the other pursuits of life (τοῦτο δ᾽ ἦν καὶ τοῦ νόμου καὶ τῶν ἄλλων ἐπιτηδευμάτων ἀκριβὴς ἐπιμελεία, § 187). Similarly *Ag.Ap.* 2:194: the high priest, along with his colleagues, safeguards the laws (φυλάξει τοὺς νόμους). In the ideal Jewish theocracy that Josephus portrays to his Gentile audience, it is the priests who have supreme responsibility for the communal goal of ἀκρίβεια.

Small wonder, then, that Josephus frequently points to his own priestly credentials as he reiterates his constant goal of ἀκρίβεια (*Ag.Ap.* 1:54; *Ant.* 20:264ff.; *Life* 1-9). Nor is this a late development in his think-ing, for we find the connection between his priestly credentials and his knowledge of the Scriptures already in *War* 3:352:

> He [Josephus] was an interpreter of dreams and skilled in divining the meaning of ambiguous utterances of the Deity; *a priest himself and of priestly descent*, he was not ignorant of the prophecies in the sacred books (τῶν γε μὴν ἱερῶν βίβλων οὐκ ἠγνόει τὰς προφητείας ὡς ἂν αὐτός τε ὢν ἱερεὺς καὶ ἱερέων ἔγγονος). (Thackeray)

Indeed, the possibility of a dramatic development in Josephus's thinking on the priestly prerogative in scriptural exegesis is excluded by a com-parison of this, his first writing, with his last work (*Ag.Ap.* 1:54):

> I have rendered the sacred writings, being a priest by birth and trained in the philosophy of their writings (ἐκ τῶν ἱερῶν γραμμάτων μεθηρμήνευκα γεγονὼς ἱερεὺς ἐκ γένους καὶ μετεσχηκὼς τῆς φιλοσοφίας τῆς ἐν ἐκείνοις τοῖς γράμμασι).

---

[25] E.g., *Ag.Ap.* 1:29, 32, 36, 54.

In both passages, the point being made and the ἱερεύς/ἱερός word-play are almost identical. We may also recall that Josephus opens *War* by claiming historical ἀκρίβεια and citing his priestly credentials side by side (1:2-3, 6). Finally, in *War* 2:411f-417, he claims that the leaders of the people, the chief priests, and the leading Pharisees called on "priestly experts on the traditions" (τοὺς ἐμπείρους τῶν πατρίων ἱερεῖς) to prove that the Jews had always accepted sacrifices from foreigners.[26] Thus, one can hardly doubt that Josephus always associated the priesthood with ἀκρίβεια in the interpretation of the laws.[27]

Josephus's position accords conspicuously well with what Lauterbach sees as the pre-Pharisaic, priestly view of the Law. That scholar remarks:

> The position held by priest and laity alike, before that group of lay-teachers, the Pharisees to be, started on their progressive march towards advanced Pharisaism, was that the authority of the Torah was supreme and binding upon the people, and that every one of its laws had to be carried out strictly and scrupulously.[28]

The motivation behind this strict observance, Lauterbach argues, was the "primitive" mechanism of the oath, as described in Deut. 29:9-30:20 and Neh. 10:1, 29-30.[29] We may note that Josephus, although he freely omits material from the Bible that might be offensive to his readers,[30] does not hesitate to describe the oath that Moses made the people swear, complete with the consequences of blessings and cursings (*Ant.* 4:305-310). Josephus appears, therefore, to embrace a classic "pre-Pharisaic" (therefore non-Pharisaic) view of the function of the Law.

To summarize: scrupulous adherence to one's traditional laws is, for Josephus, a universal responsibility, binding on all nations. The Jews, he maintains, take this task especially seriously. Since the original promulgation of their Law by Moses, they have sworn to study it and to obey its precepts with diligence. Although ἀκρίβεια with respect to the laws is the common goal of Jewish life, certain individuals and groups are reputed to excel in this area (e.g., the Pharisees, Eleazar, and certain

---

[26] As will become clear below, τὰ πάτρια is a favourite Josephan term, and designates the whole of Jewish law and custom.

[27] The importance of Josephus's priesthood for his world-view has often been noted by scholars; cf. Laqueur, *Historiker*, 34, 131; S. Rappaport, *Agada und Exegese bei Flavius Josephus* (Vienna: A. Kohut Memorial Foundation, 1930), *passim*; B. Heller, "Grundzüge der Aggada des Flavius Josephus", *MGWJ*, 80 (1936), 237-246, esp. 238f.; Lindner, *Geschichtsauffassung*, 75f., 146 n.2; and Rajak, *Josephus*, 18-20. It is seldom if ever realized, however, that Josephus's priestly view of the Law effectively precludes a Pharisaic outlook.

[28] Lauterbach, *HUCA*, 94.

[29] Ibid., 95.

[30] Heller, "Grundzüge", 241f.

Jerusalemites). In Josephus's own view, however, it is the priests who are the real adepts in accurate scriptural exegesis. He forthrightly and repeatedly makes his own claim to ἀκρίβεια on the basis of his priestly descent and training.

E. Νόμοι, "customs, conventions, laws". It has been enough so far to speak of "the Law" or "laws" as the object of Pharisaic exactitude in Josephus's definition: σύνταγμά τι 'Ιουδαίων δοκοῦν . . . τοὺς νόμους ἀκριβέστερον ἀφηγεῖσθαι. The meaning of νόμοι for Josephus, however, requires somewhat closer attention.

Now it is clear that Josephus views the νόμοι as the centre of Jewish life. He claims that Jews hold observance of the νόμοι to be dearer than life;[31] that the education of Jewish children begins with the νόμοι;[32] and that among Jews, accurate knowledge of the νόμοι is the sole criterion of wisdom or piety.[33] He reports that the Pharisees and other groups were especially renowned for (or pretended to) such expert knowledge. Since the νόμοι play a central role in Josephus's thought, it is crucial for us to specify as closely as possible what he means by this term.

We can do this by examining Josephus's definitions and summaries of the νόμοι, as well as contextual indicators such as qualifiers and synonyms for νόμος.

The Νόμοι of the Gentiles

More than one fifth of the 507 occurrences of νόμος in Josephus have to do with something other than Jewish νόμοι.[34] He speaks, for example, of the νόμοι of war,[35] of history,[36] and of Nature.[37] Each of the Gentile nations has its own νόμοι.[38] These passages evince a considerable fluidity in Josephus's conception of νόμος. They show, first, that he does not reserve νόμος, as a technical term, for something peculiar to Judaism; the νόμοι of the Jews are (at least formally) comparable to the νόμοι of the nations. Consider Josephus's caustic judgement of the anti-Semitic propagandist Apion:

---

[31] E.g., *Ant.* 3:317; 18:274; *Ag.Ap.* 1:42, 190, 2:219.

[32] *Ant.* 4:211; *Ag.Ap.* 1:60; 2:204.

[33] *Ant.* 20:265.

[34] By my count, about 376 of the 507 occurrences of νόμος (or the plural) denote the Jewish Law.

[35] *War* 2:90: 3:103, 363; 5:332; 6:346; *Ant.* 1:315; 6:69; 9:58; 14:304; 15:157.

[36] *War* 1:11; 5:20.

[37] *War* 3:370; 4:382; 5:367; *Ant.* 4:322; 17:95.

[38] *Ant.* 4:139; 10:257; 11:191ff.; 14:153; 16:277; 19:168ff.; *Ag.Ap.* 1:167; 2:143, 225, 257ff.

It is the duty of wise men scrupulously to adhere to their native laws concerning piety (τοῖς οἰκείοις νόμοις περὶ τὴν εὐσέβειαν ἀκριβῶς ἐμμένειν) and not to abuse those of others. Apion was delinquent in respect of his own country's laws and told lies about ours. (*Ag.Ap.* 2:144)

Indeed, Josephus's entire apologetic purpose is to demonstrate that, of all of the systems of νόμοι in the world, that of the Jews is the most perfect.

Notice, second, that the νόμοι of the Gentiles are not merely legislated decrees. They can also be customs or conventions. Although, for example, the νόμοι of historiography or of war may have been taught in the Hellenistic world as binding, they were approved practices rather than statutory laws. Josephus speaks of the inattention to Caligula's corpse immediately after his assassination as something inconsistent with Roman νόμοι, by which he evidently means "custom" (*Ant.* 19:195). On the other hand, however, he can use the word νέμοι to indicate statutory laws enacted by governing authorities such as the Babylonian Darius (*Ant.* 10:258), the Spartan Lycurgus (*Ag.Ap.* 2:225), Herod the Great (*Ant.* 16:1), and Gaius Caligula (*War* 2:195). Outside of the Jewish context, then, Josephus evokes the full range of Greek conceptions behind the word νόμος, from custom or convention to "law" in the most proper sense.[39]

We turn now to Josephus's use of νόμος in the context of Judaism.

The Νόμοι of the Jews

Josephus leaves no doubt, in the first place, that he regards the νόμοι of the Jews as the laws received and delivered by Moses at Sinai. Moses was the lawgiver (νομοθέτης);[40] his laws provided the Jews with a constitution (πολιτεία).[41] Although Josephus is always willing to recognize the divine inspiration of the laws,[42] he is more often concerned to demonstrate to his pagan readers the wisdom and forethought of the lawgiver Moses.[43] Once Josephus has introduced the laws, he often calls them οἱ Μωυσέος νόμοι.[44]

---

[39] Cf. C.H. Dodd, *Greeks*, 25-41; and H. Kleinknecht and W. Gutbrod, "Νόμος", *TDNT*, IV, 1023ff., 1044ff.

[40] *Ant.* 1:118, 95, 240; *Ag.Ap.* 2:165, 173, 279.

[41] Josephus sometimes pairs νόμοι καὶ πολιτεία, e.g., *Ant.* 3:332; 4:198; 310.

[42] *Ant.* 3:93, 213, 322; 5:107; 7:338; *Ag.Ap.* 2:184.

[43] *Ant.* 1:18-26; 3:317ff.; *Ag.Ap.* 2:157-163.

[44] *Ant.* 4:243, 302, 331; 7:338; 8:191, 395; 9:187; 10:59, 63, 72; 11:17, 76, 108, 121, 154: 13:74, 79, 297; 17:159; 18:81; 20:44, 115; *Life* 134.

So far, then, it seems clear enough that the phrase οἱ νόμοι refers to the Mosaic legislation embodied in Scripture. Analyzing the twenty-two "approved books" among the Jews, Josephus explains that:

> Of these, five are the books of Moses, which comprise *the laws* (ἃ τοὺς νόμους περιέχει) and the tradition [for the period] from the original man until his [Moses'] death. (*Ag.Ap.* 1:38f.)

Indeed, Josephus frequently uses νόμος/νόμοι to mean the first and central books of the Scriptures.[45] It is in this sense that he tells of a Roman soldier's taking τὸν ἱερὸν νόμον and tearing it in pieces (*War* 2:229) and of the Caesarean Jews who, having "snatched up" τοὺς νόμους, removed them from that city (*War* 2:291). Likewise in Josephus's account of the Septuagint translation effort, ὁ νόμος appears consistently as a document that can be handled and translated.[46]

If some of the contextual indicators point to such a specific meaning, however, other considerations indicate that Josephus is unable to distinguish the original Mosaic νόμος from its later elaborations in Judaism. In several places, for example, he summarizes the content of the Jewish νόμοι for his pagan readers. These summaries, found in the third and fourth books of the *Ant.* and in the second book of *Ag.Ap.*,[47] contain many departures from the letter of the Mosaic Law as we know it.[48]

In *Ant.* 3:224-386, which details the sacrificial system, Josephus frequently qualifies or elaborates the biblical prescriptions in some way. For the season coinciding with the *Sukkot* festival, he claims, Moses instructed the people to set up tents, indefinitely, as protection against inclement weather.[49] His understanding of the year of jubilee also differs notably from the scriptural presentation.[50] Yet he closes this section with the remark:

---

[45] Cf. *Ant.* 1:12; Ptolemy II was not able to receive, for the LXX translation, πᾶσαν τὴν ἀναγραφήν but only τὸν νόμον; cf. *Ag.Ap.* 1:43; (οἱ νόμοι) καὶ αἱ μετὰ τούτων ἀναγραφαί.

[46] *Ant.* 12:11, 20, 21, 39, 48, 49, 55, 56, 57, 87, 89, 90, 104, 106-111.

[47] The summaries are given at *Ant.* 3:213, 224-286; 4:196-301; *Ag.Ap.* 2:150, 163, 190-219.

[48] Cf. Thackeray's notes to these passages in the LCL edition; he draws heavily from the commentary by M. Weill in T. Reinach's French edition of Josephus. Cf. also H. W. Attridge, *Interpretation*, *passim*; and N. G. Cohen, "Josephus and Scripture . . .", *JQR* 54 (1963-64), 311-332.

[49] *Ant.* 3:244. According to Lev. 23:42f., the practice of erecting tents was to commemorate the Hebrews' wilderness wanderings.

[50] *Ant.* 3:282-285. Among other things, he has debts being resolved in that year and views slavery as a punishment for transgressing some aspect of the Law; neither of these is biblical.

Such was the code of laws (τὴν διάταξιν τῶν νόμων) which Moses, while keeping his army encamped beneath Mount Sinai, learnt from the mouth of God (ἐξεμάθη παρὰ τοῦ θεοῦ) and transmitted in writing to the Hebrews. (*Ant.* 3:286)

Josephus evidently believes that his understanding of the laws, in which the modern reader can find influences of post-biblical tradition, corresponds exactly to the content or intention of the Mosaic legislation.

Likewise, in *Ant.* 4:196-301, Josephus insists: "All is here written as he left it: nothing have we added for the sake of embellishment, nothing which has not been bequeathed by Moses" (*Ant.* 4:196). Yet he has Moses calling for a twice-daily prayer[51] and for a judicial body of seven men in each city,[52] neither of which is enjoined in Scripture. Further embellishments are: the disqualification of evidence from women and slaves in court,[53] the offering of rewards for information about murderers,[54] the custom of taking fourth-year produce to Jerusalem,[55] the punishment of thirty-nine (rather than forty) lashes,[56] the practice of burning alive an impure daughter of a priest,[57] and so on.[58]

Finally, in the summary of the νόμοι found in *Ag.Ap.*, Josephus again elaborates the Mosaic Law in significant ways. A few examples are the claims: that sexual intercourse is envisaged for only procreation;[59] that abortion is forbidden, as the destruction of a soul;[60] that all who pass a funeral procession must join it;[61] that friendship requires absolute frankness;[62] and that those who faithfully observe the laws will receive "a renewed existence (γενέσθαι πάλιν) and in the revolution (of the ages) the gift of a better life (βίον ἀμείνω)".[63]

In all of these elaborations of Mosaic Law, it is difficult to find a single explanatory logic. Several items are attested in talmudic tradition;[64]

---

[51] *Ant.* 4:212.

[52] *Ant.* 4:214.

[53] *Ant.* 4:219.

[54] *Ant.* 4:220.

[55] *Ant.* 4:227.

[56] *Ant.* 4:238; but Deut. 25:3.

[57] *Ant.* 4:248.

[58] Several other examples are given by Thackeray; cf. especially *Ant.* 4:212-214, on the rules for war.

[59] *Ag.Ap.* 2:199.

[60] *Ag.Ap.* 2:202.

[61] *Ag.Ap.* 2:205.

[62] *Ag.Ap.* 2:207.

[63] *Ag.Ap.* 2:218. For a discussion of Josephus's intriguing references to the afterlife in Jewish belief, cf. chapter 6, below.

[64] E.g., *Ant.* 3:237, 242, 250 (which reflects Pharisaic views about the date of Pentecost; but these already appear in the LXX translations and in Philo), 251; 4:205, 219, 227, 238 (Makkot 3:10ff.); 248 (b. Ket 45b), 252, 278 (b. BKamma 83b); *Ag.Ap.* 2:205.

others do not appear there[65] and some even disagree with talmudic practices.[66] Several items are paralleled in Josephus's description of Essene teachings[67] and some accord with Alexandrian exegesis.[68]

For our purpose, the crucial point is this: although Josephus identifies the νόμοι of the Jews with the Mosaic Law, he evidently sees that Law only through the filter of post-biblical tradition and current practices familiar to him, which he finds already implicit in the Law. It seems likely that, as a full participant in his own historical setting, Josephus was unable to draw a clear distinction between the letter of the Law and its traditional application. It is the undifferentiated amalgam of statute and custom that Josephus attributes to Moses when he says (Ag.Ap. 2:173):

> Our legislator, on the other hand, took great care to combine both systems [sc. instruction by precept and by practical exercise]. . . . Starting from the very beginning with the food of which we partake from infancy and the private life of the home, he left nothing, however insignificant, to the discretion and caprice of the individual.

Here as elsewhere[69] Josephus presents Moses as the author of a complete and practical programme for living. To be sure, such passages are intended to serve his idealizing apologetic. Nevertheless, in light of his summaries of the Jewish code, discussed above, we must conclude that Josephus really believed that his own knowledge of legal practice was already implicit in the Mosaic code.

That Josephus cannot distinguish between the original statutes and their current application in his experience is corroborated further by the variety of terms that he can use interchangeably, hence more or less synonymously, with νόμος. As the following selective list shows, he seems to use ὁ νόμος, οἱ νόμοι, τὰ ἔθη, οἱ ἐθισμοί, τὰ νόμιμα, τὰ πάτρια, and various combinations of these phrases as practical equivalents.

---

[65] *Ant.* 3:244 (purpose of tents at Sukkot), 262.

[66] *Ant.* 3:242f. (sprinkling the blood of a kid; cf. Yoma 5:4, 5); *Ant.* 4:209 (high priest as reader of laws; cf. Sotah 7:8); 4:212 (twice-daily prayer; tradition has it thrice daily); 4:263 (οὔτε θυγατέρα is an embellishment of Scripture); 4:287 (tribunal of seven men). Cf. B. Revel, "Some Anti-Traditional Laws of Josephus", *JQR* n. s. 14 (1923-24), 293-301. Attridge (*Interpretation*, 179 n. 1) remarks, "Examination of the legal passages in *Antiquities* is somewhat disappointing . . . [He then lists much of the pertinent secondary literature.] These studies show no consistent relation between Josephus and later halachic tradition."

[67] *Ag.Ap.* 2:199 (sex for procreation only; cf. *War* 2:161), 203 (the suffering of souls in bodies; cf. *War* 2:154f.) and 207 (the frankness of friends; cf. *War* 2:141).

[68] *Ant.* 4:207; *Ag.Ap.* 2:237 (not reviling gods of other countries; cf. Ex. 22:28 [27, LXX] and Philo, *Life of Moses* 2:26, 205; *Special Laws* 1:7, 53); *Ant.* 4:285 (παρακαταθήκην . . . ἱερόν . . . χρῆμα ; cf. Philo, *Moses* 2:341.)

[69] Cf. *Ant.* 3:213.

(a) We have noted Josephus's report that the Pharisees were famous for their erudition and accurate exegesis. But the object of the Pharisees' exegesis is described variously as οἱ νόμοι (*War* 1:110), τὰ νόμιμα (*War* 2:162), τὰ πάτρια νόμιμα (*Life* 191), and τὸ πάτριον καὶ (οἱ) νόμοι (*Ant.* 17:41). Presumably, Josephus holds these terms to be equivalent.

(b) In *War* 1:648ff., we have the famous story of the two scholars who incited their students to pull down the golden eagle from Herods' temple. The scholars are described as δοκοῦντες ἀκριβοῦν τὰ πάτρια and consequently as enjoying a great reputation among the people. In the next sentence, however, we learn that these scholars attracted large crowds to their ἐξηγουμένοις τοὺς νόμους (649). Further, the scholars advise their students to remove the eagle because it violates τοὺς πατρίους νόμους (649)—a combination of the two phrases; they encourage their hearers even to die for τοῦ πατρίου νόμου (650).[70]

From this episode, we see that Josephus can use ὁ νόμος (1:654), οἱ νόμοι (649), ὁ πάτριος νόμος (650, 653), οἱ πάτριοι νόμοι (649, 2:6), and simply τὰ πάτρια, substantively (1:648), as equivalents.

(c) In *War* 2:169f., it is reported that Pilate's introduction of standards with effigies of Caesar into Jerusalem offended the Jews, who felt that οἱ νόμοι had been violated; in 171, they beseech Pilate to remove the standards and thereby to maintain τὰ πάτρια.

(d) In *War* 4:99, John of Gischala requests that Titus give him the Sabbath to rest, in deference to τῷ Ἰουδαίων νόμῳ. In doing so, says John (102), Titus would spare the Jews transgressing τῶν πατρίων ἐθῶν and would be therefore preserving τοὺς νόμους.

(e) In *Life* 198, Josephus describes the charge that was given to the delegation sent to relieve him of command in the Galilee: if the Galileans remained loyal to him because of his expertise in the *laws* (διὰ τὴν ἐμπειρίαν τῶν νόμων), then the Jerusalem delegation should respond that they themselves were by no means ignorant of the ancestral customs (μηδ' αὐτοὺς ἀγνοεῖν ἔθη τὰ πάτρια).

(f) David counsels his son Solomon to keep God's τὰς ἐντολὰς καὶ τοὺς νόμους, οὓς αὐτὸς διὰ Μωυσέος κατέπεμψεν ἡμῖν (*Ant.* 7:384) because (γάρ), if he should transgress τι τῶν νομίμων, he will lose divine favour. Likewise in 9:2, we are told that Josaphat (Jehoshaphat) διδάσκειν τὰ νόμιμα τὰ διὰ Μωυσέος . . . δοθέντα. But in 8:395, what Josaphat teaches are τοὺς Μωυσέος νόμους.

---

[70] Cf. also *War* 1:653 (ὁ πάτριος νόμος), 654 (ὁ νόμος), and 2:6 (οἱ πάτριοι νόμοι), which all refer back to the same episode.

(g) Solomon, according to *Ant.* 8:190, ended his life abandoning τὴν τῶν πατρίων ἐθισμῶν φυλακήν, on account of his numerous marriages to foreigners; but this failure is described in the next sentence as the transgressing of τοὺς Μωυσέος νόμους (191).

(h) Notice in *Ant.* 9:95 that the verb used to describe Joram's (= Jehoram's) and his predecessors' offences against τὰ πάτρια ἔθη (ancestral customs) is παρανομέω. In 12:286, we have the same verb used with τὰ πάτρια as object: Judah Maccabee did away with τοὺς παρανομήσαντας εἰς τὰ πάτρια.

(i) Mattathias the Hasmonean admonishes his sons that it is better to die ὑπὲρ τῶν πατρίων νόμων than to live ingloriously (*Ant.* 12:267). He then actualizes this principle (271) with the charge: "Whoever is zealous for the ancestral customs (εἴ τις ζηλωτής ἐστιν τῶν πατρίων ἐθῶν [Marcus translates "laws"!]), . . . let him come with me!" The practical equivalence of "laws" and "customs" here is unmistakable.

(j) Finally, some things commanded in the Law are said by Josephus to be "traditional", such as the prohibition of work on the Sabbath (*Ant.* 18:312; cf. Ex. 30:13)[71] and the half-shekel tax (*Ant.* 18:312; cf. Ex. 30:13). On the other hand, the *traditional* practices of repentance in sackcloth and of prostrating oneself for prayer he calls practices τῷ πατρίῳ νόμῳ (*Ant.* 11:231; *Ant.* 19:349).

Dozens of other instances of Josephus's substituting synonyms for ὁ νόμος can be cited.[72] These, however, will suffice to show that he does not regard νόμος as an irreplaceable technical term. He can and does alternate freely between ὁ νόμος, οἱ νόμοι, τὰ ἔθη, οἱ ἐθισμοί, τὰ νόμιμα, τὰ πάτρια, and various combinations of these (usually πάτριος used attributively with one of the other substantives). Other interchangeable terms for οἱ νόμοι are ἡ (πάτριος) εὐσέβεια[73]/ θρήσκεια[74]/ συνηθεία[75]/ and πολιτεία.[76]

It would be overstating the case to say that the above terms are identical for Josephus, that he is insensitive to any differences of nuance be-

---

[71] Indeed, in *Ant.* 12:276, Sabbath observance is called a νόμιμον.

[72] οἱ νόμοι + τὰ πάτρια, cf. *War* 1:34, 108; 2:393; *Ant.* 18:266// 276, 281; 20:24// 226. οἱ νόμοι + τὰ πάτρια ἔθη, cf. *Ant.* 5:101// 108; 11:338// 339; 14:263// 264; 15:328; 16:1// 3; 19:290; *Ag.Ap.* 1:317. οἱ νόμοι + τὰ νόμιμα, cf. *Ant.* 3:282; 4:181; 8:96, 195, 208, 256, 280, 290, 297; 9:157,168, 222; 12:14, 276; 3:243, 297; 18:38, etc. τὰ πάτρια + τὰ ἔθη, cf. *Ant.* 15:281; 16:35; τὰ πάτρια νόμιμα + οἱ ἐπιχωρίοι ἐθισμοί + τὰ πάτρια, cf. *Ant.* 9:95/96/99.

[73] *Ant.* 13:243.

[74] *Ant.* 8:229; 12:364, 384; 19:283.

[75] *Ant.* 10:72; 13:4, 121.

[76] *Ant.* 3:213; 4:45, 193, 194, 198, 292, 310; 5:132; 10:275; 11:140; *Ag.Ap.* 2:287.

tween them.[77] What is clear, however, is that he often juxtaposes these terms in what appears to be an attempt to avoid repetitiveness. In such cases the juxtaposed terms must be tolerably equivalent for him. And that equivalence betrays the comprehensiveness of οἱ νόμοι in his thought.

If we have correctly interpreted the (πάτριοι) νόμοι of Josephus as the all-embracing Mosaic code (from Josephus's perspective), which is really an undifferentiated mass of original law and subsequent tradition (from our perspective), then his usage finds significant parallels in the politics of ancient Greece. J. Schreiner, C. Hignett, A. Fuks, and M. I. Finley, among others, have shown that the Athenians could use πάτριοι νόμοι or πάτριος πολιτεία with similar elasticity.[78] To reproduce the evidence here would be superfluous, but one of Finley's observations is particularly germane to our discussion. The first known official document produced after the Athenian return to democracy was the Decree of Theisamenos (403 BC).[79] This document called for a reinstatement of the "laws of Solon and Draco", the seventh-century Athenian lawgivers. Finley observes:

> By the 'laws of Solon and Draco' the decree meant the law of Athens as it stood in 403, some of it indeed going back to the ancient lawgivers but much of it either revised or wholly new legislation promulgated in the two centuries since Solon. . . . After the year 403/2 no earlier law was valid unless it had been incorporated into the code; yet advocates went on cheerfully citing in the courts what they called 'a law of Solon', even when it was blatantly impossible for the enactment to have been very ancient.[80]

The unrefined historical consciousness that has been discovered among the Athenians is exactly what we find in Josephus: he makes no clear distinction between statute and precedent.

One of the questions to be broached by this study is whether Josephus's νόμος-conception implies anything about his party allegiance. Although a proper answer must await the examination of *Ant.* 13:297-298 below, a preliminary statement is demanded by the assertion of some commentators that Josephus's inclusion of "custom" in his presentation of "Law" indicates a Pharisaic viewpoint. The tacit

---

[77] E.g., at *Ant.* 14:258 (ἔθη), *War* 2:417 (τὰ πάτρια), and *War* 4:136 (πάτρια ἔθη), the meanings seem more restricted.

[78] J. Schreiner, *De corpore iuris Atheniensium*, (1913), 49ff., cited in C. Hignett, *A History of the Athenian Constitution* (Oxford: Clarendon Press, 1952), 18f.; A. Fuks, *The Ancestral Constitution* (London: Chatto & Windus, 1953) 39f., who refers also to one Linforth, *Solon the Athenian* (1919), appendix 4 (inaccessible to me); and M. I. Finley, *The Use and Abuse of History* (London: Chatto & Windus, 1975), 35-40.

[79] So Fuks, *Constitution*, 37. The decree is given by Andokides, 1:83f.

[80] Finley, *Use and Abuse*, 39.

premise here is Josephus's claim (*Ant.* 13:297) that the Pharisees were distinguished by their recognition of a body of normative tradition, in addition to the pentateuchal law. W. Gutbrod's *TDNT* article on νόμος, for example, observes: "Customs are part of the Law. . . . This shows his [Josephus's] orientation to Pharisaism."[81]

Such an inference is excluded, however, by the facts that have emerged so far. First, several of Josephus's embellishments either are unattested in rabbinic halakhah or actually contradict the tradition. H. W. Attridge, after reviewing scholarly analyses of Josephus's νόμοι, concludes, "These studies show no consistent relation between Josephus and later halachic tradition."[82] Without pronouncing on the larger problem of the correspondence between Pharisaic tradition and rabbinic halakhah, we can say that there is no positive basis in the content of Josephus's νόμοι for considering him a Pharisee.

Second, it is a well-attested phenomenon that groups who recognize authoritative texts tend to believe that their own developed ideas are already implicit (or explicit) in those texts. What was true in Athens was true in Judaism: we now have the Temple Scroll as proof that at least one non-Pharisaic group earnestly believed its own teachings to have come from Moses.[83] It should occasion no surprise if every Jew, no matter what his party allegiance, identified his accustomed interpretation of the Mosaic code with the code itself.[84]

Most important, finally, Josephus disallows any formal distinction between the written code of Moses and the customs or traditions of the Jews. It needs to be emphasized that the Mosaic πολιτεία in which Josephus exults is a *written* code. Moses wrote (γράφω) his constitution in books[85] and Josephus now endeavours to translate the account as he finds it ἐν ταῖς ἱεραῖς βίβλοις ἀναγεγραμμένα.[86] It is the written code of Moses that "the Hebrew nation" continues to observe in Josephus's

---

[81] H. Kleinknecht and W. Gutbrod, "νόμος", *TDNT*, IV, 1051. Cf. already H. Paret ("Pharisäismus", 825f.) for this claim.

[82] Attridge, *Interpretation*, 179 n.1.

[83] Cf. for example, B. Z. Wacholder, *The Dawn of Qumran* (Cincinnati: Hebrew Union College Press, 1983), xii.

[84] Analogous phenomena in the religious sphere would seem to include the Protestant oversight by which the Reformation slogan *sola scriptura* sanctions even those doctrines that were formulated in the fourth and fifth centuries, and after bitter controversy. Likewise J. Ross (*The Jewish Conception of Immortality and the Life Hereafter: An Anthology* [Belfast: Belfast News-Letter, 1948], 1-3) infers the doctrines of resurrection and immortality from the Pentateuch. Finley (*Use and Abuse*, 40-44) cites parallels to this sort of "ellipsis" from modern political argumentation.

[85] Cf. *Ant.* 1:20; 3:213; *4:193f.*, 302; *Ag.Ap.* 1:39; 2:45.

[86] Cf. *Ant.* 1:26; 2:34; 4:196ff.; 9:208, 214.

own day.[87] The point is made with special force in *Ag.Ap.* 2:155-156. Arguing the superiority of the Mosaic code to the laws of the Greeks, Josephus points out there that the Greek laws were, for a long time, merely unwritten customs (ἔθη ἄγραφα), subject to change. He explicitly contrasts the Jewish laws (ὁ δ' ἡμέτερος νομοθέτης) on the ground that Moses delivered a single, comprehensive (ὅλην τοῦ βίου) code, which has never been altered since the day of its inauguration.[88] It is this written πολιτεία that tells Jews how they should act in all circumstances (*Ant.* 3:92f.) and that leaves nothing, not even the slightest detail (οὐδὲ τῶν βραχυτάτων), to individual discretion (*Ag.Ap.* 2:173).[89] Not only does Josephus fail to mention any distinction between written law and custom (or between written and oral law); his positive portrayal of Moses' πολιτεία excludes this distinction.

There is nothing, then, in Josephus's hundreds of references to the νόμοι to indicate that he was a Pharisee.

Summary of οἱ Νόμοι in Josephus

To summarize thus far: for Josephus, νόμος is a generic or universal category; every nation has its own νόμοι. Moreover, in discussing both Jewish and Gentile laws, Josephus can use synonyms for οἱ νόμοι, such as οἱ πάτριοι νόμοι, τὰ πάτρια, and ἔθη.[90] This circumstance warns against any attempt to read νόμος In Josephus as a technical term for some exclusively Jewish concept.

Our findings reflect Josephus's starting point. All of his works are addressed to pagan audiences. When he speaks of νόμοι, therefore, the term does not in the first instance reflect any specifically Jewish content. As an apologist,[91] Josephus argues from general conceptions that his readers will understand to specific conclusions about Judaism. That explains the generic use of νόμοι. Josephus wants his readers to accept the premise that, no matter which nation is concerned, adherence to one's πάτριοι

---

[87] Cf. *Ant.* 4:308; *Ag.Ap.* 1:42; 2:153, 156, 169.

[88] Cf. *Ant.* 3:282; 8:395; 20:264; *Life* 9, 74; *Ag.Ap.* 1:165; 2:272.

[89] It is worth noting that when Josephus uses compounds like νόμοι καὶ ἔθη, as he occasionally does (*War* 2:160, 195; 5:237; *Ant.* 10:72 [συνήθεια]; 12:203; 14:216. 15:254. 328; 16:43, 172; *Ag.Ap.* 2:164), the relationship between the two terms is either one of hendiadys (as also with αἱ ἐντολαὶ καὶ οἱ νόμοι, *Ant.* 7:338, 384) or it is epexegetical (as also with οἱ νόμοι καὶ ἡ πολιτεία [*Ant.* 1:10; 12:240]). The ἔθη are seen as embodied in the written code; they are not a distinct category.

[90] Thus, τὰ πάτρια of Adiabene (*Ant.* 20:75, 81), of Commagene (*Ant.* 18:53), and of the Greeks (*Ant.* 18:41); ἔθη of the Greeks (*Ag.Ap.* 2:155); and νόμιμα of Egypt (*Ant.* 1:166) and of Parthia (*Ant.* 18:344)

[91] Cf. *Ant.* 1:5-24; 14:186f.; 16:174; *Ag.Ap.* 1:1-2.

νόμοι is supremely virtuous.[92] Once that premise is secure he can set out
to show, in numerous ways, that the Jewish νόμοι are especially ad-
mirable and that the Jews as a people adhere scrupulously to them even
in the face of death. This apology for the Jewish νόμοι, if only fully ex-
plicated in *Ag.Ap.*, is unmistakably present in *Ant.*[93] and in *War.*[94]

When Josephus speaks of the νόμοι of the Jews, therefore, the term has
the same comprehensiveness as when it is used of other nations. The
πολιτεία instituted by Moses governs every detail of Jewish conduct and
requires nothing more than simple (and scrupulous) obedience. Josephus
presents as a seamless whole what we should distinguish as legislation
and convention, or law and custom. He apparently knows the Mosaic
νόμοι only through the filter of tradition. Most significant: outside of *Ant.*
13:297f., to be considered later, Josephus never hints at any intramural
distinctions on this point:[95] the Jewish νόμοι are shared by all Jews.

F. The verb ἀφηγέομαι occurs 25 times in Josephus, the noun ἀφήγησις
9 times. Josephus employs the verb in two distinct senses, namely: (i)
to conduct, lead, or execute[96] and (ii) to narrate, report, set forth, or explain.[97] Although a meaning something like "administer the laws" is
conceivable in this passage, parallel constructions (with respect to both
the Pharisees and others)[98] strongly suggest the expositional sense: the
Pharisees are reputed to expound the traditional laws more accurately
than others do.

G. Δοκέω is the verb on which the whole definition of the Pharisees
in *War* 1:110 hinges.

As is well known, δοκέω bears two main senses, depending on its subject.[99] With a personal subject, the verb usually has the meaning: "to
think, suppose, imagine, purpose, or resolve". With an impersonal sub-

---

[92] Cf. especially *Ag.Ap.* 2:226, 257, where Josephus cites Plato to this effect.

[93] In *Ant.* Josephus consistently enthuses over Moses, the νόμοι, and Jewish zeal for
the νόμοι (1:6, 14: 7:338; 9:2; 14:65; 15:267, *et passim*).

[94] Exaltation of the νόμοι receives less space in *War* but is undeniably present throughout. Cf. the descriptions of Alexandra and the Pharisees (1:108, 110); the story of the
golden eagle (1:648-653; 2:6f.)—an unabashed apology for the νόμοι; the triumph of τὰ
πάτρια over Pilate (2:170ff.); Jewish zeal for the Law (2:228ff., 289ff.), to name only a
few episodes.

[95] The sole exception, so far as I can tell, is in the references to the special, extra-
biblical νόμιμα of the Pharisees (*Ant.* 13:297, 408), which will be discussed below.

[96] *War* 1:50, 52, 367; 2:168, 219, 443, 578: 3:56; *Life* 288.

[97] *War* 1:3, 69; 2:417, 469, 580; 4:476; 7:54; *Ant.* 13:300; 16:404; 18:24, 307, 373;
30:105; *Life* 310; *Ag.Ap.* 1:131. It is striking that Josephus can use the same phrase—
ἀφήγησις πραγμάτων—in *both* senses, viz: "narrative of events" (*War* 5:20; *Ant.* 1:26) and
"conduct of affairs" (*War* 1:226); the latter is probably taken over from his source.

[98] Of the Pharisees, *War* 2:162 (ἐξηγεῖσθαι); of a Jewish scoundrel in Rome, *Ant.* 18:81
(ἐξηγεῖσθαι).

[99] Cf. LSJ and the Thackeray/Marcus *Lexicon* to Josephus.

ject it means: "to seem, appear, or seem good". In the one case the verb indicates an action *of* the mind, in the other an action's impinging *upon* the mind. Sometimes, however, the two senses become blurred, especially when a personal subject takes δοκέω as an auxiliary verb, followed by a main verb (often εἶναι) attributing some quality to the subject. In that case, δοκέω may have the sense "to be regarded (as) or reputed (to)". For simplicity, I have so far rendered δοκέω in *War* 1:110 in keeping with this last sense because that is how the passage is all but universally rendered by commentators: the Pharisees *have the reputation of being* more pious than the others and of expounding the laws more accurately (δοκοῦν εὐσεβέστερον εἶναι. . . καὶ ἀκριβέστερον ἀφηγεῖσθαι).[100]

Among the few dissenters from this reading are G. F. Moore and R. H. Pfeiffer, who render the definition: "a body of Jews *who profess* to be more religious than the rest/others, and to explain the laws more precisely/accurately".[101] These translations take up the first option mentioned above: the Pharisees suppose or imagine that they have superior ἀκρίβεια. Neither Moore nor Pfeiffer is concerned to argue the case for such a translation, however, and so the evidence *pro* and *contra* must now be considered. Granted that both interpretations are possible in Greek and that both fit the syntax of this passage, the deciding factors must be Josephan usage and the immediate context.

An initial difficulty is that Josephus uses δοκέω of a personal subject and with an infinitive main verb in both senses. On the one hand, we are told that Aristobulus saw fit to transform (μεταθεῖναι δόξας) the government into a kingdom (*Ant.* 13:301), that Herod thought he had (ἔδοξε ἔχειν) sufficient ground to accuse his sons (*Ant.* 16:251), and that the brigands did not think it impious (οὐδὲ δοκοῦντες ἀσεβεῖν) to slaughter their enemies in the Temple (*Ant.* 20:165).[102] On the other hand, however, Josephus speaks of one who "is regarded as evil and untrustworthy" (πονηρὸς εἶναι δοκεῖ καὶ ἄπιστος, *War* 3:327) and of himself as a child, "gaining a reputation for an excellent memory and understanding" (μνήμῃ τε καὶ συνέσει δοκῶν διαφέρειν, *Life* 8)".[103] The construction alone, therefore, does not demand either interpretation of δοκέω.

Even if one narrows the field to the ten occurrences of δοκέω with a personal subject and an ἀκρίβεια form, in search of a formulaic pattern,

---

[100] So the major translations: Whiston, "seem/appear"; Thackeray, "with the reputation of"; Cornfeld, "were considered"; Reinach, "passe pour être"; Michel-Bauernfeind (and Schlatter, *Theologie*, 205), "im Ruf stehen"; cf. Rivkin (*Revolution*, 54f.), "are deemed".

[101] Moore, *Judaism*, I, 64, 66; Pfeiffer, *New Testament Times*, 54.

[102] Cf. also *War* 1:497; 3:144, 319; 5:437; 6:320; *Ant.* 15:101, 16:125, 211, 244, 386.

[103] Cf. also *War* 2:119; 4:207; *Ant.* 16:319; *Ag.Ap.* 1:232.

the ambiguity remains. On one side, Josephus remarks that the Spartans "saw fit strictly to observe their laws (ἀκριβῶς ἔδοξαν τοὺς νόμους διαφυλάττειν)" only so long as they retained their independence (*Ag.Ap.* 2:227). And this use of δοκέω as an action of the mind has intriguing parallels in the use of προσποιοῦμαι in *Ant.* 17:41 and 18:81. Liddell and Scott cite several cases in which the subjective sense of δοκέω approximates the meaning "to pretend or seem . . . ";[104] the eighth edition of that work even suggests προσποιοῦμαι and the Latin *simulo* as synonyms for δοκέω in this sense. But in *Ant.* 17:41 Josephus describes the Pharisees as:

μόριόν τι, 'Ιουδαικῶν ἀνθρώπων ἐπ' ἐξακριβώσει μέγα φρονοῦν τοῦ πατρίου καὶ νομῶν οἷς χαίρει τὸ θεῖον *προσποιούμενον*.

In *Ant.* 18:81f., in much the same vein, he describes a certain Jew in Rome, who was evil in every way (πονηρὸς εἰς τὰ πάντα), with these words: προσεποιεῖτο μὲν ἐξηγεῖσθαι σοφίαν νόμων τῶν Μωυσέος. Both of these passages have obvious similarities to *War* 1:110; the Pharisees, the νόμοι, and "exegesis" are common terms. This similarity, taken together with *Ag.Ap.* 2:227, supports the subjective, volitional reading of δοκέω in *War* 1:110: the Pharisees profess (or, pretend) to interpret the laws with accuracy.

On the other side of the ledger, however, are the other six occurrences of δοκέω with a personal subject and an ἀκρίβεια form.[105] Four of the six include not only δοκέω and ἀκρίβεια but also a reference to the νόμοι/νόμιμα/πάτρια. They are as follows:

War 1:648[106] speaks of two σοφισταί in Jerusalem "with a reputation for their superior precision with the national laws (μάλιστα δοκοῦντες ἀκριβοῦν τὰ πάτρια) who consequently enjoyed the highest esteem (μεγίστης δόξης) of the whole nation. The meaning of δοκέω here is fixed by the occurrence of δόξα in the following clause: their *reputation* is the point under discussion.

Ant. 19:332: While discussing the virtues of King Agrippa, Josephus mentions a certain Simon from Jerusalem who, ἐξακριβάζειν δοκῶν τὰ νόμιμα, claimed that the King was unclean. Although both senses of δοκέω would fit here, the fact that this man gained a considerable

---

[104] Cf. Herodotus 1:110; Aristotle, *Politics* 5.11.19, and Euripides, *Hippolytus* 462, for this usage.

[105] That is, not counting the three that concern the Pharisees or *Ag.Ap.* 2:227 (already considered).

[106] The parallel (*Ant.* 17:149) lacks δοκέω: the teachers *were*, Josephus says there, ἐξηγηταὶ τῶν πατρίων νόμων, indicating his agreement with their reputation.

audience for his charges[107] probably suggests that his reputation is intended.

Ant. 20:43 tells of one Eleazar from Galilee, περὶ τὰ πάτρια δοκῶν ἀκριβὴς εἶναι.[108] In contrast to the opinion of an earlier authority, Eleazar advised the proselyte King Izates to be circumcised in accordance with the Law. The meaning of δοκέω here could go either way.

Ant. 20:201: Recounting the savage stoning of Jesus' brother James, Josephus allows that ὅσοι δὲ ἐδόκουν ἐπιεικέστατοι . . . εἶναι καὶ περὶ τοὺς νόμους ἀκριβεῖς were offended. Since the people involved are shown by the sequel to be religious leaders in Jerusalem,[109] δοκέω evidently indicates their reputation more than their intention.

The two passages that combine δοκέω and ἀκρίβεια but do not refer to the νόμοι are nonetheless helpful for comparison. In one, Josephus is pointing out the frequent contradictions among Greek historians and he remarks that even Thucydides, καίτοι δοκῶν ἀκριβέστατα τὴν κατ' αὐτὸν ἱστορίαν συγγράφειν, has been accused of error (*Ag.Ap.* 1:18). In the other passage, continuing the same theme, he charges that even those reputed to be the most exact historians (οἱ δοκοῦντες ἀκριβέστατοι συγγραφεῖς) have made egregious geographical errors (*Ag.Ap.* 1:67). Since the whole point of Josephus's discussion is to challenge the widely held *belief* that Greek historians are the most accurate, δοκέω in these passages must refer to their reputation.[110]

If there is anything like a formulaic meaning of δοκέω with ἀκρίβεια, it would appear to be "reputed to . . . with accuracy"; *Ag.Ap.* 2:227, however, destroys this consistency. There may be something like a formula, however, in those passages that include reference to the νόμοι/νόμιμα/πάτρια. The meaning of δοκέω in those cases uniformly has to do with "reputation".

Decisive for the sense of δοκέω in *War* 1:110 must be its immediate context. Within the preceding narrative we have already noted two significant occurrences of δοκέω or δόξα. Alexander Janneus came to the throne with a (mistaken) reputation for moderation (μετριότητι προύχειν δοκοῦντα, *War* 1:85). His wife Alexandra come to power easily because

---

[107] He assembled the people (πλῆθος εἰς ἐκκλησίαν ἁλίσας), we are told, in order to make his assertions.

[108] The fact that one MS (M) reads εὐσεβής here is interesting in light of our earlier discussion of the relationship between the two concepts.

[109] They are familiar with the Roman legal principles behind the high-priestly administration, they correspond with royalty, they even send a delegation to the new procurator (20:201-203).

[110] An interesting parallel is found in Polybius (12.26d.3), who asserts that Timaeus, when he makes everyone think (δοκεῖν) that he has tested the ἀκρίβεια of everything, is making a pretense.

of a (well-founded) reputation for piety (διὰ δόξαν εὐσεβείας, 1:108). These clear references in the immediate context to the *reputations* of leaders create a strong predisposition to interpret the δοκέω of *War* 1:110 in the same way. It was the Pharisees' reputation for piety that won them the support of Alexandra Salome. Moreover, to anticipate coming analyses, Josephus repeatedly alludes to the prominent role of the Pharisees in public life (*War* 2:162; *Ant.* 13:288, 298, 401; 18:15) and this popularity would accord well with a reputation for superior accuracy in the interpretation of the laws.

It appears, then, that the usual reading of δοκέω in *War* 1:110 as a reference to the Pharisees' reputation is justified. The reading of Moore and Pfeiffer, tantalizing as it is with the support of προσποιοῦμαι in *Ant.* 17:41, has somewhat less plausibility in the context. It may be that Josephus intended a double meaning: the Pharisees professed to be, and were indeed believed to be, precise interpreters of the laws.

III. *Interpretation of War 1:110-114*

With the analysis of the key terms now complete, we are in a position to offer an interpretation of Josephus's first definition of the Pharisees.

In recounting the history of the Hasmonean dynasty, Josephus has claimed that its days of glory ended with John Hyrcanus, whose eldest son Aristobulus presided over a year-long καταστροφή (1:69). Alexander Janneus came to power with a reputation for moderation (1:85) but he turned out to be an impious tyrant. His wife Alexandra, on the contrary, took the throne with a well-deserved (δή, § 108) reputation for piety. By the end of *War* 1:109, the situation once again looks promising for the Hasmonean house.

Enter the Pharisees. If Alexandra's reputation for εὐσέβεια was based on the fact that she ἠκρίβου μάλιστα τὰ πάτρια, the Pharisees were a certain group of Jews δοκοῦν εὐσεβέστερον εἶναι τῶν ἄλλων καὶ τοὺς νόμους ἀκριβέστερον ἀφηγεῖσθαι (§ 110). This was a group, therefore, that appeared to share the religious outlook and goals of the Queen. The question now is: Did the Pharisees' reputation turn out to be well founded, like that of Alexandra, or baseless, like that of her late husband?

Elsewhere, when Josephus speaks of someone's reputation for ἀκρίβεια, he always goes on, in the immediate context, either to substantiate it (as with the two σοφισταί, Eleazar of Galilee, and the religious leaders of Jerusalem) or to debunk it (as with the Greek historians and Simon of Jerusalem). The concept of ἀκρίβεια, both in historical writing and in religion, is central to Josephus's vision of things. With his belief that the priests hold something of a monopoly on these virtues, he considers himself authorized to point out which other groups among his co-religionists come close to the Jewish ideals and which are mere pretenders.

In the case of the Pharisees, the reader is not left in doubt for very long. Josephus's judgement is that the alliance between Alexandra and the Pharisees was singularly unfortunate. She was a sincere woman but they were wolves in sheep's clothing: being herself genuinely pious (σεσοβημένη περὶ τὸ θεῖον), Alexandra paid far too much heed to the Pharisees (τούτοις περισσὸν δή τι προσεῖχεν, § 111). On their part, the Pharisees increasingly exploited (ὑπιέναι) this ingenuous woman (ἁπλότης); they encroached upon her authority (cf. παραφύομαι, § 110) to the point that they became the *de facto* managers of public life (διοικηταὶ τῶν ὅλων ἐγίνοντο) even exploiting the judicial system to punish their enemies! Although Alexandra held her own in foreign policy (§§ 112, 115f.), on domestic issues she deferred entirely to the Pharisees, to the point that they controlled (ἐκράτει) her (§ 112). In their caprice, they killed one of the distinguished citizens (τῶν ἐπισήμων) and then others (§ 113), on the charge that these had encouraged Janneus in his atrocities. In all of this, claims Josephus, Alexandra's superstition (δεισιδαιμονία) rendered her a helpless pawn; her "pious" co-regents proceeded to kill whomever they wished on false charges.

If we have correctly understood Josephus as contrasting the real (δή) scrupulosity of Queen Alexandra with the Pharisees' groundless reputation (δοκοῦσιν) for ἀκρίβεια, then he is here evoking a standard theme of Hellenistic moral philosophy, namely, the contrast between "seeming" (δοκεῖν) and "being" (εἶναι). Among the diatribes of the Cynic Teles (c. 242 BC), for example, is a piece entitled "On Seeming and Being" (Περὶ τοῦ δοκεῖν καὶ τοῦ εἶναι).[111] By noting the unpleasant consequences that might result from merely seeming to have some ability (whether musical, acting, or military), Teles tries to persuade his interlocutor that one must seek really to be just (δίκαιος), not merely to seem so, as the politicians (ῥήτορες) do! Having a reputation for δικαιοσύνη, argues Teles, is worth nothing unless that reputation is deserved. Josephus seems to be making the same point about the Pharisees, only now the issue is εὐσέβεια and ἀκρίβεια.

Several other writers of the period invoke the contrast between "seeming" and "being" in such a way as to suggest that it was a commonplace of popular morality. Sextus (2d. cent. AD), who compiled a list of ethical τόποι in his day,[112] offered the maxim:

---

[111] Cf. E. O'Neil, *Teles (the Cynic Teacher)*, "SBL Texts and Translations", 11; "Graeco-Roman Religion Series", 3 (Missoula: Scholars Press, 1977), 2-5.

[112] These *sententiae* have close parallels in neoplatonic, neopythagorean, and Christian texts, which means that they were ethical commonplaces. Cf. H. Chadwick, *The Sentences*

ἀσκεῖ μὴ τὸ δοκεῖν ἀλλὰ τὸ εἶναι δίκαιος
τὸ δοκεῖν γὰρ ἕκαστον τοῦ εἶναι ἀφαιρεῖται (§ 64).

In his *Dialogues of the Dead*, Lucian of Samosata (2d. cent. AD) turned the δοκεῖν/εἶναι contrast against the pretentiousness of Alexander the Great. Lucian has Philip of Macedon chastising his son for having passed himself off as divine. Philip muses:

> For you were supposed to be a god (θεὸς γὰρ εἶναι δοκῶν) and any time you were wounded and seen being carried out of the fighting on a litter, streaming with blood and groaning from a wound, the onlookers were amused to see how Ammon was shown up as an impostor (γόης. . . ἠλέγχετο). . . . For now that you are dead, don't you think that there are many who wax witty about that pretence (προσποίησις) of yours?

Notice here the connection between δοκέω and προσποίησις, which we have already noted in the case of Josephus's Pharisees, and which confirms our suspicion that δοκέω can mean *both* ''suppose/ pretend'' (subjective) *and* ''seem'' (objective) in the same context.

The Christian Paul was doubtless drawing upon the same stock theme when he called the Jerusalem apostles οἱ δοκοῦντες and wrote:

> From those who were reputed to be something—whatever they were makes no difference to me; God does not consider a person's image—the famous men contributed nothing to me . . . . ('Απὸ δὲ τῶν δοκούντων εἶναί τι,—ὁποῖοί ποτε ἦσαν οὐδέν μοι διαφέρει πρόσωπον θεὸς ἀνθρώπου οὐ λαμβάνει—ἐμοὶ γὰρ οἱ δοκοῦντες οὐδὲν προσανέθεντο.)

These examples illustrate the wide currency of the δοκεῖν/ εἶναι contrast in Hellenistic thought. It is this contrast that Josephus employs against the historical ἀκρίβεια of the Greeks and the religious ἀκρίβεια of the Pharisees.

Although,· then, the Pharisees do not play a major role in *War* as a whole, their function in the history of the Hasmonean house is significant. The downward spiral that began after John Hyrcanus, with Aristobulus and Alexander Janneus, was to reach its nadir in the internecine strife between Alexandra's sons.[113] Alexandra's own rule, though a potential turning point because of her genuine piety, was fatally damaged by her association with the Pharisees. This group, says

---

of Sextus: a contribution to the history of early Christian ethics (Cambridge: University Press, 1959), 139f., 144-146.

[113] Josephus reveals the importance of this moment in Jewish history at *War* 5:396: Whence did our servitude arise? Was it not from party strife among our forefathers, when the madness (μανία) of Aristobulus and Hyrcanus and their mutual dissension brought Pompey against the city, and God subjected to the Romans those who were unworthy of liberty? (Thackeray)

Josephus, although they enjoyed a reputation for piety and scrupulous faithfulness to the laws, turned out to be a manipulative band of counterfeits. Their outrages drove many leading citizens to enlist the protection of Aristobulus (§ 114), who was thus enabled to seize power before his mother's death (§ 117), thereby initiating the fateful struggle with his older brother Hyrcanus.

Josephus's first definition of the Pharisees is not a friendly one. In a society that exalted precise knowledge of the laws, they had acquired a reputation for piety. Their actions in the time of Alexandra, however, gave the lie to their reputation.

IV. *The Source of War 1:110*

G. Hölscher, the greatest of the Josephan source critics, assigned *War* 1:110f. to the pen of Nicolaus of Damascus. His argument was: (a) that for various reasons,[114] the whole of *War* 1:31 - 2:116 appears to come from Nicolaus; (b) that *War* 1:110f. in particular gives "höchst unjüdische Urteile . . . über die Pharisäer",[115] where "höchst unjüdisch" apparently means "recht unfreundlich";[116] and (c) that, therefore, this passage also comes directly from Nicolaus. The view that *War* 1:110 is a quotation from Nicolaus has won significant, if by no means universal, support.[117]

Against that view, we have already noted certain *a priori* considerations, especially: (a) that Josephus knew the Pharisees first-hand and (b) that he was perfectly capable, in other respects, of stamping his own ideas upon his work.[118] To these observations we may now add the following *a posteriori* judgements. (c) *War* 1:110 bears a close verbal resemblance to descriptions of the Pharisees in *War* 2:162 and *Life* 191, neither of which is usually attributed to Nicolaus (and the latter cannot be). (d) *War* 1:110 is one of ten passages in Josephus's writings that combine δοκέω and a form of ἀκρίβεια to describe a group or individual. Of these ten, seven also include some reference to the νόμοι or νόμιμα. The combinations of these words seem to be Josephan constructions. (e) Finally, all of the key terms in the definition of the Pharisees in *War* 1:110—ἀκρίβεια, εὐσέβεια, νόμοι—are elements of Josephus's characteristic vocabulary; clearly, they are theologically charged and he uses them with conscious intent.

---

[114] Cf. chapter 2, above.
[115] Hölscher, *PWRE*, 1945.
[116] Ibid., 1936 and n. + + thereto.
[117] Cf. Moore, *Judaism*, I, 62 n. 4 and 65 n. 3; Pfeiffer, *New Testament Times*, 22. 54; Michel-Bauernfeind, I, XXVf.
[118] Cf. chapter 2, above.

Although, then, Josephus may well have taken the basic content of the
Hasmonean history from Nicolaus, perhaps including some reference to
the Pharisees' actions under Alexandra, it is Josephus himself who has
formulated the portrayal of the Pharisees in *War* 1:110. Nor is that the
extent of his activity, for we have seen that the description at 1:110 is
an integral part of the story line and that it depends for its meaning on
the prior descriptions of Janneus (§ 85) and especially of Alexandra (§
108). That Josephus has shaped this whole section of narrative seems a
necessary conclusion.

Conclusion

The foregoing analysis of *War* 1:110 illustrates the severe limitations of
the usual approach to Josephus on the Pharisees. That approach, endorsed by Schürer and maintained to the present day, regards
Josephus's descriptions of the Pharisees as more or less "raw material",
as Rivkin puts it, that can be substantially understood in their own right.
That such a view is theoretically flawed has been argued above;[119] in addition, we now have tangible evidence that the context of the Pharisee
passages is determinative of their meaning. "Context" here refers
equally to (a) the immediately surrounding narrative, (b) the concerns
and themes of the work as a whole, and (c) the author's thought in
general.

To illustrate: A. Guttmann makes the assertion, "When Josephus
states that the Pharisees 'are considered the most accurate interpreters
of the laws' he speaks as a Pharisaic Jew."[120] A. Schlatter and H.-F.
Weiss[121] likewise believe that such a description is honorific.

One can only hold that conclusion, however, if one takes the statement out of its context and therefore out of Josephus's own mouth. For
the foregoing analysis has shown that Josephus's intention was to
debunk the Pharisees' reputation for embodying superior piety and for
expounding the laws with particular accuracy. Terms like ἀκρίβεια and
εὐσέβεια represent worlds of religious meaning for him. He views these
areas as priestly responsibilities or concerns. Although he allows that certain others have well-deserved reputations for excellence in these
respects, the Pharisees are not among them.

---

[119] Cf. chapter 1, above.
[120] Guttmann, *Rabbinic Judaism*, 127.
[121] Schlatter, *Theologie*, 204f; H. F. Weiss, "Pharisäismus und Hellenismus: zur
Darstellung des Judentums im Geschichtswerk des jüdischen Historikers Flavius
Josephus", *Orientalistische Literarzeitung* 74 (1979), 425.

Nor does it seem plausible, to give a further example, that Josephus chose the word ἀκρίβεια to describe the Pharisees because of its currency as an interpretation of the name פרושים.[122] Sufficient explanation of Josephus's usage of the word is his characteristic vocabulary, in which ἀκρίβεια occupies a conspicuous place. That ἀκρίβεια did circulate as an interpretation of פרושים is of course possible but must be shown by other evidence.[123]

In short: Josephus's statements on the Pharisees only have full meaning when they are read as his statements and as products of his analysis and thought.

---

[122] *Contra* A. I. Baumgarten, "Name", 413ff.

[123] The hypothesis would face very serious objections if it could be argued that Luke-Acts, Baumgarten's other key witness, uses ἀκρίβεια of the Pharisees under the influence of Josephus; cf. especially M. Krenkel, *Josephus und Lukas: der schiftstellerische Einfluss des jüdischen Geschichtschreibers auf den christlichen nachgewiesen* (Leipzig: H. Haessel, 1894).

CHAPTER FIVE

WAR 1:571: THE PHARISEES AT HEROD'S COURT, I

After Josephus has introduced the Pharisees in *War* 1:110-114, the reader next meets them in a passing reference at 1:571. Here, Josephus is recounting the intrigues of Herod's family against the king. Herod, he says, accused his sister-in-law of plotting against him in several ways, one of which was her rewarding of Pharisaic opposition to him (ὅτι τε Φαρισαίοις μὲν χορηγήσειεν μισθοὺς κατ' αὐτοῦ). This bare notice, which is nowhere elaborated in *War*, has little importance in the narrative; Josephus clearly does not intend here to say much about the Pharisees. Nevertheless, since the incident will also be recounted in *Ant.* (17:42f.), some brief account of its treatment in *War* is necessary.

I. *The Context of War 1:571*

Fundamental is the observation that *War* in general presents Herod the Great very favourably.[1] He appears as generous and large-spirited (1:397), pious (1:400), humane (1:42ff.), a loyal friend (1:391), brave (1:429), and affectionate toward his family (1:417ff.). All of his domestic problems were brought on by the women in his court, we are told, beginning with his second wife Mariamne and her sons (1:431ff.). Indeed, Herod's home life develops along the lines of a tragedy, in which he is the largely innocent victim of plots and intrigues.

One such disturbance was instigated by the wife of Pheroras, who capitalized on the rising fortunes of Herod's son Antipater to establish her own power and dominate the Herodian court. Herod is informed of her surreptitious activities (1:569f.) and it is in his subsequent denunciation of this woman (§ 571) that we hear of her payments to the Pharisees.

II. *Key Terms*

The two key terms of the brief clause, χορηγέω and μισθός, are both elements of Josephus's usual vocabulary.

A. Χορηγέω: "to supply, furnish, procure, grant". Josephus employs

---

[1] This was a major factor in Hölscher's attribution of *War* 1:31-2:116 to Nicolaus, Herod's court historian, *PWRE*, 1947; cf. also Michel-Bauernfeind, *De Bello Judaico*, I, XXVf., and Cohen, *Josephus*, 111.

the verb and its cognates (χορηγία, χορηγός) some 64 times throughout *War* and *Ant.*[2] The verb has a stronger meaning than, say, δίδωμι; it is generally used in contexts of liberality or abundance,[3] sometimes with the supplement ἀφθονίᾳ—the subject supplies something lavishly.[4] This may, but does not necessarily,[5] suggest that the woman's support of the Pharisees was ample.

B. Μισθός: "payment, reward, money, compensation". This noun is evenly distributed throughout Josephus's four works,[6] occurring a total of 42 times.

III. *Interpretation of War 1:571*

The salient features of this brief notice may be summarized in three observations.

First, the remark obviously puts the Pharisees in a negative light. It is not clear from the wording whether Pheroras's wife actually initiated Pharisaic opposition to Herod by offering money to the group or whether she simply encouraged an already present opposition by financial reward. Alon[7] and Cornfeld,[8] working at the historical level, adduce rabbinic evidence of principled Pharisaic opposition to Herod, which would suggest the latter option. Likewise *Ant.* 17:41, if it is a true parallel,[9] claims that Pheroras's wife merely paid the fine imposed on the Pharisees by Herod for their refusal to swear an oath of allegiance to himself and Caesar. In *War* 1:571 itself, however, it is the woman's mercenary tactics and not so much the Pharisees' actions that are in question. In either case, the Pharisees turn up on the wrong (= anti-Herodian) side of the dispute. If Herod appears in *War* as a victim, then the Pharisees must be counted among his victimizers.

---

[2] Χορηγέω appears 10 times in *War*, 30 times in *Ant.*; χορηγία appears 5 times in *War*, 14 times in *Ant.*; χορηγός appears 4 times in *War*, once in *Ant.*

[3] E.g., at *War* 1:424; 3:519; 4:56, 471; 6:23; *Ant.* 2:272; 6:350; 7:231, 279; 8:113, 396; 10:156, 193.

[4] *Ant.* 1:181; 4:116, 237; 12:58, 105; 13:224; cf. also 10:193; 12:84, 138 for χορηγία with ἀφθονία.

[5] In at least two cases, χορηγέω has a restrictive sense—people are "supplied" only (μόνος) with bread and water (*Ant.* 8:330, 410)—but this is probably sarcastic.

[6] It occurs 7 times in *War*, 28 times in *Ant.*, 4 times in *Life*, and 3 times in *Ag.Ap.*

[7] Alon, *Jews*, 35f.

[8] Cornfeld, *Jewish War*, 110f.

[9] Reinach (*Oeuvres*, V, 116, n. 2), Michel-Bauernfeind (*De Bello Judaico*, I, 151, 424 n. 264), and Thackeray (LCL edn., I, 270f. n. *b*.) all make the connection; so also D. Schwartz, "Josephus and Nicolaus", 160f. Feldman (LCL edn., VIII, 391 n. *b*.) thinks that the author of *Ant.* 17:41f. (Nicolaus, in his view) has confused Essenes with Pharisees; this would seem to break any parallel with *War* 1:571 (which is also, however, from Nicolaus!).

Second, association of the Pharisees with monetary gain also damages their image before the reader. Suggestions of such impropriety occur throughout Josephus's writings. Already in *War* 1:111 we have read that, while the Pharisees were enjoying all the benefits and prerogatives (ἀπολαύσεις) of royalty, the expenses (ἀναλώματα) were falling to Queen Alexandra. Further, to anticipate future analyses: in *Ant.* 17:42f. the Pharisees are said to have manufactured false predictions in return for money; in *Life* 195f. a prominent Pharisee bribes the high priest to act unfairly. Thus, the association of the Pharisees with financial impropriety is fairly common in Josephus.

Linking one's opponents with the love of money was a common slander in antiquity.[10] Notice, however, that Josephus does not resort to stock, generalizing phrases like φιλάργυροι, which is used of the Pharisees by the author of Luke-Acts (Lk. 16:14).[11] Josephus only makes the charge of financial impropriety against the Pharisees in specific, historically plausible cases. Without actually calling them ''lovers of money'' he manages to insinuate the same point in a narrative context.

Third, Josephus continues to represent the Pharisees as an influential group. This is clear from the fact that the woman's financing of Pharisaic opposition is ranked in its enormity with her alienation of Herod's own brother and her insulting of Herod's own (cf. ἑαυτοῦ) daughters. That Josephus chooses to mention these three offences as only the most heinous examples among *many* misdeeds seems to indicate that Herod felt the antagonism of the Pharisees very keenly. The impact of this antagonism on Herod, Josephus implies, was roughly on a par with that generated by the abuse of his daughters or by the opposition of his brother. To be sure, the Pharisees no longer have the mechanism of government in their hands, as they did under Alexandra, but Josephus's remark at *War* 1:571 presupposes their continued influence: their opposition to Herod appears as a matter of great concern to him.

IV. *The Source of War 1:571*

We have seen that the two key terms are elements of Josephus's natural vocabulary. In *Ant.* 13:129, furthermore, they also appear together as verb and direct object. Any doubt that the formulation is Josephus's own, therefore, seems unwarranted.

---

[10] Cf., e.g., R. J. Karris, ''The Background and Significance of the Polemic of the Pastoral Epistles'', *JBL* 92 (1973), 549-564, esp. 552. He gives numerous references, from Plato to Tatian, to document the widespread use of this charge.

[11] Cf. the charge of φιλαργυρία levelled against opponents in the Pastoral letters of the NT: I Tim. 6:10; 2 Tim. 3:2; Titus 1:11.

With respect to content, on the other hand, it is entirely likely that Josephus received his information—about Pheroras's wife's sponsorship of Pharisaic opposition to Herod—from Nicolaus of Damascus, who would have been in a position to know the inner workings of Herod's court.

Summary

Although *War* 1:571 is an incidental reference to the Pharisees—and one ought not, therefore, to expect from it a wealth of insight—two points emerge clearly. First, the author presents the Pharisees as an influential group. Second, however, he reveals his lack of sympathy for them. They have a part in the undoing of the tragic victim Herod and they are vulnerable to the lure of money. Both of these points—the Pharisees' influence and Josephus's antipathy toward them—continue themes already introduced in *War* 1:110-114.

CHAPTER SIX

WAR 2:162-166: THE PHARISEES AMONG
THE JEWISH SCHOOLS, I

From the standpoint of Josephus's intention, *War* 2:119-166 is his crucial description of the Jewish groups, including the Pharisees. For when he writes in *Ant.* of the distinctive groups within Judaism, he refers the reader back to his "accurately detailed" (ἀκριβῶς δεδήλωται) presentation in *War* 2.[1] Clearly, Josephus views this lengthy passage as his standard treatment, to which the later discussions are supplementary.[2]

Furthermore, *War* 2:119-166 is unique in that Josephus is free here to say whatever he wishes about the Pharisees, Sadducees, and Essenes, without being subject to narrative pressures. His main source for *War* 1:31-2:116, Nicolaus of Damascus, has probably expired with the deposition of Herod's son Archelaus.[3] After that, Josephus gives only a cursory outline of events to the time of Agrippa (2:167-187), a period as long as Herod's reign! Again the narrative moves quickly through the following twenty years (2:220-276) to the events preceding the revolt. Whereas all of Josephus's other references to the Pharisees, therefore, come in the midst of a flowing narrative, where Josephus can only say enough about the groups to make his narrative intelligible,[4] in *War* 2:119-166 he has no story-line to pursue. On the contrary, his discussion of the three Jewish groups provides him an opportunity to compensate for the sparseness of his history of Judea under the prefects.[5] This freedom from narrative constraints may well have accounted for his decision to give his definitive descriptions of the Jewish αἱρέσεις here.

---

[1] The *War* passage is recalled in the following ways: ἐν τῇ δευτέρᾳ βίβλῳ τῆς Ἰουδαικῆς πραγματείας (*Ant.* 13:173); ἐν τῇ δευτέρᾳ μου τῶν Ἰουδαικῶν (*Ant.* 13:298); and ἐν τῷ βίβλῳ τοῦ Ἰουδαικοῦ πολέμου (*Ant.* 18:11).

[2] The question as to whether his later treatments of the Pharisees are intended as revisions or corrections of *War* material will be discussed in Part III, below.

[3] Cf. Hölscher, "Josephus", 1944-49; Safrai and Stern, *Jewish People*, 23f.; Michel-Bauernfeind, *De Bello Judaico* I, XXVf.; Thackeray, LCL edn., II, xxiif.

[4] Even the parallel to our passage in *Ant.* (18:11-25) is subject to narrative pressures. There Josephus only introduces the three φιλοσοφίαι as background for his discussion of the fourth philosophy. This is not the case in *War* 2, where the discussion of the schools is open-ended.

[5] Whether this sparseness was deliberate or forced upon him by a lack of source material is both impossible to decide and irrelevant here. Cf. n. 95 to chapter 3 (on the purpose of *War*).

I. *Context*

Josephus seems uninterested in discussing—or, perhaps, lacks material to discuss—the early years of the history of Judea as a Roman province. He barely mentions that the ethnarchy of Archelaus, on the deposition of that tyrant in AD 6, passed under direct Roman rule, with Coponius as governor (*War* 2:117).[6] Likewise, after his treatment of the three groups he refers only briefly to the status of the other portions of Herod's old kingdom (2:167) and then moves immediately to the death of Augustus in AD 14.

This departure from his usual emphasis on the details of political history allows Josephus to develop a major theme of his work. In the preface, it will be recalled, he announced his thesis that his homeland owed its destruction to a faction of tyrants among the people and not to the δῆμος itself (1:10). So, it seems, he introduces the material of 2:119-166 as an early attempt to establish that theme, well before the narrative of the revolt itself begins. Thus we learn that the passing of Judea[7] into Roman hands caused a certain Judas to come forward, who "urged revolt (ἀπόστασιν) on his countrymen, calling them cowards if they consented to pay tribute to the Romans and endured mortal masters after having served God".

Having so described the rebel's position—a position that would find no sympathy among Roman readers—Josephus goes on immediately to disavow it, not only for himself but also for Jews in general:

> This man represented a peculiar school of thought (ἰδίας αἱρέσεως), which was not even remotely similar to the others (οὐδὲν τοῖς ἄλλοις προσεοικώς, § 118). For among the Jews, philosophy takes three [customary][8] forms (τρία γὰρ παρὰ Ἰουδαίοις εἴδη φιλοσοφεῖται, § 119).

Quite early in his narrative, therefore, Josephus takes the opportunity to show his readers that the whole mentality of ἀπόστασις is foreign to "mainstream" Jewish ways of thinking. The point is significant because Judas will turn out to be something of a patriarch to the rebel family that included Menahem (*War* 2:433) and Eleazar ben Yair, of Masada fame (*War* 2:447; 7:253).

---

[6] Josephus uses ἐπίτροπος (procurator) to describe Coponius' office. A. N. Sherwin-White, however (*Roman Society and Roman Law in the New Testament*, 6), points out that equestrian governors before Claudius had the title of *praefectus* and not *procurator*.

[7] Idumea and Samaria were also included in the ethnarchy of Archelaus (2:96), as were the cities of Caesarea, Sebaste, and Joppa (2:97).

[8] The emphasis is on τρία. Thackeray captures this by rendering: "Jewish philosophy, in fact, takes three forms."

We can see, then, a clear rationale for Josephus's introduction of
2:119-166, which deals extensively with the three εἴδη of Jewish thinking:
he wants to dissociate mainstream Judaism from the rebel psychology.
This observation does not imply that every item in the narrative must
somehow demonstrate the docility or peacefulness of the Jews. On the
subject of the Essenes, for example, much of the material would have
had an intrinsic interest for his Hellenistic-Roman readers.[9] Nevertheless, we should expect to find clear indications in 2:119-166 that recognized Judaism, in its three forms, does not equate the service of God
with ἀπόστασις from all earthly masters.

Although the Pharisees are introduced at the outset (§ 119) as one of
the three forms of Jewish thought, they do not receive full attention until
the end of the passage (162-166). It is the famous description of the
Essenes—which has become an important aid for interpreting the Dead
Sea Scrolls[10]— that dominates our passage. Some brief discussion of the
Essene narrative is necessary, both to provide insight into the function
of 2:119-166 and as a basis for interpreting the description of the
Pharisees (§ 162-166).

The first thing that Josephus says about the Essenes sets the tone for
his entire description: they are renowned for their cultivation of solem-
nity (δοκεῖ σεμνότητα ἀσκεῖν, § 119); they hold self-control (τὴν ἐγκράτειαν),
or the refusal to surrender to the passions (τὸ μὴ τοῖς πάθεσιν ὑποπίπτειν),
to be a virtue (§ 120). Although the πάθη are described primarily in sexual terms, a broader range of meaning is evoked: in contrast to the αἵρεσις
of Judas, which draws its energy from self-assertion, the Essenes are self-
controlled and disciplined. We read further: "In their dress and com-
posure they are like children being trained in fear" (μετὰ φόβου
παιδαγωγουμένοις παισίν, § 126). And that is the tenor of the whole Essene
passage: these men are ascetics, whose every waking moment is ordered
according to a strict discipline (§§ 128-134, 137-149). Thus: "Holding
justified anger in check, they are masters of their temper, champions of
faithfulness, ministers of peace" (§ 135, Thackeray).[11] This image of ex-

[9] On the appeal of esoteric Eastern groups to cultured Romans, cf. F. Cumont, *Orien-
tal Religions in Roman Paganism* (New York: Dover, 1956 [1911]), esp. 28ff.; also M.
Hadas, *Hellenistic Culture* (New York: Columbia University Press, 1959), chapter 9; and
M. Smith, "Palestinian Judaism", 75.

[10] Although Josephus's description of the Essenes does not always harmonize with the
Scrolls, the use of Josephus to interpret the Qumran find is well-nigh universal. Cf. the
authors and works cited in chapter 2, n.45. For a commentary on *War*'s portrayal of the
Essenes in the light of Qumran, cf. Michel-Bauernfeind, *De Bello Judaico*, I, 431-440
(nn. 35-92).

[11] My translation here draws heavily on Thackeray's.

treme discipline contrasts starkly with the independence and rebellious-
ness of Judas.

Most striking is Josephus's description of the many oaths that the candidates must take before admission to full membership (§§ 139-142).
Among them is the promise ''to keep faith (τὸ πιστὸν παρέξειν) always
with all men, *especially with those who are ruling* (μάλιστα δὲ τοῖς κρατοῦσιν)
since no one acquires the position of ruler without God'' (οὐ γὰρ δίχα θεοῦ
περιγενέσθαι τινὶ τὸ ἄρχειν, § 140). Here Josephus provides clear evidence
for his assertion that the mainstream Jewish groups differ radically from
Judas's philosophy of freedom: the Essenes, for one, believe in
faithfulness to the ruling authorities.[12]

Beyond that, the Essenes appear as an esoteric group, preoccupied
with their own rites and teachings. They are concerned with prayers (§
128), strenuous labour (§ 129), ancient writings, medicinal substances
and stones (§ 136), and their own sectarian books, secrets, and names
of the angels (§ 142). These esoteric pursuits contribute to the image of
the Essenes as a harmless element in Jewish society. Josephus presents
them in such a way as to foster admiration for their discipline, self-
control, and quiet manner or life. So the Essenes are not in the slightest
degree (οὐδὲν προσεοικώς) comparable to the group represented by
Judas.[13]

Thus in coming to the description of the Pharisees in §§ 162-166, we
already possess two major interpretive clues, both furnished by the context. First, by including this group among the three εἴδη of Jewish
thought, in contrast to that of Judas, Josephus acknowledges the historic
legitimacy of the Pharisees: they, along with the Essenes and Sadducees,
are true representatives of Judaism, at least to the extent that they do
not demand complete political independence.

Second, however, by proportioning his narrative as he does, Josephus
makes it plain that he is much more interested in describing the Essenes
than the other two groups. In contrast to his expansive portrayal of the
Essenes, he dispenses with the Pharisees and Sadducees in three
sentences, which comprise two μέν . . . δέ constructions, comparing these
two schools of thought only on matters of belief and practice.

---

[12] Josephus does not explain how some Essenes found themselves in conflict with
Rome (*War* 2:152f.) or why one of the regional commanders of the revolt was an Essene
(2:567; 3:11).

[13] Michel-Bauernfeind (*De Bello Judaico*, I, 436, n.65) see also in *War* 2:142 a reference
to the Essenes' refusal to engage in armed revolt. There, the Essene candidate vows to
abstain from λῃστεία. Since he has already sworn not to steal (cf. κλοπή, 2·141), the commentators propose a more political sense for λῃστεία, in accord with Josephus's usage of
this word-group elsewhere.

II. *Five Statements About the Pharisees*

Within Josephus's portrayal of the Pharisees, we may distinguish five statements:

Δύο δὲ τῶν προτέρων (sc. ταγμάτων, § 161) Φαρισαῖοι μὲν οἱ

(2:161)   a. μετ' ἀκριβείας δοκοῦντες ἐξηγεῖσθαι τὰ νόμιμα

           b. καὶ τὴν πρώτην ἀπάγοντες αἵρεσιν

(2:163)   c. εἱμαρμένη τε καὶ θεῷ προσάπτουσι πάντα καὶ τὸ μὲν
              πράττειν τὰ δίκαια καὶ μὴ κατὰ τὸ πλεῖστον ἐπὶ τοῖς
              ἀνθρώποις κεῖσθαι, βοηθεῖν δὲ εἰς ἕκαστον καὶ τὴν
              εἱμαρμένην.

           d. ψυχήν τε πᾶσαν μὲν ἄφθαρτον,
              μεταβαίνειν δὲ εἰς ἕτερον σῶμα
                     τὴν τῶν ἀγαθῶν μόνην,
              τὰς δὲ τῶν φαύλων ἀιδίῳ τιμωρίᾳ κολάζεσθαι

(2:166a)   e. καὶ Φαρισαῖοι μὲν φιλάλληλοί τε καὶ τὴν
              εἰς τὸ κοινὸν ὁμόνοιαν ἀσκοῦντες.

We shall take each statement in turn and analyze its key terms.

A. οἱ μετ' ἀκριβείας δοκοῦντες ἐξηγεῖσθαι τὰ νόμιμα

This opening statement corresponds closely to the second half of the definition in 1:110: δοκοῦν . . . τοὺς νόμους ἀκριβέστερον ἀφηγεῖσθαι. The changes are as follows.

(1) τὰ νόμιμα for οἱ νόμοι. In discussing *War* 1:110, we observed that οἱ νόμοι has no technical meaning for Josephus; he uses it interchangeably with τὰ νόμιμα. Later he will speak of special Pharisaic νόμιμα (*Ant.* 13:296, 297, 408), but he will clearly designate those as non-Mosaic ordinances, originating with the fathers (ἐκ πατέρων . . . οὐκ ἀναγέγραπται ἐν τοῖς Μωυσέος νόμοις, 13:297; κατὰ τὴν πατρῴαν παράδοσιν, 13:408). In all of the other 53 cases in which Josephus uses τὰ νόμιμα (or the singular) substantively, the term is practically synonymous with οἱ νόμοι[14] or with τὰ ἔθη.[15] Thus, since τὰ νόμιμα in our passage stands without qualification, we have no reason to suppose that it means anything other than the νόμιμα τὰ γεγραμμένα (*Ant.* 13:297) and that it is equivalent to the νόμοι of *War* 1:110. Whatever distinctive νόμιμα the Pharisees may have, then, in *War* Josephus claims only that they are experts in the νόμιμα common to all Jews.

---

[14] E.g., *Ant.* 8:395, where φυλάσσειν τοὺς νόμους = τηρεῖν τὰ νόμιμα. Cf. also *Ant.* 7:384f.; 8:208, 256; 12:276; 14:173f.; 18:274. The interchangeability may also be indicated by the textual variants at *Ant.* 13:257 and 18:55.

[15] Cf. *Ant.* 9:95-99; 15:328-30; 14:213-216.

(2) ἐξηγεῖσθαι for ἀφηγεῖσθαι. The two verbs are virtually synonymous, as the similarity between the prefixes ἐκ and ἀπό suggests. Two basic meanings apply to both: the primary sense, "to lead (out), direct, administer", and the more abstract, "to interpret, relate, expound" Josephus uses both verbs in both senses.[16] Here, as in 1:110, the idea of exposition or "exegesis" is intended.

B. (οἱ) καὶ τὴν πρώτην ἀπάγοντες αἵρεσιν

The second statement in *War* 2:161 is a *crux interpretum*, created by uncertainty about the significance of πρώτη, ἀπάγω, and αἵρεσις. We shall look first at αἵρεσις.

(1) The rendering of αἵρεσις by "sect" was enshrined by W. Whiston and has survived into the twentieth century in all of the major translations, those of Reinach ("*secte*"), Thackeray ("*sect*"), and Michel-Bauernfeind ("*Sekte*").[17] In the influential Loeb edition, Thackeray even supplies the marginal heading for our passage: "the three Jewish sects". This translation is congenial to those, like Smith and Neusner, who portray the Pharisees as a small, closed society.[18] The English word sect, like its French[19] and German equivalents, may have connotations of exclusivity, rigid organization, novelty, comparative smallness, and perhaps even deviance from a larger body (cf. "heresy").[20] Although not necessarily implied by all modern translators of Josephus,[21] such connotations have naturally drawn criticism from those scholars who understand Pharisaism as a mass movement within Judaism.[22] Rivkin, for example, proposes the abandonment of "sect" as a translation of αἵρεσις, preferring rather "school of thought", as introduced by R. Marcus in his portion of the Loeb translation (*Ant.* 13:171, 288).[23] The possible implications call for special care in the translation of αἵρεσις.

Josephus uses the word 31 times, in three distinct senses. Eight times it means the taking or capture of something, often a town.[24] Eight times it signifies an option or choice.[25] These meanings derive, respectively,

---

[16] Rengstorf gives 16 occurrences of ἀφηγέομαι with the sense "report or narrate" and 9 with the sense "lead (out), direct". For ἐξηγέομαι, the figures are 9 and 11, respectively.

[17] Cf., e.g., all of these translations at *War* 2:162.

[18] See chapter 1, n. 9.

[19] Cf. LeMoyne, *Les Sadducéens*, 33.

[20] Cf., e.g., *The Houghton-Mifflin Canadian Dictionary*, ad loc.

[21] The *Oxford English Dictionary* and *Webster's* suggest also more neutral connotations.

[22] E.g., G. Alon, A. Guttmann, and E. Rivkin; cf. chapter 1, above.

[23] Rivkin, *Revolution*, 317f.

[24] *Ant.* 7:160; 10:79, 133, 247; 12:363; 13:122, 231, 233; cf. Herodotus 4:1.

[25] *War* 1:99; 6:352; 7:326; *Ant.* 1:69; 6:71, 91; 7:321, 322.

from the active ("to take") and middle ("to choose") voices of αἱρέω.²⁶ In 15 of its 31 occurrences, however, αἵρεσις signifies the *object* of one's choice, namely, a philosophy, school, party, or faction.²⁷ In 13 of these 15 cases the word designates one or more of the various groups within Judaism—viz., Pharisees, Sadducees, Essenes, or that of Judas the Galilean.

What precisely does Josephus mean by calling these groups αἱρέσεις? At first glance he seems to use the word to designate very different sorts of groups. On the one hand, Judas represents a αἵρεσις that Josephus ostracizes from mainstream Judaism (*War* 2:118); on the other hand, the mainstream groups themselves are also αἱρέσεις (*loc. cit.*; cf. 2:162; *Ant.* 13:171ff.; *Life* 10), so the word itself cannot be taken to imply any deviance or "sectarianism".²⁸ The Essenes, who hold to stringent rules for the initiation and conduct of their members (*War* 2:128-153), are called a αἵρεσις (2:122, 137, 142); but so is a group of men united by nothing more than their opposition to a particular candidate for the throne (*Ant.* 7:347). The only common denominator in all of these αἱρέσεις appears to be the constituents' agreement on a given issue. No inference about their size or degree of organization can be drawn from the word itself.²⁹

Nevertheless, it must be significant that Josephus reserves αἵρεσις almost exclusively for the Pharisees, Sadducees, Essenes, and the faction of Judas. Of its 15 occurrences, 13 are found in the relatively few references to these groups within the Josephan corpus. If αἵρεσις could be used of *any* discernible group, one would expect to see it hundreds of times in the major stretches of narrative dealing with other matters. Other words for "group" such as τάγμα, μοῖρα, and γένος, which Josephus also uses of the αἱρέσεις, occur hundreds of times in other passages. But αἵρεσις appears only twice in those contexts. This special use of αἵρεσις spans Josephus's entire literary career and appears in three works of very different character (*War* 2:118, 162; *Ant.* 13:171; 20:199; *Life* 10, 191, 197), so it cannot be attributed to a source. Since αἵρεσις, when it denotes a group of people, almost always refers to the Pharisees, Sadducees, Essenes, and partisans of Judas, one must ask what these groups have in common that might have attracted this particular designation.

---

²⁶ See the discussions in Thackeray, *Lexicon*, and LSJ, *s.v.*; and H. Schlier, "αἵρεσις", *TDNT*, I.

²⁷ *War* 2:118, 122, 137, 142, 162; *Ant.* 13:171, 288, 293; 20:199; *Ant.* 7:347; 15:6; *Life* 10, 12, 191, 197.

²⁸ As LeMoyne, *Les Sadducéens*, 33, points out.

²⁹ Thus far, Rivkin's judgment is correct: "*hairesis* is neutral with respect to number, deviation, and denomination" (*Revolution*, 318).

Two points stand out. First, the groups are consistently presented as engaged in "philosophical" pursuits. At the beginning of our passage, Josephus explains that τρία παρὰ 'Ιουδαίοις εἴδη φιλοσοφεῖται (2:119). In the previous sentence, Judas has been called a σοφιστής. And Josephus closes his entire discussion of the three αἱρέσεις with the words: "Such is what I have to say περὶ τῶν ἐν 'Ιουδαίοις φιλοσοφούντων" (§ 166). These statements identify the αἱρέσεις as philosophizing groups. In *Ant.* 18:11-25, which is parallel to our passage, Josephus will even substitute φιλοσοφία for αἵρεσις (18:11, 23, 25). Nor does this surprise the reader, since Josephus regularly presents the focal point of debate between the αἱρέσεις as a philosophical issue, namely: the relationship between fate (εἱμαρμένη) and free will (*War* 2:162-166; *Ant.* 13:171-173; 18:11-25). So Josephus's αἱρέσεις are motivated by philosophical concerns.

Second, the αἱρέσεις are groups with more or less formal memberships. For example, Josephus's approximate figures for the size of both the Essene and Pharisaic followings—4,000[30] and 6,000[31] respectively—suggest defined constituencies. Further, he employs many substitutes[32] for αἵρεσις that seem to highlight the physical constitution of the groups, such as: μόριον, τάγμα, γένος, σύνταγμα, and μοῖρα.[33] In our passage, the Essenes are described both as a αἵρεσις (2:122, 137, 142) and as a τάγμα or "order" (2:122, 125, 143, 160, 161), with the two terms being fully interchangeable (cf. 122, 142f.). At the end of our passage, the Pharisees are designated ἡ πρώτη αἵρεσις (§ 162) and the Sadducees τὸ δεύτερον τάγμα (§ 164). The fact that Josephus can employ these terms as substitutes for αἵρεσις indicates that he envisioned identifiable groups with recognizable memberships.

To summarize: Josephus's reservation of αἵρεσις for the Pharisees, Sadducees, Essenes, and Judas's faction implies that the word denotes not merely a "group" but a philosophical school with an identifiable membership. Although Josephus nowhere implies that a αἵρεσις is peculiar or deviant (so Rivkin), he does suggest that the αἱρέσεις organized themselves to some extent and possessed a visible constituency (*contra* Rivkin). Each had its *raison d'être* in a certain "philosophical" position.

---

[30] *Ant.* 18:20.

[31] *Ant.* 17:42.

[32] Rivkin, *Revolution*, 318, errs when he claims that φιλοσοφία is the only synonym.

[33] Cf. the table in LeMoyne, *Sadducéens*, 32. These terms are used of religious groups as follows: μόριον, *Ant.* 17:41 (Pharisees); τάγμα, *War* 2:122, 125, 143, 160, 161 (Essenes), 164 (Sadducees); σύνταγμα, *War* 1:110 (Pharisees); γένος, *Ant.* 13:297 (Sadducees); *War* 1:78; 2:113; *Ant.* 13:172, 311; 15:371; 17:346 (Essenes); and μοῖρα, *Ant.* 13:296 (Sadducees).

Josephus's use of αἵρεσις accords well with common usage in the Hellenistic world. Polybius and Dionysius of Halicarnassus, for example, refer to the Greek philosophical schools (the Academy, Peripatos, Stoa, and later schools) as αἱρέσεις.[34] Philo used the word of both the Greek schools[35] and the Jewish Therapeutics.[36] When, therefore, Josephus calls the Palestinian religious groups αἱρέσεις, he not only marks them out as philosophical schools but he implies at least a formal similarity to the Greek schools. Indeed, he will later claim that the Essenes follow Pythagorean teachings (*Ant.* 15:371) and that the Pharisees are like the Stoics (*Life* 12).

The author of Acts also reflects Josephus's vocabulary closely at this point. He calls both the Pharisees and the Sadducees αἱρέσεις (15:5; 5:17) and even has Paul say that he lived as a Pharisee κατὰ τὴν ἀκριβεστάτην αἵρεσιν τῆς ἡμετέρας θρησκείας (26:5).[37] Likewise, Eusebius introduces a citation from Hegesippus, in which the latter refers to the Palestinian groups as "various opinions (γνῶμαι διάφοροι) among the circumcision", as a description of the αἱρέσεις.[38]

The historical question, as to whether Josephus was justified in calling the Pharisees a "philosophical school", is still debated.[39] We shall consider something of that debate when we examine the fate/free will question. Suffice it here to note that Josephus, an eyewitness who intends factuality, does describe them by such a term.

(2) and (3). The ordinal πρώτη obviously means "first". It is unclear, however, whether Josephus means that the Pharisees were the "first αἵρεσις" with respect to their age, their prominence in society, or simply their place in the earlier listing of the schools (2:119).

---

[34] Cf. Polybius 5.93.8; Dionysius, *Composition* 2; Diogenes Laertius 1:19; 7:191; Sextus Empiricus (c. AD 200), *Pyrrhonic Elements* 1:16, 185, 237.

[35] Philo, *On Noah's Work as a Planter*, 151.

[36] *Contemplative Life*, 129.

[37] The possibility of a literary relationship has long been debated; cf. M. Krenkel, *Josephus und Lukas, passim*; Foakes Jackson, *Josephus and the Jews*, 259-274; A. Ehrhardt, "The Construction and Purpose of Acts", *Studia Theologica* 12 (1958), 64; and E. Haenchen, *The Acts of the Apostles*, trans. R. McL. Wilson (Oxford: Basil Blackwell, 1982), 257; also G. Lüdemann, *Paul, Apostle to the Gentiles*, trans. F. S. Jones (Philadelphia: Fortress, 1984), 8-11.

[38] *Eccl.Hist.* 4.22.7.

[39] Older scholarship, assuming a rigid division between Greek and Jewish thought patterns, suspected Josephus of rank distortion; cf. Moore, "Fate", 283f.; Rasp, "Religionsparteien", 28; Bousset, *Die Religion des Judentums*, 187. But see now, *inter alia*, M. Smith, "Palestinian Judaism", and E. Bickerman, "La chaîne de la tradition pharisienne", *Studies in Jewish and Christian History*, Part II (Leiden: E. J. Brill, 1980), 256-269.

Ἀπάγοντες is likewise deceptively simple: ἄγω + ἀπό = "lead away/off". Josephus uses the verb some 45 times, and elsewhere it always bears a simple meaning:[40] to "lead away, divert, carry off, abduct, withdraw", or the like.[41] It often appears in descriptions of battles, where it refers to the *capturing* of prisoners,[42] or of cattle,[43] or to the withdrawal of troops from a siege.[44] The problem is what it could possibly mean with reference to the Pharisees: they are those who ἀπάγοντες τὴν πρώτην αἵρεσιν.

One may visualize the problems created by πρώτη and ἀπάγω by comparing three standard critical translations of *War* 2:162: those of Reinach, Thackeray, and Michel-Bauernfeind.

Reinach gives:

> Des deux sectes plus anciennes les Pharisiens (Δύο δὲ τῶν προτέρων Φαρισαῖοι μὲν οἱ), considérés comme les interpretes exacts des lois et comme les createurs de la premiere école (τὴν πρώτην ἀπάγοντες αἵρεσιν). . . .

He takes the προτέρων, πρώτη, and δεύτερον (§ 164) to refer to the *age* of the schools. Both Pharisees and Sadducees are older than the Essenes (*plus anciennes*) and of these two, the Pharisees are older: they created the first school.

Reinach's translation has the virtue of providing plausible meanings for both of the troublesome words. If chronology is the issue, then πρώτη explains itself simply. One can also understand ἀπάγω by envisioning, at some point in the past, an undifferentiated body of Jews, some of whom the Pharisees "draw away" in order to create or constitute the first school. This interpretation seems to be supported by the old Latin: et primae *apud Iudaios* sectae auctoris erant. If Reinach's translation is valid, then Josephus in *War* 2:162 provides a unique and historically valuable claim about the origins of the Jewish groups in Palestine.

That uniqueness, however, also poses difficulties for Reinach's translation. For elsewhere, when Josephus refers to the antiquity of the schools, he implies a roughly contemporaneous point of origin for all three. In *Ant.* 13:171 he dates them all to the mid-second century BC, the time of Jonathan the Hasmonean. In *Ant.* 18:11, he claims: "The Jews, from the most ancient times (ἐκ τοῦ πάνυ ἀρχαίου), had three

---

[40] If ἀπάξειν were the correct reading at *Ant.* 15:374, as in the (10th. century?) Epitome, its meaning would also be problematic. But this variant is unlikely. Cf. G. C. Richards and R. J. H. Shutt, "Critical Notes on Josephus' *Antiquities*", *CQ* 31 (1937), 174.

[41] E.g., *War* 1:46, 297; *Ant.* 2:307, 311; 20:152.

[42] *Ant.* 10:83, 98; 11:61.

[43] *War* 3:452; 5:65; *Ant.* 5:167; 8:294; 9:191.

[44] *Ant.* 7:290, 393; 8:365.

philosophies pertaining to their traditions.'' These statements suggest that Josephus regarded all three groups as of similar antiquity.

Further, the present participle ἀπάγοντες ought to denote a continuing action of the present rather than an action of the past. Indeed, the whole discussion of Essenes, Pharisees, and Sadducees should be considered in the present tense. So it would seem more reasonable to give πρώτη a meaning consonant with the overwhelming present sense of the context rather than to force everything else (especially the parallel δοκοῦντες) into a "historical present" on the basis of a presumed chronological sense for πρώτη. Whatever ἀπάγω means, it seems to be an action in which the Pharisees are presently engaged.

Finally, with respect to context, Reinach seems to ignore the fact that *War* 2:119-166, though lacking somewhat in symmetry, is a single literary unit. In reading προτέρων, πρώτη, and δεύτερον as chronological references, he fails to establish any connection with the topic sentence of the entire pericope, which begins:

> τρία γὰρ παρ' Ἰουδαίοις εἴδη φιλοσοφεῖται, καὶ τοῦ μὲν αἱρετισταὶ Φαρισαῖοι, τοῦ δὲ Σαδδουκαῖοι, τρίτον δὲ . . . Ἐσσηνοί.

Michel and Bauernfeind, on the other hand, seize upon these contextual indicators and so render the passage, "Von den beiden früher gennanten Sekten . . . stellen [die Pharisäer] die erste Sekte dar.'' An end-note makes the interpretation clear: "Josephus schliesst hier an § 119 an".[45] Michel and Bauernfeind thus take προτέρων, πρώτη, and δεύτερον (§ 164) as simple references back to the original list of § 119—a reminder that would be helpful to the reader after the long description of the Essenes (§§ 119-161).

On this reading, however, ἀπάγοντες lacks a clear sense. Michel-Bauernfeind suggest *darstellen*: "the Pharisees represent the first school [on the above list]". Yet how this renders ἀπάγοντες is not clear. If Josephus wants merely to recall his initial list of schools in § 119, he has chosen an awkward way to do so. The opening words of § 162 suffice to evoke the earlier topic sentence: Δύο δὲ τῶν προτέρων (sc. ταγμάτων, cf. § 161). Then follows in apposition this two-pronged description of the Pharisees:

οἱ (a) μετ' ἀκριβείας δοκοῦντες ἐξηγεῖσθαι τὰ νόμιμα καὶ
     (b) τὴν πρώτην ἀπάγοντες αἵρεσιν

If the German critics are right, the second strand in this pair refers yet again to the list at § 119. It seems clear, however, that ἀπάγοντες stands

---

[45] Michel-Bauernfeind, *De Bello Judaico*, I, 439 n. 86.

in some sort of parallel relationship to δοχοῦντες. Both have the same form and share a common article. This implies a correspondence of meaning. Therefore the way in which the Pharisees "constitute the first school" ought to be related somehow to their reputation for (or profession of) ἀκρίβεια.

Thackeray's translation takes into account both the contextual necessity that προτέρων refer back to § 119 and the fact that the first two statements of § 162 are related in sense. He proposes:

> Of the two first-named schools, the Pharisees, who are considered the most accurate interpreters of the laws, and hold the position of the leading sect
> . . . .

That the Pharisees' reputation for ἀκρίβεια enabled them to become the leading (πρώτη) school accords well with Josephus's vision of Judaism, as we have seen. For he declares elsewhere that among the Jews, accurate interpretation of the laws is the communal goal and, consequently, the sole criterion by which one acquires fame (*Ag.Ap.* 2:149, 175; *Ant.* 20:264; *Life* 8f.). As the reader of *War* has already been told, Queen Alexandra was able to take firm control of the government because of her reputation for ἀκρίβεια (1:108). Likewise, two teachers of the πάτρια acquired a reputation for ἀκρίβεια and "consequently (διὰ τοῦτο) enjoyed the highest esteem of the whole nation" (1:649). So it fits perfectly with Josephan usage that he should claim that the Pharisees, "who are considered the most accurate interpreters of the laws, . . . hold the position of the leading school".

Thackeray, however, concedes that the verb ἀπάγω is puzzling.[46] The difficulty lies in the prefix ἀπό, which suggests a movement away from something (the centre, or main body?) and therefore does not seem to fit with the idea that the Pharisees are the dominant (πρώτη) school. To justify his translation, Thackeray opts for the emendation of ἀπάγω to ἐπάγω, without manuscript support;[47] this allows for a greater range of positive associations.

One must ask whether the scholars' difficulties with ἀπάγω do not arise merely from the common presupposition, shared by Thackeray,[48] that Josephus was himself a Pharisee. One would not expect a committed Pharisee to speak of his group as "leading astray the foremost school", as the most obvious sense of ἀπάγω might suggest. A full discussion of Josephus's alleged Pharisaism must await Part IV of this study. We may observe, however, that Josephus has said nothing so far to give the

---

[46] *Lexicon,* "ἀπαγεῖν".
[47] *Lexicon, s.v..* The emendation was suggested by Hudson.
[48] LCL edn., I, viif.; cf. his *Josephus,* 7.

slightest hint of any Pharisaic allegiance on his part. On the contrary, in *War* 1:110 he demolished the Pharisees' reputation for superior ἀκρίβεια and εὐσέβεια, presenting them rather as frauds and deceivers. Second, although the Pharisees in the present passage are listed first (§ 119) and are called "the foremost school" (§ 162), they receive only perfunctory attention—two Niese sections, in contrast to the fifty-two sections allotted to the Essenes. It is the Essenes who love one another more than do the other groups (§§ 120, 125), who are just and most scrupulous (ἀκριβέστατοι) in their judgements (§ 145), who shun wealth and privilege (§§ 122ff., 140), who love the truth (§ 141), and who "irresistibly attract all who have once tasted their philosophy" (§ 158). But if Josephus regards the Essenes as the fullest specimens of Judaism, whose virtues excel those of other Jews, what must he think of the fact that the Pharisees are the dominant school? This consideration, together with his earlier denunciation of the Pharisees, seems to warrant the retention of ἀπάγω in its ordinary sense, thus: the Pharisees are "leading away/astray" the foremost school of thought among the Jews. Such an interpretation shares all the advantages of Thackeray's proposal, without the disadvantage of relying on a conjectural emendation of ἀπάγω.

C. Josephus's third statement about the Pharisees concerns fate and free will:

(1) εἱμαρμένῃ τε καὶ θεῷ προσάπτουσι πάντα
(2) καὶ τὸ μὲν πράττειν τὰ δίκαια καὶ μὴ κατὰ τὸ πλεῖστον ἐπὶ τοῖς ἀνθρώποις κεῖσθαι,
(3) βοηθεῖν δὲ εἰς ἕκαστον καὶ τὴν εἱμαρμένην.

Here we finally encounter the main verb of the passage. For the participles δοκοῦντες and ἀπάγοντες have merely summarized what was already said about the Pharisees at 1:110, 571. They are strictly preliminary to the main issue in 2:162ff., which now comes clearly into view, namely: the Pharisees' position on εἱμαρμένη and voluntary action. By isolating the main verb (προσάπτουσι), we have also found the central issue in the comparison (μὲν . . . δέ) between Pharisees and Sadducees in §§ 162-165. The two schools differ about whether "fate" is a factor in human life.

That the central issue of the passage is that of fate and free will is confirmed by Josephus's first summary description of the three Jewish αἱρέσεις in *Ant.* (13:171-173). There he reports that these groups "held different opinions περὶ τῶν ἀνθρωπίνων πραγμάτων", that is, as to what resides in the power of fate and what resides in human power. In *Ant.* 18:13, 18, again, Josephus will raise the issue in connection with the Pharisees and Essenes.

The obvious prominence of the fate/free will issue in Josephus's description of the αἱρέσεις[49] prompts both literary and historical questions, viz.: (a) What did Josephus mean to say about fate and free will in Jewish thought? and (b) what historical reality was he describing? We cannot examine here the extensive body of secondary literature that has grown up around these questions because the literature tends to consider together: (i) all of the passages on fate and free will among the schools (usually focusing on *Ant.* 13:171-173); (ii) the question of parallels (i.e., "Was Josephus more Jewish or more Greek?"); and (iii) the question of Josephus's sources. The format of the present study, however, demands that passages be treated individually. Further, our interest is confined to the question of Josephus's intention: "What did he mean to say?" For a review of the scholarly discussion *in situ* the reader is referred to Appendix B; views presented there will only be mentioned here in the notes.

1. *Key Terms*

(a) Josephus uses εἱμαρμένη 20 times:[50] 12 times in *War*, 7 times in *Ant.*, and once in *Ag.Ap.* Seven of these occurrences, however, fall within the school passages now under discussion. Subtracting these, the word occurs in other contexts 9 times in *War*, 3 times in *Ant.*, and once in *Ag.Ap.* One may distinguish at the outset two senses of εἱμαρμένη, the one subjective (i.e., Fate as a power) and the other objective (i.e., what is "fated", "allotted", or "decreed").[51]

---

[49] This prominence should not be overstated. Schlatter calls the Pharisaic position on fate and free will "das Wesentliche" in Josephus's portrayal of the group (*Theologie*, 209; so also Maier, *Mensch und freier Wille*, 3). It is true that whenever the Pharisees are compared to the Sadducees and Essenes (*War* 2:162ff.; *Ant.* 13:17ff.; 18:11ff.), this issue is usually central (but cf. *Ant.* 13:297f., which compares Pharisaic and Sadducean views of the laws). Nevertheless, when the Pharisees are described on their own, it is their reputation for exegetical ability that consistently comes to the fore (*War* 1:110; 2:162; *Ant.* 13:288f.; 17:41; *Life* 191).

[50] The verb εἴμαρτο occus at *War* 1:79 and 4:257.

[51] For this general distinction and for the history of the term, see: LSJ, "εἱμαρμένη"; W. Gundel, "Heimarmene", *PWRE*, XIII, 2622-2645; St. G. Stock, "Fate (Greek and Roman)", *ERE* V, 786-790; I. Kajanto, *God and Fate in Livy* (Turku: Turun Yliopiston Kustantama, 1957), esp. 11-23; W. D. Greene, *Moira: Fate, Good, and Evil in Greek Thought* (Cambridge, Mass: Harvard Univ. Press, 1944); and D. Amand, *Fatalisme et Liberté dans l'Antiquité Grecque* (Louvain: Bibliotheque de l'Université, 1945), esp. 1-28. It is now widely agreed that εἱμαρμένη is a perfect passive feminine participle of μείρομαι, "to divide", in contrast to ancient etymologies. Cf. Stock, "Fate", 789; B. C. Dietrich, *Death, Fate, and the Gods* (London: Athlone, 1965), 11; D. J. Furley, "Aristotle and Epicurus on Voluntary Action", in his *Two Studies in Greek Atomism* (Princeton: Princeton University Press, 1967), 174; W. Theiler, "Tacitus und die antike Schicksalslehre," in *Phyllobolia: für P. von der Muhll* (Basel: Benno Schwabe & Co., 1946), 43 and n. 1.

In its objective sense, εἱμαρμένη almost always refers to the idea of an appointed and unavoidable time, place, or manner of death.[52] Thus Herod complains of his ἄδικον εἱμαρμένην, when he perceives that his family wants his death (1:628); later, he tries to anticipate τὴν εἱμαρμένην by suicide (1:662). When Matthias (= Mattathias) the Hasmonean dies, he allows that he is going "the destined way" (τὴν εἱμαρμένην πορείαν— adjectival usage, *Ant.* 12:279). Notice also *War* 1:79, where Judas the Essene speaks of the place appointed or "predestined" (χωρίον . . . εἵμαρτο) for the death of Antigonus the Hasmonean.

In the majority of cases, however, Josephus employs εἱμαρμένη as a subject, as he does in the school passages. And it is these instances that can be expected to shed the most light on our problem.

(i) In *War* 6:84, εἱμαρμένη as subject comes very close to the usual objective meaning of "one's allotted time and place of death". The Roman hero Julianus, we are told, although he had fought valiantly, was pursued by Fate (ἐδιώκετο . . . ὑπὸ τῆς εἱμαρμένης), "which every mortal is powerless to escape" (ἣν ἀμήχανον διαφυγεῖν θνητὸν ὄντα), and met an unfortunate death.

(ii) Generally, however, εἱμαρμένη as a subject in Josephus appears in close proximity to θεός. This is true, for example, of the six occurrences of the word in *War* in the context of the destruction of the Temple. Reporting on the various factions in Jerusalem, Josephus notes that both the bellicose Idumeans and the moderates under Ananus thought that God (ὁ θεός) was on their own side (*War* 4:288). One reads on, however, to find that they had mistakenly read the future (§ 289) and that the "decree of Fate" (στρατηγούσης τῆς εἱμαρμένης) brought about the deaths of Ananus and his sentries (297). Εἱμαρμένη here executes the will of God.

(iii) In a speech outside the Temple precincts, Josephus calls on the intransigent John of Gischala to quit the revolt before the Temple is destroyed (*War* 6:96ff.). At the end of his speech, Josephus confesses his own foolishness "for offering advice in *fate*'s despite" (ὃς ἀντικρὺς εἱμαρμένης τι παραινῶ) and "for struggling to save those whom *God* has condemned" (τοὺς ὑπὸ τοῦ θεοῦ κατακρίτους, § 108; Thackeray). The synonymous parallelism between fate and God is clear. It is confirmed by the sequel: "God it is then, God himself (θεὸς αὐτός), who with the Romans is bringing the fire" (§ 110; Thackeray).

(iv) Concerning the day of the Temple's destruction, Josephus writes:

---

[52] Cf. V. Cioffari, "Fortune, Fate, and Chance", in *Dictionary of the History of Ideas*, ed. P. P. Wiener (New York: Charles Scribner's Sons, 1973), II, 226: "The notion of Fate may very well have arisen from the observation of the inexorability of death."

That building, however, God (ὁ θεός), indeed long since, had sentenced to the flames; but now . . . had arrived the fated day (ἡ εἱμαρμένη ἡμέρα) . . . the day on which of old it had been burnt by the king of Babylon. (§ 250; Thackeray).

To be "fated", therefore, is to be decreed by God. A few sentences later Josephus comments:

> Deeply as one must mourn for the most marvelous edifice which we have ever seen or heard of, . . . yet we may draw very great consolation from the thought that there is no escape from Fate (τὴν εἱμαρμένην, ἄφιχτον οὖσαν, § 267; Thackeray).

Josephus marvels at the ἀκρίβεια of Fate, by which she chose the very date of the Temple's former destruction for its present catastrophe (§ 268). The whole narrative is of one piece, so the εἱμαρμένη from which Josephus draws consolation (or explanation[53]) is nothing other than the will of God being acted out.[54]

(v) Likewise, when Josephus claims that εἱμαρμένη had shut up a larger than usual number of people in Jerusalem at the outbreak of the revolt, during Passover (6:428), the reader has not had time to forget Titus's words: "God indeed has been with us in the war" (6:411; Thackeray). And the reader will soon be assured that *God* meted out retribution to the tyrants who caused all of the suffering and destruction (§ 433).

(vi) The thesis of *War* is that God is on the Roman side,[55] which explains Josephus's remark about Vespasian:

> Now that fortune (ἡ τύχη)[56] was everywhere furthering his wishes and that circumstances had for the most part conspired in his favour, Vespasian was led to think that divine providence (δαιμονία πρόνοια) had assisted him to grasp the empire and that some just destiny (δικαία τις εἱμαρμένη) had placed the sovereignty of the world in his hands (4:622; Thackeray).

The indefinite pronoun τις, being indefinite, reflects Vespasian's dawning awareness that he is receiving divine aid (although Josephus himself knows very well *who* is bringing the Roman victory) and, being personal,

---

[53] For "explanation" or "solution" as a meaning of παραθυμία, see LSJ (,9th. edn.).

[54] How Wächter ("unterschiedliche Haltung", 101f.) can interpret εἱμαρμένη in these passages to mean an autonomous power is not clear.

[55] Cf. esp. 2:390; 5:2, 367, where τύχη and God are said to be on the Roman side. Cf. Lindner, *Geschichtsauffassung*, 22f., 29, 40ff.

[56] Josephus uses τύχη some 137 times (71 of these in *War*). Though rich in its associations, the word never appears in a discussion of the Pharisees and is, therefore, beyond the scope of our study. Lindner (*Geschichtsauffassung*, 42-48 and 85-94) finds that Josephus's own tendency is to present τύχη as one aspect of the biblical-Jewish God (p. 92), but that Greek and Roman views of τύχη also survive in his work. Cf. also Kajanto, *God and Fate*, 11-23.

solidifies the parallel with δαιμονία πρόνοια and the other references to God's assistance to the Romans (e.g., 2:390; 5:367; 6:411).

(vii) The words put into the mouth of King Agrippa, who is about to die in retribution for his acceptance of worship as a god, are also noteworthy:

> Fate (εἱμαρμένη) brings immediate refutation of the lying words lately addressed to me . . . . But I must accept my lot (τὴν πεπρωμένην) as God (θεός) wills it. (*Ant.* 19:347; Feldman)

Here ἡ πεπρωμένη is what God has decreed; εἱμαρμένη, again, is the execution of that decree.

(viii) The only other passage in which Josephus discusses εἱμαρμένη in connection with θεός is *Ag.Ap.* 2:245. There he ridicules the way in which the Greek θεοί are presented by Homer, for Zeus is "so completely at the mercy of Destiny (κρατούμενος ὑπὸ τῆς εἱμαρμένης) that he cannot either rescue his own offspring or restrain his tears at their death"[57] (Thackeray). Such an idea, Josephus claims, reflects a misapprehension of the true nature of God (*Ag.Ap.* 2:250).[58]

In all of these passages Josephus presents a clear and consistent view of the relationship between εἱμαρμένη and θεός. Εἱμαρμένη is never a supreme or even autonomous entity.[59] Often used interchangeably with θεός, it is simply the executive aspect of the divine will.

The frequent juxtaposition of εἱμαρμένη and θεός in Josephus's writings has obvious implications for the question of how and where he used sources. Several commentators have thought that the tandem εἱμαρμένη καὶ θεῷ in *War* 2:163 requires explanation, either as Josephus's attempt to explain the Jewish sense of θεός to Hellenistic readers (by adding εἱμαρμένη)[60] or as Josephus's superficial attempt to judaize a Hellenistic description of the schools, which contained only εἱμαρμένη.[61] But once it is observed that Josephus regularly combines θεός and εἱμαρμένη in his own writing (and thought!), such stratagems become

---

[57] The charge is based on passages like Homer's *Iliad*, 16:433-461; 19:95-133 (where Zeus is trapped by an oath); and 22:168-185. Notice that Lucian (*Zeus Catechized*, 4-11) launches a similar attack on the notion that Zeus, if he is a god, should be limited by Fate.

[58] Greene, *Moira*, 16, argues that it was only the poets, not the philosophers, who followed Homer in subordinating Zeus to Fate. Cf. A. Leach, "Fate and Free Will in Greek Literature", in *The Greek Genius and its Influence*, ed. L. Cooper (New Haven: Yale University Press, 1917), 134-155, who denies in general that the Greek gods were seen as bound by Fate; also Kajanto, *God and Fate*, 20.

[59] *Contra* Wächter, "Die unterschiedliche Haltung", 101f. and Martin, "Josephus's Use of *Heimarmene*", 133f. Cf. Nötscher, *Aufsätze*, 7, for an accurate assessment.

[60] So L. Wächter, "unterschiedliche Haltung", 107.

[61] So G. Maier, *freier Wille*, 11f., who thinks that Josephus's source was a description of the Pharisees by Nicolaus of Damascus.

superfluous. It is wholly in keeping with Josephan usage, further, that in 2:164, the Sadducees' abolition of εἱμαρμένη is parallel to their "removal of God (θεός) from the sphere of human action".[62] The fact that he himself can substitute θεός for εἱμαρμένη in various descriptions of the Essenes (*Ant.* 18:18; cf. 13:172) ought to have been sufficient to preclude extravagant source hypotheses.

Does Josephus's use of εἱμαρμένη accord with any particular philosophical currents in the Hellenistic world? Although the idea of a predetermined order was present in Greece from earliest times,[63] εἱμαρμένη itself only came into its own with the Greek philosophers.[64] According to Diogenes Laertius (9:7), it was Heraclitus (503 BC) who introduced the term into Greek philosophical discussion, with the aphorism πάντα τε γίνεσθαι καθ' εἱμαρμένην.[65] Notice the striking similarities to this dictum in what Josephus ascribes to the Pharisees (εἱμαρμένη προσάπτουσι πάντα, *War* 2:163[66]), to the Essenes (μηδὲν ὃ μὴ κατ' ἐκείνης [sc. εἱμαρμένης] ψῆφον ἀνθρώποις ἀπαντᾷ, *Ant.* 13:172), and to himself (καλοῦμεν αὐτὴν εἱμαρμένην, ὡς οὐδενὸς ὄντος ὃ μὴ δι' αὐτὴν γίνεται, *Ant.* 16:397; cf. *War* 6:84). Yet some 600 years separate Josephus from Heraclitus, and the idea of εἱμαρμένη was to become more popular and nuanced during that time.

In Plato's thought, W. Gundel sees a radical shift in the use of εἱμαρμένη.[67] In his earlier works Plato ridicules as effeminate the idea that εἱμαρμένη cannot be avoided;[68] his later works, however, reveal an increasing acceptance of—even an emphasis on—the idea of fate.[69] Thus in the tenth book of his *Republic* Plato tries to effect a symbiosis between fate and free will, which he does by resorting to the Myth of Er.[70]

---

[62] Josephus's Sadducees *do* distinguish between God and fate. They utterly reject the latter, but (only) severely limit the former (*War* 2:164). This disavowal of fate, however, means that they deny the "executive" aspect of God's nature, his involvement in the world. Josephus, for his part (*Ant.* 10:280), censures those who divorce divine activity (πρόνοια, which is linked with εἱμαρμένη at *War* 4:622) from God's existence.

[63] Terms associated with this idea were αἶσα, ἀνάγκη, μοῖρα, μόρσιμον, πέπρωται, κήρ, and δαίμων, all of which occur in Homer. By Hesiod's time (*Theogony* 218f.) we have the three Μοῖραι (Fates), who dispense good and evil at birth. Cf. Stock, "Fate", 786f.; Gundel, "Heimarmene", 2623; and Greene, *Moira*, 8f.

[64] Gundel, "Heimarmene", 2622f.; Stock, "Fate", 789.

[65] Stobaeus, I, 178.

[66] Cf. *Ant.* 18:13: πράσσεσθαι εἱμαρμένη τὰ πάντα.

[67] Gundel, "Heimarmene", 2626f.

[68] *Gorgias* 512E: "It is believed by the women that no one can escape Fate". Cf. *Phaedo* 115A and Stock, "Fate", 789.

[69] Gundel, "Heimarmene", 2627, finds two different nuances of the term in the mature Plato, *viz.*: (a) an individual's fate and (b) fate as cosmic law (*Weltgesetz*). Amand, *Fatalisme et Liberté*, 4f., distinguishes four senses of the word in Plato.

[70] See the discussion below.

It was Stoicism, however, that reclaimed the heritage of Heraclitus and elevated εἱμαρμένη to a central role.[71] Being a monistic philosophy, Stoicism could not hypostatize εἱμαρμένη or distinguish it ontologically from the one World-Soul, the Logos.[72] Thus the Stoics identified Εἱμαρμένη with Θεός, Φύσις, Λόγος, Πρόνοια, and all of the other terms that they used for the World-Soul, as the following examples show:

(i) Diogenes Laertius 7:135, on the Stoics: "God is one and the same with Reason, Fate, and Zeus; he is also called by many other names" (῞Εν τ᾽ εἶναι θεὸν καὶ νοῦν καὶ εἱμαρμένην καὶ Δία; πολλάς τ᾽ ἑτέρας ὀνομασίας προσονομάξεσθαι).

(ii) Zeno is reported to have wholly identified εἱμαρμένη with πρόνοια and φύσις: (τὴν εἱμαρμένην) δύναμιν κινητικὴν τῆς ὕλης . . . μὴ διαφέρειν πρόνοιαν καὶ φύσιν καλεῖν (Stobaeus, Ecl., I, 178 = SVF I, 176).

(iii) Chrysippus, the third head of the Stoic school, apparently wrote in several places (including his lost work Περὶ τῆς Εἱμαρμένης): εἱμαρμένη ἐστὶν ὁ τοῦ κόσμου λόγος (Stobaeus, Ecl., I, 180).

(iv) The Stoic Seneca likewise identifies Jupiter with *fatum*, *providentia*, and *natura* (*Benefits* 4.7.2; *Natural Questions* 2.45.2).

(v) Plutarch, the first-century adversary of the Stoics, writes: "that the universal nature (ἡ κοινὴ φύσις) and the universal reason of nature (ὁ κοινὸς τῆς φύσεως λόγος) are destiny (εἱμαρμένη) and providence (πρόνοια) and Zeus, of this not even the Antipodes are unaware, for the Stoics keep harping on this everywhere." (*Stoic Self-Contradictions* 1050 B; Cherniss, LCL edn.)

(vi) Finally, Augustine (*City of God* 5:8) notes that the Stoics call Jove Fate.[73]

As the Stoics used εἱμαρμένη to describe the unavoidable chain of cause and effect empowered by the Logos/God, so Josephus uses the term as a synonym for, or complement to, θεός when speaking of God's activity in the world. By presenting the Pharisees as those who attribute everything to εἱμαρμένη καὶ θεῷ,[74] Josephus may be anticipating one of

---

[71] Cf. Stock, "Fate", 789; Gundel, "Heimarmene", 2628; W. Windelband, *A History of Philosophy*, trans. J. H. Tufts (New York: Macmillan, 1910), 192f.; Amand, *Fatalisme et Liberté*, 6f.; Greene, *Moira*, 338f.; Cioffari, "Fortune", 228; and Kajanto, *God and Fate*, 13.

[72] Cioffari, "Fortune", 226; Theiler, "Tacitus", 45f.; and Kajanto, *God and Fate*, 13.

[73] Further examples may be found in *SVF*, II, 1024, 1076, and in Theiler, "Tacitus", 46 n. 2.

[74] It is strange that Maier (*freier Wille*, 12) thinks this combination *ungewöhnlich* for Stoicism. In proposing καὶ θεῷ to be a Josephan addition, intended to connect Nicolaus's εἱμαρμένη with Jewish monotheism, he overlooks both normal Stoic and normal Josephan usage.

the bases on which he will later compare the Pharisees to the Stoics (*Life* 12).[75]

Not only the pairing of εἱμαρμένη and θεός but also the ascription of everything (πάντα) to εἱμαρμένη recalls a Stoic position. Cicero describes as Stoic the view that *omnia fato fiunt* (*On Fate*, 40f.). Diogenes Laertius likewise describes the views of leading Stoics:

> That all things happen by fate or destiny (καθ' εἱμαρμένην δὲ οἆσι τὰ πάντα γίγνεσθαι) is maintained by Chrysippus in his treatise *De fato*, by Posidonius in his *De fato*, book ii, by Zeno and by Boethus in his *De fato*, book i (7:149).

Such a view was unavoidable because of the Stoic equation of εἱμαρμένη with λόγος. Here, then, is a further parallel between Josephus's Pharisees and the Stoics.

Yet although Stoicism became the dominant philosophical system of the hellenistic world by the first century AD,[76] its own concept of εἱμαρμένη was not the one that ultimately captured the popular imagination. That honour went to the astrological conception of εἱμαρμένη as the operation of planets and stars on the course of earthly life.[77] In the free flow of ideas that characterized the Hellenistic period, this "Chaldean" philosophy drew strength and rational support from the Stoic doctrine of συμπάθεια in the universe.[78] Under the dual sponsorship of Stoicism and astrology, therefore, εἱμαρμένη acquired a central place in Hellenistic speculations, both learned and popular.

Nevertheless, the Stoic-philosophical understanding of fate was still

---

[75] A. Posnanski (*Über die religionsphilosophischen Anschauungen des Flavius Josephus* [Breslau: T. Schatzby, 1887], 11), notes that we have here only a terminological parallel. Josephus does not advance any particular Stoic doctrines for the Pharisees, such as that of the λόγος σπερματικός. It is worth noting, however, that Josephus himself comes close to this Stoic teaching when, in his speech against suicide at Jotapata, he speaks of the soul as a "portion of God" (θεοῦ μοῖρα, *War* 3:372).

[76] Sandbach, *The Stoics*, 16; Long, *Hellenistic Philosophy*, 107.

[77] Tacitus, *Annals* 6:22, records the struggle between the philosophical and popular (astrological) conceptions of Fate in his own time; cf. Theiler, "Tacitus", 42f.; Gundel, "Heimarmene", 2632-34; Amand, *Fatalisme et Liberté*, 11f.; Nock, *Conversion*, 99f. By the time of Augustine, the struggle was long over. Says he: "Ordinarily, when people hear the word fate they think of nothing but the position of the stars at the moment of one's birth or conception" (*City of God* 5:1, Walsh/Zema).

[78] Gundel, "Heimarmene", 263ff.; Amand, *Fatalisme et Liberté*, 11f. It is sometimes argued that Stoicism, like astrology, had a Semitic origin and that this common origin encouraged cross-fertilization (so Amand, 12f., drawing on Cumont). The case of Posidonius of Apamea (first century BC), who was both a Stoic teacher and an astrologer (so Augustine, *City of God* 5:15) is famous. Cf. also J. Bergman, "I Overcome Fate, Fate Hearkens to Me", in *Fatalistic Beliefs in Religion, Folklore, and Literature*, ed. H. Ringgren (Stockholm: Almqvist & Ringgren, 1967), 42.

very much alive among the educated class in the first century AD.[79]
After Chrysippus' Περὶ τῆς Εἱμαρμένης came many works on the same
subject, most of which are now lost.[80] And it is in the Stoic understanding of fate that we find the background to Josephus's own use of
the term in his portrayal of the Pharisees, for he never hints at any
astrological notions in this connection.

To speak of a Jewish background for Josephus's use of εἱμαρμένη is difficult because the word does not appear at all in the LXX. Nor is it to
be found in the NT, which springs from a largely Jewish milieu. Even
Philo uses the word only 8 times.[81] But Posnanski was probably correct
when he said that Josephus:

> unter εἱμαρμένη nichts anderes als den Ratschluss Gottes versteht, der als
> Herr der Welt über alles frei verfügt und ohne den nichts geschehen
> kann.[82]

So we conclude that Josephus's use of εἱμαρμένη most closely parallels
that of Stoicism, not astral fatalism,[83] and that it could well be understood by a Hellenistic readership. Josephus does not, however, attribute
to any of the Jewish schools, or to himself, a belief in any of the other
particular Stoic doctrines.[84]

Most interesting for the interpretation of *War* 2:163 are four passages
in which Josephus seems to be divulging his own views about the relationship between fate (εἱμαρμένη) and human action (τὰ ἀνθρώπινα
πράγματα).

(i) *Ant.* 3:314: "From these events [God's destruction of the impious
kings of Israel] one may learn how close a watch the Deity keeps over
human affairs (ὅσην τὸ θεῖον ἐπιστροφὴν ἔχει τῶν ἀνθρωπίνων πραγμάτων)
and how He loves good men but hates the wicked, whom He destroys
root and branch." (Thackeray/Marcus)

---

[79] Theiler, "Tacitus", 42f. (although he calls the "philosophical" definition of fate
"Platonistic", 67-81). Tacitus, *Annals* 6:22, presents the philosophical view of fate as a
common one in his day. Augustine still recognizes and respects it, albeit as a minority
view: "There are some, however, who define fate, not as the arrangement of stars at
conception, . . . but as the total series of causes which brings about all that happens"
(*City of God* 5:8, cf. 5:1). So Posidonius's influence on Stoicism was not decisive (Greene,
Moira, 354); he did not cause that school to reinterpret εἱμαρμένη in astrological terms.
[80] Gundel, "Heimarmene", 2625, lists many of these works, which are known either
through extant fragments or through secondary testimony. Only a few of the later ones
(e.g., those by John Chrysostom and Gregory of Nyssa) survive intact.
[81] Cohn-Wendland cite eight occurrences.
[82] Posnanski, *Anschauungen*, 12.
[83] So Posnanski, *Anschauungen*, 11; *contra* L. H. Martin, "Josephus's Use of
Heimarmene", 127-137.
[84] Cf. Posnanski, *Anschauungen*, 11 *et passim*.

(ii) *Ant.* 10:277-280. Having discussed the remarkable fulfillment of Daniel's prophecies, Josephus asserts that anyone reading them must:

> learn from these facts how mistaken are the Epicureans, who exclude Providence from life and refuse to believe that God governs its affairs (οἳ τήν τε πρόνοιαν ἐκβάλλουσι τοῦ βίου καὶ θεὸν οὐκ ἀξιοῦσιν ἐπιτροπεύειν τῶν πραγμάτων).

He goes on to castigate "those who judge there to be no foreknowledge (πρόνοια) of human affairs (περὶ τῶν ἀνθρωπίνων) with God" (§ 280).

(iii) *Ag.Ap.* 2:180, where Josephus criticizes those who do away with the foreknowledge (πρόνοια) of God. The Law, says Josephus, teaches that all things are under the eye of God (πάντα . . . ἐκεῖνον ἐφορᾶν, § 181). Contrast these tenets of Josephus with the views that he attributes to the Sadducees in *War* 2:164, who "do away with fate entirely" (τὴν μὲν εἱμαρμένην παντάπασιν ἀναιροῦσιν) "and place God beyond the threshold of doing or even observing anything" (καὶ τὸν θεὸν ἔξω τοῦ δρᾶν τι ἢ ἐφορᾶν τίθενται). L. Wächter is doubtless correct in finding here a harsh assessment of the Sadducees.[85]

(iv) *Ant.* 16:395-404, where Josephus discusses in some detail the relation between fate/providence and human responsibility. Prior to this passage he has recounted the long period of mistrust and intrigue between Herod and two of his sons, which ended in the deaths of the sons. Now Josephus reflects upon the causes of this tragedy and considers three possibilities: (a) the intransigence of the sons (§ 395); (b) the vanity of Herod (§ 296); and (c) Fortune (ἡ τύχη). Of the last he writes:

> who has a power greater than all prudent reflection. For which reason we are persuaded that human actions (τὰς ἀνθρωπίνας πράξεις) are dedicated by her beforehand to the necessity of taking place inevitably, and we call her Fate (εἱμαρμένην) on the ground that there is nothing that is not brought about by her (οὐδενὸς ὄντος ὃ μὴ δι' αὐτὴν γίνεται). (§ 397; Marcus/Wikgren)

Yet he does not leave the matter there—thereby making τύχη/εἱμαρμένη the culprit—but continues:

> It will be enough, so I think, to weigh this tenet against that which attributes something also to us ourselves and renders us not unaccountable for the differences in our behaviour, and which has been philosophically expounded before our time in the Law. (§ 398)

> τοῦτον μὲν οὖν τὸν λόγον, ὡς νομίζω, πρὸς ἐκεῖνον ἀρκέσει κρίνειν ἡμῖν τε αὐτοῖς ἀποδιδόντας τι καὶ τὰς διαφορὰς τῶν ἐπιτηδευμάτων οὐκ ἀναπευθύνους ποιοῦντας, ἃ πρὸ ἡμῶν ἤδη πεφιλοσόφηται καὶ τῷ νόμῳ.

---

[85] L. Wächter, "Unterschiedliche Haltung", 99f.

The meaning of this statement is not immediately clear, but appears to hinge on the sense of κρίνειν. It cannot mean "decide in favour of [the fatalist position]" because Josephus will presently return to the human causes (§§ 399-404) of Herod's problems and will ultimately lay most of the blame on Herod.[86] Nor can it mean "decide against, condemn [the fatalist position]" because: (a) this would make nonsense of the preceding words, which extol the omnipotence of fate; (b) elsewhere, as we have seen, there is ample evidence of Josephus's belief in the inexorability of fate; and (c) neither the verb ἀρκέσει ("it will be enough") nor the present tense of κρίνειν implies any finality; both rather suggest an ongoing tension between the two λόγοι of fate and human responsibility. Hence my translation "weigh against".[87] Josephus wants simply to balance his belief in "fate" with a statement of human responsibility.

To summarize: Josephus believes that God observes (ἐφορᾶν) and directs human affairs; he calls God's direction εἱμαρμένη or πρόνοια.[88] God's superintendence, however, does not exclude human responsibility. Josephus declines the opportunity to reconcile human responsibility and divine providence, deferring instead to the "philosophical" treatment in the Law.

(b) τὸ πράττειν τὰ δίκαια καὶ μή. We may set some parameters for our discussion of δίκαιος in Josephus by citing Dodd's summary of the relationship between the Hebrew and Greek conceptions associated with this word:

> Where within this field δικαιοσύνη differs from צדק, it is not a matter of difference in the meaning of the terms, but of different conceptions of the content of 'righteousness'. Thus the fact that צדק is always related to God and His law, rather than to social customs and institutions as such, . . . gives a different colour to its use. . . . Where the Hebrew conception of righteousness differs from the popular Greek conception, we may put it thus, that whereas for the Greek δικαιοσύνη is always being pulled over from

---

[86] It is difficult to see how Wächter ("unterschiedliche Haltung", 101f.) and Stählin ("Schicksal", 337) can say that Josephus here makes fate all-powerful and autonomous from God, since Herod catches most of the blame for what happened with his sons. My reading (that fate is here an aspect of God's nature) agrees with Posnanski's (Anschauungen, 13 n. 17); he evidently had a similar difficulty understanding his predecessor Langen.

[87] This interpretation would still hold, and would perhaps be strengthened, if the reading κινεῖν instead of κρίνειν were accepted, as Niese has it. Marcus/Wikgren follow the reading of T. Terry.

[88] Πρόνοια is a favourite term of Josephus's. He uses it some 159 times and the verb προνέω about 89 times. Although πρόνοια is much more common than εἱμαρμένη in his vocabulary, he never uses it to describe the beliefs of the schools. This is doubtless an accommodation to the terms of the contemporary debate. On πρόνοια and its significance, cf. Attridge, Interpretation, 71-78.

the broad sense of 'righteousness' to the narrower sense of 'justice', the pull in Hebrew is in the opposite direction.⁸⁹

In assessing Josephus's use of δίκαιος, we shall need to decide whether it is more "Greek" or more "Jewish", according to Dodd's criteria.

Josephus is partial to the δικ-word group and uses δίκαιος as an adjective, substantive, or adverb (δικαίως) a total of 354 times: 48 times in *War*, 284 in *Ant.*, 7 in *Life*, and 15 in *Ag.Ap.*⁹⁰ We have already observed that in the frequent pair εὐσεβῆς καὶ δίκαιος, the former term is oriented πρὸς τὸν θεόν and the latter πρὸς ἀνθρώπους.⁹¹ That observation may now be supplemented by other data that indicate the human and social orientation of δίκαιος in Josephus.

Since the phrase under discussion is built around τὰ δίκαια, our main concern is with the articular substantives τὸ δίκαιον and τὰ δίκαια.

Generally speaking, the singular τὸ δίκαιον denotes the abstraction "justice".⁹² For example, in *Ant.* 4:214-218 Josephus summarizes the provisions of the Mosaic Law concerning magistrates. Four times within this paragraph τὸ δίκαιον appears as the goal of the magistrates in their trial of cases; it is most clearly related to their avoidance of partiality (§ 217). Herod, we are told, manipulated his own trial so as to outrage τὸ δίκαιον (*Ant.* 14:173). And Josephus claims that when he functioned as a magistrate in Galilee, he tried to avoid rash decisions and all forms of bribery so as to preserve τὸ δίκαιον (*Life* 79). The word does not always require such a formal legal sense, to be sure, and often means simply "justice, fairness, or propriety" in mundane affairs (*Ant.* 15:218; 16:264; 17:118, 191, 298; 20:181).

When the standard of fairness or propriety is articulated by law, and when the law in question is conceived of as the gift of God to mankind, as in Judaism, then just behaviour toward one's fellows will *ipso facto* please God also.⁹³ Josephus says as much in two places. First:

μεθ' ὧν γὰρ τὸ δίκαιόν ἐστι⁹⁴
μετ' ἐκείνων ὁ θεός. (*Ant.* 15:138)

---

⁸⁹ C. H. Dodd, *The Bible and the Greeks* (London: Hodder & Stoughton, 1935), 44f. So also J. A. Ziesler, *The Meaning of Righteousness in Paul* (Cambridge: University Press, 1972), 47.

⁹⁰ Δικαιοσύνη appears 39 times, but δικαιόω only 9 times (all in *Ant.*). Δίκη appears 158 times.

⁹¹ See chapter 4, above.

⁹² On Josephus's use of this word-group, cf. "δίκαιος" in the Thackeray/Marcus *Lexicon*, and Ziesler, *Righteousness*, 110.

⁹³ So Schlatter, *Theologie*, 159.

⁹⁴ That τὸ δίκαιον here means "justice" or "fair dealings" is clear from the context: Herod's envoys visit the Arabs to discuss a "just settlement" (*Ant.* 15:137, Marcus/Wikgren, for τὸ δίκαιον) but are killed by them.

For with whom justice is,
With them God is.

Then in *Ant.* 16:177 he emphasizes that justice toward mankind is the requirement of the Jewish law:

> And it is most profitable for all men, Greeks and Barbarians alike, to practise justice (τὸ δίκαιον), about which our laws are most concerned and, if we sincerely abide by them, they make us well disposed and friendly (εὔνους καὶ φίλους; Marcus/Wikgren)

Since the divinely appointed law enjoins justice, the exercise of justice brings divine favour. Nevertheless, in both of these cases τὸ δίκαιον is primarily right behaviour towards others.

In two other cases, Josephus comes very close to the sense of "righteousness" for τὸ δίκαιον. First, he uses the phrase to describe the goal of the Essenes, in *Ant.* 18:18, where the context deals only with matters of the cult.[95] And when he says that because the Jews admire τὸ δίκαιον rather than glory (δόξα), they refused to flatter Herod (*Ant.* 16:158), he may be suggesting the nuance "righteousness", but this is not clear. The context would seem to allow also "propriety/justice".[96]

Yet aside from these two ambiguous cases, τὸ δίκαιον in Josephus bears the simple meaning of "justice" or "propriety" in human affairs.

Decisive for the interpretation of our phrase must be the plural τὰ δίκαια, which occurs substantively 25 times outside of *War* 2:163. In practically all of these instances, the term bears no particular theological significance but rather denotes human fairness or justice. We may distinguish three specific nuances:

(1) Twice, τὰ δίκαια are ties of family or race (*War* 1:508; 2:211).

(2) In nine instances τὰ δίκαια may be literally translated "rights", as, for example, in the "merits or rights of a (legal) case" (*War* 1:136) or "the rights of citizenship" (τὰ δίκαια τὰ τῆς πολιτείας, *Ant.* 12:121). Most of the occurrences with this sense are in passages where Josephus cites pro-Jewish decrees and edicts from various Greco-Roman rulers concerning the legal rights (τὰ δίκαια) of Jews in various parts of the world.[97]

(3) In the remaining cases (about fourteen), τὰ δίκαια may simply be rendered "what is right, just, fair, or proper (in human affairs)". Thus the Essenes swear an oath τὰ πρὸς ἀνθρώπους δίκαια φυλάξειν (*War* 2:139).

---

[95] It is worth noting that in the parallel account in *War* (2:145), the Essenes are said to be "scrupulously careful and just in their trial of cases" (περὶ . . . τὰς κρίσεις ἀκρι-, βέστατοι καὶ δίκαιοι). Here δίκαιος clearly refers to human affairs.

[96] Marcus/Wikgren choose "righteousness", but the alternative seems just as appropriate.

[97] *Ant.* 14:208, 211, 265 (Josephus's words); 16:29 (Josephus's words); 19:282, 285, 288.

Josephus accuses John of Gischala of having done away with all those in Jerusalem who proposed "just and salutary measures" (Thackeray, for τὰ δίκαια καὶ συμφέροντα, *War* 7:263). *Ant.* 3:72 speaks of τὰ δίκαια in the trial of cases; 5:232 reports that Gideon the judge administered τὰ δίκαια; in 8:23 Solomon prays that he might judge (κρίνοιμι) the people on the basis of τὰ δίκαια; and 8:296 foresees a time when there will be no priest to administer (χρηματίζων) τὰ δίκαια. In the same vein, *Ant.* 13:126 records Demetrius II's pleasure that the Jews have fulfilled their "just obligations" (τὰ δίκαια) toward the Seleucids and 15:108 notes that the Nabatean king failed to perform the same (τὰ δίκαια) toward Herod.

As with the singular, a few instances of τὰ δίκαια in Josephus suggest more directly the idea of "righteousness" or pleasing God. One example is *Ant.* 9:167-169, where King Joash is said to have transgressed (πλημμελεῖν) against what was right (εἰς τὰ δίκαια) and the prophet is sent by God (§ 169) to admonish him to do the right (τὰ δίκαια πράττειν). In *Ant.* 11:56 Zerubbabel praises truth (ἡ ἀλήθεια) as that which provides "what is just and lawful" (τὰ δίκαια καὶ τὰ νόμιμα)[98] and thereby keeps away what is unjust (τὰ ἄδικα). Although these examples show that ultimately it is God's Law that sets the standard for justice, they do not change the fact that τὰ δίκαια in Josephus suggests primarily "doing the right thing by one's fellows" rather than "obeying the divine Law" *per se*.[99] The meaning is generally closer to "justice" than to "righteousness".[100]

That Josephus intended τὰ δίκαια καὶ μή as a simple ethical choice—"to do good or not"—is made absolutely clear by the latter half of the μέν . . . δέ construction in our passage. For whereas the Pharisees say that τὸ πράττειν τὰ δίκαια καὶ μή rests κατὰ τὸ πλεῖστον ἐπὶ τοῖς ἀνθρώποις, but that fate assists in each case, the Sadducees (§ 164) do away with fate entirely and maintain (§ 165) that ἐπ' ἀνθρώπων ἐκλογῇ τό τε καλὸν καὶ τὸ κακόν; the latter phrase must be more or less equivalent to τὸ πράττειν τὰ δίκαια καὶ μή. Josephus's meaning, then, seems clear enough. When he speaks of τὸ πράττειν τὰ δίκαια καὶ μή he is evoking the ethical alternatives of "doing what is right or not".[101]

---

[98] Cf. *Ant.* 7:151.

[99] In *Ant.* 12:121 and 14:315, τὰ δίκαια is paired with τὰ θεσεβεῖς and τὰ εὐσεβεῖς, respectively. In these combinations it probably refers to the man-ward side of just behaviour, just as δίκαιος in the complementary pair εὐσεβὴς καὶ δίκαιος.

[100] The Thackeray/Marcus *Lexicon* counts 59 instances in which the neuter adjective (singular and plural) occurs substantively with the meaning "justice".

[101] Note also the parellel in *Ant.* 18:14, where the Pharisees are said to believe in rewards or punishments for those who have led lives of virtue or vice (ἀρετὴ ἢ κακία). These terms likewise denote ethical action in the human sphere.

The concept of justice/righteousness (δικαιοσύνη, צדקה, and related terms) has a rich history in Jewish, Greek, and early Christian worlds of thought.[102] The number of potential parallels that might illuminate τὰ δίκαια in *War* 2:163 is enormous. It is impossible to attempt here even the barest summary of the relevant primary (not to mention secondary) literature. Yet some account must be taken of how Josephus's use of τὰ δίκαια relates to Jewish and Hellenistic conceptions in his own day.

A useful starting point is the recent proposal of G. Maier that the phrase τὸ πράττειν τὰ δίκαια καὶ μή (*War* 2:163) is part of Josephus's attempt to judaize a description of the Pharisees given to him by his source (Nicolaus). Asserting the ultimately Jewish character of *War* 2:162-166, Maier remarks:

> Das gilt vor allem für die von vornherein religiös und ethisch geführte Fragestellung nach dem 'Tun des Rechten', welche die 'Gerechtigkeit' nicht als eine der vier kardinaltugenden, sondern als Inbegriff des Geforderten, als das dem Menschen gesetzte Leitbild voraussetzt; *hinter dem griechischen πράττειν τὰ δίκαια entdeckt man ohne weiteres das hebräische* עשׂה צדקה des AT und der Qumranschriften, das in den Ps Sol und im NT mit ποιεῖν δικαιοσύνην wiedergegeben wird.[103] (emphasis added)

For Maier, then, Josephus's discussion of τὸ πράττειν τὰ δίκαια καὶ μή presupposes a biblical-Jewish view of τὰ δίκαια as the fulfillment of the divine commandments. Curiously, Maier does not investigate the meaning of δίκαιος/τὰ δίκαια elsewhere in Josephus; he is exclusively concerned with external parallels from the Old and New Testaments and the Community Rule (1QS) of Qumran, while apparently discounting any Greek parallels *a priori*.

In response to Maier, it is necessary to say the following.

(i) The interpretation of any term in Josephus must begin with, or at least include, an analysis of his own usage. We have seen that Josephus

---

[102] For general treatments of the concept in both Greek and Hebrew thought, cf. Dodd, *The Bible and the Greeks*, 42-59; W. Schrenk, "δίκαιος", *TDNT*, II, 181ff. For the OT, cf. A. R. Gordon, "Righteousness (OT)", *ERE* and the literature cited on p. 784; Ziesler, *Righteousness*, 17-45; B. Johnson, "Der Bedeutungsunterschied zwischen *sadaq* und *sedaqa*", *Annual of the Swedish Theological Institute* 11 (1978-79), 31-39; B. Przybylski, *Righteousness in Matthew* (Cambridge: University Press, 1980), 8-12. For the intertestamental and rabbinic literature, cf. J. Abelson, "Righteousness (Jewish)", *ERE*; Ziesler, *Righteousness*, 52-126; E. P. Sanders, *Paul*, 198-205; Przybylski, *Righteousness*, 13-76. For the Greek and hellenistic literature, cf. P. Shorey, "Righteousness (Greek and Roman)", *ERE*; R. Hirzel, *Themis, Dike, und Verwandtes* (Leipzig: S. Hirzel, 1907); M. Salomon, *Der Begriff der Gerechtigkeit bei Aristoteles* (Leiden: E. J. Brill, 1937); W. Siegfried, *Der Rechtsgedanke bei Aristoteles* (Zurich: Schulthess, 1947); P. Trude, *Der Begriff der Gerechtigkeit in der aristotelischen Rechts- und Staatsphilosphie* (Berlin: W. de Gruyter, 1955); and E. A. Havelock, *The Greek Concept of Justice: From its Shadow in Homer to its Substance in Plato* (Cambridge, Mass.-London: Harvard University Press, 1978).

[103] Maier, *freier Wille*, 12.

uses τὰ δίκαια (and the singular) elsewhere in his writings to refer to simple justice in human affairs, whether in the trial of cases or with reference to the rights of the Jews. He nowhere denies that this kind of justice pleases God and he sometimes connects it with faithfulness to the law. But religious ideas are usually secondary to the main idea of social propriety. So the usefulness of any outside "parallels" will be directly proportional to their correspondence to this Josephan sense.

(ii) It cannot be denied that the root צדק plays an important role in the OT and in later Judaism.[104] Insofar as the biblical conception has to do with what might be called simple ethics—"fair weights and balances, standard wages and prices"[105]—or lawful behaviour, Maier is justified in linking it with Josephan usage. It now seems clear, however, that for the OT and Judaism generally, צדקה refers to human action within the scope of the covenant: one is צדיק when one fulfills one's covenant obligations toward God.[106] This emphasis, however, is not significant in Josephus's use of τὰ δίκαια. Indeed, as H. W. Attridge has shown, Josephus has a marked tendency to omit the idea of covenant from his biblical paraphrase.[107]

(iii) Notice that the LXX translators seem to have perceived a significant difference between צדקה and δικαιοσύνη. For in the LXX, δίκαιος-forms occur much more frequently in the books with universal themes—the wisdom literature—than in the more covenantal books. The word-group appears only 25 times in all of the Pentateuch, but 94 times in Proverbs alone, where gnomic wisdom is discussed. It occurs 142 times in Job, Proverbs, and Ecclesiastes together. All five cases of the neuter substantive in Proverbs have the sense of common justice (16:7, 33; 18:5; 21:7; 29:6). This suggests that the LXX translators perceived important differences between צדקה (as covenantal) and δικαιοσύνη (social/relational).[108]

---

[104] Ziesler, *Righteousness*, 18 counts this word group some 504 times in Kittel's OT text. Cf. Przybylski, *Righteousness*, 8ff., and Sanders, *Paul*, 198ff.

[105] Quoting A. R. Gordon, *ERE*, 781, who is summarizing Amos's usage. Cf. Dodd, *Greeks*, 44.

[106] Ziesler (*Righteousness*, 42) says for the OT: "When we turn to man's righteousness, it is clearly a possibility only within the covenant. . . . Being within the covenant involves doing God's will . . . and it is loyalty to the covenant and therefore righteousness. So also right judging, right governing, right worshipping, and gracious activity, are all covenantal and righteous, despite their diversity."

Sanders (*Paul*, 204) concludes, with respect to the tannaitic literature: "on the one hand, that *the righteous are those who are saved* . . . . On the other hand, *the righteous are those who obey the Torah and atone for transgression.* . . . One who accepts the covenant and remains within it is 'righteous' . . . ." So also Przybylski, *Righteousness*, 76.

[107] Attridge, *Interpretation*, 79f.

[108] Cf. also R. B. Y. Scott, *Proverbs, Ecclesiastes*, "Anchor Bible", vol. 18 (Garden City: Doubleday, 1965), xvif.

Further, the LXX phrases that come closest to Josephus's τὸ πράττειν τὰ δίκαια are τὸ ποιεῖν τὰ δίκαια (Prov. 16:7), which has no Hebrew original, and πράσσειν τὰ δίκαια (Prov. 21:7), which stands for the Hebrew עֲשׂה מִשְׁפָּט and has nothing to do with צדק. This would seem to cast considerable doubt on Maier's assumption that τὸ πράττειν τὰ δίκαια "ohne weiteres" reflects a Hebrew-Jewish conception.

(iv) On the other hand, one can hardly dismiss the Greek parallels to Josephus's usage. That the Greeks personified Δίκη and Θέμις as deities in the time of Homer (and before) indicates their early reverence for norms of behaviour.[109] By the time of Plato, δικαιοσύνη is not only one of the four virtues;[110] it is the chief virtue that subsumes all the others.[111] The entire *Republic* of Plato has been described as "a literary monument to the celebration of justice".[112] Aristotle, similarly, devotes the fifth book of his *Nicomachean Ethics* to an analysis of δικαιοσύνη.[113] Furthermore, the Stoic Chrysippus is said to have written a widely read treatise "On Justice".[114] Thus the concept of justice/righteousness played a large role in Greek thought.

It is not possible here to give any sort of exposition of the nuances of δικαιοσύνη for individual Greek writers.[115] We may note, however, that the Greek concept was fundamentally social and not religious in content.[116] So Dodd: "We may take it that the Greek-speaking public, on the whole, meant by δικαιοσύνη doing the right thing by your neighbour, however the right thing might be conceived."[117] Aristotle offers as a common definition (πάντας ... λέγειν) of τὸ δίκαιον: "The just (τὸ δίκαιον), then, means the *lawful* (τὸ νόμιμον) and the *equitable* (τὸ ἴσον)" (*N.E.* 5.1.8.). Or again:

> The term 'just' is applied to anything that produces and preserves the happiness (εὐδαιμονία), or the component parts of the happiness, of the political community (τῇ πολιτικῇ κοινωνίᾳ). (5.1.13.)[118]

[109] Hirzel, *Themis*, 18f., 138f.

[110] *Republic* 432b. Schrenk (*TDNT*, II, 182 n. 2) finds righteousness among the virtues already in Aeschylus.

[111] So already Theognis 147: "In Justice (δικαιοσύνη) is all virtue found in sum" (quoted by Aristotle, *N.E.* 5.1.15, trans. Rackham).

[112] Havelock, *Greek Concept*, 308f.

[113] The richness of the Aristotelian conception of δικαιοσύνη has inspired the monographs of Salomon, Siegfried, and Trude (n. 102 above).

[114] So Plutarch, *On Common Conceptions*, 1070D; cf. P. Shorey, "Righteousness", 804.

[115] See n. 102 above.

[116] That is not to say that the Greeks did not also use δικαιοσύνη in the context of one's obligations to the gods (cf. Ziesler, *Righteousness*, 50f.). It is rather a matter of emphasis.

[117] Dodd, *Greeks*, 43. Cf. also Schrenk, *TDNT*, II, 182, who cites many examples, and Ziesler, *Righteousness*, 44f.

[118] Cf. also *N.E.* 5.1.3 and 15, where Aristotle likewise cites the common understanding of δικαιοσύνη (introduced by λέγεται. . . or πολλάκις εἶναι δοκεῖ. . .).

Observe how Rackham summarizes τὰ δίκαια in Aristotle:

> Τὰ δίκαια means sometimes 'just acts' in the English sense, sometimes any acts in conformity with the law, sometimes 'rights' or 'claims', i.e., any consideration which by law, equity, or custom, certain persons have a right to expect from others.

The senses identified here for τὰ δίκαια in Aristotle correspond exactly to those discovered in Josephus above.

Given the high degree of semantic overlap between δίκαιος and צדק, noted by Dodd at the outset, it seems unwise to claim that when Josephus used the phrase τὸ πράττειν τὰ δίκαια καὶ μή he was thinking of an exclusively Hebrew conception or an exclusively Greek one. What is clear is: (a) that Josephus's δικαιοσύνη generally lacks any connection with the idea of covenant; (b) that the phrase in *War* 2:163 refers to a straightforward ethical problem—"to do right or not"; (c) that the ethical discussion of τὰ δίκαια had had a long and venerable history in Greek thought before Josephus's time; and (d) that his Hellenistic readers could have been expected to understand his meaning.[119] Maier's proposal overlooks entirely the primacy of ethics in Greek thought.[120]

Josephus presents the Pharisees as a philosophical school concerned about relations between God/εἱμαρμένη and τὸ ἐπὶ τοῖς ἀνθρώποις in the "doing of what is right or not".[121] This means that Josephus's use of δίκαιος parallels his use of such other terms as εὐσέβεια, νόμοι/νόμιμα/πάτρια, ἀκρίβεια, αἵρεσις, and εἱμαρμένη. None reflects a uniquely Jewish category; all are drawn from the ordinary vocabulary of Hellenism.

(c) ἐπὶ τοῖς ἀνθρώποις κεῖσθαι. This phrase seems straightforward. The verb κεῖμαι with ἐν or ἐπί and a dative occurs at least 8 other times in Josephus with the meaning "to be in the power of someone or something".[122] Thus Josephus claims here that the Pharisees hold that "the doing of right or not" lies mainly with men.

---

[119] Schrenk (*TDNT*, II, 183) comments on Josephus's frequent use of δίκαιος in conjunction with ἀγαθός, χρηστός, etc., that these lists of virtues "display not the slightest difference from current hellenistic usage". (For these pairs, cf. *Ant.* 3:71; 4:134; 6:21, 93, 147; 7:151, 386; 8:248; 9:100, 132, 216; 10:246, etc.).

[120] Cf. Diogenes Laertius' claim that Socrates introduced ethics (2:16); also Greene, *Moira*, 221ff. (on the importance of ethics for the earlier philosopher), 331, 333 (for Stoics and Epicureans); Armstrong, "Greek Philosophy", 210 (on the later Stoics); and Sandbach, *Stoics*, 11f. (on ancient philosophy in general).

[121] Even the equation of δίκαιος with νόμιμος, which Josephus implies several times (e.g., *Ant.* 6:165; 7:151; 8:208; 11:56; 13:291; *Ap.* 2:293), though it certainly accords with biblical-Jewish conceptions, is also native to Greek thought, as we have seen in the definitions from Aristotle.

[122] *War* 3:389, 396; 5:59; *Ant.* 1:178; 5:110; 13:355; 18:215; 19:167.

Josephus uses ἐπὶ τοῖς ἀνθρώποις here to speak of both the Pharisaic (§ 163) and the Sadducean (§ 165) positions; the Sadducees φασὶν δ' ἐπ' ἀνθρώπων ἐκλογῇ τὸ καλὸν καὶ τὸ κακὸν προκεῖσθαι. In the parallel at *Ant.* 13:171-173, however, the phrase is ἐφ' ἡμῖν: the Sadducees believe ἅπαντα δὲ ἐφ' ἡμῖν αὐτοῖς κεῖσθαι (§ 173).[123]

Two observations are pertinent here. First, the phrase τὸ ἐφ' ἡμῖν had taken on, long before Josephus's time, a quasi-technical sense in Greek ethical discussions having to do with the causes of human action. In the third book of his *Nicomachean Ethics* Aristotle is concerned to distinguish voluntary (ἑκούσιος) from involuntary (ἀκούσιος) actions.[124] Near the beginning of this discussion he observes that, "when the origin of an action is in oneself (ὧν δ' ἐν αὐτῷ ἡ ἀρχή), it is in one's power to do it or not" (ἐπ' αὐτῷ καὶ τὸ πράττειν καὶ μή, 3.1.6; Rackham). Further along in his discussion, Aristotle begins regularly to use the phrase ἐφ' ἡμῖν for "what is in our power'. Especially suggestive of parallels for Josephus is 3.5.2:

ἐφ' ἡμῖν δὴ καὶ ἡ ἀρετή. ὁμοίως δὲ καὶ ἡ κακία. ἐν οἷς γὰρ ἐφ' ἡμῖν τὸ πράττειν, καὶ τὸ μὴ πράττειν. . . . ὥστ' εἰ τὸ πράττειν καλὸν ὂν ἐφ' ἡμῖν ἐστί, καὶ τὸ μὴ πράττειν ἐφ' ἡμῖν ἔσται αἰσχρὸν ὄν.

Therefore virtue depends on ourselves. And so also does vice. For where we are free to act we are also free to refrain from acting . . . ; if therefore we are responsible for doing a thing when to do it is right, we are also responsible for not doing it when not to do it is wrong. (Rackham)[125]

Here we have, as in Josephus: a discussion of the cause of human actions; the use of τὸ πράττειν . . . καὶ μή[126] as a term for ethical action; and the use of ἐπ' αὐτῷ/ἐφ' ἡμῖν to designate "what lies in human power".[127] Once Aristotle had conventionalized the phrase ἐφ' ἡμῖν, it took a permanent place in ethical discussion concerning voluntariness in human action.[128]

Second, that Josephus uses ἐπὶ (τοῖς) ἀνθρώποις in *War* 2:163-166 rather than ἐφ' ἡμῖν (as in *Ant.* 13:171-173) may be due simply to caprice.[129] It is worth noting, however, that the pronoun ἡμεῖς, when

---

[123] In describing the Pharisaic position (13:172), the MSS LAMWE support ἐφ' ἡμῖν αὐτοῖς.

[124] *N.E.* 3.1.1.

[125] Cf. also *N.E.* 3.5.3, 6, 7, 16, 21, 22, *passim*.

[126] Δίκαιος and ἄδικος also appear in the discussion, *N.E.*, 3.5.12, 14.

[127] Notice the pairing of ἀρετή and κακία here and at 3.5.19. Compare Josephus on the Pharisees, *Ant.* 18:13, 14.

[128] Cf., e.g., Epiphanius, *Against Heresies* 3.2.9, on Zeno (in H. Diels, *Doxographi Graeci*, p. 592, no. 36); Eusebius, *Preparation for the Gospel* 4:3, on Chrysippus (in *SVF* II, 939); and examples given by Greene, *Moira*, 350.

[129] Epicurus, for example, uses τὸ παρ' ἡμᾶς for the same conception, *Letter to Menoeceus* 133, cited in Furley, *Two Studies*, 184.

used by Josephus himself in editorial or reflective contexts, usually means "we *Jews*".[130] Since in *War* 2:163-166 he is describing Jewish philosophical schools (παρ' Ἰουδαίοις, § 119) it might have caused some vagueness if he had used the usual ἐφ' ἡμῖν here. In *Ant.* 13:171ff., however, the situation is different, because he begins by defining the debate as περὶ τῶν ἀνθρωπίνων πραγμάτων (§ 171). There, ἐφ' ἡμῖν would naturally be understood as "in *human* power". In any case, the phrase chosen by Josephus in *War* 2:163 would, it seems, have been understood by Hellenistic readers as referring to the discussion of human voluntariness and culpability that had become prominent with Aristotle.

(d) The meaning of βοηθεῖν also seems clear in its context: although the doing of right and wrong rests mainly with men, εἱμαρμένη *assists* in each case. The verb βοηθέω is at home in Josephan vocabulary. It occurs a total of 60 times: 19 in *War*, 38 in *Ant.*, 1 in *Life*, and 2 in *Ag.Ap.* The abstract noun βοήθεια is likewise evenly distributed thoughout his writings, for a total of 67 occurrences.[131]

What is striking about βοηθέω in this context is that it recalls one particular position in the philosophical debate on human voluntariness and culpability, namely, that of Chrysippus the Stoic.[132] Chrysippus tried to identify the area left for human will by Stoic doctrine, which seemed (to its opponents) to exclude true volition with its claim that everything (τὰ πάντα) happens by fate (= providence).[133] Part of his solution, according to Cicero, was to distinguish two sorts of causes in any action: an antecedent or main cause (*causae perfectae et principales*) and a "helping" or proximate cause (*causae adiuvantes et proximae*). His argument was that only the latter sort of cause is attributable to εἱμαρμένη, whereas the main cause of an action lies within the nature of the person or thing that acts.[134] Thus when someone sets a drum rolling down a hill, the principal cause of its rolling is its own nature, its "rollability".[135] The initial impetus

---

[130] E.g., *War* 1:6, 16; 5:137; 7:454; *Ant.* 1:4, 5, 9, 11, 18, 33, 129, etc.; 14:63, 65, 77, 186ff., 265ff., 304, 323; 15:7, 50, 259, 267, 371, 391, 398, 419, 425; 16:404; 17:14. *Life* 1, 2, 7, 10, etc.; *Ag.Ap.* 1:1, 2, 4, 5, 6, 8, 27, 29, 32, etc.; 2:1, 2, 4, 7, 8, 31, 32, etc. Hölscher claimed ("Josephus", 1982) that this use of ἡμεῖς in *Ant.* 13-20 indicated the Jewish character of Josephus's "intermediate source". But the use is typically Josephan.

[131] 18 times in *War*, 46 in *Ant.*, 3 in *Life*, 1 in *Ag.Ap.*

[132] As reported by Cicero in *On Fate*, 39ff. The parallel was noted already by G. F. Moore, "Fate", 238f., and was one of the factors in his attribution of our passage to Nicolaus.

[133] For the Stoic belief that everything happens by fate, cf. Diogenes Laertius 7:149.

[134] Cf. the discusions of Chrysippus in Long, *Hellenistic Philosophy*, 166f.; Rist, *Stoic Philosophy*, 121f.; Hicks, *Stoic and Epicurean*, 345d.; Sandbach, *Stoics*, 101f.; Windelband, 9ff.; Greene, *Moira*, 348; and Moore, "Fate", 376ff.

[135] Cicero, *On Fate*, 42.

from outside that makes possible the rolling movement is only an auxiliary or "adjuvant" cause—which is the role played by fate in human
affairs.[136] So Chrysippus' distinction of causes allowed him to maintain
the Stoic doctrine *omnia fato fiunt*[137] while at the same time offering a
basis for human volition.[138]

Our purpose is only to observe the correspondence at this point between the Chrysippean doctrine and Josephus's description of the
Pharisaic position: in both, εἱμαρμένη is a cause auxiliary (*adiuvo* =
βοηθέω) to human volition. That the correspondence is exact as far as it
goes does not mean, however, that it is comprehensive. For just as
Josephus does not make God a world-soul, so he does not elaborate ideas
of principal and auxiliary causes.

2. *Interpretation*

Having examined the key terms in the passage, we must now interpret
Josephus's remarks on the Pharisees, fate, and free will. To do so, it is
necessary to bring into view the larger μέν . . . δέ construction of §§ 162-
165, in which the Pharisees and Sadducees are compared.

After his long and loving description of the Essenes, Josephus
dispenses with the Pharisees and Sadducees by comparing their views on
several points. The first concerns their respective views of εἱμαρμένη.
Here Josephus presents the two positions as polar opposites, characterized by contradictory propositions, namely:

Pharisees	*Sadducees*
(163) εἱμαρμένη τε καὶ θεῷ προσάπ-τουσι πάντα	(164) τὴν . . . εἱμαρμένην παντάπασιν ἀναιροῦσιν καὶ τὸν θεὸν ἔξω . . . τίθενται

This contrast makes clear theat the emphasis in 162b-163a is on the
Pharisaic belief in εἱμαρμένη and not on the recognition of human volition. The latter is clearly concessive: "Although (in their view) doing
what is right or not rests mainly with men, in each case (εἰς ἕκαστον) fate
assists."

This recognition that fate always assists reasserts the original proposition that everything goes back to fate, although Josephus has now

---

[136] Ibid., 41.
[137] Ibid., 40f.
[138] Whether this stratagem gives adequate credit to human volition is another question. Cicero (*On Fate*, 39) did not think so. Nor do some modern commentators, e.g.,
Amand, *Fatalisme et Liberté*, 14; Greene, *Moira*, 348; Gundel, "Heimarmene", 2630.

granted some room within this scheme for human volition.[139] On the other hand, since the Sadducees do away with fate altogether, their position gives man unfettered choice (ἐκλογή) on the basis of his own will (κατὰ γνώμην ἕκαστον) to do good or evil (τὸ καλὸν καὶ τὸ κακόν. . . προσιέναι, § 165). Thus the Pharisees and Sadducees represent opposite poles of thought on εἱμαρμένη: the Pharisees find it everywhere; the Sadducees reject it entirely.

On a literary level our passage presents no special difficulties. All of the key terms reflect typical Josephan usage. The syntax seems clear, as does the main point. It is not made plain in what way the Pharisees believe that fate "assists" each action, so that one may ascribe everything to fate while at the same time recognizing human volition. But it is clear that in each action fate does not assist and that, therefore, everything for the Pharisees is at least partially attributable to fate, whereas for the Sadducees fate does not enter into the discussion at all.

On the historical level, scholars have found our passage to be quite problematic because Josephus's ascription to the Pharisees of a strong belief in εἱμαρμένη does not sound very Jewish.[140] The present study does not intend to solve the problem of the historical reality of the Pharisees, but only to interpret Josephus's statements as his first readers might have understood them. In that respect, the following observations are pertinent.

From at least the time of Socrates, Greek philosophers were absorbed with the ethical question of how one comes to act rightly or wrongly.[141] For Socrates, the answer lay in knowledge: one who knows what is good will naturally do what is good.[142] This means, however, that the ignorant man acts involuntarily (or, not freely) because he does not know any better.[143] Plato continued this emphasis on environmental factors that tend to commit one *a priori* to a particular life pattern (sometimes calling these

---

[139] Maier (*freier Wille*, 13) acknowledges this as a possible reading of our passage, but argues that the free-will clause may be intended to designate one exception to the otherwise complete rule of fate, namely, the area of ethics/*Soteriologie*, in which man remains wholly free. This reading, however, fails to account for the final fate clause (βοηθεῖν εἰς ἕκαστον τὴν εἱμαρμένην), which restates the original proposition, with no exceptions. Maier also neglects the μέν. . . δέ comparison with the Sadducees, which seems to require that precisely on the issue of ethics the two parties disagree about the cause of human action, with the Sadducees making human volition the cause.

[140] Moore, "Fate", 375, 397f.; Maier, *freier Wille*, 3. Cf. Appendix B at the end of this study.

[141] Diogenes Laertius 2:16 ("Socrates introduced ethics"); Greene, *Moira*, 223; Windelband, *History of Philosophy*, 191.

[142] Windelband, *History of Philosophy*, 191.

[143] Ibid.

factors ἀνάγκη and εἱμαρμένη).[144] He emphasized at the same time, however, the responsibility of man for his choices and the ability of man to overcome environmental prejudices.[145] Particularly in his Myth of Er, Plato attempts a reconciliation of the two ideas.[146] Souls standing before the three Fates are presented with life patterns to choose from, and Plato remarks through the prophet: "The responsibility belongs to him who chooses; God is not responsible" (Rep. 617e).[147] Once the choice of life pattern is made, however, a δαίμων is assigned to the soul and the soul's destiny is ratified by the Fates: he is now bound by necessity (ἀνάγκη) to live out the chosen life (Rep. 620d-621b). The goal of this life, then, is for man to learn how to distinguish the good from the bad so that he can take this knowledge with him after death, when he must choose another life-pattern (Rep. 618b-619a).[148]

Aristotle takes up the problem of τὸ πράττειν (τὰ δίκαια) καὶ μή in his Nicomachean Ethics. Having conceded that much is due to nature (φύσις), necessity (ἀνάγκη), and chance (τύχη), and is therefore beyond our control (N.E. 3.3.3-10), he nevertheless locates the cause of virtue and vice (ἀρετὴ καὶ κακία) squarely in ourselves (ἐφ' ἡμῖν; N.E. 3.5.2).[149] Already with these pillars of Greek philosophy the exploration of the relationship between environmental factors (or fate) and volition in the matter of ethics had made a solid beginning.

It was with the Stoics, however, that the problem became acute, due principally to their understanding of fate as the world-soul itself, the Λόγος.[150] Windelband comments:

> Since this theory of fate made man, like all other creatures, determined in all his external and internal formation and in all that he does and suffers, by the all-animating World-power, personality ceased to be the true

---

[144] Phaedo 80d-81d; cf. Amand, Fatalisme et Liberté, 4; Windelband, History of Philosophy, 191.

[145] Greene, Moira, 313f. In Laws 904, Plato insists that the gods leave the decision for virtue or vice to men's own souls.

[146] Republic 614b-621b. For commentary on this passage, see Amand, Fatalisme et Liberté, 5; Gundel, "Heimarmene", 2627; Greene, Moira, 313ff.; and Cioffari, "Fortune", 227.

[147] Cf. Timaeus 41d, 42d, 91de, in which it is said that one determines the quality of one's reinarnation by one's actions.

[148] Greene, Moira, 315, comments on the Myth of Er: "The allotment of human destinies is described in terms that emphasize both the lement of encompassing necessity or determinism and, within it, that of human freedom of choice."

[149] Cf. the discussions of Aristotle on this point in Amand, Fatalisme et Liberté, 6; Windelband, History of Philosophy, 192f.; Greene, Moira, 338, 348ff.

[150] Cf. Greene, Moira, 338, 348ff.; Windelband, History of Philosphy, 192f.; Amand, Fatalisme et Liberté, 6f.

ground (ἀρχή) of his actions and these appeared to be . . . but the predetermined and unavoidably necessary operations of the God-Nature.[151]

We have seen one of the ways in which the Stoic Chrysippus tried to
mitigate this problem. For the Epicureans, Academics, and Peripatetics
the problem was not as severe because they did not accept the monistic
premise of universal causality.[152] Still, the problem of fate and free will
has persisted wherever belief in an all-powerful God has been maintained.[153]

What all of this shows is that Josephus's description of the Pharisees
would have been readily intelligible to an educated Hellenistic reader.
The Pharisees, he says, are the leading philosophical school among the
Jews, and, like the leading Hellenistic school (the Stoics), they attribute
everything to fate or God. Also like the Stoics, the Pharisees both concede that virtuous action lies in man's power and insist that εἱμαρμένη
cooperates (βοηθέω/adiuvo) in each action.

It is beyond the scope of this study to decide whether or not Josephus
was right.[154] Suffice it here to note: (a) that Josephus knew a good deal
more about the Pharisees, and probably about the Stoics, than does
modern scholarship;[155] (b) that he considered the Pharisees and Stoics to
be alike in some respects (cf. παραπλήσιος, Life 12); (c) that outside
observers of ancient Judaism sometimes described it in Stoic terms;[156]

---

[151] Windelband, History of Philosophy, 192f.

[152] Cf. Diogenes Laertius 10:133 on the Epicureans; Windelband, History of Philosphy,
194f.; Greene, Moira, 334ff.

[153] Christian theology has made famous attempts to tackle the problem. Milton writes
of the fallen angels who:

      reasoned high
  Of Providence, foreknowledge, will and fate,
  Fixed fate, free will, foreknowledge absolute;
  And formed no end, in wandering mazes lost.
                Paradise Lost 2:557f., cited in Greene. Moira, 397.

[154] Several attempts have been made to decide the question historically; cf. Appendix
B. Maier and Wächter both conclude that Josephus's portrayal of the schools is at least
tolerably accurate.

[155] The Pharisees left no literary remains except the brief Megillat Ta'anit. The situation is better for later Stoicism, but authentic statements in context for the earlier
teachers (Zeno, Cleanthes, Chrysippus) are also scarce. Cf. Sandbach, Stoics, 18.

[156] Cf. T. Reinach, Textes d'Autres Grecs et Romains relatifs au Judaïsm (Hildesheim: G.
Olms, 1963 [1895]), pp. 11, 16, 99, 242. In one passage, Hecataeus of Aodera credits
Moses with a belief that τὸν οὐρανὸν μόνον εἶναι θεὸν καὶ τῶν ἐλων κύριον (p. 16). Likewise
Strabo has Moses insisting that images cannot be made of the deity because the deity
is everywhere (τὸ περίεχον ἡμᾶς ἅπαντας καὶ γῆν καὶ θάλατταν, ὃ καλοῦμεν οὐρανὸν καὶ
κόσμον καὶ τὴν . . . φύσιν). Suffrin, "Fate", 793, remarks: "It is possible that the Stoic
philosophy lent a colouring to Jewish speculations on Divine Providence. We know that
the ethics of Stoicism agree in many points with those of the Haggada [cf. e.g., M.
Avot], betraying some acquaintance, on the part of the Rabbis, with that school."

and (d) that monism and monotheism, insofar as they both posit a single ultimate being, must share certain common features.

D. Josephus's fourth statement about the Pharisees concerns their views on the soul:

    (i) ψυχήν τε πᾶσαν μὲν ἄφθαρτον,

    (ii) μεταβαίνειν δὲ εἰς ἕτερον σῶμα τὴν τῶν ἀγαθῶν μόνην,

    (iii) τὰς δὲ τῶν φαύλων ἀιδίῳ τιμωρίᾳ κολάζεσθαι.

With the question of the soul's immortality we reach the second part of the μέν. . . δέ construction that governs our passage. As with the fate/free will issue, Josephus describes the Pharisaic position first with a summary proposition and then follows with two elaborative clauses: "every soul is immortal; only that of the good, however, passes into another body, whereas the wicked suffer endless punishment". The Sadducees, however, dispense with (ἀναιροῦσιν) all three of these points. Josephus's use of ἀναιρέω to describe their positions on both fate (§ 164) and immortality (§ 165) makes clear that he is trying to schematize the views of the two groups as polar opposites: the Pharisees affirm; the Sadducees deny.

1. Analysis of Terms and Concepts

To determine how this description of the Pharisees fits into the context of Josephus's thought, it would be of limited usefulness to examine the discrete occurrences of such common words as μεταβαίνω, σῶμα, ψυχή, ἀγαθός, or τιμωρία elsewhere in his writings.[157] Our interest here is only in how these terms illuminate Josephus's meaning with respect to the Pharisaic belief in immortality. This consideration limits the following analysis to those passages in Josephus that deal with the immortality of the soul. They fall into three groups: (a) those that concern the teachings of the Pharisees and the Essenes; (b) those that claim to reflect

---

J. Bergmann ("Die stoische Philosophie und die jüdische Frömmigkeit", in *Judaica: Festschrift zu H. Cohens siebzigstem Geburtstage*, edd. I. Elbogen, B. Kellerman, E. Mittwoch [New York: Arno, 1980 (Berlin: B. Cassirer, 1912)], 145-166) is able to list some twenty-six significant parallels between Stoic and ancient Jewish teaching, three of which he attributes to direct influence (popular teaching form, comparison between God and the soul, the point at which the soul occupies the body). Writing before the recent discoveries of wide-ranging Hellenistic influence on Palestine, Bergmann proposes that Stoic influence was mediated through such means as the Greek cities in Palestine, the pilgrimage visits of both diaspora Jewry and proselytes, and Greeks' visiting Herod's games in Jerusalem (147f.).

[157] For source-critical purposes, however, it will be necessary to ask whether these words are characteristically Josephan.

Josephus's own views; and (c) those that attribute beliefs to other individuals or groups.

a) The Teachings of the Pharisees and the Essenes

Shortly before our passage (*War* 2:163f.) Josephus writes of the Essenes
(2:154-158):

> For among them the view is vigorously maintained that bodies are corrup-
> tible and their constituent matter impermanent (φθαρτὰ μὲν εἶναι τὰ σώματα
> καὶ τὴν ὕλην οὐ μόνιμον αὐτῶν) but that souls are immortal and imperishable
> (τὰς δὲ ψυχὰς ἀθανάτους ἀεὶ διαμένειν). Emanating from the finest ether, these
> souls become entangled, as it were, in the prison-house of the body (εἱρκταῖς
> τοῖς σώμασιν) to which they are dragged down by a sort of natural spell; but
> when once they are released from the bonds of the flesh (σάρκα δεσμῶν),
> then, as though liberated from a long servitude, they rejoice and are borne
> aloft. Sharing the belief of the sons of Greece, they maintain that for vir-
> tuous (ἀγαθαῖς) souls there is reserved an abode beyond the ocean, a place
> which is not oppressed by rain or snow or heat, but is refreshed by the ever
> gentle breath of the west wind coming in from the ocean; while they
> relegate base (φαύλαις) souls to a murky and tempestuous dungeon big with
> never-ending punishments (τιμωριῶν ἀδιαλείπτων). . . . Such are the
> theological views of the Essenes concerning the soul, whereby they ir-
> resistibly attract all who have once tasted their philosophy. (Thackeray, ex-
> cept first sentence.)

Of the three points in the Pharisaic credo (2:163), then, the Essenes accept (i) the immortality of the soul and (iii) the everlasting punishment
(τιμωρία) of the wicked (φαύλοι). On the destiny of the ἀγαθοί, however,
two different pictures emerge: the Pharisees have the good passing into
other bodies; the Essenes, viewing the body as a prison, believe in a
special home "beyond the ocean" for freed souls.

In the only direct parallel to these descriptions (*Ant.* 18) Josephus says
of the Essenes simply, "They regard souls as immortal" (ἀθανατίζουσιν
τὰς ψυχάς, 18:18). For the Pharisees, he recalls his three-point scheme in
War 2: (i) souls are immortal (ἀθάνατον for ἄφθαρτον); (ii) eternal imprisonment awaits those who have lived lives of vice (εἱργμὸν ἀίδιον for
ἀίδιος τιμωρία); and (iii) virtuous souls find ease to live again (ῥᾳστώνην
τοῦ ἀναβιοῦν instead of μεταβαίνειν εἰς ἕτερον σῶμα). It would appear,
then, that Josephus understands the Pharisaic and Essene views of immortality to be quite similar. The only noticeable difference is on the
question whether the soul after death goes to an idyllic heavenly location
or enters a new body; and we shall see that even these two views do not
necessarily exclude each other.

b) Josephus's Own View of the Afterlife

Four passages purport to give Josephus's own views about immortality. First, in his description of the Essene belief (discussed above), he reflects:

> For the good (ἀγαθοί) are made better in their lifetime by the hope of a reward (τιμῆς) after death, and the passions of the wicked (κακῶν) are restrained by the fear that, even though they escape detection while alive, they will undergo never-ending punishment (ἀθάνατον τιμωρίαν) after their decease. (*War* 2:157; Thackeray)

This recognition of the social utility of a belief in immortality combines with Josephus's statement on the irresistible appeal of Essene teachings (2:158) to suggest that he himself endorsed their position.

The second passage comes during Josephus's speech against suicide at Jotapata, where his zealous comrades-in-arms, about to be overrun by the Romans, want to take their own (and his) lives (*War* 3:335f.). His argument, in effect, is that although it is proper to die in combat, it is improper to take one's own life; one must leave to God, the giver of life, the decision to take it away (3:362-371). He continues:

> All of us, it is true, have mortal bodies (σώματα θνητά), composed of perishable matter (φθαρτῆς ὕλης), but the soul lives forever, immortal (ψυχὴ δὲ ἀθάνατος ἀεί): it is a portion of the Deity (θεοῦ μοῖρα) housed in our bodies . . . . Know you not that they who depart this life in accordance with the law of nature . . . win eternal renown . . . that their souls, remaining spotless and obedient, are allotted the most holy place in heaven (χῶρον οὐράνιον), whence, in the revolution of the ages (ἐκ περιτροπῆς αἰώνων), they return to find in chaste bodies a new habitation (ἁγνοῖς πάλιν ἀντενοικίζονται σώμασιν)? But as for those who have laid mad hands upon themselves, the darker regions of the nether world receive their souls (ᾅδης δέχεται τὰς ψυχὰς σκοτεινότερος) . . . . (3:372-375; Thackeray)

Third, Josephus justifies his inclusion of a story about a post-mortem appearance by claiming that it provides an instance (παράδειγμα) in support of the truth of the immortality of the soul (*Ant.* 17:349-354).

In the final passage, *Ag.Ap.* 2:217f., Josephus claims that the ideas of an afterlife and final judgement are clearly taught in the Mosaic Law:

> For those who live in accordance with our laws (τοῖς νομίμως βιοῦσι) the prize is not silver or gold. . . . No, each individual, relying on the witness of his own conscience and the lawgiver's prophecy, confirmed by the sure testimony of God, is firmly persuaded that to those who observe the laws (τοῖς τοὺς νόμους διαφυλάξαι) and, if they must needs die for them, willingly meet death (προθύμως ἀποθανοῦσι), God has granted a renewed existence (δέδωκεν ὁ θεὸς γενέσθαι πάλιν) and in the revolution [of the ages] (ἐκ περιτροπῆς) the gift of a better life (βίον ἀμείνω λαβεῖν). (Thackeray)

Compare now Josephus's own views about the afterlife, given here, with those that he sets out for both the Pharisees and the Essenes:

<table>
<tr><td colspan="2" align="center">Pharisees</td><td align="center">Josephus</td></tr>
<tr><td>(i)</td><td>ψυχὴν ἄφθαρτον (War 2:163) ἀθάνατον ἰσχὺν ταῖς ψυχαῖς (Ant. 18:14)</td><td>ψυχὴ ἀθάνατος ἀεί (War 3:372)</td></tr>
<tr><td>(ii)</td><td>Souls of the ἅγίοι μεταβαίνειν εἰς ἕτερον σῶμα (War 2:163)
Souls of the virtuous find ῥαστώνην τοῦ ἀναβιοῦν (Ant. 18:14)</td><td>Those who observe and die for the laws are granted γενέσθαι πάλιν καὶ βίον ἀμείνω λάβειν ἐκ περιτροπῆς (Ag.Ap. 2:218)
Those who die naturally ἁγνοῖς πάλιν ἀντενοικίζονται σώμασιν (War 3:374)</td></tr>
<tr><td>(iii)</td><td>The souls of the φαῦλοι suffer ἀιδίῳ τιμωρίᾳ after death (War 2:163)</td><td>The souls of the κάκοι meet with ἀθάνατον τιμωρίαν after death (War 2:157)</td></tr>
</table>

<table>
<tr><td colspan="2" align="center">Essenes</td><td align="center">Josephus</td></tr>
<tr><td>(i)</td><td>φθάρτα εἶναι τὰ σώματα καὶ τὴν ὕλην οὐ μόνιμον (War 2:154)</td><td>τὰ σώματα θνητὰ πᾶσιν καὶ ἐκ φθαρτῆς ὕλης (War 3:372)</td></tr>
<tr><td>(ii)</td><td>τὰς δὲ ψυχὰς ἀθανάτους ἀεί (War 2:154)</td><td>ψυχὴ δὲ ἀθάνατος ἀεί (War 3:372)</td></tr>
<tr><td>(iii)</td><td>Souls emanate from the ether (ἐκ τοῦ λεπτοτάτου αἰθέρος) and become trapped in the prison of the body (εἰρκταῖς τοῖς σώμασιν) (War 2:154)</td><td>A soul is a portion of God housed in a body (θεοῦ μοῖρα τοῖς σώμασιν ἐνοικίζεται) (War 3:372)</td></tr>
<tr><td>(iv)</td><td>For virtuous (ἀγαθοί) souls, after death there is a δίαιτα beyond the ocean, a χῶρον οὔτε ὄμβροις οὔτε νίφετοις οὔτε καύμασι βαρυνόμενον (War 2:155)</td><td>Those who die naturally are allotted the χῶρον οὐράνιον τὸν ἁγιώτατον (War 3:374)</td></tr>
<tr><td>(v)</td><td>The souls of the φαῦλοι after death go to a dungeon (μυχός) filled with τιμωριῶν ἀδιαλείπτων (War 2:155)</td><td>The souls of the κάκοι meet with ἀθάνατον τιμωρίαν (War 2:157)</td></tr>
</table>

As to whether Josephus's own views on immortality are closer to those of the Pharisees or those of the Essenes, the following observations are pertinent:

(i) The similarities between Josephus's own statements and his description of Essene teachings are more extensive and verbally closer (cf. esp. *War* 2:154//3:372) than are his agreements with Pharisaic positions. Further, the fact that he introduces his own reflections on the subject at *War* 2:157, in the course of his warm description of Essene views, reveals his sympathy with that group. He makes his feelings clear by concluding the passage: "Such are the theological views of the Essenes concerning the soul, whereby they irresistibly attract (ἄφυκτον. . . καθίεντες) all who have once tasted their philosophy" (*War* 2:158; Thackeray).

(ii) Since he will also attribute Pharisaic popularity in some measure to their belief in the afterlife (*Ant.* 18:15), he seems to believe that the idea of post-mortem rewards and punishments is an attractive one, whether held by Pharisees or Essenes.

(iii) On the point that distinguishes Pharisees from Essenes—viz., the nature of the reward for the good—Josephus appears to agree with the Pharisaic belief in "reincarnation",[158] which does not appear among Essene beliefs. One must exercise caution, however, for bodily immortality and (at least temporary) disembodied bliss are not mutually exclusive ideas. Josephus himself combines them when he asserts that "[good] souls . . . are allotted the most holy place in heaven, whence (ἔνθεν), in the revolution of the ages, they return to find in chaste bodies a new habitation" (*War* 3:374). Nevertheless, inasmuch as the Essenes envision a permanent disembodied state, Josephus's own belief is closer to that of the Pharisees.

It appears, then, that Josephus agrees with both the Pharisees and the Essenes on the immortality of the soul. Like the Pharisees, he envisions a new body for the future state, but he also includes an interim state of disembodiment. In *War* 2, however, it is the Essene view that receives his enthusiastic support (2:154-159), whereas the Pharisaic view (2:163) is somewhat anti-climactic.

c) Other References in Josephus to Immortality

For the sake of completeness, we may note briefly other references to immortality in Josephus. Two of his characters assert that an honourable death (θάνατος) is better than immortality (ἀθανασία).[159] Two others allow that heroic death merits a superior form of immortality.[160] Mattathias the Hasmonean, however, calls for a willingness to die heroically on the ground that one can achieve immortal rank in the memory of one's deeds (τῇ δὲ τῶν ἔργων μνήμῃ τάξιν ἀθανασίας λαμβάνομεν)—a comparatively weak conception![161] Finally, in Eleazar's speech at Masada, the rebel leader tries to convince his comrades that life in the body is inappropriate to the soul and should be ended forthwith.[162] The principle of conflict between body and soul bears some affinities to the Essene

---

[158] I use the term, for now, in its broader sense—the entry of a soul into another body. A more nuanced analysis follows below.

[159] *War* 1:58; 2:151.

[160] *War* 1:650 (re: Judas and Mattathias); *War* 6:46-48 (re: Titus).

[161] *Ant.* 12:282.

[162] *War* 7:341-357.

view,[163] although the corollary of suicide is foreign to both the Essenes and Josephus.[164]

Since, however, none of the views expressed in these passages can safely be attributed to the Pharisees, the Essenes, or Josephus himself, they can serve only to illustrate other possible views of the afterlife. It is the views that he attributes to the Pharisees and the Essenes, together with those he sets out as his own, that are most pertinent to our study.

2. Interpretation

All three elements in Josephus's description of the Pharisees at *War* 2:163 seem clear enough. All of them accord with his own thoughts on the soul, namely: every soul is immortal; eternal punishment awaits the wicked; and a new body awaits the good. Interpretation is frustrated somewhat, however, by Josephus's failure to elaborate on the final clause. His language is everywhere vague: souls pass into ἕτερον σῶμα, or will simply ἀναβιοῦν, say the Pharisees; in his own words, souls will γενέσθαι πάλιν, βίον ἀμείνω λαβεῖν, or they ἁγνοῖς πάλιν ἀντενοικίζονται σώμασιν. Remaining unanswered are the questions: Where does the new body come from? What is it like? How long will it last? Where does it live? How long is the interval between death and "reincarnation"? Josephus does offer some clues about these matters, but they can only be adequately interpreted against the background of commonly held beliefs in the Hellenistic world.

The idea of the soul's passing at death into another body was not at all strange to ancient thought.[165] Although some sort of belief in the

---

[163] Especially with the idea that the body is a prison, an inappropriate vehicle for the soul, *War* 7:344, cf. 2:154f.

[164] Josephus, *War* 3:362-382, speaks against suicide. Lindner (*Geschichtsauffassung*, 39) accurately points out that Eleazar functions in the narrative of *War* as an implacable opponent of Josephus's view. His call for suicide is meant to illustrate the hopeless outcome of the rebels, who have defied God's will and therefore deserve to die. The speech does not reflect Josephus's own views about suicide.

[165] Cf. F. Cumont, *After Life in Roman Paganism* (New Haven: Yale University Press, 1922); W. Stettner, *Die Seelenwanderung bei Griechen und Römern* (Stuttgart: W. Kohlhammer, 1933); C. H. Moore, *Pagan Ideas of Immortality During the Roman Period* (Cambridge, Mass.: Harvard University Press, 1918); idem, *Ancient Beliefs in the Immortality of the Soul* (New York: Cooper Square, 1963 [c. 1930]); T. F. Glasson, *Greek Influence in Jewish Eschatology* (London: S.P.C.K., 1961); W. F. Jackson Knight, *Elysion* (London: Reider & Co., 1970); H. S. Long, "Plato's Doctrine of Metempsychosis and its Source", *Classical Quarterly* 41 (1948) 149-155; Büchsel, "παλιγγενεσία", *TDNT*, I, 686-689; Blumenthal, "Palingenesia", *PWRE*, XVIII, 139-148; and J. Head and S. L. Cranston, *Reincarnation in World Thought* (New York: Julian Press, 1967). This last work gives, albeit in translation and without clear identification, many of the pertinent texts from our period.

soul's immortality goes back to Homer and beyond,[166] the conviction
that the soul both leaves the body at death and passes into another body
can only be securely attributed to Pythagoras (6th century BC).[167]
Herodotus (mid-5th century) describes a view current among Greeks in
his time that a man's soul at death begins a cycle in which it passes
through all the creatures of the land, sea, and air until it once again
enters a human body—a cycle of 3,000 years (2:123). It may have been
this theory of inevitable metempsychosis, a sort of law of nature, which
was held by Pythagoras.[168]

At some early point, however, this belief was modified by the injection
of a strong moral element: metempsychosis was no longer a permanent,
natural process, but a punishment. The soul was trapped in the body as
in a prison or grave, and its goal was to escape back to its true home.[169]
Such a view was present already in Pindar (early 5th century BC),[170]
who suggested that if a soul remained pure throughout three lifetimes it
would find blissful rest from bodily life.[171] It was Plato, however, who
gave definitive shape to the idea of reincarnation as a punishment.

Plato deals with reincarnation in several places and always sets it in
a moral context.[172] His various presentations do not always harmonize
in detail. The picture in the middle works, however—*Phaedo, Republic,*
and *Phaedrus*—is fairly consistent: pre-existent souls fall from their
heavenly abode because of their failure to maintain pure thought. They
become incarnated as humans. At death, the soul goes to the underworld

---

[166] C. H. Moore, *Pagan Ideas*, 8f. The eleventh book of the *Odyssey* contains the oldest known "descent into Hades" story.

[167] Moore (*Pagan Ideas*, 10ff.) attributes it to the Orphics, as do Head and Cranston (*Reincarnation*, 190). Stettner (*Seelenwanderung*, 7f.), however, follows Williamowitz in attributing this development to Pythagoras. H. S. Long ("Plato's Doctrine", 154ff.) agrees, pointing out that all of the evidence connecting metempsychosis with Orpheus is quite late.

[168] Herodotus declines to name its exponents, for he thinks that they plagiarized the idea from the Egyptians. Stettner (*Seelenwanderung*, 8f.) thinks it Pythagorean because it does not match any known Greek view. Seneca (*Epistles* 108:19) attributes such a natural view of reincarnation to Pythagoras.

[169] Stettner (*Seelenwanderung*, 19ff.). Cf. Plato (*Cratylus* 400c and *Phaedo* 81d f.), for whom reincarnation is not for the ἀγαθοί, but is a punishment (δίκη) for the φαύλοι.

[170] *Olympian Odes* 2:64-80.

[171] That is, they will abide "where the ocean breezes blow around the isle of the blest". Cf. Josephus on the Essene view, *War* 2:155f.

[172] The key passages are *Meno* 81b-82e; *Cratylus* 400b-c; *Phaedo* 70c f., 80a ff.; *Republic* 10:613e ff.; *Phaedrus* 245c ff.; *Timaeus* 41d ff., 76 d f., 90e ff. Plato's arguments for immortality/reincarnation (the two are inseparable for him) have often been summarized and analyzed. Cf. Cicero, *On Old Age*, 77-81, and now R. L. Patterson, *Plato On Immortality* (University Park, PA: Penn. State Univ. Press, 1965). H. S. Long's article ("Plato's Doctrine") gives a lucid summary of Plato on reincarnation. I follow closely Stettner's interpretation of Plato (*Seelenwanderung*, 32-40) on this topic.

to face judgement for its past life. Recompense is meted out either solely in the underworld[173] or also by a new incarnation.[174] Yet even within these works there is some tension (or development); for whereas *Phaedo* 108c has the new body determined solely by the quality of the previous life (as punishment or reward), the Myth of Er (*Republic* 10:613e ff.) leaves the choice of a new body and life pattern up to the soul.[175] The process described in these works is actually παλιγγενεσία and not μετεμψύχωσις because the soul does not merely pass from one body to another but spends intervening periods in the underworld before it "becomes again".[176]

In the *Timaeus*, Plato paints a somewhat different picture. The creator-God fashions one soul for every star and assigns each to its star. Entrance into a human body is a test that is required of each soul. The soul that succeeds in mastering the body will return at death to its blissful life; the one that fails will begin a cycle of further incarnations in descending classes of beings—women, animals, birds, etc. In both of these schemes, however, life in the body is inimical to the soul and something from which it desires to be released.

It is instructive to note Plato's vocabulary on the topic of immortality. He does not himself use the noun παλιγγενεσία,[177] but he does employ the combination πάλιν γίγνεσθαι to speak of reincarnation. In *Meno* 81b he has Socrates report a view held by priests and poets that:

> The human soul is immortal (τὴν ψυχήν . . . ἀθάνατον) and although it comes to an end, which is called death, it then lives again (τότε δὲ πάλιν γίγνεσθαι) and is never destroyed.

Similarly in *Phaedo* 70c, Socrates expounds the "old view" that:

> Souls go from here to there [sc. ᾅδης] and returning here are born again (πάλιν . . . γίγνονται) from the dead. Now if this is so, that the living are born again out of the dead (πάλιν γίγνεσθαι ἐκ τῶν ἀποθανόντων τοὺς ζῶντας), are not our souls, then, there?

---

[173] *Meno* 81b-c.

[174] *Phaedo* 80e ff.; 81e/114c; 107c/113d.

[175] Stettner's observation (*Seelenwanderung*, 37).

[176] For the distinction, cf. Cumont, *After Life*, 182, and Stettner, *Seelenwanderung*, 3ff. The latter lists the occurrences of μετεμψύχωσις, μετενσωμάτωσις, and παλιγγενεσία in writers of the period. In the *Phaedrus*, 249a, Plato is describing παλιγγενεσία (by this definition) when he allows that a soul requires ten incarnations, with an interval of 1,000 years between each. (Note, however, that Philo, *On the Cherubim*, 114, seems to use παλιγγενεσία of the soul's absorption into the divine after death.)

[177] Blumenthal ("Palingenesia", 140) attributes the first known usage of the term to Pindar.

A little further on Plato introduces another term into the discussion, namely, τὸ ἀναβιώσεσθαι, "living again". He uses this term three times in the argument of *Phaedo* 71e and then in 72a substitutes again πάλιν γίγνεσθαι.

Now it is generally recognized that παλιγγενεσία and ἀναβίωσις are equivalent expressions.[178] Yet this equivalence is not always recognized by commentators on Josephus when he uses ἀναβιοῦν to describe the Pharisaic view of the afterlife (*Ant.* 18:14) and γενέσθαι πάλιν to describe his own view (*Ag.Ap.* 2:218), a point to which we shall return presently.

Speculation about the afterlife seems to have subsided after Plato. Aristotle's skepticism about personal immortality[179] corresponded to the emerging rationalism of the Hellenistic age.[180] Epicureanism rejected the soul's immortality out of hand,[181] while the older schools became generally skeptical.[182] Even for the Stoics immortality was problematic because of their thorough-going materialism: "soul" for them could only be the active principle in matter, the Λόγος.[183] It was, significantly, Posidonius, the Stoic teacher who was most open to Platonism (and so somewhat atypical), who most clearly espoused immortality.[184]

When interest in reincarnation revived in the late first century BC,[185] all of the earlier ideas from Herodotus, Pindar, Empedocles, and Plato reappeared. Ovid's *Metamorphoses* (AD 7), for example, portrays the *anima* as perpetually passing from one body to another as a sort of natural phenomenon, with no hint of moral judgement as the cause:

> Our souls are deathless, and ever, when they have left their former seat,
> do they live in new abodes and dwell in the bodies that have received them.
> . . . The spirit wanders, comes now here, now there, and occupies

---

[178] Blumenthal, "Palingenesia", 139; Büchsel, 687. The equivalence holds even when the terms are used in the Stoic context of *cosmic* rebirth. It was Stoic teaching that gave currency to both terms.

[179] Head and Cranston, *Reincarnation*, 201ff. Aristotle gives his objections in *Metaphysics* 1:9; 6:8; 12:10; 13:3. As Jackson Knight shows, however (94f.), Aristotle was both a follower and a critic of Plato, and this leaves some tension in his writings. W. Jaeger (*Aristotle: Fundamentals of History of his Development* [Oxford: Univ. Press, 1948], 50ff.), finds a development in the philosopher's thought on immortality. In his *On the Soul*, 3.4.430a, 22f., for example, Aristotle allows that mind (νοῦς) alone is immortal.

[180] P. Wendland, *Die hellenistisch-römische Kultur* (Tübingen: J. C. B. Mohr, 1912), 140ff.; Cumont, *After Life*, 6ff., Stettner, *Seelenwanderung*, 42f.

[181] Cf. especially Epicurus' "Letter to Menoecus" in Diogenes Laertius 10:124b ff., and the poem *The Nature of Things*, bk. III, by the Epicurean Lucretius (mid-first century BC).

[182] Cumont, *After Life*, 6.

[183] C. H. Moore, *Ancient Ideas*, 39: "The soul then for them was a mode or function of matter."

[184] Ibid., 41f. Cf. Hippolytus, *Philosophoumena* 1.21.3.

[185] Cumont, *After Life*, 17f.; Stettner, *Seelenwanderung*, 42f.

whatever form it pleases. From beasts it passes ito human bodies, and from our bodies into beasts, but never perishes.[186]

Seneca attributes a similar view to Pythagoras.[187] Alongside this apparently amoral view, however, the Platonic notion of reincarnation as a morally determined process also reappeared, both in the form of uninterrupted movement from body to body (μετεμψύχωσις)[138] and as periodic reincarnation, following interludes in the underworld (παλιγγενεσία)[189] The Stoic view of immortality is unclear.[190]

To summarize: it was Plato who exercised the decisive influence on the idea of reincarnation in Greco-Roman antiquity. He made it a constituent element of his philosophy and gave it a rational basis.[191] Yet even Plato was not consistent in his portrayal of the issue. In the ancient world there was no consensus about such matters as: whether reincarnation is a perpetual process or a form of atonement; whether or not the soul spends intervals between various incarnations in the underworld; how many incarnations are to be expected; how long the periods of disembodiment, and so forth. No single schema prevailed.

Clearly, Josephus's chosen terms to describe the afterlife—terms like μεταβαίνειν εἰς ἕτερον σῶμα, γενέσθαι πάλιν and ἀναβιοῦν—would have evoked among his Greco-Roman readers some sort of philosophy of reincarnation. Thackeray says simply that in these passages we find "the doctrine of the reincarnation of the soul".[192] Yet given the variety of beliefs at the time, it is necessary to define the Josephan and Pharisaic views somewhat more closely.

We begin with W. Stettner's distinction between amoral or inevitable metempsychosis, on the one hand, and reincarnation as a process deter-

---

[186] *Metamorphoses* 15:158-168, trans. F. J. Miller (LCL edn.); cf. Stettner, *Seelenwanderung*, 44f.

[187] *Epistles* 108:19.

[188] Stettner (*Seelenwanderung*, 50) cites the treatise περὶ ψυχὰς κόσμῳ, attributed to Timaios Lokros, as evidence of this view, which recalls the *Timaeus*.

[189] Stettner (*Seelenwanderung*, 50f.) adduces here the sixth book of Vergil's *Aeneid*, with its descent to Hades, and Plutarch's *The Face on the Moon*, 28-30 (= 943-944D in the LCL edn.).

[190] Cf. especially *SVF*, II, 804-22, on the views of various Stoics. Blumenthal ("Palingenesia", 149f.) points out that for the Stoics παλιγγενεσία referred not to the soul's rebirth but to that of the *cosmos*, after the conflagration. Cf. Cumont (*After Life*, 12ff.) on the problems with Stoic immortality. Stettner (*Seelenwanderung*, 66) argues that the old Stoa did not accept reincarnation but that Stoic physics (being monistic/pantheistic) lent a basis to Ovid's view of reincarnation. According to Cicero (*Tusculan Disputations* 1:79) the Stoic Panaetius vehemently denied the immortality of the soul. Cf. C. H. Moore, *Pagan Ideas*, 20ff., and Jackson Knight, *Elysion*, 120.

[191] So C. H. Moore, *Pagan Ideas*, 14ff.; Blumenthal, "Palingenesia", 141; Stettner, *Seelenwanderung*, 33, 49ff.

[192] LCL edn., II, 386 n. *a*.

mined by moral factors, on the other. Clearly, Josephus and his Pharisees espouse the latter view. He consistently claims that it is only the soul of the good person that receives a better life.[193] Nowhere does he suggest that souls of men or animals pass naturally at death into other bodies. Rather, he speaks always of "rewards and punishments" for "virtue and vice".

Yet Josephus's portrayal of the afterlife is distinctive. For fundamental to every other moral theory of reincarnation are the beliefs that: (1) the body is antithetical to the soul; (2) life in the body results from a fall; (3) good souls effect an early release from the κύκλος τῆς γενέσεως and return to their heavenly home; and (4) only the impure and contaminated souls must spend longer periods in the body. Josephus's own views and those he attributes to the Pharisees, however, reflect none of these features.

Josephus's portrayal of the Pharisaic position is perfectly clear:

μεταβαίνειν δὲ εἰς ἕτερον σῶμα τὴν ψυχὴν τῶν ἀγαθῶν μόνην, τὰς δὲ φαύλων ἀιδίῳ τιμωρίᾳ κολάζεσθαι. (War 2:163)

In the parallel passage (Ant. 18:14) he also emphasizes that to "live again" (ἀναβιοῦν) is a reward (τιμή).[194] In the Pharisaic scenario, as Josephus presents it, the wicked never enter a body again but undergo eternal (ἀίδιον) punishment/imprisonment; only the good are rewarded with a new body. One reads about heavenly realms only once, in Josephus's own description of the afterlife (War (3:374). And there, heaven is not a final goal but an intermediate stage for good souls, "whence, ἔνθεν, they return to find in chaste bodies (ἁγνοῖς σώμασιν) a new habitation". All of this runs counter to the basic principle of Greek reincarnation theory that life in the body is a necessary evil, to be overcome as quickly as possible.

Three further peculiarities in Josephus's own descriptions of the afterlife should be noted. First, we have observed that his γενέσθαι πάλιν and ἀναβιοῦν recall the Platonic πάλιν γίγνεσθαι and τὸ ἀναβιώσεσθαι. In the former case, however, Josephus uses an aorist infinitive instead of

---

[193] War 2:163: ἡ ψυχὴ τῶν ἀγαθῶν (Pharisaic position); Ant. 18:14: οἱ ἀρετῆς (Pharisees); War 3:374: those who die naturally (Josephus's position); Ag.Ap. 2:218: τοῖς τοὺς νόμους διαφυλάξασι (Josephus).

[194] This is clear whether one takes the final two clauses as elaborations of ὑπὸ χθόνος δικαιώσεις καὶ τιμάς or as additions. Feldman (LCL edn.) interprets the eternal imprisonment and passage to new life as epexegetical: they are the punishments and rewards meted out ὑπὸ χθόνος. It is possible, however, that the additional καὶ's signify a two-stage recompense, viz.: (a) reward and punishment under the earth and then (b) eternal imprisonment or a new life.

Plato's present infinitive.[195] Does the aorist suggest a single reincarnation rather than an ongoing cycle of life? Possibly, although the present infinitive ἀναβιοῦν does not help the case. It is worth noting, however, that the new body (βίον ἀμείνω) promised to the virtuous by Josephus and his Pharisees is always singular.[196]

Moreover, Josephus's references to the new body seem to suggest that it is more simply another human or animal form. Unlike practically every other ancient writer on reincarnation, he is strangely silent about the specific nature of the new σῶμα into which the soul will go. He does not say explicitly how it corresponds to the past life of the soul. What he does say is that the new body will be ἁγνός and will bring a better life. Now outside of *War* 3:374 (Josephus's portrait of the afterlife), ἁγνός occurs only four times in Josephus.[197] Each time it clearly means "holy, sacred, or consecrated". Thackeray's rendering "chaste" at *War* 3:374, then, seems peculiar. Josephus is talking about a holy or sacred body that will bring a better life.[198]

Finally, we should note that in both of Josephus's own descriptions of the afterlife he uses the intriguing phrase ἐκ περιτροπῆς (αἰώνων) to denote *the time* at which the soul enters it sacred body. Thackeray renders the phrase in both places, "in the revolution of the ages"[199]—so suggesting an ongoing process, like the turning of a wheel. One might recall the revolution of the heavenly spheres in Plato's *Phaedrus* 245c, from which souls are continually falling into incarnations because of their failure to behold the truth. Yet for Josephus this image is hardly appropriate, because: (a) for him, entrance into a holy body is a final reward for good souls, not a punishment; (b) he speaks of the revolution of αἰώνων, not of heavenly spheres; and (c) the context suggests a singular, climactic movement into a new body.

Indeed, outside of the Josephan corpus περιτροπή can mean "continuous revolution", as in the turning of a wheel.[200] But it can also refer to a sudden inversion or upheaval;[201] the verb περιτρέπω often means "to

---

[195] Plato's extra γ merely reflects the Attic reduplicaticn (LSJ, *s.v.*).

[196] *Ag.Ap.* 2:218.

[197] *Ant.* 4:80; 12:38; 15:418; 18:85.

[198] Some sort of special body would indeed be necessary if the future life is to be ἀμείνω for the soul. Josephus allows that, normally, the soul suffers (κακοπαθεῖ) when entering and leaving the body (*Ag.Ap.* 2:203).

[199] LCL edn. of *War* 3:374 and *Ag.Ap.* 2:218. Thackeray agrees here with Whiston. Cornfeld's "when the wheel of time has turned full circle" is more promising (see below).

[200] In *Theaetetus* 209e and *Republic* 546e, Plato uses περιτροπή to describe the revolution of the κύκλος of life; see also Philo, *Embassy to Gaius* 206.

[201] Cf. Philo, *On the Change of Names* 150, referring to social revolutions, and *Life of Moses* 1:42, referring to a sudden change in one's physical condition.

turn over or capsize".²⁰² All three instances of the verb in Josephus
mean "to invert or overturn".²⁰³ In its only occurrence in Josephus
outside of our passages, the noun περιτροπή means "recapitulation or
recurrence", with a single event envisioned (*Ant.* 14:487). These examples, few though they are, suffice to warrant the question whether
Josephus does not envision a single moment at which the soul will
receive a new, holy body.

Outside of Josephus, the phrases ἐκ περιτροπῆς and ἐν περιτροπῇ
generally seem to mean "in succession' or "in turn". For example: the
responsibility for an annual event falls on various groups of people "in
turn", or each member of a harem spends time with her lord "in
turn".²⁰⁴ The phrases have to do, then, not with perpetual motion but
with one change in a series or succession.

So the use of περιτροπή, περιτρέπω, and ἐκ περιτροπῆς in Josephus and
other Greek literature allows both the idea of "continuous revolution"
and that of "sudden upheaval, inversion, or succession".²⁰⁵

But Josephus's ἐκ περιτροπῆς involves the αἰῶνες. Although αἰών can
refer to periods of varying length, from a lifetime to an epoch, it practically always has the sense of a conceivable, delimited period of time.²⁰⁶
And this observation appears to support the idea of succession or change
for ἐκ περιτροπῆς, rather than a "continuous revolution": it is not that
all the aeons are somehow revolving simultaneously, but rather that
when one age comes to an end the next begins. I propose, therefore, the
translation: "in/at the succession (or change) of the ages".

Taking into account all of the above observations, we may summarize
Josephus's portrayal of the Pharisaic belief in immortality as follows. In
War 2:163 Josephus presents the Pharisees, in contrast to the Sadducees,
as believing in the immortality of the soul, with eternal punishment
awaiting the wicked and entry into another body awaiting the good. The
first two of these propositions (immortality and punishment) agree with
views that he ascribes also to the Essenes; all three of them (including

---

²⁰² Cf. Philo, *Allegorical Interpretation* 3:23 and *On the Unchangeableness of God* 129.
²⁰³ *Ant.* 9:72 (a sudden change of emotion); 10:297 (the overturning of a chariot);
14:356 (the overturning of a wagon).
²⁰⁴ Cf. Herodotus 2:168; 3:69; Dio Cassius 53.1.5; 54.19.8; Dionysius of Halicarnassus, *Rom. Ant.* 5:2.
²⁰⁵ Since my goal is to establish a plausible translation in the case of Josephus, the investigation of περιτροπή in other ancient writers has not been exhaustive.
²⁰⁶ So LSJ, "αἰών". In Josephus, the word occurs some 26 times, in five main senses:
(a) the whole time from creation to the present, or from the present onward, *War* 1:12;
5:442; *Ant.* 7:385; 18:287; 19:79, 170; (b) a single generation or lifetime, *War* 5:185,
187; 6:105 (?); *Ant.* 19:170; (c) an epoch, *Ant.* 1:16, 272, 275; (d) simply "period of
time", *Ant.* 3:56, 223; and (e) in the expression εἰς αἰῶνα for "forever", *Ant.* 7:211, 356.
In all of these cases, αἰών refers to a period of time.

a new body for the virtuous) accord with his own views. Although Josephus employs the common language of reincarnation to describe both his and the Pharisees' views, those views still seem peculiar in the Greco-Roman context, insofar as they hold the new body to be a *reward*, only for the souls of the good. Seeking to understand this anomaly better by noting subtleties in Josephus's description, we have seen: (a) that the new body is a special, holy body and will bring about a better life; (b) that only one such body seems to be envisioned, not a "cycle of becoming"; (c) that the soul will wait in heaven until its reincarnation; and (d) that this reincarnation will take place "at a succession of the aeons/ages".

The form of reincarnation attributed to the Pharisees by Josephus, then, bears many similarities to what we should call resurrection—a Pharisaic doctrine well attested in the rabbinic literature and in the New Testament.[207] A slight difficulty arises, perhaps, with Josephus's use of the adjective ἕτερον for σῶμα, which seems to conflict with the customary Jewish idea that in resurrection the bodies *of the dead* rise again. One should not, however, read too much into this, since Josephus makes plain that the new body will be different from the old with respect to its "holiness" (cf. ἀγνός)—a view shared to some extent by the ex-Pharisee Paul (1 Cor. 15:35ff.). In any case, there is no question in Josephus of a repeated exchange of one human (or animal) body for another.

It would appear, then, that at a time when many different views of the afterlife were circulating in the Greco-Roman world, Josephus added to the list a Jewish theory of resurrection by appropriating for it the language of reincarnation. He was not alone in this. The author of 2 Maccabees also applies ἀναβίωσις to resurrection (7:9).[208] Similarly, the author of Matthew adopts the term παλιγγενεσία—which commonly referred to either the rebirth of souls or (for the Stoics) the rebirth of the cosmos—to indicate the approaching kingdom of God (19:28).[209]

It is a historical question, beyond the scope of this study, whether Josephus misrepresented the Jewish doctrine of resurrection by appropriating Greek terminology for it. As an entrée to that question, how-

[207] Cf. J. Ross, *Immortality*, esp. 58-68. In the NT, cf. Acts 23:8. I thus agree with Feldman (LCL edn. of Josephus, IX, 13 n. *c.*) that Josephus attributes to the Pharisees a doctrine of resurrection. I differ from Feldman, however, in two ways: (a) I have not worked from the premise that Josephus, as a Pharisee, must have known that the group believed in resurrection; and (b) I do not think that resurrection and "reincarnation" (in its many Hellenistic modes) are mutually exclusive. Rather, Josephus apparently considered the former to be one mode—the Jewish mode—of the latter

[208] Noted by Feldman (LCL edn., IX, 13 n. *c.*), though not in this context.

[209] Cf. Büchsel, "παλιγγενεσία", 688. The Lucan parallel to Mt.'s ἐν τῇ παλιγγενεσίᾳ is ἐν τῇ βασιλείᾳ μου.

ever, we may emphasize: (a) that there was no single, authoritative
Greek view of reincarnation at the time, various scenarios being proposed; (b) that any doctrine of resurrection that has the soul leaving the
body at death and then entering either that same body or another at
some later date is *ipso facto* a form of reincarnation or παλιγγενεσία in the
broad sense; (c) that Greek ideas of reincarnation may have played a role
in the emergence of the Jewish doctrine of resurrection;[210] and (d) that
among the Jews there were also different interpretations of resurrection
and immortality.[211]

E. The final statement of Josephus on the Pharisees in *War* 2:162-166
is as follows:

Φαρισαῖοι μὲν φιλάλληλοί τε καὶ τὴν εἰς τὸ κοινὸν ὁμόνοιαν ἀσκοῦντες.

Having completed his μέν . . . δέ comparison of the Pharisees and Sadducees on the two major philosophical issues, Josephus now turns to
their behaviour: "Whereas the Pharisees are fond of one another and
cultivate harmony within the group, the Sadducees are boorish even
toward each other; their dealings with their fellows are as inconsiderate
as those with foreigners."

1. *Key Terms*

a. The word φιλάλληλος occurs only twice in Josephus, both times in *War*
2:119-166. In 2:165f. he contrasts the Pharisees favourably with the Sadducees; at 2:119, however, and this will be crucial for interpreting our
passage, he presents the Essenes as superior to all others in their concern
for one another: φιλάλληλοι δὲ καὶ τῶν ἄλλων πλέον. The mutual affection
of the Pharisees, then, is remarkable only in comparison to the rudeness
of the Sadducees. It is well known that Josephus has little sympathy for
the Sadducees.[212] In *Ant.* 18:16 he mentions again their disputatiousness
and in 20:199 he calls them "savage" (ὠμοί). It is, then, the Sadducees'

---

[210] So T. F. Glasson, *Greek Influence*, 1f., 5f., 30, who argues that Jewish eschatology
has been too quickly traced to Iran, when the political circumstances of Palestine from
the fourth century BC onward would suggest the likelihood of Greek influence.
[211] Cf. R. H. Charles, *A Critical History of the Doctrine of a Future Life* (London: Adam
and Charles Black, 1913); G. W. Nickelsburg, *Resurrection, Immortality, and Eternal Life
in Intertestamental Judaism* (Cambridge, Mass: Harvard Univ. Press, 1972), e.g., p. 180;
and H. C. C. Cavallin, *Life After Death: Paul's Argument . . . Part I: An Inquiry into the
Jewish Background* (Lund: Gleerup, 1974), 199, 212.
[212] Noted already by Paret, "Pharisäismus", 820f.

rudeness, as much as the Pharisees' affection, which seems to be the point of the passage.[213]

b. The word ὁμόνοια[214] taps the root of a theme that runs throughout all of Josephus's works, but is especially poignant in *War*. The thesis of *War*, as set out in the preface (1:10), is that the destruction of Jerusalem was due to domestic strife (στάσις οἰκεία). But στάσις is the opposite of ὁμόνοια. In failing to ὁμονοεῖν, the rebels failed to live up to their principles as Jews.

That a lack of ὁμόνοια leads to destruction is first illustrated in the case of Herod's family. Herod is portrayed as thanking Caesar for giving his sons ὁμόνοια, "something greater than a kingdom" (1:457), and he appoints advisors for each son to ensure that ὁμόνοια is maintained (1:460). He prays that God will ratify the instalment of his sons as royalty—as long as they ὁμονοεῖν (1:464). And he tells his people that it is in everyone's interest that he rule in harmony (κρατεῖν . . . ὁμονοεῖν, 1:465). Alas, however, the tragedy of Herod's reign was precisely its domestic strife and intrigue.[215]

Ten of the remaining sixteen instances of ὁμόνοια/ὁμονοεῖν in *War* have to do with the thesis of the work: the factiousness of the rebels.[216] Titus comes to Tarichaeae and, finding the Jews squabbling with each other, calls for an immediate attack, before they can restore ὁμόνοια (3:496). Conversely, when Vespasian observes the internal bickering within Jerusalem, he rejects the advice to attack before they ὁμονοήσειν (4:367), arguing rather that such an attack would drive them to ὁμόνοια; he would rather wait and let them wear themselves down (4:369). On two occasions Josephus reports that the rebels came to their senses and saw that their lack of ὁμόνοια was actually aiding the enemy (5:72, 278). Twice he remarks sardonically that the rebels expressed ὁμόνοια only in their heinous crimes toward fellow Jews (5:30, 441). He laments the party strife (τὸ φιλόνεικον) that existed in Jerusalem, which began in homes and affected those who had long worked together (τῶν ὁμονοούντων πάλαι, 4:132). The final word is given to Titus, who, upon hearing of the shocking crimes within the city, declares that he has given the Jews opportunity for freedom and peace but that "they prefer στάσις to ὁμόνοια" (6:216).

---

[213] Although the Pharisees are commended, (a) they do not receive the enthusiastic praise accorded the Essenes in 2:119-161 and (b) the commendation is governed by the μέν . . . δέ comparison with the boorish Sadducees.

[214] The noun occurs 20 times in Josephus, in every work but *Ag.Ap.*; the verb ὁμονέω appears 17 times.

[215] Cf. *War* 1:567ff., 576f., 592ff., 641ff., *passim*.

[216] The other six occurrences are at *War* 1:569, 570; 2:209, 345, 467, 609.

That this contempt for ὁμόνοια was untrue to Judaism is an important theme of *War*.[217] The point is made in a passage that explains why Jewish attempts to destroy the Roman earthworks failed:

> For, to begin with, there seemed to be no unanimity in their design (οὐδ' ὁμονοεῖν ἡ σκέψις αὐτῶν ἐῴκει): they darted out in small parties, at intervals, hesitatingly and in alarm, in short *not like Jews* (καθόλου . . . οὐκ Ἰουδαϊκῶς): the characteristics (ἴδια) of the nation . . . were all lacking. (6:17; Thackeray)

In *War*, then, the rebels are presented as traitors to the principles of Judaism. Indeed, they could not act as authentic Jews because of the illegitimacy of their cause, which alienated them from God.

Ὁμόνοια as a Jewish ideal also turns up at strategic points in *Ant*. Standing at the border of Canaan, Moses exhorts the people before they enter: "Above all, let us be one of mind" (πρὸ δὲ πάντων ὁμονοῶμεν, 3:302). In the controversy over the priesthood, Moses prays that the unjust may be punished so that ὁμόνοια and εἰρήνη might return to the people (4:50). Later in the narrative, Onias asks Ptolemy for a temple at Leontopolis, where the Jews might worship in ὁμόνοια (13:67). And Mattathias the Hasmonean, as he lies dying, charges his sons: "Above all, I urge you to be of one mind" (μάλιστα δ' ὑμῖν ὁμονοεῖν παραινῶ, 13:283). Finally, Josephus notes that when Pompey marched on Jerusalem, the people in the city had differences of opinion and were οὐχ ὁμονοούντων (14:58). Once again, therefore, we see ὁμόνοια as a Jewish ideal, the absence of which leads to collapse.[218]

This idea comes through most clearly in *Ag.Ap.*, where Josephus has no reserve about claiming ὁμόνοια as a Jewish virtue. Contrasting the ordinary Jew's thorough knowledge of the Law with the general ignorance of laws among other nations, he writes:

> To this cause above all we owe our admirable harmony (τὴν θαυμαστὴν ὁμόνοιαν ἡμῖν). Unity and identity of religious belief, perfect uniformity in habits and customs (τῷ βίῳ δὲ καὶ τοῖς ἔθεσι), produce a very beautiful concord (συμφωνίαν) in human character. Among us alone (παρ' ἡμῖν μόνοις) will be heard no contradictory statements about God, as are common among other nations. (2:179f.; Thackeray)

Josephus then lists a number of areas in which the Jewish νόμοι have been imitated by the rest of the world; among other things, he says, "they try to imitate our cooperative spirit" (τὴν πρὸς ἀλλήλους ἡμῶν

---

[217] Cf., e.g., *War* 1:10, 27; 2:345-347.
[218] *Ant.* 13:305 reports that evil men (πονηροί) wanted to destroy the ὁμόνοια between the Hasmonean brothers Artistobulus and Antigonus, from whom Josephus traces the decline of the dynasty (*War* 1:69).

ὁμόνοιαν, 2:283). Finally, in his closing remarks Josephus offers a list of ideals that he believes the Jews have introduced (εἰσάγω) into the world. Third on the list comes πρὸς ἀλλήλους ὁμονοεῖν, ''to be a prey neither to disunion in adversity, nor to arrogance and faction in prosperity'' (2:294; Thackeray).

In Josephus's works ὁμόνοια seldom appears in the pedestrian sense of ''agreement or unanimity''.[219] It is much more a theological term for him, indicating the unity of thought and behaviour that characterizes genuine Jews. The consistency of this theme highlights the low opinion that Josephus has of the rebels, who abandoned concern for ὁμόνοια.

2. Interpretation

Returning now to *War* 2:166, one can see the significance of Josephus's attribution of ὁμόνοια to the Pharisees. On the one hand, the Essenes are pre-eminent in the exercise of this basic Jewish virtue; as in other respects, the monks are in a class by themselves. On the other hand, the Sadducees are totally lacking in the harmony characteristic of Jews, even as they debunk the higher doctrines of immortality and providence. In contrast to the Sadducees, the Pharisees cultivate ὁμόνοια, at least amnong themselves (εἰς τὸ κοινόν).

III. *Interpretation of War 2:162-166 on the Pharisees*

War 2:162-166 is Josephus's fundamental description of the Pharisees. In it he sets down everything that he wants his readers to know about the Pharisees, and he refers back to it several times as his standard presentation. It is now possible to summarize our findings on Josephus's five statements about the Pharisees and to interpret them together as a whole. Our aim, once again, is both cognitive and conative: to determine both the content of the description and Josephus's attitude toward the group.

Josephus presents the Pharisees as a philosophical school (αἵρεσις), which opposes the Sadducean school on two issues: the Pharisees recognize the hand of fate/God and they accept the immortality of the soul, whereas the Sadducees deny both. The Pharisees' combination of fate and free will recalls particularly the view of the Stoic Chrysippus (as related by Cicero); but it is generally compatible with the synergism

---

[219] For *War*, cf. n. 216 above. For *Ant.*, the mundane occurrences are at 2:21; 7:213; 18:376; and 19:341.

between these two causes that was widely held in ancient thought going back to Plato and beyond. On the immortality of the soul, the Pharisaic view (via Josephus) recalls Plato's language of reincarnation. On closer examination, however, it reveals several peculiarities vis-à-vis Greek thought and suggests something like the resurrection idea known from Jewish and Christian sources. On both issues, the Sadducees hold a skeptical postion akin to that of the Epicureans.

On all three points of contrast between the Pharisees and Sadducees—the two philosophical issues and the question of behaviour—the Pharisees not only stand nearer to Josephus's own thought, they seem to replicate it more or less exactly. Like them, Josephus attributes everything to fate, juxtaposes God and fate, and emphasizes free will. Like them, he believes in the immortality of the soul, punishments for the wicked, and a new body for the good. Like them, he holds to an ideal of ὁμόνοια. Yet it must be asked what this philosophical agreement means. What does it say about Josephus's attitude toward, or relation to, the Pharisees?

One should note, first of all, that Josephus never espouses a position on the ground that it is Pharisaic. On the contrary, he exalts the Law and its accurate interpretation because he is a priest. The Pharisees happen to make the same claims. Likewise, on each of the three points of comparison between the Pharisees and Sadducees, Josephus accepts the "dogmatic" or affirmative position rather than the skeptical one because, he claims, it is taught in the Law, which means for him the Mosaic code. Thus he claims that the role of fate and free will is spelled out in the Law (*Ant.* 16:389f.); that immortality of the soul and resurrection/reincarnation is to be found in "what the lawgiver has prophesied" (*Ag.Ap.* 2:218); and that ὁμόνοια is something enjoined by the Law (*Ap.* 2:280ff.). On all of these issues, Josephus finds the skeptical position of the Sadducees to be un-Jewish and so he accepts the affirmative positions. But he never endorses the Pharisaic postion *per se*; we can only discover his agreement with them by patient analysis.

Second, it is not only the Pharisees who hold the postions espoused by Josephus, so that his belief in fate or immortality would imply Pharisaic allegiance. We know, for example, that he thought the Essenes to excel everyone else in ὁμόνοια, that he heartily endorsed their view of the afterlife, and that they too believed in εἱμαρμένη. Indeed, the Pharisees' views are those of the mainstream. Josephus says as much when he claims that their views endear them to the people (*Ant.* 18:14). Notice the order: it is not that the masses believe in fate and immortality because the Pharisees teach such things; rather, the Pharisees have the public trust because, unlike the Sadducean élite, they teach ideas that are already popular. So the fact that Josephus also shares such mainstream beliefs does not make him a Pharisee.

Third, Josephus begins *War* 2:162 by recalling his earlier, negative portrayal in 1:110-114: the Pharisees are the ones who *seem* to interpret the laws accurately, who deceived the pious Queen Alexandra, and who have "shanghaied" (ἀπάγω) the position of the leading school. In the earlier passage Josephus did not assail any Pharisaic beliefs, but rather pointed out the tension between their reputation for εὐσέβεια, on the one hand, and their unscrupulous behaviour on the other. But if Josephus's critique of the Pharisees is aimed at their behaviour in particular instances, then no amount of general ideological agreement can prove him to be a Pharisee.[220]

Fourth, one cannot escape the overwhelming contextual indicators. It is true that, over against the Sadducees, the Pharisees turn out positively on every point. But Josephus dislikes the Sadducees. The key point is that both of these groups are dispensed with in short order after the long and admiring portrayal of the Essenes. The Pharisees are credited with at least seeking harmony, for example, whereas the Sadducees do not even treat their friends well. But Josephus's heart is with the Essenes. They are more devoted φιλάλληλοι than any other group (2:119). Their admirer gives two paragraphs (2:122-127) to a discussion of their remarkable ὁμόνοια. We have also noted his warm and sympathetic discussion of the Essenes' belief in immortality (2:153-158). And it is equally obvious that Josephus agrees with their politics of submission (2:139f.). Furthermore, if the Pharisees *are reputed to* have special ἀκρίβεια, the Essenes *are* ἀκριβέστατοι in their judgments (2:145) and more careful than all other Jews in observing the Sabbath (2:147). In short, if the Pharisees are superior to the almost irreligious Sadducees, the Essenes are in a class by themselves.

All of the evidence considered above points to the conclusion that, although Josephus agreed with the Pharisees on major philosophical issues, because they represented "affirmative" mainstream positions, he is very far from unrestrained enthusiasm for the group. He acknowledges their role as the foremost Jewish sect, but he hardly exults over it.

Our investigation, however, has not turned up any further evidence to support Josephus's initial assertion (2:118f.) that the three legitimate αἱρέσεις have nothing in common with that of the Judas. That assertion

---

[220] It is perhaps worth remembering that even the Matthean Jesus agreed with Pharisaic teaching (Mt. 23:2); yet that does not make him a Pharisee (although such an identification has been made from time to time).

is supported only for the Essenes, who are featured players; one has only Josephus's word that it holds also for the Pharisees and Sadducees.

IV. *Source Criticism of War 2:162-166*

It remains to apply the results of the foregoing analysis to the question: Can the passage be traced to an author other than Josephus?

Of the older sources critics, most did not comment on *War* 2:162-166. Hölscher did, but assigned it to Josephus himself because it presents the Pharisees and Sadducees "in der üblichen Weise des J.[osephus]".[221] The recent attempt by Schwartz to revive source criticism with respect to the Pharisee passages also ends up attributing our passage to Josephus, this time on the grounds that it gives a "thoroughly positive" account of the Pharisees[222]—though that rationale is dubious, both because the account is not thoroughly positive and because the assumption that Josephus would only write postitively about the group is unwarranted.

On the other side, practically alone, stands G. F. Moore, who argues that the discussion of the Pharisees on fate and free will is non-Josephan,[223] un-Jewish,[224] and rather Stoic.[225] Moore infers from all of this that Josephus is dependent for this segment on an account of the Pharisees by Nicolaus.[226] Yet even Moore credits the rest of the passage (i.e., everything but the fate/free will notice) to Josephus. G. Maier modifies Moore's position by isolating the specific words that he believes were contributed by Josephus (e.g., καὶ θεῷ, τὸ πράττειν τὰ δίκαια καὶ μή), in support of his thesis that Josephus has judaized Nicolaus's hellenizing description of the Pharisees.[227]

We may respond: while it is true that the description of the Pharisees in *War* 2:162-166 uses language that evokes the Stoic Chrysippus (as recounted by Cicero), Josephus himself elsewhere likens the Pharisees to Stoics in some points (cf. *Life* 12). Outsiders sometimes did likewise.[228] Most important: Josephus himself employs both the viewpoint and the language that he attributes to the Pharisees several times in his own narrative. Our study has revealed that the passage as we have it is Josephan

---

[221] Hölscher, "Josephus", 1949 n.*. He takes *War* 2:119-161, however (on the Essenes), to be the work of a Greek-educated Jew, other than Josephus. That view is criticized and rightfully rejected by Maier, *freier Wille*, 6f.
[222] Schwartz, "Josephus and Nicolaus", 162f.
[223] Moore, "Fate", 375f.
[224] Ibid., 379-382.
[225] Ibid., 376-379.
[226] Ibid., 383f. See Appendix B, below.
[227] Maier, *freier Wille*, 11-13.
[228] Cf. n. 156, above.

in all of its details. It exhibits Josephus's vocabulary from first to last and it uses this vocabulary in typically Josephan style. Examples are: ἀκρίβεια; τὰ νόμιμα; ἀκρίβεια with δοκέω, ἐξηγεῖσθαι, and τὰ νόμιμα; αἵρεσις; εἱμαρμένη; juxtaposition of εἱμαρμένη and θεός; τὰ δίκαια; κεῖσθαι;[229] the attribution of decisions to human volition; ψυχὴ πᾶσα ἄφθαρτον; reincarnation as a reward for the good alone; ἀίδια τιμωρία for the wicked; and ὁμόνοια. There can, therefore, be no reasonable doubt that Josephus authored this passage from beginning to end.[230]

Although one might wish to attribute the negative judgements on the Pharisees to Nicolaus rather than to Josephus (a mistake, I have argued), one cannot easily use this option, as Moore does, to explain apparent errors of fact. For Nicolaus lived in the Herodian court, which was based in Jerusalem, for at least ten years—perhaps twenty years or more—of his adult life.[231] He must have known the Pharisees at least as well as Josephus did, since our author was captured at age thirty and lived the rest of his life in Rome.

---

[229] With ἐν, ἐπί, or a simple dative, meaning "to be in one's power, to depend on someone/something". *War* 5:59; *Ant.* 1:78; 5:110; 13:355; 18:215; 19:167.

[230] Incidentally, we have also noted data that suggest Josephus's final authorship of the Essene passage (*War* 2:119-161), e.g., the references to their political harmlessness, the terms φιλάλληλοι (2:119), εὐσέβεια toward God, ἀκρίβεια toward men (2:139), and the immortality of the soul passage (2:154f.; cf. Josephus's own views in 3:372-374). Cf. also Maier's arguments (*freier Wille*, 7ff.) and Appendix B, below.

[231] Nicolaus was already a confidante (φίλος) of Herod's in 14 BC (*Ant.* 16:16ff.). He remained with the family until 4 BC, when he supported Archelaus's bid for succession in Rome (*Ant.* 17:240ff.). Cf. R. Laqueur, "Nicolaus (Damask.)", *PWRE*, XVII:1, 362-424, esp. 365-372. Laqueur theorizes (*Historiker*, 366f.) that Nicolaus had joined Herod already in 40 BC. B. Z. Wacholder (*Nicolaus of Damascus* [Berkely-Los Angeles: U. of California Press, 1962], 22ff.) argues more cogently that Nicolaus was in Herod's service by 20 BC and may have joined it in the early or mid-twenties. That still gives Nicolaus twenty years or more in Judea.

PART THREE

THE PHARISEES IN THE *JEWISH ANTIQUITIES*

CHAPTER SEVEN

THE PURPOSE AND OUTLOOK OF *ANTIQUITIES*

Fifteen to twenty years after the publication of *War*, Josephus completed his *Jewish Antiquities*.[1] Comprising twenty books, this work was his *magnum opus*; accordingly, it has provided the basis for many analyses of his thought and literary technique.[2] A general introduction to *Ant.* would be out of place in this study because (a) such introductions are already plentiful and easily accessible[3] and (b) much of the material would have marginal relevance to our topic, since the Pharisees appear only in the last third (books 13-18) of the work.[4] It is possible here only to summarize what has been ascertained about the purpose of *Ant.* and to specify those themes that might bear on the interpretation of the Pharisee passages.

We shall begin with the purpose and outlook of *Ant.* as a self-contained work. Since, however, the final third of *Ant.* substantially parallels the first two books of *War*, and since the Pharisee passages of both works fall within this parallel material,[5] we must also ask about the relationship between *War* and *Ant.* in general terms. Finally, we shall survey the

---

[1] The common English title comes from the Latin *Antiquitates Judaicae*. Josephus called the work Ἰουδαϊκὴ Ἀρχαιολογία (cf. *Ant.* 1:5; *Ag.Ap.* 1:54), probably, as Thackeray suggests (*Josephus*, 56f.), in imitation of the Ῥωμαϊκὴ Ἀρχαιολογία in twenty books by Dionysius of Halicarnassus.

Josephus dates *Ant.* in 20:267, where he defines the "present day" as (a) the thirteenth year of Domitian's reign and (b) the fifty-sixth year of his own life. Since Josephus was born in the year of Caligula's accession, AD 37/38 (cf. *Life* 5), both of these data put the completion of *Ant.* in AD 93/94. The chief difficulties with this dating arise in connection with the appendix, *Life*, and will be considered in Part IV, below.

[2] Part of the great appeal of *Ant.* for source and redaction critics derives from the fact that we possess many of its sources, e.g., the LXX, *Aristeas*, 1 Maccabees, and *War*. A comparison of Josephus with his sources has generated much material for studies such as those of Bloch, Destinon, Hölscher, Pelletier, Franxman, and Attridge. Further, *Ant.* is so long that it affords copious material for a study of Josephus's literary technique (cf. Thackeray, *Josephus*, 100ff.; Shutt, *Studies*) and of his exegetical principles (cf. Olitzki, Rappaport, and Heller).

[3] Cf., e.g., Schürer, *Geschichte*, I, 79-85; Niese, *HZ*, 21?-219; idem, *ERE*, VII, 572-575; Thackeray, *Josephus*, 51-74, also 75-124; idem, LCL edn., IV, vii-xix; Foakes Jackson, *Josephus*, 246-258; Franxman, *Genesis*, 5-8; Attridge, *Interpretation*, 29-70.

[4] The Pharisees appear as a group in *Ant.* 13:171-173, 288-298, 400-431; 17:41-45; and 18:11-25. Individual Pharisees are mentioned in 15:3-4, 371; cf. 14:172-176.

[5] Nevertheless, most of the material in the Pharisee passages in *Ant.* is not paralleled in *War* (i.e., 13:171-173, 288-289, 400-406; 15:3-4, 371; 17:41-45, except for the brief notice at *War* 1:571).

attempts that have been made to interpret the Pharisee passages of *Ant.* in terms of that work's goals and major themes.

I. *Preface and Dominant Themes*

A. *Josephus an Apologist for Judaism*

Scholarship has generally taken the proem to *Ant.* much more seriously than its counterpart in *War*. Since *War* is usually viewed as a work of Roman propaganda, its programmatic statements about truthfulness and about the author's sorrow over the fate of Jerusalem are often ignored or depreciated in favour of a hypothetical reconstruction of the work's real (= ulterior) motive.[6] With *Ant.* the situation is different. Josephus declares at the outset, and repeatedly thereafter, that he has an apologetic purpose: he wants to convince his Greco-Roman readers of the nobleness of Jewish origins, beliefs, and practices. Scholars have usually believed him.

After some opening reflections on his motives for having written *War* (*Ant.* 1:1-4), Josephus turns to the work at hand (1:5):

> So also I have now taken up the present work, believing that it will impress the Greek world as worthy of serious consideration (νομίζων ἅπασι φανεῖσθαι τοῖς ῞Ελλησιν ἀξίαν σπουδῆς).

That Josephus expects a Greek-pagan readership for *Ant.* is clear at several points in the narrative[7] and is spelled out again in the conclusion (20:262): ''no one else would have been able to produce such an accurate work as this for the Greeks (εἰς ῞Ελληνας)''.[8]

What does Josephus want to tell the Greeks about the Jews? He goes on to sketch the content of the work (1:5):

> It will embrace our entire ancient history (παρ' ἡμῖν ἀρχαιολογίαν) and political constitution (διάταξιν τοῦ πολιτεύματος), translated from the Hebrew records (ἐκ τῶν ἑβραικῶν μεθηρμηνευμένην). (Thackeray)

But this material is not merely of academic interest. Josephus presents as the hypothesis of *Ant.* the virtue (ἀρετή) of the Mosaic code and its superiority to pagan mythology. He invites the reader critically to assess (δοκιμάζειν) the worthiness (εἰ ἀξίως) of Moses' teachings about God (1:15), which teachings lie at the heart of Jewish life and history. Josephus is convinced that what the Jews have is good and ought not to

---

[6] Cf. my discussion of *War* in chapter 3, above.
[7] E.g., *Ant.* 1:29; 2:247; 16:174.
[8] Cf. Niese, *HZ* 213f.

be hidden from the Greeks (1:11). *Ant.* is motivated, then, by an apologetic purpose.

In the preface and throughout the entire work, our author declares his intention to combat both ignorance and error about Jewish history. In 14:186ff., for example, he reveals something of the hostility with which other historians had depicted the Jews:

> And here it seems to me necessary to make public all the honours given our nation. . . . Since many persons, however, out of enmity to us refuse to believe what has been written about us by Persians and Macedonians, . . . while against the decrees of the Romans nothing can be said, . . . from these same documents I will furnish proof of my statements. (Marcus)

He comments later, again in connection with the pro-Jewish decrees (16:174f.):

> Now it was necessary for me to cite these decrees since this account of our history is chiefly meant to reach the Greeks in order to show them that in former times we were treated with all respect. . . . And if I frequently mention these decrees, *it is to reconcile the other nations to us and to remove the causes for hatred* (μίσους αἰτίας) which have taken root in thoughtless persons among us as well as among them. (Marcus/Wikgren; emphasis added)

That Josephus intended the *Ant.* as an ἀπολογία for Judaism is clear, finally, from his last extant work, *Against Apion*. In that treatise he undertakes a systematic refutation of pagan errors about the Jews and their history. This is necessary, he insists, because:

> a considerable number of persons influenced by the malicious calumnies of certain individuals, discredit the statements in my history concerning our antiquity. (*Ag.Ap.* 1:1-2; Thackeray)

Because *Ant.* was not entirely successful in eradicating false ideas Josephus wrote *Ag.Ap.* Thus his programmatic statements about *Ant.* are consistent from first to last in presenting the work as a defence of Jewish history, beliefs, and values.

That such apologies were needed in the late first century AD has long been recognized by commentators.[9] Contemporary literary evidence abundantly attests the widespread misinformation about the Jews that *Ant.* presupposes.[10] We have good reason to believe that ordinary hostility toward the Jews, caused by ignorance and xenophobia, was

---

[9] E.g., H. Bloch, *Quellen*, 4f.; Niese, *HZ*, 212ff., 213 n. 1; idem, *EKE*, VII, 572.

[10] Cf. T. Reinach, *Textes* (1963 [1985]); M. Stern, *Greek and Latin Authors on Jews and Judaism*, I: *From Herodotus to Plutarch* (Jerusalem: Israel Academy of Sciences and Humanities, 1974); and now M. Whittaker, *Jews and Christians: Graeco-Roman Views* (Cambridge: University Press, 1984).

compounded by the revolt in Judea[11] and then again by the severe policies of the Emperor Domitian, in whose reign Josephus wrote *Ant.*[12]

In light of the contemporary situation, the consistency of *Ant.*'s programmatic statements, and the character of the work as a whole, scholars have come to accept the preface to *Ant.* as a forthright declaration of purpose.[13] To be sure, they have often dismissed as benign exaggeration Josephus's claim to have translated the scriptures without embellishment or omission (1:17).[14] Nevertheless, his avowed intention to write as a Jew about Jewish origins and history, to serve therefore as an apologist to the Greek world, has impressed critics as a fair statement of the work's goals. Thackeray's assessment of *Ant.*, for example, corresponds closely to the emphasis of the preface: "Its design was to magnify the Jewish race in the eyes of the Greco-Roman world by a record of its ancient and glorious history."[15]

B. *Specific Themes; Judaism as a Philosophy*

We must now specify, as nearly as possible, the particular themes that Josephus wanted to impress on his readers in the effort to convince them of the worthiness of Judaism.

H. W. Attridge has demonstrated that two themes introduced in the preface serve Josephus as interpretive keys in his paraphrase of the Bible, which occupies about the first ten books of *Ant.*[16] The first theme is that of God's watchful care (πρόνοια) for the world. In 1:14, 20, Josephus declares that the main lesson (τὸ σύνολον, τὸ παίδευμα) of *Ant.* is that God rewards obedience to his Law with happiness (εὐδαιμονία) but punishes disobedience. Attridge shows that God's intervention in human affairs to reward and punish individuals is indeed a consistent emphasis of Josephus's biblical paraphrase.[17]

---

[11] Farmer, *Maccabees*, 11: Whittaker, *Jews and Christians*, 12; cf. Dio Cassius, *History of Rome* 45.7.2.; Philostratus, *Apollonius of Tyana* 5:33; Fronto, *Parthian War* 2; Minucius Felix, *Octavius* 10:4 (on the later revolts, under Trajan and Hadrian).

[12] Suetonius, *Domitian* 12.

[13] In addition to the scholars cited in n. 3 above, cf. Laqueur, *Historiker*, 136, 228ff.

[14] Cf. H. Bloch, *Quellen*, 6: Attridge, *Interpretation*, 58; Cohen, *Josephus*, 28f. But W. C. van Unnik has offered a new interpretation of this promise in his lecture, "Die Formel 'nichts wegnehmen, nichts hinzufügen' bei Josephus", in his *Schriftsteller*, 26-40; (cf. 28-32 on previous scholarship). He argues that Josephus does not promise a *verbatim* reproduction of scripture but rather a true presentation of its sense; in particular, he will not alter that sense out of hatred or flattery.

[15] Thackeray, LCL edn, IV, vii; cf. his *Josephus*, 52.

[16] Attridge, *Interpretation*, 67-70.

[17] Ibid., 71-107.

The second interpretive key discovered by Attridge is a "moralizing" tendency.[18] Josephus claims in the preface (1:23) that Moses presented God as the perfect expression of virtue (ἀρετή) and taught that men should strive to participate (μεταλαμβάνειν) in this moral attribute. Josephus develops this motif in his biblical paraphrase by reworking his source so as to highlight the virtues (εὐσέβεια, δικαιοσύνη, ἀνδρεία, σωφροσύνη, etc.) of those figures in Jewish history who pleased God and the vices of those who did not. He illustrates everywhere the ruinous consequences of unchecked emotion (especially greed and lust) and offers, by contrast, the example of Moses as a model of virtue.[19]

Attridge's study is a welcome exploration of Josephus's thought in *Ant.* One aspect of his analysis, however, requires further elaboration, namely, the identification of happiness (εὐδαιμονία) as a significant term. In both 1:14 and 1:20, Josephus declares his thesis to be that God rewards obedience to the Law with εὐδαιμονία (or εὐδαίμονα βίον). One indication of the importance of this theme is that, although the word εὐδαιμονία is entirely absent from the LXX, Josephus introduces it no less than 47 times into his biblical paraphrase (*Ant.* 1-11).[20]

Now H.-F. Weiss has pointed out that εὐδαιμονία was precisely the goal of Hellenistic philosophy.[21] Aristotle declared that it was the chief end (τέλος) of man.[22] The quest for εὐδαιμονία motivated both Stoic and Epicurean philosophy.[23] Therefore, by setting out to prove that God grants happiness to those who observe his Law, Josephus effectively enters Judaism as a serious option in the Hellenistic philosophical discussion.[24]

Indeed, throughout *Ant.* Josephus presents Judaism as a philosophy. In the preface he challenges the reader (1:25):

> Should any further desire to consider the reasons (τὰς αἰτίας) for every article in our creed, he would find the inquiry highly philosophical (λίαν φιλόσοφος). (Thackeray)

Everything that he is going to relate, Josephus explains, depends on the σοφία of Moses (1:18). Not only Moses but also Abraham and Solomon appear as great philosophers.[25] We have already seen that in his discus-

---

[18] Ibid., 68f.
[19] Ibid., 121-140.
[20] Cf. esp. *Ant.* 2:7-8; 4:186, 195; 6:93; 7:380.
[21] Weiss, "Pharisäismus und Hellenismus", 427f.
[22] *NE* 10.6.1ff.; cf. Greene, *Moira*, 324f.
[23] Weiss, "Pharisäismus und Hellenismus", 427f.; cf. Sextus Empiricus, *adv. math.* 12:69 (on Epicurus); Epictetus, *Dissertations* 1.4.32 (on the Stoics).
[24] Weiss, "Pharisäismus und Hellenismus", 427f.
[25] Weiss, "Pharisäismus und Hellenismus", 427f.; cf. *Ant.* 1:154ff., 151. 167f. (on Abraham); 8:42-44 (on Solomon).

sions of the Jewish αἱρέσεις, he says explicitly that the Jews do philosophize.[26] The point becomes especially clear in *Ag.Ap.*, which is a sequel to *Ant.*[27] We are bound, therefore, to conclude with Weiss:

> Das Judentum ist nach Josephus also insgesamt und seinem Wesen nach 'Philopsphie', und zwar die auf dem Gesetz beruhende, durch das Gesetz gelehrte Philosophie. Das Gesetz ist die Grundlage der Philosophie des Judentums.[28]

It is not possible in the framework of this introductory chapter to examine all that Josephus might have meant by describing Judaism as a philosophy. Several scholars have reminded us, however, that the connotations of "philosophy" in the ancient world were at once broader and more concrete than the modern use of the word suggests.[29] Philosophy after Socrates was not a technical academic discipline but rather a comprehensive "way of life";[30] a metaphysical basis was important, to be sure, but the emphasis was on ethics and behaviour.[31] In this context, Josephus's portrayal of Judaism as a philosophy is not surprising.

To summarize: a longstanding scholarly consensus has accepted Josephus's presentation of his motives for writing *Ant.* He is an apologist, writing to combat widespread ignorance and misunderstanding about Jewish origins, history, beliefs, and practices. Josephus presents Judaism as a philosophy that offers a definite response to the human quest for εὐδαιμονία. Happiness is granted by God to those who observe his laws.

II. *The Relationship Between War and Antiquities*

Because the Pharisee passages of *Ant.* fall within the portion of that work that is paralleled in *War*, it is necessary here to ask how Josephus understood the relationship between the two narratives. Since R. Laqueur's study of Josephus (1920) it has been a common view that *War*, as a vehicle of Roman propaganda, had a purpose and outlook very different from those of *Ant.*[32] A recent manual of Jewish history in the New Testament period echoes the general opinion that:

---

[26] E.g., at *War* 2:119, 166; cf. *Ant.* 13:289; 18:9, 11, 23, 25.
[27] Cf. esp. 1:54, 165; 2:47.
[28] Weiss, "Pharisäismus und Hellenismus", 428.
[29] E. Bickerman, "La chaîne", 262f.; M. Smith, "Palestinian Judaism", 79f.; and Weiss, "Pharisäismus und Hellenismus", 428.
[30] Weiss, "Pharisäismus und Hellenismus", 428.
[31] Cf. chapter 6, n. 120, above.
[32] So Laqueur, Rasp, Thackeray, M. Smith, Neusner, and Cohen, who will be discussed below; in addition, see the works cited in chapter 3, n. 16.

whereas in his first work Josephus was a spokesman for the Roman Empire and the Flavian dynasty, in the *Antiquities* he is first and foremost the apologist for Judaism.[33]

In what follows I shall argue that Laqueur's theory, although it accurately identifies some major differences of outlook between *War* and *Ant.*, tends to obscure Josephus's own literary intention, which is to link together the goals of the two works.

A. *Differences of Outlook Between* War *and* Antiquities

Critics have long realized that comparison of *Ant.* 13-20 with the parallel material in *War* 1-2 reveals many differences of perspective.[34] Most conspicuous is the revision of Josephus's attitude toward Herod the Great: whereas *War* had given a very sympathetic portrayal,[35] *Ant.* often attacks his character and accuses him of impiety.[36] Other public figures such as Salome Alexandra,[37] King Agrippa and Agrippa II,[38] the high priest Ananus,[39] and the Roman procurators[40] have likewise been re-

---

[33] S. Safrai and M. Stern (edd.), *The Jewish People*, I, 24.

[34] The problem of the literary relationship between *Ant.* 13-20 and *War* 1-2 is a thorny one. For the history of scholarship on this question, see Lindner, *Geschichtsauffassung*, 3-8. For a deft analysis of the issues see Cohen, *Josephus*, 48-66. He proposes a novel solution to the effect that *Ant.* 13-14 closely follow *War*; books 15-16 revert to *War*'s source; book 17 uses both *War* and the source; and books 18-20 are erratic.

[35] Cohen aptly remarks (*Josephus*, 111) that *War*'s portrait of Herod "is almost an encomium (or a biography) rather than a history"; cf. Hölscher, "Josephus", 1947; Michel-Bauernfeind, *De Bello Judaico*, I, XXV f.; Thackeray, *Josephus*, 65.

[36] Notice, e.g., the following passages: (a) *War* 1:208f has Herod accused of impropriety by certain malicious (βάσκανοι) persons; but *Ant.* 14:167 asserts that Herod "violated *our* Law"; (b) *Ant.* 15:8f., on the popular hatred of Herod; (c) *Ant.* 15:174-182, which accuses Herod of lying, deceitfulness, and injustice in the death of Hyrcanus; (d) *Ant.* 15:267, on Herod's departure from τὰ πάτρια, which was the cause of later judgement on the Jews; (e) *Ant.* 15:328f., in which Herod's lavish gift-giving are said to evince his departure from Jewish ἔθη and νόμιμα; (f) *Ant.* 16:150-159, on Herod's extreme vanity, which violated Jewish law; (g) *Ant.* 16:183-187, which takes issue with Nicolaus's flattery of Herod; (h) and *Ant.* 16:400-404, which attributes to Herod a "murderous mind that cannot be turned from evil" (Marcus/Wikgren); cf. also 17:151, 207; 19:329; 20:247ff., and Laqueur, *Historiker*, 171-221.

[37] Cf. *War* 1:108f. with *Ant.* 13:430ff. See chapter 10, below.

[38] Cf. Laqueur, *Historiker*, 261.

[39] Cf. *War* 4:319-321 with *Ant.* 20:199; also Cohen, *Josephus*, 150f.

[40] On Felix, cf. *War* 2:253-260 with *Ant.* 20:160-161; also Foakes Jackson, *Josephus*, 166f. It is the portrayal in *Ant.* that corresponds more closely to Tacitus's accounts (*Histories* 5:9; *Annals* 12:54). On Festus, cf. *War* 2:271 with *Ant.* 20:188. The portrait of Albinus in *Ant.* 20:197, 204, 215 is not as hostile as *War* 2:273-276; cf. Cohen, *Josephus*, 60ff. On Gessius Florus, the last procurator, both *War* (2:277-279) and *Ant.* (20:252-257) are unforgiving.

Along with the generally intensified hostility toward the procurators in *Ant.* goes an

evaluated. Some critics have argued, finally, that *Ant.* has reversed *War*'s negative portrayal of the Pharisees.[41] It is the last question that interests us most directly but we cannot treat that issue in isolation from the larger problem of explaining Josephus's new outlook.

1. The Source Critics and Niese

The old source-critical movement sought to explain all of Josephus's attitudes as the attitudes of his sources.[42] Thus Schürer, for example, in noting that the Josephus of *Ant.* sometimes disagrees with Nicolaus and judges Herod an evil man, theorized that Josephus must have used a new, "dem Herodes ungünstige", source for the later work.[43] Destinon's solution was to attribute the anti-Herodian remarks in *Ant.* to Nicolaus of Damascus.[44] He argued that Nicolaus, but not Josephus, was capable of such a critical attitude.[45] This theory limited Josephus's role to the absurd castigation of Nicolaus for his excessive flattery of Herod (*Ant.* 16:183ff.), a charge of which Nicolaus was innocent.[46] Hölscher explained both *Ant.*'s judgement of Herod and its conflict with Nicolaus by positing an intermediate source for 13:212-17:355, a Jewish pro-Hasmonean reworking of Nicolaus, which Josephus simply copied.[47] The source critics, then, tended to attribute Josephus's changed attitude to his sources.

We may note, incidentally, that none of these critics perceived any major shift in the portrayal of the Pharisees between *War* as a whole and *Ant.* as a whole.[48] Rather, they attributed the individual Pharisee-pericopae within each of the books to discrete sources.

---

increased emphasis (also in *Life*) on the willingness of the Jews to fight the Romans (cf. *Ant.* 20:257 and Cohen, *Josephus*, 155f).

[41] E.g., Rasp, Smith/Neusner, and Cohen. See the discussion below and also chapter 2, above.

[42] See chapter 2, above.

[43] Schürer, *Geschichte*, I, 84. We may note that Bloch, though a source critic, was not given to this sort of wholesale dissolution of Josephus's personality but left some room for the historian's own activity, at least as an intelligent compiler. Thus (*Quellen*, 112f., 140ff.), he insisted that Josephus himself had consulted the *Memoirs* of Herod and personally disagreed with them, albeit on the basis of other sources.

[44] Destinon, *Quellen*, 91-20.

[45] Ibid., 96f.

[46] Ibid., 120.

[47] Hölscher, "Josephus", 1971f., 1977f.

[48] The only source critics who have expressd a consistent interest in the Pharisee passages are Hölscher and, now, Schwartz. Hölscher found within *Ant.* a variety of attitudes toward the Pharisees ("Josephus", 1936 and n. + +). Schwartz explicitly refutes the theory that *Ant.* intends an improved portrait of the Pharisees over against *War* ("Josephus and Nicolaus", 165f.).

More than many of his contemporaries, B. Niese was sensitive to Josephus's own literary interests as a significant cause of the differences between *War* and *Ant.*. This sensitivity is reflected in Niese's willingness to believe that Josephus made direct use of *War* in the composition of *Ant.* 13-20.[49] Such a theory, which was rejected by most source critics, requires that Josephus was intelligently involved in the composition of the later work. It was he who supplemented *War* with an array of new materials, including citations of pagan authors, Jewish traditions, and the pro-Jewish decrees of various rulers.[50] It was he, also, who worked diligently to vary the style of *War*, while generally preserving its content intact.[51] Finally, if *Ant.* used *War* then Josephus himself must have developed new attitudes toward certain parties in the interim between the works. Niese cites the case of Ananus, noted above, but *not* that of the Pharisees.[52] Nor does he elaborate on the possible reasons for such changes.

2. Laqueur and Thackeray

It was this shift in Josephus's attitudes, which Niese had mentioned only in passing, that consumed R. Laqueur in his watershed study of Josephus (1920).[53] Repudiating a source criticism that had practically annihilated Josephus's character, Laqueur set out to explain many of the differences between *War* and *Ant.* by demonstrating a development in the historian's outlook.[54] Laqueur believed that *Ant.*, "nichts anderes ist als eine tendenziöse Zurechtmachung der im bellum überlieferten Tatsachen".[55] Laqueur thinks that *Ant.*'s revision of *War*, especially on Herod and his family, represents Josephus's attempt to redeem his Jewish heritage after his years in the service of Roman propaganda.[56]

---

[49] *HZ*, 218f.; *ERE*, VII, 574. The common view was based on the belief that *War*, with its thematic treatment of Herod's life, for example, was secondary to the more detailed chronological, account in *Ant.* Cf. Laqueur *Historiker*, 133. Niese, however, held that *War* was 'too much of a unity, too coherent to be a mere epitome or reworking of a source'. He thought it impossible to get behind *War* to posit an earlier source.

[50] *HZ*, 220-222; *ERE*, VIII, 574f.

[51] *HZ*, 223; *ERE*, VII, 575. The change in style is on the whole toward simplicity, Niese observes, but is also influenced by a desire to imitate Thucydides, especially in books 16 to 19.

[52] *ERE*, VII, 575.

[53] See my discussion of Laqueur in chapter 2, above.

[54] Laqueur notes (*Historiker*, 234), that his interpretation of Josephus corroborates his earlier analysis of Polybius's method.

[55] Laqueur, *Historiker*, 133f.

[56] Ibid., 136, 228ff., 239ff., and especially 258ff. These last pages fall within chapter 8, "Der Werdegang des Josephus," which is now reprinted in Schalit, *Zur Josephus-Forschung*.

That *Ant.* contains several anti-Herodian passages not found in *War* was already well-known by Laqueur's time, as we have seen. His particular contributions were two. First, he examined the nature of the divergence between *War* and *Ant.* on Herod, in order to show that it could not be explained by source hypotheses alone. Comparing *War* 1 and *Ant.* 14, he demonstrated that the re-evaluation of Herod's family is subtly woven into the narrative of *Ant.*, even in passages where the later work reproduces the vocabulary of *War*.[57] It is not, therefore, a question of new material.[58] Roles are reversed so that, for example, the valiant Antipater (Herod's father) of *War* becomes a malicious troublemaker in *Ant.*[59] Conversely, Antipater's Hasmonean opponent Aristobulus receives much better treatment in *Ant.* than he had in *War*.[60] Again, although the conflict between Hyrcanus and Herod appears in both *War* and *Ant.*, and although a similar course of events is described, the roles of the protagonists are reversed to accord with Josephus's new denigration of Herod.[61] Laqueur points out that in these cases it is not the content but the colouring (Färbung) that is new in *Ant.*: "Die Darstellung der Arch. (*sc. Ant.*) ist also nur erklärlich aus der systematischen politischen Umarbeitung des bellum heraus."[62] So the anti-Herodian polemic comes from Josephus himself.

Why should Josephus have reversed himself so dramatically between *War* and *Ant.*? What inspired his revision of the Herodian history? Laqueur's second contribution to our problem was his proposal that between *War* and *Ant.* Josephus's attitude changed as a result of his altered circumstances. Namely: Josephus had written *War* as a vehicle of Roman propaganda. Called upon by his Falvian protectors, this *Römling* wrote an account of the Jewish revolt that was calculated to persuade the rest of the world to submit to the *Pax Romana*.[63] Because this history used Roman source material and propounded a Roman outlook, it presented

---

[57] Ibid., 128-230.

[58] Laqueur was fully cognizant of the fact that *Ant.* employs new sources over against *War* (*Historiker*, 141, 171, 241). He even allowed (138, 148-155) that Josephus culd use a new source (e.g., the *Memoirs* of Herod) to substantiate *Ant.*'s new view of Herod's family. What Laqueur denied was that Josephus merely copied from the new sources, as others had claimed. Laqueur wanted to prove that Josephus carefully altered his earlier narrative to incorporate his anti-Herodian views and that the new views are, therefore, Josephus's own.

[59] Laqueur, *Historiker*, 138ff., esp. 140. Cf. also 166f.

[60] Ibid., 143., 146f., 158f.

[61] Ibid., 171ff.

[62] Ibid., 168.

[63] Ibid., 255ff. Cf. chapter 3, above, on Laqueur's intepretation of *War* as an instrument of Roman policy.

Roman leaders (Vespasian and Titus) and Roman appointees (Herod's family) in a glowing light.[64]

Naturally enough, argued Laqueur, *War* was seen by world Jewry of the day as Josephus's ultimate betrayal of his people; the former rebel leader had sold his soul to his new patrons.[65] The many attempts of Jews to dislodge the traitor from his life of privilege have left clear tracks in Josephus's writings.[66] But while Vespasian and Titus lived, imperial favour guaranteed Josephus's security.[67]

With the accession of Domitian, however, Jewish measures against Josephus were renewed, this time with a degree of success because of that emperor's distaste for the policies of his father and brother.[68] Josephus lost his favoured court position and this placed him "zwischen zwei Stühle": he had been stripped of his right to speak for Rome but he had also forfeited the support of his compatriots. In these circumstances, he turned to one Epaphroditus (the patron of *Ant.* and *Life*) and found in him a politically neutral sponsor.[69] Now relieved of his obligations to the authorities, Josephus was free to give expression to his natural Jewish instincts.[70] Hence the negative portrayal of Herod and his family in *Ant.*[71] *War* had belonged to Josephus's "Roman period"; *Ant.* was the creation of Josephus as Jewish apologist, now free to express his nationalistic sentiments.

Although Laqueur was content to interpret the Jewish apologetic of *Ant.* as mere self-expression on Josephus's part, he also raised the question whether this apologetic was calculated to effect a certain *Rehabilitation* between the erstwhile traitor and his compatriots.[72] This possibility Laqueur only mentioned and did not explore further.

Thackeray, who was everywhere influenced by Laqueur, rejected the latter's suggestion that in *Ant.* Josephus "was prompted by self-interested motives, hoping to rehabilitate himself with his offended countrymen".[73] But this proposal was merely an afterthought on Laqueur's part and not crucial to his theory. That Thackeray in fact took over the substance of Laqueur's view of *Ant.* is clear from his remark that Josephus:

---

[64] Laqueur, *Historiker*, 258.
[65] Ibid., 258.
[66] Ibid. Laqueur points to *War* 7:442, 447f., which indicate that Josephus was (falsely) accused of inspiring the revolt in Cyrene (AD 73).
[67] Ibid.
[68] Ibid., 258f.
[69] Ibid., 259f.
[70] Ibid., 260f.
[71] Laqueur, *Historiker*, 260f.
[72] Ibid.
[73] Thackeray, *Josephus*, 52.

deprived of his former patrons, . . . seems finally to have severed his con-
nexion with Roman political propaganda, and henceforth figures solely as
Jewish historian and apologist.[74]

This observation distinctly echoes Laqueur's view of Josephus's development between *War* and *Ant.* Thackeray once again became a medium of
Laqueur's insights. The combined influence of these two scholars on
subsequent Josephan scholarship is impressive.

Before we consider the ways in which the Laqueur/Thackeray theory
has been adapted to interpret the Pharisee passages of *Ant.*, some brief
critical observations on that theory are in order.

B. The Apologetic Purpose Common to War and Antiquities

Scholars have not always believed that *War* and *Ant.* sprang from two opposite motives, Roman propaganda and Jewish apologetic. For example,
Benedictus Niese, the great Halle classicist, formed his judgement before
and independently of Laqueur. Niese remarks:

> As in the *BJ* [*War*], so in the *AJ* [*Ant.*], the object of Josephus is to furnish
> the Hellenes with an accurate dilineation of Israelitic and Jewish history in
> place of the misrepresentation of unfriendly or malevolent chroniclers.[75]

In our discussion of *War* (chapter 3, above), we saw that Josephus claims
there to be presenting an accurate eyewitness account of the revolt in
order to refute the current anti-Jewish reports of the conflict. We may
now observe that whenever he speaks of *Ant.* and *War* together, he takes
some trouble to spell out that the two works have a similar motivation.

1. Josephus begins *Ant.* (1:1-3) by describing four motives that cause
historians to write, namely: (a) egotism; (b) flattery of important persons; (c) participation in great events; and (d) the desire to replace ignorance with accurate knowledge. Of these four, he claims, only the last
two influenced his writing of *War* (1:4). But he is not speaking only of
War: by means of a μέν . . . δέ construction in 1:4-5, he states explicitly
that the same motives that led him to write *War*—the recounting of great
events and the refutation of those who "disfigure the truth"—now move
him to write *Ant.*

2. He goes on to claim that he had contemplated including the ancient
history when he wrote *War*[76] but had decided against it because there

---

[74] Ibid.

[75] Niese, *ERE*, VII, 542; cf. *HZ*, 212f.; and Franxman, *Genesis*, 5.

[76] So Thackeray, *Josephus*, 52f.; but this is denied by Niese, *HZ*, 212f., and Attridge,
Interpretation, 44ff., 46.

was too much material. He chose rather to devote a separate work to the Jewish ἀρχαιολογία. According to Josephus, then, the only difference between *War* and *Ant.* is in their subject matter. Both are designed to refute anti-Jewish presentations of history: *War* deals with the revolt, *Ant.* with the more distant past.

3. Both works employ the ἀλήθεια/ἀκρίβεια theme often and in the same way: Josephus is writing the truth over against the misrepresentations of others.[77] Both works link this theme with Josephus's priestly status.[78]

4. Finally, in *Ag.Ap.* 1:53-56 Josephus reflects on *War* and *Ant.* and again attributes to both of them the goal of ἀλήθεια: "I believe that I have fully accomplished this in both works (περὶ ἀμφοτέρας . . . πραγματείας)."

To summarize: Josephus does not see, or he does not wish the reader to see, any significant difference of purpose between *War* and *Ant.* Both works, he claims, have apologetic goals. They set out to combat error, ignorance, and slander among Greco-Roman readers, whether in relation to the Jewish revolt (*War*) or to earlier Jewish history (*Ant.*).

Although, then, one cannot deny Laqueur's conclusion that Josephus changes some of his *attitudes* between *War* and *Ant.*, one must doubt his explanation of those changes as the result of a radical shift in the *purpose* of the two works, from Roman propaganda to Jewish apologetic.

III. *The Pharisees in Antiquities*

In his characterization of the change in Josephus's outlook between *War* and *Ant.*, Laqueur omitted any mention of the Pharisee passages in either work. This may be because his analysis focused on *Ant.* 14, which lacks any reference to the Pharisees, or it may be because he did not see any clear development between the two works on this subject. Other critics, however, would soon argue that *Ant.* revises *War's* portrayal of the Pharisees to accord with the later work's apologetic thrust. We have already examined the proposals of these scholars in some detail (chapter 2, above)[79] and may now simply recall their views with brief summaries.

If Thackeray discounted Laqueur's suggestion that Josephus's new nationalism in *Ant.* was a self-serving attempt to re-establish his credentials with his countrymen, H. Rasp (1924) seized on the idea as a means

---

[77] On *War*, cf. chapter 3, above.
[78] See the discussion in chapter 3, above.
[79] See chapter 2, above.

of intepreting the Pharisee passages in that work. Rasp was particularly
impressed by what he considered to be a development between *War*
2:119ff. and *Ant.* 18:11ff. He thought that the latter passage, with its
diminished praise of the Essenes and its emphasis on the Pharisees'
political clout, represented Josephus's attempt to make amends with the
Pharisees, who had now achieved power in post-war Palestine. The ever-
adaptable historian even tried now to present himself as a member of this
group (*Life* 12).

Smith (1956) and Neusner (1972) have found in *Ant.* a similar revision
of Pharisaic history but interpret it somewhat differently. They locate the
heart of the development in *Ant.* 13:401ff., in Alexander Janneus's
deathbed plea to his wife that, if her adminstration is to be a success, she
must yield power to the Pharisees. Smith and Neusner argue that the
words put in Janneus's mouth, along with *Ant.*'s other references to
Pharisaic popularity (13:298, 18:15), were intended by Josephus as a
signal to the Roman government that it should endorse the Pharisees as
the new aristocracy in post-war Palestine. This recommendation would
naturally facilitate Josephus's reconciliation with the Pharisees, in keeping with Rasp's view, but Smith and Neusner understand *Ant.*'s respect
for Pharisaic power to be directed first of all toward the Romans. Like
Rasp, these American scholars consider Josephus's claim to be a
Pharisee (*Life* 12) as clear proof of *Ant.*'s pro-Pharisaic apologetic. Their
interpretation of *Ant.*'s portrayal of the Pharisees has won significant
support.[80]

Cohen (1987) follows both Rasp and Smith/Neusner. On the one
hand, he thinks that the (allegedly) pro-Pharisaic tone of *Ant./Life* is part
of an overall religious apologetic in these works, which was intended to
rehabilitate Josephus in the eyes of Jewish readers.[81] On the other hand,
Cohen finds in *Ant.* an appeal to the Romans, "that the Pharisees had
always been prominent and therefore deserve Roman support".[82]

In all of these scholars one can easily detect the Laqueurian approach
to Josephus.[83] Whereas, however, Laqueur had observed the new
nationalistic-religious spirit primarily in *Ant.*'s revision of Herodian
history, these scholars think that the Pharisee passages of *Ant.* are also
important instances of the new outlook. They claim that, for one reason
or another—whether to make amends with the Yavnean leaders or to

---

[80] See chapter 2, n. 101.
[81] Cohen, *Josephus*, 144ff.
[82] Ibid., 237f.
[83] It is not clear, however, that Smith and Neusner have any direct knowledge of Laqueur or Rasp.

assist the Roman administration—Josephus has improved the image of
the Pharisees *vis-à-vis War*.

Summary and Conclusion: the Task of Part Three

Josephus intended to present *Ant.* and *War* as two parts of a whole. Both
were written, he says, to counter ignorance and misinformation about
the Jews; the ἀκρίβεια motif is constant throughout both works. As
Josephus presents it, the major difference between *War* and *Ant.* is their
subject matter. The latter is an ἀρχαιολογία whereas the former deals
primarily with the revolt against Rome. Josephus does not suggest that
his outlook has changed between the two works.

Nevertheless, it is now widely accepted that Josephus did alter his
point of view between *War* and *Ant.*, especially on the subject of Herod
and his family. The problem that remains to be solved is the relationship
between the Pharisee passages of *Ant.* and those of *War*. A few influential
scholars have argued that the Pharisee material of *Ant.* is a clear and important example of Josephus's new outlook in that work. Unlike the
revolution in his attitude toward the Herodians, however, which was
already noted and explained by the source critics, his volte-face on the
Pharisees has been perceived by few commentators. It did not occur to
the source critics (Bloch, Destinon, Hölscher, or Schwartz) to posit a
shift between *War* and *Ant.* on the Pharisees. Even Laqueur and
Thackeray, who recognized a shift on other issues, did not connect the
Pharisee pericopae with it. As Neusner remarks (in praise of Smith's
originality), the idea was practically unheard of before his own 1972 article.[84] It is, therefore, an open question whether Josephus intended, in
Ant., to reverse or significantly alter *War*'s portrait of the Pharisees.

In addition to the usual interpretive considerations, we shall need to
classify each of the Pharisee passages of *Ant.* in one of the following
categories: (a) the same basic content as *War*, with the same attitude expressed; (b) the same content, but reformulated so as to express a new
attitude; (c) new material added, but in a way that confirms *War*'s viewpoint; or (d) new material that brings with it a new attitude toward the
Pharisees.

---

[84] He wrote in 1972 ("Josephus's Pharisees", 225): "Apart from Feldman [who published an annotated bibliography, *Scholarship on Philo and Josephus*, in 1963]. . . I know
of no significant attempt to confront, let alone make use of, Smith's discoveries."

CHAPTER EIGHT

ANT. 13:171-173:
THE PHARISEES AMONG THE JEWISH SCHOOLS, II

Josephus introduces the Pharisees to the reader of *Ant.* in the course of his description of events under Jonathan, the second Hasmonean στρατηγός and high priest.[1] This early reference to the Pharisees has no parallel in *War*, which first mentions the group's activities under Alexandra Salome, some seventy-five years later.[2] In our passage, the Pharisees appear as one of the three Jewish αἱρέσεις:

171. Now at this time (κατὰ δὲ τὸν χρόνον τοῦτον) were three schools among the Jews, which thought differently about human actions (αἳ περὶ τῶν ἀνθρωπίνων πραγμάτων διαφόρως ὑπελάμβανον); the first of these were called Pharisees, the second Sadducees, and the third Essenes.

172. The Pharisees, for their part, say that certain events, but not all, are the work of fate; with others it depends on ourselves whether they shall take place or not (οἱ μὲν οὖν Φαρισαῖοι τινὰ καὶ οὐ πάντα τῆς εἱμαρμένης ἔργον εἶναι λέγουσι, τινὰ δ᾽ ἐφ᾽ ἑαυτοῖς ὑπάρχειν συμβαίνειν τε καὶ μὴ γίνεσθαι). The sect (γένος) of the Essenes, however, declares fate the mistress of all things (πάντων τὴν εἱμαρμένην κυρίαν) and says that nothing befalls men unless it be in accordance with her decree.

173. But the Sadducees do away with fate, believing that it is nothing and that human actions are not achieved in accordance with her decree, but that all things lie within our own power (ἅπαντα δὲ ἐφ᾽ ἡμῖν αὐτοῖς κεῖσθαι), so that we ourselves are responsible for our well-being, while we suffer misfortune through our own thoughtlessness. Of these matters, however, I have given a more detailed account in the second book of the *Jewish History*.[3]

---

[1] According to Josephus, Judas had become the first Hasmonean high priest after the death of the apostate Alcimus (*Ant.* 12:413; cf. 12:419). The accuracy of these notices is widely disputed, for they contradict *Ant.* 20:237, and *Life* 4, according to which there was no high priest between Alcimus (= Jacimus) and Jonathan. Cf. Schwartz, ''Josephus and Nicolaus'', 162 n.16, and the literature cited there. Jonathan was appointed στρατηγός when he took up the mission of his slain brother (*Ant.* 13:6), and high priest somewhat later (13:42, 124), as the result of an internal Seleucid power struggle.

[2] Jonathan became high priest in 152 BC; Alexandra succeeded her husband to the throne in 75 BC.

[3] I have given the LCL translation (by Marcus) except for minor changes in 171.

I. *Context*

At *Ant.* 12:240, Josephus begins to make extensive use of 1 Maccabees as a source of the Hasmonean revolt and for the early years of Hasmonean rule. Book 13 of *Ant.* recounts the military and diplomatic achievements of Jonathan. Taking advantage of the uncertain leadership of the Seleucid regime, we are told, Jonathan was able to win a measure of autonomy for the nation. To enhance this autonomy, he sent envoys to Rome, to renew the alliance that his brother Judas had made with the great power of the West;[4] he also sought to strengthen ties with Sparta. This narrative takes us to *Ant.* 13:170, which corresponds to 1 Macc. 12:23. Between his paraphrase of 1 Macc 12:23 and 24, Josephus splices into his narrative our passage on the Jewish schools. *Ant.* 13:174ff., following 1 Macc. 12:24, carries on with the political history of Jonathan's time.

Commentators have long puzzled over Josephus's decision to include our passage, on the philosophical schools, in the course of a narrative to which it seems unrelated. Schwartz bluntly states, "As it stands, the function of this passage is incomprehensible".[5] At least five proposals have emerged to account for the perceived irrelevance of *Ant.* 13:171-173.

Whether Hölscher was aware of the problem is difficult to know. In any case, his sourse analysis absolved Josephus of all responsibility: it was the intermediate source, the pro-Hasmonean polemicist, who had already combined the school passage with the narrative from 1 Maccabees.[6] Hölscher's theory of intermediate sources, however, has long been out of favour.[7]

Rasp suggested that the pericope has a preparatory function for the next discussion of the Pharisees (*Ant.* 13:288f.).[8] In support of this suggestion we may note that 13:288 will refer to the Pharisees as, "one of the Jewish schools, as we have related above (ὡς καὶ ἐν τοῖς ἐπάνω δεδηλώκαμεν)".[9] This seems like a direct reference back to our passage. Nevertheless, Moore has pointed out that in the later account, which concerns John Hyracanus and the Pharisees, Josephus takes time again to discuss the Pharisees and Sadducees. And he says there that the point

---

[4] On the Hasmonean alliances with Rome, see E. M. Smallwood, *The Jews Under Roman Rule: From Pompey to Diocletian* (Leiden: E. J. Brill, 1976), 4-11.
[5] Schwartz, "Josephus and Nicolaus", 161. Cf. Moore, "Fate", 371f. and Rivkin, *Revolution*, 34f.
[6] Hölscher, "Josephus", 1973.
[7] See the Excursus to Part I above.
[8] Rasp, "Religionsparteien", 31.
[9] Marcus's translation (LCL).

of contention between these groups is not fate and free will but rather the problem of authoritative νόμιμα.[10] This difference of portrayal leads Moore to exclude a preparatory function for *Ant.* 13:171-173; he tries to solve the problem of the tension between §§ 171-173 and §§ 288-298 by assigning the former to another author.[11]

Since, however, Josephus will explicitly refer back to an "above" passage at 13:288, one ought to hesitate before denying a preparatory function to 13:171-173. Although the tension that Moore points out between the two passages cannot be ignored, two considerations help to put it in perspective. First, we have already seen in *War* that Josephus himself can describe the Pharisees in very different ways. In 1:110, he mentions only their reputation for ἀκρίβεια with respect to the νόμοι, which might sound like a very Jewish portrayal; but at 2:162f., he both recapitulates this earlier definition and continues on in the same sentence to describe the Pharisees' view of fate, a description that has been considered very "Greek".[12] We know that both kinds of descriptions are Josephus's own, because of their Josephan themes and vocabulary.[13] This demonstrable flexibility in Josephus's presentation prevents us from assuming that he could not have intentionally inserted *Ant.* 13:171-173 as a preparation for 13:288-298. Second, we shall see that the description of the Pharisee-Sadducee dispute in 13:297f. has something like footnote status; it is an afterthought that arises out of the narrative (§§ 288-296) and does not, therefore, compete with 13:171-173 as an intentional statement by Josephus about the schools. Thus we are compelled to accept Josephus's own statement that *Ant.* 13:288-298 assumes the reader's acquaintance with an earlier passage in *Ant.* and to infer that our passage is the one in question.

Moore proposes that our passage is intended as "a purely chronological notice".[14] Josephus inserted this material (taken from another source) merely in order to date the schools to about 150 BC. Rivkin, likewise, draws attention to the connective κατὰ δὲ τὸν χρόνον τοῦτον (§ 171) and remarks:

> By introducing the three *haireseis* here as fully functioning in the times of Jonathan, Josephus is alerting us to the fact that he must have had [*sic.*] some other source than I or II Maccabees recording the existence of the

---

[10] Moore, "Fate", 372.
[11] See the section on "source analysis" of this passage below.
[12] So, e.g., Moore and Maier; cf. Appendix B.
[13] See above, chapters 4 and 6.
[14] Moore, "Fate", 372.

Pharisees. Since he had found this chronological connection in some other source, Josephus felt constrained to insert this datum into his history.[15]

Although it is a dubious assumption that Josephus took his description of the Jewish schools from a source, the view that he is trying here to date the origins of the schools does seem to be a natural interpretation of the introductory phrase.

Schwartz, however, has recently contended that Josephus uses phrases like κατὰ τοῦτον τὸν χρόνον in an irresponsible way:

> True, he justifies the insertion [of Ant. 13:171-173] by introducing it by 'At this time', but this need be no more than a convenient way of linking otherwise irrelevant sources.[16]

Schwartz goes on to elaborate a highly speculative hypothesis as to Josephus's real motivation for including our passage in its present context, denying that the connective phrase κατὰ τοῦτον τὸν χρόνον has any real significance for assessing Josephus's intention. That denial, if it is being made, is remarkable and demands further investigation.

Schwartz refers the reader back to an earlier article of his, in which he had tried to show that the anti-Agrippa passages of Ant. 20 were copied by Josephus from an auxiliary source on Agrippa II.[17] The first step in his argument there had been to show that Josephus regularly uses chronological connective phrases, especially κατὰ τοῦτον τὸν χρόνον (which often introduces the anti-Agrippa passages), to splice material from an auxiliary source into a narrative that is based on a main source. Schwartz establishes this point by listing eighteen pericopae in Josephus that (a) begin with such a chronological connective phrase and (b) are believed on other grounds to come from a *Nebenquelle*.[18] Ant. 13:17ff. is one of those eighteen passages; the ''other grounds'' that Schwartz appeals to in this case are Moore's arguments for Nicolaus's authorship,[19] which we shall consider below.[20]

It is, however, difficult to see how Schwartz's observations on Josephus's use of chronological connectives to insert material from auxiliary sources (in the earlier article) justify his dismissal of a chronological intention on Josephus's part (in the later article). Surely the choice of a chronological connective, rather than some other sort,

---

[15] Rivkin, *Revolution*, 34.

[16] Schwartz, ''Josephus and Nicolaus'', 161.

[17] D. Schwartz, ''KATA TOYTON TON KAIPON: Josephus' Source on Agrippa II'', *JQR* 62 (1982), 241-268.

[18] Schwartz, ''Josephus and Nicolaus'', 246-254.

[19] Ibid., 249 and n. 27 thereto.

[20] Under ''Source Analysis''.

indicates precisely Josephus's intention to link events chronologically. One must then ask, in each case, what right Josephus had to make the connection. One cannot dismiss the validity of all the chronological connectives for the simple reason that Josephus uses them frequently.

More important still: Schwartz's assessment of Josephus's use of chronological connectives is far too narrow. For Josephus uses phrases like κατὰ τοῦτον (ἐκεῖνον/αὐτὸν) τὸν καιρόν (χρόνον) almost 100 times in his writings, and in many different situations. For example: (a) while following a single source, the Septuagint, Josephus regularly substitutes his chronological connectives for the biblical phrases καὶ ἐγένετο, ἐγενήθη ἐν ταῖς ἡμέραις, ἐγένετο δέ, or the simple καί.[21] (b) He finds these phrases especially useful when he has slightly rearranged events vis-à-vis the biblical narrative and must therefore return to an event that occurred "about that time".[22] (c) Most interesting for our purpose, Josephus frequently uses the phrases in question to connect events that he recalls from his own experience, which do not come from any written source.[23] We notice this particularly in the Life, where he links together events from his career as Galilean commander with the phrase κατὰ τοῦτον τὸν καιρόν.[24]

Thus Josephus's use of κατὰ τοῦτον τὸν χρόνον to introduce Ant. 13:171-173 should not predispose us to think that he is splicing material from an auxiliary written source into his narrative, for his usage of chronological connectives is not so restricted. Whenever he knows of two events that are chronologically related (no matter how he knows of them), he is apt to use a bridge like κατὰ τοῦτον τὸν χρόνον to connect them. Throughout, his goal is obviously chronological—he wants to date some events in relation to others.

Schwartz's own theory as to why Josephus located Ant. 13:171-173 where he did starts with the (debatable) premise that the Essenes and Sadducees were opposed to the early Hasmonean high-priesthood.[25] From this perspective, Schwartz asks why a brief passage about Essenes and Sadducees (and Pharisees) should have been placed, for no obvious reason, in the middle of a narrative about the first Hasmonean high

---

[21] Cf., e.g., Ant. 1:71; 5:352; 6:30, 213, 271, 292, 325; 7:21, 117, 298, 383; 8:328, 363; 9:7, 97, 178; 10:15, 96.

[22] Cf. Ant. 1:194; 8:176; 9:28, 258; 13:18; 16:36.

[23] War 2:595; 7:41, 54, 216; Ant. 1:174; cf. 11:32 and n.d. in the LCL edn., VI, 329.

[24] Life 112, 216, 271, 373, 398.

[25] In "Josephus and Nicolaus", 161 n. 15, Schwartz cites various scholars in support of this claim. He also appeals to the "legitimist" name of the Sadducees (>Zadok) as an indicator of their early opposition to non-Zadokite high priests. For the opposite view, that the Pharisees opposed the Hasmoneans from the start, see Wellhausen, Pharisäer und Sadducäer, 90-120.

priest. He conjectures that the passage originally stood in a larger narrative, composed by Nicolaus of Damascus, which made reference to the anti-Hasmonean stance of the Essenes and Sadducees. That original content of the passage led Josephus to include it in his narrative about Jonathan; rather ineptly, however, he deleted the material about the conflict because of his own pro-Hasmonean bias, thereby rendering the passage "utterly incomprehensible" in its present context.[25]

Problems with this hypothesis include the following. (a) Regardless of "what actually happened", Josephus's own narrative has made it clear (to this point) that Judas, not Jonathan, was the first Hasmonean high priest.[27] If Schwartz's assessment of his motives were correct, therefore, Josephus should have inserted the passage earlier, in the context of Judas's achievements. (b) The form and content of *Ant.* 13:171-173, as we presently have it, do not suggest that it was excerpted from a larger narrative on the political inclinations of the Essenes and Sadducees. What we have is a concise, balanced pericope that describes the views of the (three!) schools on a single philosophical issue. The passage gives the appearance of completeness within itself. Schwartz's theory, then, is both untenable and unnecessary.

Only L. H. Martin, it seems, has found a way to connect *Ant.* 13:171-173 thematically with its context.[28] He contends that Josephus wants to develop an "apologetic contrast" between the Hellenistic world's enslavement to εἱμαρμένη (astrologically interpreted, 13:171-173!) and Jewish submission to the πρόνοια of God (13:163f.), which submission liberates mankind from fate. As Martin notes, this view makes Josephus a Jewish counterpart to the apostle Paul.[29] I have tried to show elsewhere, however, that Martin's theory hinges on misinterpretations—both of εἱμαρμένη in Josephus and of our passage in particular.[30]

Although is it not yet possible to spell out the function of *Ant.* 13:171-173 in its context, we have made some headway already. We have seen, namely, that Josephus used the connective phrase "at about this time" to introduce our passage because he believed, or wished his readers to believe, that the Jewish schools were in existence at the time of the Hasmonean Jonathan. Whence he acquired this knowledge we do not know. Perhaps it came from Nicolaus, perhaps from Josephus's early education; perhaps it was merely a common belief in his days.

[26] Schwartz, "Josephus and Nicolaus", 161f.
[27] Cf. n. 1 above.
[28] L. H. Martin, "Josephus' use of *Heimarene* in the *Jewish Antiquities* XIII, 171-3", *Numen* 28 (1981), 127-135.
[29] Ibid., 134.
[30] See Appendix B, below.

Placing the pericope where he does, Josephus prepares the way for his next reference to the Pharisees, which comes at 13:288-298. Further ways in which the passage assists his larger narrative will become apparent in the course of the following interpretation.

II. *Key Terms*

All of the key terms in the definition of the Pharisees at *Ant.* 13:172a have already been analyzed in chapter 6 above. Αἴρεσις in Josephus means "philosophical school"; εἱμαρμένη refers to God's providential or executive aspect; and τὸ ἐφ' ἡμῖν (ἑαυτοῖς)[31] was the usual term in ethical discussion of the period for that which originates in, or depends on, the individual.

III. *Interpretation*

As with all of the Pharisee passages of *Ant.*, our interpretation of 13:172a must consider both the passage in itself and its relation to the Pharisee passages of *War*.

Ant. 13:171-173 is a self-contained unit that, taken by itself, presents a clear statement. The topic, announced in § 171, is the various views of the Jewish philosophical schools on "human actions" (ἀνθρώπινα πράγματα). The issue, we discover, is that of the causes of good and evil actions, or the relative roles of fate and human volition. It was a discussion that lay at the heart of Greek-Hellenistic ethical thought.[32] Josephus's treatment is anything but profound. He draws a lucid spectrum and locates the three schools, respectively, at the middle and either end. The Essenes attribute everything (πάντων) to fate; the Sadducees attribute everything to human volition (ἄπαντα. . . ἐφ' ἡμῖν αὐτοῖς); the Pharisees attribute some things (τινά) to the one factor and some (τινά) to the other. The vagueness of the language defies serious conceptualization; we can only conclude that Josephus's purpose is limited to that of sharp, simple schematization.

This kind of schematization has a fairly close parallel in Cicero's presentation, to his Roman readership, of the Greek philosophical schools on the very same issue of fate and free will:

---

[31] The MSS LAMWE support the inclusion of ἡμῖν. Marcus, in omitting the pronoun, presumably follows the PFV reading. It matters little, since the sequel (§ 173)— ἄπαντα δὲ ἐφ' ἡμῖν αὐτοῖς κεῖσθαι—gives the force of the phrase.

[32] See Chapter 6, above.

There were among the old philosophers two schools of thought: the one held the view that everything is determined by fate—that this fate entails a necessary force . . . . The others were of the conviction that the soul's promptings are determined by the will, without any influence from fate. Between these contending options, Chrysippus [the Stoic] wanted to arbitrate by finding a middle way. (*On Fate* 39)[33]

In a similar way Tacitus (*Annals* 6:22) reflects on the problem of fate and free will by summarizing the views of: (a) those who dismiss fate altogether from the sphere of human activity; (b) those who accept fate but also give man freedom to choose;[34] and (c) those (the majority) who attribute everything to fate, in its astrological sense.[35] To instruct the Roman world about Jewish philosophy, Josephus employs the same simple outline that Cicero and Tacitus had chosen: only the representatives of the three positions are different.

Ant. 13:171-173 serves well the apologetic purpose of *Ant.*, as Rasp and Weiss have shown.[36] We have seen that in this work Josephus tries to establish Judaism as a serious participant in the Hellenistic discussion about how one achieves εὐδαιμονία (chapter 7, above). It can only help this general argument that Josephus is able to show in 13:171-173 that the Jews possess philosophical αἱρέσεις of long standing (cf. κατὰ τοῦτον τὸν χρόνον) and that these schools concern themselves with the same fundamental issues as the Hellenistic schools.

Although the function and the sense of our passage seem clear enough, the reader is struck by two differences between its portrayal of the schools and that given in *War* 2:119-166. The first difference is structural. Of paramount interest in the *War* passage are the Essenes (2:119-161). Josephus dispenses with the Pharisees and Sadducees by contrasting their views on fate and immortality (§§ 162-165). Since the Essenes do not figure in that final comparison, he can present the Pharisees and Sadducees as polar opposites: the Pharisees affirm fate and immortality; the Sadducees deny both. In our passage, the situation is different. Josephus has chosen the single issue of fate and free will to illustrate the beliefs of the schools. He has also decided to include the

---

[33] My translation draws heavily on the German rendering by K. Bayer, *Über das Fatum*, by M. Tullius Cicero (2d. edn.; Munich: Heimeran, 1976 [1959]), *ad loc.*

[34] Groups (a) and (b), it seems generally agreed, are the Epicureans and Stoics, respectively. Cf. J. Jackson, LCL edn., p. 190 nn.1-2; also C. W. Mendell, *Tacitus: the Man and his Work* (New Haven: Yale University Press, 1957), 57f. Theiler ("Tacitus", 37) accepts the usual identification for (a) but argues (56-58, 80f.) that (b) is a Platonist view.

[35] Tacitus is apparently the first (extant) witness to have distinguished between the astrological and philosophical interpretations of fate; so Theiler, "Tacitus", 43.

[36] Rasp, "Religionsparteien", 31; H.-F. Weiss, "Pharisäismus und Hellenismus", 421-433, esp. 427f.

Essenes in the comparison. To accomplish this, he removes the Pharisees
from their polar position and replaces them with the Essenes, who now
become the "pan-heimarmenists". The Sadducees retain their position
on the extreme left[37] and the Pharisees are now given a place in the middle of the spectrum.

Intertwined with the structural change is a substantive one. Josephus
no longer has the Pharisees ascribing everything to fate, as in *War* 2, for
that is now the Essene position (πάντων τὴν εἱμαρμένην κυρίαν ἀποφαίν-
εται). The Pharisees now say that some things but not all (τινὰ καὶ οὐ
πάντα) fall within the sphere of fate and that some depend on human
volition (τινὰ δ' ἐφ' ἡμῖν ἑαυτοῖς). The phrase καὶ οὐ πάντα, which is made
redundant by the second clause, seems almost like a pointed correction
of *War* 2:263. In the earlier passage, Josephus had the Pharisees espous-
ing a Chrysippean model: although they acknowledged the key role of
human volition in moral actions, they nevertheless attributed *every* action
(πάντα, ἕκαστον) to fate. In our pericope, the Pharisees are said to
distinguish two spheres of actions: only some are caused by fate; others
depend on human will.

How to explain the development? Most commentators on the
Pharisees or on fate and free will in Josephus seem to have overlooked
the difference between *War* 2:163 and *Ant.* 13:172.[38] G. Maier notes the
problem but explains it as follows. He thinks that *War* 2:163 can be interpreted *either* in the Chrysippean sense *or* in such a way that the clause
τὸ πράττειν τὰ δίκαια καὶ μὴ κατὰ τὸ πλεῖστον ἐπὶ τοῖς ἀνθρώποις κεῖσθαι im-
poses a restriction on the preceding εἱμαρμένῃ προσάπτουσι πάντα.[39] He
suggests that Josephus deliberately left the description ambiguous so that
it could be interpreted both in the Chrysippean sense, for the benefit of
Greco-Roman readers, and in a properly Jewish sense, to the effect that
some things are in fate's power, but others depend on human choice. In
Ant. 13:172, according to Maier, Josephus has taken over another
Chrysippean portrayal of the Pharisees from his source (Nicolaus of
Damascus) and has attempted to judaize it by inserting the phrase καὶ
οὐ πάντα.[40]

I have already argued against Maier's proposal that *War* 2:163 can
plausibly be interpreted in the "Jewish" sense—i.e., as distinguishing

---

[37] Or "right", depending on one's perspective.
[38] I find no reference to the problem in, for example: Moore, "Fate"; Rasp,
"Religionsparteien"; Wächter, "Die unterschiedliche Haltung"; Rivkin, *Revolution*;
Neusner, "Josephus's Pharisees"; Pines, "A Platonistic Model"; Schwartz, "Josephus
and Nicolaus"; or Martin, *"Heimarmene"*.
[39] Maier, *freier Wille*, 13.
[40] Ibid., 14f.

between the spheres in which fate and human will are dominant;[41] on the contrary, the Pharisees there ascribe everything to fate, while at the same time acknowledging human volition. I would now suggest further that καὶ οὐ πάντα in *Ant.* 13:172 is not likely an interpolation because its removal would not alter the sense of the passage. Even without this phrase, we should have a clear statement that the Pharisees attribute some things (τινά) to fate and others (τινά) to human will. So Maier's attempt to distinguish Josephus's redaction from his source material does not resolve the tension between *War* 2:162f. and *Ant.* 13:172. One has still to explain the difference between Josephus's Chrysippean formulation of Pharisaic belief in *War* 2:163 and his distinction of spheres in *Ant.* 13:172.

It is important to realize first that the difference, although unmistakable, is not major. Both passages have the Pharisees combining fate and free will in *some* way, unlike the Sadducees and Essenes. The difference lies only in the manner in which the Pharisees are said to combine the two factors, whether by means of the Chrysippean "co-operation" model or by distinguishing the sphere of fate from that of human volition. Moreover: (a) *Ant.* 18:13 will return the Pharisees to the co-operation or fusion (κρᾶσις) model of *War* 2 and (b) at the end of our passage, Josephus refers the reader back to *War* 2:119-166 as a more adequate (ἀκριβεστέραν) account. Evidently, then, Josephus does not think that his self-contradiction is significant.

Taking into account both these observations and our earlier conclusions (in chapter 6), I submit the following proposal as a means of explaining the different portrayals of Pharisaic belief in *War* 2:162f. and *Ant.* 13:172. Josephus always becomes vague when he speaks of the relationship between fate and free will, whether he is describing his own position or that of the Pharisees. For himself, as we have seen, he insists that "it will be enough" to juxtapose the two factors, without further discussion.[42] In *War* 2:163 he gives not the slightest indication of the way in which fate "assists (βοηθεῖν) in each case". *Ant.* 18:13 looks like an attempt to say something more substantive on the issue, but the result is a notorious *crux interpretum*.[43] It fits with his general tendency that in our passage Josephus should content himself with the marvelous simplicity of the double τινά.

Nor should this resort to vagueness occasion surprise or cause the critic to belittle Josephus's philosophical talents. For the problem of the

---

[41] See Appendix B, below, and chapter 6.

[42] *Ant.* 16:398: τοῦτον μὲν οὖν τὸν λόγον (*sc.* the doctrine of the universal causality of fate), ὡς νομίζω, πρὸς ἐκεῖνον ἀρκέσει κρίνειν (or κινεῖν) ἡμῖν τε αὐτοῖς; cf. chapter 6, above.

[43] Cf. chapter 12, below.

relation between fate and free will has exercised the greatest minds of
Greek philosophy and of Christian, Jewish, and Muslim theology; the
issue survives in our own time in both philosophical and psychological
formulations. Common throughout the history of Western thought has
been the attempt to work out a model that allows for both determinism
and human responsibility. As Augustine insists, "the religious mind
chooses both, confesses both, and maintains both by the faith of
piety".[44] Josephus carves out a niche for the Jewish schools on this issue
and asserts that it is the Pharisees who take up the mediating position;
he is appropriately modest about explaining the details of the position.

If Josephus wants only to make the limited point that the Pharisees,
unlike the Sadducees and Essenes, do effect a compromise between fate
and free will, then it is probably the difference of structure between *War*
2:119-166 and *Ant* 13:171-173 that causes him to report that compromise
differently. In *War* 2, where he has only the Pharisees and Sadducees to
deal with, it lends simplicity and mnemonic value to his presentation
that he can portray the one as dogmatic and the other as skeptical on the
issues of fate and immortality. The Chrysippean language allows him to
present the Pharisees there as pan-heimarmenic—in contrast to the Sadducees, who reject fate out of hand (ἀναιροῦσιν)—while at the same time
noting their provision for human will. In *Ant.* 13:171-173, however, the
Chrysippean language is no longer useful because it would require
Josephus to present both Essenes and Pharisees as pan-heimarmenists,
which would detract from the terse clarity of the passage. Evidently,
Josephus believed that the Essenes were more suited to the pan-
heimarmenic position than were the Pharisees; so in order to preserve
the compromise position of the Pharisees, he now shunts them into the
middle of the philosophical spectrum. This requires the removal of all
πάντα-language from the description of their view, so Josephus replaces
the Chrysippean model with another, in which certain areas (τινά)
belong to fate and others belong to human volition.[45] He can do this, apparently, because the *fact* that the Pharisees effect a compromise between

---

[44] *City of God* 5:9 (trans. M. Dods). Augustine speaks of God's foreknowledge rather
than fate, because of the common astrological sense of the latter; he does accept the *fatum*
terminology, however, in its philosophical sense (5:8). Cf. also the comment of Stock
("Fate", 787) on the *Odyssey* 1:32-36, where Homer effects a compromise between fate
and free will: "Some evils, we are led to suppose, come from the gods, whereas there
are others which men bring upon themselves by their own infatuation . . . . This is a
sound judgment to which common sense responds". Cf. also Theiler, "Tacitus", 56f.
and, on Homer in general, Greene, *Moira*, 20f.
[45] In *Ant.* 18:13ff., Josephus will abandon his efforts at a point-by-point comparison
of the schools. This will allow him to return to the fusion model for the Pharisaic teaching
on fate.

fate and free will is more important for his schematic purposes than the nature of that compromise.

It is often noted that the alleged Pharisaic distinction between two spheres, one for fate and other for human will, corresponds to certain later rabbinic dicta, especially the famous maxim: "Everything is in the hands of God except the fear of God".[46] Maier goes so far as to claim that this is the truly Jewish view of fate and free will; and he uses that identification to determine the extent of Josephus's contribution to *Ant.* 13:171-173 (which, he thinks, comes essentially from Nicolaus).[47]

Although the late rabbinic parallels are in order, however, one ought to note that Josephus's language is vague enough to match a host of Greek-Hellenistic parallels as well. We need only mention Plato's Myth of Er, in which one role is assigned to human choice (the selection of a life-pattern) and another to fate (the confirmation and execution of the life-pattern).[48] Many other writers, from Homer to Aristotle to various Platonists,[49] could be said to ascribe "some things to fate and others to human will". Perhaps the closest parallel to the Pharisaic view described by Josephus is Epiphanius's interpretation of the position held by Zeno, the founder of Stoicism. The latter, we are told, considered τὰς δὲ αἰτίας τῶν πραγμάτων πῇ μὲν ἐφ' ἡμῖν, πῇ δὲ οὐκ ἐφ' ἡμῖν.[50] The verbal parallels with our passage—πράγματα (§ 171), ἐφ' ἡμῖν, αἰτία (§ 173)—and the general similarity of sense are obvious. Once again we see, then, that Josephus is not describing the Pharisees in special, intramural Jewish language. He portrays them in terms that his Hellenistic readers will easily understand.

IV. *Source Analysis*

It has often been claimed that *Ant.* 13:171-173 comes from someone other than Josephus. Hölscher thought that it originated in Jewish tradition and that it was taken over by the pro-Hasmonean polemicist who authored almost the entire second half of *Ant.*, whom Josephus merely

---

[46] b.Niddah 16b; b.Ber. 33a.

[47] Maier, *freier Wille*, 13f., 15.

[48] *Republic* 619c.; cf. chapter 6, above, and Greene, *Moira*, 313f.

[49] For Homer, see n. 44 above. I mention Aristotle because, although he is famous for his emphasis on human responsibility (*NE* 3.315; cf. Windelband, *History of Philosophy*, 192; Greene, *Moira*, 321ff.) and although he eschews the term εἱμαρμένη (Gundel, "Heimarmene", 2627), he does recognize certain areas of life that come about by necessity (ἀνάγκη) and are unalterable by human volition (*NE* 3.3.3-6; 3 5.14f.). Cf. chapter 6, above. On the Platonists, see Theiler, "Tacitus", 67ff.

[50] *Against Heresies* 2.3.9 (= Diels, *Doxagraphi Graeci*, 592, 24-26) cited in Greene, *Moira*, 350. One might also consider Aetius's comparison of the Stoics with Plato; they both, he says, give place to εἱμαρμένη and ἡ παρ' ἡμᾶς αἰτία (*SVF* II, 976); cf. Greene, 350.

copied.[51] A more common view attributes the passage to Nicolaus of Damascus.[52] In this final section we shall assess the grounds for attributing our passage to someone other than Josephus.

The case for Nicolaus's authorship of *Ant.* 13:171-173 was made by G. F. Moore, who offered four lines of evidence. His chief point, which he adduced for all of the school passages, was that the author of *Ant.* 13:171-173 uses εἱμαρμένη in a way that is "un-Jewish" and sounds rather Stoic.[53] We may respond to this point: (a) that the broad question of the influence of Hellenistic thought on Palestinian Judaism is still *sub judice*;[54] (b) that the use of εἱμαρμένη in the school passages matches Josephus's own usage (Josephus the Jew does not hesitate to employ the term and even hints at his own sympathy with Stoic views);[55] and (c) that Josephus's use of Hellenistic categories to describe Judaism, regardless of its historical justification, fits squarely with his apologetic-didactic purpose; he consistently uses terms in ways that will be intelligible to his readers, as we have seen with νόμος, εὐσέβεια, ἀκρίβεια, αἵρεσις, δικαιοσύνη, and τὸ ἐφ' ἡμῖν, among others.[56] His use of εἱμαρμένη fits this pattern perfectly.

Moore's other three reasons for assigning *Ant.* 13:171-173 to Nicolaus may be quoted *en bloc*, as he summarizes them:

> I have pointed out that it is irrelevant in its present context; that it mentions no other peculiarities of the sects than their different doctrines about Fate; and that it makes the Essenes thoroughgoing fatalists, of which there is in Josephus elsewhere no suggestion. All these things would be explicable enough in a general historian in Herod's time [?], who was trying to give his readers a brief account of Jewish sects in terms of current Greek philosophical controversies.[57]

Moore's first comment ignores his own acknowledgement, noted above, that the passage is rescued from irrelevance to "its present context" by

---

[51] Hölscher, "Josephus", 1973. He gives no reason for the specific attribution of this passage to Jewish tradition.

[52] Cf. Moore, "Fate", 383; Marcus, LCL edn., VII, 311 n.*f.*; LeMoyne, *Les Sadducéens*, 38; Maier, *freier Wille*, 14; Schwartz, "Josephus and Nicolaus", 161f.

[53] Moore, "Fate", 375ff.; cf. my fuller discussion of Moore on the schools in Appendix B, below.

[54] Cf. esp. Lieberman, *Greek in Jewish Palestine*; idem, *Hellenism in Jewish Palestine*; M. Smith, "Palestinian Judaism in the First Century"; Hengel, *Judaism and Hellenism*; H. A. Fischel, "Story and History: Observations on Greco-Roman Rhetoric and Pharisaism", in *American Oriental Society— Middle West Branch: Semi Centennial Volume*, ed. D. Siñor (Bloomington-London: Indiana University Press, 1969), 59-88; and Weiss, "Pharisäismus und Hellenismus", 427f.

[55] Cf. *Ant* 16:397f. and chapter 6, above; also *Life* 12c and *Ag.Ap.* 2:168 on his inclination toward Stoicism.

[56] See chapter 6, above; also Attridge, *Interpretation*, 145-176.

[57] Moore, "Fate", 384.

the chronological connective phrase: the author includes it in order to date the emergence of the schools. And in any case, *Ant.* 13:171 occurs in the middle of Josephus's paraphrase of 1 Maccabees 12. However irrevelant it may appear, therefore, we can only blame (or credit) Josephus himself for its present location.[58] One can hardly exploit that apparent irrelevance, which was caused by Josephus, as an argument against Josephus's authorship.

The significance of Moore's second observation, that the schools are compared here on only one issue, is hard to see. In 13:297-298 Josephus will compare the Pharisees and Sadducees on the single issue of the νόμιμα. Does this datum also speak for Nicolaus's authorship? Nicolaus, as we have seen,[59] lived at least twenty years of his adult life in Jerusalem and probably knew a good deal about the Pharisees. As Moore himself remarks in a footnote, "Nicolaus was not unacquainted with other characteristics of the Pharisees as a party".[60] And we know that the particular issue in question here—the role of fate in human affairs—was one to which Josephus had devoted some thought.[61] How, then, does the fact that the schools are compared on the single issue of fate and free will suggest that Nicolaus rather than Josephus was the author of *Ant.* 13:171-173? If Josephus was the author, the choice of a single issue is easily explained by narrative constraints. He wanted to date the Jewish schools, in preparation for 13:288-298, but he had to keep this interruption of his political history as brief as possible. He therefore chose only one topic, whose philosophical significance would be evident to the reader, on which to compare the schools.

Moore's final claim, that only *Ant.* 13:172 describes the Essenes as pan-heimarmenic, is once again inaccurate. *Ant.* 18:18 will tell us that "The doctrine of the Essenes is wont to leave everything in the hands of God (θεῷ καταλείπειν. . . τὰ πάντα).[62] Given that it is characteristic of Josephus to use θεός and εἱμαρμένη interchangeably,[63] this passage provides a close parallel to our own. Even if *Ant.* 13:172 were unique, it would not follow that this information ought to be ascribed to someone other than Josephus.

In short: it is unclear how any of the points enumerated by Moore speaks either against Josephan authorship of *Ant.* 13:171-173 or for that

---

[58] That is, discounting Hölscher's theory of an intermediate source; cf. the excursus to Part I.
[59] Chapter 6, n. 234.
[60] Moore, "Fate", 384 n. 56.
[61] Cf., e.g., *Ant.* 8:419f.; 16:395ff. and chapter 6, above.
[62] Feldman's translation, LCL edn.
[63] Cf. chapter 6, above.

of a "general historian in Herod's time". Moore is doubtless correct in his judgement that the author of this pericope "was trying to give his readers a brief account of Jewish sects in terms of current Greek philosophical controversies". But that author was Josephus.

In view of their shared themes and vocabulary, it would seem most reasonable to assign all three "school passages" in Josephus (*War* 2:162-166; *Ant.* 13:171-173; 18:11-25) to the same author. All three present the Pharisees, Sadducees, and Essenes as philosophical schools concerned with philosophical issues of the day, especially with the causes of good and evil in human actions. These general similarities are enhanced by many parallels of vocabulary. Common to all three are the essential terms of the debate: εἱμαρμένη, τὰ πάντα, and some form of τὸ ἐφ' ἡμῖν. Compare, especially, *War* 2 and *Ant.* 13 on the Sadducees:

War 2:164f.	*Ant.* 13:173
Σαδδουκαῖοι δέ, . . .τὴν μὲν εἱμαρμένην παντάπασιν ἀναιροῦσιν . . . . φασὶν δ' ἐπ' ἀνθρώπων ἐκλογῇ	Σαδδουκαῖοι δὲ τὴν μὲν εἱμαρμένην ἀναιροῦσιν, οὐδὲν εἶναι ταύτην ἀξιοῦντες, οὐδὲ κατ' αὐτὴν τὰ ἀνθρώπινα τέλος λαμβάνειν, ἅπαντα δὲ ἐφ' ἡμῖν αὐτοῖς κεῖσθαι
τό τε καλὸν καὶ τὸ κακὸν προκεῖσθαι καὶ κατὰ γνώμην ἑκάστου τούτων ἑκάτερον προσιέναι	ὡς καὶ τῶν ἀγαθῶν αἰτίους ἡμᾶς αὐτοὺς γινομένους καὶ τὰ χείρω παρὰ τὴν ἡμετέραν ἀβουλίαν λαμβάνοντας

It is incredible that source critics could assign these two descriptions to different authors.[64] The thought-world is the same in both, although exact verbal agreement is limited. The fact that we have two presentations of the same content, in similar language but differently constructed, speaks for Josephan authorship; it fits with his usual practice in *Ant.* 13-14 of reformulating the narrative of *War*.[65] The unity of the school passages would seem to exclude the theories of both Hölscher and Schwartz, who assign *War* 2:162-166 to Josephus himself and *Ant.* 13:171-173 to someone else.

Having established the unity of the school passages,[66] we may proceed to one further point. One of those passages (*War* 2:162-166) incorporates, along with its discussion of philosophical issues, a statement about the Pharisees' reputation for ἀκρίβεια with respect to the laws (2:162). Since this statement, on the one hand, is part and parcel of the school passage and since, on the other hand, it closely parallels

---

[64] Hölscher ("Josephus", 1973) assigns our passage to Jewish tradition, taken over by the polemicist, but *War* 2:162-166 to Josephus himself ("Josephus", 1999 n.*). Schwartz ("Josephus and Nicolaus", 162f.) likewise assigns *War* 2:162-166 to Josephus, but he thinks that our passage comes from Nicolaus.

[65] Cf. Niese, *HZ*, 223f; Cohen, *Josephus*, 50f.

[66] Cf. also the evidence of Maier, *freier Wille*, 7-10.

Josephus's own statements in *War* 1:110 and *Life* 191 (and, indeed, Josephus's ἀκρίβεια-theme in general), one is bound to conclude that Josephus also wrote the school passages.

Summary and Conclusion

Josephus wrote and situated *Ant.* 13:171-173 in such a way that it would serve the apologetic-didactic interests of *Ant.* He wanted his readers to know that the Jews had philosophical schools, that these schools had existed for a long time, and that they occupied themselves largely with that area in which metaphysics interfaces with ethics, viz.: the respective roles of fate and human volition as causes of human actions. Of the three schools, he says, the Pharisees represent the middle position on the spectrum: they attribute certain actions to fate and others to human will. In Hellenistic philosophy, the middle position was taken by Platonists and Stoics.

That the Pharisees give place to both fate and human volition, unlike the Sadducees, is a point made in both *War* 2:163 and our passage. The nature of the compromise is explained differently in the two places, but that disparity seems to be a function of different structures: *Ant.* 13:171-173 must make room for the Essenes. That Josephus does not intend our passage as a correction of *War* 2 is made clear by: (a) his referral of the reader back to the ἀκριβεστέραν δήλωσιν ἐν τῇ δευτέρᾳ βίβλῳ τῆς Ἰουδαικῆς πραγματείας; (b) his close reproduction here of the Sadducean position as given in *War* 2:164f.; and (c) the fact that in *Ant.* 18:13 he will return to the ''cooperation'' model of fate and free will that he had given in *War* 2. Josephus is evidently committed only to the proposition that the Pharisees do combine fate and free will; the way in which they combine these factors he can explain differently, depending on the context.

If we ask, finally, what *Ant.* 13:172a reveals about Josephus's attitude toward the Pharisees, we shall have to answer: very little. Writing for a Gentile audience, he wants only to show that the Jews *have* philosophical schools. The tone of his portrayal of all three schools, therefore, is positive. If Josephus's favour can be inferred from a school's recognition of fate's importance (cf. *Ant.* 10:277ff.), then the Essenes are his favourites, for they make fate the κυρία of all things. If Josephus devotes the most space to his favourite school, or has them duly emphasize the Law's teaching on human responsibility (cf. *Ant.* 16:398ff.), then the Sadducees are his favourites. If, finally, he gives his favourite school first place in the discussion, or attributes to them the virtue of moderation, then the Pharisees have his support. And we have seen (chapter 6) that the Pharisaic juxtaposition of fate and free will in fact comes closest to Josephus's own view of the matter. But the pericope under discussion, in keeping with its context and function, presents all three schools (even the Sadducees!) in a favourable or at least neutral light.

CHAPTER NINE

ANT. 13:288-298: THE PHARISEES AND JOHN HYRCANUS

Of all of Josephus's descriptions of the Pharisees, his story of the rupture between them and John Hyrcanus is perhaps the most controversial. Predictably, most of the learned controversy relates to the historical question: Did it really happen? Josephus's detractors range all the way from Wellhausen, who claimed that the Pharisees were opposed to the Hasmoneans from the outset,[1] to C. Rabin, who argues that the Pharisees and Hasmoneans never had serious differences.[2] Several commentators, following a rabbinic account, connect the episode with Alexander Janneus rather than John Hyrcanus.[3] And even those who accept Josephus's allegation that there was a rift between the Pharisees and John Hyrcanus often dismiss his explanation of it.[4] But that is the historical question.

Josephus's narrative aims in *Ant.* 13:288-298 have received comparatively scant attention. Critics have usually confined their interest to two aspects of the literary question, namely, (a) the problem of sources and (b) the interpretation of 13:297f., on the distinctive Pharisaic νόμιμα. Both issues will be important for this study, but we shall also need to understand the story within the context of *Ant.* and of Josephus's larger vision of things.

In view of the unusual significance of source criticism for the interpretation of *Ant.* 13:288-298, it will be necessary in this chapter to rework our usual format. The distinction of sources must here become an integral part of the interpretive effort. After a consideration of the context, we shall proceed to discuss the literary problems of our passage and their usual solutions. I intend to show that a reasonably secure verdict on the source question is within our reach and that this verdict has clear implications for Josephus's view of the Pharisees. A final section will deal with the famous "footnote" on the Pharisaic νόμιμα (§§ 297f.).

---

[1] Wellhausen, *Pharisäer*, 90ff.

[2] Rabin, "Alexander Janneus and the Pharisees", *JJS* 7 (1956), 5ff.

[3] J. Friedlander, "The Rupture Between Alexander Jannai and the Pharisees", *JQR* n.s. 4 (1913-1914), 443ff.; Alon, *Jews*, 7ff.; M. J. Geller, "Alexander Jannaeus and the Pharisees' Rift", *JJS* 30 (1979), 203ff. These scholars prefer the account in b. Kaddushin 66a.

[4] E.g., Herford, *Pharisees*, 29ff.; Dubnow, *Weltgeschichte*, II, 148.

I. *Context*

At *Ant.* 13:214 (= 1 Macc. 13:42)[5], Josephus gives up his use of 1 Maccabees as a source for the history of the Hasmonean period. From then on, he reverts to *War* itself[6] and/or to the sources that he had used for *War* 1-2 (especially Nicolaus);[7] this material he supplements with various kinds of new information.[8] For the tenure of John Hyrcanus, Josephus reproduces *War* 1:56-66 but stretches it into a narrative that is about six times as long (*Ant.* 13:230-287), as the table below demonstrates. Where *Ant.* parallels *War*, the reproduction is more or less exact with respect to content but the formulation is new.[9]

WAR AND *ANTIQUITIES* ON THE REIGN OF JOHN HYRCANUS

War 1:56-66		*Ant.* 13:230-287
(a) 1:56-61a	Hyrcanus's attempt to free his mother and brothers at Dagon; attack by Antiochus Sidetes.	13:230-237a
	Dealings with Antiochus Sidetes (This expansion drastically alters the sense of *War* 1:61f.)	13:237b-248, 250-253
(b) 1:61b	Hyrcanus opens David's tomb, to bribe Antiochus (*War*)[10] or to raise a mercenary army (*Ant.*).	13:249
(c) 1:62-63	Hyrcanus's campaigns in Idumea and Samaria.	13:254-257a
	Hyrcanus judaizes Idumea.	13:257b-258
	He renews friendship with Rome.	13:267-274
	Summary of relations between Hyrcanus and various Seleucid rulers.	13:267-274

---

[5] He has not, however, exhausted 1 Maccabees as we know it and this raises the question whether the version that he knew was defective or whether he had some other motive for leaving his source prematurely. Cf. Hölscher, "Josephus", 1951 n. + ; Thackeray, *Josephus*, 86; and Marcus, LCL edn., VII, 334f. n. *d.*

[6] So the later Niese, "Historiker", 223f.; cf. S. J. D. Cohen, *Josephus*, 50f.

[7] So Destinon, *Quellen*, 11f.

[8] Cf., e.g. H. Bloch, *Quellen*, 90ff.; Destinon, *Quellen*, 19f.; Niese, *HZ*, 220f.; Hölscher, "Josephus", 1973ff.

[9] We observed the same phenomenon in the case of *Ant.* 13:173 (on the Sadducees), *vis-à-vis War* 2:162.

[10] As also at *Ant.* 7:393.

(d) 1:64-65a	Hyrcanus besieges the city of Samaria.	13:275-277
	Expansion of the Samaritan episode.	13:275-277
(e) 1:65b	Hyrcanus captures and razes Samaria.	13:281
	Legend about Hyrcanus.	13:282-283
	Note on the Jews of Alexandria, Egypt and Cyprus (from Strabo).	13:284-287

Although the new material in *Ant.* 13:230-277 contradicts the sense of *War* in one notable case,[11] Josephus manages on the whole to maintain the sense of the earlier account. Just as *War* 1:56-66 serves to document the "prosperous fortunes" (τὰς εὐπραγίας) of Hyrcanus (1:67-69), whose rule preceded the decline of the Hasmonean dynasty (1:69), so also *Ant.* 13:230ff. climaxes with a discussion of this high priest's εὐπραγία, which his sons will never recapture (13:288, 299f.). But this brings us to our passage, *Ant.* 13:288-298.

The story of the rift between John Hyrcanus and the Pharisees has no parallel in *War*. It is one of the new elements that Josephus introduces in *Ant.* to fill out *War*'s account of Hyrcanus's tenure. In keeping with his usual practice in *Ant.* 13 (see table above) Josephus splices the whole story of the rift into what is, at *War* 1:67-69, his concluding paragraph on Hyrcanus. The following comparison between that paragraph and the material surrounding our pericope illuminates Josephus's procedure:

War 1:67-69

67. πρὸς δὲ τὰς εὐπραγίας αὐτοῦ τε Ἰωάννου καὶ τῶν παίδων φθόνος ἐγείρει στάσιν τῶν ἐπιχωρίων μέχρι καὶ πρὸς φανερὸν πόλεμον ἐκριπισθέντες ἡττῶνται.

68. τὸ λοιπὸν δ' ἐπιβιοὺς ἐν εὐδαιμονίᾳ Ἰωάννης καὶ τὰ κατὰ τὴν ἀρχὴν κάλλιστα διοικήσας ἑνὶ καὶ τριάκοντα ὅλοις ἔτεσιν ἐπὶ πέντε υἱοῖς τελευτᾷ, τρία γοῦν τὰ κρατιστεύοντα μόνος εἶχεν, τήν τε ἀρχὴν τοῦ ἔθνους καὶ τὴν ἀρχιερωσύνην καὶ προφητείαν.
69. . . . ὧν τὴν καταστροφὴν ἄξιον ἀφηγέσασθαι, παρ' ὅσον τῆς πατρῴας εὐδαιμονίας ἀπέκλιναν.

Ant. 13:288-300

288. Ὑρκανῷ δὲ φθόνον ἐκίνησε παρὰ τῶν Ἰουδαίων ἥ τε αὐτοῦ καὶ τῶν υἱῶν εὐπραγία.

[Insert (289-298): the Pharisees and Hyrcanus]

299. Ὑρκανὸς δὲ παύσας τὴν στάσιν καὶ μετ' αὐτὴν βιώσας εὐδαιμόνως, καὶ τὴν ἀρχὴν διοικησάμενος τὸν ἄριστον τρόπον ἔτεσιν ἑνὶ καὶ τριάκοντα, τελευτᾷ καταλιπὼν υἱοὺς πέντε, τριῶν τῶν μεγίστων ἄξιος ἀρχῆς τοῦ ἔθνους, καὶ τῆς ἀρχιερατικῆς τιμῆς καὶ προφητείας.
300 . . . ὧν τὴν καταστροφὴν εἰς τὸ πάθειν ὅσον τῆς τοῦ πατρὸς ὑπέβησαν εὐτυχίας ἄξιον ἀφηγήσασθαι

---

[11] That is, in *Ant.* 13:237b ff., on Antiochus Sidetes; cf. *War* 1:61.

So Josephus has inserted the story of John Hyrcanus's break with the Pharisees into a narrative that is indistinguishable from *War* 1:67-69. This is confirmed by *Ant.*13:299, which has Hyrcanus quelling a στάσις that is not mentioned in *Ant.* but only in the *War* parallel (1:67).[12]

Our passage falls, then, in a context in which Josephus wants to illustrate the successes of John Hyrcanus. The εὐπραγία motif is taken over from *War* and all of the other supplementary material in this part of *Ant.* 13 seems to contribute to it. We now proceed to examine the story of Hyrcanus and the Pharisees, to determine its meaning and its function in the narrative.

II. *Literary Problems and Solutions*

A. *Topic Paragraph*

288. As for Hyrcanus, his own success (εὐπραγία) and that of his sons aroused jealousy (φθόνον ἐκίνησε) among the Jews; the Pharisees, who are one of the Jewish schools, as we have explained above, were especially hostile toward him (μάλιστα δὲ οἱ Φαρισαῖοι κακῶς πρὸς αὐτὸν εἶχον). Their power with the populace is such that, even when they speak against a king and against a high priest, they are immediately credited! (τοσαύτην δὲ ἔχουσι τὴν ἰσχὺν παρὰ τῷ πλήθει ὡς καὶ κατὰ βασιλέως τι λέγοντες καὶ κατ' ἀρχιερέως εὐθὺς πιστεύεσθαι.)

B. *Body of the Passage*

(i) 289-290a. Now Hyrcanus was also one of their disciples (μαθητής) and he was greatly loved (σφόδρα ἠγαπᾶτο) by them. Accordingly, he invited them to a feast and entertained them hospitably. When he saw how delighted (σφόδρα ἡδομένους) they were, he began to speak with them along the following lines. They knew, he said, of his desire to be righteous (εἶναι δίκαιον) and to do all things so as to please God and them (for the Pharisees advocate a certain way of life [οἱ γὰρ Φαρισαῖοι φιλοσοφοῦσιν]); nevertheless, he requested that, if they should notice him doing anything wrong and veering from the path of righteousness (τῆς ὁδοῦ τῆς δικαίας ἐκτρεπόμενον), they were to lead him back (ἐπανάγειν) and restore him (ἐπανορθοῦν) to it.

(ii) 290-292. Now the Pharisees attested to his consummate virtue and he was pleased by their compliments, but one of the guests (τις τῶν κατα-κειμένων), by the name of Eleazar, who was malicious by nature and revelled in discord, said, "Since you asked to know the truth, if you

[12] Cf. Schwartz, "Josephus and Nicolaus", 158f.

want 'to be righteous' (εἶναι δίκαιον), then relinquish the high priesthood and be satisfied with ruling the people'' (τὸ ἄρχειν τοῦ λαοῦ).
When Hyrcanus asked him the reason why he should relinquish the
high priesthood he replied, ''because we hear from the elders that
your mother was a captive in the reign of Antiochus Epiphanes''. But
the story was false. Hyrcanus became furious with the man and the
Pharisees were all very angry (καὶ πάντες δ' οἱ Φαρισαῖοι σφοδρῶς
ἠγανάκτησαν).

(iii) 293-296. Then someone from the school (αἵρεσις) of the Sadducees,
who espouse a view opposed to that of the Pharisees (οἱ τὴν ἐναντίαν
τοῖς Φαρισαίοις προαίρεσιν ἔχουσιν), a certain Jonathan, who was
among the close friends of Hyrcanus, began to say that Eleazar had
uttered his slanders in agreement with the collective opinion of all the
Pharisees (τῇ κοινῇ πάντων Φαρισαίων γνώμῃ). And this would become
clear to him, Jonathan said, if he asked them what punishment was
appropriate for what had been said. When Hyrcanus asked the Pharisees what they considered a worthy punishment (for he would be persuaded that the slanders had not been made with their approval, he
said, if they advocated punishing Eleazar with a commensurate
penalty), they proposed lashes and chains; for it did not seem right
to punish someone with death on account of verbal abuse and, in any
case, the Pharisees are naturally merciful in the matter of punishments (φύσει πρὸς τὰς κολάσεις ἐπιεικῶς ἔχουσιν οἱ Φαρισαῖοι). At this
response, Hyrcanus became very angry and assumed (ἐνόμισεν) that
the man had slandered him with their approval. Jonathan exacer-
bated his anger greatly and achieved the following result: he induced
Hyrcanus to join the party of the Sadducees, to abandon the
Pharisees, to repeal the ordinances that they had established among
the people (τὰ τε ὑπ' αὐτῶν κατασταθέντα νόμιμα τῇ δήμῳ καταλύσαι),
and to punish those who observed these ordinances. This is the
reason, then (οὖν ἐντεῦθεν), that hatred developed among the populace
toward him and his sons. But we shall speak of these matters below.

C. *Footnote: the Pharisaic Νόμιμα*

297-298. I want to explain here that the Pharisees passed on to the
people certain ordinances from a succession of fathers, which are not
written down in the laws of Moses. For this reason the party of the
Sadducees dismisses these ordinances, averring that one need only
recognize the written ordinances, whereas those from the tradition of
the fathers need not be observed. Conflicts and major differences
developed between the two groups over these matters. The Sadducees

persuade only the wealthy, however, and have no popular following, whereas the Pharisees have the support of the populace. But these two groups and also the Essenes have been described with detailed accuracy in the second book of my *Judaica*.

(νῦν δὲ δηλῶσαι βούλομαι ὅτι νόμιμα τινὰ παρέδοσαν τῷ δήμῳ οἱ Φαρισαῖοι ἐκ πατέρων διαδοχῆς, ἅπερ οὐκ ἀναγέγραπται ἐν τοῖς Μωυσέος νόμοις, καὶ διὰ τοῦτο ταῦτα τὸ τῶν Σαδδουκαίων γένος ἐκβάλλει, λέγον ἐκεῖνα δεῖν ἡγεῖσθαι νόμιμα τὰ γεγραμμένα, τὰ δ' ἐκ παραδόσεως τῶν πατέρων μὴ τηρεῖν. καὶ περὶ τούτων ζητήσεις αὐτοῖς καὶ διαφορὰς γινέσθαι συνέβαινε μεγάλας, τῶν δὲ Σαδδουκαίων τοὺς εὐπόρους μόνον πειθόντων τὸ δὲ δημοτικὸν οὐκ ἐπόμενον αὐτοῖς ἐχόντων, τῶν δὲ Φαρισαίων τὸ πλῆθος σύμμαχον ἐχόντων.)

As it stands in its present context this story creates several well-known problems for the interpreter.

A. Although Josephus casually refers the reader to both *Ant.* 13:171-173 (§ 288) and the "precise" account in *War* 2:119-166 (§ 298), he discusses here a major difference between the Pharisees and Sadducees that the earlier passages did not mention at all.[13]

B. The topic paragraph (§ 288) describes an initial hostility between Hyrcanus and the Pharisees that the sequel (§§ 289-296) fails to demonstrate. On the contrary, the Pharisees appear throughout as friends of the high priest. On the basis of § 288, the reader expects to see evidence of Pharisaic envy and hatred but instead it turns out that they love Hyrcanus greatly (§ 289), they praise his virtue (§ 290), and they *all* become indignant when someone speaks against him (§ 292).[14] The Eleazar who utters the slanders is not identified as a Pharisee but merely as "one of the guests".[15] And Hyrcanus only abandons the Pharisees in the end as a result of the machinations of his Sadducean friend.[16]

C. The story provides no evidence, as the topic paragraph leads us to expect, of the Pharisees' speaking against a public figure and finding automatic support among the people. Their public following is illustrated by the popular outcry that follows the annulment of their νόμιμα (§ 296) but we see nothing of their alleged impertinence. It is Hyrcanus who takes the initiative against the Pharisees.[17]

---

[13] Cf. G. F. Moore, "Fate", 372.

[14] Schwartz, "Josephus and Nicolaus", 158f.

[15] So Rivkin, *Revolution*, 40. The phrase that describes Eleazar is τις τῶν κατακειμένων, "one of those at table" (13:290). Hölscher, however, views him as a Pharisee ("Josephus", 1975 n.*).

[16] Cf. Rivkin, *Revolution*, 40, and Schwartz, "Josephus and Nicolaus", 158.

[17] Cf. Rivkin, *Revolution*, 40.

D. Finally, § 288 agrees with *War* 1:67 in attributing the popular hatred of Hyrcanus to the Jews' *envy* (φθόνος) of his success. The story concludes, however (§ 296), by flatly contradicting that notice. The populace comes to hate Hyrcanus because he abolished the much-loved Pharisaic ordinances. Since the story makes it clear that this occurred only because of a misunderstanding, the pro-Pharisaic masses appear as the victims of an injustice and not as "envious" of their leader's successes.

To summarize: in addition to the obvious difference in content between *Ant.* 13:297-298 and the other Pharisee-Sadducee comparisons in Josephus, the reader is struck by several tensions within our passage itself. These all hinge on the dissonance between the topic paragraph (§ 288) and the story that it introduces (§§ 289-296). The topic paragraph is favourable toward Hyrcanus but is markedly anti-Pharisaic,[18] whereas the actual story is favourable toward the Pharisees, the people, and Hyrcanus; only the malicious Eleazar and the Sadducee Jonathan are villains.[19]

It has been rightly understood by scholars who have broached these problems that their solution is to be sought in Josephus's (or an intermediate author's) imperfect redactions of disparate sources. A virtual consensus obtains that the main body of the story (§§ 189-296) originated in Jewish tradition, whether that tradition be understood as a chronicle of Hyrcanus's reign,[20] an extensive written narrative,[21] or an orally transmitted legend.[22] The Jewish character of the tradition is usually surmised from (a) its favourable presentation of both Hyrcanus and the Pharisees[23] and (b) a parallel story in the Babylonian Talmud, which tells in similar terms of a break between Alexander Jannaeus and the Pharisees.[24]

We are now able to confirm the traditional Jewish provenance of *Ant.* 13:289-296 with two further observations.

(c) First, within the short space of 13:288-291, the adjective δίκαιος occurs three times. We have observed above[25] that Josephus uses forms of this word hundreds of times but that it generally lacks any of the specially Jewish, covenantal nuances of צדק. On the contrary, Josephus uses the word group in its ordinary Hellenistic sense, to mean "justice";

---

[18] Schwartz, "Josephus and Nicolaus", 158.
[19] Rivkin, *Revolution*, 40.
[20] H. Bloch, *Quellen*, 90-92.
[21] Destinon, *Quellen*, 41-44.
[22] Hölscher, "Josephus", 1974f. Cf. also Niese, "Historiker", 221.
[23] E.g., H. Bloch, *Quellen*, 90, and Schwartz, "Josephus and Nicolaus", 158.
[24] The rabbinic story is in b. Kaddushin 66a.
[25] Chapter 6, above.

and this usage is reinforced by his omission of covenant themes from his biblical paraphrase.[26] In the passage before us, however, δίκαιος has precisely the covenantal sense of pleasing God by fulfilling his Law. Thus Hyrcanus claims that he wants εἶναι δίκαιον καὶ πάντα ποιοῦντα ἐξ ὧν ἀρέσειεν ἂν τῷ θεῷ (§ 289). Eleazar throws his claim back at him (§ 291) with the remark that in order "to be righteous" Hyrcanus would need to give up the high priesthood; for his mother's alleged captivity disqualifies him (according to the Law)[27] from serving as high priest. The sense of δίκαιος here is not that of simply "doing the right thing by one's neighbour", as with Josephus elsewhere; it has rather the biblical-Jewish force of "pleasing God by keeping his commandments".

(d) The occurrence of δίκαιος in our passage is especially noteworthy because the adjective qualifies ὁδός. Hyrcanus expresses his wish not to stray from "the righteous path" (τῆς ὁδοῦ τῆς δικαίας). But it is well known that the use of "way" (דרך) as a metaphor for the course of one's life is biblical.[28]

For example, Moses is instructed by Jethro (Ex. 18:20):

> And you shall teach them the statutes (את־החקים) and the decisions and make them know the way in which they must walk (את־דרך ילכו בה) and what they must do.[29]

In Psalm 119, a panegyric on the Law, the psalmist often prays that his "way" will please God, inasmuch as he fulfills the Law. The theme is announced in 119:1:

> Blessed are those whose way is blameless,
> אשרי תמימי־דרך
> who walk in the law of the Lord![30]
> ההלכים בתורת יהוה

Although there are many possible ways, it is the way of obedience, or the "righteous path", that one ought to seek.[31] In the LXX, the phrase ἡ ὁδὸς τῆς δικαιοσύνης, which is very close to our ἡ ὁδὸς ἡ δικαία, occurs several times.[32] We may note, finally, that the idea of obedience to God's law as a "way" stands behind the rabbinic term הלכה. Thus the

---

[26] Cf. Attridge, *Interpretation*, 79ff.

[27] Lev. 21:14f.; the assumption was that a captive woman had been raped; cf. *Ag.Ap.* 1:35.

[28] Cf. Michaelis, "ὁδός", *TDNT*, V, esp. 48ff.

[29] RSV trans. Cf. also Ex. 32:8; Deut. 5:23; 1 Sam. 12:23; 22:22; Prov. 16:7; Jer. 7:28.

[30] RSV trans. Cf. also Ps. 119:5, 9, 10, 15, 29, 32, 35, 59, 101, 105, 128, 133.

[31] Cf. Ps. 37:5; Prov. 12:28.

[32] Prov. 12:28; 21:16, 21; Job 24:13; Mt. 21:32. The familiar Ps. 23:3 (LXX Ps. 22:3) has ἐπὶ τρίβους δικαιοσύνης.

"righteous way" to which Hyrcanus aspires is a biblical-Jewish conception.

Notice in particular the shepherd imagery that Hyrcanus evokes when he requests that the Pharisees restore him if he should stray (ἐκτρέπομαι) from the righteous path. One thinks easily of the sheep metaphor in (deutero-) Isaiah, "All we like sheep have *gone astray*; we have turned every one to his own *way*" (53:6),[33] or perhaps again of Psalms 23 and 119.[34] The imagery is biblical and Palestinian.[35] Outside of our passage, Josephus uses ὁδός some 182 times, but practically always in a literal, mundane sense.[36] It will suffice to quote Michaelis's contrast between biblical usage, on the one hand, and Josephan usage on the other. Of the former he remarks, "The fig[urative] use of ὁδός is very common in all parts of the LXX, including the apocrypha".[37] Of the latter he notes, "In Joseph[us], as is to be expected in a historian, ὁδός is always used in the lit[eral] sense."[38]

Since the connotations of δίκαιος and ὁδός in *Ant.* 13:239-296 are foreign to Josephus's usual style, but thoroughly compatible with biblical-Jewish themes, we may safely confirm the usual attribution of the story to an *einheimischer jüdischen Quelle*. This conclusion does not, however, prevent us from looking for traces of Josephus's redactional influence, as we shall see presently.

Some critics do not distinguish the discussion of the Pharisaic νόμιμα in *Ant.* 13:297f. from the body of the story.[39] Those who do tend to see it as Josephus's own elaboration.[40] Even Hölscher credits Josephus with this notice.[41] His reasoning seems to be that, unlike most of Josephus's other Pharisee passages, which either portray the group unfavourably[42] or seem to misrepresent all the Jewish parties as philosophical schools,[43] this notice about the νόμιμα reflects the insights and positive evaluation of the Pharisees that one would expect from a Pharisaic Jew such as

---

33 RSV trans.

34 Cf. Ps. 119:10, 176.

35 Cf. Jesus' parable of the "lost sheep", Lk. 15:4-10.

36 A figurative sense does occur in *War* 5:402, 415 (in a speech by Josephus) and in *Ant.* 6:34, but this last is taken over from the LXX, "1 Kings" (= 1 Sam.) 8:3, 5.

37 Michaelis, "ὁδός", 49.

38 Ibid., 64. As Michaelis later concedes (p. 65), the "always" is slightly hyperbolic.

39 E.g., Bloch, *Quellen*, 90ff.; Destinon, *Quellen*, 41, 44; Niese, *HZ*, 221f.

40 Hölscher, "Josephus", 1936 n. + + ; G. F. Moore, "Fate", 372; Rivkin, *Revolution*, 41.

41 Hölscher, "Josephus", 1936 n. + + .

42 E.g., *War* 1:110; *Ant.* 17:41-45.

43 E.g., *War* 2:162-166; *Ant.* 13:171-173.

Josephus.[44] We may confirm the conventional view in this matter by pointing out (rather) that: (a) since the explanatory note is intended to enlighten Greco-Roman readers about the conflicts between Pharisees and Sadducees, it must have been added by the person who edited the story for Greco-Roman readers (therefore, by Josephus); (b) the author refers the reader back (§ 198) to the discussion of Pharisees, Sadducees, and Essenes in *War* 2; and (c) the language in the footnote, as we shall see below, is typically Josephan. We sustain, therefore, the conventional view of the provenance of both the story itself (§§ 289-296) and the explanatory footnote (§§ 297-298).

Since, however, the major difficulties in *Ant.* 13:288-298 arise from tensions between the topic paragraph (§ 288) and the body of the story (§§ 289-296), it is crucial for us to identify, if possible, the author of the opening paragraph. And on this question we must part company with the conventional view.

Among those inclined toward thoroughgoing source criticism, it is widely agreed that Nicolaus of Damascus was responsible for the topic paragraph of our passage (§ 288).[45] Three lines of reasoning produce this conclusion. (a) First, it has long been recognized that Nicolaus was Josephus's major (or exclusive) source for *War* 1:30-2:116 and that he also contributed much of *Ant.* 13-17.[46] Moreover, where *War* and *Ant.* give parallel accounts, *Ant.* is usually thought to reflect Nicolaus more closely. Two of the reasons for this judgement are: (i) that although *Ant.* frequently gives the fuller description, it does not look like an expansion of *War*,[47] and (ii) *War* 1:30-2:116 gives many indications of being an excerpt (*Abzug*) rather than an original account.[48] Now, as we have seen above, *Ant.* 13:288a closely resembles *War* 1:67a in vocabulary. Schwartz theorizes that Josephus took *Ant.* 13:288 directly from Nicolaus's account, whereas in *War* 1 he had cropped Nicolaus's account so as to omit any mention of the Pharisees.[49] Thus, *Ant.* 13:288 reflects *Nicolaus's* unsympathetic view of the Pharisees.

---

[44] Hölscher, "Josephus", 1936 n. + +: "Sein [Josephus's] eigener pharisäischer Standpunkt kommt etwa ant. XIII 297f.; vita 191 zur Geltung".

[45] E.g., Reinach, *Oeuvres*, III, 177 n. 3; Marcus, LCL edn., VII, 373 n. *d.*; Schwartz, "Josephus and Nicolaus", 158f.

[46] Cf. Hölscher, "Josephus", 1944-1948; Michel-Bauernfeind, *De Bello Judaico*, I, xxvf.; and S. Safrai and M. Stern, *The Jewish People in the First Century*, I, 23f.

[47] Destinon, *Quellen*, 11-13. An example is the story of Antiochus Sidetes and Hyrcanus (see the table above). The *Ant.* account is not only much fuller; it also accords better with the accounts of other historians (cf. Marcus, LCL edn., VII, 340 n. *c.*, 353 n. *f*); Josephus himself quotes Nicolaus in favour of the *Ant.* version (*Ant.* 13:250f.).

[48] Hölscher, "Josephus", 1944f.

[49] Schwartz, "Josephus and Nicolaus", 159.

We may respond that, since the overthrow of Hölscher's theory of monolithic intermediate sources for *Ant.*,[50] the degree of Josephus's authorial freedom in that work has become an open question that can only be resolved on a case-by-case basis. One cannot argue from general theories of how Josephus used his sources to conclusions about specific passages. We shall see that § 288 betrays Josephus's own hand.

(b) A second argument for Nicolaus's authorship of *Ant.* 13:288 deals with the second sentence of the topic paragraph: the Pharisees' influence is so great that "even when they say something against a king and against a high priest (ὡς καὶ κατὰ βασιλέως . . . καὶ κατ' ἀρχιερέως) they are immediately credited". According to Reinach, who is followed by Marcus and Schwartz,[51] the "distinction" made here between the offices of king and high priest was not one that suited Josephus's own time of writing (after 70), nor did it match the Hasmonean period; it can only reflect, they claim, the time of Herod (and Nicolaus), in which the king and the high priest were two different individuals.

It is not at all clear, however, why the phrase must be taken to refer to two distinct individuals rather than two offices held by the same person. Hyrcanus is not yet called βασιλεύς, to be sure, but the whole story hinges on the fact that he *has* both the ἀρχιερωσύνην and the ἄρχειν τοῦ λαοῦ. That is the point of Eleazar's charge (§ 291), to the effect that Hyrcanus should give up the former and be content with the latter. After the story, further, Josephus reflects that Hyrcanus was counted uniquely worthy by God to enjoy τὴν ἀρχὴν τοῦ ἔθνους, τὴν ἀρχιερατικὴν τιμήν, and προφητεία (§ 299), thereby evoking the familiar triad of prophet, priest, and king.[52] If Hyrcanus himself did not take the official

---

[50] See the excursus to Part I, above.

[51] See n. 45, above.

[52] These were, as is well known, the three outstanding public offices of biblical Israel, which later provided much fuel for messianic speculation. Cf. e.g., the "Messianic Anthology" from Qumran, in G. Vermes, *The Dead Sea Scrolls in English* (Harmondsworth: Penguin, 1962), 247ff.; also 1QS 9:11; 1QSa 2:12ff.; *Test. Levi* 8:11-15; *Test. Simeon* 7:1-2. Of a vast secondary literature on these texts, and on the Qumran expectation of both a royal and a priestly Messiah as well as the "prophet", see G. R. Beasley-Murray, "The Two Messiahs in the Testaments of the Twelve Patriarchs", *JTS* 48 (1947), 1-12; Millar Burrows, "Messiahs of Aaron and Israel", *ATR* 34 (1952), 202-206; R. W. Klein, "Aspects of Intertestamental Messianism", *Concordia Theological Monthly* 43 (1972), 507-517; R. B. Laurin, "The Problem of Two Messiahs in the Qumran Scrolls", *Revue de Qumran* 4 (1963), 39-52; J. Liver, "The Doctrine of Two Messiahs in Sectarian Literature in the Time of the Second Commonwealth", *HTR* 52 (1959), 149-185; M. Smith, "What is Implied by the Variety of Messianic Figures?" *JBL* 88 (1959), 66-72. For the application of all three offices to Jesus, cf. Eusebius, *Eccl. Hist.* 1.3.7-9.

title of βασιλεύς, his oldest son Aristobulus did,[53] immediately after Hyrcanus's death, which suggests that Hyrcanus had already been a *de facto*
king. What is more, Josephus implies elsewhere that all of his Hasmonean ancestors were kings: "the sons of Asamoneus served for the
longest time as both high priests and kings".[54] Loose language this may
be; but it takes all the force from Reinach's claim that the author of §
288 must have lived when the king and high priest were different individuals, in the time of Herod the Great.

Nor is it difficult to speculate as to why the author of § 288 should
have exaggerated Hyrcanus's ἀρχὴ τοῦ λαοῦ into full-fledged kingship.
The author is clearly partial to Hyrcanus and is also anti-Pharisaic.[55] It
lends a sense of enormity to his opening description of the Pharisees that
he can declare: "even when they speak against a *king* [rather than a mere
'leader' or the like] and a high priest they are credited!" The present
participle λέγοντες indicates that the Pharisees' speaking against high
priests and kings (= Hasmoneans) was not an isolated occurrence; in the
sequel (*Ant.* 13:401f.) we find that the Pharisees continue to wield their
popular support against the priestly dynasty. So the second sentence of
the topic paragraph has clearly been added by the narrative editor to introduce the story of Hyrcanus's rift with the Pharisees (§§ 289-296);
there is no need to attribute it to Nicolaus.

(c) Finally, Schwartz recognizes that the author of § 288, unlike the
author of §§ 289-296, is openly hostile toward the Pharisees.[56] This disqualifies Josephus, according to Schwartz, because in *Life* 12 Josephus
declares himself to be a Pharisee. I shall try to demonstrate in Part IV,
however, how unlikely it is that Josephus ever wished to be thought of
as a Pharisee.

In response to the arguments adduced in favour of Nicolaus's authorship of *Ant.* 13:288, I have argued that the second sentence of the
paragraph was introduced in order to create a framework for the traditional story that follows (§§ 289-296). Although its anti-Pharisaic tone
contradicts the story, it does introduce the high priest/ruler scheme that

---

[53] According to Josephus, at least. Once again, the fact that Josephus may have erred
historically (cf. Marcus, LCL edn., 379 n. *c.*) does not affect our understanding of his
narrative as narrative.

[54] Cf. *Ant.* 16:187: ἡμεῖς . . . τῶν ἐξ Ἀσαμωναίου Βασιλέων; *Life* 2: οἱ γὰρ Ἀσαμωναίου
παῖδες . . . ἐπὶ μήκιστον χρόνον ἠρχιεράτευσαν καὶ ἐβασίλευσαν. In *Ant.* 13:406 we are told
that Alexander Janneus, the second Hasmonean "king" by Josephus's reckoning
(13:301), received a more splendid funeral than any of the *kings* before him (τινὰ τῶν πρὸ
αὐτοῦ βασιλέων). And in 15:403, we are told that the fortress called Baris was built by
the "kings and high priests of the Hasmonean family (τοῦ Ἀσαμωναίων γένους βασιλεῖς
καὶ ἀρχιερεῖς)". But the Baris antedated John Hyrcanus (*War* 1:75)!

[55] Hölscher, "Josephus", 197f.; Schwartz, "Josephus and Nicolaus", 158.

[56] Schwartz, "Josephus and Nicolaus", 158.

lies at the heart of the story and appears again in Josephus's summary remarks on Hyrcanus.

We may now add that the rueful recognition of Pharisaic popularity that appears in § 288 is a trademark of Josephus's own portrayal of the group. We saw it in *War* 1:110-114, where it was implied that Queen Alexandra and the masses were deceived by the Pharisees' reputation for ἀκρίβεια, and in *War* 2:162, where the Pharisees are said to lead astray (ἀπάγω) the foremost school. We shall encounter the same attitude again in *Ant.* 13:400-432; 17:41-45; 18:17; and *Life* 191-198. Josephus, like the author of *Ant.* 13:288, acknowledges but regrets the great fame and influence of the Pharisees.

Three other considerations seem to confirm that the author of § 288 is Josephus himself. First is the obvious point that he refers the reader back to his earlier presentation on the Jewish αἱρέσεις (ὡς καὶ ἐν τοῖς ἐπάνω δεδηλώκαμεν). The "above" description is evidently *Ant.* 13:171-173,[57] which comes from Josephus himself.

Second, the author of the paragraph reveals by his praise of Hyrcanus that he is pro-Hasmonean.[58] Yet we know Josephus to be a proud scion of the Hasmonean dynasty.[59] Indeed, John Hyrcanus was something of a hero to Josephus, and our author likes to point out his own prophetic and priestly qualifications as well as his royal lineage.[60] Was it coincidental that Josephus named his first son Hyrcanus?[61] In both *War* and *Ant.*, as we have seen, this ruler marks the apogee of Hasmonean glory; the decline of the dynasty begins with the sons of Hyrcanus.[62] Josephus, then, eminently satisfies the requirement that the author of § 288 be pro-Hasmonean and an admirer of John Hyrcanus.

Decisive for our question, however, is the vocabulary used in § 288, especially the pairing of "success" (εὐπραγία) and "envy" (φθόνος). With these terms, which occur also in the *War* parallel (1:67), we hit upon a characteristic Josephan theme.

In keeping with the well-known tendency of Hellenistic historiography to analyze the psychological motivations of historical figures,[63] Josephus

[57] So Marcus, LCL edn., VII, 373 n. *c*.
[58] Cf. Hölscher, "Josephus", 1974f.
[59] *Ant.* 16:187; 20:266; *Life* 1ff.
[60] On prophecy and priesthood, cf. *War* 3:351ff. and J. Blenkinsopp, "Prophecy and Priesthood in Josephus", *JJS* 25 (1974), 239-262. On Josephus's royal lineage, cf. *Ant.* 16:187; *Life* 2.
[61] *Life* 5.
[62] *War* 1:68f/*Ant.* 13:300.
[63] Cf. Collingwood, *Idea*, 39f. (on Tacitus) and 41f.; M. Hadas, *Hellenistic Culture: Fusion and Diffusion* (New York: Columbia Univ. Press, 1959), chapter 10: "Historiography"; M. Braun, *Griechischer Roman und Hellenistische Geschichtsschreibung* (Frankfurt: N. Klostermann, 1934); H.R. Moehring, ' Novelistic Elements in the

often makes the observation that the success of some public person
"caused envy" in someone else. The first time we meet this claim is in
War 1:67, with respect to John Hyrcanus, but after that it becomes a
significant theme in all of Josephus's works.[64]

One might initially suppose that the editorial remarks on the theme
of envy in *War* 1 and 2 were copied from Josephus's source, Nicolaus
of Damascus. Such remarks occur at 1:77 (cf. *Ant.* 13:310): "of our better feelings (πάθη), none is strong enough to hold out interminably
against envy (φθόνος)".[65] Especially close to our passage is 1:208, "But
it is impossible in prosperity (εὐπραγία) to escape envy (φθόνος)". These
editorial reflections are, however, perfectly consistent with Josephus's
own narrative tendencies. With respect to his own career in the Galilee,
for example, Josephus claims frequently that his brilliance and
popularity aroused the envy of his opponents, especially John of
Gischala.[66] He reflects (*Life* 80):

> I was now about thirty years old, at a time of life when, even if one
> restrains his lawless passions, it is hard, especially in a position of high
> authority, to escape the calumnies of envy (φθόνος).

Compare also *Life* 122. Josephus tells us that John of Gischala heard
about his εὔνοια among his supporters and, "believing that my success
(τὴν ἐμὴν εὐπραγίαν) involved his own ruin, gave way to immoderate
envy (εἰς φθόνον οὔτι μέτριον)". As in our passage, εὐπραγία calls forth
φθόνος. By what criteria could one distinguish these remarks of Josephus
from those in the early part of *War* or in *Ant.* 13:288?

In his biblical paraphrase, moreover, Josephus consistently introduces
the theme of envy where it is absent from his LXX source. Thus we
learn that Joseph was envied by his brothers because of Jacob's special
affection for him;[67] that Korah "envied" Moses;[68] that Saul delayed telling his family about his selection as king in order to prevent envy;[69] and
that Saul himself became envious of David's accomplishments and
fame.[70] In all of these cases Josephus introduces the theme of φθόνος to

Writings of Flavius Josephus", (Dissertation, Chicago, 1957), e.g. 99, 143ff.; E.
Milokenski, *Der Neid in der griechischen Philosophie* (Wiesbaden: Steiner, 1964).
  [64] E.g., *War* 1:72, 84, 463, 633f.; 2:82, 181; 4:393; 5:97; 7:027; *Ant.* 2:27; 4:14; 6:59,
193; 10:212, 250, 256; 13:402; 15:130, 349; 16:248; 18:240f.; 20:21; *Life* 85, 122, 204,
423; *Ag.Ap.* 1:213.
  [65] The following quotations, illustrative of the φθόνος theme, are taken from the LCL
translation.
  [66] *War* 2:614, 620, 627; *Life* 80, 85, 122, 204, cf. 423. Cf. Pt. IV, below.
  [67] *Ant.* 2:10//Gen. 37:3; 2:13//37:9; 2:27//37:22.
  [68] *Ant.* 4:14//Num. 16:1ff.
  [69] *Ant.* 6:59//1 Sam. 10:13.
  [70] *Ant.* 6:193//1 Sam. 18:8.

his LXX source. Notice, finally, Josephus's reflection on Daniel, who
(he says) was envied both by Nebuchadnezzar and by the Babylonian
nobility:[71]

> And so Daniel, being held in such great honour and dazzling favour by
> Darius, . . . became a prey to envy (παραλαμβανόμενος ἐφθονήθη), for men
> are jealous (βασκαίνουσι) when they see others held by kings in greater
> honour than themselves.[72] (Marcus/Wikgren)

Since Josephus has reformulated the biblical narrative so as to thematize
envy and since he reflects on that theme frequently in all of his writings,
we are compelled to attribute the same theme in *Ant.* 13:288 (= *War*
1:67) to Josephus himself.

Notice, finally, that (a) the combination of φθόνος and μῖσος, as in our
passage (§ 288/ § 296), is fairly common in Josephus[73] and (b) the exact
phrase φθόνον ἐκίνησε at § 288 is also paralleled elsewhere in his
writings.[74]

To summarize: since the author of *Ant.* 13:288 is pro-Hasmonean,
praises John Hyrcanus, regrets the fame and influence of the Pharisees,
refers the reader back to *Ant.* 13:171-173 (a Josephan pericope), and uses
language that is characteristic of Josephus, that author can only be identified as Josephus. This conclusion incidentally confirms our earlier
judgement that *War* 1:110-114 and the narrative preceding it were
decisively shaped by Josephus so as to express his own view of Hasmonean history and his own themes (e.g., δοκέω/ ἀκρίβεια). Without denying that Nicolaus provided a historical substructure, therefore, one must
concede that the final formulation comes from Josephus, in the cases that
we have tested. This conclusion, in turn, fits with Josephus's
demonstrable procedure in the case of the LXX.[75]

III. *Interpretation of Ant. 13:288-296*

The above source analysis has revealed that Josephus took over a traditional Jewish story about a rift between the Pharisees and John Hyrcanus (*Ant.* 13:289-296) and included it in his narrative of events under
that high priest. In order to provide a framework for it, he took over *War*
1:67a (his earlier formulation) and expanded it. Since the outcome of the
story was the abolition of certain νόμιμα that had been established by the

[71] *Ant.* 10:212, 256.
[72] *Ant.* 10:250, absent from Dan. 6:1ff.
[73] E.g., *War* 2:82; 4:566; *Ant.* 2:10; 6:193; 20:29; cf. 13:401-402.
[74] *Ant.* 2:10; 15:50.
[75] Cf. Attridge, *Interpretation, passim.*

Pharisees (§ 296), which ordinances Josephus had never before mentioned to his Greco-Roman audience, he appended a brief elaboration on this matter in §§ 297f.

These are not the only adjustments that Josephus has made to his narrative in order to accommodate the traditional story. First, having shown that Hyrcanus repealed the Pharisaic νόμιμα, he must later note that these ordinances were reinstated under Alexandra Salome (13:408), a point that is lacking (because unnecessary) in the *War* parallel (1:110-114).

Second, it is likely that Josephus has retouched the story itself, even though he did not alter the δίκαιος and ὁδός language. Especially suggestive of his hand are the parenthetical remarks on the Pharisees and Sadducees, which, like the "footnote" in §§ 297f., elaborate on some particular point. In order to explain Hyrcanus's aspiration to please the Pharisees by his conduct, Josephus reminds his readers that οἱ Φαρισαῖοι φιλοσοφοῦσιν (§ 289). This statement is perfectly in character for Josephus[76] and recalls his earlier portrayals of the Pharisees. Similarly, his notice that the αἵρεσις of the Sadducees espouses a view opposite to that of the Pharisees recalls previous discussions (§ 293). And finally, after reading that the Pharisees thought the death penalty too severe a punishment for careless speech, which notice is a sufficient explanation of the narrative, we meet the further generalization, "In any case, the Pharisees are naturally merciful (ἐπιεικῶς ἔχουσιν) in the matter of punishments."[77] Since all of these remarks: (a) are explanations for a Greco-Roman audience; (b) are parenthetical observations, in the *present* tense; and (c) accord with Josephus's own tendencies, we should probably attribute them to his redactional efforts.

A more thorough analysis would doubtless uncover other minor Josephan traits in §§ 289-296. The above suffice to establish that our author has gone some way toward making the traditional story his own.

---

[76] We have seen that Josephus characteristically describes the Jewish religious groups as (philosophical) αἱρέσεις. On φιλοσοφέω/φιλοσοφία, used of the Jewish schools (including the Pharisees), cf. *War* 2:119, 166; *Ant.* 18:11, 23, 25 (cf. *Ant.* 18:9).

[77] The mildness of the Pharisees is, it should be noted, relative to the harsh position of the Sadducees. Josephus will tell us later (20:199) that the Sadducees are more savage (ὠμοί) in their punishments than any other Jews, "as we have already explained (καθὼς ἤδη δεδηλώκαμεν)". Cf. Hölscher, 1974. The reference seems to be back to the comment in our passage (so Feldman, LCL edn, X, 107 n.*g*), which confirms that this earlier statement comes from Josephus. Josephus's acknowledgement of the (relative) mildness of the Pharisees ought not, then, to be construed as outright praise.

Rivkin, *Revolution*, 40 n.*, suggests that the basis for the Sadducean position was a conflation of Ex. 22:38 (prohibition of cursing God *or a ruler*) and Lev. 24:15f. (death penalty for cursing God).

That endeavour was not entirely successful, however, as our original observations on the tensions within *Ant.* 13:288-298 indicate. The tensions that remain suggest the following redactional scenario. Josephus was a proud descendant of the Hasmoneans and a particular admirer of John Hyrcanus. In his efforts to fill out the brief account of Hyrcanus's tenure that he had given in *War*, he came across a traditional story about a rift between the high priest and the Pharisees. The story itself was sympathetic to both Hyrcanus and the Pharisees; it attributed the rupture to Eleazar's impertinence and to the machinations of a certain Sadducee.[78] Nevertheless, Eleazar appeared in the company of the Pharisees and the story ended in a break between Hyrcanus and his erstwhile religious advisors. For Josephus, with his anti-Pharisaic animus, there was no question about which party was to blame. He could not, however, clearly demonstrate the Pharisees' guilt from the story itself, so he fell back on the familiar *topos* that he had used in *War* 1:67: the Pharisees and their popular supporters were moved to envy (φθόνος), he declares, by the success (εὐπραγία) of Hyrcanus and his sons.[79] To this favourite (but here inappropriate!) theme he adds a reference to the Pharisees' hostility (οἱ Φαρισαῖοι κακῶς πρὸς αὐτὸν εἶχον) and he laments their malign influence, with which they are able to arouse the masses even against one who is both high priest and "king". Thus, Josephus's pro-Hasmonean and anti-Pharisaic instincts have led him to misrepresent, in his topic paragraph (§ 288), the traditional story that follows (§§ 289-296).

Josephus's redactional failure is perhaps most obvious in the case of Eleazar; the reader is left in doubt as to whether this *provocateur* is or is not a Pharisee. Hölscher confidently states, "In der Gesellschaft der Pharisäer ist der Zänker Eleazar".[80] But the only hint of any link between Eleazar and the Pharisees comes in the Sadducee Jonathan's allegation that the man had spoken in agreement with the common consent of all the Pharisees (τῇ κοινῇ πάντων Φαρισαίων γνώμῃ, § 293). All of the other evidence dissociates Eleazar from the Pharisees. For example, the genitive absolute in §§ 290f. distinguishes the Pharisees' commendation of Hyrcanus from Eleazar's calumny. Then, Eleazar is described not as τις τῶν Φαρισαίων but simply as τις τῶν κατακειμένων;

---

[78] The traditional story may already represent the attempt of a pro-Hasmonean and pro-Pharisaic tradition to explain how the rift between Hyrcanus and the Pharisees came about—neither was at fault! If so, we have strong evidence that the rupture did in fact take place (against the views of those scholars mentioned in nn. 1-3, above).

[79] That Josephus already employed the φθόνος motif in such an unconvincing way in *War* 1:67—why should a nation be *envious* of its leader's successes (on its behalf)?—might indicate that the story of the rift was in his mind when he composed the *War* account.

[80] Hölscher, "Josephus", 1975 n.*.

and we know that at least one non-Pharisee (Jonathan) was included among the guests. Further, when Eleazar does utter his charge, *all* of the Pharisees (πάντες οἱ Φαρισαῖοι) are said to have become indignant. No one, therefore, suspects that Eleazar spoke with Pharisaic approval until Jonathan makes the allegation. Rivkin correctly observes:

> The story . . . puts the blame for the slander on a single individual, Eleazar, who is described as having an evil nature. The Pharisees as such are not held responsible for the charge.[81]

Indeed, read without the topic paragraph, the story seems to say that Jonathan's accusation of the Pharisees was a shrewd piece of "disinformation", not an accurate statement of the facts.

Josephus's introductory remarks (§ 288) only make sense, however, on the identification of Eleazar as a Pharisee, for we are told that "the Pharisees" speak against a high priest. Thus we see that Josephus's anti-Pharisaic introduction (§ 288) contradicts the sense of the traditional story (§§ 289-296). His zeal to promote Hyrcanus and to denigrate the Pharisees has led to a redaction that is somewhat clumsy.[82]

IV. *The Pharisaic Νόμιμα*

The outcome of Eleazar's affront and Jonathan's craftiness, the story tells us, was that John Hyrcanus became a Sadducee; he abandoned the Pharisees and repealed "the ordinances that they had established among the people (τά τε ὑπ' αὐτῶν κατασταθέντα νόμιμα τῷ δήμῳ)". At the conclusion of the story (§§ 297-298), Josephus pauses to explain to his Greco-Roman readership what these Pharisaic νόμιμα were. This brief discussion has taken on considerable significance in the secondary literature because (a) it is almost universally accepted as Josephus's own contribution, unlike most of the other Pharisee passages, and (b) it is sometimes thought to provide early and independent attestation of the later rabbinic teaching of the "Oral Law".[83] The importance of the passage demands a careful attempt to capture Josephus's intended sense.

The first half of the statement contains the decisive information and the key terms: τὰ νόμιμα, ἀναγράφω, οἱ πατέρες, παραδίδωμι/παράδοσις, and διαδοχή. An examination of these terms will help provide some fixed points for our interpretation of the passage.

---

[81] Rivkin, *Revolution*, 40.

[82] The imperfect redaction of *Ant.* has long been recognized; cf. Bloch, *Quellen*, 112f.; 28ff.; Hölscher, "Josephus", 1971 n.*.

[83] So, e.g., Rivkin, *Revolution*, 41ff., J.M. Baumgarten, "The Unwritten Law in the Pre-Rabbinic Period", *JSJ* 3 (1972), esp. 12-14, and the literature cited in his notes (much of which is in Hebrew).

A. *Key Terms*

1. τὰ νόμιμα. Josephus's use of τὰ νόμιμα we have discussed above, in chapter 4. Outside of the present passage and its sequel (13:408), Josephus uses τὰ πάτρια νόμιμα as a simple substitute for οἱ Μωυσέος/πάτριοι νόμοι. Written in longhand, that is to say, "the ordinances" are τὰ νόμιμα τὰ διὰ Μωυσέος ὑπὸ τοῦ θεοῦ δοθέντα (*Ant.* 9:2). Although the modern critic can discern many traditional elements in the νόμοι/νόμιμα, Josephus insists that they all go back to the all-embracing legal system devised by Moses, which prescribes clear rules of conduct from the cradle to the grave. It is precisely because Josephus has never before mentioned any νόμιμα . . . ἅπερ οὐκ ἀναγέγραπται ἐν τοῖς Μωυσέος νόμοις that he must now explain this special case to the reader.

2. ἀναγράφω. Josephus uses the verb ἀναγράφω in its usual restricted sense, "to record or write down officially". He can use the word, therefore, with respect to decrees, public records and historical writings, including his own.[84] About a dozen times, we find the perfect passive verb or participle (as in our passage), denoting what "stands written" in the scriptures. Often this meaning is spelled out by the phrase, ἐν ταῖς ἱεραῖς βίβλοις ἀναγέγραπται;[85] in our passage we have the qualifier ἐν τοῖς Μωυσέος νόμοις. Nevertheless, Josephus can also use the perfect passive without qualification, to mean what is "written (in the scriptures)", where the context is sufficiently clear.[86] In his paraphrase of *Aristeas* 56 (*Ant.* 12:63), for example, he designates the biblical prescriptions with the simple phrase τὰ ἀναγεγραμμένα, in place of his source's ὅσα διὰ γραπτῶν. This usage may shed some light on the phrase (ἐκεῖνα) νόμιμα τὰ γεγραμμένα in our passage (297).

3. οἱ πατέρες. Josephus explains in *Ant.* 13:297 that the Pharisees handed on (παρέδοσαν) to the people certain νόμιμα ἐκ πατέρων διαδοχῆς; he then characterizes these νόμιμα as τὰ ἐκ παραδόσεως τῶν πατέρων. In 13:408, he will also refer back to the νόμιμα that the Pharisees introduced (εἰσήνεγκαν) as κατὰ τὴν πατρῴαν παράδοσιν. We must now ask whether the terms οἱ πατέρες and παράδοσις/παραδίδωμι have any fixed or special meaning for Josephus.

The short answer is that they do not. Although Josephus uses ὁ πατήρ hundreds of times in his writings, the plural occurs only about 42 times; and half of those instances have the mundane sense of "fathers" or "fatherhood" in a familial context. Only in 21 cases does Josephus use

---

[84] *War* 1:1, 30; *Ant.* 1:93, 203; 8:324; 11:99; 13:12; 14:144; *Life* 6, 40, 339, 413; *Ag.Ap.* 1:49, 92, 106, 109, 128, 143.

[85] *Ant.* 1:26, 82; 3:81, 105; 9:28, 208.

[86] Cf. *Ant.* 8:129; 9:214.

the phrases οἱ πατέρες (without qualification) and οἱ πατέρες ἡμῶν. He refers to "the fathers" or "our fathers" in three particular contexts; the category does not have any clear or significant function in his thought.

First, in *War* 5, Josephus makes a speech before the walls of Jerusalem, in which he attempts to prove that the Jews have always received divine support, without resort to arms, when their cause has been just. To prove this thesis, he cites several examples of οἱ πατέρες (ἡμῶν). The identity of these forefathers ranges all the way from Abraham (5:377ff.) to the Jews of the first century BC (at least), who willingly paid tribute to Rome (5:405). In between are mentioned the "fathers" who entered Egypt (5:382), those who left Egypt (388), those who recovered the ark from the Philistines (386), and those who returned from the Babylonian exile (390). In this speech, the "fathers" are all the Jews and Israelites of past generations.

A second block of references to the πατέρες comes in the two brief books *Against Apion*. All six occurrences there take the form οἱ πατέρες ἡμῶν. Since Josephus's apologetic and polemic in these books are devoted largely to the question of Jewish origins, he usually refers to "our forefathers" as those who left Egypt in the Exodus.[87] Otherwise, the term refers simply to the Hebrews of the earliest times, who were ignored by Herodotus and Thucydides.[88]

Finally, we have six references to the "fathers" scattered through the later books of *Ant*. Once the term denotes pre-exilic Israel in general (11:143), once it refers to the patriarchs (11:169), and once to the participants in the Exodus (20:230). In book 15, the term occurs twice in a speech by Herod, where it refers to those who rebuilt the Temple after the exile (15:385, 386), and once in Josephus's retelling of a legend handed down *from Herod's time* by οἱ πατέρες ἡμῶν (15:425).

For Josephus, then, οἱ πατέρες ἡμῶν does not denote any specific group of men but rather all the Israelites and Jews of the past, from the very earliest times until recent generations. His "fathers" are all in the Jewish mainstream and most of them are biblical figures. The category "fathers" is not prominent in his thought.

Josephus's infrequent and flexible use of οἱ πατέρες (ἡμῶν) contrasts markedly with his descriptions of the Pharisaic νόμιμα. In the short space of *Ant*. 13:297 and its sequel 13:408, these νόμιμα are described three times. They are always qualified with (τῶν) πατέρων or with πατρῷος. He never describes the Pharisaic νόμιμα without reference to "the fathers".

---

[87] *Ag.Ap.* 1:232, 280; 2:8, 122.
[88] *Ag.Ap.* 1:62; 2:117.

The possibilities would seem to be: (a) that Josephus himself considered πατέρων a particularly illuminating qualifier and therefore supplied it, or (b) that he has taken over a formulaic description of the Pharisaic ordinances that was current in his day.[89] Against (a) is the fact that Josephus's own usage of οἱ πατέρες is too flexible to be illuminating. In favour of (b) are the well-known external parallels, especially: (i) the apostle Paul's description of his former Pharisaic zeal for τῶν πατρικῶν μου παραδόσεων[90] and (ii) the Mishnah tractate Avot, which contains the sayings of Pharisaic "fathers" through several generations.[91] If Josephus did take over the qualifier τῶν πατέρων from a standard contemporary description of the Pharisaic νόμιμα, then the "fathers" in question would be whomever the Pharisees designated as such.

4. ἡ παράδοσις/παραδίδωμι. Our suspicion that Josephus took over his designation of the Pharisaic νόμιμα from contemporary usage is confirmed by an analysis of the word παράδοσις. Each of the three descriptions of the Pharisaic ordinances (13:297, 408) contains either παράδοσις or παραδίδωμι. He will use the verb again in Ant. 18:12 to describe Pharisaic beliefs: ὧν τε ὁ λόγος κρίνας παρέδωκεν ἀγαθῶν ἕπονται.

In ordinary Josephan usage, however, παράδοσις is not a theologically charged term. Of its 27 occurrences, 13 are in War; in 12 of these the word means the "surrender", of a city or fort.[92] In the other case (War 2:579), it means the "transmission" of field signals in the army. The 8 occurrences in the Life and Ag.Ap. refer to Josephus's historical productions.[93] The noun occurs only 4 times in Ant. (outside of our passages): once meaning "surrender" (10:10), once meaning "historical report" (20:259), and once meaning the "giving" of a password (19:187).

In the remaining case, Ant. 10:51, we are told that the twelve-year-old king Josiah was guided by τῇ τῶν πρεσβυτέρων συμβουλίᾳ καὶ παραδόσει. This construction might seem at first to correspond to the Gospels' description of Pharisaic teaching as ἡ παράδοσις τῶν πρεσβυτέρων.[94] The context in Josephus, however, disallows the idea of Pharisaic tradition. If the phrase τῶν πρεσβυτέρων ought to be there at all,[95] it derives its

---

[89] Cf. J. M. Baumgarten, "Unwritten Law", 13ff.
[90] Gal. 1:14.
[91] On Avot, see especially E.J. Bickerman, "La chaîne de la tradition pharisienne", Studies in Jewish and Christian History, "AGAJU" 9 (Leiden: E.J. Brill, 1980), II, 256-269.
[92] War 1:174, 414; 4:86, 146, 414, 519; 5:336; 6:378; 7:195, 201, 205, 414.
[93] Life 361, 364; Ag.Ap. 1:8, 28, 39, 50, 53; 2:287.
[94] Mk. 7:3, 5//Mt. 15:2.
[95] The MSS ROLV, an important group (Thackeray, LCL edn. IV, xvii; cf. Richards and Shutt, "Critical Notes I", 170), omit the phrase in which πρεσβυτέρων stands. Marcus follows SP at this point and includes the phrase.

significance from the youthfulness of Josiah: he combined *his* innate wisdom and understanding with the counsel (συμβουλία) and advice (παράδοσις) of his elders. The parallel with συμβουλία makes it clear that the παράδοσις of the elders is here a present influence and not a "tradition".[96] In any case, the biblical king predates the Pharisaic elders/fathers by several centuries, so there is no question of his adherence to a Pharisaic νόμιμα.

Thus Josephus never uses παράδοσις, outside of *Ant.* 13:297, 408, in the religious-legal sense that these passages imply.

The verb παραδίδωμι presents a slightly different case. It occurs some 238 times in Josephus. Although the verb almost always has a sense cognate to that of παράδοσις in Josephus, such as "to surrender, give up, yield, betray", or "record as history", we have perhaps 15 occurrences with the meaning "to pass on as a tradition". But only 8 or 9 of these have to do with the Jewish νόμοι. What we find in these cases, interestingly enough, is that Josephus uses παραδίδωμι of Moses' giving the written Law to the Hebrews. For example:

(a) *Ant.* 3:280: "These [laws], then, which were already in place during his lifetime, Moses passed on (παρέδωκε)."

(b) *Ant.* 3:286: "This code of laws Moses . . . . learned from the mouth of God (ἐξέμαθε) and passed on in writing (γεγραμμένην παραδίδωσιν) to the Hebrews.

(c) *Ant.* 4:295 (Moses speaks): "May you persevere in your observance of the laws that God has deemed good and now delivers (παραδίδωσι) to you."

(d) *Ant.* 4:302: "Such, then, is the constitution that Moses left; he passed on (παραδίδωσι) still other laws that he had written forty years before."

(e) *Ant.* 4:304: "These books [= the laws] he [Moses] then gave over (παραδίδωσι) to the priests."

(f) *Ag.Ap.* 2:279: "Since the passage of time is in all matters recognized as the surest criterion, I should appoint time as a witness to the virtue of our lawgiver and of the revelation concerning God handed down (παραδοθείσης) by him."

These passages[97] make it clear that when Josephus employs παραδίδωμι in the context of Jewish laws, which is hardly ever, he means by it Moses' act of passing on the Law, which Moses, in turn, had received from God.

---

[96] Marcus's rendering "translations" is misleading, for the reason given.

[97] Cf. also *Ag.Ap.* 1:60, where παραδίδωμι is used of the εὐσέβεια implicit in the Mosaic νόμοι.

Josephus's normal usage of παράδοσις and παραδίδωμι is wide-ranging and, for the most part, mundane. Outside of our passage, he neither appeals to nor even mentions any extra-biblical legal tradition handed down from "the fathers". This confirms our suspicion that his consistent descriptions of the Pharisaic νόμιμα in *Ant.* 13:297, 408 are not his own formulations but derive from fixed expressions of his day. Further support for this judgement comes in the several references outside Josephus to a Pharisaic παράδοσις[98] and in the parallels between παραδίδωμι/ παραλαμβάνω and the "transmission" terminology of Avot.[99]

5. ἡ διαδοχή. In the first of his three definitions of the Pharisaic νόμιμα, Josephus allows that the Pharisees derived their ordinances "from (or out of) a 'succession of fathers' (ἐκ πατέρων διαδοχῆς)".[100] This is the only place where Josephus combines the idea of "succession" with the category "fathers", which may suggest again that the combination is not his own creation. Nevertheless, his own usage of διαδοχή is worth noting, as it illuminates certain aspects of his thought.

Josephus intends, especially in *Ant.* and *Ag.Ap.* to present Judaism as a "philosophy" and Moses as its founding philosopher. Now, C. H. Turner and E. J. Bickerman have drawn attention to the important role that "succession" (διαδοχή) came to play in all of the Hellenistic schools of philosophy.[101] Plato, Aristotle, Epicurus, and Zeno all passed the direction of their schools on to "successors", who viewed their task as the preservation and exposition of the master's original philosophy.[102] The test of any single teacher's competence was his degree of faithfulness to the school's foundational principles.[103] Lists of διάδοχοι became the bases for histories of Greek philosophy in the Hellenistic world.[104]

Against this background, Josephus's use of διαδοχή, διάδοχος, and δια-δέχομαι takes on special interest. He often employs these words to speak

---

[98] E.g., Gal. 1:14; Mk. 7:3, 5; Eusebius, *Eccl. Hist.*, IV. 22.8.

[99] For קיבל and מסר as technical terms in Avot 1, cf. W. Bacher, *Tradition und Tradenten in den Schulen Palästinas und Babyloniens* (Leipzig: Gustav Pock, 1914), esp. 1ff. I owe the insight that παπάδοσις/παραδίδωμι corresponds to מסרה/מסר to Prof. A. I. Baumgarten of McMaster and Bar Ilan Universities.

[100] *Ant.* 13:297.

[101] C.H. Turner, "Note on 'Succession' Language in non-Christian Sources", in H. B. Swete, *Essays on the Early History of the Church and the Ministry* (London: Macmillan & Co., 1918), 197-199; Bickerman, "La chaîne", 262f.; cf. the literature he cites in n. 3.

[102] Says Bickerman, ("La chaîne", 269): "Les *diadochoi* d'une école étaient . . . les continuateurs de la sagesse du fondateur de cette philosophie. Leur rôle était de transmettre et d'interpréter cette sagesse et pas innover."

[103] Bickerman cites, e.g., Diogenes Laertius 4:4; 9:115f; Cicero, *Acad* 1:34.

[104] Bickerman cites as examples Sotion, whom he dates to 200 BC; Suidas on Epicurus; Diogenes Laertius 10:9; and various secondary works ("La chaîne", 262 n. 31).

of the strife that surrounded the succession to Herod's throne.[105] Several more are general, insignificant references to royal or other succession.[106] In the framework of Jewish history and religion, however, Josephus employs the idea of "succession" in three notable contexts.

The first is that of the high priesthood. Josephus's material on the διαδοχή τῶν ἀρχιερέων has long interested scholars. Most of the scholarly interest, however, has been with the historical and source-critical problems that his succession lists create.[107] Our concern, on the other hand, is with the question why the high-priestly succession was so important to Josephus. He takes pains, both in the body of *Ant.*[108] and again in a final summary,[109] to trace the high priesthood from its inception down to his time. That the endeavour was significant to him he reveals in *Ant.* 20:261, where, in a very brief summary of the contents of *Ant.* (259-261), he specifically notes, "I have tried also to preserve the record of those high priests who have served throughout two thousand years."

Josephus's overriding concern with the high-priestly succession explains itself when we recall that, in his vision of things, the priests are the guardians and interpreters of the Mosaic Law.[110] When Moses completed the Law, we are told, he entrusted it (παρέδωκε) to the priests (*Ant.* 4:304).[111] Since then, the priests have exercised scrupulous care in their preservation of the Law exactly as Moses delivered it (*Ag.Ap.* 2:187).[112] The one who supervises the priests in their task is the high priest (*Ag.Ap.* 2:185). If, therefore, Judaism is a philosophical system, established (under God) by Moses and enshrined in his laws, then the high priests who carefully preserve and expound those laws from generation to generation are the διάδοχοι of the Mosaic philosophy. In order to prove his thesis that Judaism is a superior philosophy, Josephus must demonstrate not only that Moses taught an excellent way of life, but also that the original teaching has been preserved accurately up to the present

---

[105] διάδοχος, διαδοχή occur some 121 times in total. Of these, approximately 35 refer to Herod's throne, occurring especially in *War* 1-2 and *Ant.* 16-17. The verb occurs 70 times; only 3 of these refer to the struggle for Herod's throne.

[106] E.g., *War* 2:121; 3:212; 4:463; 5:482; *Ant.* 1:215; 5:276; 8:113; 18:112, 35, 186, 224, 261; 19:174, 209, 20:1, 27, 93f., 182, 215, 252.

[107] Cf. H. Bloch, *Quellen*, 147ff.; J. von Destinon, *Quellen*, 29-39; G. Hölscher, "Josephus", 1989f.; and the relevant notes in the LCL edn.

[108] E.g., *Ant.* 5:362; 10:152, 153; 11:158, 297, 302; 12:43, 225; 13:78; 18:35; 20:16, 103, 197, 213, 229, 231, 237, 240.

[109] *Ant.* 20:224-251. It is well known that this final list often disagrees with the details of the earlier presentation, especially up to 13:212.

[110] Cf. *Ag.Ap.* 1:29, 32, 36, 54; 2:184-187, 194.

[111] Notice that both the LXX and MT say (Deut. 31:9) that Moses gave the book of the law to the priests *and* to the "elders of Israel", a detail that Josephus omits.

[112] Cf. *Ag.Ap.* 1:29, 42.

day. The latter task he accomplishes, in part, by tracing an unbroken line of high priestly διάδοχοι.

It seems likely that Josephus's remarks on the διαδοχή of the Hebrew kings are also intended to establish continuity between the origins of Judaism (with Moses) and his own day. The word διαδοχή is entirely absent from the Septuagint; διάδοχος appears only three times and then with the sense of "deputy" rather than "successor".[113] Josephus, however, often paraphrases the Septuagint so as to describe a new king as a διάδοχος, where his source has the phrase ἐβασίλευσε . . . ἀντ' αὐτοῦ.[114] He introduces the unscriptural detail of Hezekiah's anxiety about the possible failure of a legitimate succession (γνησίας διαδοχῆς) to the throne of Judah.[115] Finally, in the same brief summary of *Ant.* that we noted above (20:259-261), Josephus takes the trouble to spell out that he has recorded accurately τὴν περὶ τοὺς βασιλεῖς διαδοχήν, along with the period of rule by the Judges.

It is striking that Josephus should tie these two succession lists—of kings and high priests—together in his closing remarks in *Ant.* The opening paragraphs of *Life* show that this concern with succession has a personal application: he claims that his own διαδοχή (Thackeray: "pedigree") makes him an heir to both kings and high priests; he is a descendant of the Hasmonean rulers, who "were for the longest time (ἐπὶ μήκιστον χρόνον) high priests and kings of our nation".[116]

Josephus completes the familiar triad in *Ag.Ap.* 1:41, when he refers also to a succession of prophets.[117] He argues there that only prophets were eligible to write the Jewish sacred books (1:37). Accordingly, Moses wrote the first five (1:39) and the prophets after him wrote the later books (1:40).[118] The works that have been written since, we are told, dealing with post-exilic history, do not have the same status "because the exact succession of the prophets failed (διὰ τὸ μὴ γενέσθαι

---

[113] I Chron. 18:17; 2 Chron. 26:11, 28:7.
[114] E.g., *Ant.* 8:197, 250, 9:45, 160, 233, 257. The verb, also absent in the LXX parallels, occurs at *Ant.* 7:244, 334, 337, 371; 8:50, 212, 264, 274, 286, 287, 313, 315, 420; 9:172, 204, 215; 10:37, 81, 98.
[115] *Ant.* 10:25; cf. Marcus's n. *e.*, p. 171 (LCL edn., VI).
[116] *Life* 2f., 6; cf. *Ant.* 16:187.
[117] As Bickerman, "La chaîne", 263f. and n. 38, points out, the idea of a prophetic succession, though unbiblical, is not original with Josephus. It may have been conceived by Eupolemus (ca. 150 BCE), he suggests, who is the earliest witness to it (cf. Eusebius, *Prep. Evang.* 9.30.447a).
[118] Josephus follows the Bible in presenting Moses as a prophet (*Ant.* 4:165, 303, 313, 320, 329; cf. Deut. 18:15, 18). But Deuteronomy emphasizes that, even though Moses passed on his general responsibilities to Joshua (34:9), there never was a prophet like Moses again (οὐκ ἀνέστη ἔτι προφήτης ἐν Ἰσραὴλ ὡς Μωυσῆς, 34:10). Josephus, on the other hand, specifies that Joshua was a διάδοχος to Moses ἐπὶ ταῖς προφητείαις (*Ant.* 4:165).

τὴν τῶν προφητῶν ἀκριβῆ διαδοχήν)''. The implication is that the prophetic διαδοχή guaranteed the accuracy of Jewish law and history as it
appears in the Scripture.[119]

It would seem too much to infer that Josephus, even though he
unreservedly claims ἀκρίβεια for his own treatment of Jewish history, is
here placing his own works on the same level as Scripture.[120] Nevertheless, it is clear from *War* 3:352ff., 399ff.; 4:629, that he did consider
himself a prophet, at least in certain respects.[121] In these passages, moreover, Josephus explicitly links his prophetic abilities with his priestly
status.[122]

In summary: Josephus's concern with the succession of high priests,
kings, and prophets appears to serve both his apologetic for Judaism and
his self-representation. That all three biblical offices were handed down
from generation to generation, especially that of the high priest, supports
Josephus's claim that the original Mosaic teaching has been preserved
with accuracy.[123] Although he presents his favourite, John Hyrcanus, as
the only one who ever combined τὴν ἀρχὴν, τὴν ἀρχιερεωσύνην, and τὴν
προφητείαν in one person, Josephus is eager to point out his own combination of royal and high priestly lineage and, in *War*, he also claims
to be an accomplished prophet.

Returning now to our passage: it is clear that the "succession of
fathers" from which the Pharisaic ordinances derive has no place in
Josephus's vision of things. Since Josephus never explains such a
διαδοχή, one must ask, again, whether the phrase is his own.

We have seen that the terms οἱ πατέρες and παράδοσις, which Josephus
uses of the Pharisaic teachings, have solid parallels in Paul, the Gospels,
and the Mishnah tractate Avot. It may now be significant that Avot
begins by recalling a list of *successive* Pharisaic teachers (= "fathers"),
who lived between the time of the Great Assembly and that of Rabbi
Judah.[124] The common view among rabbinic scholars seems to be that
Avot's list of fathers is based on a very early (pre-70) list that included
at least the five "pairs" (זוגות), from the two Yose's to Hillel and Sham-

---

[119] Cf. W. C. Van Unnik, *Schriftsteller*, 98.

[120] Cf. J. Blenkinsopp, "Prophecy and Priesthood in Josephus", *JJS* 25 (1974), 246f.

[121] Cf. H. Lindner, *Geschichtsauffassung*, 52ff., 137ff., esp. 141; W. C. van Unnik,
"Die Prophetie bei Josephus", in his *Schriftsteller*, 41-45; and Blenkinsopp, "Prophecy",
239-262.

[122] Cf. Blenkinsopp, "Prophecy", 250ff.; cf. also *War* 3:352; *Ant.* 7:72 and n. *f.* to
LCL edn., V, 397; 8:296, 10:79f.

[123] To his credit, perhaps, Josephus acknowledges ruptures and abuses along the way.
E.g., *Ant.* 20:15f., 237, 247, 249 (cf. 226), on the high priests and *Ag.Ap.* 1:41, on the
prophets.

[124] Avot 1:2-2:1.

mai (Avot 1:4-12, 15).[125] Bickerman argues that the Pharisees' purpose in formulating a list of their "fathers" was to establish themselves as a philosophical school by setting forth their διάδοχοι in Hellenistic fashion.[126] Each of the pairs is said, in the Mishnah, to have received (קיבל) the Law from its predecessors and to have passed it on (מסר) to the next pair.[127] If the list of pairs was already current before 70, as seems likely, then Josephus, who certainly knew many Pharisees, was probably familiar with it. In that case, his description of the Pharisaic ordinances as ἐκ πατέρων διαδοχῆς was a well-chosen allusion to their fundamental justification.[128]

To summarize thus far: (a) Josephus's normal usage of the five terms investigated here adds some nuance to our portrait of his world-view. At the foundation of this world-view stands Moses, who passed on (παρέδωκε) to the Jews in writing the all-encompassing body of laws (νόμοι/νόμιμα) that God had revealed to him. These laws, inviolable for all time, Moses entrusted to the stewardship of the priests. (b) Since the terms οἱ πατέρες and παράδοσις have no special significance for Josephus; since he uses them, however, in all three of his descriptions of the Pharisaic νόμιμα; and since, finally, the combination of these terms occurs in other (non-Josephan) discussions of Pharisaic teaching, we may reasonably suppose that he took over these elements of his portrayal from contemporary usage. (c) Although the concept "succession" (διαδοχή) does play a significant role in Josephus's thought, it is the succession of high priests, kings, and prophets that interests him, in accord with the world-view described in (a) and with his apologetic purposes. The phrase "succession of fathers", which occurs only in *Ant.* 13:297, probably comes from current usage among the Pharisees themselves. (d) His description of the Pharisaic νόμιμα as "not written down in the laws

[125] Bickerman, "La chaîne", 260f., 264. The diverse arguments that have been used to support an early dating of the pairs list may be summarized under two broad rubrics, viz., (a) multiple attestation (cf. m. Hagigah 2:2; m. Peah 2:6; tos. Hagigah 2:8; Avot de Rabbi Nathan, I and II) and its tradition-historical implications and (b) literary- or form-critical considerations within Avot 1-2 itself. On the latter, cf. J. Neusner, *The Rabbinic Traditions about the Pharisees Before 70* (Leiden: E.J. Brill, 1971), I, 11-23, esp. 15-21. On the former, cf. Neusner, Ibid.; L. Finkelstein, "Introductory Study to Pirke Abot", *JBL* 57 (1938), 13-50, esp. 14, 17-20; and the literature cited by Finkelstein, 14 n. 2.
[126] Bickerman, "La chaîne", 261. I have adapted Bickerman's theory, as the reader will have noticed, to interpret Josephus's concern with the high-priestly διαδοχή.
[127] See n. 99 above.
[128] As Bickerman, "La chaîne", 268 suggests. If Bickerman's interpretation of Avot 1 is correct, incidentally, then we have positive evidence that Josephus's presentation of the Pharisees as a αἵρεσις (cf. also Acts 15:5; 26:5; 5:17) derived from their own self-understanding.

of Moses'' reflects his strenuous effort to distinguish these νόμιμα from those that he ordinarily talks about.

B. *Interpretation of Ant. 13:297-298*

With the above discussion of the key terms in *Ant.* 13:297f., we have gone some way toward an interpretation. Turning now to the passage itself, we see that the main point is delivered in 297a. It is elaborated in 297b and then two subsidiary points are made in 298.

297a. νῦν δὲ δηλῶσαι βούλομαι ὅτι νόμιμα τινὰ παρέδοσαν τῷ δήμῳ οἱ Φαρισαῖοι ἐκ πατέρων διαδοχῆς, ἅπερ οὐκ ἀναγέγραπται ἐν τοῖς Μωυσέος νόμοις, καὶ διὰ τοῦτο ταῦτα τὸ τῶν Σαδδουκαίων γένος ἐκβάλλει.

This statement is already complete in itself. The story of John Hyrcanus reported that, in becoming a Sadducee, he repealed the νόμιμα that had been established among the people by the Pharisees. We now learn the reason. The Pharisaic νόμιμα are special (hence: τινα); they derive from a ''succession of fathers'' and are not among the written laws of Moses. For this reason (διὰ τοῦτο) the Sadducees dismiss them out of hand. So far as it goes, this explanation poses no difficulty. The only νόμιμα that Josephus has ever talked about (or that he will ever talk about again) are those ἀναγέγραπται ἐν τοῖς Μωυσέος νόμοις, those that comprise the all-sufficient Mosaic code. When he explains that the Pharisaic νόμιμα were not of this sort and were therefore rejected by the Sadducees, the reader ought to understand. Unless Josephus has entirely misrepresented his own view, he too would have rejected these non-Mosaic νόμιμα.

In order to illuminate the Sadducean position, Josephus adds 297b. The Sadducean group rejects the Pharisaic νόμιμα:

297b. λέγον ἐκεῖνα δεῖν ἡγεῖσθαι νόμιμα τὰ γεγραμμένα, τὰ δ' ἐκ παραδόσεως τῶν πατέρων μὴ τηρεῖν.

These two clauses have generated some debate among scholars. Some rabbinists, like E. Rivkin and J. M. Baumgarten, find here an early attestation, among the Pharisees, of the rabbinic doctrine of the Oral or Unwritten Law.[129] As is well known, the corpus of rabbinic halakhah came to be called the Oral Law (תורה שבעל פה), for it was believed by the rabbis to have been delivered at Sinai, along with the Written Law (תורה שבכתב).

---

[129] Rivkin, *Revolution*, 41f.; J. M. Baumgarten, ''Unwritten Law'', 12-14.

The Oral Law, however, was the unique possession of Israel, inaccessible to the Gentiles.[130] Certain *beraitot* in the Babylonian Talmud already proclaim an interdict on the writing of *halakhot*.[131] The question is how early this interdict was in force, that is, whether the Pharisees before 70 already transmitted their teachings in oral form.[132]

The scholars mentioned above interpret ἐκεῖνα νόμιμα τὰ γεγραμμένα in an absolute sense, so that the Sadducees rejected the Pharisaic νόμιμα because they were not written down; in recognizing only "laws that had been written down", they rejected the *principle* of an Oral Law. Thus Rivkin:

> Josephus is as explicit as he can be: the Pharisees and Sadducees were hostile to each other because they violently disagreed as to the authority of the so-called Unwritten Law. The Unwritten Law was championed by the Pharisees. The Laws were not to be found in the Laws of Moses. They were laws that had been *transmitted in unwritten form*.[133]

Baumgarten also thinks that this sense is quite obvious. He argues:

> If he [Josephus] had known of the existence of authoritative halakhic texts, *his stress on the contrast in form* between them (οὐκ ἀναγέγραπται) and the written ordinances (τὰ γεγραμμένα) would be pointless. The issue would rather be whether the Torah was the only source of law or whether these texts, too, were to be acknowledged as authoritative.[134]

These scholars believe, then, that Josephus intends to draw a contrast between the written laws of Moses and the oral/unwritten laws of the Pharisees.

Against this view, J. N. Epstein interprets Josephus's statement to mean only that the Pharisaic νόμιμα "were not written in the Laws of Moses; it does not say anything about their external form . . . and it is possible that they were written."[135] Marcus indicates his agreement with this view by supplying the parenthetical phrase "in Scripture" after "written down" (§ 297b) in the Loeb translation. Most recently, J. Neusner has added his voice, asserting, "If we had no preconception about oral tradition, this passage would not have led us to such an

---

[130] Cf. G. F. Moore, *Judaism*, II, 68; S. Sandmel, *Judaism and Christian Beginnings* (New York: Oxford Univ. Press, 1978), 55f., 180f., 183f.; J. M. Baumgarten, "Unwritten Law", 7ff.

[131] E.g., b. Gittin 60b and b. Terumah 14b; cf. j. Megillot 4:74b.

[132] Because much of the scholarly discussion is in modern Hebrew, a fact that precludes my serious interaction, I mention only the most accessible representatives of the two interpretations of our passage.

[133] *Revolution*, 41; emphasis added.

[134] J. M. Baumgarten, "Unwritten Law", 13; emphasis added.

[135] Epstein, *Mavo le-Nusah ha Mishnah*, 697; cited in Baumgarten, "Unwritten Law", 13.

idea.''[136] I do not know of any attempt, however, specifically to challenge the Rivkin/Baumgarten interpretation of *Ant.* 13:297. To make good the deficiency, I offer the following considerations.

Josephus does not make, much less stress, the direct contrast ''in form'' between οὐx ἀναγέγραπται and τὰ γεγραμμένα that Baumgarten infers. The former phrase occurs in 297a, where the contrast is between ἐx πατέρων διαδοχῆς and ἐν τοῖς Μωυσέος νόμοις as two possible sources of νόμιμα. The Sadducees reject the Pharisaic ordinances because they are not written *in the laws of Moses.* The conflict is over provenance, not form.

The latter phrase cited by Baumgarten, τὰ γεγραμμένα, occurs in a second contrast, introduced in 297b. Josephus has just told us what the Pharisees accept and the Sadducees reject; now he will elaborate on the Sadducean position, by explaining what they accept and reject. The two contrasts may be viewed synoptically as follows:

"A"	"B"
Pharisees Accept:	*Sadducees Reject:*
297a. νόμιμα τινὰ	ἅπερ οὐx ἀναγέγραπται
ἐx πατέρων διαδοχῆς	ἐν τοῖς Μωυσέος νόμοις

"C"	"D"
Sadducees Accept:	*Sadducees Reject:*
297b. ἐxεῖνα νόμιμα	τὰ (νόμιμα) ἐx
τὰ γεγραμμένα	παραδόσεως τῶν πατέρων

Clearly, the second contrast (C-D) is Josephus's attempt to elaborate on the Sadducean position given in the first (A-B); the participle λέγον makes the connection obvious. He is not introducing some new area of conflict but is only restating what he has said in § 297a.

Given that C-D elaborates upon A-B, the problem is to ascertain the meaning of the new term "C". The Rivkin/Baumgarten view requires that C mean ''written laws in general'', for only this meaning would justify the Sadducees' exclusion of a Pharisaic tradition because it was oral. Such a meaning for C is, however, implausible. First, the definite article and demonstrative pronoun indicate that Josephus is talking about specific written laws; it is not that the Sadducees recognize any and all written laws (as a simple νόμιμα γεγραμμένα might have suggested). Second, the context requires that A = B = D and that C be understood as the opposite of A, B, and D. This means that τὰ γεγραμμένα in C refers to what is written down *in Scripture,* since A, B, and D all

---

[136] Neusner, *Rabbinic Traditions,* II, 163; cf. 177.

stress the non-Mosaic provenance of Pharisaic tradition.[137] We are bound, therefore, to conclude in favour of Epstein, Marcus, and Neusner.

It should be noted that this interpretation of *Ant.* 13:297 says nothing whatsoever about the question whether the Pharisees actually transmitted their teachings orally or in writing. Our conclusion is only that Josephus has nothing to say about the matter. His point is that the Pharisaic ordinances were not part of the written Law of Moses and that for this reason they were rejected by the Sadducees. I submit that this explanation would have been easily understood by the Gentile reader of *Ant.* Josephus has repeatedly emphasized in that work the authoritative status and inviolability of the all-sufficient Mosaic code. He needs only to explain that the Pharisaic ordinances were something different and not part of the recorded Mosaic laws for the reader to understand why the Sadducees did not observe them.

Ant. 13:298 goes on to point out the significance of this dispute between the Pharisees and Sadducees. It makes the two points: (a) that their disagreement led to "conflicts and major differences" and (b) that the Sadducees appeal only to the wealthy, whereas the Pharisees have a massive public following.[138] This notice explains why Hyrcanus's abrogation of the Pharisaic νόμιμα called forth the hatred (μῖσος) of the masses, as the story has said (§ 296). That the Pharisees have a mass following is indicated throughout Josephus's writings.

Josephus's notice about the Pharisees' popularity raises once again the question of his attitude toward the group. A modern reader is apt to see in the acknowledgement of their "demotic" appeal Josephus's own commendation. That would, however, be a hasty inference. It is true that Josephus can sing the praises of "the people." We see this especially in *War*, which sets out to distinguish the self-controlled δῆμος from the few outrageous τύραννοι.[139] Nevertheless, we are dealing here with a member of the priestly aristocracy, whose sympathies are not necessarily always with τὸ πλῆθος. In the absence of a thorough study of Josephus's view of "the people" or "the masses", we may at least note: (a) that, as we have seen and shall see again, he consistently laments the fame and popularity of the Pharisees[140] and (b) that the opening paragraph of our passage (§ 288) distinctly pits him against both the Pharisees and the people, who are both moved by envy (φθόνος). Hölscher correctly

[137] Note again the parallel phrase τὰ ἀναγεγραμμένα in *Ant.* 12:63, which is used of scriptural prescriptions.
[138] Cf. *War* 1:110; 2:162; *Ant.* 13:400ff.; 18:12ff.; *Life* 191.
[139] So *War* 1:10.
[140] *War* 1:110ff.; 2:162; *Ant.* 13:400ff.; 18:17; *Life* 191ff.

observes, concerning the author of § 288, "Mit den bei den Massen in Gunst stehenden Pharisäern identifiziert er sich offenbar nicht."[141] It is far from clear, therefore, that Josephus's acknowledgement of Pharisaic popularity in § 298 is a commendation. We do know that, on the question of which νόμιμα are authoritative, his sympathies would lie entirely with the Sadducees.

It remains, finally, to comment on one of the problems that we noted at the outset of this chapter. Josephus claims in *Ant.* 13:297f. that the dispute over the νόμιμα caused major differences between the Pharisees and Sadducees. In *War* 2:162-166 and *Ant.* 13:171-173, however, he has implied that their differences on "philosophical" issues, especially on fate and free will, were decisive. How to explain the disparity? We have seen that it is often resolved by source-critical means, with the school passages being assigned to some other author.[142] We have also seen that this solution is unacceptable; the school passages are Josephus's own.

A more plausible solution is suggested by contextual considerations. The school passages, especially *War* 2:119-166, are free Josephan formulations. As he himself concludes one of them, "This is what I had to say (τοιαῦτα. . . εἶχον εἰπεῖν) about those among the Jews who discuss philosophy" (*War* 2:166). Similarly in *Ant.* 13:171-173 we have discovered a definite apologetic purpose. When Josephus has the freedom to do so, then, he represents the religious groups as the Jewish counterparts to Hellenistic philosophic schools.

Ant. 13:297-298, however, is not a free Josephan formulation. The traditional story of the rift between Hyrcanus and the Pharisees (§§ 289-296), which he has decided to recount in order to fill out his record of Hyrcanus's tenure, climaxed with the high priest's abrogation of the Pharisaic νόμιμα. Since Josephus has never before mentioned any Pharisaic νόμιμα, he is now compelled to explain to the reader what these were and why their annulment should have caused such an upheaval. As Rivkin says of 13:297f.:

> It takes the form of a descriptive aside, for the narrative is temporarily halted so as to clarify for the reader the significance of John Hyrcanus' break with the Pharisees and his adherence to the Sadducees.[143]

In modern English style, Josephus might have used a footnote to give his brief explanation of the conflict. This explanation is forced upon him by the traditional story and is not part of what he volunteers about the

---

[141] Hölscher, "Josephus", 1947f.
[142] Cf. chapters 6 and 8 above, and Appendix B, below.
[143] *Revolution*, 41.

religious groups; that information was conveyed in the ἀκριβῶς δεδήλωται account in *War* 2, to which he ultimately refers the reader (*Ant.* 13:298).

Summary and Conclusion

The pericope *Ant.* 13:288-298 had its genesis in a traditional story concerning a rupture between John Hyrcanus and the Pharisees (§§ 289-296). In the story, which was originally favourable to both Hyrcanus and the Pharisees, the rift was blamed on a troublemaker named Eleazar and a Sadducee named Jonathan. When Josephus took over the story, however, his anti-Pharisaic predisposition apparently caused him to overlook the pro-Pharisaic tone of the story. This admirer of Hyrcanus apparently noticed only that the Pharisees were with Eleazar at the banquet where the outrage took place and that the outcome was a rift between the Pharisees and Hyrcanus. For when he placed the story in his narrative, he furnished it with a bitter introduction (§ 288) that accused the Pharisees and their popular supporters of envy and malice toward Hyrcanus. Although we have several indications of his efforts to edit the story for a Greco-Roman audience, we see that he never managed to correct this fundamental oversight.

Josephus's most obvious effort at editing the passage for non-Jewish readers is the digression on the Pharisaic νόμιμα (§§ 297-298). His chief point there is that these ordinances were peculiar; they were not the same as the νόμιμα ἐν τοῖς Μωυσέος νόμοις, which are the only ones that he has told the reader about elsewhere. The Pharisaic νόμιμα derive rather from a "succession of fathers", a phrase that Josephus probably took over from contemporary descriptions of the Pharisees (or from their own self-descriptions). The Sadducees, he explains, do not recognize any such non-Mosaic ordinances.

The disagreement over the νόμιμα was very serious, Josephus tells the reader, and the Pharisees were able to win massive popular support for their ordinances. That is why Hyrcanus's move brought on him the hatred (μῖσος) of the people (§ 196).

CHAPTER TEN

ANT. 13:400-432: THE PHARISEES AND ALEXANDRA SALOME, II

In both *War* and *Ant.* Josephus describes the involvement of the Pharisees in the reign of Alexandra Salome. That story has enormous significance for our study because it offers the only example of a Pharisee passage in *Ant.* (13:400-432) that has an extended parallel in *War* (1:107-119). One of the questions behind the present investigation is that of a possible shift between *War* and *Ant.* in Josephus's attitude toward the Pharisees; his dual account of Alexandra's rule ought to provide a good test case for this question. The significance of *Ant.* 13:400-432 is not lost on Smith and Neusner, who both believe that it evinces Josephus's dramatic re-evaluation of the Pharisees *vis-à-vis War.*[1] The purpose of this chapter will be to interpret Josephus's portrayal of the Pharisees in *Ant.* 13:400-432, both in itself and in comparison with *War* 1:107-119.

In accord with this purpose, we shall determine first the degree to which the content and function of our passage correspond to those of *War* 1:107-119. We shall then undertake a point-by-point comparison in order to judge whether Josephus has changed his portrait in particular areas, by way of omission, by the reformulation of the earlier material in a new sense, or by the addition of new material. Source-critical questions will be dealt with as they arise.

I. *Context*

In chapter 4, above, we summarized *War*'s presentation of the Hasmonean dynasty somewhat as follows.[2] The δυναστεία of the Hasmoneans had a noble and heroic origin as the leading resistance movement during the persecution by Antiochus Epiphanes (*War* 1:34-37). The glory of the house passed from Judas to Jonathan to Simon and reached its apogee with John Hyrcanus, who ruled excellently (κάλλιστα) for "thirty-one whole years" (1:68). By a gift of prophecy, however, this great high priest was allowed to see that his successors would forfeit the government. Josephus proceeds to outline the ways in which this happened,

---

[1] Smith, "Palestinian Judaism", 75f.; Neusner, "Josephus's Pharisees", 238ff.
[2] Chapter 4, above.

namely:[3] the tragedy of Aristobulus I;[4] the brutality of Alexander Janneus;[5] the naive piety of Queen Alexandra, whose reign was spoiled by her deference to the Pharisees;[6] and the "mad squabbling" of Hyrcanus II and Aristobulus II.[7]

In the preceding chapter we saw that, although he fills out considerably his account of John Hyrcanus's tenure, Josephus manages to retain the fundamental scheme of *War*. John Hyrcanus still marks the apex of the Hasmonean dynasty; his sons, we are again told, would lose his good fortune (13:300).

The tragic story of Aristobulus (*Ant.*13:301-318a) is a paraphrase of the *War* account, although Josephus appends a seemingly inappropriate eulogy on this king's beneficent rule (εὐεργετήσας), which he supports by a quotation from Strabo.[8] This new discussion of Aristobulus's accomplishments on behalf of the Jews, which included the conquest and circumcision of the Itureans,[9] has the effect of revising *War*'s account by pointing out the king's good side. This, in turn, serves to heighten the sense of tragedy: a *good* king was the victim of forces beyond his control. Aristobulus's love for his brother was sabotaged by conspirators, among whom was his wife.[10] Nevertheless, the reader still realizes that this son of Hyrcanus did indeed lose his father's εὐτυχία.

The account of Alexander Janneus's reign in *Ant.* likewise offers a small but significant qualification of *War*. To be sure, it includes the earlier work's notices that Alexander slew 6,000 Jews at one time, 50,000 at another, and, most heinous of all, that he crucified 800 of his domestic opponents while slaughtering their families before their eyes.[11] And the new material on Alexander's dealings with the Seleucids and Ptolemies does nothing to soften his image as a vindictive tyrant;[12] only the courage of his enemies and victims is praised. Notice, however, that *Ant.* adds the following reflection to its account of the crucifixion incident:

> This was the revenge he [Alexander] took for the injuries he had suffered; but the penalty he exacted was inhuman for all that, even though he had,

---

[3] *War* 1:69.
[4] *War* 1:70ff.
[5] *War* 1:85ff.
[6] *War* 1:107ff.
[7] *War* 1:120ff., cf. 5:396.
[8] *Ant.* 13:318f. (but cf. 13:302).
[9] That the circumcision is described as κατὰ τοὺς Ἰουδαίους νόμους also accords with *Ant.*'s oft-noted religious-nationalistic tendencies; see chapter 7, above.
[10] *Ant.* 13:305, 308; cf. *War* 1:74.
[11] *Ant.* 13:373, 376, 380.
[12] *Ant.* 13:334, 360ff.

as was natural, gone through very great hardships in the wars he had
fought against them [*sc.* the Jews], and had finally found himself in danger
of losing both his life and his throne, for they were not satisfied to carry
on the struggle by themselves but brought foreigners as well. . . . But still
he seems to have done this thing unnecessarily, and as a result of his excessive cruelty he was nicknamed Thrakidas (the 'Cossack') by the Jews.
(*Ant.* 13:381f.)[13]

We have here an equivocation. As in the case of Aristobulus, the author
has introduced a new tone of pathos *vis-à-vis War*,[14] even though he does
not remove any of the earlier work's grisly details. It is still clear that
Alexander fell from the εὐτυχία of his father, but now he is not exclusively to blame. What he did was wrong but, to some degree, understandable in the circumstances.

II. *Interpretation*

When we come now to the reign of Alexandra Salome we shall need to
ask in what ways, if at all, Josephus has altered her image. She was
already portrayed positively in *War*, as a pious woman; it was only her
gullibility, which allowed the Pharisees to exploit her, that brought her
reign to a sad conclusion. Has Josephus modified this portrayal in *Ant.*?
We shall proceed with our interpretation by dividing the lengthy narrative into six parts and considering each in turn.

A. *Alexandra and Alexander (Ant. 13:399-406)*

A major difference from *War* is the way in which Alexandra is introduced. In *War*, the reader knew only the discrete facts (a) that
Aristobulus's (unidentified) wife had released Alexander Janneus from
prison (1:85) and (b) that Alexander's wife, Alexandra, had succeeded
her husband as ruler. Being pious and gentle, and opposed to her husband's brutality (1:107), the woman had opened a promising new
chapter in the Hasmonean succession. In *Ant.*, however, all of this
changes.

First, Josephus tells us that Aristobulus's widow, who released Janneus from prison and gave him the throne, was named Salina (or Salo-

---

[13] Throughout this chapter I am following the LCL translation of *Ant.* 13, by R.
Marcus, except where noted. The parenthetical "the Cossack" is Marcus's attempt to
give the sense of *Thrakidas* (LCL edn., p. 418 n. *d*).

[14] Since the new tone comes through particularly in reflective asides and since it is
pro-Hasmonean in tendency (cf. *Ant.* 16:187; *Life* 1-2), the natural assumption is that
it comes from Josephus himself.

me) Alexandra (13:320).[15] Although Josephus does not explicitly say so, most interpreters infer from his account that this Alexandra was the one who became Alexander's wife—the one with whom we are concerned.[16] If that is the case, however, we already have some disturbing new information about our Queen: it was she who, while married to Aristobulus, had conspired with the πονηροί to set that king against his brother Antigonus (13:308). Such actions hardly accord with *War*'s description of her as gentle, frail, and pious.

Indeed, *Ant.* omits altogether *War*'s lavish praise of the Queen's virtues. Gone is the notice that "she was indeed most precise" (ἠκρίβου δὴ μάλιστα) in her treatment of the laws and that she used to expel offenders from office (*War* 1:111). Gone also is the clear distinction between her husband and herself. Whereas *War* 1:107 had spoken of her "utter lack of her husband's brutality" (τῆς ὠμότητος αὐτοῦ μακρὰν ἀποδέουσα) and of her "opposition to his crimes" (ταῖς παρανομίαις ἀνθισταμένη), *Ant.* concedes only that Alexandra "was thought to disapprove" (τὸ δοκεῖν . . . δυσχεραίειν) of her husband's misdeeds (13:407).

War's insistence on a clean separation between Alexandra and Alexander is shattered, finally, by the opening paragraphs of our story (§§ 399-406). Whereas *War* had claimed that the woman's innocent religious disposition made her easy prey for the Pharisees (cf. ἁπλότης, 1:111), we now see her carefully plotting, on the advice of her dying husband, how to placate the nation's hatred; the solution, they decide, is to court the Pharisees. Alexandra thus appears as a calculating politician.

The planning for the Queen's succession begins when Alexander, exhausted with disease and recurring fever, lies dying while besieging a fortress east of the Jordan (§ 398). A furious Alexandra visits the site in order to castigate him for his lack of responsibility: he will soon be gone but she and her sons will be left to face a hostile nation! To mollify his wife, the King cudgels his fading wits and offers a solution (§ 399). First, she should keep silent about his death and proceed herself to capture the fortress:

> And then, he said, on her return to Jerusalem as from a splendid victory, she should yield a certain amount of power to the Pharisees (τοῖς Φαρισαίοις ἐξουσίαν τινὰ παρασχεῖν), for if they praised her in return for this sign of regard, they would dispose the nation favourably toward her. These men, he assured her, had so much influence with their fellow-Jews that they could injure those whom they hated (τούτους μισοῦντας) and help those to

whom they were friendly; for they had the complete confidence of the
masses when they spoke harshly of any person, even when they did so out
of envy (μάλιστα γὰρ πιστεύεσθαι παρὰ τῷ πλήθει περὶ ὧν κἂν φθονοῦντες τι
χαλεπὸν λέγωσιν); and he himself, he added, had come into conflict with the
nation because these men had been badly treated by him. (13:400-402)

Schwartz[17] has pointed out some of the strong verbal parallels between
this speech, put into Janneus's mouth, and the editorial remarks in *Ant.*
13:288 (considered in the previous chapter). The parallels include:
φθονοῦντες/φθόνος, παρὰ τῷ πλήθει, πιστεύεσθαι, τι χαλεπὸν λέγωσιν/τι
λέγοντες κατά, μάλιστα. Both passages must come from the same author.
For reasons outlined in chapter 9, Schwartz believes that author to have
been Nicolaus of Damascus. We should rather suggest that, since the
anti-Pharisaic and pro-Hasmonean tone (cf. *War* 1:110-114; *Ant.*17:41-
45; *Life* 189-198; and *Ant.* 13:288; 16:187; *Life* 1-2, respectively), along
with the μῖσος/φθόνος theme (cf. *War* 2:82; 4:566; *Ant.* 2:10; 6:193;
13:288/296; 20:29), are characteristically Josephan, Josephus must have
formulated (or freely invented) Alexander's deathbed speech.

It is in this paragraph that Smith and Neusner find the most compelling evidence for their theory that *Ant.* attempts to commend the
Pharisees to the Romans. Neusner observes that the relationship between Alexandra and the Pharisees is portrayed very differently from the
War parallel, and he attributes the change to a new, positive presentation
of the Pharisees:

> No longer do the Pharisees take advantage of the woman's ingenuousness.
> Now they are essential to her exercise of power. . . . In place of a credulous
> queen, we have a supine one. In place of conniving Pharisees, we have
> powerful leaders of the whole nation.[18]

Josephus offers the new account because he now wants the Romans to
install the Pharisees as the new aristocracy in Palestine.

Although Neusner has correctly discerned a change in the relationship
between Alexandra and the Pharisees, however, he misses entirely the
anti-Pharisaic thrust of the passage in *Ant.* As we shall see, all of *War*'s
details about their despotic actions are taken over and expanded in *Ant.*
Their relationship to Alexandra has changed because she has changed;
they are no better. Rather than commending the Pharisees, *Ant.* 13:400-
432 makes it very clear that their participation in power was a disaster
and sealed the doom of the Hasmonean house. Alexandra should have
prevented it.

[17] Schwartz, ''Josephus and Nicolaus'', 159.
[18] ''Josephus's Pharisees'', 238.

We return to the passage. Since the source of Alexander's troubles has been his mistreatment of the Pharisees, he advises his wife to share power with this group. Then she will have the support of the people. The reader's question is: Does the plan work? The rest of the narrative answers this question with a resounding "No!"

Notice the cynicism in Alexander's assessment of the Pharisees. Until now he has been their determined opponent. What they really want, he claims, is power. If Alexandra will only give the Pharisees some ἐξουσία they will be happy. No principles are at stake here. Thus the King advises his wife to present his corpse to the Pharisees, for them to abuse as they wish (§ 403). He calculates that this pre-emptive show of generosity will placate their anger and even inspire them to give him a magnificent funeral. Further, she is to promise them that she will make no decisions without their approval (μηδὲν δίχα τῆς ἐκεινῶν γνώμης διαπράξεσθαι).

So these opening sentences explain the logic and basis of Queen Alexandra's reign in *Ant.* On her husband's advice, she will attempt to rescue the dynasty by throwing in her lot with the Pharisees. It will be an experiment in pragmatic politics.

In the event, Alexander's cynical view of the Pharisees is proven correct. After his death Alexandra places everything (πάντα) in their hands. The delighted Pharisees act as predicted. They instantly become "well-wishers and friends" of Alexandra. They go around the country declaring what a just (δίχαιος) king they had lost and move the people to deep mourning! As hoped, they provide a funeral for Alexander that is unprecedented in splendour (§§ 405f.). The author of the passage agrees, then, with Alexander's view of the Pharisees: they *are* unprincipled power-mongers.

The Pharisees' euphoria at coming into sudden power and their manipulation of popular feeling in support of Alexandra are, however, only the beginning of the story.

B. *Alexandra's Sons (13:407-408, 417)*

Because the Queen has given absolute power to the Pharisees, she has little left for the two sons that we now hear about, Hyrcanus and Aristobulus. There is still, however, the high priesthood and this she bestows on Hyrcanus, the older son.

Notice how differently this action is presented in *War* and *Ant.* In *War*, Alexandra was commended for her judicious treatment of her sons. She gave the high priesthood to Hyrcanus because he was older and more subdued (νωθέστερον). Aristobulus, by contrast, was a "hot-head" (θερμότητα, 1:109, 117) and would have been unsuitable for office. In *Ant.*, the Queen's decision is differently evaluated:

> Now although Alexander had left two sons, Hyrcanus and Aristobulus, he had bequeathed the royal power to Alexandra. Of these sons the one, Hyrcanus, was incompetent ('Ὑρκανὸς μὲν ἀσθενὴς ἦν πράγματα διοικεῖν) to govern and in addition much preferred a quiet life, while the younger, Aristobulus, was a man of action (δραστήριος) and high spirit (θαρσαλέος). Alexandra then appointed Hyrcanus as high priest because of his greater age but more especially because of his lack of energy (διὰ τὸ ἄπραγμον). (§§ 407-408a)

Two modifications of *War* are: (a) the note of surprise that although he left sons, Alexander gave the rule to his wife, and (b) the new claim that it was Hyrcanus, not Aristobulus, who was unfit for office.[19] Hyrcanus was "weak". Aristobulus is no longer seen as a hot-head; he was a "doer", a courageous man. The implication is that Aristobulus ought to have been given the executive power.

Josephus will later make this point in plain terms. Describing the injustices suffered by victims of the Pharisees, he will reflect:

> But still they themselves were to blame for their misfortunes, in allowing a woman to reign who madly desired it in her unreasonable love of power (κατὰ φιλαρχίαν ἐκλελυσσηκυίᾳ γυναικί παρὰ τὸ εἰκὸς βασιλεύειν), and when her sons were in the prime of life (ἐν ἀκμῇ οὔσης). (13:417)

This reflection sums up Josephus's new attitude toward both Alexandra and her sons. In the interest of maintaining her own power, the old woman[20] sacrificed propriety and left her sons (especially Aristobulus) out of her reign. Josephus will reiterate this judgement in his closing remarks on Alexandra (13:430-432).

So far, then, we have seen that Josephus reversed his attitudes toward both Alexandra and her sons between *War* and *Ant.* In *War*, she gave the Pharisees power because her religious devotion blinded her to their real nature; in *Ant.*, she invites them to sponsor her regime as part of a clever scheme for maintaining her own power. In *War*, her decision to confine the upstart Aristobulus to private life was a wise one; in *Ant.*, she is castigated for having silenced such a vigorous and courageous young man. The question now is whether Josephus's attitude toward the Pharisees has also changed between *War* and *Ant.*.

---

[19] *Ant.*'s denigration of Hyrcanus becomes obvious later in the narrative. Confronted by Herod, we shall be told, "he was incompetent to do anything, because of his cowardice and folly" (14:179). *War* 1:213, by contrast, had allowed only that Hyrcanus did not know what to do because he was outmatched by Herod.

[20] According to *Ant.* 13:430, Alexandra was about 64 years of age at her accession.

C. *The Pharisees' Actions and the Reaction (13:408-417)*

In *War*, we were told that the effects of the Pharisees' coming into power were felt mainly in the judicial sphere. They took over the penal system: they banished and recalled from exile whomever they wished (οὓς ἐθέλοιεν); they were free to incarcerate or release from prison; and they even had a *de facto* power of capital punishment. By influencing Alexandra, they were able to do away with whomever they wished (again, οὓς ἐθέλοιεν, 1:111-113).

Neusner, in his attempt to show that *Ant.* commends the Pharisees to the Romans, claims that our passage tones down the Pharisaic reign of terror under Alexandra: "The mass slaughter of *War*, in which the Pharisees killed anyone they wanted, is shaded into a mild persecution of the Pharisees' opposition."[21] It is, however, impossible to accept Neusner's interpretation at this point.

War's account of the Pharisees' actions and the reaction that they evoked took up four Niese sections (1:111-114). *Ant.* expands the same topic to ten sections (13:408-417); and none of the new material improves the image of the Pharisees. They personally engage, we are now told, in a systematic slaughter of their enemies; what is more, the author takes considerable space to dilate on the justice of their victims' cause. Consider the following excerpts:

> Alexandra permitted the Pharisees to do as they liked in all matters (πάντα τοῖς Φαρισαίοις ἐπιτρέπει ποιεῖν), and also commanded the people to obey them. . . . And so, while she had the title of sovereign (τὸ ὄνομα τῆς βασιλείας), the Pharisees had the power (τὴν δύναμιν). For example, they recalled exiles and freed prisoners, and, in a word, in no way differed from absolute rulers (οὐδὲν δεσποτῶν διέφερον). [Then follows a notice on the Queen's competence in *foreign* affairs.] And throughout the country there was quiet except for the Pharisees; for they worked upon the feelings of the queen and tried to persuade her to kill those who had urged Alexander to put the eight hundred to death. Later they themselves slaughtered[22] one of them (εἶτα αὐτοὶ τούτων ἕνα σφάττουσι), named Diogenes, and his death was followed by that of one after another (καὶ μετ' αὐτὸν ἄλλους ἐπ' ἄλλαις), until the leading citizens (οἱ δυνατοί) came to the palace. . . and they reminded her of all that they achieved in the face of danger, whereby they had shown their unwavering loyalty to their master [*sc.* Alexander Janneus]. . . . And they begged her not to crush their hopes completely, for, they said, after escaping the dangers of war, they were now being slaughtered at home like cattle (δίκην βοσκημάτων κόπτεσθαι) by their foes [*sc.* the Pharisees], and there was no one to avenge them. (408b-412)

---

21 "Josephus's Pharisees", 240.
22 Marcus, *ad loc*, has "cut down"; but cf. his n. *d*.

Nothing in this passage suggests a "shading" of the Pharisees' pogrom into a "mild persecution". If anything, the imagery used to describe their actions (σφάττουσι, βοσκημάτων) is more vivid in *Ant.* The Pharisees are no longer content, as in *War*, to get rid of their enemies merely by influencing Alexandra to act; Josephus now claims emphatically that they themselves (αὐτοὶ τούτων) behaved viciously, at least in the case of Diogenes. Finally, whereas *War* had only briefly noted the plight of the eminent citizens (οἱ δοκοῦντες) and their appeal to the Queen (1:114), *Ant.* tells us the details of what they said to Alexandra (§§ 411-416) and thereby pleads their cause before the reader.

The thrust of the speech made by the δυνατοί is that Alexandra has betrayed them. They had always been loyal to her husband's policies and so they at least deserved her protection. Their only goal has been faithfulness to the Hasmonean house and they are also loyal to her; but now they are being slaughtered by her husband's enemies, evidently with her support (§§ 411-413)! The δυνατοί close their speech by calling on the δαίμονας of Alexander to take pity on their plight, at which the bystanders burst into tears. The courageous young Aristobulus, who deplores his mother's betrayal of these men,[23] "denounces her bitterly" (πολλὰ κακίζων).

It is perfectly clear that Josephus sides with Aristobulus and the leading citizens against Alexandra and her Pharisaic sponsors. As Hölscher long ago observed, the passage "steht mit ihrer Sympathie sichtlich auf der Seite der Vornehmen und betrachtet das Pharisäerregiment unter Alexandra offenbar nicht als ideal".[24] Before Smith and Neusner, one never imagined that the author of *Ant.* 13:400-432 was trying to recommend that the Romans entrust any sort of power to the Pharisees.

D. *Alexandra's Foreign Policy (13:418-421)*

We come now to a brief account of Alexandra's foreign policy, which elaborates a little on *War* 1:115-116. The thrust is that, although she made no significant gains, the Queen managed at least to maintain the

---

[23] Cf. also 13:411.

[24] Hölscher, "Josephus", 1975, n.*. Since he considered Josephus to have been a Pharisee, on the basis of *Life* 12 (cf. p. 1936, n. ++), Hölscher had to attribute these sentiments to a hypothetical intermediate source, which he thought to be pro-priestly and pro-Hasmonean. I shall argue in Part IV, however, that Josephus does not claim Pharisaic allegiance in *Life* 12. I see no reason, therefore, to deny that the anti-Pharisaic sentiments of our passage reflect Josephus's own viewpoint, which we know to be priestly and pro-Hasmonean (*Ant.* 16:187; 20:266; *Life* 1-9).

status quo. This was itself an accomplishment, however, in the face of external threats such as that posed by Tigranes, King of Armenia.

Most significant for us, Alexandra's foreign policy is the only aspect of her reign that Josephus finds praiseworthy; and it is the only area in which the Pharisees apparently had no influence. After detailing the absolute domestic powers given to the Pharisees, Josephus makes the point:

> Nevertheless the queen took precautions (ἐποιεῖτο. . . τῆς βασιλείας πρόνοιαν)[25] for the kingdom and recruited a large force of mercenaries and also made her own force twice as large, with the result that she struck terror into the local rulers around her and received hostages from them. And throughout the entire country there was quiet except for the Pharisees; for they worked upon the feelings of the queen (ἠρέμει δὲ ἡ χώρα πᾶσα πάρεξ τῶν Φαρισαίων. οὗτοι γὰρ ἐπετάραττον τὴν βασίλισσαν). (13:409)

Notice the contrast. Where she was left to herself, Alexandra at least maintained quiet; where the Pharisees held sway, there was trouble. The bulk of our passage is devoted to the unhappy results of their malign influence.

E. *Aristobulus's Revolt (13:422-429)*

Ant.'s description of Aristobulus's reaction to his mother's policies again reflects Josephus's shift in perspective since *War*. In the earlier work the whole matter had been summed up as follows: when Alexandra became sick, her impetuous younger son seized the fortresses and proclaimed himself king. His followers were attracted to him solely because of his colourful personality (πάντας εὔνους διὰ τὴν θερμότητα, 1:117). We were told that Alexandra moved to prevent this *coup* by taking Aristobulus's family hostage but that she died before the outcome was known (1:118).

Ant. expands the account considerably. In the process it omits (again) any reference to Alexander's recklessness. Instead, it highlights his devotion to his family. When his mother became sick, we are now told, he visited the fortresses to which she had sent his father's persecuted friends (to protect them from the Pharisees). And these men now support Aristobulus not διὰ τὴν θερμότητα, as *War* would have it, but because he has consistently championed their cause. Aristobulus's reason for making his move is now given as follows:

---

[25] Marcus renders "took thought for the welfare of the kingdom". Since, however, the overriding point is that Alexandra's reckless policies caused the kingdom to be lost (§§ 430-432), we should probably read πρόνοια in a minimalist sense, as referring to the single area in which the author concedes that the Queen did act properly, viz., in her defence policy.

> For while he had long resented the things his mother was doing, he was just then especially fearful that on her death their whole family might come under the rule of the Pharisees (ἔδεισε μὴ ἀποθανούσης ἐπὶ τοῖς Φαρισαίοις τὸ πᾶν γένος αὐτοῖς ὑπάρξειεν), for he saw the incapacity (τὸ ἀδύνατον) of his brother [sc. Hyrcanus], who was destined to succeed the throne. (13:423)

The disclosure of this motive entirely changes *War*'s picture. Aristobulus is not out for personal gain; he wants to preserve the royal family and to protect it from being swallowed up by the Pharisees.

That the author sides with Aristobulus is clear from the above notice and from what follows. When the Queen learns of Aristobulus's revolt, both she and the "people" (τὸ ἔθνος) become extremely anxious (ἐν μεγίσταις ταραχαῖς ὑπῆρχεν):

> For they knew that Aristobulus was not far from being able to seize the throne for himself, and they were very much afraid that he might exact satisfaction for the excesses which they had practised on his house (ὧν παρῴνησαν αὐτῷ τὸν οἶκον). (13:426)

The author has the people confessing that they have "played drunken games" (παροινέω > οἶνος) with the Hasmonean house! His sympathies are patent.

Notice the curious identification here of the people with the Pharisees. We have been told all along that it was the Pharisees who persecuted the friends of Alexander and Aristobulus; now it is "the people" who are afraid of retribution. But this equation is not new. It is merely the reverse case of what happened in the narrative of Alexander's reign. The account of his atrocities against "the people" never once mentioned the Pharisees. When he is dying, however, he confesses that he has badly mistreated this group[26] and we are told that the Pharisees demanded satisfaction for Alexander's crucifixion of the eight hundred.[27] Evidently, Josephus considers the Pharisees and the people to be so closely related that he expects the reader to understand that "Pharisaic" actions have the support of the people. Only thus can he implicate τὸ ἔθνος in the Pharisees' wrongdoing under Alexandra.

As in *War*, *Ant.*'s account of Alexandra's reign ends without mentioning any decisive response to Aristobulus's move. The "elders of the Jews", representing the popular/Pharisaic viewpoint, join Hyrcanus in protesting Aristobulus's move to the Queen. But she is too weak to respond and, having given them permission to do as they see fit, she dies (§§ 420f.).

---

[26] *Ant.* 13:402.
[27] *Ant.* 13:410.

F. *Josephus's Final Remarks on Alexandra (13:430-432)*

Josephus does not leave the reader in any final doubt about his assessment of Alexandra's reign but concludes with a reflective paragraph in which he spells out his views. It is significant that this paragraph closes book 13 of *Ant.*, which has recounted the fortunes of the Hasmoneans from the death of Judas onward. Josephus will tell us now that it was Alexandra's misguided policy of keeping power from her sons (especially Aristobulus) and giving it instead to the Pharisees that caused the downfall of the Hasmonean δυναστεία. Since these closing remarks are crucial for the interpretation of our passage, I quote them in full:

> She was a woman who showed none of the weakness of her sex, for being one of those inordinately desirous of the power to rule (δεινὴ γὰρ εἰς τὸ φίλαρχον), she showed by her deeds the ability to carry out her plans, and at the same time she exposed the folly of those men who continually fail to maintain sovereign power. For she valued the present more than the future, and making everything else secondary to absolute rule (πάντα δεύτερα τιθεμένη τοῦ ἐγκρατῶς ἄρχειν), she had, on account of this, no consideration for either decency or justice (οὔτε καλοῦ οὔτε δικαίου). At least matters turned out so unfortunately for her house that the sovereign power (δυναστεία) which it had acquired in the face of the greatest dangers and difficulties was not long afterwards taken from it (ἀφαιρεθῆναι) because of her desire for things unbecoming a woman, and because she expressed the same opinions as did those [*sc.* the Pharisees] who were hostile to her family (τοῖς μὲν δυσμενῶς ἔχουσιν πρὸς τὸ γένος αὐτῶν τὴν αὐτὴν γνώμην προθεῖσα), and also because she left the kingdom without anyone who had their interests at heart. And even after her death she caused the palace to be filled with misfortunes and disturbances (συμφορῶν καὶ ταραχῆς) which arose from the public measures taken during her lifetime. Nevertheless, in spite of reigning in this manner, she had kept the nation at peace.

With these words, Josephus gives his final verdict on the experiment that Alexander had conceived in order to deflect his wife's anger at being left with a hostile kingdom. She was obsessed with power, Josephus tells us, and this was inappropriate to a woman. Her obsession prevented her from handing over the dynasty to Aristobulus, who was in his prime and had the interests of the family at heart (cf. § 417). Instead, she opted to preserve her own place of honour by sharing power with the enemies of her husband, the Pharisees. Although this strategy enabled her to retain the title of sovereign while she lived, its implications for the Hasmonean house were catastrophic. The old woman's folly caused the δυναστεία to be removed from the once glorious family. In short, Alexandra's domestic policy, which was based on wholesale submission to the Pharisees, was an unqualified disaster.

It is worth emphasizing, perhaps, that we are now dealing only with

Josephus's interpretation of events. Judgements of success and failure depend entirely on the criteria of the one who judges. It is obvious from Josephus's account that Alexandra's rule had the strong support of the ἔθνος and we know that Queen "Shalom-Zion" is honoured in Jewish tradition. Josephus, however, is an aristocrat and not a democrat. He mourns the loss of the Hasmonean dynasty, in which he finds his own roots (*Life* 1-2; *Ant.* 16:187). And he attributes the loss, in large measure, to Alexandra's collusion with the Pharisees.

Summary and Conclusion

In both *War* and *Ant.*, the story of Alexandra Salome's reign is an account of the interaction between three parties: the Queen, her sons, and the Pharisees. The Smith/Neusner hypothesis deals only with the last of these; it holds that *Ant.* revises *War* so as to commend the Pharisees to the Romans, by drawing attention to their massive popular support. An analysis of the roles played by all three parties, however, excludes such a reading.

In *Ant.*, Alexandra is no longer a frail, religiously devout woman. She has become an aggressive schemer, willing to sacrifice posterity to her immediate ambitions. It is only this new portrayal of Alexandra that changes her relationship to the Pharisees. She can no longer appear as their hapless victim because she has conspired with her husband to manipulate them by taking advantage of their lust for power. It is because *Ant.* says nothing about Alexandra's piety, moreover, that it omits *War*'s notice about the Pharisees' reputation for εὐσέβεια and ἀκρίβεια (1:110); this information has no point in the new context, since Alexandra is no longer deceived by the Pharisees' reputation.

The Pharisees themselves have not improved one bit. If anything, the new material in *Ant.* heightens the enormity of their actions. It also leads the reader to sympathize with their aristocratic victims, who were loyal to the Queen's husband. Josephus certainly acknowledges the Pharisees' fame and public support, as he had in *War* 1:110, but he (still) abhors this state of affairs.[28]

Josephus has revised his opinion of Alexandra's sons. Whereas *War* had presented Aristobulus as an upstart and had applauded the Queen's appointment of the lethargic Hyrcanus to the high priesthood, *Ant.*

---

[28] Indeed, the rueful recognition of Pharisaic power is a consistent feature of all of Josephus's writings. Cf. also *War* 1:571; 2:162f., 411-418; *Ant.* 13:288-298; 17:41ff.; *Life* 189ff. But if Josephus raises the issue of Pharisaic predominance only in order to express his regrets about it, he can hardly have invented the idea that they were in fact predominant.

stands squarely behind Aristobulus: he is the only one who is concerned about the integrity of his family. Hyrcanus has moved from docility to utter impotence.

Our conclusion is that Josephus, in *Ant.*, has radically redrawn his portrait of Alexandra Salome's reign, as Smith and Neusner rightly perceive. This development, however, affects everything but the image of the Pharisees. One can only marvel at Josephus's ability to take over the substance of the *War* account and yet give it a completely new sense. One is impressed by his determination, even while changing the roles of all of the other players, to keep the role of the Pharisees as villains constant. It is impossible to see in *Ant.* 13:400-432 a commendation of the Pharisees.

If we now step back to compare the main lines of Hasmonean history in *War* and *Ant.*, we discover the following similarities and differences. Both narratives locate the high point of the dynasty in the long reign of John Hyrcanus. Both accounts declare that his successors lost his εὐδαιμονία or εὐτυχία. The sequel, however, is differently reported. In *War*, we have a steady degeneration from Aristobulus I to Alexander Janneus. Alexandra opens a new chapter and, because of her piety, offers a ray of hope; but the entrance of the Pharisees sets the downward spiral in motion again. *Ant.*, by contrast, is somewhat kinder to both Aristobulus and Alexander. They still represent a degeneration but the fault is not exclusively their own. We now hear about Aristobulus's basic goodness and about the hardships faced by Alexander. Queen Alexandra, on the other hand, is now completely out of order and it is she who plunges the dynasty into irreversible straits. The reason is that she betrayed her house to its Pharisaic opponents.

In both scenarios, then, the Pharisees play a major and destructive role in the collapse of the Hasmonean rule. For that reason, if for no other, they have earned the contempt of the pro-Hasmonean Josephus.

CHAPTER ELEVEN

ANT. 17:41-45: THE PHARISEES AT HEROD'S COURT, II

In the last chapter we saw that, although *Ant.* reworks *War*'s explanation of the downfall of the Hasmoneans, the role of the Pharisees in both accounts is similar. *Ant.* reappraises both Alexandra Salome and her two sons but it continues to present the Pharisees as a destructive force. In the present chapter, we shall discover that Josephus's reevaluation of Herod in *Ant.* likewise does not lead to any improvement in the image of the Pharisees. Josephus will again attack their claims to superior ἀκρίβεια and he will add the new charge that they have issued fraudulent predictions.

That *Ant.* 17:41-45 is hostile toward the Pharisees is universally recognized, because it is obvious. Most scholars, however, insist that the passage is a direct reproduction of some source (often thought to be Nicolaus of Damascus) and that it does not reflect Josephus's own sentiments. The following analysis will challenge this widespread assumption. Before engaging in source criticism, however, we shall need to ensure that our understanding of the passage in its present context is adequate.

I. *Context*

By the opening of *Ant.* 17, the Hasmoneans have long since lost their δυναστεία.[1] A Roman appointee, Herod the Idumean, has now ruled the Jews for over three decades. He has enjoyed outstanding political success but has fallen progressively deeper into domestic strife. A complex network of ambitions, jealousies, and misunderstandings, both his own and others', have led him to execute one of his wives and two of his sons.[2] But that did not end his troubles. A powerful clique, headed by Herod's sister-in-law (Pheroras's wife), and his oldest son (Antipater), is now plotting against the king.[3] It is in the course of his discussion of these conspirators that Josephus introduces the Pharisees (*Ant.* 17:41-45). The passage has a brief parallel in *War* 1:571, which we considered above (chapter 5).

---

[1] Cf. *Ant.* 14:490f.
[2] *Ant.* 15:232-236, 16:320ff., 392ff.
[3] *Ant.* 17:32-40.

A few remarks on the general portrayal of Herod in *Ant.* will help to provide a context for our interpretation. It is now well known that, on the whole, Herod receives kinder treatment in *War* than he does in *Ant.*[4] At several points the later work introduces direct criticism of the Idumean king for his vanity and for his violation of the Jewish πάτρια,[5] criticism which was largely absent from *War*.[6] Equally effective in their cumulative force are the many small changes that *Ant.* makes in *War*'s narrative that vitiate *War*'s flattering portraits of the king, his father (Antipater), and his descendants.[7]

It needs to be emphasized here that the shift in attitude is not simply from a "pro-Herodian" stance in *War* to an "anti-Herodian" stance in *Ant.* The later presentation, rather, is highly nuanced. Josephus now offers a psychological profile of Herod, in order to explain the roots of both his viciousness and his amazing generosity.[8] Our author still frankly acknowledges Herod's valour,[9] beneficence,[10] devotion to his family,[11] and even his piety, in certain contexts.[12] Most important, *Ant.* is still full of condemnation for the meanness and impiety of those within Herod's family and court who conspired against him.[13] It does not follow, then, because *War* had praised Herod and denounced his opponents, that *Ant.*, which is more critical of the king, must automatically treat his enemies more kindly. Josephus now seems prepared to point out the injustices both of Herod and of his opponents.

Ant. consistently presents the Pharisees as Herod's opponents. While he was still governor of the Galilee,[14] we are told, Herod incurred the wrath of the Jewish leaders by, among other things, executing many of the local bandits without the due process that was enshrined in Jewish

---

[4] Cf. Laqueur, *Josephus*, 171ff.; Hölscher, "Josephus", 1947; Thackeray, *Josephus* 65ff.; Michel-Bauernfeind, *De Bello Judaico*, I, XXV f.; Cohen, *Josephus*, iii; and chapter 7, above.

[5] E.g., *Ant.* 14:173; 15:182, 267, 280ff., 291, 299, 328f.; 16:1f., 159.

[6] Herod's violation of the laws is, however, implicit in the story of Judas and Mattathias, esp. *War* 1:648-650, 653; 2:6-7. It is an interesting coincidence, if nothing more, that Herod's serious illness follows immediately on his execution of the pious offenders (cf. 1:656, ἔνθεν, and the parallel *Ant.* 17:168).

[7] Cf. chapter 7, above.

[8] *Ant.* 16:150-159.

[9] *Ant.* 14:430, 439-444, 462-464.

[10] *Ant.* 14:377; 15:305-316, 380-425.

[11] *Ant.* 14:348ff., 451ff.

[12] *Ant.* 14:482f.; 15:380-425, esp. 381-387, 421-423.

[13] Cf. e.g., *Ant.* 15:81, 213, 232-235 (Alexandra), 255f. (Costobarus); 16:3f., 66-77, 206 (Salome); 16:78-86, 87-90, 244-250, 302, 305-307; 319; 17:1-7, 32-35 (Antipater).

[14] Cf. *Ant.* 14:158f.; on the proper titles of Herod and his father Antipater, see 14:143f. and LCL edn., VII, 514 n. *d*.

law.[15] At the ensuing trial, however, the members of the Sanhedrin were overawed by Herod's presence and were afraid to speak against him. The only exception was a certain Samaias, "an upright man (δίκαιος ἀνήρ) and for that reason superior to fear" (14:172). This man berated the Sanhedrin and the king (Hyrcanus)[16] for allowing the impertinent Idumean to mock Jewish law. He predicted that Herod, though acquitted, would one day punish both Hyrcanus and the Sanhedrin (14:174). Josephus remarks that this prophecy was to be fulfilled: when Herod became king, he killed Hyrcanus and all of the sanhedrists *except* for Samaias. Herod spared this one, Josephus claims, for two reasons. First, he respected Samaias's uprightness (δικαιοσύνη). Second, when Herod arrived to assume his royal position, Samaias:

> exhorted the people to admit Herod, having stated that because of (their) sins, they would not be able to escape him (διὰ τὰς ἁμαρτίας οὐ δύνασθαι διαφυγεῖν αὐτόν). (*Ant.* 14:176).

Samaias, then, is appalled by Herod's lawlessness and views his royal appointment as a divine punishment of the Jews.[17] Herod, for his part, respects his adversary's integrity and is grateful for his support, whatever its motivation.

The next time we hear of Samaias, we discover that he was a Pharisee. In *Ant.* 15:3-4, Josephus is explaining that Herod, once he became king of Judea, rewarded those who had taken his side while he was still a commoner. Among those so rewarded were "the Pharisee Pollion and his disciple Samaias,[18] for during the siege of Jerusalem these men [had] counseled the citizens to admit Herod". Thus, Pollion is now included as one who also recommended submission when Herod arrived to take Jerusalem. To Pollion also is attributed the prediction (of Samaias! 14:176) that Herod would one day persecute his erstwhile judges (15:4).[19] We now learn, therefore, that at least two Pharisees were opposed to Herod from the start; ironically, Herod honoured them because their call for submission, though motivated by the view that Herod's reign was an inescapable punishment, served his ends well.

---

[15] *Ant.* 14:163-167.

[16] On Hyrcanus II's title at this point, cf. *Ant.* 14:151 and LCL edn., VII, 523 n. *f*.

[17] Samaias's acquiesence in this punishment recalls Josephus's own rationale for submitting to Rome, as he elaborates in it in *War* e.g., 4:323; 5:17-19, 401-404, 442-445; 6:110; 7:330-332); cf. Lindner, *Geschichtsauffassung*, 41ff.

[18] On the various proposals for identifying Pollion and Samaias, see the discussion and literature cited in Blenkinsopp, "Prophecy", 257 n. 81. Neusner, however, considers such attempts "primitive and pointless" (*Rabbinic Traditions*, I, 5).

[19] The Epitome and the Latin have "Samaias" at 15:4, which fits with 14:176. But the major MSS support "Pollion", which also seems to be the *lectio difficilior*.

In 15:370, we hear yet again of Herod's favour toward Pollion and Samaias in spite of their opposition to him. Concerned about the faithfulness of his subjects, Josephus narrates, Herod took steps to ensure their loyalty: he banned public meetings, sent out spies, and demanded from everyone an oath of fidelity (15:366-368). Those who resisted the oath were done away with by every means possible (παντὶ τρόπῳ ἐκποδὼν ἐποιεῖτο). Although Herod was pushing for the Pharisees Pollion and Samaias and their colleagues to take the oath:

> they did not consent to do so; yet they were not punished in the same ways as those [others] who refused (οὔθ᾽ ὁμοίως τοῖς ἀρνησαμένοις ἐκολάσθησαν) for they were given respect on account of Pollion. (*Ant.* 15:370)

What this means, evidently, is that Herod's regard for Pollion prevented him from punishing the Pharisees with death "by every possible means", which is what the other protestors received; it would not seem to exclude lesser punishments. We see here again that the Pharisees oppose Herod but that he favours them.

To summarize: incidental references to the Pharisees in *Ant.* 14 and 15 establish several themes and topics that will occur again in 17:41-45. First, individual Pharisees have been engaged in prediction or prophecy. Second, they have acquired a position of influence with Herod. Third, they are opposed to Herod because of his violation of Jewish law. Fourth, they have refused to take an oath of allegiance to the king. All of these points will be reprised in *Ant.* 17:41-45.

II. *Key Terms*

In keeping with his common procedure, Josephus constructs our passage from a topic paragraph (17:41), which contains a summary characterization of the Pharisees, followed by a brief narrative of events in which they were involved (17:42-45), which narrative elaborates on his summary remarks. The opening statement of our passage reads:

> There was also a certain segment of Jews that prided itself greatly on its extremely precise observance of the ancestral heritage and pretended [to observe] laws with which the Deity is pleased; by them the female faction was directed. Called Pharisees, these men were entirely capable of issuing predictions for the king's benefit, and yet, evidently, they rose up to combat and injure [him].
> καὶ ἦν γὰρ μόριόν τι Ἰουδαικῶν ἀνθρώπων ἐπ᾽ ἐξακριβώσει μέγα φρονοῦν τοῦ πατρίου καὶ νόμων οἷς χαίρει τὸ θεῖον προσποιούμενον, οἷς ὑπῆκτο ἡ γυναικωνῖτις, Φαρισαῖοι καλοῦνται, βασιλεῖ δυνάμενοι μάλιστα πράσσειν προμηθεῖς, καὶ τοῦ προὔπτου εἰς τὸ πολεμεῖν τε καὶ βλάπτειν ἐπηρμένοι.

Several terms call for comment.

A. μόριον. The word occurs in Josephus only here and at *Ant.* 3:182, where he counts seventy elements or sections (μόρια) in the candelabrum of the Tabernacle. Significantly, however, Thucydides has μόριον 8 times in his narrative. He uses it to mean "segment, portion, part, or division";[20] four times he has the phrase βραχεῖ μορίῳ, "a small portion".[21] This parallel is significant because it is widely recognized that books 17-19 of *Ant.* imitate Thucydidean vocabulary and style.[22] If 17:41 also recalls Thucydides, then we have some reason to connect this passage with the books in which it appears, and this connection must have some bearing on the question of authorship.

B. ἐπ᾽ ἐξακριβώσει μέγα φρόνουν. The noun ἐξακρίβωσις occurs only here in Josephus. Nevertheless, it is built on the stem ἀκριβ—which is ubiquitous in our author.[23] As noted above, this stem occurs in several of Josephus's descriptions of the Pharisees:[24] they are among those who are reputed to (or profess to) exercise superior ἀκρίβεια with respect to the νόμοι. Further, in *Ant.* 19:332, we read of a certain Simon from Jerusalem who ἐξακριβάζειν[25] δοκῶν τὰ νόμιμα, which gives us the verbal cognate of our noun in conjunction with "the laws". Notice again the connection between our passage and this entire section of *Ant.*

Although the noun is unique, the phrase μέγα φρονοῦν, "priding oneself greatly", occurs a dozen times in Josephus; in almost every case, we are certainly dealing with his own style.[26] In 8 of these instances, moreover, Josephus has the whole construction, ἐπὶ τινὶ μέγα φρονοῦν.[27] In *War* 7:383, for example, Eleazar b. Yair, faced with the unwillingness of his followers to kill themselves, exhorts, "But we, priding ourselves greatly on our courage (ἐπ᾽ ἀνδρείᾳ μέγα φρονοῦντες), revolted from Rome". Josephus uses the same phrase when he speaks of the Philistines who, though they prided themselves greatly on their courage (μέγα ἐπ᾽ ἀνδρείᾳ φρονούντων), were killed by David's army (*Ant.* 7:301). Others are said "to pride themselves greatly" on their successes,[28] on the laws,[29] or simply on "themselves".[30]

---

[20] Cf. Thucydides 1.85.1, 45.7, 2.39, 65.12; 6.86.5, 92.5; 7.58.2; 8.46.2.
[21] Thucydides 1.85.1, 45.7; 6.92.5; 8.46.2.
[22] Thackeray, *Josephus*, 110ff. Cf. the discussion in chapter 12, below.
[23] Cf. chapter 4, above.
[24] Cf. *War* 1:110, 2:162; *Life* 191; also A. I. Baumgarten, "Name", 414ff.
[25] The Epitome has ἐξακριβοῦν.
[26] *War* 7:383; *Ant.* 3:83; 4:100; 6:298; 7:301; 15:10, 372, (μεῖζον φρόνων); *Life* 43, 52; *Ag.Ap.* 1:99; 2:136, 286.
[27] *War* 7:383, *Ant.* 4:100; 6:298; 7:301; 15:372 *Ag.Ap.* 1:99; 2:136. 286.
[28] *Ag.Ap.* 1:99. This comes in a citation of Manetho, but Josephus may have retouched his source.
[29] *Ag.Ap.* 1:286.
[30] *Ag.Ap.* 4:100.

It is, therefore, entirely in keeping with Josephan usage that the Pharisees should be said to have "prided themselves greatly on their extreme precision". We note that Thucydides has the phrase ἐφ' ἑαυτῷ μέγα φρονοῦντα for one who "has a high opinion of himself" (6.16.4).

C. τοῦ πατρίου καὶ νόμων. Also in keeping with Josephan usage elsewhere, the object of the Pharisees' alleged ἀκρίβεια is τὸ πάτριον and οἱ νόμοι. In *War* 1:110, it was οἱ νόμοι, in *War* 2:162, τὰ νόμιμα, and in *Life* 191, τὰ πάτρια νόμιμα. As we have seen, the juxtaposition of πάτρια and νόμοι in reference to the Jewish laws is characteristic of our author.[31]

D. προσποιοῦμαι. In keeping with established practice, Josephus regularly uses the middle voice of προσποιέω in the sense, "to pretend, feign, or act".[32] Ordinarily, he supplies an infinitive to indicate the nature of the pretence.[33] One of the syntactical (and perhaps textual) difficulties with our passage is the absence of such an infinitive.[34] Marcus and Wikgren must be correct in supplying a verb like "observe", which I have also adopted for the above translation.

Nevertheless, the idea of pretending to ἀκρίβεια in the laws, which is what the Pharisees are here said to do, is quite at home in Josephus. A certain Jew in Rome, he tells us, was completely evil (πονηρός εἰς τὰ πάντα) but "*pretended* to interpret the wisdom of the laws of Moses" (προσεποιεῖτο μὲν ἐξηγεῖσθαι σοφίαν νόμων τῶν Μωυσέος; *Ant.* 18:81). Although Josephus more commonly correlates δοκέω with ἀκρίβεια, there is a significant semantic overlap between δοκέω (with a personal subject) and προσποιοῦμαι.[35] When he claims, therefore, that the Pharisees pretend (προσποιούμενοι) to observe the laws with ἀκρίβεια, he is not saying something new but is rather emphasizing the subjective or volitional aspect that was already latent in δοκέω, when he said that the Pharisees δοκοῦσιν ἐξηγεῖσθαι τὰ νόμιμα μετ' ἀκριβείας.[36]

E. ἡ γυναικωνῖτις. The "female faction" that is controlled (ὑπῆκτο) by the Pharisees was introduced at 17:33ff. In his efforts to build his power base, we are told, Herod's son Antipater wanted to bring his uncle

---

[31] Cf. chapter 4, above. At *Ant.* 17:41, a variant reading is τοῦ πατρίου νόμου (WE Lat.), which is followed by Reinach. This would conform even more closely to Josephan usage.

[32] See LSJ and BAG, s.v. on "established practice" and A. I. Baumgarten, "Name", 414f., on Josephan usage.

[33] Cf., e.g., *Ant.* 13:102; *Life* 319; *Ag.Ap.* 1:5.

[34] Holwerda conjectures that the infinitive γεραίρειν, "to honour", originally stood after χαίρει but (presumably) dropped out in the course of transmission, by *parablepsis* (cf. LCL edn. VII, 390 n. 8). Thus, the Pharisees "pretended to honour laws with which the Deity was pleased".

[35] Cf. chapter 4.

[36] So *War* 1:110; 2:162; *Life* 191.

Pheroras on side. In order to accomplish this, he cultivated the loyalty of Pheroras's wife, mother-in-law, and sister-in-law. These three, along with Antipater's own mother, acted in concert and constituted a γυναικωνῖτις, which Antipater had entirely under his control (ὥστε παντοίως ὁ ᾿Αντίπατρος ὑπῆκτο αὐτάς, 17:35). Against the co-ordinated actions of the women, Josephus allows, Pheroras was powerless to act independently (17:34).

It was these female opponents of Herod whom the Pharisees were able to manipulate, as the sequel also shows.[37] Pheroras's wife (one of the band) pays their fine for refusing to swear allegiance to Herod and they, in turn, manufacture predictions that please her.

E. προμηθεῖς. Both the meaning and the syntactical function of προμηθεῖς are problematic. Marcus and Wikgren (LCL) take the word to mean "foresight" but offer as an alternative "prediction". In favour of their adopted reading is the fact that 8 of the other 9 occurrences of προμηθής in Josephus have the sense of "caution, precaution, prudence, or foresight".[38] Only once does the word mean "divination" of the future. Tiberius regrets that he has resorted to augury (τοῦ προμηθοῦς) because now he must die knowing what will befall his grandson (Ant. 18:218).

Yet the context in 17:41 would seem to require that προμηθεῖς mean "predictions"—the alternate sense given by Marcus and Wikgren. One of the few things said about the Pharisees under Herod to this point has been that their leaders (Samaias and/or Pollion) predicted what the Idumean would do with the Sanhedrin when he came to power (14:176; 15:4). Even more important, Ant. 17:41 introduces a passage in which the major theme is the Pharisees' reputation for foreknowledge (πρόγνωσις, 17:43) and their issuing of fraudulent predictions. They promise (προλέγω) Pheroras and his wife that they and their children will assume the throne in place of Herod's line. They also predict that a certain eunuch named Bagoas will sire a king who will restore his reproductive capacity (17:43-95). These considerations suggest that προμηθεῖς in 17:41 refers to the Pharisees' predictions: although they could have used their talents of divination for the king's benefit, they chose instead to use them against him.

On the syntactical problem: Marcus and Wikgren seem to take πράσσειν as intransitive and προμηθεῖς attributively, so that the Pharisees, being prudent, or "having foresight", were able to help the king greatly. In the translation offered above, on the other hand, I have supposed that

---

[37] Josephus does not intend to say that the Pharisees were distinguished by "their influence with women" (contra Rivkin, Revolution, 323).

[38] War 1:367, 499, 539, 611; 3:70, Ant. 17:23, 18:176, 19:91. Five of these cases are attributive in function; three are substantive.

πράσσειν is transitive and that προμηθεῖς, as an accusative, is its direct object. Thus, "the Pharisees were entirely capable of issuing predictions for the king's benefit (βασιλεῖ δυνάμενοι μάλιστα πράσσειν προμηθεῖς)" but chose instead to combat and injure him by these means. In this reading, βασιλεῖ is a dative of "advantage and disadvantage". In view of the uncertain state of the text throughout 17:41, however, it would be unwise to place too much weight on any particular syntactical construction.

With the terms προμηθής, προλέγω, and πρόγνωσις, we encounter an important theme in Josephus. Since he has a considerable interest in the idea of prophecy or prediction, we ought briefly to consider his view of this matter before proceeding with our interpretation of *Ant.* 17:41-45.

III. *The Meaning of Prophecy for Josephus*

Only in recent years have scholars begun seriously to deal with the theme of prophecy in Josephus.[39] Particularly significant are two articles by J. Blenkinsopp and W. C. van Unnik.[40] In the following sketch of the meaning and significance of prophecy for Josephus, I can do little more than summarize the pertinent aspects of these studies.

Although Josephus uses the words προφήτης, προφητεία, and προφητεύω more than 300 times in total, he reserves them almost exclusively for the biblical prophets.[41] The two exceptions are: (a) Josephus's favorite, John Hyrcanus, who is said to have been capable of προφητεία and, indeed, to have prophesied (προφητεύσεν) the downfall of the Hasmonean house,[42] and (b) the various false prophets who arose before and during the revolt.[43] These men claimed to be prophets (προφητὴς ἔλεγεν εἶναι, *Ant.* 20:97) but were not.

We may add that the verb προλέγω, which is used of the Pharisees in our passage, has a similar restriction. It occurs 37 times in Josephus. In 34 of those instances the sense is "to predict",[44] and 31 of these occurrences, in *Ant.* 1-11, refer to the activity of the biblical prophets. It is God himself[45] or a prophet[46] who predicts (προλέγει). The three excep-

---

[39] The theme was broached already by Paret in 1856, pp. 834-838, but then only very sporadically until the 1970's; cf. W. C. van Unnik, *Schriftsteller*, 41 n. 1 and 46 n. 16, and J. Blenkinsopp, "Prophecy", 239 n. 2, on the history of scholarship.

[40] See previous note. Cf. also D. E. Aune, "Critical Notes: the Use of ΠΡΟΦΗΤΗΣ in Josephus", *JBL* 101 (1982), 419-421.

[41] Blenkinsopp, "Prophecy", 240, 246.

[42] *War* 1:68-69; *Ant.* 13:299.

[43] *War* 2:261; 6:286; *Ant.* 20:97, 169.

[44] That is, not counting *War* 7:353; *Ant.* 12:342; 19:31, which all lack the sense of "prediction".

[45] *Ant.* 8:232, 319, 9:189; 10:53, 178; 11:96.

[46] Cf. esp. *Ant.* 8:420; 9:169, 265, 281; 10:13, 60, 89, 268.

tions are (a) John Hyrcanus (again! *Ant.* 13:300); (b) the Essenes (*Ant.* 13:311), whom Josephus clearly admires[47] and (c) the Pharisees, in our passage (*Ant.* 17:43).

Josephus's treatment of the biblical prophets is noteworthy in several respects. First, as Paret lamented,[48] he reduces their prophetic activity more or less to that of prediction[49] and minimizes their didactic and hortatory roles.[50] In keeping with this tendency, he expresses the greatest interest in those prophets who have left written records of events to come;[51] of these, Jeremiah and Daniel (as well as the "prophet" Moses) figure prominently.[52] Remarkably, Josephus describes Daniel as "one of the greatest prophets (εἷς τις τῶν μεγίστων προφητῶν)"[53] and as one who "conversed with God".[54] The main reason for Daniel's greatness, we are told, is that he left behind a written timetable of future events, which allows us to test the accuracy of his prophecies (ὅθεν ἡμῖν τὸ τῆς προφητείας αὐτοῦ ἀκριβὲς . . . ἐποίησε δῆλον).[55] This appreciation of Daniel illustrates Josephus's understanding of "prophecy" as essentially predictive.

Josephus repeatedly claims that all of the events of his own day were foretold by the prophets. Isaiah, for example:

> wrote down in books all that he had prophesied
> and left them to be recognized as true from the
> event by men of future ages. And not only this
> prophet, but also others, twelve in number, did
> the same, and *whatever happens to us* whether for
> good or ill *comes about in accordance with their
> prophecies* (κατὰ τὴν ἐκείνων προφητείαν).[56]

---

[47] Cf. *Ant.* 15:371-379.

[48] Paret, "Pharisäismus", 836f.

[49] Cf. *Ant.* 10:33-35; 13:65 (on Isaiah); 4:303 (on Moses); also Blenkinsopp, "Prophecy", 242f.

[50] Paret, "Pharisäismus" 837f., believed that this "misunderstanding" of the prophets indicated Josephus's (narrow) Pharisaic perspective!

[51] Van Unnik, *Schriftsteller*, 51, 52f.

[52] Van Unnik, *Schriftsteller*, 52ff.; Blenkinsopp, "Prophecy", 244f.

[53] Remarkably, because the Hebrew canon does not even list Daniel among the prophets but rather with the "writings". The rabbis, as Ginzberg (*Legends*, VI, 413) shows, disagreed as to whether or not Daniel should even be considered a prophet.

[54] *Ant.* 10:266f.

[55] *Ant.* 10, 267, 269, 276; cf. Paret, "Pharisäismus", 837. Josephus also remarks that, unlike the other prophets, Daniel proclaimed *good* news; *Ant.* 10:268; cf. van Unnik, *Scriftsteller*, 49f.

[56] *Ant.* 10:35, trans. Marcus (LCL edn.) emphasis added; cf. *Ant.* 4:303, 313; 8:418-420; 10:142, 280.

Since the prophecies of Jeremiah and Daniel were particularly relevant to the events of Josephus's time, his special interest in them is understandable.[57]

In a famous passage, discussed briefly in the previous chapter, Josephus speaks about "the failure of the exact succession of prophets" (μὴ γενέσθαι τὴν τῶν προφητῶν ἀκριβῆ διαδοχήν) soon after the Exile.[58] Blenkinsopp interprets the passage, in keeping with Josephus's restricted use of the προφητ–word group, to mean that prophecy ceased altogether at that time.[59] Paret and van Unnik, on the other hand, emphasize the adjective; they argue that it was only the exact succession that failed and that prophets continued to appear sporadically in Josephus's time.[60] Since, however, everyone agrees that the activity of predicting the future was, according to Josephus, widespread in his day, the debate is inconsequential for our purposes. Josephus claims that he himself,[61] many Essenes,[62] and some Pharisees[63] accurately predict the future.

Josephus asserts his ability to tell the future in the context of his impending capture at Jotapata (*War* 3:350ff). Unsure whether to die voluntarily with his comrades or to surrender to the Romans (so he says), he suddenly recalled "those nightly dreams" in which God had foretold to him the fate of the Jews and the destinies of Vespasian and Titus. For, he allows, he could interpret dreams and was able to determine the meaning of ambiguous divine utterances, being a priest. Now bound by a sense of solemn obligation, as God's servant (διάκονος), to convey his predictions to Vespasian, Josephus is compelled to decline the offer of death and he surrenders to the Romans.

Rajak, understandably, doubts that this account is anything more than a desperate stratagem to explain Josephus's embarrassing flight to the enemy.[64] Van Unnik, however, rejects this possibility because: (1) Josephus's prophecy before Vespasian is independently attested in other comtemporary sources[65] and (2) Josephus's writings contain many indications that he thought of himself as a prophet.[66] In the sequel to the

---

[57] Cf. *Ant.* 10:79., 142 (on Jeremiah); 10:276 (on Daniel); also Blenkinsopp, "Prophecy', 244f.

[58] *Ag.Ap.* 1:41.

[59] Blenkinsopp, "Prophecy", 240. This view also corresponds to several rabbinic statements, *loc. cit.* n. 4.

[60] Paret, "Pharisäismus", 834f; van Unnik, *Schriftsteller*, 48.

[61] *War* 3:352-354.

[62] *Ant.* 13:311f. (cf. *War* 1:78); 15:371-379; 17:346 (cf. *War* 2:113).

[63] *Ant.* 14:174; 15:4.

[64] Rajak, *Josephus*, 18f.

[65] Van Unnik, *Schriftsteller*, 42; cf. Suetonius, *Vespasian* 4, and Tacitus, *Histories* 5:13; also Lindner, *Geschichtsauffassung*, 71ff.

[66] Van Unnik, *Schriftsteller*, 42ff.

Jotapata story, for example, Josephus claims that he had accurately predicted other events (as well as Vespasian's rise), including the fall of Jotapata and his own captivity.[67] Further indications of Josephus's prophetic self-understanding are: (3) his occasional reformulation of the biblical narrative so as to enhance the role of prophets;[68] (4) the parallels that he insinuates between his own career and that of Jeremiah;[69] (5) his reflections on the present value of prophecy;[70] (6) his consistent correlation of prophecy with the priesthood;[71] (7) his omission, in his paraphrase of 1 Maccabees, of that work's lament over the absence of authorized prophets;[72] and (8) his stated intention to begin writing *War* at the point where "the prophets" ended their accounts.[73] There can be little doubt, in view of van Unnik's and Blenkinsopp's work, that Josephus "wünschte sich, als Prophet angesehen zu wissen".[74] He counts himself (doubtless not the least) among the modern-day seers.

A final pertinent observation arising from the work of van Unnik and Blenkinsopp is that Josephus and his fellow-seers claim a dual basis for their predictions, namely, scriptural exegesis and immediate divine inspiration.[75] Because the authorized prophets had recorded all the events of the future, the seer of Josephus's day had to begin with a thorough knowledge of the ancient prophetic texts. This principle explains Josephus's remark that he is an interpreter of dreams and skilled in divination, being a priest (ὢν ἱερεύς) and thus being familiar with the prophecies in the sacred scriptures (τὰς προφητείας τῶν ἱερῶν βίβλων).[76] It is his knowledge of biblical prophecy that enables him to interpret

---

[67] *War* 3:405-408. Notice also the imperfect ἦν at *War* 3:352: Josephus presents his predictive activities as ongoing.

[68] Cf. van Unnik, *Schriftsteller*, 49f.

[69] Cf. van Unnik, *Schriftsteller*, 52f.; Blenkinsopp, "Prophecy", 244: "Jeremiah in particular seems to have served as a model for Josephus—at least retrospectively. . . . As a true prophet he foretold the destruction but was rejected by the religious leaders who were misled by the pseudoprophets." See Lindner, *Geschichtsauffassung*, 133-140, who compares the lament theme in *War* with (Jeremiah's) Lamentations; also R. Mayer and C. Möller, "Josephus—Politiker und Prophet", in O. Betz, M. Hengel, K. Haacker, *Josephus-Studien* (Göttingen: Vandenhoeck & Ruprecht, 1974), 284.

[70] Cf. *Ant.* 8:418-420; 10:142.

[71] See Blenkinsopp, "Prophecy", esp. 250ff. and e.g., *Ant.* 3:192 (Aaron's prophetic gift qualifies him to be a high priest); 7:72 (David orders the high priest to prophesy, a detail not found in scripture); 8:296 (an unscriptural prediction of the future exile, in which *no prophet or priest* would be found among the people); 10:79f. (notice that both Ezekiel and Jeremiah were priests by birth); *Ag.Ap.* 1:29; 37-41 (cf. 30-36).

[72] That is, 1 Macc. 4:46; 9:27 (cf. 14:41). Notice especially the way in which *Ant.* 13:5 reworks I Macc. 9:27, which is pointed out by van Unnik, *Schriftsteller*, 48 n. 23.

[73] *War* 1:18, cf. Blenkinsopp, "Prophecy", 241.

[74] Van Unnik, *Schriftsteller*, 42.

[75] Cf. Blenkinsopp, "Prophecy", 246f. and van Unnik, *Schriftsteller*, 43.

[76] *War* 3:352.

dreams and other signs. Similarly, he tells us that some of the Essenes undertake to tell the future, "being lifelong students of sacred scripture . ... . and of the sayings of prophets" (βίβλοις ἱεραῖς. . . καὶ προφητῶν ἀποφθέγμασιν ἐμπαιδοτριβούμενοι).[77] This kind of scriptural study may also be alluded to in the curious notice that one day Judas the Essene was offering "instruction on predicting the future" (διδασκαλίας. . . τοῦ προλέγειν τὰ μέλλοντα).[78] Finally, in *Ant.* 17:41-45 the Pharisees' ability to predict the future seems to be tied to their claim to superior ἀκρίβεια with respect to scripture.[79]

In addition to scriptural exegesis, the post-biblical seer is often engaged, like his biblical predecessors,[80] in the interpretation of immediate divine manifestations, especially dreams. Josephus and the Essenes both interpret the future by interpreting dreams.[81] In our passage, likewise, the Pharisees "had been credited with knowing the future *through manifestations of God* (πρόγνωσιν δὲ ἐπεπίστευντο ἐπιφοιτήσει τοῦ θεοῦ)".[82]

Josephus makes it clear, however, that divine appearances come only to those who are worthy. He says, as proof of John Hyrcanus's unique virtue, "For the Deity conversed with him so closely that he was never unaware of the future".[83] Josephus claims that the Essene Menahem's πρόγνωσις τῶν μελλόντων was proof of his virtue (καλοκαγαθία μαρτυρούμενος)[84] and that the Essenes in general were granted knowledge of "divine things" because of their virtue (ὑπὸ καλοκαγαθίας).[85]

This brief overview of prophecy in Josephus is enough to show that our author has a sustained interest in the topic. That interest arises in part from his self-understanding as a modern heir of the prophets. As his denunciations of contemporary false prophets show, he considers himself a qualified critic in the field. Let van Unnik summarize the importance of these observations for the interpretation of *Ant.* 17:41-45:

> Es sollte nun klar sein, dass wir, wenn wir über Prophetie bei Josephus sprechen, über eine Sache reden, die Josephus nicht nur objektiv, historich, sondern auch subjektiv und ganz persönlich aufs stärkste interessiert hat.[86]

---

[77] *War* 2:159.
[78] *Ant.* 13:311. So Blenkinsopp, "Prophecy", 258.
[79] The parallel is drawn by Blenkinsopp, "Prophecy", 247.
[80] Cf. e.g., *Ant.* 2:11-16, 64-73, 84-86 (Joseph); 10:250 (Daniel); Blenkinsopp, "Prophecy", 245.
[81] *War* 3:352 (Josephus); *Ant.* 17:345-348 (Simon the Essene).
[82] *Ant.* 17:43.
[83] *War* 1:69; cf. *Ant.* 13:300 (and 282).
[84] *Ant.* 15:373.
[85] *Ant.* 15:379.
[86] Van Unnik, *Schriftsteller*, 47.

Josephus's discussion of the Pharisees' prophetic activities under Herod the Great, like his earlier discussions of their reputation for scriptural expertise, comes from a qualified and interested critic.

IV. *Interpretation*

It is now possible to bring together all of the above considerations, with respect to context, key terms, and the prophecy motif, in an effort to interpret *Ant.* 17:41-45.

We have noted that the passage is built from a topic sentence (§ 41) and an elaborative story (§§ 42-45). The thrust of the topic sentence is that the Pharisees, who prided themselves greatly on their exegetical prowess, were perfectly able to issue predictions (πράσσειν προμηθεῖς) that would benefit the king but they chose, rather, to employ their talents to the king's detriment.

Notice that the phrase "issuing predictions for the king's benefit" need not imply the manufacturing of false or flattering prophecies. On the contrary, Josephus has earlier described the benefit of prophecy and foreknowledge as the awareness of "what to guard against" (*Ant.* 8:418). He has also presented Herod as one who was eager to know the future; the Essene Menahem helped him in this quest (*Ant.* 15:377ff.). According to our passage, the Pharisees also had the ability to assist Herod in this way but they opted instead to use their abilities against him, by encouraging his opponents with false predictions. They were, it now appears, a major force behind the "gang of women" assembled by Antipater to oppose his father.

The postpositive γοῦν in 17:42 suggests that the story to follow will substantiate the claim that the Pharisees used προμηθεῖς against the king, which is indeed what we find: the following narrative (§§ 42-45) recounts two instances of the Pharisees' unscrupulous use of prophecy. The first sentence of the story provides the background: when the "whole Jewish people" swore an oath of loyalty to Caesar and to the policies (πράγμασιν) of Herod, the Pharisees refused. Their intransigence earned them a fine but this was paid for them by Pheroras's wife, who was one member of the γυναικωνῖτις that they controlled.[87]

This event provides the context for the first example of the Pharisees' using προμηθεῖς against the king (17:43):

> As a reward for her kindness they predicted—for [the Pharisees] had been credited with knowing the future through divine manifestations (πρόγνωσιν

---

[87] On the suggestion that the mention of this fine contradicts *Ant.* 15:370, see the source-critical discussion below.

δὲ ἐπεπίστευντο ἐπιφοιτήσει τοῦ θεοῦ)—that a cessation of Herod's rule, his and his family's after him, had been decreed by God and that the kingdom would devolve on her and Pheroras and on any children they might have.

Now declining an oath of allegiance to Herod's policies was one thing. If the reader knows anything about Herod from *War* 1 and from *Ant.* 15-17, however, it is that he was obsessed with his own power and would not tolerate any opposition, whether real or imagined.[88] He was even prepared to execute his own sons on the suspicion that they were conspiring against him.[89] Particularly in the last years of his life, in which our passage falls, the king was beset by all sorts of morbid fears.[90] His response to the Pharisees' prediction, therefore, is perfectly in character. When he learns of their actions from his sister Salome, who also tells him that the Pharisees have corrupted or perverted (διαφθείρω) some people in his court, "the king put to death (ἀναιρεῖ) the chief culprits among the Pharisees" (τῶν Φαρισαίων τοὺς αἰτιωτάτους τινας) (17:44). Among those "corrupted" members of the court who were killed along with the guilty Pharisees were: a eunuch named Bagoas, a certain Karos,[91] and everyone in the king's household (τοῦ οἰκείου) who supported "what the Pharisee said" (οἷς ὁ Φαρισαῖος ἔλεγεν)—a curious phrase to which we shall return.[92]

Josephus now explains what happened in the case of Bagoas the eunuch and this provides his second example of a Pharisaic προμηθής that injured the king:

> Now Bagoas had been taken in by them (ἦρτο δὲ ὁ βαγώας ὑπ' αὐτῶν), being led to believe that he would be named father and benefactor of the one who should be on high with the title of king (τοῦ ἐπικατασταθησομένου προρρήσει βασιλέως); for everything would be in the hands of that one (κατὰ χεῖρα γὰρ ἐκείνῳ τὰ πάντ' εἶναι), and he would grant Bagoas potency for marriage and for the production of his own children. (*Ant.* 17:45)

The future passive participle (ἐπικατασταθησόμενος), indicating that an omnipotent king would "be appointed above" (by God?), suggests a messianic figure. Marcus and Wikgren point out that Isaiah 56:3-5 seems to offer an eschatological hope for eunuchs.[93] Regardless of how one interprets the royal figure, however, the point of the passage is that

---

[88] E.g., *Ant.* 15:173-178, 247-252, 262-266, 280-289, 365-369; 16:235ff.
[89] *Ant.* 16:320, 392ff.
[90] Cf. *Ant.* 16:241, 244.
[91] This Karos appears to have been an object of the King's pederasty (cf. παιδικὰ ὄντα αὐτοῦ, 17:44).
[92] See the source-critical discussion below.
[93] LCL edn. VIII, 393 n.*b*.

this Pharisaic prediction implied a disruption of Herod's rule within the lifetime of Bagoas. The infuriated king did away with Bagoas, who had set his hopes on such an outcome.

Josephus makes it clear that the Pharisees' predictions in this case were mere flattery and nonsense. Bagoas dies immediately, childless, and Pheroras follows soon after (17:58f., 61). Contrary to the Pharisees' prophecies, Herod rules until his death, at which point the kingdom passes to his sons (17:189-192). Josephus, who considers himself adept in the art of prediction, has remarked earlier in *Ant.*:

> Nor should we think the things which are said to flatter us (τὰ πρὸς ἡδονήν) or please us more worthy of belief than the truth, but should realize that nothing is more beneficial than prophecy and the foreknowledge which it gives (ὅτι προφητείας καὶ τῆς διὰ τῶν τοιούτων προγνώσεως οὐδέν ἐστι συμφορώτερον), for in this way God enables us to know what to guard against. (*Ant.* 8:418; Thackeray/Marcus)

In *Ant.* 17:41-45, he is presenting the Pharisees as false prophets, as those who sent out to make flattering predictions in place of the truth. Although Josephus can be critical of Herod in *Ant.*, he is also quick to point out the many injustices that the king faced. In our passage he portrays the Pharisaic seers as major players in the perpetration of those injustices. Allied with the king's enemies, they abused prophecy in a scandalous way, to flatter their friends (in reward for financial support) and to injure the king.

In *War* 1:110-114 we saw that Josephus takes issue with the Pharisees' reputation for (or profession of) ἀκρίβεια and εὐσέβεια. As a priest, an official guardian of the nation's εὐσέβεια and ἀκρίβεια, he has a personal interest in these concepts. His procedure in that passage was to state the Pharisees' reputation and then to attack it with examples of their impious behaviour. *Ant.* 17:41-45 has a similar effect, though now in the context of prophecy. Josephus views himself not only as a priest but also as an heir of the prophets. He reflects much on the theme of prophecy and considers himself both an able seer and a qualified critic of other seers. In connection with their pretence to ἐξακρίβωσις, he now tells us, the Pharisees were also believed to have foreknowledge. In our passage, however, he gives examples of the Pharisees' predictions in order to show that their reputation for πρόγνωσις, like their reputation for ἀκρίβεια, is ill-founded.

V. *Source Analysis*

No other Pharisee passage in Josephus's writings has been as confidently and universally attributed to some other author as *Ant.* 17:41-45. Rivkin is so sure of its non-Josephan origin that he omits it altogether from his otherwise complete survey of Josephus's Pharisee passages.[94] The scholarly consensus is so strong that A. I. Baumgarten can cite *Ant.* 17:41 as *independent* evidence (that is, in addition to Josephus's own testimony!) that the Pharisees considered themselves the party of ἀκρίβεια.[95] Our final task in this chapter is to examine the basis on which the conventional view rests.

Before proceeding, we may note that the identity of the "real" author of *Ant.* 17:41-45 is not agreed upon by those who deny Josephan authorship. Nicolaus of Damascus is the favoured candidate chiefly because he was Herod's court historian and the reported incidents took place in Herod's court.[96] Hölscher, however, proposed that the passage came from a biography of Herod, perhaps written by Ptolemaeus of Ashkelon.[97] Rivkin seems to believe that a Hebrew account was the basis of *Ant.* 17:41-45 and that a misrepresentation of פרושים as Φαρισαῖοι resulted in our (alleged) present difficulties.[98] On the question of the real author, we are obviously in the realm of speculation. What all of these scholars agree on is that, whoever wrote *Ant.* 17:41-45, it was not Josephus. It is the criteria for this judgement that must concern us.

A. *Arguments Against Josephan Authorship of Ant. 17:41-45*

At least ten reasons for denying Josephan authorship have been proposed in the scholarly literature.

1. The author was obviously hostile toward the Pharisees and could not, therefore, have been Josephus.[99] This objection presupposes, of course, that Josephus himself was partial toward the Pharisees. But Josephus's view of the Pharisees is the question in our study; so far, we have seen no reason to believe that he favoured the group.

2. Some critics perceive a tension between *Ant.* 15:370, in which the Pharisees are (allegedly) excused from an oath of allegiance, and 17:42 in which they are fined for their disobedience.[100] We respond: (a) that

---

[94] Rivkin explains this omission in an end-note, *Revolution*, 321-324; we shall consider his reasons presently.

[95] A.I. Baumgarten, "Name", 415f.

[96] H. Bloch, *Quellen*, 169; Destinon, *Quelllen*, 120; Schwartz, "Josephus and Nicolaus", 160; A. I. Baumgarten, "Name", 414f.

[97] Hölscher, "Josephus", 1977, 1979, 1981.

[98] *Revolution*, 324.

[99] Bousset, *Religion des Judentums*, 187; Hölscher, "Josephus", 1974 n.** (the author is "sicher ein Nichtjude").

[100] Hölscher, "Josephus", 1974 n.**; Schwartz, "Josephus and Nicolaus", 160; Rivkin, *Revolution*, 323.

the narrative implies that these were two different oaths, separated by fifteen years or so[101] and (b) that even if the same oath were being described, *Ant.* 15:370 says only that the Pharisees were not punished in the same way as the others who refused (ὁμοίως τοῖς ἀρνησαμένοις), that is, with death. This does not exclude the possibility of a fine.

3. That the author of our passage describes the Pharisees as if for the first time—καὶ ἦν γὰρ μόριόν τι Ἰουδαικῶν ἀνθρώπων . . .—has led some to argue that the passage is lifted directly from a source that first mentions the Pharisees here.[102] But it is not uncommon for Josephus to introduce previously discussed topics, such as the Jewish schools, as if he had never mentioned them. *War* 2:119-166 offered a completely new portrayal of the Pharisees, with no indication that they had been mentioned before (but cf. *War* 1:110-114); so does *Life* 191, although it comes in an appendix to *Ant.*, which often discusses the Pharisees. Even *Ant.* 13:171-173, 297f. and 18:11-25, although they acknowledge earlier treatments, proceed as if these did not exist.

4. The use of the third person—μόριόν τι Ἰουδαικῶν ἀνθρώπων (17:41)—according to Schwartz, "sounds strange for Josephus".[103] He thinks the expression more suited to a Gentile author (Nicolaus). Although Josephus can use the first person (ἡμεῖς) when speaking of the Jews, however, he often uses the third person, as in "the Jews"[104] or "the Jewish laws", in what is unquestionably his own writing.[105] He even speaks of himself in the third person![106] So the force of this objection is not at all clear.

---

[101] The first oath took place in about 20 BC (Herod's seventeenth year), according to 15:354 and 365 (τότε). The later oath took place after the execution of Herod's two sons (7 BC). The whole story of the Pharisees' fine and its payment by Pheroras's wife is firmly connected to the emergence of the female cabal (ἡ γυναικωνῖτις, 17:41) under Antipater, which only occurred in the final years of Herod's life (17:32ff) when he had lost control of affairs. The parallel in *War* (1:567ff.) makes this absolutely clear. Schwartz's claim that *Ant.* 17:42 is "simply recalling the earlier event" ("Josephus and Nicolaus", 160 n. 12) seems to me to ignore all of the narrative indications. My position evidently agrees with those of A. Schalit and I. L. Levine (published in Hebrew); cf. Schwartz, *loc cit.*

[102] Hölscher, "Josephus", 1974 n.**; Bousset, *Religion des Judentums*, 182, I. Lévy, *Pythagore*, 236f., 244f.

[103] Schwartz, "Josephus and Nicolaus", 159.

[104] A glance at Schalit, *Supplementband* to the Rengstorf *Concordance*, *s.v.*, shows that the third person "Jew" occurs thousands of times in Josephus. It is spread evenly throughout every book *except Ant.* 1-11, which comprises the biblical paraphrase. In those books, the third person Ἑβραικός is correspondingly frequent. Cf., e.g., *War* 1:1, 7, 17, 60; 2:119, 166; 5:51, 99; *Ant.* 1:6; *Life* 416, 424; *Ag.Ap* 1:42.

[105] Cf. Schalit, *Supplementband*, *s.v.*; e.g., *Ant.* 13:243, 397; 16:158, 18:55, 81; 20:34, 41.

[106] E.g., *War* 2:568, 569, 575, 585, 590, *et passim.*

5. The Pharisees' opposition to Herod is described in terms (πολεμεῖν, βλάπτειν, 17:41) that recall earlier accounts of their opposition to John Hyrcanus (πόλεμος, *War* 1:67) and to other rulers (βλάψαι, *Ant.* 13:401). Since Schwartz attributes the earlier narratives to Nicolaus of Damascus, he does the same with *Ant.* 17:41-45.[107] Our analysis of the earlier passages concluded, however, that they came from Josephus himself: therefore the verbal parallels speak in favour of, rather than against, Josephan authorship of *Ant.* 17:41.[108]

Another five criteria are proposed by Rivkin alone.[109]

6. He asks why Josephus would use the term μόριον instead of his usual αἵρεσις to describe the Pharisees. We note: although αἵρεσις appears most often, Josephus can also call the Pharisees a σύνταγμα, a τάγμα, or a φιλοσοφία.[110] Why not μόριον?

7. Rivkin remarks that the Pharisees of our passage:

> are described as laying claim to being exact observers of the country's laws, and not expounders [sic] or interpreters of the laws. This is in contrast with Josephus's reiterations that the Pharisees were the most accurate expounders of the laws.

Rivkin seems to be concerned about the absence of a verb like ἐξηγέομαι or ἀφηγέομαι (cf. *War* 1:110; 2:162). We note, however, that the description of the Pharisees in *Life* 191, which is clearly Josephus's own, also lacks such a verb.[111] Further, Josephus nowhere claims that "the Pharisees *were* the most accurate expounders", but only that they seemed, professed, or were reputed to be (δοκοῦσιν) such. The difference is monumental. Our passage fits squarely with his ordinary usage.

8. Rivkin avers that:

> among the characteristics of these *pharisaoi* [sic] are their influence with women and their foreknowledge of things to come. The Pharisees elsewhere in Josephus do not share these characteristics.[112]

We respond, first, that the passage says nothing about the Pharisees' "influence with women" as a general trait; it claims only that they controlled the four-woman cabal (ἡ γυναικωνῖτις) that was plotting against Herod. Moreover, in *Ant.* 14:174f. and 15:3f., Josephus *does* claim that certain Pharisees predicted the future.

---

[107] Schwartz, "Josephus and Nicolaus", 160.
[108] See chapters 9 and 10.
[109] *Revolution*, 323.
[110] σύνταγμα, *War* 1:110; τάγμα, *War* 2:164; φιλοσοφία, *Ant.* 18:11.
[111] Thus: οἱ περὶ τὰ πάτρια νόμιμα δοκοῦσιν τῶν ἄλλων ἀκριβείᾳ διαφέρειν.
[112] Rivkin, *loc. cit.*

9. According to Rivkin, the Pharisaic opposition to Herod in *Ant.* 17:41-45 "contrasts sharply with Pollion [*sic.*] and Samaias' positive relationship with Herod". We respond: if these two Pharisees had a "positive relationship" with Herod, it was entirely the king's doing, as Josephus presents the matter. For Pollion and Samaias opposed Herod from the start; they regarded him as a serious offender against Jewish law (*Ant.* 14:172-174). Samaias accepts Herod's rule only as a *punishment* from God (14:176). It was Herod, we are told, who respected Pollion and Samaias, not they who respected Herod (15:3).

10. Finally, Rivkin thinks it significant that the Pharisees of *Ant.* 17:41-45 "are not juxtaposed to the Sadducees or Essenes". We simply note that the same is true of the discussions of the Pharisees at *War* 1:110-114; *Ant.* 13:400-432; and *Life* 191-198.[113]

B. *Considerations that Favour Josephan Authorship*

The foregoing study has attempted to interpret *Ant.* 17:41 in the context of both the surrounding narrative and Josephus's thought in general. That it was possible to do this (if the effort was successful) indicates that Josephus has made the passage his own. It will be helpful here to spell out those results of the study that have direct significance for the source-critical question.

1. The opening characterization of the Pharisees as a group priding itself on ἐξακριβώσις is thoroughly Josephan (cf. *War* 1:110; *Life* 191), as are also: the construction ἐπὶ τινὶ μέγα φρονοῦν, the reference to τὸ πάτριον καὶ οἱ νόμοι (or ὁ πάτριος νόμος), and the verb προσποιοῦμαι in this context (cf. *Ant.* 18:81 and δοκέω).

2. The format of the pericope—an opening claim refuted by the story that follows—matches other Pharisee passages in Josephus very well (cf. *War* 1:110-114; *Life* 191-198).

3. As Schwartz has noted, the use of πολεμεῖν and βλάπτειν in our

---

[113] The most obvious tension, it seems to me, between the earlier descriptions of the Pharisees under Herod and *Ant.* 17:41ff. has apparently not impressed many others. Namely, 14:172 describes Samaias as an upright man (δίκαιος ἀνήρ) and superior to fear, whereas our passage presents the Pharisees as scoundrels. Notice, however, that when Josephus is talking about Samaias's virtues, he does *not* mention that the man was a Pharisee; that datum does not appear until somewhat later (15:3f.), by which time the reader might have forgotten the earlier praise. In 14:172, Josephus wants to contrast the lawless Herod and the cowardly Sanhedrin with an upright man who was not afraid to voice the truth. If his source told him that the man was Samaias, he could not very well suppress that fact; what he could do and did do was to omit the datum that Samaias was a Pharisee.

passage to describe the Pharisees' actions toward rulers fits with other passages in Josephus (*War* 1:67; *Ant.* 13: 401).

4. The entire theme of our passage, that of foretelling the future, is important to Josephus. His connection between the Pharisees' prophetic abilities and their claim to ἀκρίβεια accords with his usage elsewhere.[114] That the Pharisees should acquire their foreknowledge through divine manifestations (17:43) also fits with his overall presentation.[115] Finally, the juxtaposition of πρόγνωσις and προλέγω (17:43) is paralleled elsewhere in Josephus.

5. We noted above the peculiar phrase οἷς ὁ Φαρισαῖος ἔλεγεν (17:44). What is peculiar is that the Pharisees should be referred to by a collective singular. One wonders whether this figure of speech, as the English term "the Taxman", conveys a certain resentment at the inexorability and pervasiveness of the institution in question. However that may be, precisely the same phrase appears in *Ant.* 18:17. Josephus will report there that among the Sadducees are "men of the highest standing" but that they are compelled by popular sentiment to follow "what the Pharisee says (οἷς ὁ Φαρισαῖος λέγει)". But notice that Schwartz himself attributes *Ant.* 18:17 to Josephus[116] and that Hölscher allows a degree of Josephan influence there.[117] Further, the context in 18:17 seems to confirm the interpretation of the phrase suggested above: the author laments the power of the Pharisees. And that is precisely the attitude we have discovered in Josephus.[118] It is difficult to escape the conclusion that the rueful phrase οἷς ὁ Φαρισαῖος ἔλεγεν in *Ant.* 17:44 comes from Josephus himself.

6. A final indication of Josephan authorship is the author's evident familiarity with eschatological themes, which the Bagoas incident reveals. We know, however, that Josephus was intensely interested in the prophets and especially in those, like Jeremiah and Daniel, who predicted the upheavals and events of his own day.[119]

To conclude: except where he was prepared to invent stories *ex nihilo*, Josephus had to rely on sources of some kind for all of the events that occurred before his own time. No one will deny that he relied heavily on sources for his narrative. Nevertheless, we have no basis on which to assume that, where he follows a source, he does so mechanically and

---

[114] Cf. Blenkinsopp, "Prophecy", 247; *War* 3:352; 2:159.
[115] Cf. Blenkinsopp, "Prophecy", 254f., 258; van Unnik, *Schriftsteller*, 43; *War* 3:352; *Ant.* 17:345ff.
[116] "Josephus and Nicolaus", 162f.
[117] Hölscher, "Josephus", 1991.
[118] Cf. *War* 1:110 ff.; 2:162 (ἀπάγοντες); *Ant.* 13:288, 401; cf. *Life* 191ff.
[119] Cf. Blenkinsopp, "Prophecy", 244ff.; van Unnik, *Schriftsteller*, 52f.

without imparting his own perspective. This must be proven in any given case and, in the light of recent studies, it is an increasingly difficult position to sustain. We have seen, for example, that Josephus consistently reworks his LXX source so as to convey his own themes and interests. He likewise makes the Hasmonean history his own, although some elements are less perfectly redacted than others. The foregoing analysis has sought to show that the description of the Pharisees in *Ant.* 17:41-45 is wholly intelligible as Josephus's own considered formulation. With all of its obvious hostility toward the Pharisees, the passage comes from Josephus himself.

CHAPTER TWELVE

ANT. 18:12-15: THE PHARISEES AMONG THE JEWISH SCHOOLS, III

Josephus's most ambitious portrait of the Pharisees comes in his final description of the three Jewish philosophical schools, *Ant.* 18:11-23. It is in this passage that Rasp finds the most compelling evidence of *Ant.*'s positive re-evaluation of the Pharisees.[1] The purpose of the present chapter is to interpret the description of the Pharisees in *Ant.* 18:12-15 and thereby to determine its relationship to the other Pharisee passages in Josephus.

An initial difficulty is that our passage falls within the section of *Ant.* (books 17-19) that contains some of Josephus's most difficult Greek. Thackeray attributed those books to an inept literary assistant, whom he designated the "Thucydidean hack".[2] Of him Thackeray remarked:

> This journalistic hack is verbose and prefers two or more words to one. . . . The commonplace word is studiously shunned and replaced by the unusual and *bizarre*.[3]

Although Thackeray's particular explanation of the shortcomings of these books as the work of a literary assistant has not proven durable,[4] his perception of the difficulties stands as a caution to the interpreter.[5] The passage on the schools in *Ant.* 18 shares the problematic language and syntax of books 17-19;[6] the explanation of the Pharisees' view of fate and free will, for example, poses famous problems.[7]

In view of these difficulties, one's interpretive aims can only have a respectable chance of fulfillment if they are modest. It will suffice if we are able to ascertain: (a) the function of the Pharisee passage in its context; (b) the main points that Josephus is making in his description of

---

[1] Rasp, "Religionsparteien", 29f., 32ff.

[2] Thackeray *Josephus*, 110f.

[3] Ibid., 111f.

[4] Cf. Richards, "Composition", 39; Peterson, "Literary Projects", 261 n. 5; Shutt, *Studies*, Rajak, *Josephus*, 233ff; Moehring, "Novelistic Elements", 145f.; and the excursus to Part I, above.

[5] Cf. Richards, "Composition", 37f.

[6] Cf. Rivkin's discussion, *Revolution*, 318f. We are grateful to him for soliciting independent translations of *Ant.* 18:11-15 by S. Topping and by A. Damico and M. Yaffe, 320f.

[7] Cf. Schlatter, *Theologie*, 209f. n. 1 and Thackeray, "On Josephus' Statement of the Pharisees' Doctrine of Fate (Antiq. xviii, 1, 3)", *HTR* 25 (1932), 93.

the group; (c) whether each of these points is new or repetitive of earlier discussions, with respect to both content and attitude; and (d) whether Josephus himself is the author.

I. *Context*

In *Ant.* 18:11-23, Josephus offers a description of three Jewish philosophical schools (φιλοσοφίαι): Pharisees, Sadducees, and Essenes. This passage has almost exactly the same position and function in the narrative as *War* 2:119-166 had in the earlier work. Judea has just become a Roman province, under the prefecture of Coponius (*War* 2:117/*Ant.* 18:1f.). This development provokes a certain Judas and his followers to ἀπόστασις (*War* 2:118/*Ant.* 18:4), for they refuse to become subservient to Rome.

New details in *Ant.* are: (a) that the particular aggravation was an appraisal of Jewish property conducted by the new governor of Syria (Quirinius); (b) that the Jews in general were offended by this move (18:3); (c) that most of the people, however, were pacified by the counsel of the high priest Joazar (18:3); and (d) that Judas, a determined hold-out, won the support of Saddok, a Pharisee. Together, these additions have the effect of making the school of Judas more intelligible to the reader; we have already observed in *Ant.* a tendency to explain the motives of all parties involved in a given event.[8] Nevertheless, in both *War* 2 and *Ant.* 18 Josephus introduces the three "recognized" Jewish schools as a means of exposing the novelty and strangeness of Judas's philosophy of unconditional freedom.

A. *The Pharisees and the Philosophy of Judas*

The parallel accounts in *War* and *Ant.* of the relationship (or lack thereof) between Judas's followers and the accredited philosophies of Judaism have given rise to a problem that bears significantly on our topic. In *War* 2:118, namely, Josephus claimed that the αἵρεσις of Judas had nothing at all in common with the others (οὐδὲν τοῖς ἄλλοις προσεοικώς). In *Ant.* 18, after discussing the other three schools, he returns to Judas's following and remarks:

> This school agrees in all other respects with the opinions of the Pharisees, except that they have a passion for liberty that is almost unconquerable, since they are convinced that God alone is their leader and master. (*Ant.* 18:23; Feldman)

---

[8] Cf. *Ant.* 13:318f. (on Aristobulus), 381f. (on Alexander Janneus), 423f. (on Aristobulus); 16:150ff. (on Herod). All of these passages are absent from *War*.

τὰ μὲν λοιπὰ πάντα γνώμῃ τῶν Φαρισαίων ὁμολογοῦσι δυσνίκητος δὲ τοῦ
ἐλευθέρου ἔρως ἐστὶν αὐτοῖς μόνον ἡγεμόνα καὶ δεσπότην τὸν θεὸν ὑπειληφόσιν.

It is a scholarly commonplace that these two passages are plainly contradictory.[9] The prevailing view is that *War* 2:118 was motivated by
Josephus's desire to cover up the involvement of his own party (i.e., the
Pharisees) in the revolt; by the time he writes *Ant.*, however, he can af-
ford to divulge the truth of the matter, which is that the followers of
Judas were simply a "radical wing" of the Pharisees.[10] Rasp gives this
view a peculiar twist. He argues that in *War* Josephus denigrated the
party of Judas in order to disguise his own past as a rebel; but in *Ant.*,
his work of repentance, Josephus raises the stature of the rebels by linking them with the Pharisees, whom he now praises:[11]

> Worte der Anerkennung und Verehrung widmet er aber den Anhängern
> des Judas. Sie stimmen auch, wie er nun hervorhebt, mit den Pharisäern
> in den meisten Stücken überein.[12]

So in Rasp's view, *Ant.* 18 honours the Pharisees, and the followers of
Judas benefit by their association, newly conceded, with the favoured
group.

In the present study we cannot attempt to resolve the historical
problems of the origin and identity of Judas's followers.[13] We are concerned, however, with the correct interpretation of Josephus on the
Pharisees. To that end, I submit the following observations.

1. In *War* 2:118, the αἵρεσις of Judas was presented as a single-issue
party and it was in the context of that one issue—unconditional freedom
from earthly rulers—that, Josephus claimed, they had nothing in common with the other schools.[14] In *Ant.* 18, Josephus says nothing to modify
his earlier claim.

2. The parallel to *War* 2:118 in *Ant.* 18 is not § 23 but rather §§ 4-10.
But in those sentences Josephus expands and even intensifies his earlier
claim that the philosophy of Judas was entirely foreign to the mainstream
of Jewish thought.[15] Consider the following representative excerpts:

---

[9] So, e.g., Paret, "Pharisäismus", 818; Rasp, "Religionsparteien", 39, 44, 47;
Farmer, *Maccabees*, 33f. n. 23; Weiss, "Pharisäismus", 425; Blenkinsopp, 'Prophecy',
260; Black, "Judas", 50; Hengel, *Zeloten*, 83f., 89f.

[10] So Paret, "Pharisäismus", 818; Black, "Judas of Galilee and Josephus's 'Fourth
Philosophy'", *Josephus-Studien*, edd. O. Betz, K. Haacker, P. Schäfer, 50; Hengel,
Zeloten, 89f.; Alon, *Jews*, 44ff.; R. Meyer, *Tradition and Neuschöpfung*, 52 n. 4, 54ff.

[11] Rasp, "Religionsparteien", 39, 44, 47.

[12] *Ibid.*, 47.

[13] But see the studies by Farmer, Hengel, and Black.

[14] See chapter 6, above.

[15] Of all of the commentators, Hengel is the most sensitive to the importance of the
context; he concludes that the contradiction is only apparent (*scheinbar*), *Zeloten*, 91.

these men sowed the seed of every kind of misery, which so afflicted the
nation that words are inadequate . . . . Here is a lesson that an innovation
and reform in ancestral traditions (ἡ τῶν πατρίων καίνισις καὶ μεταβολή)
weighs heavily in the scale in leading to the destruction of the congregation
of the people. In this case certainly, Judas and Saddok started among us
an intrusive fourth school of philosophy (τετάρτην φιλοσοφίαν ἐπείσακτον ἡμῖν
ἐγείραντες). . . . They filled the body politic immediately with tumult, also
planting the seeds of those troubles which subsequently overtook it, all
because of the novelty of this hitherto unknown philosophy (τῷ ἀσυνήθει
πρότερον φιλοσοφίας). . . . (Feldman)

It is difficult to imagine how Josephus could assert any more clearly the
novelty and strangeness of Judas's philosophy! Since this passage is considerably longer and more forceful than the *War* parallel, it can hardly
be interpreted as "words of recognition and esteem" for the party of
Judas.

3. When Josephus does come to say that, "for the rest" (τὰ λοιπά),
the fourth philosophy agrees with the Pharisees, he is patently talking
about their non-distinctive teachings (18:23).[16] But this statement means
little, since the question of how one responds to Roman rule was the
crucial question of the day and the *raison d'être* of Judas's party. Moreover, Josephus consistently presents the Pharisees as exponents of
popular beliefs.[17] That the fourth philosophy, in its non-distinctive
teachings, should agree with these common beliefs (e.g., the immortality
of souls) and not with those of either the high-born Sadducees or the sectarian Essenes is neither surprising nor very illuminating.

Indeed, one is tempted to stand Rasp's theory on its head. Given
Josephus's abiding distaste for the rebel party, one must ask whether his
new insinuation of links between them and the Pharisees, on minor
points of philosophy, does not involve a gratuitous vilification of the
Pharisees.[18] The same question arises with respect to Josephus's new
claim that a Pharisee named Saddok was a co-founder of the wretched
freedom-loving school (18:4). Since he makes clear his distaste for the
rebels, what else does he achieve by connecting them with the Pharisees?
If these notices do imply a denigration of the Pharisees, they accord with
the sentiments that Josephus has expressed about the group thus far in
Ant.[19]

To summarize: the context of *Ant.* 18:11-23, on the three Jewish
schools, is very similar to that of the parallel in *War* 2. Josephus repeats
and intensifies his portrayal of Judas's programme as the result of an

---

[16] Cf. Hengel, *Zeloten*, 90f.
[17] Cf. *War* 2:162; *Ant.* 13:296-298; and now 18:15.
[18] As Hölscher, "Josephus", 1991, seems also to think.
[19] As in 13:388, 400-432; 17:41-45.

aberrant philosophy. That he is willing to exploit inconsequential details[20] to insinuate links between the rebels and the Pharisees probably indicates his antipathy toward the latter. Why Josephus did not include these anti-Pharisaic notices (18:4,23) in *War* is a matter for speculation.[21]

B. *The Pharisees Among the Three Schools*

Josephus opens his discussion of the three recognized schools with the observation that:

> Among the Jews from earliest times (ἐκ τοῦ πάνυ ἀρχαίου) there were three philosophies of the ancestral traditions (τῶν πατρίων): that of the Essenes, that of the Sadducees, and third, those who are called Pharisees also engaged in philosophy. (18:11)

In its context the phrase ἐκ τοῦ πάνυ ἀρχαίου is less an attempt to date the origin of the schools than it is a contrast to ἡ τῶν πατρίων καίνισις (18:9), which phrase describes the school of Judas.[22] This contrast focuses the whole point of the discussion. The three recognized schools, unlike that of Judas, are ancient and therefore authorized "sub-philosophies" of the national philosophy.

Notice that the order of the schools in the opening list (18:11) is reversed *vis-à-vis War* 2:119 and *Ant.* 13:171, so that the Essenes now appear first and the Pharisees last. On the other hand, in the order of discussion the Pharisees appear first and the Essenes last. In *War* 2, the Essenes were discussed first and in *Ant.* 13:171ff. they were discussed second. Rasp finds particular significance in the gradual slippage of the Essenes in the order of discussion; he thinks that it reflects Josephus's

---

[20] Inconsequential, because he has to admit that the philosophy of unconditional freedom is entirely alien to all of the major schools, including the Pharisees.

[21] If we have correctly assessed the allusions to Pharisaic links with the fourth philosophy as rather wild insinuations, their absence from *War* may result from that work's greater discipline of style and content, on which see Niese, *HZ*, 207f., and Thackeray, LCL edn., II, xiiif.

[22] The noun καίνισις, "innovation", occurs only here in Josephus but several cognates, such as καινοποιέω, καινός, καινοτομέω, καινουργέω, and καινουργία do appear throughout his writings, often with pejorative connotations. He is able to exploit the double meaning of the root καιν—as "revolution" (cf. *War* 6:343; 7:410; *Ant.* 7:362) and as "innovation" in the laws (*War* 5:402; 7:259; *Ant.* 8:245; 9:96, 250; 20:216-218; *Ap.* 2:250-252)—to emphasize that, for the Jews, revolution *is* an innovation. In *War* 2:414, he makes the converse point that innovation (the cessation of sacrifice for the Romans) is tantamount to revolution. Josephus's exploitation of the shift between "innovation" and "revolution" is even more striking in his use of νεωτερίζω/νεωτερισμός and cognates; cf. Rengstorf, *Concordance*, s.v., esp. *Ant.* 18:10. For Josephus, with his conviction that Jewish law and custom were prescribed by Moses and fixed for all time, "new" is a term of abuse.

changing attitudes toward the group.[23] Since Josephus refers the reader (18:11) back to *War* 2, Rasp infers that he intends a subtle correction of his earlier portrayal.[24] Similarly, both Rasp and Neusner believe that the Pharisees of *Ant.* 18 receive much better exposure than they had in *War* 2, at the expense of the Essenes; the latter are "cut down to size".[25] Neusner attributes this re-evaluation to Josephus's (alleged) new, pro-Pharisaic outlook in *Ant.-Life.*

There is good reason to doubt, however, that the order in which the schools are discussed, the amount of space devoted to each, or the tone of Josephus's remarks indicate any re-evaluation in favour of the Pharisees. First, although the Essenes do receive much less space than they had in the remarkable panegyric of *War* 2:119-161, they still merit fuller coverage than either the Pharisees or the Sadducees.[26] More important is the tone of the description, which includes such remarks as the following:

> They [the Essenes] deserve admiration in contrast to all others who claim their share of virtue (ἄξιον δ' αὐτῶν θαυμάσαι παρὰ πάντας τοὺς ἀρετῆς μεταποιουμένους)[27] because such qualities as theirs were never found before among any Greek or barbarian[28] people, nay, not even briefly, but have been among them in constant practice and never interrupted since they adopted them from of old.

We have here unqualified, unrestrained praise on the part of Josephus. It is wholly consistent with the tenor of his portrayal of the Essenes in *War* 2:119-161 and *Ant.* 15:373, 379. Equally consistent with his earlier presentations are his remarks on the Pharisees (18:12-15). Nowhere does Josephus express direct approval or commendation of this group; he always says that they seem to be, are reputed to be, or pretend to be (δοκέω, προσποιοῦμαι) the most faithful adherents to the laws. Accordingly, in our passage he acknowledges only their massive popularity with the people (οἱ δῆμοι) and the cities (αἱ πόλεις).[29] It is extremely doubtful, however, that this aristocrat shares the popular enthusiasm (see below).

---

[23] Rasp, "Religionsparteien", 29ff.

[24] Rasp, "Religionsparteien", 31: "Die Verschiedenartigkeit der neuen Schilderung in Verbindung mit dem Hinweis [to *War* 2] lässt sich nur erklären aus dem Wunsch des Autors, die ältere Darstellung zu korrigieren."

[25] Neusner, "Josephus's Pharisees", 232; cf. Rasp, "Religionsparteien", 33f.

[26] The Essenes receive 5 Niese sections (= 25 lines of Greek); the Pharisees get 4 sections (= 22 lines of Greek); and the Sadducees get 2 sections (= 11 lines of Greek).

[27] Similar phrases occur at *Ant.* 3:58 and 18:278. They echo Thucydides 2.51.5.

[28] Notice that Josephus distinctly includes the Jews among the "Barbarians" (*War* 1:3, 16; *Ag.Ap.* 1:6-14, esp. 8); cf. Collomp, "Platz", 292f.

[29] *Ant.* 18:15.

The fact that Josephus discusses the Essenes last and the Pharisees first probably indicates nothing more than his tendency to vary his style and presentation in *Ant.* over against *War*; this tendency is well-documented by Niese, who cites our passage as an example.[30] In any case, the order of discussion in *Ant.* 18 corresponds exactly to the order of the schools in the lists at *War* 2:119 and *Ant.* 13:171. One is hard pressed to find any development here.

All of these contextual issues will be significant for the interpretation of *Ant.* 18:12-15 on the Pharisees. We may now proceed directly to the passage itself.

II. *Five Statements About the Pharisees*

As in *War* 2:162-166, the description of the Pharisees in our passage comprises several statements on discrete topics. It will facilitate our interpretation if we consider each of the five items in turn. Four of the five statements repeat points made earlier. It would be superfluous to rehearse the background and parallel material in these cases but we shall need to be sensitive to any changes of vocabulary or construction.

A. *Avoidance of Luxury (18:12a)*

12a. οἵ τε γὰρ Φαρισαῖοι τὴν δίαιταν ἐξευτελίζουσιν οὐδὲν ἐς τὸ μαλακώτερον ἐνδίδοντες. . . .

1. Key Terms

(a) The main verb, ἐξευτελίζω, occurs only here and at *Ant.* 6:8, in a reflective comment by Josephus. Although the word is not characteristic of his vocabulary, therefore, he is able to use it. The Pharisees "restrict", "restrain", or "simplify" (Feldman) their style of living.

(b) Δίαιτα appears some 72 times in our author's writings, with a range of meanings from "place of abode", "necessaries of life", or "daily routine", to simply "manner of life". He has used the word several times previously of the Essene lifestyle.[31] When used of these groups and of the Jews as a nation, *vis-à-vis* the pagan world,[32] δίαιτα has the sense of a special, peculiar, or perhaps "philosophical" way of life.

---

[30] Niese, *HZ*, 223f.
[31] *War* 2:137, 138, 151, 155, 160; *Ant.* 15:371.
[32] E.g., *Ant.* 13:245, 258; *Ag.Ap.* 1:185.

(c) Μαλακός occurs 18 times throughout *War* and *Ant.*, though never as the neuter substantive τὸ μαλακώτερον, "softness", "luxury", or "the more luxurious", as in our passage. G. C. Richards observes, "The *neuter article* with adj. or participle is an overdone idiom in (*Ant.*) XVII-XIX."[33] He argues that this could not be the work of a native speaker of Greek (or of Thackeray's Greek assistant) and that it doubtless comes from Josephus.

(d) Ἐνδίδωμι occurs about 62 times in Josephus, most frequently in the final books of *War*, with the meaning "surrender". In our passage, the sense is either that the Pharisees are not "inclined toward" luxury or that they do not "yield" to its lure.

2. Interpretation

The meaning of Josephus's opening statement on the Pharisees is more or less clear: "their lifestyle is one of restraint (or "they disparage the accoutrements of life"); they do not yield at all to the softer side." The second clause merely restates and emphasizes the first. This is the only element of *Ant.* 18:12-15, as we shall see, that is entirely new; Josephus has never before mentioned the austerity of the Pharisees. His assertion is paralleled, however, in a rabbinic tradition that contrasts the Sadducees' enjoyment of silver and gold vessels with the Pharisees' rejection of such in anticipation of the world to come.[34]

B. *The Pharisaic Tradition*

12b.   ὧν τε ὁ λόγος κρίνας παρέδωκεν ἀγαθῶν
            ἕπονται τῇ ἡγεμονίᾳ
        περιμάχητον ἡγούμενοι τὴν φυλακὴν ὧν
            ὑπαγορεύειν ἠθέλησεν.
12c.   τιμῆς γε τοῖς ἡλικίᾳ προήχουσιν
            παραχωροῦσιν
        οὐδ' ἐπ' ἀντιλέξει τῶν εἰσηγηθέντων
            θράσει ἐπαιρόμενοι.

The next two statements, which seem to be linked in sense, have the same form as 12a: they comprise a main clause with a main verb (pres. ind. 3p. pl.), followed by a subordinate clause with a plural present participle. In each case, the subordinate clause reiterates the point of the main clause.

---

[33] Richards, "Composition", 37.
[34] Avot de Rabbi Natan 5.

1. Key Terms

(a) Λόγος occurs about 588 times in Josephus's writings, usually in the ordinary sense of "word" or "utterance". Its meaning here, however, is fixed by its occurrence also in the following descriptions of the Sadducees (18:16) and Essenes (18:18).[35] Each of the three schools has its own λόγος. This is a basic structural component of the passage and must refer to the "teaching" or "doctrine" of each group. Whiston's translation "reason", which was congenial to those like Lauterbach, who saw the Pharisees as an eminently "reasonable" or progressive group,[36] is excluded by this contextual fact. (Lauterbach's view of the Pharisees is, of course, still possible if otherwise demonstrable.)

(b) With the verb παραδίδωμι we meet the first clear reminiscence of an earlier portrait of the Pharisees. In *Ant.* 13:297f., namely, Josephus has told us about special Pharisaic ordinances "handed down from a succession of fathers". Although there is no mention here of either νόμιμα or the διαδοχή, the use of παραδίδωμι with respect to the Pharisaic teachings can hardly be coincidental.

If παραδίδωμι had no special meaning here, if it did not designate a body of extra-biblical tradition as in 13:297, then all the verbiage of § 12b would tell us nothing more than the self-evident fact that "the Pharisees follow their (own) teachings". That Josephus does use the word deliberately, however, is shown first of all by § 12c, which will claim that the Pharisees do not contradict "what was introduced (τῶν εἰσηγηθέντων)" and that they defer to those "preceding them in age (τοῖς ἡλικίᾳ προήκουσιν)". These phrases, though admittedly periphrastic, seem to point to a special Pharisaic tradition, *introduced* in addition to the laws. This reading is confirmed by the following description of the Sadducees (18:16), who are "on guard that there be no 'additional claim' whatsoever, outside the laws (φυλακῇ δὲ οὐδαμῶς τινων μεταποίησις αὐτοῖς ἡ τῶν νόμων)". The context thus confirms that Josephus uses παραδίδωμι deliberately, as something of a technical term, to evoke the special Pharisaic tradition handed down from the fathers (cf. *Ant.* 13:297f.).

(c) The main verb, ἕπομαι, is common in Josephus; most of its 125 occurrences have the literal sense "to follow". Nevertheless, Josephus can use it figuratively, to speak of following God, or the laws, or virtue; in an earlier passage he spoke of the Sadducees' (lack of) following (*Ant.* 13:298). The peculiar construction here, "they follow the authority

---

[35] So Feldman, LCL edn. IX, 10f. n. *c.*, following Thackeray.
[36] Lauterbach, *HUCA*, 99f.; cf. G. F. Moore, "Fate", 374.

(ἕπονται τῇ ἡγεμονίᾳ)" of what has been transmitted, is unique in Josephus.

(d) The subordinate clause is built on the odd phrase περιμάχητον ἡγούμενοι, which seems to mean something like "they consider worth fighting for"[37] or, more mildly, "they take very seriously". This phrase fits with the awkward style of *Ant.* 17-19. In 18:280, Petronius is declaring his support for the Jews' refusal to accept a statue of Gaius Caligula in the Temple. He agrees that they are only acting in accord with the standards of their law, "which, being your heritage, you regard as worth defending (περιμάχητον ἡγεῖσθε)". The speech is doubtless a Josephan creation.[38] The same phrase is used of the Essenes, who περιμάχητον ἡγούμενοι τοῦ δικαίου τὸν πρόσοδον (18:18). In these cases, as with the Pharisees, the phrase is used of the central, non-negotiable tenet of the group.

(e) What the Pharisees regard so highly is "the observance [or "protection"] of those things that it [their λόγος] wished to propagate (τὴν φυλακὴν ὧν ὑπαγορεύειν ἠθέλησεν)". If ὧν ὑπαγορεύειν ἠθέλησεν is here equivalent to ὧν ὁ λόγος κρίνας παρέδωκεν ἀγαθῶν in the main clause, as seems likely from the structure, then the two clauses stand in synonymous parallelism.

The noun φυλακή is interesting because it touches on a major theme of *Ant.*, that those who *observe* the divine laws are rewarded with εὐδαιμονία.[39] Throughout *Ant.*, Josephus frequently speaks of ἡ φυλακὴ τῶν (πατρίων) νόμων[40] as a Jewish virtue. Notice, however that in our passage the Pharisaic *Schwerpunkt* is not the observance of τῶν νόμων in general but rather "of things that their λόγος deemed good and transmitted (παρέδωκεν)", or "what their λόγος saw fit (ἠθέλησεν) to dictate". In this regard, the Pharisees are explicitly contrasted to the Sadducees, who maintain a guard (φυλακῇ) against such claims (or perhaps "after-creations", μεταποίησις) apart from the laws (ἢ τῶν νόμων). As in *Ant.* 13:297f., therefore, it is the Sadducees' position that accords with Josephus's view of the laws. The Pharisees proclaim and defend an additional, extra-biblical body of teachings.

(f) The verb ὑπαγορεύω occurs 13 times in Josephus and has the sense, "dictate", "advise", or "prescribe". Three times he uses the phrase

---

[37] The word occurs in Thucydides (7.84.5) with this literal sense.

[38] As is well known, speeches were commonly used by hellenistic historians to carry their own themes. The view expressed by Petronius, which is absent from *War*, accords well with Josephus's consistent emphasis on adherence to the πάτριον.

[39] Cf. *Ant.* 1:14, 20 and chapter 7, above.

[40] E.g., *Ant.* 4:306, 309; 8:21, 191, 195, 290; 9:157; 11:152; 14:165; 17:152; 18:59, 84, 267; cf. *Ag.Ap.* 1:212.

ὑπαγορεύε τὸ πάθος to indicate that someone acted as "emotion dictated".⁴¹ Four times he speaks of what God or "the Deity" has dictated, namely the laws.⁴² In our passage, the Pharisees are said to place the greatest emphasis upon what their λόγος chose to prescribe for them.

(g) Who are οἱ ἡλικίᾳ προήκοντες, to whom the Pharisees defer out of honour or esteem (τιμῆς)? The phrase does not occur elsewhere in Josephus; the verb appears only at *War* 3:184, where it means to "reach before-hand", and at *Ant.* 3:226, where it means to "be older". But we have three major clues about the meaning of the phrase in our context.

First, it appears that these elders are somehow connected with τῶν εἰσηγηθέντων. This is suggested by the equivalent verbal constructions τιμῆς παραχωροῦσιν (of the elders) and οὐδ' ἐπ' ἀντιλέξει θράσει ἐπαιρόμενοι (of the things introduced). Moreover, the conjunction οὐδέ implies a close connection. I infer, with Feldman (LCL edn.), that οἱ ἡλικίᾳ προήκοντες are the ones responsible for τῶν εἰσηγηθέντων.

Second, all three of the earlier references to the Pharisaic tradition in *Ant.* include some reference to the "fathers" (τῶν πατέρων or πατρῷος).⁴³ These are the ones who have generated and transmitted the νόμιμα that the Pharisees prize so highly. It would be easy to assume that οἱ ἡλικίᾳ προήκοντες in our passage is a crabbed reference to these Pharisaic fathers.

It may be worth noting also that the designation seems to include the Pharisees' present elders. This is suggested by (a) the present participle and (b) the contrast with the Sadducees, who "reckon it a virtue to contradict the teachers of wisdom" (18:16). We note that the "fathers" of Mishnah Avot include contemporary teachers; even the son of Rabbi Judah is mentioned (Avot 2:2).

(h) The Pharisees are not emboldened to contradict τὰ εἰσηγηθέντα. The verb εἰσηγέομαι occurs a dozen times in Josephus. It usually has the sense, "to introduce" or "to bring in" (something new), often in the context of new legislation.⁴⁴ At *Ant.* 3:266, it is equivalent to νομοθετέω. The word is also used of Ahab's "introduction" of new gods (*Ant.* 9:135) and of a new proposal for a special day of public fasting (*Life* 290).⁴⁵ Twice, however, the verb appears to mean only "instruct" or "counsel".⁴⁶ Do the Pharisees, then, observe "the things counseled" by the elders or "the things introduced" by them? The nuance is important.

---

⁴¹ *War* 1:277, 544; *Ant.* 8:325.
⁴² *Ant.* 3:84; 4:121, 183, 193.
⁴³ *Ant.* 13:297 (twice), 401.
⁴⁴ *Ant.* 3:266; 14:152, 256, 259, 262.
⁴⁵ Cf. also *Ant.* 18:332, "to produce" or "bring forth".
⁴⁶ *Ant.* 4:186; *Ag.Ap.* 1:261.

The context places some emphasis on the novelty of Pharisaic teaching. They believe what their λόγος has deemed good and handed down, or what *it* chose to dictate. By contrast, the Sadducees (18:16) observe only the laws and guard against any μεταποίησις—"pretence" or perhaps "additional claim".[47] The context would appear to justify the translation of τὰ εἰσηγηθέντα as "the things that were introduced".

In further support of this translation, we may note that in all of the earlier descriptions of the Pharisaic tradition, it was said to be embodied in certain special νόμιμα. If one looks for an equivalent in our passage, one must wonder whether τὰ εἰσηγηθέντα and μεταποίησις are not merely periphrastic for τὰ νόμιμα ἅπερ οὐκ ἀναγέγραπται ἐν τοῖς Μωυσέος νόμοις. Such extreme periphrasis is characteristic of *Ant.* 17-19.

(i) Finally, ἀντιλέξις occurs only 3 times in Josephus and only in *Ant.* 17-19. Both of the other passages (17:126; 18:286) speak of the strength (ἰσχύς) required to contradict someone; they appear to come from the same author. Moreover, 17:126 shares with our passage the construction ἐπ' ἀντιλέξει, which again points to a common author. Once again we see that *Ant.* 18:11-23 is stylistically at home in *Ant.* 17-19.

2. Interpretation

For the sentences § 12b and § 12c Josephus continues the structure that he employed for 12a; the main clause (with a finite verb) expresses the central point, which is then restated in a subordinate clause. The following "amplified" translation results:

12b.   [The Pharisees] follow [or submit to] the
        authority of those things that their
        teaching deemed good and handed down;
        They regard as indispensable the observance
        [or protection] of those things that it
        saw fit to dictate.

12c.   Out of honour they yield to those who go
        before them in age,
        Nor are they inclined boldly to contradict
        the things that were introduced.

All of this seems to be little more than a verbose repetition of the crisp notice in *Ant.* 13:297: "the Pharisees passed on (παρέδοσαν) to the people

---

[47] The noun μεταποίησις occurs only twice outside our passage. In *Ant.* 3:58 it means "aspiration" and in 18:242 it means "claim". The verb μεταποιοῦμαι at 18:20 and 278, as in Thucydides 1.140.1; 2.51.5, also means "to claim".

certain ordinances (νόμιμα) from a succession of fathers (ἐκ πατέρων) which do not stand written in the laws of Moses''. In our passage, evidently, § 12b describes the παράδοσις; § 12c refers to the fathers as ''those who precede in age'' and to the non-Mosaic νόμιμα, which ''were introduced''. Just as the Sadducees were earlier said to reject (ἐκβάλλει) these non-Mosaic ordinances, we now learn that this school was on its guard against any such μεταποίησις in addition to the laws (18:16).

What is new in our passage is Josephus's emphasis on the centrality of the special tradition among the Pharisaic beliefs. In 13:298, it is true, we were told that the Pharisaic νόμιμα were the object of controversies (ζητήσεις) and serious differences (διαφορὰς μεγάλας) between them and the Sadducees. In 18:12, however, Josephus restates the Pharisees' devotion to their tradition in four equivalent ways: they follow it as an authority (ἡγεμονία); they consider it indispensable (or ''worth fighting for''); they yield in honour to the bearers of the tradition; and they do not contradict it. Josephus seems to be emphasizing that this special extra-biblical tradition is the cornerstone of Pharisaic understanding.

This new emphasis marks a certain development in Josephus's presentation of the Pharisees. In the earlier descriptions (*War* 2:162-166; *Ant.* 13:171-173) he chose only to contrast their ''philosophical'' views with those of the other schools. Perhaps he considered the dispute over the νόμιμα unreportable to a Greco-Roman readership. In 13:297f., however, he was compelled to explain the preceding narrative by pointing out that the Pharisees had a special tradition and that this was the root of much conflict between them and the Sadducees. Now, in 18:12, he stresses the importance of that tradition to the Pharisees and gives it first place among their tenets.

C. *Fate and Free Will*

13a.   πράσσεσθαί τε εἱμαρμένῃ τὰ πάντα ἀξιοῦντες
13b.   οὐδὲ τοῦ ἀνθρωπείου τὸ βουλόμενον
          τῆς ἐπὶ αὐτοῖς ὁρμῆς ἀφαιροῦνται
13c.   δοκῆσαν τῷ θεῷ κρᾶσιν γενέσθαι
          καὶ τῷ ἐκείνης βουλευτηρίῳ
          καὶ τῶν ἀνθρώπων τὸ (τῷ) ἐθελῆσαν(τι)
          προσχωρεῖν μετ' ἀρετῆς ἢ κακίας.

In 18:13 Josephus abandons the repetitive format of § 12. The first two propositions in this sentence are fairly clear statements on fate and free will, but § 13c poses famous difficulties.

1. Key Terms

(a) Εἱμαρμένη was discussed above, in connection with *War* 2:162-166.

(b) The common verb ἀξιόω was used in *Ant.* 13:173 in connection with the Sadducean view of fate and free will. It introduces the views or postulates of any particular school.

(c) Τὸ ἀνθρωπεῖον, a neuter substantive, is one of the "overdone" idioms that Richards finds in this section of *Ant.* and attributes to Josephus.[48] It occurs 12 times in *Ant.* 17-19[49] and perhaps 3 times earlier in *Ant.*[50] Its occurrence here, in the context of fate and free will, recalls earlier references to τὰ ἀνθρώπινα (πράγματα) in discussions of fate and free will.[51]

(d) A conspicuous barbarism in *Ant.* 17-19 is the use of a neuter participle to govern a genitive substantive, which is what we have in τοῦ ἀνθρωπείου τὸ βουλόμενον, "the willing of the human sphere" (= "human will"?). Richards remarks, "Here Josephus seems to go astray in his desperate effort to improve his style."[52]

(e) The reading ἐπ' αὐτοῖς is given by the Epitome and is followed by Niese and Feldman (LCL edn.) as the *lectio difficilior*. Our problem is to find the antecedent of the pronoun.[53] Thackeray connects it with τὰ πάντα, so that the human will is involved in every action.[54] Some manuscripts have apparently attempted to remove the awkwardness by reading ἀπ' αὐτῆς, whereby the human will itself becomes a function of εἱμαρμένη.[55] Schlatter conjectures ἀπ' αὐτοῦ, which would simply clarify that the ὁρμή springs from human will.[56]

We may note that Josephus's other two discussions of the schools on fate and free will both contain phrases like ἐπὶ τοῖς ἀνθρώποις (*War* 2:163) and ἐφ' ἡμῖν ἑαυτοῖς (*Ant.* 13:172f.) for that which resides "in *human power*". This raises the question whether ἐπ' αὐτοῖς in our passage does not refer back to τὸ ἀνθρώπειον, taken as a collective noun, as Feldman's translation (LCL edn.) supposes. The syntax is awkward[57] but the reading has manuscript support; moreover, its awkwardness explains the

---

[48] Richards, "Composition", 87.
[49] *Ant.* 17:60, 118, 150, 180, 309, 354, 18:13, 30, 128, 281, 19:41, 171.
[50] *Ant.* 4:229, 293, 16:99, plus several variants.
[51] *Ant.* 13:171, 173; 16:397.
[52] Richards, "Composition", 37. The phrase τὸ βουλόμενον occurs with the meaning "will" or "purpose" in Thucydides 1.90.2.
[53] Cf. Schlatter, *Theologie*, 209f. n. 1.
[54] Thackeray, *HTR*, 93.
[55] I follow here Schlatter's explanation of the textual tradition, *Theologie*, 209f. n. 1.
[56] Ibid.
[57] Schlatter, *loc. cit.*, suggests that the phrase should be ἐφ' αὐτοῖς on this reading.

development ἀπ' αὐτῆς and it accords with Josephus's usage in the other school passages. Thus: the Pharisees do not deprive the human will of the initiative (ὁρμή) that rests in their (i.e. human) power.

(f) The noun ὁρμή, which occurs some 118 times in Josephus, is about seven times more frequent in *War* than in *Ant.*, since it often refers to an "attack" or "assault", or to the "emotions" of war. Here, however, the word must mean "initiative" or "impulse". It is significant because, as G. F. Moore points out, it is equivalent to the Latin *adpetitus*, which appears in Cicero's description of Chrysippus's view of fate and free will.[58] We shall see that in this passage Josephus returns to a Chrysippean model to describe the Pharisaic position, as in *War* 2:162-166.

(g) The Loeb edition follows the manuscripts MWE in rendering χρᾶσις in 18:12: it pleased God that there should be a "fusion" between fate and free will. This word appears elsewhere in Josephus only at *War* 5:212 and 7:298; in both cases it has the mundane sense of "mixture" or "alloy". Niese and Schlatter follow the manuscript A in our passage and read χρίσις. Schlatter thinks that the reference is to the New Year's day (1. Tishri) *judgement* mentioned in rabbinic haggadah, at which time God determines a person's fate for the coming year.[59] We may note, however, that at 16:398 Josephus uses the verb χρίνειν of the relationship between fate and free will. The meaning there was not "to judge" but "to weigh"; fate and free will are simply balanced against each other.[60] If χρίσις were the reading in 18:13, this sense would fit the context well, since the Pharisees, like Josephus, are said to accept both fate and free will as causes.

On this interpretation of χρίσις it makes little difference whether the Loeb reading χρᾶσις is substituted. Either way, the context demands some sort of blending or balancing between fate and free will.

(h) The noun τὸ βουλευτήριον occurs 7 times in Josephus, with the sense either of "council hall" or "council meeting". The difficulty is to determine *whose* council meeting/chamber is intended by the demonstrative ἐκείνης. Thackeray, Feldman, Yaffe/Damico, and Topping all take the antecedent to be εἱμαρμένη.[61] Schlatter thinks that this is too distant and he therefore conjectures the emendation ἐκείνου, as a reference back to θεῷ.[62] Since Josephus normally uses θεός and εἱμαρμένη inter-

---

[58] G. F. Moore, "Fate", 378, 384.
[59] Schlatter, *Theologie*, 210 n. 1.
[60] See chapter 6, above.
[61] For the translations suggested by S. Topping, M. Yaffe, and A. Damico, cf. Rivkin, *Revolution*, 320f.
[62] Schlatter, *Theologie*, 219 n. 1.

changeably, however, as also in this passage, the difference is not significant for our purpose. He is speaking figuratively of the council chamber
of God or of fate.

(i) The Epitome gives the neuter aorist participle τὸ ἐθελῆσαν in the
nominative, which is followed by Feldman (LCL edn.). The manuscripts AMW give the dative, τῷ ἐθελήσαντι, which better parallels τῷ
βουλευτηρίῳ.[63] It is not clear, on either reading, why Josephus chooses
the neuter "that which has willed (of man)" or what the precise meaning
is, in combination with προσχωρεῖν. Since the thrust of § 13ab is clear
enough, however, a complete resolution of this *crux* is unnecessary: we
know that Josephus wants to balance fate with human will.

(j) The pair ἀρετὴ ἢ κακία touches the root of a major theme in *Ant.*
Of the 291 occurrences of ἀρετή in Josephus, a disproportionate 238 are
in *Ant.* We have already seen that the preface to this work establishes
"virtue" as a major theme of the biblical paraphrase (1:20).

> God, as the universal father and Lord who beholds all things, grants to
> such as follow him a life of bliss (τοῖς ἑπομένοις αὐτῷ δίδωσιν εὐδαίμονα βίον),
> but involves in dire calamities those who step outside the path of virtue
> (τοὺς ἔξω δὲ βαίνοντας ἀρετῆς). (Thackeray)

In this construction, ἀρετή means concretely obedience to God and his
laws. Moses teaches that God is the perfection of ἀρετή and that men are
to participate in this attribute (1:23). In accord with this theme,
Josephus employs the word ἀρετή some 116 times in the course of his
biblical paraphrase; by contrast, the entire canonical Septuagint has it
a bare 8 times, and mainly in the prophetic books, which Josephus does
not use.[64] He speaks of the virtue of Moses, of the laws, and of those who
obey the laws.[65] As in our passage, ἀρετή is sometimes contrasted with
κακία.[66]

It is significant that, of the 238 occurrences of ἀρετή in the twenty
books of *Ant.*, 96 instances (or about two fifths) are in books 17-19. This
disproportion indicates that the word is also part of the peculiar
vocabulary that Josephus adopts in these books. In the passage on the
schools (18:11-23) ἀρετή is one of several terms, such as λόγος, φυλακή,
περιμάχητον ἡγούμενοι, ἐθέλω, and τυγχάνω, that appear two or more
times. The phrase ἀρετὴ ἢ κακία, therefore, helps to bond the description

[63] Schlatter, *Theologie*, 210 n. 1.
[64] Esther 4:17; Prov. 1:7; Hab. 3:3; Zech. 6:13; Isa. 42:8, 12; 43:21; 63:7.
[65] *Ant.* 4:320, 321, 326; 5:73; 18:280; 19:57, 202; cf. *Ag.Ap.* 2:226, 278, 279.
[66] *War* 2:156; 4:387; *Ant.* 6:93; 8:252; 17:101; 19:16; *Ag.Ap.* 2:145. It is not clear in
our passage whether the phrase qualifies ἀνθρώπων, τὸ ἐθέλησαν, or προσχωρεῖν.

of the Pharisees to the entire passage on the schools, to books 17-19, and to *Ant.* as a whole.

2. Interpretation

The first two strands of our statement, §§ 13ab, are reasonably clear: "the Pharisees reckon that everything is effected by fate but they do not thereby deprive the human will of the initiative that resides in their [*sc.* human] power." This paradoxical statement is very similar to the description of the Pharisees' view in *War* 2:163, which said that εἱμαρμένῃ καὶ θεῷ προσάπτουσι πάντα, καὶ τὸ μὲν πράττειν . . . ἐπὶ τοῖς ἀνθρώποις κεῖσθαι. Josephus has given up the τινα/τινα model of *Ant.* 13:172 in favour of his original "cooperation" model, which, as we have seen, bears a marked similarity to the view of Chrysippus reported by Cicero. Fate or God is the universal cause but human volition is still active throughout.

The real difficulties begin in § 13c. Josephus is no longer content with the statement that fate "assists" (βοηθέω) in each case as he had said in *War* 2:162. He now attempts a fuller explanation by resorting to metaphor.

Fate, he says, has a council chamber or holds a council meeting (βουλευτήριον). Somehow, at this meeting or chamber, a settlement is effected between fate and human will (§ 13ab), such that Josephus can speak of a "weighing" (κρίσις) or "blending" (κρᾶσις) of the two causes. Seemingly intractable problems, however, are: (a) the textual certainty of τὸ ἐθελῆσαν, (b) the syntax of τῶν ἀνθρώπων τὸ ἐθελῆσαν προσχωρεῖν,[67] and (c) the relationship of μετ' ἀρετῆς ἢ κακίας to the rest.[68]

Thus Josephus's intended explanation of the Pharisaic view has succeeded in baffling both medieval copyists and modern scholars. Fortunately, for our purpose it is enough to establish that he presents a cooperation or "fusion" model of the roles of fate and free will. One must reckon seriously with the possibility that he did not know exactly what to say about this perennial puzzle.

D. *The Immortality of Souls*

14a.   ἀθάνατόν τε ἰσχὺν ταῖς ψυχαῖς
        πίστις αὐτοῖς εἶναι

---

[67] Cf. Schlatter, *Theologie*, 209f. n. 1.

[68] One is tempted to conjecture that the phrase entered the text by a dittography of ἀρετῆς ἢ κακίας. Schlatter (*Theologie*, 209f. n. 1) explains the double τυγχάνουσιν by a similar means.

14b.　καὶ ὑπὸ χθονὸς δικαιώσεις τε καὶ τιμὰς
　　　　οἷς ἀρετῆς ἢ κακίας ἐπιτήδευσις
　　　　ἐν τῷ βίῳ γέγονεν,
14c.　καὶ ταῖς μὲν εἱργμὸν ἀΐδιον προτίθεσθαι,
14d.　ταῖς δὲ ῥᾳστώνην τοῦ ἀναβιοῦν.

This description of the Pharisees' conception of immortality is very similar to other passages in Josephus that describe his own view, the Essene view, and also the Pharisaic view. Because of these obvious similarities, it was necessary to consider the salient features of our passage above, in our analysis of *War* 2:163. We discovered there that Josephus presents the Pharisaic position (and also his own) as a belief in a peculiar form of reincarnation, in which a new body is promised only to the good as a reward for virtuous conduct; the new and better life will be granted at the "succession of ages".

It remains to supplement our earlier discussion with a few remarks on the distinctive vocabulary of *Ant.* 18:14.

1. Key Terms

(a) Ὑπὸ χθονός. The word χθών, "(surface of the) earth", occurs only here in Josephus.[69] Indeed, as a poetic term, it is very rare in ancient Greek prose in general.[70] The phrase ὑπὸ χθονός does, however, occur in Homer, Aeschylus, and Sophocles[71] as a poetic designation of the nether-world, which is more prosaically called Ἅιδης.[72]

In *War* 2:163 Josephus referred to the Pharisaic belief in the eternal punishment of the wicked but he did not mention the venue for this punishment. He did, however, tell us that the Sadducees do away with τὰς καθ' ᾅδου τιμωρίας καὶ τιμάς (2:165),[73] a phrase that must reflect their opposition to the Pharisaic view. In our passage, Josephus's experiment with high style leads him to seize on the more poetic expression but the meaning is the same. Rewards and punishments, according to the Pharisees, are meted out in the nether-world.

---

[69] But cf. χθόνιος at *War* 1:377.
[70] Cf. LSJ, *s.v.*
[71] Homer, *Iliad* 8:14; Aeschylus, *Choephor* 833; Sophocles, *Antigone* 65.
[72] E.g., Plato, *Meno* 81bc; *Phaedo* 107c.
[73] So the Loeb text, after C (11th cent.). The rest of the MSS have "universal (καθόλου) punishments and rewards". Even if the Loeb reading were incorrect, we should still know from *War* 2:155 and 3:375 that the Essenes and Josephus, respectively, assign the wicked to subterranean punishments. We have seen that the views of Josephus and those of the Pharisees on the afterlife are also very close (chapter 6, above).

(b) Ἐπιτήδευσις is another unusual word for Josephus. Of its 7 occurrences in his writings, 4 fall within *Ant.* 17-19 and 2 within his description of the Pharisees here. The word is Thucydidean, as is the phrase ἐπιτήδευσις ἀρετής.[74] The word denotes one's "striving" or "conduct" in life; here, it refers to the striving after virtue or vice.

(c) The noun ῥᾳστώνη is, again, characteristic of *Ant.* 17-19. Of its 11 occurrences in Josephus 6 are in these books. In our passage the word is used in contrast to the eternal imprisonment (εἱργμόν) that awaits the wicked; we may render "freedom (from restriction)".

(d) Finally, ἀναβιόω occurs only here in Josephus. Rasp ventures the hypothesis that by using this word, Josephus intends to *correct* his earlier presentation of the Pharisaic belief in immortality: it is not metempsychosis that the Pharisees espouse, as he had erroneously reported in *War*, but resurrection.[75] We have seen, however, that phrases like πάλιν γίγνεσθαι and τὸ ἀναβιώσασθαι are equivalent in Plato: they both mean "to live again". It is doubtful that Josephus intended his readers to perceive any difference between these terms, or between them and μεταβαίνειν εἰς ἕτερον σῶμα (*War* 2:163).[76]

In all of these cases, it appears that Josephus has merely altered the vocabulary and construction of his earlier statement, as is his usual practice in *Ant.* over against *War*; the sense, however, remains the same. In addition, this passage is affected by the experiment with grandiose vocabulary and syntax that Josephus conducts through *Ant.* 17-19.

2. Interpretation

The general thrust of *Ant.* 18:14 is clear enough, even though the syntax is difficult in the absence of a main finite verb:

14a.   That souls have an immortal power is a
           conviction among them
14b.   and subterranean punishments and rewards
           come to those whose conduct in life
           has been either of virtue or vice;
14c.   for some, eternal imprisonment is prepared
14d.   but for others, freedom to live again.

---

[74] Cf. Thucydides 7.86.5 and also *Ant.* 19:49.
[75] Rasp, "Religionsparteien", 32.
[76] Cf. chapter 6, above, and Moore, "Fate", 385 n. 57.

As in *War* 2:165, the Sadducees are now said to reject the Pharisaic belief. A new detail is that their teaching "dissipates (συναφανίζει) the soul along with the body".

E. *The Influence of the Pharisees*

15a. καὶ δι' αὐτὰ τοῖς δὲ δήμοις πιθανώτατοι
      τυγχάνουσιν
15b. καὶ ὁπόσα θεῖα εὐχῶν τε ἔχεται καὶ
      ἱερῶν ποιήσεως ἐξηγήσει τῇ
      ἐκείνων τυγχάνουσιν πρασσόμενα.
15c. εἰς τοσόνδε ἀρετῆς αὐτοῖς αἱ πόλεις
      ἐμαρτύρησαν ἐπιτηδεύσει τοῦ ἐπὶ
      πᾶσι κρείσσονος ἔν τε διαίτῃ
      τοῦ βίου καὶ λόγοις.

1. Key Terms

(a) The adjective πιθανός is a favourite word in *Ant.* 17-19. Although it occurs 47 times throughout Josephus's writings, fully one third of those occurrences (i.e., 16) are concentrated in *Ant.* 18-19. The Pharisees happen to be "most convincing" to the people (Yaffe/Damico: "to the vulgar"). We note that this statement does not imply Josephus's approval of the Pharisees' popularity; he also tells us of certain deceivers that were πιθανοί.[77] We have seen throughout our study that he consistently acknowledges the Pharisees' influence but, just as consistently, deplores it.

The phrase τοῖς δήμοις πιθανώτατοι is reminiscent of Thucydides, who uses this superlative three times and always with the indirect objects τῷ δήμῳ (3.36.6), τῷ πλήθει (4.21.3), or τοῖς πολλοῖς (6.35.2). Notice, first, that for Thucydides, who provides the literary model for *Ant.* 17-19, these indirect objects are interchangeable.[78] This fact militates against Schwartz's proposal that Josephus, by making the Pharisees now popular with τοῖς δήμοις instead of with τῷ πλήθει (as at *Ant.* 13:288, 402), is attempting to improve their image.[79] Notice further that in two of its three occurrences, Thucydides predicates τῷ δήμῳ (πλήθει) πιθανώτατος of one Cleon, son of Cleaenetus, whom the historian

---

[77] *Ant.* 18:41, 69, 85f.
[78] Thucydides 3.36.3 and 4.21.3 speak of the same person, a certain Cleon, son of Cleaenetus.
[79] Schwartz, "Josephus and Nicolaus", 163. We await a comprehensive study of δῆμος and πλῆθος in Josephus.

describes as immoderate and most violent (βιαιότατος). Thucydides' acknowledgment of this man's influence with the public is by no means a commendation.

(b) The verb τυγχάνω is typically Josephan: it occurs 439 times throughout his writings and its 40 occurrences in books 17-19 are proportionate to the others. That it appears twice within our statement about the Pharisees' popularity is striking; Schlatter excises the latter occurrence as a dittography.[80]

Because τυγχάνω is often little more than a "spice word" for Josephus, it is difficult to know how, or whether, to translate it. Feldman takes it emphatically, to mean, "they are, as a matter of fact, extremely influential". Topping omits it altogether or, perhaps, gives it the force of εἰμί: "they are plausible to the people". Yaffe and Damico take the verb in its most literal sense (from τύχη), "they *happen to be* most persuasive to the vulgar", which is rather different in nuance from Feldman's rendering.[81] The word is common enough that one can easily find support elsewhere in Josephus for all three senses.[82]

If one takes the other Pharisee passages into consideration, however, the Yaffe/Damico translation commends itself. Josephus is not pleased with the Pharisees' influence and therefore acknowledges only that they "happen to have" the support of the people, not that they deserve it. This interpretation is also supported by the context of our passage. Josephus openly praises the Essenes as superior to all others who make any claim to virtue (18:20); he also gives *his* opinion that the Sadducees include men of the highest standing (τοὺς πρώτους τοῖς ἀξιώμασι, 18:17) but that they are compelled by popular sentiment to accept "what the Pharisee says". In view of these remarks and in the absence of any unqualified commendation of the Pharisees, it makes sense that Josephus should say that "they happen to be" the ones with the popular following.

Even if this interpretation of τυγχάνω is correct, however, we have detected only a nuance in Josephus's remarks and not an outright attack on Pharisaic influence such as we have met before.[83] His purpose here is not to attack the Pharisees but to show that they, along with the Sadducees and Essenes, represent normal Judaism, unlike the school of Judas.

(c) In the relative adjective ὁπόσα we encounter one of the clearest hallmarks of the style adopted in *Ant.* 17-19. Of 112 occurrences of this

---

[80] Schlatter, *Theologie*, 211 n. 1.
[81] For the translations of Topping and Yaffe/Damico, see Rivkin, *Revolution*, 320f.
[82] Cf. Rengstorf, *Concordance*, *s.v.*
[83] I.e., in *War* 1:110-114; *Ant.* 13:288, 401, 432; 17:41-45.

word in Josephus, a remarkable 101 are found in *Ant.* 17-19. This high frequency results, as in our passage, from an unliterary substitution of the relative adjective for the relative pronoun. This is hardly the work of a Greek *litteratus*.

(d) The adjective θεῖος, "divine", is characteristic of all of Josephus's writings; it occurs some 206 times. More than three-quarters of these instances are in the neuter substantive, τὸ θεῖον, meaning "the deity", which is Josephus's preferred circumlocution for God. Nevertheless, the adjective occurs attributively, as in our passage, more than 40 times.

(e) Yet another favoured term in *Ant.* 17-19 that turns up in our passage is ἡ ποίησις. Of its 15 occurrences in Josephus, 8 are in these three books. Significantly, in his description of the Sadducean view Josephus also includes the word μεταποίησις, which occurs again at 18:242 and only once elsewhere (3:58); this accords with the general repetitiveness of the vocabulary in our passage.

(f) The noun ἐξήγησις occurs only 8 times in Josephus. Four times it refers to the "interpretation" of dreams.[84] Once it refers to Josephus's own "narrative" in *War*,[85] once to the "translation" of the Septuagint,[86] and once to the Persians' "exposition" of their laws.[87] Only in our passage does ἐξήγησις refer to a particular exposition or interpretation of the Jewish laws.

Nevertheless, the cognate verb ἐξηγέομαι does occur in this connection several times. Most interesting for us: in *War* 2:162 the Pharisees are said to be reputed μετ' ἀκριβείας. . . . ἐξηγεῖσθαι τὰ νόμιμα.

(g) The meaning of ἀρετή in the final sentence is problematic because it is connected with εἰς τοσόνδε, which seems to be retrospective. But Josephus has not yet spoken of any moral "virtue" on the Pharisees' part. Indeed, all of his earlier accounts of the Pharisees' activities alleged that these men were singularly lacking in moral principle (*War* 1:110-114, 571; *Ant.* 13:288-298, 400-432; 17:41-45). If, then, εἰς τοσόνδε ἀρετή is retrospective, the ἀρετή in question must be the "power" or "influence" of the Pharisees (rather than their moral virtue), for that is what Josephus has just spoken about.[88]

Ἀρετή was an extremely malleable term in classical and Hellenistic usage.[89] Like the English "virtue" (> Lat. *virtus*), its original sense was

---

[84] *Ant.* 2:69, 75, 77, 93.
[85] *War* 1:30.
[86] *Ant.* 1:12.
[87] *Ant.* 11:192.
[88] Thus Yaffe/Damico (in Rivkin, *Revolution*, 320f.).
[89] Cf. LSJ, *s.v.*, the specialized lexica to the classics, and O. Bauernfeind, "ἀρετή", *TDNT*, I, 457-461.

not moral but referred to "manly strength, martial valour, prowess, potency, skill, capacity", and thence "accomplishment, eminence, fame, success". These are the only senses in which Homer used ἀρετή;[90] interestingly enough, he sometimes used the word as a synonym for δόξα, to mean "success" or "prosperity".[91] Indeed, the non-moral connotations of ἀρετή were paramount in Attic usage generally.[92] Even the LXX consistently uses ἀρετή, in Homeric fashion, as a synonym for δόξα, to render the Hebrew הוד ("glory") and תהלה ("praise").[93] Thus, long after the philosophers had transformed ἀρετή into an ethical *Leitmotif*, writers continued to use it non-moral senses as well—not least the philosophers themselves.[94] This is what we find in Josephus: on the one hand, as we have seen, he makes ἀρετὴ καὶ κακία into a major moralizing theme of *Ant.*; yet on the other hand, he can still use ἀρετή in the old non-moral sense of "prowess" or "power".[95] So it is an open question what he means by ἀρετή when he uses it of the Pharisees.

Since *Ant.* 17-19 slavishly imitates Thucydidean style, it is worth asking how Thucydides uses ἀρετή, and the answer to that question is most illuminating. Although the exact meaning of ἀρετή in particular passages of Thucydides is a matter of debate, recent commentators agree that he uses the word in a wide range of senses, evoking both moral and non-moral nuances.[96] Especially pertinent, however, is his description of Antiphon, who appears in his narrative as "both a subverter of the constitution and a traitor".[97] For Thucydides describes this morally dubious figure as:

> a man inferior to none of the Athenians of his day in ἀρετή and one who had proved himself most able both to formulate a plan and to set forth his conclusions in speech. (8.68.1)

---

[90] Cf. *Iliad* 3:411; 8:535; 13:257; 15:642; 20:242; 23:276; *Odyssey* 4:725; 8:239; 13:45; 14:212, 402; 18:133, 251.

[91] *Odyssey* 13:45; 14:402; 18:133.

[92] Pindar, *Odes* 7:163; Xenophon, *Memorabilia* 2:1, 21; Sophocles, *Ph.* 1420; Thucydides 1:33; Lysias 193:12; cf. LSJ, *s.v.* and Bauernfeind, "ἀρετή", 458.

[93] Isa. 42:8, 12; Hab. 3:3; Zech. 6:13.

[94] Although Plato is the one who established the ethical sense of ἀρετή (*Republic* 500d; *Laws* 963c), he also continues to use it in non-moral contexts (*Republic* 335b, 601d, 618d; *Symposium* 208d; *Protagoras* 322d).

[95] Cf. *War* 3:380; *Ant.* 17:130. Bauernfeind, "ἀρετή", 458 n.6, finds the non-moral sense "commonly" in Josephus, but I think that is an overstatement.

[96] Cf. J. T. Hooker, "Χάρις and ἀρετή in Thucydides", 165-169, esp. 168; J. L. Creed, "Moral Values in the Age of Thucydides", *CQ* 23 (1973), 213-231; A. W. Gomme, A. Andrewes, and K. J. Dover, *A Historical Commentary on Thucydides* (5 vols; Oxford: Clarendon, 1981), V, 171f.; W. R. Connor, *Thucydides* (Princeton: Princeton University Press, 1984), 224f. n. 30

[97] Andrewes, *Thucydides*, 171.

C. F. Smith translates ἀρετή here (LCL edn.) as "force of character";
and now A. Andrewes agrees that it means practically φύσεως ἰσχύς or
δύναμις.⁹⁸ W. R. Connor remarks, "It is a mistake, I believe, to infer
that the word indicates Thucydides' own moral approval."⁹⁹ So for
Thucydides, Josephus's literary model, it was perfectly possible to use
ἀρετή in senses devoid of moral affirmation, to speak objectively of someone's "prowess, skill, or power".

We give the last word to Josephus's contemporary, Plutarch.
Although the style of *Ant.* 17-19 can hardly be described as poetic, it is
clearly a bungled attempt at elegant prose. But Plutarch claims that the
"poets" like to give new meanings to ἀρετή, and that they "make good
repute (εὐδοξία) and influence (ἡ δύναμις) to be ἀρετή".¹⁰⁰

Given the variety of possible meanings for ἀρετή in Josephus's day,
and given the context in *Ant.* 18:15, where it is the influence of the
Pharisees that is under discussion and not any moral virtue, it would
seem reasonable to take ἀρετή here as a synonym for (after Plutarch)
εὐδοξία and δύναμις. This interpretation would fit squarely with
Josephus's many notices about the Pharisees' public influence, on account of their reputation for piety.¹⁰¹

(h) Similarly, the interpreter must decide whether the comparative
κρείσσων is intended to have any moral significance in this context, as in
"more excellent" or "superior", or whether it simply acknowledges that
Pharisaic teaching is "more influential", "predominant", or
"prevalent". Josephus employs the word some 121 times and in both
senses.¹⁰² In our passage, the context would seem to require that τοῦ ἐπὶ
πᾶσι κρείσσονος refer to the Pharisees' "predominance over all" and not
their "excellence" above all (*contra* Feldman), since: (i) Josephus clearly
makes the Essenes superior to all who claim (μεταποιοῦμαι) some share
of virtue (§ 18); (ii) he describes the Pharisees' influence as merely a
matter of chance (cf. τυγχάνω); and (iii) he speaks in a resigned way
about how eminent Sadducees must yield to "what the Pharisee says"
(§ 17).¹⁰³ It is difficult to interpret this phrase as Josephus's advocacy of

---

⁹⁸ Andrewes, *Thucydides*, V, 172.
⁹⁹ Connor, *Thucydides*, 224 n. 30.
¹⁰⁰ Plutarch, *How to Study Poetry* 24d.
¹⁰¹ One could wish that Josephus had not used ἀρετή in two different senses within
the same passage, but one should note that Thucydides, the literary model in this case,
stands accused of the same fault; cf. Hooker, "Χάρις and ἀρετή", 169.
¹⁰² The amoral, non-evaluative sense of the word is well attested in Josephus, e.g.,
War 1:88, 91, 654; 4:640; 5:176; 7:88, 158, 330, 360; *Ant.* 1:244; 4:195; 5:139, 64, 66;
6:231, 328; 7:20, 127 *et passim*; *Life* 45.
¹⁰³ Notice the tendency in *Ant.* 17-19 to spell κρείσσων (as also πράσσω) with a double
sigma, in imitation of Thucydides, rather than with the atticizing double *tau*, which

Pharisaic moral superiority. Further, the neuter substantive of κρείσσων is Thucydidean; in Thucydides it also lacks a moral-evaluative sense.[104]

The rest of the vocabulary, if not the syntax, of 18:15 is fairly straightforward. Much of it is repetitive, such as τυγχάνουσι, ἐπιτήδευσις, βίος, and λόγος.

2. Interpretation

Our passage begins with a clear opening statement about the Pharisees' popularity (§ 15a), which is followed by an elaboration on the particular areas of their influence (§ 15b). The final sentence (§ 15c) is difficult but seems to be a summary statement emphasizing the pervasiveness of Pharisaic views. Thus:

15a.   On account of these (views) they happen
             to be most persuasive to the people;
15b.   of prayers and sacred rites, whatever is
             considered divine happens to be conducted
             according to their interpretation.
15c.   This much of their influence the cities
             have demonstrated, in both manner of
             life and discourse, by their pursuit
             of [or "adherence to"] the way that
             prevails over all.

In several earlier passages Josephus has indicated that the Pharisees have the support of the people (*War* 1:110, 571; 2:162; *Ant.* 13:288, 296-298, 400-432), that they are instantly credited, even when they speak against authorities (*Ant.* 13:288, 401), and that the annulment of their special ordinances created an uproar (*Ant.* 13:296-298, 402). The passage before us recapitulates this theme and explains it in part by the appeal of the Pharisees' philosophical views, especially that of immortality (cf. δι' αὐτά).

The explanation is significant because we know that Josephus himself holds a view of immortality that is very close to that of the Pharisees. He also agrees with their accommodation of fate and free will. He seems

---

prevails elsewhere in Josephus. Cf. L. R. Palmer, *The Greek Language* (London-Boston: Faber and Faber, 1980), 167.
[104] Thucydides 1.77.4; 3.45.4.

to say here that these were popular views and that, because the Pharisees espoused them (unlike the Sadducees), that group attracted the good will of the people.

In the earlier Pharisee passages, we have noted, Josephus regularly conveys his regret over the extent of Pharisaic power. If such regret is present in our passage, it is not obvious but must be looked for in subtleties, for example: (a) in Josephus's emphasis on the verb τυγχάνω in his discussion of the Pharisees' influence; (b) in his open commendation of the Sadducees and, especially, the Essenes; and (c) in his notice that the Sadducees, though capable and competent, must abide by οἷς ὁ Φαρισαῖος λέγει, which phrase connotes a feeling of resignation rather than enthusiasm.

III. *Source Analysis*

Ant. 18:12-15 is one of only two Pharisee passages that Schwartz attributes to Josephus himself; the other is the *War* parallel (2:162-166). Schwartz's reasoning is that, "both passages present thoroughly positive accounts of the Pharisees".[105] Hölscher is not so sure. He acknowledges that Josephus has already pointed ahead to this passage in *Ant.* 15:371, which implies some degree of forethought and involvement as an author. Ultimately, however, Hölscher cannot accept that the author of our passage was a Pharisee.[106] First, he draws attention to the phrase τοῖς δήμοις πιθανώτατοι τυγχάνουσιν, which, he observes, hardly depicts the Pharisees' influence as praiseworthy. Second, Hölscher doubts that a Pharisee could have named a Pharisee as co-founder of the school of Judas, in view of what is said about the rebel school in our passage.

Both of Hölscher's observations on the anti-Pharisaic nuances are accurate and important. The only weak link in his argument is the premise that Josephus was a Pharisee and could not, therefore, have written the passage. We shall discuss this widely endorsed assumption in Part IV, below.

On the other hand, the foregoing study has made three discoveries that seem to require Josephan authorship. First, *Ant.* 18:12-15 is basically a restatement of four points that Josephus himself has repeatedly made about the Pharisees in earlier discussions. So the content is Josephan. Second, some of Josephus's usual vocabulary—such as τυγχάνω, φυλακή, θεός as an equivalent of εἱμαρμένη, and the pair ἀρετὴ ἢ κακία—turns up in our passage. Most significant, however, is our

105 Schwartz, "Josephus and Nicolaus", 162f.
106 Hölscher, "Josephus", 1991.

discovery that the author of *Ant.* 18:12-15 is the same person who wrote *Ant.* 17-19 as a whole. Our passage is laced with the terminology and stylistic features that characterize these books, such as: ὁπόσα, πιθανός, ποίησις, ἐπιτήδευσις, περιμάχητον ἡγέομαι, ῥᾳστώνη, ἀρετή, ἀντιλέξις, and the neuter participle governing a genitive. Our passage, like the rest of *Ant.* 17-19, is characterized by the attempt to imitate the archaic Attic prose of Thucydides.[107]

It is possible to deny Josephan authorship of *Ant.* 18:12-15, therefore, only if one also denies his authorship of *Ant.* 17-19 in its entirety. The closest that any scholar has come to such an unlikely view was Thackeray's proposal that Josephus commissioned a literary assistant to write these books. But that proposal has been thoroughly repudiated, with many cogent arguments.[108] One of these arguments, as we have seen, is that the solecisms found in *Ant.* 17-19 are more easily attributed to the Palestinian Josephus than to someone who was hired for his literary abilities in Greek! Further, Josephus's own characteristic vocabulary is intermingled with the more pretentious style.[109]

Why Josephus chose to alter his style so dramatically in *Ant.* 17-19 is not, I concede, clear. It may be that he was studying Thucydides at the time and threw himself into a programme of devoted imitation.[110] It may be that these books alone benefited (or suffered) from a revision of *Ant.* that Josephus was not able to carry through the whole work.[111] Whatever his reasons for the literary experimentation, however, we may be sure that he exercised final control over the content of *Ant.* 18:12-15.

Summary and Conclusion

In his final statement on the Pharisees in *Ant.* Josephus sets out to contrast them, along with the Sadducees and Essenes, to the school of Judas. He wants, therefore, to put all three schools in the best possible light and to downplay any negative feelings that he might have toward any of them.

---

[107] Palmer, *Greek Language*, 159, describes the distinctive features of the old Attic style: "poetical colouring, forced and strange expressions, bold new coinages and substantivized neuters of participles and adjectives".

[108] See the excursus to Part I above.

[109] Cf. Richards, "Composition", 39. Nor does Hölscher's own theory of intermediate sources explain the linguistic data, since he posits the same intermediate source for books 18-20 as for books 13-17, thus overriding the distinctive features of 17-19.

[110] So Niese, *HZ*, 225; Peterson, "Literary Projects", 260f. n. 5; Shutt *Studies*, 62ff.; Rajak, *Josephus*, 233f.

[111] So Richards, "Composition", 40.

His description of the Pharisees begins, accordingly, with an approving notice about their distaste for luxury. He follows this with a three-point summary of tenets that he has mentioned previously. At the head of these he now puts their allegiance to a special extra-biblical tradition (cf. *Ant.* 13:296-298). Then come the philosophical issues of fate/free will and immortality (cf. *War* 2:162f.). Finally, he talks about the Pharisees' major role in public and religious life.

The theory of Rasp, Smith, Neusner, and others that *Ant.* 18 dramatically improves the Pharisees' image over against *War*, or that Josephus deliberately corrects *War* (Rasp), seems to lack any basis whatsoever. It is true that much of the vocabulary is new, but this accords perfectly with (a) Josephus's consistent tendency in *Ant.* to vary *War*'s presentation and (b) the well-known peculiarities of *Ant.* 17-19.

Most important, one can still detect a tone of resentment on the part of Josephus toward the Pharisees, as Hölscher already perceived. Josephus connects the Pharisees twice with the school of Judas, which he dislikes intensely; he allows only that the Pharisees "happen to be" or "chance to be" most popular with the people; and he seems to regret that the finest Sadducees, when they assume leadership positions, are compelled to follow "what the Pharisee says".

PART FOUR

THE PHARISEES IN THE *LIFE*

Among all of his discussions of the Pharisees, it is only in the *Life* that Josephus implies any personal affiliation with the group (§ 12). The attempt will be made in Part Four to ascertain the nature of that affiliation and to interpret Josephus's other remarks on the Pharisees in this short "autobiography". After considering the purpose and outlook of *Life*, we shall focus our attention on *Life* 10-12, which describes Josephus's experience with all three schools and his final alignment (of some sort) with the Pharisees, and on *Life* 191ff., where he describes the involvement of certain Pharisees in an episode of his career as Galilean commander.

CHAPTER THIRTEEN

PURPOSE AND OUTLOOK OF THE *LIFE*

Some brief remarks on the famous problem of dating the *Life* will serve
to introduce the analysis of its purpose and outlook.

I. *Date*

The problem of dating the *Life*, in brief, is as follows. On the one hand,
Life was clearly written as an appendix to *Ant.*[1] It even lacks any introduction of its own, beginning rather with the conjunction δέ. It was introduced, however, at the end of *Ant.*, where Josephus remarked
(20:266):

> Perhaps it will not arouse jealousy or strike ordinary folk as gauche if I
> review briefly my own ancestry and the events of my life while there are
> still those living who can refute or support [me].[2]

And *Life* closes with a word to the patron of *Ant.*:[3]

> Having now, most excellent Epaphroditus, rendered a complete account of
> our *antiquities* (τὴν πᾶσαν τῆς ἀρχαιολογίας), I shall here . . . conclude my
> narrative. (Thackeray)

So the *Life* is apparently intended as the final section of *Ant.* All of the
manuscripts but one unite the two works[4] and Eusebius quotes from *Life*
as if it were part of *Ant.*[5] That *Life* was written as an appendix to *Ant.*
seems undeniable.

On the other hand, the two works appear to date themselves differently. According to *Ant.* 20:267, that treatise was completed "in the
thirteenth year of the reign of Domitian Caesar and the fifty-sixth year
of my life" (Feldman), both of which data point to the year AD 93/94.[6]

---

[1] For fuller discussions of the issue cf. Schürer, *Geschichte*, I, 87; Niese, *HZ*, 226; T.
Frankfort, "La date de l'autobiographie de Flavius Josephe et des oeuvres de Justus de
Tiberiade, *Revue Belge de Philologie* 39 (1961), 52-58; Rajak, "Justus", 354 n. 1; and S.
J. D. Cohen, *Josephus*, 175.

[2] Schürer, *Geschichte*, I, 87, denies that *Ant.* 20 introduces *Life*; but he seems to have
overlooked this passage (cf. n. 10 below).

[3] Cf. *Ant.* 1:8.

[4] Cf. Schreckenberg, *Tradition*, 11.

[5] *Eccl. Hist.* 3.10.8f.

[6] Josephus, *Life* 5, states that he was born in the year of Gaius Caligula's accession
(= AD 37/38).

Life, however, presupposes the death of Agrippa II (§§ 359f.), which the tenth-century patriarch Photius puts at AD 100.[7] The challenge in dating the *Life*, therefore, is to explain how it can be a part of *Ant.* and yet have been written after the death of Agrippa II.

Four main solutions have been advanced in the literature. Perhaps the simplest was that of Schürer (1867),[8] who proposed that *Life*, in spite of its association with *Ant.*, was not written until several years later.[9] Schürer argued, on the basis of *Ant.* 20:267,[10] that Josephus was intending to write a supplementary account of the war, but not an autobiography, when he finished *Ant.*[11] His decision to write the *Life* instead was caused by the appearance of a rival account of the war by Justus of Tiberias. This rival account embarrassed Josephus in Rome by making him out to have been the champion of the revolt in Galilee, rather than the voice of moderation that he had claimed to be. Josephus had to respond with the *Life*, which deals mainly with a six-month period in his Galilean command.[12]

In support of the date for Agrippa's death given by Photius, Schürer points to numismatic evidence that the king lived at least until 95 (and therefore somewhat later than the completion date of *Ant.*);[13] he dates coins referring to the ''35th year of Agrippa'' from an era beginning in AD 61.

By the time of Schürer's so-called ''third-fourth edition'' (1901), however, most scholars had come to think that the best solution to the problem was to give up Photius's dating and to put both *Ant.* and *Life* at 93/94.[14] This view won the support of B. Niese, H. Luther, and G. Hölscher,[15] and has re-emerged in recent times as one of the few points of agreement between T. Rajak and S. J. D. Cohen.[16]

---

[7] That is, the third year of Trajan; in his *Bibliotheca*, 33, given by Jacoby, *Fragmente*, 734 T. 2. Cf. the ET by Cohen, *Josephus*, 142.

[8] I do not have access to the first edition of Schürer, *Geschichte* (1867), but only the ''third-fourth'' (1901ff.); he claims there, however (I, p. III), that, though he has enlarged his earlier work, he has not otherwise altered it much.

[9] Schürer, *Geschichte*, I, 77, 87f.

[10] *Ant.* 20:267: ὑπομνήσω πάλιν τοῦ ἐκ πολέμου.

[11] Schürer, *Geschichte*, I, 87f. The renowned German scholar seems, unaccountably, to have overlooked *Ant.* 20:266, which promises an account of Josephus's life.

[12] Schürer, *Geschichte*, I, 87f.

[13] *Ibid.*, I, 88 n. 20; 597-599. An inscription unknown in Schürer's time refers to the ''37th year of Agrippa''. This would put the king's death later than AD 97; cf. Cohen, *Josephus*, 173.

[14] Schürer, *Geschichte*, I, 88 n. 20, acknowledges this as a common opinion (in 1901). H. Luther, writing in 1910, designates it the prevailing view of his time, in *Josephus and Justus von Tiberias* (Halle: Wischan and Burkhardt, 1910), 54.

[15] B. Niese, *HZ*, 226f.; Luther, *Josephus und Justus*, 54ff.; Hölscher, ''Josephus'', 1941 n.Ḥ.

[16] Rajak, ''Justus'', 361, who draws on Frankfort (see n. 1. above) and Cohen, *Josephus*, 170-180.

Against Schürer, Niese (1896) maintained that Josephus's obvious linkage of *Ant.* and *Life* has greater probative value than the late notice of Photius.[17] He insisted, on the basis of *Ant.* 20:266 (which Schürer does not explain) that Josephus had planned from the start to append an account of his life to *Ant.*[18] Furthermore, Niese pointed to *Life* 428f., in which Josephus expresses his gratitude to Vespasian, Titus, and especially Domitian (and his wife) for their many kindnesses.[19] Niese took this to be a clear indication that Josephus was writing in Domitian's reign, not Trajan's; for it was incredible, he thought, that Josephus would praise a previous dynasty without even mentioning the incumbent ruler.[20]

To these considerations Niese's student Luther (1910) added three others. First, he argued that several unflattering remarks about both Agrippa II and his father in *Ant.* are only explicable if the king was already dead when *Ant.* was written; but if *Ant.* and *Life* both presuppose Agrippa's death, there is no need to separate them.[21] Second, he discounted Schürer's numismatic evidence on the basis of its many irregularities.[22]

The decisive argument, according to Luther, concerned the identity of the patron of *Ant.* and *Life*, Epaphroditus.[23] The two prime candidates, he thought, were the secretary of Nero, who was executed by Domitian in 95, and a grammarian of the same name from Chaironea. Whereas Schürer had favoured the latter because Nero's secretary died too early for Schürer's dating of *Life*, Luther pointed out that even the latter Epaphroditus seems to have died in the reign of Nerva (96-98), which would still be too early for Schürer's dating of the *Life*.[24] And Luther argued that much of the language that Josephus uses of Epaphro-

---

[17] Niese, *HZ*, 226f. (On the other hand, Cohen, *Josephus*, 176, is properly cautious, noting that even though *Life* was written as an appendix to *Ant.*, it may not have appeared immediately.)

[18] Niese, *HZ*, 226 n. 1. Luther, *Josephus und Justus*, 59f., distinguishes between the autobiography, which *Ant.* 20:266 introduces as work that will follow immediately, and the three works mentioned in 20:267, which are only planned.

[19] Ibid., 227.

[20] Luther, *Josephus und Justus*, 63, adds that such praise would have been out of step with popular feeling, which regarded Domitian's demise as a godsend because his reign had ended in terror (AD 93-96). Cf. also Frankfort, "La date", 57, on the references to emperors in *Life*.

[21] Luther, *Josephus und Justus*, 54-59. Cf., e.g., *Ant.* 18:145f., 153f., on Agrippa I, and *Ant.* 20:145 on Agrippa II. Cf. now also Cohen, *Josephus*, 177f., for a list of such passages.

[22] Ibid., 64f. He points out, for example, that among the various coins from "the 14th year of Agrippa", three different emperors are mentioned as incumbents.

[23] Luther, *Josephus und Justus*, 61-63.

[24] Ibid.

ditus is suited better (or only) to Nero's secretary.[25] But if Nero's secretary was the patron of *Ant.-Life*, then both volumes were written before AD 95.

Hölscher (1916), in making his case for the rejection of the Photius datum, took over the Niese/Luther arguments.[26]

A considerable hiatus in the popularity of this view was caused, however, by R. Laqueur's watershed study (1920).[27] For Laqueur found a way to retain both the Photius datum (with Schürer)[28] and the close connection between *Life* and *Ant.* (with Niese/Luther); he proposed that *Ant.* was published in two editions and that only the second of these, written after 100, included *Life* as an appendix. This re-edition would account, he argued, for the apparent double ending of *Ant.*, at 20:259ff. and 20:267ff.[29] Laqueur's now famous theory was that the latter ending served for a first edition of *Ant.* in AD 93/94, which was indeed the thirteenth year of Domitian, but several years before Agrippa's death (100). After Agrippa's death, Josephus wrote *Life* (in response to the work of Justus) and at the same time reissued *Ant.* with a new ending (20:259ff.) to introduce the appendix; the textual tradition, however, combined the two endings.[30] Laqueur's theory gained considerable prestige in the English-speaking world through its endorsement by Thackeray (1926).[31]

Still another way of salvaging the Photius datum, already suggested as improbable by Hölscher (1916),[32] was sponsored by B. Motzo (1924).[33] This was the theory that Josephus wrote two editions of the *Life*: the first one, purely autobiographical, accompanied *Ant.* (93/94); the second appeared on its own and incorporated the defence against Justus (soon after 100).

Obviously, the proposal of a second edition of either *Ant.* or *Life* is only justified if the Photius datum is indeed worth saving. In recent

---

[25] Ibid.

[26] Hölscher, "Josephus", 1941., n.*.

[27] Laqueur, *Historiker*, 1-6.

[28] Laqueur, *Historiker*, 1f., thought it unacceptable to reject the Photius datum solely on the ground of its inconvenience for dating *Life*.

[29] *Ant.* 20:259: παύσεται δ' ἐνταῦθά μοι τὰ τῆς ἀρχαιολογίας. *Ant.* 20:267 has: Ἐπὶ τούτοις δὲ καταπαύσω τὴν ἀρχαιολογίαν.

[30] Laqueur, *Historiker*, 5f. In his composition of *Life* against Justus, Laqueur proposes, Josephus used an account of his own activities that he had written many years earlier, in 66/67.

[31] LCL edn. of Josephus, I, xiiif.; M. Gelzer, "Die Vita des Josephus", *Hermes* 80 (1952), 67f. also follows Laqueur. Cf. D. Barish, "The Autobiography of Josephus and the Hypothesis of a Second Edition", *HTR* 71 (1978), 62 n. 11, for other adherents to Laqueur's theory.

[32] Hölscher, "Josephus", 1941 n.*.

[33] B. Motzo, *Saggi di Storia e Letteratura Guideo-Ellenistica* (Florence, 1924), 217-219. I am dependent on Rajak, "Justus", 361 n. 4, for a summary of Motzo.

times, however, T. Frankfort (1961), T. Rajak (1973), D. A. Barish (1978), and S. J. D. Cohen (1979) have mounted another formidable attack on the accuracy of that notice. These scholars revive most of the Niese/Luther arguments,[34] although the identity of Epaphroditus is no longer thought to be recoverable with any probability. Barish argues,[35] further, for the literary unity of the conclusion to *Ant.*, in which Laqueur had distinguished two endings.[36] The major contribution of these scholars, however, has been to turn the numismatic and epigraphical evidence for Agrippa's death decisively against the Photius datum.[37] This they accomplish by redating the era of Agrippa, against which his coins and inscriptions are dated, from AD 61 (which Schürer accepted) to 50 (Frankfort)[38] or 56 (Barish and Cohen).[39] The result is that no coin or inscription dates Agrippa any later than 92/93;[40] thus the Photius datum is completely isolated.

After summarizing the evidence for abandoning Photius's dating of Agrippa's death, Cohen expresses the present scholarly mood:

> It is unjustified to reject all of this in favour of elaborate theories of second editions . . . etc., whose only purpose is to defend the honor of a tenth century patriarch.[41]

Every attempt to maintain a date of AD 100 for the death of Agrippa II, then, seems to run aground on both the internal evidence of *Ant.* and *Life* and the external evidence from coins and inscriptions. This evidence indicates that Agrippa died not much later than 92/93 and that *Life* was written between the completion of *Ant.* (93/94) and the death of Domitian (96).[42]

We have made only a cursory examination of the problem of dating *Life* because (a) the matter has been treated in detail elsewhere[43] and (b) although one must have some idea of the place of this work in Josephus's literary career, our topic does not require an exact date for it. What is

---

[34] Cf. Frankfort, "La date", 54f., on the remarks unkind to the Agrippas in *Ant.*, and 57, on *Life*'s praise of the Flavian emperors (*Life* 428f.). Cf. also Cohen, *Josephus*, 174ff.

[35] Frankfort, "La date", 56f.

[36] Barish, "*Autobiography*", 66-71.

[37] Frankfort, "La date", 55f.; Rajak, "Justus", 361 and notes 4 and 5 thereto; Barish, "*Autobiography*", 71-74; Cohen, *Josephus*, 173f.

[38] Frankfort, "La date", 55f.

[39] Barish, "*Autobiography*", 73 and Cohen, *Josephus*, 173, follow H. Seyrig, "Monnaies Hellenistiques", *Revue Numismatique*, 6th ser. 6 (1964), 55-65, and appeal to the widespread acceptance of this scheme in numismatic scholarship.

[40] Frankfort, "La date", 58; Rajak, "Justus", 361; Barish, "*Autobiography*", 73f.; Cohen, *Josephus*, 173. The latest inscription is of "the 37th year of Agrippa".

[41] Cohen, *Josephus*, 180.

[42] Frankfort, "La date", 58; Cohen, *Josephus*, 180.

[43] Of the modern discussions, those of Frankfort and Cohen are especially helpful.

important for us is that, whenever it appeared, *Life* was intended as an appendix to *Ant.* This connection is important because some scholars find in it the key to interpreting the Pharisee passages of both *Ant.* and *Life*.

II. *Occasion, Purpose and Outlook*[44]

The most striking feature of the *Life* is its lack of proportion. Josephus introduces and concludes the work as if it were a complete autobiography[45] and, it is true, he does include some comments on his ancestry (§§ 1-6), childhood (§§ 7-12), and post-war activities (§§ 414-430). The bulk of the work, however (§§ 28-406), portrays in detail a five-month period in Josephus's life, the time of his leadership in Galilee before Vespasian's arrival.[46] This massive disproportion, along with a combative narrative tone,[47] makes the work appear as a defence of Josephus's conduct during the period in question. The author confirms this impression by devoting an excursus (παρέκβασις) to the refutation of one Justus of Tiberias (§§ 336-367), who has composed a rival account of the events in Galilee.[48]

In order to ascertain more exactly the purpose of the *Life*, it is necessary to examine: (a) the extent to which the conflict with Justus determines the content of this work; (b) the nature of that conflict; and (c) other motives that Josephus might have had for writing *Life*.

---

[44] The *Life* has stimulated a great deal of secondary literature. Most of it, however, is occupied with the parallel questions of (a) the literary relationship between *Life* and *War* and (b) the historical truth about Josephus's activities in the Galilee. Cf. Luther, *Josephus und Justus*, 5-9; Laqueur, *Historiker*, 96-107; Gelzer, "Vita", 68ff.; and Cohen, *Josephus*, 1-18. Although of great intrinsic interest, these questions do not directly concern us. In any case, it would be hard to improve on Cohen's survey of the literature, *Josephus*, 8-23. He traces the shifts in scholarly opinion from early attempts to harmonize *Life* and *War*, to a preference for *War*, then back (under Laqueur's influence) to a preference for *Life*.

[45] *Ant.* 20:266: περὶ τῶν κατὰ τὸν βίον πράξεων; *Life* 430: διὰ παντὸς τοῦ βίου.

[46] The detailed period extends from a point after the defeat of Cestius Gallus (end of November, AD 66) to a time before Vespasian's arrival (May, 67). Cf. Gelzer, "Vita", 68.

[47] E.g., *Life* 1, 6 ("would-be detractors of my family"), 20, 40f. (ruin was due mainly to Justus), 67 (looting was contrary to Josephus's intention), 80ff. (insistence on Josephus's moderation and self-control), 361ff. (his commendations from emperors and kings).

[48] Josephus claims at first to be addressing other historians as well (§ 336) but he singles out Justus and confronts him in the second person. Cf. Cohen, *Josephus*, 114.

A. *The Conventional View and R. Laqueur*

Josephus's remarks about Justus are not confined to the excursus. He introduces this character quite early (§ 34) as a factional leader in Tiberias who "had a strain of madness in his nature" (Thackeray) and to whose depravity and duplicity the Jewish loss was largely due (§§ 40f). Josephus mentions Justus repeatedly throughout the narrative (see below) and always in an accusing tone. From this ongoing current of antipathy it has commonly been inferred that Josephus wrote *Life* simply as a response to the account by Justus. This was the view of Schürer, Niese, Luther, Hölscher, Laqueur, Thackeray, Schalit, and the "earlier Rajak".[49] Rajak, for example, claims that *Life* "was cast in the form of a reply to Justus".[50]

It is not always clear whether the critics who support this view see only the main body of *Life* (§§ 28-413) as a response to Justus or whether they would also include the remarks about Josephus's youth (and thus an important Pharisee passage, §§ 10-12) and post-war activities. Most seem willing to free the peripheral sections from any apologetic intent, for they designate §§ 1-27 and §§ 414-430 simply "introduction and conclusion" or "nur wie Einleitung und Schluss".[51]

Laqueur, however, also takes *Life* 10-12, which tells of Josephus's experience with the three schools and of his alignment with the Pharisees, to be distinctly polemical: Josephus wants to present himself as a true representative of Jewish tradition over against the hellenizing Justus, in order to save his reputation as an author in the face of Justus's attacks:

> so ist dieses ganze Material nur gegeben, um das eigene Werk gegen Justus retten zu können dadurch, dass Josephus gegenüber dem hellenisierenden Justus als Bewahrer der jüdischen Überlieferung erwiesen wird.[52]

---

[49] Schürer, *Geschichte*, I, 59, 97; Niese, *HZ*, 227; Hölscher, 1994; A. Schalit, "Josephus and Justus", *Klio* 26 (1933), 67-95. As Luther, *Josephus und Justus*, 7, puts it: "Als Antwort auf diese Angriffe des Justus schrieb Josephus seine Selbstbiographie". I include Laqueur among this group because we are only concerned with the final extant version of *Life*, which he thinks was written in response to Justus (*Historiker*, 78ff., 83). As is well-known, he considers the final *Life* to be an adaption of an earlier account of Josephus's activities. Cf. also Thackeray LCL edn. I, xivf.

[50] Rajak, "Justus", 354.

[51] Schürer, *Geschichte*, I, 87; Niese, *HZ*, 227; Hölscher, "Josephus", 1994; Rajak, "Justus", 354: "Only a brief introduction and conclusion about the rest of Josephus' life were added."

[52] Laqueur, *Historiker*, 246. How this analysis explains *Life* 10-12, with its emphasis on Josephus's three years in the desert in the company of an ascetic and its comparison of Stoics and Pharisees, is not at all clear. Cf. my analysis of the passage below.

Laqueur can only interpret *Life* 10-12 as part of the polemic against
Justus because he has a peculiar view of the issues involved in Justus's
attack on Josephus.

Most interpreters have taken their cue from Josephus's response to
Justus in the excursus:

> How then, Justus . . . can I and the Galileans be held responsible for the
> insurrection of your native city against the Romans and against the king
> [Agrippa II] . . . ?

And again:

> But, you maintain (ὡς σὺ φῇς), it was I who was responsible (αἴτιος ἐγώ) for
> your revolt at that time. (350; Thackeray)

The straightforward inference is that Justus has accused Josephus of
fomenting revolt in Tiberias and, by implication, in the rest of the
Galilee.[53] Most of the excursus responds directly to this charge[54] and
much of the rest of *Life* seems calculated to present Josephus as a pro-
Roman moderate and Justus as the instigator of revolt in Tiberias.[55] The
common view, then, is that Justus wrote an account of the war in which
he portrayed Josephus as the one who had incited revolt in the Galilee;
Josephus, living in Rome, was acutely embarrassed by these charges and
responded with the *Life*.

Laqueur, by contrast, understands the conflict between Justus and
Josephus to have been essentially historiographical. Josephus's actions in
the Galilee, he argues, could no longer have been an issue when
Josephus was in Rome, for he had long since made his peace with the
Romans.[56] Nor could he have recounted events in such detail thirty
years after the fact.[57] The defence of his Galilean command that we see
in *Life* must have come from a much earlier account that Josephus had
written in self-vindication, probably to the Jerusalem authorities, before
the war had broken out in earnest (early 67).[58] Laqueur locates the
polemic against Justus, on the other hand, in the last section of the excursus against that author (§§ 357-367), where Josephus claims superior
accuracy for his own *War*.[59] Justus had evidently claimed to have written
the definitive work on the war (§ 357), disparaging the works of Josephus

---

[53] So Schürer, *Geschichte*, I, 87; Luther, *Josephus und Justus*, 7, 67; Hölscher, 1994; Rajak "Justus", Cohen, *Josephus*, 118.
[54] Cf. Cohen, *Josephus*, 114.
[55] E.g., on Josephus: *Life* 17-23, 28f., 78, 126-131. On Justus: 36, 42, 87f., 391.
[56] Laqueur, *Historiker*, 7-9.
[57] Ibid.
[58] Ibid., 122.
[59] Ibid., 16ff. Laqueur compares *Ag.Ap.* 1:46ff. and argues that this is also directed
against Justus.

and others, and this was ruining the market for Josephus's account.[60]
Josephus responded with *Life*, which defended not only his accuracy but
also his character and credibility as a writer: hence his alleged affiliation
with Pharisaism (*Life* 12).

Cohen successfully refutes this theory of the nature of Justus's accusa-
tions by several arguments,[61] the most telling of which are: (a) that Laqueur overlooks the bulk of the excursus, which explicitly attributes to
Justus the charge that Josephus incited revolt,[62] and (b) that Josephus
would hardly have chosen to make his earlier detailed report to
Jerusalem about his Galilean command the basis of his response to
Justus if Justus's accusations had concerned something else entirely.[63]
And if Laqueur's reading of Justus's accusations is incorrect, then so is
his interpretation of *Life* 10-12 as part of Josephus's apologetic.

B. *S. J. D. Cohen and T. Rajak*

Cohen, for his part, tries to refine the conventional view by delineating
more closely the extent to which Justus's work was responsible for *Life*.
He begins with the excursus, because that is clearly addressed to Justus,
and finds Josephus there responding to accusations about his character
and his actions in Tiberias: Justus has blamed Josephus for the anti-
Roman activities of Tiberias and has charged him with brutality toward
the populace.[64] Cohen, therefore, agrees in the main with the common
view of Justus's accusations.[65] Having isolated these issues, Cohen attributes their emergence elsewhere in *Life* also to the provocation of
Justus's rival account.[66]

But this procedure still leaves several passages and themes outside the
excursus unexplained. Cohen identifies five such extraneous themes:
"Josephus's Pedigree", "Josephus and the Pharisees", "Josephus
fought the Romans", "Josephus was Pro-Roman",[67] and "Philip son

---

[60] Ibid., 21ff.
[61] Cohen, *Josephus*, 129-132.
[62] Ibid., 129.
[63] Laqueur, *Historiker*, 130.
[64] Ibid., 118.
[65] Cohen's difference with the conventional view of the nature of Justus's accusations
is as follows. Because the excursus only refers to affairs in Tiberias, he concludes that
Justus did not accuse Josephus of being a rebel *per se*, but only of specific rebellious activities in Tiberias.
[66] Ibid., 121-137.
[67] Ibid., 153f. Note that, since Cohen does not think that Justus accused Josephus in
general of being anti-Roman, he cannot view the theme of pro-Romanism as a response
to Justus.

of Jacimus''.[68] Pointing out that Josephus admits to having many accusers (*Life* 424ff., 428ff.), Cohen maintains that "we cannot assume that V's [*sc. Life's*] every apologetic element is a response to the Tiberian".[69] He finds no unifying logic in the five specified items and thinks that they might well have no connection with Justus.[70] Although, then, Cohen supports the conventional view of Justus's accusations, he finds much in the *Life*, including the Pharisee passages, that is unrelated to the conflict with Josephus.

Rajak (1983) has recently revised her position along similar, perhaps more extreme, lines.[71] She now thinks that only the excursus responds directly to Justus[72] and that the rest of *Life* addresses the concerns of, "the surviving or regenerated Jewish aristocracy in the years after 70, and especially that part of it which was to be found in the Diaspora".[73] Those diaspora concerns Rajak identifies as: (a) whether the revolt could not have been prevented and (b) whether, if it had to happen, the moderates could not have maintained orderly control.[74] These are the questions that *Life* answers, Rajak argues, with its detailed explanations of Josephus's failure to master the Galilee and of his rejection by the Jerusalem authorities.[75] Thus the later Rajak also finds much in *Life* that is extraneous to Josephus's response to Justus.

Space does not permit a detailed analysis of all of the extraneous themes proposed by Cohen and Rajak. Of special interest for this study, however, is Cohen's designation of "Josephus and the Pharisees" as an apologetic theme independent of those inspired by Justus.[76] He links together *Life* 10-12 (on Josephus's alignment with the Pharisees) with §§ 191-198 (on Simon the Pharisee) and with all of the religious nuances in *Life* that are absent from the parallels in *War*, to document what he thinks is a "religious apologetic" in *Life*.[77] He connects this apologetic with the heightened "nationalism" of *Ant.*, *vis-à-vis War*,[78] and with an alleged tendency in the later work to improve the image of the Phari-

---

[68] Cohen takes up the five themes on pp. 144-170 of his *Josephus*.

[69] Cohen, *Josephus*, 144.

[70] Ibid., 169f.

[71] On p. 14, however, she has suggested that *Life's* introductory remarks about Josephus's upbringing are also intended to deflect Justus's charge of irresponsibility.

[72] Ibid., 154.

[73] Ibid.

[74] Ibid.

[75] Ibid.

[76] Cohen, *Josephus*, 144-151.

[77] Ibid., 144-147.

[78] An oft-noted feature of *Ant.*; cf. the discussion of Laqueur and Rasp in chapter 7, above.

sees.[79] All of this leads him to the conclusion that, in writing *Ant.-Life*, Josephus was throwing in his lot with the rising fortunes of the Pharisees and was assuming the role of a Pharisaic advocate in Rome.[30] According to Cohen, Josephus contends in *Ant.* "that the Pharisees had always been prominent and therefore deserve Roman support".[81] *Life*, furthermore, "makes the ultimate commitment to this Pharisaic bias and declares the Josephus had always been, since his youth, a loyal follower of the Pharisees."[82] Josephus probably was not a Pharisee at all,[83] Cohen argues, but boldly claimed to be one in the service of his "religious-Pharisaic" (and finally political) apologetic.

We have seen that Cohen's interpretation cf *Ant.* on the Pharisees, which he inherits from Rasp and (especially) Smith/Neusner,[84] is entirely without support. In the following chapters we shall ask whether his interpretation of *Life* 12 as an audacious claim to Pharisaic allegiance (also shared with Rasp, Smith, and Neusner) is really defensible.

Summary and Critique of Scholarly Views

Everyone agrees that the *Life* is a work of apologetic and polemic and that it is directed, at least in part, against Justus of Tiberias, who wrote a rival account of the war. Matters still debated are: (a) the issues at stake in the conflict with Justus; (b) the extent to which *Life* is a response to him; and (c) other factors that entered into the composition of *Life*. Questions (a) and (b) are mutually dependent; question (c) depends on one's solution to (a) and (b).

The conventional view (Schürer, Niese, Luther, Hölscher, Schalit, the earlier Rajak) is: (a) that Justus accused Josephus of inciting revolt in the Galilee, especially in Tiberias; (b) that the whole body of *Life* (§§ 28-413) responds to this charge by recounting in detail Josephus's actions during his first five months in the region; and (c) that *Life* 1-27 and 414-430 function simply as an introduction and conclusion to this piece of polemic.

Laqueur, Cohen, and Rajak have all attempted to modify the conventional view: Laqueur, by changing altogether the terms of the conflict between Justus and Josephus; Cohen, by restricting that conflict to Tiberian affairs and then discovering other apologetic themes in *Life*

---

[79] Ibid., 148-151. He follows here the Smith/Neusner proposal.
[80] Ibid., 237f.
[81] Ibid.
[82] Ibid., 238.
[83] Ibid., 107.
[84] Cohen, *Josephus*, 144 n. 150.

independent of Justus; and Rajak, by positing a diaspora-Jewish readership for the work. Laqueur's attempt, as we have seen, was unsuccessful.
In defence of the conventional view against the modifications of Cohen
and Rajak, I would urge the following considerations.

(1) Despite its literary defects,[85] *Life* appears to have a single overriding purpose, namely, to defend Josephus's actions during the first five
or so months of his leadership in the Galilee. The body of the work (§§
28-413) is obviously dedicated to this goal.

(2) The body of the work opens with a sharply drawn contrast between
Josephus and Justus of Tiberius (§§ 28-42). Josephus, committed to a
policy of submission to Rome (§§ 17-23), goes to Galilee in order to ensure peace in the region by disarming the rebels (§§ 28f.). A major
obstacle to his programme, however, is the city of Tiberias, which he
finds already in a state of revolt (§§ 32ff.). Josephus attributes this situation wholly to the influence of Justus, whom he characterizes at some
length as a crazed and reckless tyrant (§§ 36-42). This Tiberian, we
learn, has written his own account of "these events" (τῶν πραγμάτων
τούτων); but the reader is warned that it obfuscates the truth (§ 40).
Josephus promises to prove his allegations about Justus "as the narrative
unfolds" (προιόντος τοῦ λόγου, § 40) and does indeed return to his opponent several times (§§ 87f., 279, 336-367, 390f., 410). At the outset of
the narrative, then, Josephus characterizes Justus both as a physical opponent who worked against his pacific mission and as a literary opponent
who in later times has distorted the facts about his Galilean command.

(3) Justus's account, to which Josephus objects, manifestly included
more than Tiberian affairs. The phrase τῶν πραγμάτων in *Life* 40 would
seem to include the whole Galilean situation before the revolt (§§ 37-40).
The similar phrase in § 336 appears to include all of the events covered
to that point by Josephus's narrative.[86] Finally, § 338 claims that Justus
has written about τὰς περὶ τοῦτον πράξεις τὸν πόλεμον, "the events related
to this war". So the rival account was not limited to Tiberian affairs.

All of these considerations would seem to warrant the conventional
assumption that Justus of Tiberias was the main antagonist that
Josephus had in mind when he composed his self-vindicating *Life*. That
is not to deny that Josephus included dramatic elements or items of

---

[85] These are well known. Cf. Cohen, *Josephus*, 110-113, for a brief overview.

[86] Josephus begins (*Life* 336): "Having reached this point in my narrative, I propose
to address a few words to Justus, who has produced his own account of these affairs (τὴν
περὶ τούτων πραγματείαν γεγραφότα)." Since he has just concluded a lengthy account of
his dealings with the delegation sent to replace him (§§ 189-335), Justus's work must at
least have discussed these events.

intrinsic interest to fill out the narrative:[87] one need not see every point
as a direct response to Justus. Nevertheless it does seem clear that the
whole five-month period came into serious question primarily because of
Justus's rival account, which portrayed Josephus as an instigator of
revolt.

If it is the body of *Life* (28-413) that contains the controversial material, then the conventional view is also correct in designating the rest of
the work (§§ 1-27, 414-430) "nur wie Einleitung und Schluss". To be
sure, Josephus chose to include those aspects of his youth and post-war
experience that would portray him in the best light; he hopes that the
details of his "whole life" will lead the reader to a favourable judgement
of his character (§ 430). But that is a very general aim. In giving the
details of his "life", he had no choice but to mention something of his
family background, youth, and post-war situation;[88] it is not clear that
any of these elements—whether his marriages and children or his experimentation with the Jewish philosophies—represents a specific
apologetic.[89]

Both Cohen and Rajak argue that significant aspects of the *Life* were
written for a Jewish readership. According to Cohen, the theme of
Josephus's staunch "religious-Pharisaic" observance was meant to catch
the eyes of the Yavnean rabbis; according to Rajak, Josephus wrote *Life*
mainly for the benefit of diaspora Jewry. The idea that Josephus wrote
Life for Jewish readers is, however, problematic because the work seems
to expect a Gentile audience.[90] From its opening words, Josephus has to
explain Jewish values[91] and Palestinian geography.[92] He uses ἡμεῖς, in
his characteristic way, to mean "we *Jews*" (in contrast to Gentiles).[93]

---

[87] One might think of, e.g., Josephus's dramatic escapes (94ff., 136ff., 145ff., 299ff.),
his dream (208ff.), and his ingenious strategies (e.g. 163ff.).

[88] Recall that the pedigree and education passage (*Life* 1ff.) was introduced in *Ant.*
20:266 in support of Josephus's claim to ἀκρίβεια.

[89] Cohen justifies his assumption of a multiple apologetic on the ground that the
themes unrelated to Justus lack a unifying principle; such are: (a) Josephus's pedigree,
(b) his alignment with the Pharisees, (c) his pro-Romanism, and (d) his participation
against the Romans. If, however, one denies that (a) and (b) have any apologetic role
in *Life*, since they stand in the introduction (though they are related to the argument of
Ant. 20:265f.), then they do not create a problem. If, further, one is prepared to accept
a certain ambiguity in Josephus's position *vis-à-vis* Rome, then the difficulty disappears.

[90] Remarkably, both Cohen, *Josephus*, 147, and Rajak, *Josephus*, 14, concede this.

[91] *Life* 1 (importance of the priesthood to Jews), 65 (images of animals forbidden), 162
(Sabbath explained), 12 (Pharisees likened to Stoics), 191 (Pharisees explained, again).

[92] *Life* 31 (Dora, a city of Phoenicia), 42 (location of Gadara and Hippos), 123
(Tiberias, Sepphoris, and Gabara: chief cities of Galilee), 157 (location of Tarichaeae),
232 (Sepphoris: largest city in Galilee), 269 (Jerusalem, three days' journey from
Galilee), 348 (Jerusalem, the largest city).

[93] *Life* 1, 26, 128, 275, 279.

Most important, *Life* is part of *Ant.*, which was written for Gentiles (*Ant.* 1:9); both are dedicated to the Gentile Epaphroditus (*Ant.* 1:8f.; *Life* 430). Although it is not unlikely that Jews would also have read his works, Josephus wrote in order to persuade Gentiles. It would seem hazardous, therefore, to suppose that any particular portions of *Life*, let alone the bulk of the work, were written specifically for Jewish readers.

In short, the attempts by Laqueur, Cohen, and Rajak to modify the conventional interpretation of *Life*—that it is a response to Justus of Tiberias, with an introduction and conclusion added—seem to lack solid support. Our only qualification of the conventional view is that the introduction to *Life*, with its description of Josephus's priestly pedigree, education, and experimentation with the Jewish schools, grew out of his claim to ἀκρίβεια in *Ant.* 20:266. It seems, however, to be independent of the dispute with Justus, to which the body of the *Life* is devoted.

CHAPTER FOURTEEN

THE PHARISAIC ALLEGIANCE OF JOSEPHUS
IN MODERN SCHOLARSHIP

Although interpreters of Josephus differ among themselves on practically every major issue,[1] they are almost unanimous in their belief that he intended to present himself as a devoted Pharisee.[2] Even here, it is true, one can distinguish two schools of thought. The majority of scholars[3] accept Josephus's Pharisaic allegiance as a fundamental datum for their interpretation; a skeptical minority[4] (for want of a better adjective) view the claim to Pharisaic allegiance as a political ploy, by which Josephus hoped to identify himself with the new power-brokers in Palestine. Both schools, however, maintain that Josephus *wanted* to be understood as a Pharisee. Indeed, all of the foundational scholarship on Josephus and all of the major modern translations of his works[5] have been done by critics who believed him to have been a Pharisee.

This chapter will begin by demonstrating the important role that Josephus's Pharisaic allegiance plays in modern analyses of his works. A survey of the arguments commonly offered in support of Josephus's Pharisaic affiliation will reveal, however, that an enormous burden rests on a particular interpretation of a single sentence in *Life* (12b). This conclusion will prepare for the following chapter, in which we shall examine *Life* 12b in some detail.

---

[1] E.g., on Josephus's historical reliability, his degree of nationalistic and religious commitment, the extent of his dependence on sources, and his linguistic and literary competence, to name a few important issues.

[2] The notable exception is E. Gerlach, *Die Weissagungen des alten Testaments in den Schriften des Flavius Josephus* (Berlin: Hertz, 1863), 1-18, who thought that Josephus was an Essene.

[3] E.g., H. Paret, "Pharisäismus"; J. A. Montgomery, "The Religion of Flavius Josephus", *JQR* n.s. 11 (1921), 280ff., E. Schürer (1867), B. Niese (1896), B. Brüne (1913), G. Hölscher (1916), H. St. J. Thackeray (1926, 1929), A. Schlatter (1923, 1932), R. J. H. Shutt (1961), E. Rivkin (1969, 1976, 1978), H.-F. Weiss (1979), and T. Rajak (1983). Specific references are given in the notes to the following discussion.

[4] R. Laqueur (1920), H. Rasp (1924), M. Smith (1956), J. Neusner (1972f.), and S. J. D. Cohen (1979).

[5] Cf. the usual translations of *Life* 12, discussed in chapter 16, below.

I. *The Importance of Josephus's Pharisaic Allegiance*
in Modern Scholarship

Interpreters have always come to Josephus from disparate perspectives
and with widely differing aims and interests. At least four types of interpretation can be identified, however, that all rely heavily on Josephus's
Pharisaic connection. The first three of these have been discussed
already in the course of the study and need only to be recalled.

A. *Theological Interpretations of Josephus*

Much of the early work on Josephus was done by scholars who were
primarily looking for insight into the background and origins of Christianity; it will suffice to mention Paret, Schürer, Brüne, and Schlatter.
Although all of these scholars acknowledged the Pharisaic allegiance of
Josephus, Paret and Schlatter placed particular value on it as the key to
his significance.

Paret (1856) suggested that, since the infant Church was still very
close to Pharisaic teachings in the first century, any information about
the latter would be welcome.[6] He devoted an article to proving that
Josephus was a Pharisee, on the premise that such proof would greatly
enhance the value of Josephus's writings:

> aber wenn nun, wie in Josephus, ein palästinensischer Jude des
> apostolischen Zeitalters selbst vor uns steht, der uns nicht bloss die
> wichtigste Nachrichten über die jüdischen Religionsparteien gibt, sondern
> sich selbst ausdrücklich als Pharisäer bekennt, so ist es gewiss nicht ohne
> Interesse, ihn *gerade als solchen* ins Auge zu fassen.[7]

Schlatter, writing several decades later (1910, 1932), no longer
thought it necessary to prove by sustained argument that Josephus was
a Pharisee.[8] Nevertheless, like Paret, he believed that the chief
significance of Josephus's writings for the New Testament exegete lay in
their author's Pharisaic affiliation.[9] Unlike the mystical Hellenist Philo,
Schlatter contends, Josephus shows us *Pharisäismus*, which was the dominant movement in Judaism.[10] An examination of Josephus's Pharisaism,
he suggests, will help the New Testament scholar to understand why this
religious outlook was opposed by Jesus and Paul.[11]

---

[6] Paret, "Pharisäismus", 810f.
[7] Ibid.
[8] He does, however, adduce particular points in the course of his analysis; see below.
[9] *Wie sprach Josephus von Gott?* (Gütersloh: C. Bertelsmann, 1910), 7; *Theologie*, p. V.
[10] Ibid. Cf. chapter 2, above.
[11] *Theologie*, p. VI.

Jewish scholars have generally tended to look outside Josephus (to the rabbinic corpus) for their understanding of Pharisaic thought. Nevertheless, A. Guttmann ranks Josephus alongside the Talmud as a first-rate source for Pharisaism.[12] And Rivkin cites Josephus's Pharisaic allegiance as proof that the ancient author's portrayal of the Pharisees is credible.[13]

B. *Source-Critical Interpretations*

For source critics of Josephus, his Pharisaic allegiance has always been the major criterion for determining what he could or could not have said about the group.

It was one of Hölscher's working assumptions that Josephus was a Pharisee and that, therefore, most of his accounts of the group, which are often negative, must not be his own but "je nach den von ihm ausgeschriebenen Quellen."[14] We see the principle at work in Hölscher's analysis of *Ant.* 18:11-25. The author of this passage cannot be a Pharisee, we learn, because his treatment of the group is not especially *ruhmenswert* and because he links Pharisees and Zealots together.[15] Hölscher even cites Josephus's Pharisaic education as proof that he could not have known the Greek authors cited in *Ant.*[16]

G. F. Moore followed the same procedure of attributing passages hostile to the Pharisees to someone other than Josephus.[17] More recently, D. R. Schwartz has made a thorough application of this approach to the Pharisee passages. One of his major criteria for assigning passages to Nicolaus rather than Josephus is their hostility toward the Pharisees.[18] When he does assign two passages to Josephus it is because they "present thoroughly positive accounts of the Pharisees . . . . All of these improvements in the image of the Pharisees show that it is Josephus who is speaking."[19]

C. *Biographical Interpretations*

In chapter 2, I have summarized the interpretations of the Pharisee passages offered by H. Rasp, M. Smith, and J. Neusner, who develop

---

[12] Guttmann, *Rabbinic Judaism*, 124f.
[13] Rivkin, *Revolution*, 32, 66f.
[14] Hölscher, "Josephus", 1936, cf. also n. + + .
[15] Ibid., 1991.
[16] Ibid., 1957.
[17] Moore, *Judaism*, I, 64 n. 4, 65 n. 3, 66 n. 1.
[18] Schwartz, "Josephus and Nicolaus", 158.
[19] Ibid., 163.

(whether consciously or not) Laqueur's thesis that Josephus altered his nationalistic and religious sensitivities between *War* and *Ant*.[20] Common to these scholars and also to S. J. D. Cohen[21] is the belief that *Ant*. represents an improvement over *War* in its descriptions of the Pharisees: this improvement they interpret as Josephus's attempt to make amends with the group that was coming to power in Palestine. Notwithstanding the evidence that these scholars imagine they find in *Ant*. itself, they all depend very heavily on *Life* 12; they view this sentence as Josephus's audacious attempt to pass himself off as a devoted Pharisee.

Rasp's comment to this effect I have quoted above:[22] Josephus has the nerve to portray himself before the whole world as a true Pharisee of long standing! Similarly Neusner points to the importance of *Life* 12:

> To understand the additions [in *Ant*. *vis-à-vis* Josephus's portrait of the Pharisees in *War*], we must recall that at the same time he wrote *Ant*., Josephus was claiming he himself was a Pharisee.[23]

Cohen adds his voice to the chorus by proposing that *Life* 12 "makes the ultimate commitment to this Pharisaic bias [in *Ant*.]".[24]

The importance of *Life* 12 for this group, then, is not (as with Schlatter or Hölscher) that it says something true about Josephus. On the contrary, it is interpreted as a crucial indicator of his *Tendenz* in *Ant.*-*Life*: he wants to be seen as a Pharisee for practical reasons.

D. *Cultural/Sociological Interpretations*

Two recent attempts to identify different cultural and social elements within Josephus's thought likewise rely heavily on the premise that Josephus was a Pharisee.

A 1979 article by H. F. Weiss sets out to clarify the nature of the marriage between "Pharisäismus and Hellenismus."[25] Granted that the two categories may no longer be considered mutually exclusive, he argues, it is necessary to define the way in which they unite in Josephus. Weiss first demonstrates by several arguments that Josephus was indeed a Pharisee[26] and then that he was genuinely and deeply influenced by Hellenistic concerns and concepts, especially by Stoicism.[27] Never-

---

[20] Cf. Laqueur, *Historiker*, 128ff.
[21] Cohen, *Josephus*, 144-151, esp. 148. See my discussion of Cohen in chapter 13.
[22] See chapter 2, above.
[23] Neusner, "Josephus's Pharisees," 231.
[24] Cohen, *Josephus*, 238, cited in full in the previous chapter.
[25] H.-F. Weiss, "Pharisäismus", 421-433.
[26] Ibid., 423-426.
[27] Ibid., 427-431.

theless, Josephus retains a critical stance toward Hellenistic philosophies; he does not endorse Stoicism as a whole but presents Judaism, based on the Law of Moses, as the true philosophy.[28] Weiss concludes that Josephus was trying to work out his Pharisaic commitment in Hellenistic terms, by offering the Hellenistic world a true picture of Judaism.[29]

Rajak's recent study, *Josephus: The Historian and his Society* (1983), is an attempt to use Josephus as a entrée into "the cultural and social history of the Roman empire".[30] Specifically, this scholar wants to explore the tension between Jewish tradition and Greek culture that she finds in Josephus:

> Through his early life, we can learn from the inside about the upper echelons of the Palestinian priesthood, an outward-looking, flexible group, yet strict in its religious practices and prescriptions; a group which vanished with the fall of the Temple in A.D. 70.[31]

Rajak attributes this tension to the two major influences on Josephus's life: he was an aristocratic priest by birth but a Pharisee by education. The priestly heritage gave him a cosmopolitan outlook; the Pharisaic training made him fiercely defensive of his Jewish tradition.[32]

Unlike most commentators,[33] Rajak does not think that Josephus's Pharisaic education began with his alignment with the group at age nineteen (*Life* 12). She contends that his early education was already Pharisaic.[34] We shall consider her arguments below. Here it is simply to be noted that Josephus's Pharisaic education and allegiance is a key factor in Rajak's interpretation of him. He claimed to be a Pharisee because he was a Pharisee (*contra* Rasp, Smith, Neusner, and Cohen) and this deeply ingrained tradition, combined with his aristocratic heritage, created many ambiguities in his position, especially when the war against Rome broke out.[35]

---

[28] Ibid., 431f.

[29] Ibid., 432f.

[30] Rajak, *Josephus*, 6.

[31] Ibid., 8.

[32] Ibid., 3.

[33] Hölscher may have had a similar view. He describes Josephus as, "der Jerusalemer Priestersohn, der bis zum 33. Lebensjahr in der Luft pharisäischer Gesetzesfrömmigkeit aufgewachsen ist" (1956f). Most commentators, however, interpret *Life* 12 to mean that Josephus became a Pharisee only at age 19 (see chapter 15, below).

[34] Rajak, *Josephus*, 29ff.

[35] Cf. also Rajak, *Josephus*, 102f., 116ff., and 185.

Summary

Practically every interpreter of Josephus has held that the Jewish historian wanted to be thought of as a Pharisee. For some, it is true, acknowledgement of this claim has little consequence.[36] The above synopsis reveals, however, that the major conventional approaches to Josephus not only acknowledge Josephus's claim to Pharisaic allegiance but depend upon it as an interpretive key.

II. *Arguments Offered in Support of Josephus's Pharisaic Allegiance*

If it is true that Josephus's claim to be a Pharisee underlies most modern scholarship on our author, then it is clear that *Life* 12b—the only sentence in Josephus's thirty extant books that even hints at any connection between Josephus and the Pharisees—is of crucial importance to the whole enterprise. In chapter 15, below, we shall seek to understand that sentence in its context. Other arguments, however, have sometimes been offered as proof of Josephus's Pharisaic affiliation. The following survey is intended to show that none of these ancillary arguments is compelling; this conclusion renders all the more important one's interpretation of *Life* 12b.

A. *Josephus's View of the Law*

Under this heading several alleged proofs of Josephus's Pharisaic leanings may be gathered: (1) his exaltation of the Law;[37] (2) his inclusion of extra-biblical material within the concept νόμοι;[38] (3) his alleged agreement with the *halakhah* and *haggadah*;[39] and (4) his alleged acceptance of the unwritten νόμιμα of the Pharisees.[40] All of these points have been

---

[36] Especially Lindner, *Geschichtsauffassung*, 75; Attridge, *Interpretation*, 178ff., 184; and M. Hengel, *Judentum*, 315; idem, *Zeloten* 6 nn. 2/3, 378 n. 3.

[37] Paret, "Pharisäismus", 823f.; Montgomery, "Religion", 295, Schlatter, *Theologie*, 210; Weiss; "Pharisäismus", 425.

[38] Gutbrod, *TDNT*, IV, 1051.

[39] M. Olitzki, *Flavius Josephus und die Halacha* (Berlin: H. Iskowski, 1885), 6-93; Rajak, *Josephus*, 32f. and n. 63. Rajak comments: "When it comes to the *Antiquities*, few would deny that Josephus's conceptions are on the whole Pharisaic. It is enough here simply to recall that in many small points of *halakhah* (law) and *aggadah* (extra-legal tradition) Josephus agrees with the Rabbis". D. Goldenberg ("The Halakha in Josephus and in Tannaitic Literature," *JQR* 67 [1976], 30-43) analyses four *halakhot* that Josephus shares with the traditional law of the period.

[40] Paret, "Pharisäismus", 826f.; Hölscher, "Josephus", 1936 n. + + ; Weiss, "Pharisäismus", 425.; Schlatter, *Theologie*, 210; Rivkin, *Revolution*, 67.

dealt with in the course of the study; it is necessary here only to summarize and supplement our earlier conclusions.

(1) and (2) are accurate observations but do not link Josephus with Pharisaism. For Josephus praises the Law as a priest. He portrays the whole Jewish community as one that is devoted to a strict observance of the laws, under the supervision of the priests.[41] Further, exaltation of the "laws" was native to Greek thought[42] and was fundamental to Judaism after the exile.[43] Philo and 4 Maccabees praise the Law.[44] So love for the Law was not peculiar to Pharisees.

That Josephus includes extra-biblical precepts in the term νόμος is clear to modern-day critics but was not to him; he claims to give only what Moses left in writing.[45] It is antecedently probable that all of the Jewish groups traced their beliefs to Moses; indeed the Temple Scroll from Qumran and the rabbinic doctrine of the Oral Law prove this for two cases.[46] None of this makes Josephus a Pharisee.

With respect to (4), it is far from obvious that Josephus accepted the special Pharisaic νόμιμα, which οὐκ ἀναγέγραπται ἐν τοῖς Μωθσέος νόμοις (Ant. 13:297); he consistently uses νόμιμα as an equivalent of νόμοι and always attributes these laws to the written Mosaic code.[47]

Josephus's agreement with halakhah and haggadah (3) is doubly problematic as a proof of his Pharisaic mindset. First, the rabbinic legal and hortatory material is not strictly "Pharisaic"; it may well reflect also non-Pharisaic traditions from before 70[48] and certainly contains much post-70 development. On the other hand, Josephus does not consistently agree with the halakhah.[49] Sometimes he agrees, against tradition, with the

---

[41] Cf. chapter 4, above.

[42] So, e.g., Herodotus 3:38, appropriating Pindar, "Nomos is king of all". Cf. Greene, Moira, 226.

[43] Cf. Neh. 8:1ff. and perhaps Ps. 119.

[44] On 4 Maccabees, cf. Appendix A, below. In Philo, cf. Life of Moses 2:44; Special Laws 2:189; and Decalogue 41. I am grateful to Dr. A. Reinhartz, of McMaster University, for permission to consult her paper "The Meaning of Nomos in Philo's Exposition of the Law", read at the 1985 conference of the Canadian Society of Biblical Studies.

[45] See chapter 4, above.

[46] See chapter 4. Josephus implies the same for the Sadducees: they "own no observance of any sort apart from the laws" (Ant. 18:16; cf. 13:297). Yet it is impossible that they could have conducted the Temple ritual, for example, without some sort of tradition to take care of the omissions and contradictions of the biblical text. We know from Megillat Ta' anit, furthermore, that the Sadducees possessed a "Book of Decrees", whatever that was.

[47] See chapter 4 and Ant. 3:286; 4:196; Ag.Ap. 1:39; 2:171ff. Cf. especially Ag.Ap. 2:155f., where he explicitly contrasts the ἔθη ἄγραφα of the Greeks with the Mosaic code.

[48] Cf. Neusner, "Pharisaic-Rabbinic Judaism: A Clarification", History of Religions 12 (1973), 250-270.

[49] See chapter 4, above. Revel, e.g., begins ("Anti-Traditional Laws", 293): "In the exposition of biblical texts and laws, Josephus often deviates from their traditional interpretation". Cf. Attridge, Interpretation, 179 n. 1.

Essenes, sometimes with Philo, and sometimes with positions later endorsed by the literalist Karaites.[50] Given our lack of knowledge of pre-70
traditions, it seems bizarre to maintain that these deviations must be due
to Josephus's imperfect knowledge, faulty memory, and tendentious
reworking of the tradition.[51] Do they not rather suggest that Josephus
understood some of the laws differently from the later tradition? Studies
of Josephus's non-legal elaboration of the Bible (*haggadah*), moreover,
point to a priestly, not Pharisaic, inclination.[52]

Two recent studies of Josephus's thought demonstrate (within their
respective frames of reference) that it is not obviously conditioned by
Pharisaic concerns. Lindner's analysis of Josephus's view of history in
War uncovers a strong priestly emphasis: the Jews are being punished
by God for their profanation of the Temple, God's shrine, of which they
were the appointed guardians.[53] In addition, Lindner notes that
Josephus describes his revelation from God, on the basis of which he
went over to the Romans, as the result of a dream; but the rabbis rejected dreams as sources of guidance.[54] Finally, when Josephus makes a
claim to exegetical prowess, he bases it solely on his priestly heritage.[55]
All of this, says Lindner, is "ganz unpharisäisch".[56] Thus he summarizes Josephus's debt to Pharisaism:

> Die Wurzeln seines Denkens liegen nicht in Pharisäismus, und die Angabe
> (vita 12), dass er sich nach Anschluss seiner Ausbildungszeit den
> Pharisäern angeschlossen habe, muss in ihrer Tragweite begrenzt
> bleiben.[57]

Similarly, Attridge's analysis of the manner in which Josephus interprets the Bible does not uncover any clear Pharisaic perspective. I quote
at some length from his conclusion:

> On the perennial problem of the relationship of Josephus to Pharisaism, the
> biblical interpretation provides little light. In some detailed matters, such
> as the use of the terms εὐσέβεια and δικαιοσύνη, we have noted parallels from
> Greek sources which show that Pharisaic theology need not be invoked at

---

[50] For examples of the last two, cf. Revel, "Anti-Traditional Laws", 293-301. In
general see the discussion above, chapter 4.

[51] This explanation is offered by Olitzki, *Halacha*, 8f., and is picked up by Rajak,
Josephus, 336 n. 63.

[52] Rappaport, *Agada and Exegese*, thinks that Josephus used a priestly source. B. Heller
("Grundzüge", 238f.) shows, however, that the priestly bias runs deep in Josephus's
thought. Attridge (*Interpretation*, 176f. and n. 1) thinks that the priestly perspective in
Josephus is somewhat exaggerated by these scholars.

[53] Lindner, *Geschichtsauffassung*, 142f., cf. 41.

[54] Ibid., 54, 75.

[55] Ibid.

[56] Ibid., 75.

[57] Ibid., 146 n. 2.

all. On the other hand, we have seen that many of the interpretative elements in the *Antiquities* are not inconsistent with Rabbinic Judaism, and thus perhaps with Pharisaism. These agreements, however, are not so specific that we are compelled to call Josephus a Pharisee because of them.

The precise nature of Pharisaism in the first century remains to be clarified. Where particular criteria for distinguishing the sect are available, they do not show any close conformity to the significant interpretative themes of the biblical paraphrase of the *Antiquities*.[58]

Although neither of these interpreters doubts that Josephus wanted to present himself as a Pharisee in *Life* 12, both deny that Pharisaic emphases play any significant role in his thought

If it is not possible to lay to rest once and for all the belief that Josephus's view of the Law makes him a Pharisee, it can at least be said that none of the evidence currently available points unmistakably to that conclusion.

B. *Fate/Free Will and the Immortality of the Soul*

(1) It was shown in chapter 6 that both Josephus's interpretation of εἱμαρμένη as a function of God and his juxtaposition of fate and human volition agree with teachings that he ascribes to the Pharisees; other scholars have argued that this synergism of fate and free will also concurs with "Pharisaic-Rabbinic" ideas known from the rabbinic literature.[59] Creuzer and Schlatter, among others, saw in this correspondence proof that Josephus was a Pharisee.[60] And now Rajak writes:

> It is particularly striking that Josephus rests, in his own narrative, on the same assumptions as he ascribes to the Pharisees ...: 'they hold that to act rightly or otherwise rests mainly with men, but that in each action, Fate cooperates.' We have found here another, overlooked confirmation that Josephus was, from early on, a Pharisee.[61]

In response to Creuzer, however, Paret (1865) already pointed out that a belief in Providence was basic to the scriptures and to Judaism in general: it does not make Josephus a Pharisee.[62] Others have since shown that the Qumran community combined a strong belief in Providence and election with an insistence on human choice to follow God's

---

[58] Attridge, *Interpretation*, 178f.

[59] See the previous chapter on Schlatter, Wächter, and Maier, Cf. Urbach, *Sages*, I, 268, 284; also E. P. Sanders' discussion of the rabbinic balance between election and "*doing* the Law", in *Paul*, 84-238, especially 139, 177 n. 155, and 217ff.

[60] Creuzer, "Rückblick", 907f.; Schlatter, *Theologie*, 210f.

[61] Rajak, *Josephus*, 100.

[62] Paret, "Pharisäismus", 813.

will.[63] We have seen, finally, that possible ways of combining fate and free will were much discussed in the Hellenistic world, especially under the influence of Stoicism; these discussions became enduring features of later Christian and Jewish theology. That Josephus gives room to both divine and human action, therefore, carries no weight at all in establishing his Pharisaic connections.

(2) Similarly, it was shown above that Josephus believes in the immortality of the soul, as do his Essenes and Pharisees. Although Josephus directly endorses only the Essene position (*War* 2:154-158), a close analysis of his remarks revealed also that he agrees with the Pharisaic belief in a "reincarnation" of good souls. Creuzer and Montgomery thought that Josephus's belief in immortality reflected his Pharisaic inclination;[64] Weiss also suggests that Josephus's espousal of "einer Art 'Auferstehungshoffnung'" betrays his Pharisaic standpoint.[65]

Now it is well attested, in the NT and the rabbinic literature, that the Pharisees believed in resurrection and that the Sadducees denied it.[66] Josephus confirms this. Nevertheless, one cannot regard resurrection as a purely Pharisaic distinctive. Various hopes for a future life, including that of bodily and spiritual resurrection, were embraced by the Jewish apocalyptic writers of the period;[67] the infant Church also espoused a doctrine of resurrection.[68] Thus, although Josephus is clearly unsympathetic toward the Sadducean denial of the afterlife, that does not yet establish him as a Pharisee. Their acknowledgement of fate and immortality, he says, accords with the general Jewish view.[69]

In our evaluation of the general theoretical agreements between Josephus and the Pharisees we must recall further that his critique of the group always relates to practice and not theory.[70] He never impugns their goal of ἀκρίβεια with respect to the laws, but he does challenge their reputation on this score, on the basis of their actions.[71] Since Josephus's

---

[63] E.g., Nötscher, *Aufsätze*, 33-49; Wächter, "Haltung", 109f.; and Sanders, *Paul*, 257-270. Sanders explains the two emphases as two answers to the question why God chose the community. In their prayer and worship, the Qumraners would naturally emphasize God's election, in consequence of their own unworthiness. When comparing themselves to others, however, the emphasis is on their religious deeds.

[64] Creuzer, "Rückblick", 907f.; Montgomery, "Religion", 304.

[65] Weiss, "Pharisäismus", 426.

[66] Acts 23:8; Avot de Rabbi Nathan 5.

[67] Cf. Pss. Sol. 3:3-10; 1 Enoch 45:4f.; 61:5; 108; 4 Ezra 7:37; 2 Baruch 30:2-5; 50-51; Nicklesburg, *Resurrection*, 180.

[68] 1 Cor. 15:1ff., 31ff.; 1 Thess. 4:16ff.

[69] Cf. *War* 2:158 (on the appeal of Essene views!); *Ant.* 10:277-280; 16:397-398; *Ag.Ap.* 2:180.

[70] Cf. *War* 1:110-114; *Ant.* 13:400-432; 17:41-45; *Life* 191-198.

[71] An obvious parallel is Mt. 23:1ff., in which the Matthean Jesus commends Pharisaic teaching (vv. 1-2) but condemns the group's behaviour (vv. 3ff.).

disparagement of the Pharisees always has to do with their behaviour, the fact that he holds a position similar to theirs on concepts of immortality and fate/free will cannot be taken to suggest that he was a Pharisee. It is surely significant that Josephus never connects his own beliefs in resurrection and fate with those of the Pharisees, although he explicitly (and often) endorses the Essenes' views.

C. *Opposition to the Sadducees*

Josephus presents the Pharisaic positions on resurrection and fate/free will as the "dogmatic" alternatives to Sadducean skepticism (*War* 2:162-166): the Pharisees affirm; the Sadducees deny. Since it is clear that his own sympathies are with the affirmative side (*Ant.* 10:2771ff.), and because his portrayal of the Sadducees is generally derogatory,[72] some critics have assumed that he was a Pharisee. Paret devotes several pages to a demonstration of Josephus's anti-Sadducean animus, all in order to prove that Josephus was a Pharisee.[73] And Weiss avers:

> So lässt sich also bereits aus dem durchaus negativen Urteil des Josephus über die Partei der Sadduzäer indirekt auf seinen eigenen, nämlich pharisäischen Standpunkt schliessen.[74]

It is true that all of the sources (NT, rabbis, Josephus) attest the rivalry that existed in the first century between Pharisees and Sadducees. If, therefore, Josephus were known on other grounds to have been a Pharisee, that might explain his antipathy toward the Sadducees.

One cannot assume, however, that Pharisaism and Sadduceeism were the only alternatives of the day, so that anyone who disliked the Sadducees must have been a Pharisee. The religious landscape of Palestine evidently offered many sectarian affiliations, any one of which (such as the Qumran community) might have been hostile to the Sadducees.[75] In addition, one presumably had the option of non-affiliation and private dislike of the group.

The fundamental weakness in the equation between "anti-Sadducean" and "pro-Pharisaic" is that Josephus is even more hostile toward the Pharisees than he is toward the Sadducees! He discusses the Pharisees much more often than the Sadducees, usually in order to show their nefarious influence on Jewish history. He presents them as reli-

---

[72] Cf. *War* 2:166; *Ant.* 18:16; 20:199.
[73] Paret, "Pharisäismus", 820f.: "Wirklich erhalten wir . . . aus der Feder des Pharisäers Josephus eine höchst ungünstige Schilderung jener [*sc.* the Sadducean] Relgionspartei".
[74] Weiss, "Pharisäismus", 424, Cf. also Hölscher, "Josephus", 1936.
[75] Cf., e.g., M. Smith, "Palestinian Judaism".

gious frauds and trouble-makers, opposed to all governments, whether Hasmonean or Herodian. It was largely they who precipitated the downfall of the glorious Hasmonean dynasty. This consistent anti-Pharisaic bias in Josephus precludes the assumption that his (relatively mild) repudiation of Sadducean beliefs makes him a Pharisee.

D. *Josephus's Differences from Philo*

If the diversity of the religious scene in first-century Palestine disallows the equation of "anti-Sadducean" with "Pharisaic", it also denies the old assumption that whatever was Palestinian-Jewish, and not "Hellenistic", was Pharisaic. We have noted that Schlatter valued Josephus primarily because the ancient Jew represented Pharisaism, unlike Philo, who offered a Jewish Hellenism. It was precisely in this contrast between Philo and Josephus that Schlatter found evidence of the latter's Pharisaic mindset.[76] Unlike Philo, Josephus: understands piety as the doing of God's will and not as the soul's contemplation of God;[77] lacks any aesthetic sense;[78] gives no place to a λόγος-doctrine;[79] and retains a biblical/Palestinian-Jewish anthropology.[80] All of these non-Alexandrian themes Schlatter assumes to be Pharisaic.

It is no longer possible either to distinguish rigidly between "Palestinian" and "Hellenistic" or to equate "Palestinian" and "Pharisaic", which were the two bases of Schlatter's view. Attridge comments:

> Pharisaism for Schlatter is a rather ill-defined foil to the type of Judaism represented by Philo. While it is fair to note the differences between Philo and Josephus, the designation of the latter's position as Pharisaic is not particularly illuminating.[81]

E. *Josephus's Pharisaic Teachers?*

Rajak has proposed a new and ingenious argument in favour of Josephus's Pharisaic allegiance.[82] In *Life* 196-198, Josephus tells about a plot to remove him from his Galilean command. The high priest was persuaded to send a delegation of four men to the region, whose pooled

---

[76] *Wie sprach Josephus von Gott?*, 7; *Theologie*, p. V. Cf. Attridge, *Interpretation*, 9f, on Schlatter.

[77] *Theologie*, 7, 27 n. 1. For this and the following three references, I have been aided by Attridge's notes to p. 9 of his *Interpretation*.

[78] Ibid., 4.

[79] Ibid., 1f.

[80] Ibid., 21 n. 1.

[81] Attridge, *Interpretation*, 10.

[82] Rajak, *Josephus*, 30f.

talents would at least equal those of Josephus (!), so that the Galileans might be convinced to accept their administration instead of Josephus's. The delegates, he says, differed with respect to their social class but had a similar level of education (§ 196). Two represented the popular classes and were Pharisees; one was both a priest and a Pharisee; and the youngest (νεώτατος) was of high-priestly descent (§ 197).

Rajak points out that when, somewhat later in the narrative (§ 274), Josephus encounters the delegation, its members offer him duplicitous praise, to the effect that:

> my reputation was a tribute to themselves, since *they had been my teachers* and were my fellow citizens (ὡς ἂν διδασκάλων τέ μου γενομένων καὶ πολιτῶν ὄντων).

In identifying which of the delegates might have been Josephus's teachers, Rajak assumes that "he can hardly be including the fourth and youngest member".[83] That means that his teachers were Pharisees. Rajak argues further that these men could not have taught Josephus after his final alignment with the Pharisees (because his education seems to have been complete by then), or during his experimentation with the three schools (no reason given), so they must have been responsible for his basic education before the age of sixteen (*Life* 7-8). She thinks, therefore, that Josephus was brought up a Pharisee, then experimented with other groups, and ultimately fell back on the tradition inculcated during his childhood.[84]

It must be conceded that Rajak has identified an intriguing piece of information: it appears that at least some of the delegates sent to replace Josephus had been his διδάσκαλοι. Nevertheless, the movement from that premise to the conclusion that Josephus was brought up a Pharisee involves many dubious inferences, which may be divided into two groups. First, that it was indeed the Pharisees of the delegation who had taught Josephus, and that they had done so *qua* Pharisees, is only one hypothesis among many of equal plausibility. Josephus does not say which of the delegates had taught him, and in what capacity and context.[85] It is a matter of speculation. Two of the delegates, for example, were priests. Since, as we have seen, Josephus consistently connects his expertise in the laws with his priestly heritage, and since he does so again in *Ant.* 20:259-266/*Life* 1-9, one might argue that it was the priests who

---

[83] Ibid., 31.
[84] Ibid., 30f.
[85] Rajak's disqualification of the νεώτατος seems unwarranted, since his youthfulness is clearly relative to the ages of the others.

were his teachers, *qua* priests.[86] This hypothesis seems to receive some confirmation from the instructions given to the delegation (§ 198). They are commissioned to discover the cause (αἴτιος) of the Galileans' fondness for Josephus and then to point out that they can match his three greatest qualifications, namely: (a) they are all Jerusalemites, as he is; (b) their expertise in the πάτρια ἔθη equals his (in the νόμοι); and (c) if the Galileans venerate his priestly office, then the delegates should point out that two of them are also priests. What we have here is a reprise of Josephus's own estimation of his assets, which he likes to reiterate; he is a Jerusalemite priest who interprets the laws with ἀκρίβεια (e.g., *War* 1:2f.; 3:352; *Ant.* 20:259ff.; *Life* 1ff.; *Ap.* 1:54.). Expertise in the laws is here again juxtaposed with priestly heritage. Conspicuously absent, however, is any mention of Pharisaic membership as one of Josephus's or the delegation's credentials—conspicuously because, if Josephus viewed his alleged Pharisaic training as an asset, he would presumably have mentioned it here as a point on which the delegation hoped to better him: they have *three* Pharisees.

My claim is only that it is not clear which members of the delegation had taught Josephus or in what context and capacity they did so. The hypothesis that it was the priests who had been his teachers, I have suggested, seems at least as plausible as Rajak's theory that he was taught by Pharisees.

In any case, Rajak's further argument that the Pharisees taught Josephus during his childhood contradicts the sense of his own narrative. He does not mention any Pharisaic influence in his childhood; educated in a priestly home, he was already renowned for his ἀκρίβεια by age fourteen (*Life* 1-9). If he had been brought up as a Pharisee he would hardly have needed to go out and gain personal experience (ἐμπειρίαν λαβεῖν) of that group, as of the Sadducees and Essenes, at age sixteen (*Life* 10). So if Josephus was ever taught by Pharisees, as Pharisees—and this is by no means clear, this instruction must have occurred during or after his experimentation with the Jewish schools at age 16.

F. *Josephus's Desire for Reward and his Hypocrisy*

No survey of the arguments that have been offered as proof of Josephus's Pharisaic outlook would be complete without at least a reference to the

---

[86] Another alternative interpretation: the delegates were able to congratulate themselves on Josephus's administration of the Galilee precisely because that was the subject of their instruction; they had trained him (not long before, in Jerusalem) for his new duties as administrator. Perhaps they were among the πρῶτοι (*Life* 28) who had commissioned Josephus.

claim that his ''religion of reward'' and his weakness of character were obvious products of Pharisaism. Paret made a great deal of the claim that Josephus presents Judaism as a religion of fearful (*ängstlich*), external legalism, in which the individual must struggle to observe a mass of required laws.[87] The historian, it is said further, characteristically fails to distinguish the important laws from the petty[88] and misunderstands the prophets.[89] Almost half of Paret's study is given to this sort of ''proof'' that Josephus was a true Pharisee.[90] Brüne devotes his entire discussion of Josephus's Pharisaism to the deficiencies of Josephus's religion and character.[91] This religion hypocritically rejoices in God's punishment of evildoers but nurtures self-righteousness among the observant; that explains, says Brüne, Josephus's own remarkable vanity.[92] Finally, Schlatter cites Josephus's inability to accept guilt, his evaluation of well-being as the goal of religion, and his substitution of legalism for religious conviction as proof that Josephus was a Pharisee.[93] At least until the middle of this century, then, it was possible to invoke the traditional Christian view of Pharisaism, as an institution dedicated to the promotion of hypocrisy, in order to prove Josephus's religious affiliation.

The numerous absurdities on which this argument is based —logical, psychological, sociological, and historical—are by now well known; there is nothing to be gained by further elaboration here.

Summary and Conclusion: The Importance of Life 12b

This chapter has sought to document two propositions. First: almost every interpreter of Josephus since 1850 has believed that the historian either was or wanted to be seen as a Pharisee. Most have believed that he was a Pharisee, so that his claim to be one was a natural consequence of his actual affiliation. Some have argued, however, that the claim reflects a major apologetic theme in his later works but not historical reality. In one way or another, Josephus's claim to be a Pharisee has come to serve as a crucial datum in most analyses of his writings and thought.

---

[87] Paret, ''Pharisäismus'', 823-838.
[88] Ibid., 831f.
[89] Ibid., 834f.
[90] Ibid., 842-844.
[91] Brüne, *Flavius Josephus*, 150-157.
[92] Ibid., 154f.
[93] Schlatter, *Theologie*, 211.

Second: the widespread scholarly belief that Josephus intended to present himself as a Pharisee depends entirely on one sentence of his "autobiography", *Life* 12b. Other arguments offered by scholars to demonstrate that Josephus was a Pharisee are not really proofs; they derive from evidence that could be explained at least as well if he was not a Pharisee.

Thus, the burden of proof that rests on *Life* 12b is enormous. Not only do the arguments above fail to establish Josephus's Pharisaic allegiance, but two other considerations militate strongly against it. First, he consistently portrays the Pharisees, throughout *War* and *Ant.*, in an unfavourable light. Where he reveals any feeling at all toward the group, it is one of disdain. Second, in his major works he is utterly silent about any association with the Pharisees. What makes this silence conspicuous is that Josephus repeatedly describes the Pharisees as those with a reputation for ἀκρίβεια. If he believed this reputation to be well founded, then he would view his own (putative) Pharisaic allegiance as an asset to be exploited. In all of his many discussions of his own credentials, however, including those that deal with his ἀκρίβεια, he never once gives the slightest hint of any Pharisaic background or allegiance. And this silence is particularly obvious in his later works, in which the Rasp/Smith/Neusner/Cohen view finds a bold attempt on Josephus's part to pass himself off as a Pharisee. His notable silence about any Pharisaic affiliation and his consistent disparagement of that group lead the reader of *War*, *Ant.*, and *Ag.Ap.* to conclude that he disliked the Pharisees; apart from § 12b, the *Life* itself implies the same.

So if the near universal assumption that Josephus wanted to present himself as a Pharisee is to be accepted, we shall require from *Life* 12b a clear and unequivocal statement to that effect. Those who believe that Josephus was a devoted Pharisee must reckon with the two difficulties just noted. Those who think that he merely wished to look like a Pharisee are not affected in the same degree, but must still explain why the Pharisees appear so poorly in *Ant.* 13 and 17 and in *Life* 191-198 (see chapter 16). These difficulties cannot be addressed, however (because they do not exist), until it is first shown that in *Life* 12b Josephus intends to present himself as a Pharisee.[94]

---

[94] The two most common explanations of the anti-Pharisaic thrust are: (a) the source-critical approach, which attributes the material to someone other than Josephus and (b) the proposal of Schlatter (*Theologie*, 203f.), that Josephus did praise the Pharisees, by mentioning their expertise in the laws, but that he chastised his party for its involvement in politics. This view is shared by A. Guttmann, *Rabbinic Judaism*, 124f. We may note, however: (a) Josephus consistently says that the Pharisees *are reputed to be/profess to be* (δοκέω/προσποιοῦμαι), not that they *are*, experts in the Law. The distinction is significant because: (i) Josephus is capable of saying that someone *is* a precise interpreter of the Law

(*War* 1:108—Alexandra; *Ant.* 17:149—the two doctors; *Ag.Ap.* 1:53f.—himself; cf. *War* 2:145 on the Essenes); and (ii) often, his δοκεῖ. . . ἀκριβῆς construction is followed immediately by a negation of the party's reputation (e.g. *Ag.Ap.* 1:18—Thucydides; *Ag.Ap.* 1:67—Ephorus; *War* 1:110ff.; *Life* 191ff. [cf. *Ant.* 17:41-45]—the Pharisees). It is far from clear, therefore, that Josephus did praise the Pharisees at all. (b) The rigid distinction between religion and politics, though prominent in modern American society, is of dubious validity for ancient Judaism. In any case, Josephus was himself fully involved in "politics". At age 26, he began to πολιτεύεσθαι (see chapter 15): he took a diplomatic mission to Rome and then became military commander of the Galilee.

CHAPTER FIFTEEN

LIFE 10-12: JOSEPHUS'S RELIGIOUS QUEST

Clearly, the whole basis for the scholarly consensus that Josephus wanted to be understood as a Pharisee is a single sentence in his autobiography, *Life* 12b. Josephus relates there that, having trained in the three Jewish philosophical schools (αἱρέσεις) and having then spent some time with an ascetic teacher, he returned to Jerusalem and:

ἐννεακαιδέκατον δ' ἔτος ἔχων
ἠρξάμην τε πολιτεύεσθαι
    τῇ Φαρισαίων αἱρέσει κατακολουθῶν,
ἣ παραπλήσιός ἐστι τῇ παρ' Ἕλλησι
    Στοικῇ λεγομένῃ

The purpose of this chapter is to interpret *Life* 12b and thereby to determine whether or not Josephus is here making a definitive claim to Pharisaic allegiance.

I. *Context of Life 12*

Beyond the general aim of presenting Josephus in a good light, as a man of character (cf. *Life* 430), it is not clear that the introduction and conclusion of the *Life* (1-27, 414-430) have any specific role in the apologetic against Justus of Tiberias, which governs the body of the tract. They appear to be little more than brief summaries of Josephus's youth and postwar life, respectively.[1]

Josephus has promised, in *Ant.* 20:266, to elaborate upon his lineage and the events of his life, presumably in support of his claim to superior precision (ἀκρίβεια) in the laws (20:259-265). In fulfillment of that promise, he opens the *Life* with a recital of his priestly pedigree (§§ 1-6). Then follows an account of how he came to acquire precision in the laws by the age of fourteen (§§ 7-9). Then comes the description of his adolescent religious quest (§§ 10-12), which is the focus of this chapter.

The usual interpretation of *Life* 10-12 is as follows.[2] At age sixteen, Josephus wanted to gain personal experience (ἐμπειρία) of the three

---

[1] So Schürer, *Geschichte*, I, 75; Niese, *HZ*, 227; Hölscher, "Josephus", 1994; T. Rajak, "Justus", 354. *Contra* R. Laqueur, *Historiker*, 246. Cf. chapter 13, above.

[2] Since we lack proper commentaries on Josephus, one is thrown back upon the paraphrases or summaries of *Life* 10-12 by the authors cited in the following discussion.

Jewish philosophical schools. He thought that, if he investigated all of them, he would be in a position to choose the best (ᾠόμην αἱρήσεσθαι τὴν ἀρίστην, § 10). So he embarked on an intensive programme of training in each school and, in addition, spent some time with a baptist ascetic named Bannus (§ 11). His investigation of his options now complete (τὴν ἐπιθυμίαν τελειώσας), Josephus made his decision in favour of the Pharisaic school (ἠρξάμην πολιτεύεσθαι τῇ Φαρισαίων αἱρέσει κατακολουθῶν, § 12).

Thus, for example, J. A. Montgomery wrote that Josephus:

> might flatter himself in later years that he had passed like a butterfly over the various pastures of wisdom until in maturity he lighted upon that which pleased him best. At the age of nineteen he made his choice and became a convinced Pharisee according to his own mind.[3]

And in the *Compendia* volumes H. W. Attridge comments, "The account [*Life* 10-12], which has its parallels in other stories of philosophers' quests, serves to indicate that Josephus made an informed choice in opting for the Pharisees."[4]

On the usual interpretation, then, the whole paragraph (*Life* 10-12) becomes an account of the lengthy preparations that Josephus put himself through before deciding to become a Pharisee. He had tried all of the options, so his decision to become a Pharisee was well considered and sure.

The conventional view, however, faces serious obstacles, namely: (a) it does not adequately explain the logic of the paragraph; (b) it makes *Life* 10-12 wholly incompatible with the larger context of Josephus's thought; and (c) the crucial clauses in § 12b cannot bear the weight the weight that is put on them. The first two points I shall take up immediately, since they relate to the "context" of § 12b; then I shall consider point (c) in some detail, as it is the focus of this chapter.

Few critics seem to notice that the customary reading of *Life* 10-12 renders the logic of the paragraph difficult to grasp. Josephus claims (§ 10) that there are three schools among the Jews and that his original intention (ᾠόμην) was to study each one (ἐμπειρίαν λαβεῖν) so that he

---

[3] Montgomery, "Religion", 280f.

[4] In *Jewish Writings of the Second Temple Period: Apocrypha, Pseudepigrapha, Qumran Sectarian Writings, Philo, Josephus*, ed. M. E. Stone, "Compendia Rerum Iudaicarum ad Novum Testamentum", 2:3, 186. Likewise T. W. Franxman (*Genesis*, 3): "At sixteen he [Josephus] evidently attempted to broaden his horizons by a practical sampling of life and thought among Pharisees, Sadducees, and Essenes, concluding these experiments with a three-year period spent as a hermit. By nineteen Jos seems to have been prepared to make the choice which turned out to be in favour of casting his lot with the party of the Pharisees."

might choose the best. That much is clear. But he goes on to say that
his original intention was not fulfilled. The experience he gained was not
sufficient to attract him to any of the three schools (μηδὲ τὴν ἐμπειρίαν
ἱκανὴν ἐμεαυτῷ νομίσας εἶναι, § 11). That is precisely why he went to
follow Bannus in the wilderness.

The lifestyle of this baptist ascetic, in contrast to that of the accredited
schools, was so compelling that Josephus became his devoted disciple
(ζηλωτὴς ἐγενόμην αὐτοῦ). R. Mayer and C. Möller correctly note:

> Die Persönlichkeit dieses Mannes [Bannus] sowie die Hauptelemente
> seiner Lebenshaltung scheinen den jungen Josephus stark angesprochen zu
> haben, denn er blieb drei Jahre bei ihm.[5]

Unaccountably, however, most critics dismiss this three-year retreat—
which must have occupied the bulk of Josephus's experimentation
period!—as a mere sidelight or conclusion to the main business of studying the recognized schools.

Against the conventional view, I submit that the phrase τὴν ἐπιθυμίαν
τελειώσας cannot simply refer to the completion of Josephus's originally
intended programme of preparation, as Thackeray renders it: "having
accomplished my purpose". For this translation overlooks the correspondence between the aorist participles of διατρίβω and τελέω. We
should rather translate § 12a:

> Having lived with him three years
> καὶ διατρίψας παρ' αὐτῷ ἐνιαυτοὺς τρεῖς
> and having (thereby) satisfied my yearning
> καὶ τὴν ἐπιθυμίαν τελειώσας
> I returned to the city.
> εἰς τὴν πόλιν ὑπέστρεφον.

The fulfillment of Josephus's ἐπιθυμία is clearly tied, in chronological se-
quence, to his time with Bannus. It precedes the return to Jerusalem and
the "following" of the Pharisees.

What, then, is the meaning of ἐπιθυμία? It cannot refer to Josephus's
original "purpose" as he describes it in *Life* 10, because that purpose did
not include a lengthy wilderness retreat with Bannus. The word must
refer, then, to the religious "longing" or "yearning" that spawned his
programme of study in the first place. It was that yearning that was
satisfied by the religion of Bannus.

Finally, the verb τελέω emphasizes that Josephus considers his adolescent religious quest to have closed with his period of asceticism in the
wilderness, after which he began his public career in the city (§§ 12b,

[5] R. Mayer and C. Möller, "Josephus—Politiker und Prophet", in *Josephus-Studien*,
edd. O.Betz, K. Haacker, and P. Schäfer (1974), 272.

13ff.). Josephus does *not* say that his time with Bannus made him eager to become a Pharisee. No, his decision was made in favour of Bannus: "I became his devoted disciple (ζηλωτής)". Where the regular schools had come up empty, the desert monk offered something that met Josephus's needs.

If we had only §§ 10-12a, therefore, the natural interpretation would be that Josephus originally set out to examine the three mainstream Jewish schools in order to choose the best, but that he did not find any of them to be adequate. Then he heard about Bannus and went off to investigate his programme. It was this experience that resulted in Josephus's "conversion", if that term is appropriate anywhere. He liked what he saw and stayed with Bannus three years.

Now, if § 12b really means to say that Josephus "trat definitiv zu den Pharisäern über",[6] as the climax of his religious quest, then the paragraph §§ 10-12 is quite confusing. He has already said that his experience with the schools was not satisfying and that is why he became a disciple of the anchorite. Where, then, is the rationale for a final conversion to Pharisaism? It makes no sense for him to conclude the matter by saying, in effect: "Then I returned to the city and became a Pharisee". If that is what he means to say in § 12b, then he has written an incoherent narrative.

The problem of incoherence is made acute by the circumstance that nothing Josephus has said about the Pharisees in *War* or *Ant.* would lead the reader to suppose that he was himself a member of the group. He portrays them as power-hungry opportunists, whose actions undermine their reputation for piety.[7] Indeed, he will sustain this portrayal in the *Life* itself, in his hostile characterizations of the famous Pharisee Simon ben Gamaliel (§§ 189-198) and of the Pharisees who came to relieve him of his command in the Galilee (§§ 196-335). Thus, if the six crucial words in § 12b really mean to say that Josephus chose to become a Pharisee, they are as baffling in their immediate context as they are in the larger context of Josephus's thought.

T. Rajak has noticed at least something of the incongruity of *Life* 10-12 on the usual interpretation of § 12b. She aptly points out that the reader expects some explanation of the surprise move to Pharisaism. Her solution of the problem is as follows:

> Josephus says that at the age of nineteen he began to adhere to the Pharisaic sect. He gives no reason for having done so (V 12), and describes

---

[6] So Paret, "Pharisäismus", 811.
[7] Cf. *War* 1:110-114; *Ant.* 13:288-298, 400-432; 17:41-45.

it as a matter-of-course decision. It would make good sense if we supposed that in the end he fell back upon the views with which he had been brought up.[8]

This theory runs aground, however, on Josephus's own account of his early education (*Life* 7-10), which makes no mention whatsoever of Pharisaic influences. On the contrary, he extols the virtues only of his priestly heritage. His reported decision to familiarize himself with the three Jewish schools, moreover, presupposes that he had had no serious acquaintance with them at age sixteen. He could not, then, have been raised as a Pharisee.

J. Le Moyne also remarks on the conspicuous absence of any explanation for Josephus's final conversion to Pharisaism after his happy years as a disciple of Bannus. The French scholar ventures the hypothesis that, on his return from the wilderness, Josephus "choisit un idéal de vie, celui des Pharisiens, qui lui paraît plus en rapport avec son expérience de retraite au désert que l'idéal sadducéen".[9] To be sure, if Josephus means to say that he converted to Pharisaism after his time with Bannus, then one must assume with Le Moyne that Bannus and the Pharisees had a good deal in common.

Yet nothing that Josephus says about the Pharisees elsewhere suggests any sort of anchoritic leanings on their part. He often describes their activities in the political arena, their involvement with various rulers, and their influence with the masses.[10] Recall that L. Finkelstein was able to portray the Pharisees as fundamentally *urban* ("plebeian") in outlook.[11] The Jewish school that most closely approaches a monastic ideal, in Josephus's presentation, is rather that of the Essenes (cf. *War* 2:119-161; *Ant.* 18:19-22). Le Moyne's proposal seems, therefore, to be a desperate attempt to make sense of the conventional interpretation of *Life* 12b in its context.

Since the usual understanding of *Life* 12b runs counter to its immediate context and to Josephus's overall portrayal of the Pharisees, it would seem reasonable to scrutinize the customary reading before making it the basis for one's whole understanding of Josephus's religious perspective.

---

[8] Rajak, *Josephus*, 32.
[9] J. Le Moyne, *Les Sadducéens* (1972), 28.
[10] *War* 2:411; *Ant.* 13:289, 297-298, 401; 15:3-4, 370-371; 17:41; *Life* 21.
[11] L. Finkelstein, *The Pharisees*, I, 74-76.

II. *Key Terms*

Key words in the sentence are πολιτεύεσθαι and κατακολουθῶν.

According to Liddell and Scott, πολιτεύομαι usually occurs in Greek literature with a sense that is closely related to the noun πόλις, thus: "live as a free citizen, take part in government, meddle with politics, hold public office, show public spirit". They also give, as a meaning represented largely in Jewish and Christian texts, "deal with (in private affairs), or behave".[12] Josephus, as a Jew writing in Greek, was presumably eligible to use both senses. This creates two significantly different translation possibilities for πολιτεύεσθαι in *Life* 12b. Generally speaking, German commentators have opted for the sense "to take part in public life", whereas English-language scholarship has tended to invoke the sense "to behave".

The Thompson-Price edition of Josephus (1777) rendered § 12b: "I began to apply myself to the study of civil law, for which purpose I entered the society of the Pharisees."[13] Notice the clear distinction here between the main clause ("I began to study civil law") and the subordinate clause ("for which purpose I entered the society of the Pharisees"). Other English translations, however, have ignored this distinction and have omitted any association of πολιτεύεσθαι with civil life.

The most influential has been W. Whiston's translation, which first appeared in 1737 but has gone through numerous editions and is still in print. Against Thompson and Price, he took πολιτεύεσθαι to mean something like "behave", thus: "I began to conduct myself according to the rules of the sect of the Pharisees". This rendering treats the sentence as if it were a single clause. Whiston's translation was adopted by the World Library edition (1900) and may have influenced Thackeray's rendering for the Loeb series (1926).[14] The latter has: "I began to govern my life by the rules of the Pharisees". Since the infinitive πολιτεύεσθαι combines with the aorist ἠρξάμην to form the main clause of § 12b, the Whiston/Thackeray interpretation of πολιτεύεσθαι reads the sentence as nothing other than a definitive statement of Josephus's conversion: what he "began to do" was "to conduct his life" by the rules of the Pharisees.

It is hard to gauge precisely the impact of Whiston and Thackeray on anglophone scholarship, but that impact is undeniably formidable. All of the major English-speaking commentators take the phrase ἠρξάμην πολιτεύεσθαι as a conversion statement, with the sense that Josephus

---

[12] E.g., 2 Macc. 11:25; *Aristeas* 31; Acts 23:1; Phil. 1:27.

[13] *The Works of Flavius Josephus*, 2 vols., edd. E. Thompson and W. C. Price (1777).

[14] Thackeray notes only that he has "occasionally consulted" Whiston (LCL edn., I, xx).

became a Pharisee. Since it is demonstrable that these critics are generally influenced by the Loeb translation—many cite it *verbatim*—, it is probable that their interpretations of *Life* 12b are not wholly independent.[15]

German scholars, though they also tend to see *Life* 12 as proof of Josephus's decision to become a Pharisee, have by and large taken ἠρξάμην πολιτεύεσθαι as a distinct main clause, referring to Josephus's entry into political or public life. Consider the following translations and paraphrases of *Life* 12b (emphasis added where it appears).

(a) B. Niese (1896): "Er ging bei den drei Sekten . . . um dann mit 19 Jahren *in das öffentliche Leben einzutreten*; er schloss sich den Lehren der Pharisäer an."[16]

(b) G. Hölscher (1916): "bis er als Neunzehnjähriger . . . nach Jerusalem zurückgekehrt und als Anhänger der pharisäischen αἵρεσις *in den Staatsdienst getreten sei*".[17]

(c) H. Rasp (1924): "Im neunzehnten Jahre habe er seine Vorbereitung abgeschlossen . . . und *die öffentliche Laufbahn* (πολιτεύεσθαι) als Mitglied der Pharisäersekte (τῇ Φαρισαίων αἱρέσει κατακολουθῶν) *begonnen*."[18]

(d) L. Hafaeli (1925): "Und dann mit 19 Jahren fing ich an, *mich im öffentlichen Leben zu betätigen* und zwar nach dem Programm der Pharisäersekte."[19]

(e) A. Schlatter (1932): "bis er sich 19 jährig entschloss, 'im Anschluss an die Partei der Pharisäer *zu politisieren*'".[20]

(f) E. Lohse (1971): "kehrte mit neunzehn Jahren nach Jerusalem zurück, schloss sich den Pharisäern an und *begann, sich im öffentlichen Leben zu betätigen*".[21]

(g) H.-F. Weiss (1979): "dass er als Neunzehnjähriger . . . *begonnen habe*, 'im Anschluss an die Partei der Pharisäer *zu politisieren*'".[22]

It is remarkable that the German commentators should so consistently (and independently) take πολιτεύεσθαι in the sense of public activity, while their anglophone counterparts generally refer it to Josephus's

[15] The two leading protagonists in the debate on Josephus's Pharisees, Neusner ("Josephus's Pharisees") and Rivkin (*Revolution*), both use the Loeb translation for most of their block quotations from Josephus; Attridge (*Interpretation*, 52, 58, 67, 69) follows it often. Cohen (*Josephus*, xi) acknowledges "inspiration" from the LCL edn. and Shutt (*Studies*, ix) notes his acquaintance with it.
[16] Niese, *HZ*, 194.
[17] Hölscher, "Josephus", 1936.
[18] Rasp, "Religionsparteien", 34. Cf. Laqueur, *Historiker*, 247.
[19] L. Hafaeli, *Flavius Josephus' Lebensbeschreibung* (1925), *ad loc*.
[20] Schlatter, *Theologie*, 208.
[21] E. Lohse, *Umwelt des Neuen Testaments* (1971), 102.
[22] Weiss, "Pharisäismus", 424.

ordering of his own life or behaviour. The German translations of
πολιτεύεσθαι cited above (along with Thompson-Price) give an entirely
new complexion to *Life* 12b: the main clause now means that Josephus
began to involve himself in public affairs. His connection with the
Pharisees now appears only in the four-word dependen: clause, τῇ
Φαρισαίων αἱρέσει κατακολουθῶν. This shift, as we shall see presently, is
of monumental significance.

A decision about the meaning of πολιτεύεσθαι in *Life* 12b must base
itself on (a) Josephus's usage of the word elsewhere and (b) the immediate context in this case.

The verb πολιτεύω occurs thirty times in Josephus, in all three voices;
half of these occurrences are in the middle voice. Josephus uses πολιτεύω
in the active to mean "negotiate",[23] "act officially or publicly",[24] "formulate policy",[25] or, in *Ant.* 17, "behave toward (someone)".[26] In the
passive, the verb generally means "be governed" or "live under a (particular) regime".[27]

In its fifteen occurrences outside of our passage, the middle
πολιτεύομαι is invariably predicated of a public figure. As with the active
voice, the middle occurs twice in *Ant.* 17 with the meaning "behave"
(17:103, 243). But the subjects here are the sons of Herod the Great and
the issue is their behaviour toward their father; it is a fine line that
separates their family intrigues from public affairs. In any case, all of
these occurrences of πολιτεύω with the sense "to behave or act" whether
in the active or middle voice, are conspicuously concentrated in *Ant.* 17,
which is famous for its stylistic peculiarities.[28] The material on Herod's
family struggles may even be influenced by the style of Josephus's
source.[29]

Usually, however, πολιτεύομαι in Josephus has the sense "to govern,
hold office, enact policy, act as a leader", or the like. Josephus speaks,
for example, of the "public measures" taken by Moses (ὅσα Μωυσῆς
ἐπολιτεύσατο, *Ant.* 4:13) and by Queen Alexandra Salome (*Ant.* 13:432).
He uses the word to describe the activities of the five regional governing
councils established by Gabinius (ἐπολιτεύοντο οἱ ἐν Ἱεροσολύμοις, *Ant.*

---

[23] *Ant.* 1:253.
[24] *Ant.* 18:256.
[25] *Ant.* 19:43.
[26] *Ant.* 17:16, 60, 281.
[27] *Ant.* 11:112, 279; 12:38, 142; 20:234.
[28] Cf. Thackeray, *Josephus*, 110-112; G. C. Richards, "The Composition of Josephus'
Antiquities", *Classical Quarterly* 33 (1939), 37f.
[29] If the variant πολιτεύεσθαι were accepted at *Ant.* 17:60 (so AMW), it would give one
clear example of the meaning "behave" in Josephus (again in *Ant.* 17!). Both Niese and
Marcus/Wikgren (LCL edn.), however, reject this variant.

14:91). The sons of Baba, who are described as prominent public figures,[30] are said to have followed a policy (ἐπολιτεύοντο) of endorsing Antigonus over against the young Herod (*Ant.* 15:263). Josephus remarks that the Parthian aristocracy considered it impossible to govern (πολιτεύεσθαι) without a monarchy (*Ant.* 18:44). Finally, Josephus concludes his account of the high-priestly succession with the notice: "Some of these held office (ἐπολιτεύσαντο) during the reigns of Herod and Archelaus his son" (*Ant.* 20:251).[31]

Outside of our passage, πολιτεύομαι occurs twice in the *Life*, both times in connection with Josephus's defence of his leadership in the Galilee. In § 258, he is responding to the delegation sent from Jerusalem to replace him. Rebutting the charge that he has acted as a tyrant rather than as a general (cf. § 260), Josephus appeals to the testimony of the Galileans: "Ask them how I have lived and whether I have governed (πεπολίτευμαι) here with complete dignity and virtue" (Thackeray). Josephus then (magnanimously!) offers to pardon the delegation—against the wishes of the Galileans, who have become indignant on his behalf (§ 262)—on the condition that the emissaries repent of their designs and "give a true report about my public life (περὶ τῶν ἐμοὶ πεπολιτευμένων) to those who had sent them" (Thackeray). Since the whole issue in the delegation affair is Josephus's manner of leadership in the Galilee, Thackeray must be correct in translating πολιτεύομαι here as referring to Josephus's public activities and policies.

Ordinarily, then, Josephus uses πολιτεύομαι in its primary sense, which is linked to the πόλις, thus: to govern, enact policy, show public spirit, and so forth.

That he uses the verb with this same sense in *Life* 12b —"to engage in public affairs"—is made clear by the immediate context of the sentence. Josephus has just finished describing his three years in the wilderness (ἐρημία) with Bannus (§§ 11-12a). He concludes that episode with the remark: "my yearning now satisfied, I returned to the city (εἰς τὴν πόλιν ὑπέστρεφον, § 12a). Immediately after these words comes our sentence: "And now, being nineteen years of age, ἠρξάμην πολιτεύεσθαι" (§ 12b). The proximity of πόλις and πολιτεύεσθαι suggests the following interpretation: "Following my protracted wilderness retreat, I returned to the city (πόλις) and began to engage in public affairs (πολιτεύεσθαι)." Biblical-Jewish history commonly saw the desert as the place for meeting

---

[30] According to *Ant.* 15:263, they "had a high position and great influence with the masses" (Marcus/Wikgren).
[31] Cf. also *Ant.* 14:260.

God and for preparing oneself for a public career;[32] obvious examples
are Moses (Ex. 3-4) and Jesus (Mt. 4:1-14). It would seem that Josephus
is presenting his own training in terms of this motif. His desert retreat
with Bannus prepared him for public activity (πολιτεύεσθαι).

The proposed interpretation of πολιτεύεσθαι seems to be placed beyond
doubt by the sequel. For immediately after Josephus remarks that he
began to πολιτεύεσθαι (§ 12b), he proceeds to tell of his diplomatic and
political activities (§§ 13ff.), which activities occupy the rest of the book.
First he recounts his embassy to Rome: he was chosen to go there in
order to try to free some fellow priests who had been sent to Nero on
a minor charge. On his return from Rome, Josephus was already a
public figure, by his own account (§§ 17-23). He tried to avert the inci-
pient revolt, pleading with rebel leaders and consulting the chief priests
and leading Pharisees (§ 22); indeed, by his use of ἡμεῖς in §§ 22-23, he
places himself clearly among the leaders of the city. Then, with the
failure of Cestius Gallus to quell the revolt, Josephus was dispatched to
the Galilee as a military governor (§§ 28ff.) and the rest of the story is
well known. Thus ἠρξάμην πολιτεύεσθαι in *Life* 12b marks the beginning
of Josephus's public career.

I submit, finally, that the syntax of § 12b supports the interpretation
of πολιτεύεσθαι as "engage in public affairs". If the infinitive verb meant
"govern oneself" or "behave", then the dependent participle
κατακολουθῶν would seem redundant. One would expect either
πολιτεύεσθαι with a preposition such as κατά[33] ("I began to behave/live
according to the school of the Pharisees") or the infinitive κατακολουθεῖν
by itself ("I began to follow the school of the Pharisees"). But the construction aorist verb + present infinitive + (dependent) participle is
cumbersome if it means: "I began to behave (= main clause), following
the school of the Pharisees (= dependent clause)". The proposed translation, by contrast, gives both the infinitive and the participle their own
weight, because they mean different things: "I began to engage in public
life (= main clause), following the school of the Pharisees (= dependent
clause).

All of this suggests that πολιτεύεσθαι in *Life* 12b means "to participate
in public affairs". In favour of such a reading are: (a) normal Greek
usage of the verb; (b) normal Josephan usage; (c) the immediate context
of § 12b; (d) the syntax of § 12b; and (e) the agreement of many com-

---

[32] Cf. Mayer and Möller, "Politiker", 272 and n.10 thereto.
[33] In the two cases where πολιτεύεσθαι means "behave", such qualifiers are present
(*Ant.* 17:103, ἀκράτῳ εὐνοίᾳ and πρὸς τὸν πατέρα; 17:243, οἰκείως and αὐτοῖς).

mentators who have not been influenced by Whiston and Thackeray, namely, Thompson-Price and the German critics cited earlier.

The verb κατακολουθέω is not as problematic. Liddell and Scott give the meanings "follow after, comply with, obey, emulate, and imitate". It occurs in Josephus only 20 times.

The construction of the κατακολουθέω-clause in *Life* 12b—indirect (dative) object straddling the possessive genitive + final participle/ verb—fits well with Josephan style elsewhere, for example:

(a) *Life* 12b: τῇ Φαρισαίων αἱρέσει κατακολουθῶν
(b) *Ant.* 1:14: τοῖς μὲν θεοῦ γνώμῃ κατακολουθοῦσι
(c) *Ant.* 6:147: ταῖς ἐντολαῖς αὐτοῦ κατακολουθοῦντες
(d) *Ant.* 8:271: τοῖς τοῦ βασιλέως ἀσεβήμασι κατακολούθησε

A variation has the verb as the penultimate element:

(e) *Ant.* 6:133: ταῖς Μωυσέος κατακολουθήσαντ' ἐντολαῖς
(f) *Ant.* 9:99: τοῖς τῶν Ἰσραηλιτῶν βασιλεῶν κατηκολούθησεν ἀσεβήμασι
(g) *Ant.* 9:233: τῇ τοῦ πατρὸς κατακολουθήσας ὠμότητι

One can detect at least four nuances of the verb κατακολουθέω in Josephus. Only once does it have the sense of physical "following"; that is when Samuel pursues the Philistines (*Ant.* 6:28). Once also it means "to agree with". Josephus complains that Greek historians have never agreed with one another (οὐδὲ ἀλλήλοις κατηκολουθήκασι, *Ag.Ap.* 1:17).

More commonly, the verb suggests obedience or conformity to the laws, the commandments, or to God's will. Josephus has written his *Ant.*, he says, to show that those who conform to God's will (θεοῦ γνώμῃ κατακολουθοῦσι) prosper in everything (1:14). Samuel tells Saul that all the Amalekites must be massacred, in obedience to the commands of Moses (ταῖς Μωυσέος κατακολουθησαντ' ἐντολαῖς, *Ant.* 6:133). The Deity, Samuel exhorts, is only pleased with those who obey his will and his commands (6:147). It was by following the laws (τοῖς νόμοις κατακολουθῶν) that Josiah succeeded so well in his administration. In these cases, κατακολουθέω takes an impersonal object: one obeys, or complies with, some sort of instructions or laws.[34]

The other way in which Josephus uses κατακολουθέω lacks this strong sense of obligation or duty: the idea is rather "to follow an example or model, to emulate or imitate". In this case the object is not a law but

---

[34] Cf. *Ant.* 5:73; 8:339; 12:255.

a paradigm, a person, or a person's actions. Thus Josephus relates that the people began to imitate the impious ways of King Jeroboam (*Ant.* 8:271) and that the Judean king Jehoram emulated the impious ways of his Israelite counterparts (9:99). In *Ant.* 12:269, the officers of Antiochus IV tell the Hasmonean Mattathias that if he sacrifices on their pagan altar, the other Jews will follow his example (καταχολουθήσειν αὐτῷ). In this sense, then, καταχολουθέω means to follow a personal example, precedent, or model.[35]

It is impossible to say *a priori*, therefore, precisely what καταχολουθέω means in *Life* 12b. The way in which Josephus "followed" the school of the Pharisees must be determined from the context. Crucial is the function of the verb in the sentence:

ἠρξάμην πολιτεύεσθαι

τῇ Φαρισαίων αἱρέσει καταχολουθῶν

The main clause tells us that Josephus began to involve himself in public affairs. We are obliged to assume that the dependent clause, in which καταχολουθέω stands, is dependent on the main clause for its meaning. Thus, Josephus's following of the Pharisaic school is somehow related to his career as a public figure.

III. *Interpretation of Life 12b*

In what way did Josephus's entry into public life involve him in "following" the Pharisaic school? We are not totally without clues. He has consistently asserted, in *War* and *Ant.*, that the Pharisees constitute the dominant school among the Jews (*War* 2:162; *Ant.* 13:288-298, 401; 18:15). Their influence affects not only what we should distinguish as the "religious" sphere (cf. *Ant.* 18:15—prayers and rites) but also the whole operation of the state. Thus when John Hyrcanus abrogated the Pharisaic ordinances, according to Josephus, the masses reacted with intense hostility (*Ant.* 13:297-298).

Pharisaic influence among the people is so profound, Josephus insists, that even the Sadducees are compelled to follow Pharisaic dictates. He says of the Sadducees that:

> whenever they come into a position of leadership (ἐπ' ἀρχὰς παρέλθοιεν), they defer, albeit unwillingly and by necessity (ἀκουσίως μὲν καὶ κατ' ἀνάγκας), to what the Pharisee says, because otherwise they would become intolerable to the masses. (*Ant.* 18:17)

---

[35] Cf. *Ant.* 1:19; *Ag.Ap.* 2:281.

Now if the Sadducees, who are the relentless opponents of the Pharisees, nonetheless defer (προσχωρέω) to "what the Pharisee says" when they take positions of leadership, it should occasion no surprise that the anti-Pharisaic Josephus, *when he entered public life*, also "followed the school of the Pharisees". But this does not make him a Pharisee any more than it makes the Sadducees Pharisees. The verb προσχωρέω—"to go over to, or side with"—which he uses of the Sadducees' deference to the Pharisees, would seem to be at least as strong as the vague κατακολουθέω that he uses of his own relationship to the dominant school. By his own account, concessions to the Pharisaic school were a *conditio sine qua non* of Jewish life. His adherence to Pharisaic ways, like that of the Sadducees, was both tied to and limited to (so far as we know) his public career.

The interpretation of *Life* 12b offered here agrees (independently) with the judgement of one E. Gerlach (1863), which has generally been ignored since he made it. Gerlach wrote:

> Man nimmt sie [*Life* 12] fälschlich für eine ausdrückliche Erklärung des Josephus, dass er schliesslich ein Anhänger der Pharisäer geworden sei, während sie in der That nichts weiter bezeichnet, als dass er sich im *politischen* Leben den Pharisäern angeschlossen habe.[36]

It may even be that the final words of *Life* 12b, which compare the Pharisees to the Stoics, are intended to remind the reader of what Josephus has said elsewhere about the pervasive influence of the Pharisees in Jewish society.[37]

However one interprets the Pharisee/Stoic parallel, several points in the interpretation of *Life* 12b do seem secure. Josephus's religious quest found its fulfillment in his three-year wilderness retreat with Bannus (*Life* 11-12a). After this time of preparation in the desert, Josephus returned to the πόλις (§ 12a) and embarked upon his public career (ἠρξάμην πολιτεύεσθαι, § 12b). Implicit in this public activity was a certain

---

[36] E. Gerlach, *Weissagungen*, 18.

[37] Commentators usually interpret this remark as a reference to particular agreements in doctrine or practice between the Pharisees and the Stoics (cf. G. F. Moore, "Fate", 374 and n. 20; Schlatter, *Theologie*, 198; Feldman, LCL edn., IX, 10 n. *b*). Without diminishing in the least the significance of those parallels, I should like to suggest a a further aspect of comparison.

By the first century AD, as is well known, Stoicism had become the dominant philosophical school in the Hellenistic world: its influence on the other schools and on popular thought was considerable (cf. F. H. Sandbach, *The Stoics*, 16; A. A. Long, *Hellenistic Philosophy*, 107). Since Pharisaism, according to Josephus, fulfilled a corresponding role in Jewish society, it would seem plausible that this is precisely the point of the comparison. If he is saying that the two schools have comparable functions in their respective societies, that would explain the inclusion of this clause immediately after his statement that his entry into public life entailed some deference to the Pharisaic school.

acknowledgement of, or deference to, the Pharisaic school (τῇ Φαρισαίων αἱρέσει κατακολουθῶν), a fact of life that even the Sadducees recognized (*Ant.* 18:17).

Summary and Conclusion

For anglophone scholars generally, the whole import of the sentence ἠρξάμην πολιτεύεσθαι τῇ Φαρισαίων αἱρέσει κατακολουθῶν in *Life* 12b is that Josephus chose to become a Pharisee, that he: "became a convinced Pharisee according to his own mind";[38] "attached himself to the Pharisees";[39] "chose to follow the Pharisaic rules";[40] "was a Pharisee, who had joined the group after sampling what all the current sects had to offer";[41] "began to follow the legal system of the Pharisees";[42] "chose Pharisaism";[43] "began to adhere to the Pharisaic sect".[44] All of these paraphrases probably, and most of them demonstrably, are influenced by Thackeray's translation for the Loeb series.

That translation is, however, implausible. The logic of the paragraph (§§ 10-12) militates against it. Moreover, to judge by normal Greek usage, by Josephus's usual practice, and by the context of § 12b, the main clause (ἠρξάμην πολιτεύεσθαι) refers to Josephus's entry into public life. Interpreters who are not influenced by the Loeb translation seem to agree (independently) that πολιτεύεσθαι here does not mean "behave" but rather "engage in public affairs".

In spite of this significant difference in the interpretation of πολιτεύεσθαι, everyone is agreed that *Life* 12 expresses Josephus's claim to have become a Pharisee. This conclusion has often provided the point of departure for modern scholarship on Josephus, whether source-critical, theological, sociological, or biographical. The few interpreters of Josephus who do not depend much on his "claim" to Pharisaic allegiance still believe that he made the claim; their problem is to reconcile that claim with the results of their own analyses, which do not find clear Pharisaic traits in Josephus.[45]

What is the basis of this enormous weight of scholarship? Everything depends on the four-word dependent clause in *Life* 12b: τῇ Φαρισαίων

---

[38] Montgomery, "Religion", 281.
[39] Shutt, *Studies*, 2.
[40] Neusner, "Josephus's Pharisees", 226.
[41] Attridge, *Interpretation*, 6.
[42] Rivkin, *Revolution*, 66.
[43] Cohen, *Josephus*, 106.
[44] Rajak, *Josephus*, 32.
[45] Cf. M. Hengel, *Judentum und Hellenismus*, I, 315; idem, *Zeloten*, 6 nn. 2-3, 378 n. 3; H. Lindner, *Geschichtsauffassung*, 146 n. 2; Attridge, *Interpretation*, 6, 178-180.

αἱρέσει κατακολουθῶν. But Josephus knows how to say in clear terms that he became someone's disciple, as he does with respect to Bannus: ζηλωτὴς ἐγενόμην αὐτοῦ (§ 11). If he is now saying in § 12b that he underwent a second conversion, to Pharisaism, then he has chosen an excruciatingly circuitous way of saying it.

I have argued that Josephus's "following of the Pharisaic school" was merely a necessary function of his entry into public life. It was not a deliberate choice of religious affiliation or a conversion. *Life* 12 cannot, therefore, support the weight that is customarily placed upon it. It cannot justify the attribution of anti-Pharisaic passages in Josephus to some other source, on the ground that the Pharisee Josephus could not have written them (G. Hölscher, G. F. Moore, D. R. Schwartz).[46] And it certainly cannot serve as the cornerstone of an alleged pro-Pharisaic apologetic in *Ant.-Life* (H. Rasp, M. Smith, J. Neusner, S. J. D. Cohen et al.).[47] Such an apologetic does not exist in *Ant.* If it did, *Life* 12 would not help it at all.

---

[46] *Contra* Hölscher, "Josephus", 1936 and n. + + thereto, 1957, 1991; G. F. Moore, *Judaism*, I, 64 n. 4, 65 n. 3, 66 n. 1; and now D. R. Schwartz, "Josephus and Nicolaus", 158.

[47] Cf. chapters 2 and 14, above.

CHAPTER SIXTEEN

LIFE 189-198: JOSEPHUS, SIMON, AND THE DELEGATION

Life 189-198 is significant for this study because it is the only passage in which Josephus recounts in any detail his personal dealings with specific Pharisees.[1] Furthermore, it cannot be attributed to non-Josephan sources. Here more than anywhere, then, one expects our author's real attitude toward the Pharisees to come forward. In particular: if Josephus intended *Life* 12b to be a forthright declaration of his Pharisaic allegiance, as is generally believed, we should expect *Life* 189-198 to substantiate that declaration in some way. The following analysis will reveal, however, that in this passage both the renowned Pharisee Simon ben Gamaliel and the mostly-Pharisaic delegation that is sent to replace Josephus receive distinctly hostile coverage.

Since the source question is irrelevant here and since the passage before us offers little new information about Pharisaic belief or practice, the major question for our analysis will be that of Josephus's attitude toward, and relationship to, the Pharisees. We must ask why he mentions these Pharisees when he does and what function they serve in his narrative.

I. *Context*

When Justus of Tiberias wrote his damaging account of the Jewish war, he evidently raised one matter that caused Josephus particular discomfort. That was the fact that the Jerusalem council, which included such notables as the high priest and the Pharisee Simon ben Gamaliel, had sought to relieve Josephus of his command in the Galilee. That Justus did raise the subject is clear from *Life* 336: Josephus has just given his version of these events (§§ 189-335) and now turns to address Justus, who, he says, "has produced his own account of those affairs" (τὴν περὶ τούτων πραγματείαν).[2]

---

[1] *Life* 21 mentions Josephus's meeting (again, πάλιν) with "the chief priests and leading Pharisees" (τοῖς ἀρχιερεῦσιν καὶ τοῖς πρώτοις τῶν Φαρισαίων). He implies that he was an associate of this group (cf. ἡμεῖς, § 22) and states that he and they opposed the revolt (§§ 22f.). He does not, however, mention any dealings with individual Pharisees.

[2] Cf. Cohen, *Josephus*, 125: "The delegation episode (V 190-335) in particular is replete with these themes [i.e., the kinds of issues brought up in the digression] and apparently is directed against Justus." Rajak, in proposing that only the digression itself responds directly to Justus (*Josephus*, 152-154), seems to overlook the force of *Life* 336.

The embarrassment that Justus's account caused Josephus can be measured by a comparison of *Life* with *War*. In *War* 2:626-631, Josephus had given his own brief story of the attempt to replace him as commander of the Galilee. There, he glided over the whole affair as just another of John of Gischala's nasty plots,[3] a plot that Josephus overcame by virtue of his popular support. In *War*, he did not name any of the authorities that were behind the move to oust him but referred vaguely to "the powerful and certain of the leaders" (οἱ δυνατοί . . . καὶ τῶν ἀρχόντων τινές), who had acted out of envy (κατὰ φθόνον) (2:627).

It seems clear that Justus, in his account, challenged Josephus's story by revealing the identity of these δυνατοί and ἄρχοντες, whom Josephus had so blithely dismissed. They were none other than the eminent scholar and public figure Simon ben Gamaliel and the chief priests Ananus and Jesus. Justus, it seems, would not allow Josephus simply to write off all of his opponents as "brigands" and "rebels". Whatever Justus wrote about the delegation episode must have affected Josephus considerably, for he now devotes more than one third of the main body of *Life* (§§ 189-335) to his own version of the story. To his credit, perhaps, he does not depart substantially from his earlier claims that the leaders acted from envy when they moved to replace him and that popular support was always on his side; nevertheless, he must now argue those points while at the same time conceding the stature of the leaders involved, which had been brought to light by Justus. Thus a major concern of the *Life* is to explain how it came about that the respected heads of the nation were calling for Josephus's dismissal.[4]

Despite its well-known literary shortcomings,[5] Josephus's *Life* reveals a good measure of forethought and structural arrangement. This becomes obvious, for example, in the opening words of our passage (§ 189): "Now the hatred that John, son of Levi, harboured against me because of my success (εὐπραγία) was growing steadily (προσηύξετο βαρέως)." These words evoke a theme that underlies the whole of *Life*, namely, the competition between Josephus and John of Gischala for the

---

[3] The unfavourable description of John begins at *War* 2:585.

[4] Rajak, *Josephus*, 150-154, accurately perceives the centrality of the delegation episode in *Life*. She argues from that premise that Josephus wrote the work primarily for the benefit of diaspora Jewry, for they would have been the ones most concerned about his relationship to the Jerusalem authorities. But one can imagine that Josephus would have been equally uncomfortable if his Roman readers came to think of him as a tyrant, who had acted *ultra vires* when he seized command of the Galilee. In *War*, Josephus had portrayed himself as the ideal general, sent to command the northern theatre (cf. Cohen, *Josephus*, 91ff.), and his status as a captured general doubtless helped him sell the book (cf. *War* 1:3). If he should now be exposed as a thug who had no official endorsement, his image would be severely tarnished.

[5] Cf. Thackeray, *Josephus*, 18; Cohen, *Josephus*, 110f.

allegiance of the Galilee. Josephus makes the delegation episode (§§ 189-335), which begins with our passage (§§ 189-198), the climactic phase of that struggle: the effort to have Josephus replaced was John's boldest move.

Josephus first introduced John in friendly terms: like Josephus, he had tried to restrain his compatriots from revolt against Rome (§§ 43f.).[6] When, however, his native town was attacked by neighbouring Greek cities, John abandoned that policy, armed his followers, defeated his enemies, and fortified Gischala (§ 44). When Josephus next encounters him, John has become "bent on revolution and eager for the command of the Galilee" (νεωτέρων ὀρεγόμενον πραγμάτων καὶ τῆς ἀρχῆς ἐπιθυμίαν ἔχοντα, §§ 70f.). Thus begins the theme of John's envy (φθόνος), which is woven into the narrative at strategic points (cf. §§ 70f., 84f., 122f.) so as to reach a climax with the delegation episode (§§ 189-198).

As Josephus's rival, John is everywhere concerned to persuade the Galilean cities to defect from Josephus to himself; he even tries to assassinate the Jerusalemite.[7] That he had some success in his efforts is conceded by Josephus. The latter tells us that, of the three major cities in Galilee, Gabara went over to John completely, Tiberias befriended him (but did not want to revolt), and Sepphoris rejected both suitors; in other words, it was a score of "two-nothing" for John (*Life* 123f.). Most significant is the notice that Justus of Tiberias, the author of the rival history that Josephus is here combatting, was one of John's early supporters (§§ 87f.). This datum indicates that when Justus told his account of the delegation episode, he was not giving an idiosyncratic critique of Josephus so much as he was presenting the perspective of a credible opposition party, headed by John of Gischala.

To summarize: early in Josephus's tenure as Galilean commander, the Jerusalem authorities sent a four-man delegation to replace him. When he wrote *War*, Josephus included a brief account of the episode, in order to illustrate both the strength of his own popular support and the thoroughly evil nature of his adversary, John of Gischala. Josephus easily triumphed over this knavish trick (2:626-631). Justus's account of the war, however, made a great deal more of this episode. Justus was a supporter of John and doubtless pointed out the nobler side of the man's character. He probably tried to show that John was basically a moderate, that Josephus himself had originally been friendly toward

---

[6] Cf. Luther, *Josephus und Justus*, 25f.: Josephus's opposition "ging von Johannes von Gischala aus, mit dem Josephus anfangs in gutem Einvernehmen stand". Contrast *War*, in which John appears from the first as an "intriguer . . . the most unscrupulous and crafty of all who have ever gained notoriety". (2:585, Thackeray).

[7] Cf. *Life* 82, 85ff., 122ff.

him,[8] and that John was even supported by the eminent scholar Simon ben Gamaliel in Jerusalem (perhaps also by the chief priests). That Justus argued these points is suggested by the fact that Josephus concedes them all in *Life*; the example of *War* shows that he would not voluntarily have credited his opponents in this way.

The situation facing Josephus when he writes *Life*, therefore, is a serious one. His articulate literary opponent of the 90's has demonstrated that his political opponent of the late 60's was no evil wretch but a credible public figure with major support in the Galilee and close ties to the Jerusalem authorities. In particular, John's move to have Josephus replaced could not be dismissed as an act of personal animosity but had to be seen as a determined effort by a united and powerful opposition.

The lengthy account in *Life* 189-335 is Josephus's response to this charge. Our passage, §§ 189-198, introduces the delegation episode and discusses the Pharisees' involvement in it.

II. *Interpretation*

To facilitate analysis of this lengthy passage, I shall consider it in four blocks, as follows: (a) introduction to the episode and to Simon (§§ 189-192); (b) Simon's initial bid to remove Josephus (§§ 193-195a); (c) his resort to bribery (§§ 195b-196a); and (d) the delegation and its mission (§§ 196b-198).

A. *Introduction of Simon ben Gamaliel (189-192)*

(189) Now the hatred that John, son of Levi, harboured against me because of my success was growing steadily. Determined by all means to have me removed, he fortified his native Gischala (190) and then dispatched his brother Simon, along with John, son of Sisenna, and about a hundred armed men, to Jerusalem.

He sent them to Simon, son of Gamaliel, urging him to persuade the Jerusalem assembly (τὸ κοινὸν τῶν Ἱεροσολυμιτῶν) to deprive me of the command of the Galilee (τὴν ἀρχὴν ἀφελόμενος ἐμὲ τῶν Γαλιλαίων) and to vote the office to John.

(191) This Simon was born in the city of Jerusalem; he came from a very prestigious family (γένους δὲ σφόδρα λαμπροῦ) and was from the school of

---

[8] So also Luther, *Josephus und Justus*, 75f. Luther doubts, however, that the basis of this friendship had been a mutual opposition to the revolt. He thinks rather that Josephus and John were both *rebels* originally and that Josephus invented the story in *Life* in order to explain the friendship, which Justus had pointed out.

the Pharisees, who are reputed to (or profess to) excel the others in their precision concerning the national laws (οἱ περὶ τὰ πάτρια νόμιμα δοκοῦσιν τῶν ἄλλων ἀκριβείᾳ διαφέρειν).

(192) Full of sagacity and reasoning power (πλήρης συνέσεως καὶ λογισμοῦ), this man had the ability, by his own practical wisdom, to set in order matters that were awry (πράγματα κακῶς κείμενα φρονήσει τῇ ἑαυτοῦ διορθώσασθαι). An old and close friend of John's, he was at odds with me at the time (φίλος τε παλαιὸς τῷ ᾽Ιωάννῳ καὶ συνήθης, πρὸς ἐμὲ δὲ τότε διαφόρως εἶχεν).

Most commentators on Josephus, although they read *Life* 12b as an avowal of Pharisaic allegiance, practically ignore *Life* 189-198 and whatever implications it might have for the interpretation of the earlier passage. Those who do bother to treat this story tend to focus exclusively on the above portrayal of Simon ben Gamaliel.

Neusner and Rivkin both consider our passage,[9] but both of them seem to overlook the issues of context, function, and meaning. Instead, they are concerned to find support for their respective theses about Josephus and the Pharisees.

Neusner, it will be recalled, sets out to fortify Smith's hypothesis that *Ant.-Life* commends the Pharisees to the Romans as the group most eligible to govern Palestine. Only this motive can explain Neusner's interpretive comments on *Life* 189-195, which may be quoted in full:

> The Pharisees invariably are represented as experts in the law. Of greater importance, some Pharisees come before us as important politicians, in charge of the conduct of the war, able to make or break commanders in the field. In Jerusalem they enjoyed the highest offices. Their leaders are men of great political experience and great power. So much for the Pharisees of Josephus's *Life*.[10]

These remarks are generalizations of the description of Simon in §§ 191-192. They take no account of the rest of the passage—for example, of Josephus's notice that he and Simon were at variance (§ 192). Nor does Neusner explain the context in any way. But Josephus, we have seen, is writing to defend his own cause; he is not writing to praise the Pharisees, who opposed him, or to present them as model governors.

Similarly, Rivkin ignores basic questions of context and meaning in his assessment of *Life* 189-198. He quotes the passage *en bloc* in order to support his thesis that Josephus presents the Pharisees as men of affairs,

---

[9] Neusner, ''Josephus's Pharisees'', 225; Rivkin, *Revolution*, 31f., 67.
[10] Neusner, ''Josephus's Pharisees'', 227.

who bring the "twofold Law" into every sphere of life. Following are representative excerpts from his interpretation:

> Josephus thus pictures Simon as anything but an academic recluse. We see no saintly figure here! Simon the son of Gamaliel is no quietest in Josephus' book. He had very definite ideas as to how the revolution should be conducted . . . . Simon does not cease being a Pharisee when he acts as a political leader; his vigorous actions are not out of keeping with his expertness in the laws.
>
> The Pharisees as activists emerge also in Josephus' mention of the composition of the delegation of which three Pharisees were members.[11]

Although one may deduce from *Life* 189-198 and from Josephus's writings in general that the Pharisees were involved in public life, that deduction has little to do with the specific literary intentions of our passage. Again: Josephus is writing to defend himself and to show that the fault in the delegation episode lay with his opponents, some of whom were Pharisees.

Only Cohen, it seems, has tried seriously to come to terms with the description of the Pharisees in the delegation episode.[12] He attempts to show that *Life* 189-198 does indeed reflect Josephus's new profession of Pharisaism (*Life* 12).[13] To achieve this result, Cohen focuses on the portrayal of Simon ben Gamaliel in §§ 191-192 and argues that the noted Pharisee is treated far better here than in the parallel in *War* (2:626-631). Specifically, Cohen contends: (a) that the portrayal of Simon in § 192 amounts to an encomium; (b) that the parallel in *War* had denigrated or belittled Simon by not mentioning him; and (c) that Josephus now wants to present himself to the (Jewish) reader as having "only temporarily (τότε, § 192)" been at odds with Simon. In all of this Cohen finds support for the Rasp/Smith/Neusner theory:

> Between BJ [*War*] and V [*Life*] Simon's stock rose spectacularly, as did the fortunes of the Pharisees. Their heirs were now established at Yavneh and Josephus wanted their friendship . . . .[14] The results of the new attitudes

---

[11] Rivkin, *Revolution*, 63f.

[12] Hölscher, 1936 n. + +, avers that Josephus's Pharisaic standpoint reveals itself in *Life* 191 but he does not explain this judgement. Rajak, *Josephus*, 150ff., gives what is perhaps the best assessment of the sense of the delegation episode and of its importance in *Life*. She does not, however, deal directly with our question, which is the significance of the Pharisaic involvement in the delegation.

[13] Cohen, *Josephus*, 144f.

[14] In his claim that *Life*'s pro-Pharisaic apologetic is directed toward Jews (the Yavnean rabbis), *Josephus*, 147, Cohen is closer to Rasp than to Smith/Neusner. But at pp. 237f., he also gives the Smith/Neusner line, that *Ant.* presents the Pharisees as deserving of *Roman* support; then he reiterates that *Life* is directed toward Jews. Evidently, Cohen wants to combine the theories that Josephus wrote *Ant.-Life* (a) to ingratiate himself with

are clear: glorious Simon was only temporarily (τότε, 192) ill-disposed towards Josephus. Therefore, Josephus' dispute with Simon and some Pharisees in 67 should not disqualify the historian in the eyes of the Pharisees of a later generation.[15]

The problem with Cohen's view is that, in this passage, Josephus does not appear to have the slightest concern about maintaining a good relationship with the Pharisees.

First, the description of Simon in *Life* 192 cannot be read as an unqualified encomium. It does acknowledge, and even praise, Simon's brilliance. Nevertheless, in the sequel Josephus immediately begins to accuse Simon of mean behaviour (φαύλων ἔργον, § 194), duplicity (§ 195), bribery (§ 196), and scheming (§§ 196-198). This hostile characterization is to be expected, since Simon was the major lobbyist in Jerusalem for Josephus's chief opponent.

The presentation of Simon's credentials in §§ 191-192, I have already argued, fits well with the perspective that Justus would have given in his account of the delegation episode; *he* was concerned to point out the eminent stature of Josephus's opponents. Since, then, §§ 191f. stands in tension with the remainder of the passage, it appears to be concessive in nuance; Josephus concedes, in response to Justus, that his opponent was gifted and well-respected (how could he deny it?)[16] but goes on nevertheless to insist that the two were at odds (πρὸς ἐμὲ. . . διαφόρως εἶχεν) and that Simon was to blame for this. Rajak seems closer to apprehending the sense of *Life* 192 when she observes:

> Simon ben Gamaliel, a man of great repute, was the main advocate of Josephus' dismissal: so well-known was Simon, that Josephus felt he had nothing to lose in acknowledging his opponent's distinguished descent and scholarly pre-eminence.[17]

We may add that the acknowledgement was probably forced on Josephus by Justus's account. In any case, it does not set the tone for the sequel: Josephus is concerned to exonerate himself, not Simon and the delegation. Since the whole passage is about his conflict with Simon, which resulted from Simon's underhandedness, § 192 can hardly be read as an encomium in its present context.

A major clue to the function of § 192 is its connection with the description of the Pharisees in § 191: Simon was a Pharisee and this school is

---

the newly powerful Pharisees (Rasp) and (b) to help the Romans decide who should be in power (Smith/ Neusner).

[15] Cohen, *Josephus*, 145.

[16] Simon was the son of the famous rabbi Gamaliel (cf. Acts 5:34) and father of the Yavnean Patriarch Gamaliel II.

[17] Rajak, *Josephus*, 150.

reputed to (δοχοῦσιν) interpret the laws with ἀχρίβεια. We have seen else-where (*War* 1:110-114; 2:162; *Ant.* 17:41-45) that Josephus's acknow-ledgement of the Pharisees' reputation for ἀχρίβεια implies no commitment on his part.[18] On the contrary, it consistently serves to in-troduce a negative portrayal of the group. That seems also to be the role played by *Life* 191. Certain Pharisees are about to be portrayed in quite negative terms, in spite of their reputation for ἀχρίβεια. Since the praise of Simon's intelligence in § 192 is tied to his other credentials, including Pharisaic membership (§ 191), the whole package seems to be a conces-sion, rather than Josephus's heartfelt expression of praise for Simon. The point of the passage is that, *in spite of* Simon's family background, social status, Pharisaic membership, and capability as a man of affairs, he was guilty of serious misdemeanours in his conflict with Josephus.

Especially problematic is Cohen's proposal that we compare the ac-count of the delegation episode in *War* with that in *Life*, in order to observe how dramatically ''Simon's stock rose'' between the two works.[19] He thinks it significant that the account in *War* does not men-tion Simon's name: ''The parallel passage in BJ 2:626 *did not consider Simon worthy of mention*''.[20] That *Life* not only mentions him but speaks well of his intelligence and wisdom, Cohen takes to be evidence of Josephus's newly acquired Pharisaic disposition.

The problem here is that the account of the delegation episode in *Life* (189-335) is roughly twenty times as long as the *War* parallel (2:626-631) and therefore contains a great deal of new information. *War* omits al-most everything that *Life* has, preferring to pass over the affair as one of John of Gischala's many evil plots. Josephus had good reason, as we have seen, to omit specific details about the identity and social status of his Jerusalem opponents. One cannot infer from the omission of Simon's name and personalia in *War* (N.B., the names of the high priests are also omitted) anything in particular about Josephus's attitude toward him. And the description of Simon in *Life* 189-198 does not, if read as a whole, constitute a rise in Simon's stock.

Finally, it is necessary to comment on Cohen's maximalist reading of τότε in *Life* 192. He takes the point of the passage to be that ''glorious Simon was only temporarily (τότε, 192) ill-disposed towards Josephus''.[21] This interpretation, in effect, makes τότε the key word of the passage, by supposing it to mean that, although Josephus had once

---

[18] As also with the δοχεῖ . . . ἀχριβῆς constructions of *Ag.Ap.* 1:18, 67.
[19] Cohen, *Josephus*, 145.
[20] Ibid., emphasis added.
[21] Ibid., 145.

been in conflict with Simon, he was later (by the time of writing) reconciled with the Pharisees.

The precise nuance of the particle τότε is, however, not so obvious. In my view, a more plausible sense would be that, as Josephus had once been sympathetic to the moderate aims of John of Gischala (*Life* 43f., 86), so also he had once been friendly with Simon. He tells how he conferred with the chief priests and leading Pharisees (οἱ πρῶτοι τῶν Φαρισαίων) about how to check the revolt (*Life* 21). This group doubtless included Simon, for we know that this leading Pharisee, along with the high priests, was vehemently opposed to the rebels (*War* 4:159). In their fundamental attitudes toward the revolt, apparently, Josephus and Simon were kindred spirits. Now in *Life* 192, the enmity between Josephus and Simon is clearly connected with the latter's close friendship with John:

φίλος τε παλαιὸς τῷ Ἰωάννῳ καὶ συνήθης,
πρὸς ἐμὲ δὲ τότε διαφόρως εἶχεν.

Being an old and intimate friend of John's, Simon was at that time (*ipso facto*) opposed to Josephus. This construction implies that Simon's opposition to Josephus was tied to his friendship with Josephus's opponent.

One might suppose, therefore, that Josephus, John, and Simon had all originally been associates, sharing a moderate, aristocratic outlook on the revolt.[22] At some point, however, John began to challenge Josephus for the command of the Galilee. Since John and Simon were old and close friends they pooled their efforts against Josephus. It was, therefore, only the struggle between Josephus and John that made Simon into Josephus's enemy; that development would seem to explain the τότε quite well.

However one interprets τότε, this particle can hardly serve as the basis of an entire interpretive scheme for *Life* 189-198. If Josephus had wanted to make it clear that he really was a devoted Pharisee, who had "only temporarily" been in conflict with Simon ben Gamaliel, it was not beyond his linguistic competence to do so. He would hardly have concealed this treasure in the particle τότε, hoping that his readers would interpret it as Cohen does. And he would hardly have gone on to portray Simon and the Pharisees, without apology or qualification, in the blackest possible terms.

---

[22] Cf. Rajak, *Josephus*, 22ff., 83ff., *106*, *128*ff., and *148*f., on Josephus's social position and its implications for his view of the revolt.

B. *Simon's Initial Bid to Remove Josephus (193-195a)*

We come now to Josephus's description of the actions of the great Pharisee Simon ben Gamaliel. That description, though it constitutes the heart and *raison d'être* of our pericope, is almost completely ignored by all commentators who read the passage as pro-Pharisaic.

(193) On receiving John's submission, Simon set out to persuade the high priests Ananus and Jesus, son of Gamalas, and some of their group, to put an end (ἐκκόπτειν) to my progress and not to allow me to reach the height of fame; he claimed that it would serve their interests if I were removed from the Galilee. He encouraged Ananus's party not to delay, in case I should find out [about the plan] prematurely and march on the city with a large force. (194) This was Simon's counsel, but the high priest Ananus pointed out that the task would not be so easy (ὁ μὲν Σίμων ταῦτα συνεβούλεθεν, ὁ δὲ ἀρχιερεὺς "Ανανος οὐ ῥᾴδιον. . .). Many of the chief priests and leaders of the people (πολλοὺς τῶν ἀρχιερέων καὶ τοῦ πλήθους προεστώτας) could testify that I was exercising my command well; and to accuse a man against whom no just charge could be brought (καθ᾽ οὗ μηδὲν λέγειν δύνανται δίκαιον) was a deed for uncouth men (φαύλων ἔργον). When Simon heard these things from Ananus, he requested them [the embassy from John] to keep quiet (σιωπᾶν) and not to make public what had been said (μηδ᾽ εἰς πολλοὺς ἐκφέρειν τοὺς λόγους αὐτῶν); he promised to arrange it himself (προνοήσεσθαι γὰρ αὐτὸς ἔφασκεν) that I should be quickly replaced in the Galilee.

The passage would seem to require little interpretation. In the fundamental conflict between Josephus and John of Gischala, the great Pharisee Simon sided with the latter and tried to use his influence to have Josephus removed.

Josephus's assessment of Simon's influence-peddling is clear, though he wisely leaves it to the high priest to cast doubt on Simon's uprightness. First, Ananus alleges, any move against Josephus would fly in the face of his broad popular support: many of those who are in a position to know would declare that he governs well. More seriously, the action that Simon advocates would amount to a subversion of "due process". Josephus would be removed merely out of self-interest (συνοίσειν αὐτοῖς, § 193) and not because of any just charge. Such actions, the high priest pointedly concludes, are abominable (φαύλων ἔργον).

Does Simon yield to this high-minded declaration of principle, or in any way redeem himself from the serious charges levelled by Ananus? On the contrary, his response betrays an utter disregard for justice and civility. He is determined to move ahead with his "dishonourable proceeding" (Thackeray's rendering) at any cost. Having failed to impose his will through the proper channels, he does not hesitate to transfer the whole affair into the realm of intrigue and skulduggery. Hence his admonition to John's embassy not to disclose what had taken place. Hence also his dark pledge to ensure that Josephus would be removed.

In this passage, then, Josephus evokes a clear division among the Jerusalem authorities on the matter of his leadership in the Galilee. On the side of Josephus stands the high priest, along with many of the chief priests and rulers of the people. These leaders support Josephus because he governs well (as he says); they are committed to ethical principle and civil behaviour. In the other camp stands the renowned Pharisee Simon, who has abandoned all concern for principle in this matter. Even when confronted by the high priest with the baseness of his actions, Simon shows neither remorse nor hesitation but rather plunges to new depths of treachery!

C. Simon's Resort to Bribery (195-196a)

Rebuffed by the high priest, but determined to carry his plans through, Simon ben Gamaliel decides on the following strategy:

(195b) Then he summoned John's brother and instructed him to send gifts to Ananus and his circle (προσέταξεν πέμπειν δωρεὰς τοῖς περὶ τὸν Ἄνανον), for, he said, this would likely persuade them to change their minds. (196) In the end, Simon accomplished what he had planned, for Ananus and those with him, being corrupted by material gain (χρήμασιν διαφθάρεντες), agreed to expel me from the Galilee. (This was unknown to anyone else in the city.)

Josephus advances here from mere insinuation of Simon's moral shortcomings to an outright attack on his character. The Pharisee, he alleges, had no qualms about manipulating the high priest by means of bribery![23] That Ananus should let himself be corrupted does not speak well of him either. At least, however, the high priest had a predisposition toward justice. Simon, who has consistently pursued a dishonourable course, is the villain of the piece.

---

[23] We have noted two other passages in which Josephus accuses the Pharisees of impropriety with respect to money. In *Ant.* 17:42-45 (cf. *War* 1:571) they are willing to invoke their prophetic gifts in gratitude for Pheroras's wife's payment of their fine. In *War* 1:111-114, they flaunt their power while living off the generosity of the ingenuous Alexandra.

Totally absent is any attempt on Josephus's part to mitigate the seriousness of Simon's actions, to portray him as deceived or unwitting. All we have is the stark allegation that a leading Pharisee, without just cause, undertook to remove Josephus from command of the Galilee and that he was willing to abandon all propriety in pursuit of this goal.

At this point it may be worth emphasizing that the above reading of Josephus's intention does not depend at all on the question of what actually happened. One might conjecture, for example, that the Jerusalem authorities were in fact unified in their opposition to Josephus and that Josephus invented the stories of Ananus's initial favour toward him and of the bribery scandal in order to explain away that opposition.[24] The present study, however, seeks primarily to uncover Josephus's tendencies in portraying the Pharisees. On that literary level, it is clear that Simon ben Gamaliel is painted in dark colours. He is an unprincipled, though influential, lobbyist for Josephus's major opponent.

D. *The Delegation and Its Mission (196b-198)*

Simon is not the only Pharisee who appears in our passage. As a result of his conniving, a four-member delegation is assembled and sent to replace Josephus. Three of its four members are also Pharisees:

(196b) It seemed best to them [the authorities] to send [into Galilee, as Josephus's replacements] men who differed with respect to social status but were alike in education (κατὰ γένος μὲν διαφέροντας, τῇ παιδείᾳ δ᾽ ὁμοίους).
(197) Two of those chosen, Jonathan and Ananias, were from the popular ranks and were Pharisees by affiliation (ἦσαν δ᾽ αὐτῶν οἱ μὲν δημοτικοὶ δύο, . . . Φαρισαῖοι τὴν αἵρεσιν); the third, Jozar, was of the priestly class and was also a Pharisee (ἱερατικοῦ γένους, Φαρισαῖος καὶ αὐτός); Simon, the youngest of them, was descended from the high priests (ἐξ ἀρχιερέων).
(198) These were instructed to go to the Galilean populace and to find out from them the cause of their devotion to me. If the people attributed it to my being from Jerusalem, the delegates should argue that so were all four of them; if it was because of my training in the laws (τὴν ἐμπειρίαν

---

[24] In support of this hypothetical reconstruction one might adduce (a) the vagueness of the bribery charge (the δωρεά and their reception are not described) and (b) Josephus's conspicuous insistence that the public remained totally unaware of Ananus's initial support for Josephus (§ 195a) and of the bribery episode (§ 196c: μηδενὸς ἄλλου τῶν κατὰ τὴν πόλιν τοῦτο γινώσκοντος). Claiming public ignorance, of course, frees him from the fear of contradiction.

τῶν νόμων), they should affirm that they themselves were not ignorant of the national customs (μηδ' αὐτοὺς ἀγνοεῖν ἔθη τὰ πάτρια φάσκειν); if, finally, they claimed to love me on account of the priesthood, the delegates should respond that two of them were also priests.

The reason, it now appears, that the conspirators chose four men κατὰ γένος μὲν διαφέροντας, τῇ παιδείᾳ δ' ὁμοίους was so that the delegation's combined assets could easily match whatever qualities Josephus had exploited in order to win the devotion of the Galileans, whether of παιδεία or of γένος (§ 198). Specifically: (a) the delegates were all Jerusalemites, as he was; (b) his training in the laws was matched by their knowledge; and (c) two of them even shared his priestly γένος. The strategy will have its desired effect in at least one case. Later in the narrative, Jesus, the chief magistrate of Tiberias, will appeal to his people (*Life* 278):

> It is better (ἄμεινον), O citizens, for us to submit to four men rather than one, men who are also of illustrious birth (καὶ κατὰ γένος λαμπροῖς) and intellectual distinction (καὶ κατὰ σύνεσιν οὐκ ἀδόξοις).

Significantly absent, however, from the list of assets common to both Josephus and the delegates is that of Pharisaic allegiance. We know that three of the four delegates were Pharisees and that Pharisees were known for their expertise in the laws. If, then, Josephus was also a Pharisee, the reader would have expected him to make this a point of comparison between himself and the delegates. If, that is, it turned out that the Galileans loved Josephus because of his Pharisaic learning, then the delegates could respond that three of them were also Pharisees. But Josephus never raises this as a possible point of comparison, even though he plainly states that three of the delegates were Pharisees and that their objective was to win over Galilean support by out-matching his assets. The simplest explanation of Josephus's failure to mention his Pharisaic allegiance when he had an obvious opportunity to do so is that he was not a Pharisee and could not, therefore, have compared himself with the Pharisaic delegates on this point.

Finally, it must be asked how Josephus viewed the members of the delegation, most of whom were Pharisees. That view is not hard to discern, for the envoys were his enemies, sent to retrieve him dead or alive from the Galilee (§ 202). He portrays them as cunning and deceitful (§§ 216ff., 237f., 274f., 281f., 290ff.), slanderous (§§ 245, 261), and violent (§§ 233, 301ff.). One of the Pharisaic envoys, Ananias, is called "depraved and mischievous" (Thackeray, for πονηρὸς ἀνὴρ καὶ κακοῦργος, § 290). The mostly Pharisaic delegation appears throughout in a negative light. Cohen aptly summarizes, "they swore false oaths, used sacred occasions for nefarious purposes, and violated the sanctity of the synagogue."[25]

Alone among commentators, Cohen attempts to explain how this hostile description of the delegates might be reconciled with Josephus's alleged profession of Pharisaism (in *Life* 12b). His effort: "The Pharisees who were sent to Galilee were not Pharisees of the best sort, *says Josephus.*"[26] But that is precisely what Josephus does not say. Cohen is to be commended for perceiving the tension between the unfriendly portrayal of the delegates in *Life* 198-307 and the conventional view that *Life* 12b presents Josephus as a Pharisee. His explanation, however—that Josephus regards these particular Pharisees as aberrant specimens—is totally without foundation. Josephus nowhere says anything of the kind: he makes no attempt to mitigate the scandal of the delegates' behaviour. He says only (and emphatically) that three of them *were* Pharisees.

Indeed, the actions of these Pharisees accord perfectly well with Josephus's other descriptions of Pharisaic behaviour: one need only recall the Pharisees who usurped Alexandra's power (*War* 1:110-114, *Ant.* 13:401-432), those who opposed the great John Hyrcanus (*Ant.* 13:288), those who manipulated Herod's court (*Ant.* 17:41-45), and, still fresh in the reader's mind, the unscrupulous Simon ben Gamaliel (*Life* 191-196). Cohen does not disclose the basis of his view that Josephus wished to portray the delegates as poor examples of Pharisaism. Our study points to the opposite conclusion: inasmuch as they seek to extend their own influence and achieve their partisan goals without regard for any sort of principle, the Pharisaic delegates in *Life* 198-307 are typical of Josephus's Pharisees.

Summary

Our exegesis of *Life* 10-12 found no support for the conventional view that Josephus desired to present himself as a Pharisee. One means of checking this conclusion, I proposed, was to examine Josephus's other references to Pharisees in *Life*, to see whether they reflected a new, pro-Pharisaic attitude on Josephus's part. The answer is that they do not. The eminent Pharisaic scholar Simon ben Gamaliel comes in for scathing treatment, even though Josephus first concedes the man's fame, intelligence, and good standing as a Pharisee. Our author likewise makes clear the unscrupulous character of the delegates sent to replace him,

---

[25] Cohen, *Josephus*, 238.
[26] Ibid., emphasis added.

most of whom were Pharisees. And when he enumerates the qualities that were common to himself and the delegates (§ 198), he mentions priesthood and education but not Pharisaic allegiance. In short, if one had only *Life* 189-335 to go on, one would have no grounds to suspect that Josephus was trying to pass himself off as a Pharisee. This circumstance offers still further support for the interpretation of *Life* 10-12 advanced above, to the effect that Josephus never claimed to be a Pharisee. It poses grave problems, however, for any view of *Life* 10-12 as a definitive statement of Josephus's Pharisaism.

CONCLUSION TO THE STUDY

The purpose of the foregoing study has been to develop a framework against which to interpret Josephus's testimony about the Pharisees. This was necessary because of the inadequacy of previously proposed frameworks, which did not attempt to ground themselves in the bedrock of our author's thought. The present attempt, by contrast, has employed "composition criticism", which has meant here the analysis of Josephus's remarks on the Pharisees in terms of his narrative aims and of his outlook in general. Following is a statement of our larger conclusions.

1. Josephus himself is responsible for all of the deliberate descriptions of the Pharisees that appear in his works. (a) Even in those passages that describe Pharisaic activities before his own lifetime Josephus usually includes general observations, in the present tense, on such matters as their concern for ἀκρίβεια, their philosophical beliefs, or their popularity. It is antecedently probable that such accounts were at least shaped by Josephus, since he knew the Pharisees first-hand. (b) The vocabulary in these descriptions, such as ἀκρίβεια, νόμοι/νόμιμα, εὐσέβεια, εἱμαρμένη, ὁμόνοια, φθόνος, ἀρετή, and πρόγνωσις, is characteristic of Josephus *and* is used in characteristic ways. (c) The parallels with his ordinary vocabulary extend to phrases and word associations like δοκέω/ἀκριβῆς/νόμοι/νόμιμα, εἱμαρμένη καὶ θεός, φθόνος/μῖσος/εὐπραγία/κινέω, and ἐπὶ τινι μέγα φρονοῦν. (d) The Pharisee passages thus support Schreckenberg's general conclusion about the *grundsätzliche Einheit* of Josephus's works:

> dass Sprach- und Denkmuster, Formeln und Strukturelemente aller Art, die zur unverwechselbaren Identität des Josephus gehören, verhältnismässig gleichmässig über das Gesamtwerk dieses Autors verteilt sind.[1]

Since the Pharisee passages share these marks of Josephus's identity, they cannot be detached from the rest of his narrative.

2. Josephus consistently represents the Pharisees as the dominant religious group among the Jews, who had the support of the masses. Their key role is evident at every point of Jewish history that Josephus deals with: under the Hasmoneans (*Ant.* 13:288-298; *War* 1:110-114/*Ant.* 13:400-432); under Herod (*War* 1:571/*Ant.* 17:41-45); at the incorpora-

---

[1] Schreckenberg, *Untersuchungen*, 174.

tion of Judea as a Roman province (*War* 2:162/*Ant.* 18:11-17); and at the outbreak of the revolt (*War* 2:411/*Life* 21, 191-198). It is unlikely that Josephus's assumption of Pharisaic predominance is his (post-70) invention because: (a) it is an *assumption*, which appears even in his incidental references to the Pharisees (*War* 1:571, 2:411; *Life* 21); (b) it is presupposed by stories about the Pharisees that must have had a traditional (non-Josephan) origin (e.g., *Ant.* 13:288-298, 400-432); (c) Josephus was only directly acquainted with the pre-70 state of affairs in Palestine; and (d) most important, Josephus's tendency is to *lament* the popularity and influence of the Pharisees. But this ongoing lament over Pharisaic predominance would be unnecessary—indeed it would make no sense— if the Pharisees did not hold a dominant position in pre-70 Palestine. Josephus had no discernible reason to invent their popularity, since he regarded it as an unpleasant fact of life.

3. As the source critics well realized, Josephus displays a marked and consistent antipathy toward the Pharisees. This appears in his first reference to the group (*War* 1:110-114) and continues through *Ant.* (13:288-298, 400-432; 17:41-45; 18:15, 17) and the *Life* (191-307). Although he changes his attitude toward many parties in the course of his literary career (e.g. Herod, Alexandra Salome, Hyrcanus and Aristobulus), he consistently denigrates the Pharisees.

4. The focal point of Josephus's dislike of the Pharisees is their reputation for and profession of ἀκρίβεια in the laws. He thinks that this reputation is contradicted by the Pharisees' actions (*War* 1:110-114; 2:162-166; *Ant.* 17:41-45; *Life* 191-198), so he laments their consequent popularity (*War* 2:162f.; *Ant.* 13:288, 400-432; 18:15, 17). Josephus consistently presents the Essenes as the most pious and virtuous of the schools (*War* 2:119-161; *Ant.* 15:371-379; 18:20) and therefore as deserving of praise. He even regrets that the Sadducees, whom he otherwise dislikes, must yield to "what the Pharisee says" (*Ant.* 18:17). As a priest, an accredited guardian of ἀκρίβεια and εὐσέβεια, he considers himself authorized to assess the claims of others. The Pharisees' actions, he implies, refute any claim to, or reputation for, piety.

5. Two of the reasons for Josephus's antipathy seem to be (a) that several Pharisees, including Simon ben Gamaliel, were involved in the attempt to remove him from his post in the Galilee (*Life* 191-198) and (b) that, in his view, the Pharisees played a major and destructive role in the history of the Hasmonean house (*War* 1:110-114; *Ant.* 13:288-298, 400-432), to which he traces his own priestly, royal, and prophetic heritage (*Life* 1-6). These unprincipled power-mongers tried to destroy his own career even as they had long before used their influence to attack his hero, John Hyrcanus.

6. Josephus was not, and never claimed to be, a Pharisee. He was an aristocratic priest, descended from the Hasmoneans, and he was also fascinated by hemerobaptist religion (cf. Bannus and the Essenes). He always resented the Pharisees' hold on the masses but, like the Sadducees, he accepted this influence as a fact of life. Thus he acknowledges that when he ended his blissful years of wilderness retreat with Bannus and returned to the city, he began to involve himself in public life, which meant "following the school of the Pharisees".

7. Josephus is mildest in his deprecation of the Pharisees in the "school passages" (*War* 2:119-166; *Ant.* 13:171-173; 18:11-23), where he introduces all three of the Jewish αἱρέσεις to his Hellenistic readership. Even here one can detect anti-Pharisaic undertones in Josephus's choice of words (cf. δοκέω, τυγχάνω) and in his insistence on the outstanding virtues of the Essenes; but in *Ant.* 13:171-173, at least, he achieves complete neutrality. We may, however, note several features of the school passages.

(a) They are concerned only with the philosophical beliefs of schools, not with their actions. But Josephus agrees with the Pharisaic (and Essene) *beliefs* in fate and immortality. Indeed, he seems closer to the Pharisaic view on both issues. But the Pharisees only represented the popular middle ground on these questions, which Josephus evidently shared.

(b) In the school passages *all three* schools are portrayed positively. Josephus's purpose is to map out the range of philosophical speculation among the accredited schools of Judaism; in two of the school passages, he also wants to contrast the legitimate representatives of Jewish philosophy with the novel (and false) idea of unconditional freedom espoused by Judas of Galilee. This is clearly not the place for him to vent his personal animosities toward any of the groups, and one must look for subtleties in this regard. Whenever one of the three schools comes out more favourably than the others, however, it is always that of the Essenes (*War* 2:119-161; *Ant.* 18:18-23).

(c) Most important, the school passages are part of Josephus's "ideal" portrait of Judaism. His apologetic includes the claim that the Jews received a comprehensive code of noble laws from Moses and that they have preserved and observed this code exactly ever since. He presents Judaism as a superior philosophy. Alongside this recurring theme in *Ant.*, however, he must also explain to Gentile readers how Judaism fell from its tremendous origins to become the defeated nation that it was at the end of the first century. In this story, he claims, the Pharisees have played a major role.

The difference of emphasis between the Pharisee passages, in which the group is openly vilified, and the school passages, in which Josephus discusses all three schools without obvious denigration, is traceable to this fundamental difference of purpose. On the one hand, the Pharisees can be cited as one of the Jewish groups who "philosophize" about such issues as immortality and fate. On the other hand, however, Josephus casts them as a constantly destructive force in the saga of Jewish history. Out of envy, they consistently opposed their rulers; they contributed much to the downfall of the Hasmoneans; they plotted against Herod; and, not least, they sought to oust Josephus from his command.

Both sorts of passages reflect Josephus's characteristic vocabulary and themes and they overlap in content; so there is no question of different sources accounting for the difference of emphasis. It is simply a matter of context.

8. It should perhaps be stressed, in view of the history of scholarship on early Judaism, that Josephus's antipathy toward the Pharisees had only personal causes, as far as we know. He never attacks Pharisaic piety *per se*, as a system, and indeed he shares the Pharisees' goal of ἀκρίβεια in the handling of the Mosaic Law. It would be quite illegitimate, therefore, to use the results of this study as supplementary evidence (along with, say, the Gospels and Paul) for the "defects" of Pharisaic religion. The crucial point here is that Josephus's perspective was that of a tiny minority in first-century Palestine: he was an avowed elitist. But we have seen ample evidence in his writings that the Pharisees enjoyed the steady and eager support of the ordinary people. Our author disdained both the Pharisees and the masses.

If these conclusions are valid, the present study has provided a basis for interpreting Josephus's testimony about the Pharisees. And since Josephus is probably our most valuable witness to the history of the Pharisees, an interpretation of his evidence and his biases is already a major preliminary step toward the recovery of that history.

APPENDIX A

THE HISTORIOGRAPHY OF *WAR* AND *ANTIQUITIES*: A DIALOGUE WITH H. W. ATTRIDGE

In our examination of the preface to *War*, we encountered H. W. Attridge's theory of a shift in historiographical principle between that work and *Ant*. Attridge builds on the well-known parallels between *War*'s preface and the principles of Polybius, on the one hand, and between *Ant*. and Dionysius of Halicarnassus, on the other, to propose: (a) that *War* 1:13-16 and *Ant*. 1:5-6 constitute different "programmatic statements" of historiographical principle for the works in which they appear; (b) that, therefore, Josephus changed his historiographical principles between writing *War* and writing *Ant*.; and (c) that this shift in theoretical perspective, from "critical" to "rhetorical" historiography, may well account for the choice of subject matter in *Ant*. Once exposed to rhetorical historiography, the argument goes, Josephus saw its potential for an apologetic history of Judaism and this led him to abandon his earlier principles, enunciated in *War*, which had excluded ancient history as an object of study.[1]

It is a question, however, whether Josephus really intended *War* 1:13-16 as a statement of the "critical" historiographical principles to which he was committed, which principles excluded ancient Jewish history as a proper field for investigation. Two considerations make that possibility unlikely.

1. First, by the time of Josephus, virtually *all* historiography was "rhetorical" historiography.[2] For the conflict that we see between Polybius and the rhetorical historians in the mid-second century BC was won by the rhetoricians—probably even before Polybius wrote, since his own work is not innocent of rhetorical influence.[3] It soon developed that every rhetorician felt free to engage in historical writing and everyone

---

[1] Attridge, *Interpretation*, 43f., 51ff., 56.

[2] Cf. Norden, *Kunstprosa*, I, 81ff.; Lieberich, *Proömien*, 5, 17, 20; Halbfas, *Theorie*, 7-10 *et passim*; Avenarius, *Lukians Schrift*, 81-84, 167; G. Giovannini, "Connection", 308-314; M. I. Finley, *Use and Abuse*, 12.

[3] Cf. Lieberich, *Proömien*, 20; Avenarius, *Lukians Schrift*, 20-25; and Siegfried, *Polybius*, 28f. Finley, *Use and Abuse*, 33, remarks, "It is significant. . . how quickly historians abandoned the austerity of Thucydides for the emotional appeals of the poets, how history became 'tragic history', even in Polybius who denied it so vehemently". Cf. F.W. Walbank, *Polybius* (Berkeley CA: University of California, 1972), 34-40.

who aspired to write history studied rhetoric.[4] But this victory meant less a conscious abandonment of the critical principles enunciated by Thucydides and Polybius than a development of them along rhetorical lines. The result of this evolution was a historiographical "melting-pot" in which one could draw freely on *both* the Thucydidean emphases of accuracy and eyewitness evidence *and* the rhetorical concerns for style and vividness.[5] That some historians were more critical than others is undeniable, but the distinction was one of degree *within* the pervasive sphere of rhetorical historiography and not between different historiographical "schools".

One can see the melting-pot effect in many sources. Polybius, the exemplary critical historian, does not shrink from using a rhetorical question (1.1.5) or a detailed comparison in rhetorical style (1.4.7-9).[6] Even more striking are his emphasis on the moral-pedagogical value of history (1.35.1-3, 7-10; 2.61.2-6, 11-12; 10.21.3-4) and his admission of τέρψις (delight) as a secondary goal of history, alongside truthfulness (15.36.3; 38.1.2); both of these emphases reflect the rhetorical influence of Isocrates.[7] On the other side, Dionysius, though entirely devoted to rhetorical interests, frequently speaks of the (Thucydidean-Polybian) ἀλήθεια standard for history.[8] And Lucian's essay on writing history, which represents the common rhetorical historiography of the second century AD,[9] advocates both the principles of the master historians and those of the rhetoricians, innocently juxtaposed with no hint of tension.[10]

Nor is it possible, for the first century, to attribute the writing of contemporary political history to the critical historians and that of ancient history to the rhetoricians, as if the two fields were understood to be the provinces of different kinds of historians. It is true that Thucydides and Polybius had insisted on eyewitness evidence and had thus limited their fields of inquiry to recent events. It is also true that rhetorical theory could justify writing ancient history because it could recognize originality in structure and presentation as well as in content. But the

---

[4] Norden, *Kunstprosa*, I, 81ff. and Halbfas, *Theorie*, 7f.

[5] Avenarius, *Lukians Schrift*, 167.

[6] Pointed out by Lieberich, *Proömien*, 20.

[7] Cf. Siegfried, *Polybius*, 29, and Avenarius, *Lukians Schrift*, 20ff.

[8] Cf., e.g., *Rom. Ant.* 1.1.2, 5.1-4, 6.2, 3, 5; also Halbfas, *Theorie*, 32f.

[9] Cf. P. Collomp, "Technik", 278-293, and Avenarius, *Lukians Schrift*, 165ff.

[10] Especially striking is the tension between his invocation of Thucydides as a model historian (19, 39, 42), along with his call for first-hand knowledge and painstaking investigation (47), and his overriding emphasis on literary virtues, which implies that the historian's chief responsibility is to *shape* and *stylize* his received material (16, 50: οὐ τι εἴπωσι ζητητέον αὐτοῖς ἀλλ' ὅπως εἴπωσιν). This tension is pointed out already by Avenarius, *Lukians Schrift*, 168ff.

study of ancient times was an inevitable development even among the
most sober historians.

First, if Thucydides and Polybius had emphasized the usefulness of
history as "the sovereign corrective of human nature" (Polybius 1.1.1),
as a guide for present life, then it was not difficult for Diodorus to argue
that the broader the scope of the history and the greater the variety of
situations included, the *more* useful the narrative (Diodorus 1.3.1-2).
Since history was always written in the Hellenistic world in order to
benefit its readers,[11] this argument would have had a compelling logic.

Second, as Avenarius observes, the Thucydidean/Polybian standard
of eyewitness evidence could not be sustained in the Roman empire.[12]
Whereas the earlier historians had lived in times of great upheaval and
had ready subjects for contemporary history, under the *Pax Romana* the
chances of a rhetorically-trained Roman finding himself in the middle of
a significant war were rather slight. Hence the natural focus on ancient
times. This circumstance explains the zeal with which Josephus attacks
those who write ancient history: he is keenly aware of his own privileged
status as eyewitness to a major conflict.[13]

Nor can it be said that the shift to ancient history represented an utter
disregard for the truth/accuracy standard. Thucydides already recognized the impossibility of being personally present at every significant
event, even within a single war, and so confessed his reliance on other
eyewitnesses (1.22.2-3). Likewise, Polybius allowed that the challenge
was to find trustworthy witnesses on whom to depend (12.4c.4-5).
Although Thucydides and Polybius intended that the historian cross-
examine living witnesses, it was not much of a leap from their principles
to the proposition that the *written* records of others might also be used
by a discerning historian.

Such a shift was indeed made. Lucian (§ 16) proposes that a certain
ὑπόμνημα concerning the recent Parthian war, written by a witness
named Callimorphus, could be used to good effect by a competent
historian.[14] Josephus tells us that both his account of the Jewish war and
those of his Roman competitors utilized the ὑπομνήματα of Vespasian
and Titus (*Life* 342; *Ag.Ap.* 1:56). Thus, by the middle of the first century, even historians of contemporary events were willing to draw on the

---

[11] Cf. Finley, *Use and Abuse*, 31 (on Thucydides), and Momigliano, *Essays*, 168f. (on
Thucydides and Polybius). The idea that history teaches practical lessons was fundamental to ancient historiography was and not limited to a "rhetorical" school, as Attridge,
Interpretation, 51-53, seems to suggest.
[12] Avenarius, *Lukians Schrift*, 83f.
[13] Cf. Momigliano, *Essays*, 164.
[14] Momigliano, *Essays*, 93ff.

documents of eyewitnesses to enhance their own accounts, although they were themselves eyewitnesses to the situation as a whole. This practice, inasmuch as it helped to supplement the historian's own limited perceptions, aid his memory, and check his biases, did not conflict with the claim to ἀκρίβεια but supported it.

But if historians of contemporary events could use trustworthy accounts written by others to enrich their own narratives, then the writers of ancient history could not legitimately be faulted for using the accounts of others, as long as those sources too were trustworthy. Historians of antiquity were not insensitive to this proviso. Dionysius, for example, outlines his sources in the preface to his *Roman Antiquities*: he has received oral instruction, he says, from the most learned men (λογιοτάτων ἀνδρῶν) and has employed the accounts of the most respected authors (οἱ ἐπαινούμενοι, 1.7.3, cf. 7.71.1). Livy (whose critical faculty is likewise suspect)[15] makes at least token attempts to weigh sources according to their merits on various questions of antiquity. He declares that he is following a particular source because of its author's closeness to the events or likelihood of knowing the truth (6.12.2; 8.40.3-5; 21.38.2-5; 22.7.3-4). Likewise Diodorus claims that in writing his universal history he has acquired an accurate (ἀκρίβεια) knowledge of events by means of the ὑπομνήματα that have been carefully preserved in Rome (1.4.4). He has even travelled around much of the world, he claims, incurring much hardship and danger (κακοπαθείας καὶ κινδύνων—cf. Polybius!), in order to visit the places with which his narrative is concerned (1.3.4). Though Diodorus's claim is undoubtedly exaggerated, the point remains that the principle of ἀλήθεια and ἀκρίβεια in historical reporting was not consciously discarded by those who turned to ancient history.

We have no reason, then, to doubt Josephus's suggestion that many of his contemporaries were focusing their study on ancient history. What is doubtful is his claim (*War* 1:13-15) that in doing so they were abandoning a basic concern for historical accuracy. Livy, by contrast, offers a noble motive for the concern with ancient Roman history that had become widespread by his time (the turn of the era). Namely: newer historians believed that they could improve on either the accuracy or the "rude" style of the older accounts (1.pref.2). So the concern for ἀλήθεια/ἀκρίβεια in history, which was "made a law" by Thucydides, had long since become part of the rhetorical baggage of all history-writing, whether the history concerned ancient or recent events.

By the middle of the first century BC, at any rate, ancient events and contemporary events were simply two options within the melting-pot of

---

[15] One attempt to rehabilitate him, however, is I. Kajanto, *God and Fate in Livy* (1957).

rhetorical historiography; and to write of contemporary events may have called for the greater rhetorical skill. For Cicero's "friends" it is merely a matter of personal choice whether he should write about things ancient or contemporary; the decisive point in favour of contemporary events is that it will enable him "to glorify the deeds of his friend Gnaeus" and his consulship (*Laws* 1.3.8)! This claim shatters any automatic equation of contemporary history with critical history.

About the time of Josephus, Pliny the Younger is likewise in a quandary about whether to choose an ancient or modern subject for historical treatment. His statement of the dilemma also disallows any equation of "contemporary" with "critical". The advantage of an ancient subject, Pliny reflects, is that he can use other scholars' work as a basis for his own; but the collation of this material would be extremely difficult (*sed onerosa collatio*)! And the problem with writing on a modern topic is that he would be expected to hand out lavish praise to everyone concerned and censure to no one; so the chances of pleasing his readership would be slim. In both of these examples, the choice of an ancient or modern subject is purely a matter of taste. Neither is considered more inherently truthful. The ancient topics require more work, as Diodorus and Livy also claim (Diodorus 1.4.1; Livy 1.pref.4). The φιλόπονος, *contra* Josephus (*War* 1:15), is the writer of ancient history. Modern topics lend themselves more easily to flattery and encomium.

Interesting also is Arrian's principle (mid-second century AD) of source evaluation for his history of Alexander the Great (1.1-3). He gives greatest weight to two accounts written by eyewitnesses but *after* Alexander's death, since the later composition date would diminish the tendency to lie. Once again, it is contemporary history that appears as a breeding ground for inaccuracy. The tables have been turned on Polybius!

It is difficult, therefore, to imagine a change in Josephus's thinking from some sort of "critical" historiography in *War*, little touched by rhetoric and focusing on contemporary events, to a "rhetorical" historiography in *Ant*. Indeed, *War* itself is filled with rhetorical and even tragic elements.[16] We should rather conceive of ancient historiography as a rich world of ideas—grounded in Thucydides and Polybius, but

---

[16] The tragic element is unmistakable in the narratives concerning both Herod the Great and the city of Jerusalem. Rhetorical influence reveals itself in any number of ways, from the presence of novelistic elements (cf. Moehring, "Novelistic Elements") to the style of the work, with its thorough conformity to the atticizing propensities of the day; these include the strict avoidance of hiatus, in keeping with a law of style established by the rhetorician Isocrates; cf. W. Schmid, *Der Atticismus in seinen Hauptvertretern von Dionysius von Hallicarnassus bis auf den zweiten Philostratus* (Stuttgart: W. Kohlhammer, 1887-1897, I, pp. V-VI, and III, 291f; also Niese, *HZ*, 208.

developed under rhetorical influence—that would have been at the disposal of anyone with rhetorical training.[17] Lucian's treatise on history, according to the analysis of Avenarius, summarizes this world of ideas:

> In Wahrheit vereinigen sich hier Richtlinien mannigfachen Ursprungs zu einem nicht immer harmonischen Ganzen. Lukians Anleitung für den Historiker ist somit einem Sammelbecken vergleichbar, in dem verschiedene Prinzipien zusammenströmen, die aus einzelnen schon vorhandenen Ansätzen bei Herodot und der älteren Sophistik heraus im wesentlichen von Thukydides bis in die hellenistische Zeit hinein entwickelt und formuliert worden sind.[18]

It appears, then, that the Hellenistic historian had a wealth of themes, principles, and τόποι upon which he could draw, to serve his purposes for any given situation. This circumstance seems to rule out the possibility of a conversion on Josephus's part from a school of critical, contemporary history to a rhetorical historiography geared to ancient topics.

2. Whatever may have been Josephus's feelings about Greek history, the crucial point is that he never associates the study of ancient *Jewish* history with a loss of ἀκρίβεια. Attridge's theory requires that when Josephus wrote *War* he consciously excluded the ancient history of his people on the ground of historiographical principle. All of the programmatic statements concerning *War*, however, both in the work itself and in later reflections, militate against such a view.

(a) When Josephus explains his choice of a starting point for the narrative in *War* (1:17-18), he gives two reasons for declining to ἀρχαιολογεῖν, or recount the origins and ancient history of his people (which he nevertheless briefly summarizes). First, the inclusion of such material would be untimely (ἄκαιρον) or "out of place" (Thackeray) in the present project. Second, other Jews before him have recorded the earlier events with ἀκρίβεια and this information, he says, is even accessible in tolerably accurate (οὐ πολὺ τῆς ἀληθείας διήμαρτον) Greek versions. Thus a new attempt would be superfluous (περιττόν). This appeal to the adequacy of former accounts, though it resembles one of Polybius's arguments, is somewhat less than a wholehearted endorsement of the current Greek accounts of ancient Judaism. Neither of these statements implies

---

[17] Whether Josephus had already begun his strenuous programme of τῆς γραμματικῆς, τῶν Ἑλληνικῶν γραμμάτων καὶ ποιητικῶν (*Ant.* 20:263) before he wrote *War* is a moot point (see excursus to Part I). I have argued, however, in keeping with Rajak's position, that Josephus probably knew enough Greek to control the content of the work published under his name.

[18] Avenarius, *Lukians Schrift*, 169f.

an outright exclusion of Jewish antiquity as a subject for accurate history; both leave open (and the ἄκαιρον may even suggest) the possibility of a future treatment of the theme.

Indeed, in the context, Josephus is not attacking ancient history but is rather excusing himself from including a study of Jewish origins here. He is, however, willing to include events that occurred long before his own time. These events, which occupy almost a third of his book, begin more than 200 years before his birth, in the time of Antiochus Epiphanes. So he does not discount ancient history on grounds of principle.

(b) In his preface to Ant., Josephus plainly declares that he had thought of including the ancient history of the Jews in War but had decided against it (Ant. 1:6).[19] The material was so copious (μείζων), he explains, that its inclusion would have ruined the balance and symmetry of War (1:7).[20] This claim fits squarely with the ἄκαιρον notice of War 1:17. It also excludes the possibility that Josephus only conceived of writing ancient Jewish history after he had completed War.[21] His failure in Ant. to mention the adequacy of previous Greek accounts as he did in War 1:17 is easily explained: he is now presenting the definitive history of ancient Judaism in Greek with all the ἀκρίβεια that the tradition deserves. The other accounts, whose adequacy was sufficient to excuse him from ancient history when he wrote War, cannot compare to his own present effort.

(c) Finally, the Polybian concern for first-hand knowledge that Josephus echoes in War 1:13-16 is not confined to that work but turns up again in his last extant treatise, Ag.Ap. (1:53-56). There, however, he explicitly rejects any conflict between the principle of first-hand evidence and his investigation of ancient Jewish history. He writes:

> It is the duty of one who promises to present his readers with actual facts first to obtain an exact (ἀκριβῶς) knowledge of them himself, either through having been close to the events (παρηκολουθηκότα τοῖς γεγονόσιν), or by inquiry from those who knew them (παρὰ τῶν εἰδότων πυνθανόμενον).

---

[19] Thackeray, Josephus.

[20] On the importance of τὸ σύμμετρον in hellenistic historiography, cf. Avenarius, Lukians Schrift, 105ff.

[21] Cf. also Ant. 20:259: παύσεται δ' ἐνταῦθά μοι τὰ τῆς ἀρχαιολογίας μεθ' ἣν καὶ τὸν πόλεμον ἠρξάμην γράφειν. W. Weber, Josephus und Vespasian, 2, takes this to mean that Josephus actually began writing Ant. before he wrote War. More commonly, the sentence is taken to mean either that Josephus intended a re-edition of War in AD 93-94 (Laqueur, Historiker, 1ff., 79, 263) or simply as a garbled way of saying that War covers events subsequent to those treated in Ant. (so Feldman, LCL edn., X, 137 n. d.). Weber's interpretation is, however, the most faithful to Josephus's actual words, "after which [sc. Ant.] I began to write the War".

Notice especially the following line: "That duty I consider myself to have amply fulfilled (μάλιστα. . . πεποιηκέναι) in both my works (περὶ ἀμφοτέρας. . . πραγματείας)." He has fulfilled the obligation of first-hand knowledge for *War* by being an eyewitness (αὐτόπτης) of the events, for *Ant.* by his privileged access, as a priest, to the ancient traditions that have been preserved with ἀκρίβεια (*Ag.Ap.* 1:54; cf. 1:29, 32, 36).

Whatever, then, Josephus may have said about the ineptitude of Hellenes in writing accurate history (his remarks in *War* on this point are forcefully elaborated in *Ag.Ap.* 1:6-27), he never suggests for a moment that the treatment of ancient *Jewish* history, at least by a priest such as himself, is susceptible of the same error. For the most ancient records of the Jews have been preserved, by the chief priests and prophets, with scrupulous accuracy (μετὰ πολλῆς ἀκριβείας, *Ag.Ap.* 1:29). Josephus esteems his priestly heritage precisely as a guarantor of accurate insight into the traditions; that claim is not new with *Ant.* but is already found in *War* (1:3; 3:352).

In response to Attridge, we have observed that, in spite of all the differences in subject matter, genre, style, and even opinion, between Josephus's different works, his theoretical approach to history remains quite constant. His stated goals are always ἀλήθεια and ἀκρίβεια and he believes that all of his subject matter, whether ancient or contemporary, lends itself to these goals. This constancy of historical conception throughout works of different character was made possible by the historiographical environment of the day, which was a melting pot of ideas and aspirations that had originated with Thucydides but had also been processed by rhetorical theory.

SCHOLARLY INTERPRETATIONS OF JOSEPHUS ON
FATE AND FREE WILL

At several points in the foregoing study (chapters 6, 8, and 12) we have encountered Josephus's claim that fate and free will were major topics of discussion among the Jewish schools. Because our goal has been to interpret Josephus's Pharisee passages discretely and in context, we have only been able to consider the substantial scholarly discussion of this issue in piecemeal fashion, as it relates to a given pericope. Since most of the studies treat all of the relevant passages together, our procedure has resulted in a fragmented presentation of each scholar's argument. The following pages attempt to give some perspective to those fragmentary notices by surveying the development of the scholarly debate on fate and free will in Josephus.

G. F. Moore's 1929 article, "Fate and Free Will in the Jewish Philosophies according to Josephus", has been seminal for all further discussions of the issue.[1] Moore argues that, since the three "school" passages present the Pharisees' view of fate and free will in Stoic (and not biblical or Jewish) terms, these passages must have originated with someone other than Josephus.

The cornerstone of this thesis is *Ant.* 13:171-173, which ranges the schools on a spectrum: the Essenes make εἱμαρμένη the κυρία of all things; the Sadducees do away with (ἀναιροῦσιν) εἱμαρμένην; and the Pharisees take a middle position, attributing some things, but not all (τινὰ καὶ οὐ πάντα), to fate. Moore offers several reasons for his suspicion that Josephus did not write this passage: (1) it seems to be irrelevant to its immediate context;[2] (2) its attribution of "fatalism" to the Essenes is elsewhere unsupported;[3] and (3) it does not prepare the reader well for 13:288-298, because there the issue on which Pharisees and Sadducees differ is not fate and free will but the authoritative νόμιμα.[4]

Moore also detects an inconsistency between Josephus's normal use of εἱμαρμένη and that revealed in the school passages.[5] Whereas the other occurrences of this term bear the tolerably Jewish sense of "divine fore-

---

[1] *HTR* 22 (1929), 371-372.
[2] Ibid., 371f., 384.
[3] Ibid., 372.
[4] Ibid.
[5] Ibid., 375f.

knowledge'',[6] Moore finds in the school passages an intended "philosophical definition".[7] That εἱμαρμένη appears as a philosophical term in the school passages, he argues, is clear from the context: the groups are called αἱρέσεις or φιλοσοφίαι and are concerned with an issue that had become important in Hellenistic philosophy by the first century.[8] Indeed, Moore can even point out three close verbal parallels between the Pharisaic doctrine as presented by Josephus and the teaching of Chrysippus the Stoic as reported by Cicero.[9]

Having identified this stoicizing tendency in Josephus's presentation of the Pharisees, Moore attempts to show that it was at complete variance with biblical-Jewish teaching, which always emphasized the sovereignty of God, the efficacy of repentance, and man's religious/moral responsibility.[10] Assuming that Josephus the Jew could not have erred so fundamentally, Moore offers two "guesses" as to the origin of the descriptions.[11] One possibility is that Josephus's literary assistants composed the accounts on the basis of their interpretations of what Josephus had explained to them "in his way" about Pharisaic and Sadducean distinctives.[12] Moore prefers, however, another "guess", namely, that a "foreign source" is responsible for the misleading information. He believes that Nicolaus of Damascus wrote *Ant.* 13:171-173, except for the reference back to *War* 2, and that Josephus carried over this material from Nicolaus into *War* 2:162 and *Ant.* 18:13, supplementing it with other information about the Pharisees.[13]

Just three years after the appearance of Moore's article, A. Schlatter's *Die Theologie des Judentums nach dem Bericht des Josephus* appeared.[14] Although Schlatter devotes little more than a page to our problem,[15] his presentation is useful as a contrast to Moore's. Noting that Josephus portrays distinctive Pharisaic teaching as a combination of belief in divine providence and the human power of volition, Schlatter marvels at the strength of the Greek influence in Jerusalem, which was such that Josephus could describe providence as *Schicksal*. But Schlatter does not doubt Josephus's word; he takes it to be obvious that the Pharisees in-

---

[6] Ibid. He cites *War* 4:622 and 6:250 as examples.
[7] Ibid., 376.
[8] Ibid., 376-379.
[9] Ibid., 384; viz., βοηθεῖν (*War* 2:162)//adiuvo (Cicero, *On Fate* 41); ὁρμή (*Ant.* 18:13)// adpetitus (*On Fate* 40f.); and προσχωρεῖν (*Ant.* 18:13)//assensio (*On Fate* 40).
[10] Ibid., 379-382.
[11] He defines a "guess" here as something less than a hypothesis, ' Fate'', 383.
[12] Ibid., 383.
[13] Ibid., 383f.
[14] Gütersloh: C. Bertelsmann, 1932. Cf. pp. 209f.
[15] Ibid.

herited both ideas—the foreknowledge of God and human responsibility
—from the Bible and that Josephus merely expresses the *Synergismus* with
which all Pharisees lived.

The simple acceptance of Josephus's descriptions as informed discussions of first-century Judaism, albeit in Greek "dress", is quite common. Elbogen long ago (1904) interpreted these passages in a political
sense: the Sadducees are self-reliant state-builders; the Pharisees prefer
to rely on God.[16] A. E. Suffrin (1912), I. Broyde (1925), J. Z. Lauterbach (1929), E. E. Urbach (ET, 1975), and H.-F. Weiss all accept Josephus's statements about the Pharisees on fate and free will,[17] presenting
copious evidence that the two convictions were held together throughout
the tannaitic and amoraic periods.[18] Urbach thinks also that the Dead
Sea Scrolls support Josephus's depiction of the Essenes.[19] In order to accept Josephus's statements as actually referring to Palestinian Judaism,
however, all of these scholars interpret εἱμαρμένη as simply a hellenized
reference to God or providence.[20] Suffrin, for example, remarks:

> When, therefore, Josephus makes his countrymen state their theological
> differences in philosophical language and ascribes to the Pharisees a belief
> in a εἱμαρμένη ... he does not mean by it an inflexible power to which gods
> and men must bow, but has in his mind the late Hebrew word נזרה ...
> a decree of a judge or king, or Divine decision.[21]

We are faced, then, with two very different alternatives: either
Josephus has incorporated into his narratives some very misleading
statements about the religious groups, falsely portraying the Pharisees as
near-Stoics, or he is describing the groups accurately, but in language
that his Greek readers will understand. In 1969, two German studies appeared that added some sophistication to the discussion.

L. Wächter proposes that Josephus's depiction of the Sadducees as
those who do away with fate (*War* 2:164, *Ant.* 13:173) is actually a
serious attack upon them.[22] For, according to Josephus, they not only

---

[16] Elbogen, *Anschauungen*, 14f.

[17] A. E. Suffrin, *ERE*, V, 796; I. Broyde, *Jewish Encyclopedia*, V, 351; Lauterbach,
"Pharisees", *HUCA*, 129f.; Urbach, *Sages*, I, 255; and Weiss, "Pharisäismus",
427-429.

[18] Most commonly adduced are b. Ber. 33b. m. Avot 3:15 and b. Hullin 7b.

[19] Urbach, *Sages*, I, 268.

[20] Urbach, *Sages*, I, 268; Lauterbach, *HUCA*, 129f.; Broyde, "Fatalism", 351; cf. R.
Marcus in LCL edition of *Ant.* 13:171f., VII, p. 311 n. *g.*: "Fate is here, of course, the
Greek equivalent of what we should call Providence".

[21] Suffrin, "Fate (Jewish)", 793.

[22] "Die unterschiedliche Haltung der Pharisäer, Sadduzäer und Essener zur
Heimarmene nach dem Bericht des Josephus", *ZRGG* 21 (1969), 97-114, esp. 98-106.

reject εἱμαρμένη, but remove God beyond even the observation (τὸ ἐφορᾶν, *War* 2:164) of mankind.[23] This characterization, Wächter observes, brings the Sadducees very close to the position that Josephus elsewhere attributes to the Epicureans (*Ant.* 10:278):

> who exclude Providence from human life and refuse to believe that God governs its affairs or that the universe is directed by a blessed and immortal Being to the end that the whole of it may endure, but say that the world runs by its own movement (αὐτομάτως) without knowing a guide or another's care.

Wächter concludes that Josephus implies to his readers a comparison between Sadducees and Epicureans, just as he makes explicit comparisons between Pharisees and Stoics (*Life* 12) and between Essenes and Pythagoreans (*Ant.* 15:371): the Sadducees appear as unbelievers.[24] On the historical level, however, Wächter finds such a portrayal impossible, since the Sadducees must have believed in the active God of the Bible.[25]

Wächter's treatment of the Pharisees and εἱμαρμένη is brief because he finds it quite straightforward.[26] The synergism of fate and free will he considers, with Schlatter and the others mentioned above, to be well-grounded in Pharisaic and later rabbinic belief.[27] He explains Josephus's use of εἱμαρμένη as an attempt to convey to Hellenistic readers something of the import that attached to the Jewish conception of God—Yahweh. Because θεός failed to convey this conception adequately, Josephus supplemented it with εἱμαρμένη, which probably evoked among his readers something far closer to the Jewish view of "Yahweh".[28]

On the Essenes, Wächter tries to show by an examination of documents from Qumran[29] that Josephus is correct "*im Prinzip*" in attributing to this group a strong belief in predestination. He qualifies Josephus's account, however, by proposing that (i) this predestination only applied to the Essenes themselves, as the chosen, and (ii) it was not

---

[23] With Niese, Wächter rejects the variant κακόν, so that God is "beyond either the doing of anything or even the supervision [of the world; cf. the Hebrew פקד]". Thackeray and Michel-Bauernfeind both retain κακόν with the result that God is beyond "not merely the commission, but the very sight *of evil*". Wächter's reading, however, has the Sadducees removing God entirely from the world.

[24] Ibid., 104, 106. This conclusion was already reached by G. Hölscher, *Der Sadduzäismus* (Leipzig: J. C. Hinrichs, 1906), 2. Note that for the rabbis, אפיקורוס was a term of abuse.

[25] Wächter, "Haltung", 105f.

[26] Ibid., 107-108.

[27] Ibid., 108. He notes m. Avot 3:15: "Everything is foreseen (צפוי) but freedom is given."

[28] Ibid., 107.

[29] Ibid., 108-113. He focuses especially on IQS 3:13-4:26 and CDC 2:7-14.

a general, or primarily ethical predestination, but was tied to God's plan of salvation for the community.[30]

In his conclusion, Wächter seriously doubts that the issue of fate and free will was a matter of debate among the Jewish groups, since both ideas are well grounded in the Pentateuch; rather, the Pharisees and Sadducees disagreed over the question of authoritative tradition.[31] The fate/free will issue was, however, a matter of controversy among the Hellenistic philosophies, especially with the Stoics.[32] Knowing that the issue was also discussed among the Pharisees, and wanting to present the Jewish groups as φιλοσοφίαι, Josephus presented the Pharisees as exponents of the mediating position. In the Essenes he saw a group that could legitimately represent the fatalistic/predestinarian end of the spectrum. Since no Jewish group could in reality deny providence or divine activity in life, Josephus had no one to represent the left extreme of the spectrum. For the purpose of his schematization, therefore, he chose his enemies the Sadducees to play the role of infidels. Whatever natural emphasis they may have had on human responsibility, Wächter concludes, Josephus exaggerated into an outright rejection of divine activity.[33]

Wächter's analysis bolsters the scholarly tradition that accepts as accurate Josephus's characterization of the Pharisees with respect to fate and free will. He provides a clear rationale for Josephus's use of εἱμαρμένη instead of θεός as well as for the manner in which the Sadducees and Essenes are presented.

In 1969 G. Maier completed his Tübingen dissertation on *Mensch und freier Wille* in early Jewish literature.[34] He confronts the two-fold problem already tackled by Moore and Wächter, namely: How did Josephus come to use the Greek term εἱμαρμένη—a term lacking any obvious Hebrew equivalent—as the central theme in his descriptions of the Jewish schools? And: Was he justified in doing so? Moore had argued that the presentation was unjustifiable and therefore not attributable to Josephus. Wächter claimed that the portrait is partly accurate (re: the Pharisees and Essenes) and partly not (re: the Sadducees); nevertheless he attributed the whole to Josephus. Maier, however, attempts to show that Josephus's presentation of all three schools, if understood correctly, is quite accurate and therefore is intelligible as the work of Josephus.

---

[30] For an analysis of the Qumran scrolls that emphasizes the community's freedom of choice, cf. F. Nötscher, "Schicksalsglaube in Qumran und Umwelt", in his *Vom Alten bis Neuen Testament* (Bonn: Peter Hanstein, 1962), 33-49.

[31] Wächter, "Haltung", 113.

[32] Ibid., 114.

[33] Ibid., 106, 114.

[34] This is now published as *Mensch und freier Wille: nach den jüdischen Religionsparteien zwischen Ben Sira und Paulus* (Tübingen: J. C. B. Mohr—P. Siebeck, 1981).

More clearly than the other scholars considered, Maier distinguishes the literary question—what Josephus meant, from the historical—whether he was accurate. Since our concern is solely with the former, we may focus on Maier's first chapter, which contains his literary analysis.

Maier is the first to offer a direct response to Moore's theory that Nicolaus of Damascus penned *Ant.* 13:171-173 and all such traces of that passage as appear elsewhere. He notes first of all that Hölscher's thoroughgoing source criticism would not even allow such a conclusion, but rather attributed *Ant.* 13:171-173 and 18:11-25 to the Jewish priestly "falsifier" of Nicolaus and *War* 2:119-166 to a Greek-educated Jew.[35] Yet neither of these source-critical solutions is convincing, according to Maier: Moore's because its automatic attribution of Greek philosophical language to a non-Jewish author is simplistic; Hölscher's, because any evidence that would support a Greek-educated Jewish author for *War* 2:119-166 would *ipso facto* support Josephus's own authorship.[36]

The one exception is Hölscher's claim that what is said about the Essenes in *War* 2 differs markedly from what Josephus says about them elsewhere.[37] Against this claim, however, Maier points out: (1) that in *Ant.* 13:173 and 18:11 Josephus refers back to *War* 2:119-166 as his decisive treatment of the schools, which only makes sense if he views the earlier passage as a unity for which he is responsible; (ii) that the depiction of the Sadducees in *Ant.* 13:173 and the parallel in *War* 2:163-165 exhibit clear verbal similarities;[38] and (iii) that the description of the φιλοσοφίαι in *Ant.* 18:11-25 as a whole bears many striking similarities to *War* 2:119-166 as a whole, so that the later passage often seems to be an extract of the earlier.[39] With other critics, Maier takes the presentation of the Essenes in *Ant.* 18:18-22 to be a summary of certain points from *War* 2, now supplemented by information gleaned from Philo.[40]

What Maier has shown is that the school passages cannot be treated as aberrations from Josephus's own views. They all come from the same

---

[35] Maier, *freier Wille*, 4f. In fact, however, Hölscher attributes *War* 2:162-166 to Josephus himself; cf. his "Josephus", 1949 n. He argues for non-Josephan Jewish authorship of the Essene passage (§§ 119-161), on the ground that it reflects familiarity with Jewish conceptions (e.g., ἄγγελοι, 2:142; νομοθέτης, 155f.) and is unfriendly toward the Romans, §§ 152f.

[36] Maier, *freier Wille*, 7.

[37] Hölscher, "Josephus", 1949 n.

[38] Maier, *freier Wille*, 7.

[39] Ibid., 8. He lists numerous parallels of content, as well as several close verbal agreements.

[40] Ibid., 9. Philo's discussion is in *Every Good Man is Free*, 75-91. Cf. Feldman, LCL edition of Josephus, IX, 14f. n. *d.* and M. Smith, "The Description of the Essenes".

author and that author is evidently Josephus himself.[41] That is not to deny Josephus's use of sources or even literary assistants:

> Es bedeutet aber, dass die Verantwortung für die Redaktion der betref-fenden Abschnitte bei Josephus liegt, der nicht nur die Rolle eines unbedarften Kompilators spielt.[42]

Having demonstrated Josephus's final authorship of the school passages, Maier proceeds to examine them individually.

(i) *War* 2:119-166. Although he accepts the parallel between the Pharisaic position here and the teaching of Chrysippus, Maier argues that Josephus gives the discussion a Jewish character by setting the fate/ free will question in religious-ethical terms.[43] Thus, the issue is pre-sented as τὸ πράττειν τὰ δίκαια, behind which Maier sees the עשׂה צדקה of the OT and Qumran.[44] This "righteousness" is not that of the Greek virtues but is rather a response to divine law. Moreover, he proposes that the phrase εἱμαρμένη καὶ θεῷ reflects Josephus's attempt to qualify the conception of fate in terms of Jewish monotheism. Third, Maier points to the Sadducean emphasis on ἐκλογή (§ 165) as typically Jewish and not Stoic.[45] Finally, Maier sees in the Sadducees' utter rejection of fate (§ 164) but continued discussion of God (*loc. cit.*) a distinction be-tween the two entities, such that fate is subordinate to God.[46] The whole presentation of the schools, he judges, though it may have originated with Nicolaus, is Jewish in outlook.

Maier suggests that Josephus may deliberately have described the Pharisaic position—they attribute everything (πάντα) to fate, but τὸ πράττειν τὰ δίκαια καὶ μή rests mainly with mankind—such that it could be interpreted in two ways. On the one hand, it may represent the Pharisaic/rabbinic view that "Everything is in the hands of God except the fear of God" (b. Ber. 33a); on the other hand, the Hellenistic reader-ship may interpret it in Chrysippean terms, according to which *every* ac-tion has two causes.[47]

(ii) *Ant.* 13:171-173. Maier considers this passage less judaized than *War* 2:162-166, but nevertheless finds two places where Josephus has

---

[41] Cf. also Stählin's protest against attributing Josephus's "fate" language either to sources or to literary assistants, "Schicksal", 338f. He argues that Josephus must at least have assented to the material that stands in his work.

[42] Maier, *freier Wille*, 10.

[43] Ibid., 11f.

[44] E.g., IQS 1:5; 5:3g.; 8:2. I have responded to Maier's proposals in chapter 6, above.

[45] Maier's point here (12) is not clear, since it is not usually claimed that Josephus parallels the *Sadducees* to the Stoics.

[46] Ibid., 12f.

[47] Ibid., 13f.

significantly qualified his source. First, the phrase καὶ οὐ πάντα in § 172 (οἱ Φαρισαῖοι τινὰ καὶ οὐ πάντα τῆς εἱμαρμένης ἔργον εἶναι λέγουσι) Maier takes to be a judaizing qualification of what might otherwise sound quite Stoic.[48] Second, Maier proposes that the whole clause in § 173 concerning human responsibility and ἀβουλία as a cause of misfortune[49] has been introduced by Josephus, since it reflects biblical-Jewish ideas.[50]

(iii) *Ant.* 18:11-25. In the opening statement about the Essenes— Ἐσσηνοῖς δὲ ἐπὶ μὲν θεῷ καταλείπειν φιλεῖ τὰ πάντα ὁ λόγος—Maier also finds two clear Jewish emphases. First, perhaps under Philo's influence, Josephus speaks only of God, not of fate. Second, he has the Essenes attribute all things to God; this may be seen as a correction of Philo, who has the Essenes wanting to protect God from any connection with evil.[51] Maier concedes that the description of the Pharisees' view of εἱμαρμένη (18:13) is difficult textually and grammatically and that it seems to be more Stoic than Jewish; nevertheless he finds in the reference to God's pleasure (δοκῆσαν τῷ θεῷ) and in the ethical emphasis a Jewish and therefore Josephan influence.[52]

The result of these analyses for Maier is as follows. Εἱμαρμένη does not appear in the school passages as the Stoic conception but is always subordinate to the God of the Jews. It amounts to predestination. Always present in these passages, furthermore, is the religious question of righteous or sinful action.[53] The three passages agree in portraying the Essenes as champions of predestination, the Sadducees as advocates of free will, and the Pharisees as giving priority to predestination but insisting also that the decision to do good or evil lies with man.[54] So Josephus modified the material that he found in his Greek sources, to give a truly Jewish character to the disputes between the schools.

Having so interpreted the school passages, Maier devotes the bulk of his study to the question whether or not Josephus was correct in his assertions.[55] He attempts to resolve the matter by examining three sources: the Dead Sea Scrolls for the Essenes, the Psalms of Solomon for the Pharisees, and Ben Sira for the Sadducees. Maier concludes: (i) that

---

[48] Maier, *freier Wille*, 14f. That is, by reserving one area of human conduct, presumably the religious-ethical sphere, to human choice alone, it would accord with the rabbinic maxim quoted above (b. Ber. 33a).

[49] From ὡς καί to λαμβάνοντας.

[50] Ibid., 15.

[51] Ibid., 17. Philo *op. cit.*, 4.

[52] Ibid.

[53] Ibid., 17.

[54] Ibid., 19f.

[55] Ibid., 20.

the question of free will became an issue when Hellenistic philosophy influenced some Jews to blame predestination for sin; (ii) that Ben Sira formulated a doctrine of free will in response to this crisis; (iii) that the
Sadducees maintained Ben Sira's position most closely; (iv) that the
Essenes tended toward the extreme predestinationism confronted by Ben
Sira 33:7ff.; and (v) that the Pharisees held to both predestination and
freedom of the will, the latter especially in the area of righteous or sinful
action.[56] In short, Josephus concisely and accurately represents the positions of the three Jewish schools with respect to predestination and
thereby gives stunning proof of his claim to ἀκρίβεια.[57]

Maier concedes that the issue of fate and free will was not as central
to Jewish debates as Josephus seems to imply, but argues that the real
issues were unreportable, either because they were dangerous
(apocalyptic-political themes) or because the would not be understood
(themes related to cult and Torah).[58] The fate/free will debate, on the
contrary, was both alive and eminently reportable.

By positing that Josephus took over the school passages from Nicolaus
(and Philo) and reworked them where necessary to better accord with
reality, Maier has managed to absorb many of Moore's observations
about the Stoic flavour of the descriptions, especially that of the
Pharisees. At the same time, however, he has overturned Moore's conclusions (i) that εἱμαρμένη in the school passages finally has a Stoic
nuance and (ii) that the historical reality of first-century Judaism was at
variance with Josephus's descriptions. He falls in with Schlatter, Lauterbach, Wächter, and the others in his conclusion that the Pharisees actually did maintain a synergism between "fate" and free will; he
demonstrates this, however, by examination of the *Psalms of Solomon*
rather than by the customary reference to rabbinic literature.[59] Maier
has two significant differences with Wächter: first, he accepts the portrayal of the Sadducees as an accurate statement of their position (as
found in Ben Sira)—"als habe er den Inhalt von Sir 15, 11-20 zu
beschreiben"[60]—rather than as a misrepresentation inspired by dislike.
Second, Maier sees the occurrences of θεός as Josephus's own qualifications of his source's εἱμαρμένη; Wächter, conversely, views εἱμαρμένη as
Josephus's attempt to fill θεός with content.

---

[56] Ibid., 344-46.
[57] Ibid., 347f.
[58] Ibid., 348f.
[59] He takes this route deliberately, in order to avoid the problems of dating the rabbinic traditions, cf. *freier Wille*, 23.
[60] Ibid., 347.

The two most recent discussions of the subject head in completely new directions. A 1977 article by S. Pines[61] discovers parallels between *War* 2:162 and a passage in Apuleius's (mid-2d. cert. AD) work *On Plato and his Doctrine*. Summarizing Plato's view of providence, fate, and chance,[62] Apuleius writes (1:12):

> Yet everything that happens naturally and therefore correctly is governed by providence; and the cause of any evil cannot be attributed to God. Thus Plato holds that not everything can be ascribed to fate.
>
> Sed omnia quae naturaliter et propterea recte feruntur providentiiae custodia gubernantur nec ullius mali causa deo poterit adscribi. Quare nec omnia ad fati sortem arbitratur esse referenda.

And a little further on:

> To be sure, he does not think that everything can be ascribed to the power of fate; rather something rests with us and something also with chance.[63]
>
> Nec sane omnia referenda esse ad uim fati putant, sed esse aliquid in nobis et in fortuna esse non nihil.

Pines is impressed by the fact that both the Platonist and Josephus's Pharisees attribute one sphere of events to providence and another to human volition.[64] (He thus takes καὶ τὸ πράττειν τὰ δίκαια καὶ μὴ κατὰ τὸ πλεῖστον ἐπὶ τοῖς ἀνθρώποις in *War* 2:162 to be a qualification or limitation of the preceding Φαρισαῖοι. . . εἱμαρμένῃ καὶ θεῷ προσάπτουσι πάντα.)[65] In particular he is struck by what he considers a close formal similarity: both passages begin with a general ascription of everything (πάντα/*omnia*) to fate, but then immediately qualify that statement in a way that seems contradictory at first.[66] Although Josephus's Pharisees do not have an equivalent for Apuleius's "the cause of any evil (*mali causa*) cannot be attributed to God", Pines suggests that Josephus has carried this item over to his description of the Sadducees, καὶ τὸν θεὸν ἔξω τοῦ δρᾶν τι κακὸν ἢ ἐφορᾶν τίθενται, because it did not fit with Pharisaic thought.[67]

The parallel is so compelling to Pines that he is willing to theorize as

---

[61] "A Platonistic Model for Two of Josephus's Accounts of the Doctrine of the Pharisees Concerning Providence and Man's Freedom of Action", *Immanuel* 7 (1979), 38-43, trans. L. Lown.

[62] Cf. *Symposium* 202e f. Note H. E. Butler's comment on this Platonistic work (*Oxford Classical Dictionary*, p. 74): "an exposition of the philosophy of Plato, showing neither knowledge nor understanding".

[63] For this English translation, I have compared the German by P. Siniscalo, and Pines's excerpts as rendered by Lown.

[64] Pines, "Platonistic Model", 39.

[65] But see chapter 6 above.

[66] Pines, "Platonistic Model", 40.

[67] Ibid.; on κακόν, however, see n. 23 above.

follows. Apuleius (2d. cent. AD), who wrote in Latin, relied heavily on earlier Platonistic writings in Greek.[68] Then:

> There is strong internal evidence that the report in *The Jewish War* and in *Antiquities* on the views of the Pharisees concerning the freedom of action of man is an adaptation of a philosophical text which apparently resembled the Greek original of the section by Apuleius quoted above.[69]

All that remains for Pines is to find a likely candidate for the authorship of the Greek Platonistic text used by Josephus to describe the Pharisees. He suggests the name of Antiochus of Ashkelon (early 1st. cent. BC) because of the (presumably) large role played by this philosopher in formulating late and neo-Platonic positions.[70] Pines concedes, however, that "we are dealing exclusively with probabilities".[71]

For Pines to be driven to broaden the meaning of "probabilities" as he does, one would expect the parallels between *War* 2:162 and Apuleius 1:12 to be both exact and unique. They are neither. With respect to exactness, we may note: (i) that Apuleius on Plato does not attribute everything to fate; (ii) that Pines contradicts himself by paralleling the second proposition of Apuleius (God cannot cause evil) with that of Josephus (to do right or not rests with man)[72] and then admitting that Josephus actually uses proto-Apuleius here for his description of the Sadducees, not the Pharisees;[73] (iii) that whereas Apuleius attributes events to three causes—fate, ourselves, and chance—Josephus mentions only the first two; and (iv) that Josephus's second proposition (to do right or not rests with man) does not limit the sphere of fate to non-moral events, because he emphasizes finally that fate helps in *each* case. We do not, then, have much of a parallel. Apuleius's Plato attributes some things to fate, some to ourselves, and some to chance. Josephus's Pharisees at *War* 2:162 attribute everything to fate, including our own moral choices, in which fate still assists.

With respect to uniqueness: Apuleius's three-fold attribution is already present in Plato[74] and Aristotle.[75] The position of the Pharisees in *War* 2:162, on the other hand, is much more closely paralleled, as Moore has shown, by Cicero's description of Chrysippus's theory (*On*

---

[68] Ibid., 42.
[69] Pines, "Platonistic Model", 41.
[70] Ibid., 42.
[71] Ibid.
[72] Ibid., 40.
[73] Ibid., 40.
[74] *Symposium* 202e.
[75] *Nicomachean Ethics* 3.3-10; 5.1-3.

Fate 39-41). One hardly needs to posit Josephus's use of a proto-Apuleian Greek philosophical text to explain his description of the Pharisees.

Yet another interpretation of Josephus's εἱμαρμένη-usage in his descriptions of the Jewish schools has been proposed by L. H. Martin (1981);[76] He suggests that Josephus wants to present the Jews as a nation free from the oppression of εἱμαρμένη in its astrological sense.

Martin begins with a sketch of Wächter's article,[77] mainly, it seems, in order to introduce the common view (since Moore, shared by Wächter) that Josephus's use of εἱμαρμένη parallels Stoic usage.[78] That is the issue that concerns Martin. He wants to challenge this conventional identification on the ground that, since Josephus never elaborates on related Stoic themes—such as pantheism, the regularity of nature, or the harmony of the universe—he cannot be using εἱμαρμένη in a "technical" Stoic sense.[79]

If Josephus is not using εἱμαρμένη in a technical Stoic sense, Martin proposes, one ought to consider that the term was most popular in the first century as an astrological concept.[80] Since Josephus elsewhere shows himself familiar with astrological notions,[81] it would be most natural for him to use εἱμαρμένη in the astrological sense, of the oppressive, inexorable, planetary direction of human affairs.[82] Indeed, Martin thinks he finds such a sense in *Ant.* 16:397, where τύχη is equated with εἱμαρμένη "because there is nothing that is not brought about by her (οὐδενὸς ὄντος ὅ μὴ δι' αὐτὴν γίνεται)".[83] He understands *Ant.* 16:398, where Josephus asserts that the Law calls for human responsibility, to be the historian's rejection of an astrological view of fate.[84] In this passage, Martin thinks he has uncovered the key to Josephus's εἱμαρ-

---

[76] "Josephus's Use of *Heimarmene* in the *Jewish Antiquities* XIII, 171-3", *Numen* 28 (1981), 127-135.

[77] Ibid., 129f. The sketch is defecctive. For example, Martin has Wächter arguing "the essential correctness" of Josephus on all three schools. In fact, Wächter thinks that Josephus is accurate only in the case of Pharisees, that his presentation of the Essenes needs to be qualified, and that his portrait of the Sadducees is inaccurate. See my summary of Wächter above.

[78] Martin, *"Heimarmene"*, 130.

[79] Ibid., 132.

[80] Ibid.

[81] Ibid. Martin adduces *Ant.* 1:56, 167f.; 3:179-187.

[82] Ibid.

[83] Ibid. Cf. my analysis of this passage, in chapter 6, above. It is not clear to me why this statement should be interpreted as astrological, since the Stoics also saw Fate (= Logos) as the universal cause.

[84] Martin, *"Heimarmene"*, 134. I have argued above, however (chapter 6), that such an interpretation fails to account for Josephus's *affirmation* of the omnipotence of fate.

μένη-usage: the Jewish historian, like the apostle Paul (Gal. 4:8-9), is proclaiming freedom from an oppressive, astrological "Fate".

Applying this discovery to *Ant.* 13:171-173, in which the three schools are compared with respect to their views on εἱμαρμένη, Martin finds that:

> Josephus makes a universal statement which reflects the general Hellenistic 'heimarmenic' view of human existence, and then gives, by contrast, the Jewish alternative of life in obedience to Torah in its various interpretations. In other words, a life of obedience to Torah offers man an alternative to the otherwise universal determinism of *heimarmene*, together with the subsequent freedom for directing, within the requirements of Torah, one's own life.[85]

Unlike practically every other critic, Martin is able to connect *Ant.* 13:171-173 to its context. Whereas in this passage εἱμαρμένη rules over human affairs,[86] a few sentences earlier (13:163), Josephus has noted that the πρόνοια θεοῦ was guiding the affairs of Jonathan the Hasmonean.[87] Martin finds here an intended contrast between the liberating πρόνοια θεοῦ and the oppressive Hellenistic εἱμαρμένη. Thus Josephus is writing as an apologist:

> He presents the Jews as the people who are freed from *heimarmene* by the providence of God, and who consequently exercise free will and human responsibility in and through their obedience to Torah.[88]

Martin's analysis of "Josephus' use of Heimarmene in the *Jewish Antiquities* XIII, 171-3", as the title would have it, is an extreme example of the tendency to interpret Josephus's words by every possible stratagem except Josephan usage. Martin begins well enough, by distinguishing the literary and historical questions, "What does Josephus mean by *heimarmene*?"[89] and "To what extent is Josephus correct in his use of *heimarmene* to characterize and distinguish the Jewish philosophies?"[90] He immediately falls into the trap, however, of trying to settle the question of Josephus's meaning by external parallels: he cannot accept the Stoic parallel, so he assumes an astrological parallel. He concedes that, "Josephus never uses *heimarmene* in any astrological context", but thinks that "it was not necessary" for him to do so

---

[85] Ibid. I cannot paraphrase Martin's conclusion because several readings have left me unable to comprehend its sense as an interpretation of *Ant.* 13:171-173. I am unable to find any suggestion in Josephus that the rule of εἱμαρμένη is a *pagan* view. On the contrary, it is the (beloved) *Essenes* who make fate the κυρία of all.

[86] This inference is unclear. Josephus gives three views of fate.

[87] Martin, *"Heimarmene"*, 135.

[88] Ibid.

[89] Ibid., 128.

[90] Ibid., 129.

because of the pervasiveness of the astrological sense of εἱμαρμένη at that time.[91]

That this utter disregard for Josephus's intention leads to impossible conclusions is in Martin's case obvious. If, in *Ant.* 13:171-173, Josephus is preaching Jewish freedom from εἱμαρμένη then the Sadducees must be his heroes, because they do away with it altogether, and the Essenes must be some kind of heretics, for they see fate as "the mistress (χυρία) of all things". It is well known, however, that the opposite is the case. Josephus despises the Sadducees, whom he presents as rude[92] and savage,[93] and he always has high praise for the Essenes.[94] Moreover, in *Ant.* 13:171-173 Josephus is *not* trying to present the Jewish groups as unique—but rather as philosophical schools in Hellenistic fashion, with differing views περὶ τῶν ἀνθρωπίνων πραγμάτων. Third, Martin's suggestion requires a sharp distinction between εἱμαρμένη and πρόνοια; but Josephus closely relates the two terms.[95] Finally, granted that εἱμαρμένη had acquired both a philosophical (Stoic) and a popular (astrological) sense in the first century,[96] one must wonder whether Josephus's deliberate characterization of the Jewish groups as αἱρέσεις and φιλοσοφίαι, concerned with issues such as ethics and immortality, does not suggest *a priori* a philosophical sense for the term.

Conclusion

All of the studies considered offer some useful information and insight into our problem: What does Josephus mean to say in *War* 2:162, *Ant.* 13:171f., and *Ant.* 18:13 about the Pharisees' view of fate? All of them, however, ask the historical question too quickly. This is true even of Maier's work, which ostensibly devotes its first chapter to ascertaining Josephus's meaning before preceding to ask whether he was correct. Upon examination, one finds that the three pages given there to interpreting *War* 2:162, for example, are consumed by the quest to find the Jewish (and therefore Josephan) elements in the passage. Remarkably, no attempt is made to examine Josephus's usage of εἱμαρμένη.[97] Moore, Wächter, and Martin all offer some sort of comment on other instances

---

[91] Ibid., 133. Martin has correctly apprehended the dominance of the astrological interpretation of fate in the early centuries of our era; cf. Amand, *Fatalisme*, 12ff.; Nock, *Conversion*, 99f.; Bergman, "I Overcome Fate", 42; Gundel, "Heimarmene", 2641.
[92] *War* 2:166.
[93] *Ant.* 20:199.
[94] Cf. esp. *War* 2:119-161.
[95] Cf. *Ant.* 10:247f.; *Ag.Ap.* 2:180; esp. *War* 4:622; *Ant.* 19:347; and chapter 6, above.
[96] Tacitus, *Annals* 6:22.
[97] Maier, *freier Wille*, 11-14.

of εἱμαρμένη in Josephus but their remarks on this point are of dubious validity.[98]

These studies are symptomatic of the persistent positivism that has nurtured itself in Josephan studies. The historian's words are plucked out of their setting and interpreted by means of some more or less striking parallels in some more or less contemporary literature. But this endeavour begs the question of Josephus's meaning. Before one can ask whether, where, and to what extent, Josephus's thought and vocabulary fit with those of his contemporaries, one must ascertain his meaning. And, by a fundamental axiom of interpretation, that task must first be accomplished by careful scrutiny of the author's own characteristic usage. Only when Josephus's own clues about his meaning have been exhausted and some sort of result obtained, only then can it possibly be worthwhile to ask where he fits into the many currents of Hellenistic and Jewish thought.[99]

---

[98] Moore, "Fate", 375f., distinguishes Josephus's usage of εἱμαρμένη in the school passages from his usage elsewhere. Of the former he says: "It is fair to assume that . ... Heimarmene is used in what was at least meant to be its philosophical [sc. "un-Jewish"] definition." The other occurrences, Moore claims, pose "no difficulty" (i.e., accord with "Jewish" views). Wächter likewise posits major inconsistencies in Josephus's usage of εἱμαρμένη, "Haltung", 101-103. Neither of these critics offers more than bare assertions. Cf. my analysis above, (chapter 6), in which I argue that Josephus's use of εἱμαρμένη in the school passages is consistent with his usage elsewhere.

[99] Given the high degree of cross-fertilization between Hellenism and Judaism; given the eclecticism of both Stoicism (Greene, Moira, 342) and Middle Platonism (Armstrong, "Greek Philosophy", 211) in the first century AD; and given the major deficiencies in our knowledge of both Pharisaism and Stoicism, we should be wary of tying Josephus narrowly to any particular "parallel" or current of thought. Momigliano's comment on another writer of the period well illustrates the point: "Even the trained student of today finds it difficult to disentangle the Platonic from the Stoic, the Epicurean from the Cynic element in Seneca's philosophy." Cf. "Seneca Between Political and Contemplative Life", in Momigliano, Quarto Contributo all Storial degli Classici e del Mondo Antico (Rome: Edizione di Storia et Letteratura, 1969), 240.

BIBLIOGRAPHY

I. Texts[1] and Reference Works

Apuleius. *Platon and seine Lehre*, ed. P. Siniscalo, trans. K. Albert. "Texte zur Philosophie'', 4. Sankt Augustin: Hans Richarz, 1980.

Betant, E. A., ed. *Lexicon Thucydideum*, 2 vols. Hildesheim: G. Olms, 1961 [1843].

Chadwick, H. *The Sentences of Sextus: a contribution to the study of early Christian ethics.* Cambridge: University Press, 1959.

Charles, R. H., ed. *The Apocrypha and Pseudepigrapha of the Old Testament in English*, vol. 2: *Pseudepigrapha.* Oxford: Clarendon Press, 1913.

Cicero, M. Tullius. *Über das Fatum*, 2d. edn., ed. K. Bayer. Munich: Heimeran, 1976 [1959].

Complete Works of Josephus in Ten Volumes: a new and revised edition based on Havercamp's translation. Cleveland–New York: World Syndicate Publishing Company, n. d.

Cornfeld, G., B. Mazar, and P. L. Maier, edd. *Josephus: the Jewish War.* Grand Rapids: Zondervan, 1982.

Dalman, G. H. *Aramäisch-Neuhebräisches Handwörterbuch zu Targum, Talmud und Midrasch*, 2d. edn. Frankfurt a. M.: J. Kaufmann, 1922.

———. *Grammatik des jüdisch-palästinischen Aramäisch: aramäische Dialektproben*, 2d. edn. Darmstadt: Wissenschaftliche Buchgesellschaft, 1960 [1927].

Eigler, G., ed. *Platon: Werke in acht Bänden: Griechisch und Deutsch.* Darmstadt: Wissenschaftliche Buchgesellschaft, 1977.

Essen, M. H. N. von, ed. *Index Thucydideus.* Berlin: Weidmann, 1887.

Feldman, L. H. *Josephus and Modern Scholarship (1937-1980)*, ed. W. Haase. Berlin W. de Gruyter, 1983.

———. *Studies in Judaica: Scholarship on Philo and Josephus (1937-1962).* New York: Yeshiva University, n. d.

Gesenius, W. *Hebräische Grammatik*, ed. E. Kautzsch. Hildesheim: Georg Olms, 1962 [1909].

Gomme, A. W., A. Andrewes, and K. J. Dover. *A Historical Commentary on Thucydides*, 5 vols. Oxford: Clarendon Press, 1981.

Hafaeli, L. *Flavius Josephus' Lebensbeschreibung.* "Neutestamentliche Abhandlungen'', II.4. Münster: Aschendorf, 1925.

Hartom, A. S., ed. *Ha-Sifrim ha-Hisonim*, 4 vols. Tel Aviv: Yavneh, 1958.

Jastrow, M. *A Dictionary of the Targumim the Talmud Babli and Yerushalmi, and the Midrashic Literature*, 2 vols. New York: Pardes Publishing House, 1950.

Kautzsch, E., ed. *Die Apokryphen und Pseudepigraphen des Alten Testaments*, 2 vols. Tübingen-Greibung-Leipzig: J. C. B. Mohr-P. Siebeck, 1900.

Michel, O. and O. Bauernfeind, edd. *De Bello Judaico: Der jüdische Krieg. Griechisch und Deutsch*, 4 vols. Munich: Kosel, 1959-1969.

Niese, B., ed. *Flavii Josephi Opera*, 3 vols. Berlin: Weidmann, 1887-1904.

O'Neil, E. *Teles (The Cynic Teacher).* "SBL Texts and Translations'', 11; "Graeco-Roman Religion'', 3. Missoula: Scholars Press, 1977.

Palmer, L. R. *The Greek Language.* "The Great Languages''. London, Boston: Faber and Faber, 1980.

Rappaport, U. "Bibliography of Works on Jewish History in the Hellenistic and Roman

---

[1] With the exceptions and additions noted below, I have used the LCL editions of classical texts.

Periods, 1946-1970'', in *Studies in the History of the Jewish People in the Land of Israel*, edd. B. Obed *et al.* Haifa: University of Haifa, 1972, II, 272-321.

Reinach, T., ed. *Oeuvres Completes de Flavius Josephe*, 7 vols. Paris: E. Leroux, 1900ff.

Rengstorf, K. H. *et al. A Complete Concordance to Flavius Josephus*, 4 vols. Leiden: E. J. Brill, 1973-1983. *Supplement I: Namenwörterbuch zu Flavius Josephus*, ed. A. Schalit, 1968.

Schreckenberg, H. *Bibliographie zu Flavius Josephus.* ''Arbeiten zur Literatur und Geschichte des hellenistischen Judentums'', 1. Leiden: E. J. Brill, 1968. Vol. 14: *Supplementband mit Gesamtregister*, 1979.

Segal, M. H. *A Grammar of Mishnaic Hebrew.* Oxford: Clarendon, 1958.

Stobaeus, J. *Anthologium*, 5 vols., edd. C. Wachsmuth and O. Hense. Berlin: Weidmann, 1957.

Stoicorum Veterum Fragmenta, 4 vols., ed. A. von Arnim. Leipzig: B. G. Teubner, 1903.

Thackeray, H. St. J. and R. Marcus. *A Lexicon to Josephus*, 4 vols. ''Publications of the Alexander Kohut Memorial Foundation''. Paris: Librarie Orientaliste Paul Guenther, 1930-1955.

Thackeray, H. St. J., R. Marcus, A. Wikgren, and L. Feldman, edd. *Josephus*, 10 vols. ''Loeb Classical Library''. Cambridge, Mass: Harvard University Press; London: William Heinemann, 1976-1981.

Thompson, E. and W. C. Price, edd. *The Works of Flavius Josephus*, 2 vols. London: Fielding and Walker, 1777.

Vermes, G. *The Dead Sea Scrolls in English*. Harmondsworth: Penguin, 1962.

Whiston, W. ed. *The Life and works of Flavius Josephus*. New York: Holt, Reinhart and Winston, n. d. [1737].

II. *Essays, Articles, and Books*

Abrahams, I. *Studies in Pharisaism and the Gospels*: *First and Second Series*. ''Library of Biblical Studies''. New York: Ktav, 1968 [1917 and 1924].

Alon, G. *Jews, Judaism and the Classical World*: *Studies in Jewish History in the Times of the Second Temple and Talmud*, trans. I. Abrahams. Jerusalem: Magnes, 1977.

Altheim, F. *A History of Roman Religion*, trans. H. Mattingly. London: Methuen & Co., 1938.

Amand, D. *Fatalisme et Liberté dans l'Antiquite Grecque*: *recherches sur la survivance de l'argumentation morale anti-fataliste de Carneade chez les philosphes grecs et les theologiens chretiens des quatre premiers siecles*. ''Université de Louvain, Recueil de Travoux d' Histoire et de Philologie'', 3.19. Louvain: Bibliotheque de l'Université, 1945.

Armstrong, A. H. ''Greek Philosophy from the Age of Cicero to Plotinus'', in *The Crucible of Christianity*: *Judaism, Hellenism and the Historical Background to the Christian Faith*, ed. A. Toynbee. London: Thames and Hudson, 1969.

Attridge, H. W. *The Interpretation of Biblical History in the Antiquitates Judaicae of Flavius Josephus*. ''Harvard Dissertations in Religion'', 7. Missoula: Scholars Press, 1976.

Aune, D. E. ''Critical Notes: the use of ΠΡΟΦΗΤΗΣ in Josephus'', *JBL* 101 (1982), 419-421.

Avenarius, G. *Lukians Schrift zur Geschichtsschreibung*. Meisenheim-Glan: Anton Hain, 1956.

Bacher, W. *Tradition und Tradenten in den Schulen Palästinas und Babyloniens*: *Studien und Materialen zur Entstehungsgeschichte des Talmuds*. Leipzig: Gustav Fock, 1914.

Baeck, L. *Paulus, die Pharisäer und das Neue Testament*. Frankfurt: Ner-Tamid, 1961.

——. The Pharisees and Other Essays. New York: Schocken, 1947.

Bamberger, B. J. ''The Sadducees and the Belief in Angels'', *JBL* 82 (1963), 433-435.

Barish, D. A. ''The *Autobiography* of Josephus and the Hypothesis of a Second Edition of his *Antiquities*'', *HTR* 71 (1978), 61-75.

Baron, S. W. *A Social and Religious History of the Jews*, I and II: *Ancient Times*, 2d. edn. New York: Columbia University Press, 1952.

Bauernfeind, O. and O. Michel. "Die beiden Elezarreden in Jos. Bell. 7. 323-336 und 7.341-388'', *ZNW* 58 (1967), 267-272.

Baumbach, G. "Das Sadduzäerverständnis bei Josephus Flavius und im Neuen Testament'', *Kairos* 13 (1971), 17-37.

——. "Jesus und die Pharisäer: ein Beitrag zur Frage nach dem historischen Jesus'', *Bibel und Liturgie* 41 (1968), 112-131.

Baumgarten, A. I. "The Name of the Pharisees'', *JBL* 102 (1983), 411-428.

Baumgarten, J. M. "The Pharisaic-Sadducean Controversies about Purity and the Qumran Texts", *JJS* 31 (1980), 157-170.

——. "The unwritten Law in the Pre-Rabbinic Period ', *JSJ* 3 (1972), 7-29.

Beasley-Murray, G. R. "The Two Messiahs in the Testaments of the Twelve Patriarchs'', *JTS* 48 (1947), 1-12.

Beilner, W. *Christus und die Pharisäer: exegetische Untersuchung über Grund und Verlauf der Auseinandersetzung.* Vienna: Herder, 1959.

——. "Der Ursprung des Pharisäismus'', *Biblische Zeitschrift*, n.F. 3 (1959), 235-251.

Benario, H. W. *An Introduction to Tacitus.* Athens GA: University of Georgia Press, 1975.

Bentwich, N. *Josephus.* Philadelphia: Jewish Publication Society of America, 1919.

Bergman, J. "I Overcome Fate, Fate Hearkens to Me'', in *Fatalistic Beliefs in Religion, Folklore, and Literature*, ed. H. Ringgren, Stockholm: Almquist & Wiksell, 1967, 35-51.

Bergmann, J. "Die stoische Philosophie und die jüdische Frömmigkeit'', in *Judaica: Festschrift zu Hermann Cohens siebzigstem Geburtstage*, edd. I. Elbogen, B. Kellermann and E. Mittwoch. New York: Arno, 1980 [Berlin: Bruno Cassirer, 1912], 145-166.

Betz, O., K. Haacker, and P. Schäfer, edd. *Josephus-Studien: Untersuchungen zu Josephus, dem antiken Judentum und dem Neuen Testament. Otto Michel zum 70. Geburistag gewidmet.* Göttingen: Vandenhoeck & Ruprecht, 1974.

Bickerman, E. J. "La Chaîne de la tradition pharisienne'', *Studies in Jewish and Christian History*, "Arbeiten zur Geschichte des Antiken Judentums und des Urchristenthums'', 9. Leiden: E. J. Brill, 1980, II, 256-269.

Bilde, P. "The Causes of the Jewish War According to Josephus'', *JSJ* 10 (1979), 179-202.

Black, M. "The Account of the Essenes in Hippolytus and Josephus'', in *The Background of the New Testament and its Eschatology*, edd. W. D. Davies and D. Daube. Cambridge: University Press, 1956, 172-175.

——. "Pharisees'', *IDB* III (1962), 774-781.

Blenkinsopp, J. "Prophecy and Priesthood in Josephus'', *JJS* 25 (1974), 239-262.

Bloch, H. *Die Quellen des Flavius in seiner Archäologie.* Leipzig: B. G. Teubner, 1879.

Bloch, M. *Apologie der Geschichte oder der Beruf des Historikers*, trans. S. Furtenbach, 2d. ed., rev. F. J. Lucas. Stuttgart: E. Klett-J.G. Cotta, 1974.

Blumenthal, H. von. "Palingenesia'', *PWRE* 18:3, 139-148.

Bousset, W. *Die Religion des Judentums im späthellenistischen Zeitalter*, 4th edn., ed. H. Gressmann. "Handbuch zum Neuen Testament'', 21. Tübingen: J. C. B. Mohr (Siebeck), 1966 [1926].

Bowker, J. *Jesus and the Pharisees.* Cambridge: Cambridge University Press, 1973.

Brandon, S. G. F. *The Judgment of the Dead: An Historical and Comparative Study of the Idea of a Post-Mortem Judgment in the Major Religions.* London: Weidenfeld and Nicolson, 1967.

Braun, M. *Griechischer Roman und hellenistische Geschichtsschreibung.* "Franfurter Studien zur Religion und Kultur der Antike'', 6. Frankfurt a. M.: V. Klostermann, 1934.

Brown, S. *The Origins of Christianity: A Historical Introduction to the New Testament.* "The Oxford Bible Series''. Oxford-New York: Oxford University Press, 1984.

Broyde, I., "Fatalism'', *The Jewish Encyclopedia*, V, 351. New York: Funk and Wagnalls, 1925.

Brüne, B. *Flavius Josephus und seine Schriften in ihrem Verhältnis zum Judentume, zur griechisch-römischen Welt und zum Christentum; mit griechischer Wortkonkordanz zum Neuen Testament und I. Clemensbriefe nebst sach- und Namen-Verzeichnis.* Gütersloh: Gerd Mohn, 1969 [1913].

Büchsel, F. "παλιγγενεσία", *TDNT*, I, 686-689.

Buehler, W. W. *The Pre-Herodian Civil War and Social Debate: Jewish Society in the Period 76-40 B.C. and the Social Factors Contributing to the Rise of the Pharisees and the Sadducees.* "Theologische Dissertationen", 11. Basel: Friedrich Reinhardt; 1974 [dissertation, Basel, 1964].

Burgmann, H. "Der Gründer der Pharisäergenossenschaft: der Makkabäer Simon", *JJS* 9 (1978), 153-191.

———. "The Wicked Woman: Der Makkabäer Simon?", *Revue de Qumran* 8 (1972), 323-359.

Burkitt, F. C. *The Gospel History and Its Transmission*, 2d. edn. Edinburgh: T. & T. Clark, 1907.

Burrows, M. "Messiahs of Aaron and Israel", *ATR* 34 (1952), 202-206.

———. *More Light on the Dead Sea Scrolls.* New York: Viking Press, 1958.

Byatt, A. "Josephus and Population Numbers in 1st Century Palestine", *Palestine Exploration Quarterly* 105 (1973), 51-60.

Cavallin, H. C. C. *Life After Death: Paul's Argument. . . . Part I. An Enquiry into the Jewish Background.* Lund: Gleerup, 1974.

Charles, R. H. *Eschatology: the Doctrine of a Future Life in Israel, Judaism and Christianity: a Critical History.* New York: Schocken Books, 1963 [1899].

———. *Religious Development Between The Old and The New Testaments.* "Home University Library of Modern Knowledge", 94. London-New York-Toronto: Oxford University Press, 1914.

Cioffari, V. "Fortune, Fate and Chance", *Dictionary of the History of Ideas*, II, 225-236. ed. P. P. Wiener. New York: Charles Scribner's Sons, 1973.

Cohen, J. *Les Pharisiens*, 2 vols. Paris: C. Levy, 1877.

Cohen, N. G. "Josephus and Scripture: Is Josephus' Treatment of the Scriptural Narrative Similar Throughout the *Antiquities* I-XI?", *JQR* 54 (1963-64), 311-332.

Cohen, S. J. D. *Josephus in Galilee and Rome: his Vita and Development as a Historian.* Leiden: E. J. Brill, 1979.

Collingwood, R. G. *The Idea of History.* Oxford: Clarendon Press, 1948.

Collump, P. "Der Platz des Josephus in der Technik der hellenistischen Geschichtsschreibung", *Wege der Forschung* 84 (1974), 278-293.

Connor, W. R. *Thucydides.* Princeton: Princeton University Press, 1984.

Cook, M. J. "Jesus and the Pharisees— the Problem as it Stands Today", *JES* 15 (1978), 441-460.

———. *Mark's Treatment of the Jewish Leaders.* "Supplements to Novum Testamentum", 51. Leiden: E. J. Brill, 1978.

Creed, J. L. "Moral Values in the Age of Thucydides", *CQ* 23 (1973), 213-231.

Creuzer, F. "Rückblick auf Josephus: jüdische, christliche Monumente und Personalien", *TSK* 26 (1853), 906-928.

Cross, F. M. Jr. *The Ancient Library of Qumran.* "The Haskell Lectures, 1956-1957". London: Gerald Duckworth, 1958.

Cumont, F. *After Life in Roman Paganism: Lectures delivered at Yale University on the Silliman Foundation.* New Haven: Yale University Press; London: Oxford University Press, 1922.

Cumont, F. *Oriental Religions in Roman Paganism.* New York: Dover, 1956 [1911].

Davies, W. D. *Christian Origins and Judaism.* London: Darton, Longman & Todd, 1962.

Delling, G. "Josephus und die heidnischen Religionen", *Klio*, 43 (1965), 263-269; repr. in the author's *Studien zum Neuen Testament und zum hellenistischen Judentum: Gesammelte Aufsätze 1950-68.* Göttingen: Vandenhoeck und Ruprecht, 1970, 34-42.

Derenbourg, J. *Essai sur l'Histoire et al Geographie de la Palestine: d'après les Thalmuds et les autres sources rabbiniques*, pt. I: *Histoire de la Palestine depuis Cyrus jusqu' à Adrien*. Hildesheim: H. A. Gerstenberg, 1975 [1867].

Destinon, J. von. *Die Quellen des Flavius Josephus I: Die Quellen der Archäologie Buch XII-XVII + Jüd. Krieg Buch I*. Kiel: Lipsius & Tischer, 1882.

Dexinger, F. "Die Geschichte der Pharisaer", *Bibel und Kirche* 35 (1930), 113-117.

Dietrich, B. C. *Death, Fate and the Gods: the development of a religious idea in Greek popular belief and in Homer*. "University of London Classical Studies", 3. London: Athlone, 1965.

Dietrich, E. L. "Pharisäer", in *RGG*, 3. Auflage, V, 326f.

Dodd, C. H. *The Bible and the Greeks*. London: Hodder & Stoughton, 1935.

Downing, F. G. "Common Ground with Paganism in Luke and in Josephus", *NTS* 28 (1982), 546-559.

——. "Redaction Criticism; Josephus' *Antiquities* and the Synoptic Gospels", *JSNT* 8 (1980), 46-65; 9 (1980), 29-48.

Drexler, H. "Untersuchungen zu Josephus und zur Geschichte des jüdischen Aufstandes", *Klio* 19 (1925), 277-312.

Dubnow, S. *Weltgeschichte des jüdischen Volkes: von seinen Uranfängen bis zur Gegenwart*, 70 vols. Berlin: Jüdischer Verlag, 1925-29.

Dudley, D. R. *The World of Tacitus*. London: Seeker & Warburg, 1968.

Earl, D. "Prologue-form in ancient Historiography", in *Aufstieg und Niedergang der römischen Welt. . .*, ed. H. Temporini. I: *Von den Anfangen Roms bis zum Ausgang der Republik*, vol. 2. Berlin-New York: W. de Gruyter, 1972, 842-856.

Ehrhardt, A. "The Construction and Purpose of the Acts of the Apostles", *Studia Theologica* 12 (1958), 45ff.

Ehrlich, E. L. "Zur Geschichte der Pharisäer", *Freiburger Rundbrief* 29 (1977), 46-52.

Eisler, R. *The Messiah Jesus and John the Baptist: according to Flavius Josephus' recently discovered 'Capture of Jerusalem' and other Jewish and Christian Sources*, trans. and ed. A. H. Krappe. London: Methuen & Co., 1931.

Elbogen, I. "Einige neuere Theorien uber den Ursprung der Pharisäer und Sadduzäer", in *Jewish Studies in Memory of I. Abrahams*. New York: Jewish Institute of Religion, 1927, 135-148.

——. *Die Religionsanschauungen der Pharisäer: mit besonderer Berucksichtigung der Begriffe Gott und Mensch*. "Lehranstalt fur die Wissenschaft des Judenthums", 22. Berlin: H. Itzkowski, 1904.

Farmer, W. R. *Maccabees, Zealots, and Josephus: An Inquiry into Jewish Nationalism in the Greco-Roman Period*. New York: Columbia University Press, 1956.

Feldman, L. H. "The Identity of Pollio, the Pharisee, in Josephus", *JQR* 49 (1958-59), 53-62.

——. "Josephus as an Apologist to the Roman World: his Portrait of Solomon", in *Aspects of Religious Propaganda in Judaism and Early Christianity*, ed. E. S. Fiorenza. "Studies in Judaism and Christianity in Antiquity", 2. Notre Dame-London: University of Notre Dame Press, 1976, 68-98.

Finley, M. I. *The Use and Abuse of History*. London: Chatto & Windus, 1975.

Finkel, A. *The Pharisees and the Teacher of Nazareth: A Study of their Background, their Halakhic and Midrashic Teachings, the Similarities and Differences*. "Arbeiten zur Geschichte des Spatjudentums und Urchristentums", Bd. 4. Leiden: E. J. Brill, 1964.

Finkelstein, L. "The Origin of the Pharisees", *Conservative Judaism* 23 (1969), 25-36.

——. *Pharisaism in the Making: Selected Essays*. New York: Ktav, 1972.

——. *The Pharisees and the Men of the Great Synagogue*. "Texts and Studies of the Jewish Theological Seminary of America", 15. New York: Jewish Theological Seminary, 1950.

——. *The Pharisees: The Sociological Background of their Faith*. 2 vols. "Morris Loeb Series". Philadelphia: The Jewish Publication Society of America, 1938.

——. "The Pharisees: Their Origin and their Philosophy", *HTR* 22 (1929) 185-261.

Fischel, H. A. "Story and History: Observations on Greco-Roman Historiography and Pharisaism", in *American Oriental Society—Middle West Branch: Semi-Centennial Volume*, ed. D. Sinor. "Asian Studies Research Institute Oriental Series", 3. Bloomington-London: Indiana University Press, 1969, 59-83.

Flusser, D. "Pharisäer, Sadduzäer und Essener im Pescher Nahum", in *Qumran*, edd. K. E. Krozinger *et al*. "Wege der Forschung", 410. Darmstadt: Wissenschaftliche Buchgesellschaft, 1981.

Foakes Jackson, F. J. *Josephus and the Jews: the Religion and History of the Jews as Explained by Flavius Josephus*. London: S.P.C.K., 1930.

——, K. Lake, and H. J. Cadbury. *The Beginnings of Christianity. Part I: The Acts of the Apostles*, 5 vols. London: Macmillan, 1920-1933.

Foerster, W. "Εὐσέβεια in den Pastoralbriefen", *NTS* 5 (1959), 213-218.

——. "Der Ursprung des Pharisäismus", *ZNW* 34 (1935), 35-51.

Ford, J. M. "The Christian Debt to Pharisaism", *Bridge* 5 (1970), 218-230.

Franxman, T. W. *Genesis and the 'Jewish Antiquities' of Flavius Josephus*. Rome: Biblical Institute Press, 1979.

Friedlander, J. "The Rupture Between Alexander Jannai and the Pharisees", *JQR* n. s. 4 (1913-14), 443-448.

Fuks, A. *The Ancestral Constitution: Four Studies in Athenian Party Politics at the End of the Fifth Century B.C.* London: Routledge & Kegan Paul, 1953.

Furley, D. J. *Two Studies in Greek Atomism*. Princeton: Princeton University Press, 1967.

Garrod, H. W. "Note on the Messianic Character of the Fourth Eclogue", *Classical Review* 19 (1905), 37-38.

Gaster, T. H. *The Scriptures of the Dead Sea Sect*. London: Seeker & Warburg, 1957.

Geiger, A. *Das Judenthum und seine Geschichte*, I: *bis zur Zerstörung des zweiten Tempels*, 2. Auflage. Breslau: Schletter, 1865.

——. *Urschrift und Übersetzungen der Bibel: in ihrer Abhängigkeit von der innern Entwicklung des Judentums*, 2. Auflage. Frankfurt a. M.: Madda, 1928 [1857].

Geller, M. J. "Alexander Jannaeus and the Pharisees Rift", *JJS* 30 (1979), 202-211.

Gelzer, M. "Die Vita des Josephos", *Hermes* 80 (1952), 67-90.

Gerhardsson, B. *Memory and Manuscript: Oral Tradition and Written Transmission in Rabbinic Judaism and Early Christianity*, trans. E. J. Sharpe. Uppsala: Almquist & Wiksells, 1961.

Gerlach, E. *Die Weissagungen des Alten Testaments in den Schriften des Flavius Josephus*. Berlin: Hertz, 1863.

Giovannini, G. "The Connection Between Tragedy and History in Ancient Criticism", *Philosophical Quarterly* 22 (1943), 308-314.

Glasson, T. F. "Anti-Pharisaism in St. Matthew", *JQR* 51 (1960-61), 316-320.

——. *Greek Influence in Jewish Eschatology: with special reference to the Apocalypses and Pseudepigraphs*. London: S.P.C.K. 1961.

Goldenberg, D. "Flavius Josephus or Joseph ben Mattathiah?", *JQR* 70 (1979), 178-182.

——. "The Halakha in Josephus and in Tannaitic Literature: A Comparative Study", *JQR* 67 (1976), 30-43.

Goodblatt, D. "The Origins of Roman Recognition of the Palestinian Patriarchate", *Studies in the History of the Jewish People in the Land of Israel* 4 (1978), 89-102 [Hebrew].

Graetz, H. *Geschichte der Juden von den ältesten Zeiten bis auf die Gegenwart*, 11 vols., 5th edn. Leipzig: Oskar Leiner, 1905 [1863].

Grant, M. *The Ancient Historians*. London: Weidenfeld and Nicolson, 1970.

Greene, W. C. *Moira: Fate, Good, and Evil in Greek Thought*. Cambridge, Mass: Harvard University Press, 1944.

Gruber-Magitot, C. *Jesus et les Pharisiens*. Paris: Robert Laffont, 1964.

Guignebert, Ch. *The Jewish World in the Time of Jesus*, trans. S. H. Hooke. London: Routledge & Kegan Paul; New York: E. P. Dutton, 1939.

Gundel, W. "Heimarmene", *PWRE* 13 (1910), 2622-2645.

Guttmann, A. *Rabbinic Judaism in the Making: A Chapter in the History of the Halakhah from Ezra to Judah I*. Detroit: Wayne State University Press, 1970.

Guttmann, H. *Die Darstellung der jüdischen Religion bei Flavius Josephus*. Breslau: Marcus, 1928.

Hadas, M. *Hellenistic Culture*. New York: Columbia University Press, 1959.

Haenchen, E. *The Acts of the Apostles*, trans. R. M. Wilson. Oxford: Basil Blackwell, 1982.

Halbfas, F. *Theorie und Praxis in der Geschichtschreibung bei Dionys von Halikarnass*. Münster: Westfälische Vereinsdruckerei, 1910.

Halson, B. R. "A Note on the Pharisees", *Theology* 47 (1964), 245-251.

Hanson, P. D. "Apocalypticism", *IDBS*, 28-34.

Hare, D. R. A. *The Themes of Jewish Persecution of Christians in the Gospel According to St. Matthew*. "SNTS Monograph Series", 6. Cambridge: Cambridge University Press, 1967.

Harnack, A. von. *Das Wesen des Christentums*, Neuauflage. Stuttgart: Ehrenfried Klotz, 1950 [1900].

Hata, G. "Is the Greek Version of Josephus' 'Jewish War' a Translation or a Rewriting of the First Version?", *JQR* 66 (1975), 89-108.

Havelock, E. A. *The Greek Concept of Justice: From its Shadow in Homer to its Substance in Plato*. Cambridge, Mass; London: Harvard University Press, 1978.

Head, J. and S. L. Cranston, edd. *Reincarnation in World Thought*. New York: Julian Press, 1967.

Heller, B. "Grundzüge der Aggada des Flavius Josephus", *MGWJ* 80 (1936), 237-246.

Hengel, M. *Judentum und Hellenismus*. Tübingen: J. C. B. Mohr (P. Siebeck), 1969.

——. *Die Zeloten. Untersuchungen zur jüdischen Freiheitsbewegung in der Zeit von Herodes I, bis 70 n. Chr.* Leiden: E. J. Brill, 1961.

Herford, R. T. "The Law and Pharisaism", in *Judaism and Christianity: Three Volumes in One*, edd. W. O. E. Oesterley, H. Loewe, and E. I. J. Rosenthal. New York: Ktav, 1969 [1937-38], III, 91-121.

——. *Pharisaism: Its Aim and Method*, "Crown Theological Library", 35. London: Williams & Northgate, 1912.

——. *The Pharisees*. New York: Macmillan, 1924.

Hicks, R. D. *Stoic and Epicurean*. New York: Russell & Russell, 1962 [1910].

Hignett, C. *A History of the Athenian Constitution: to the End of the Fifth Century B.C.* Oxford: Clarendon, 1952.

Hirzel, R. *Themis, Dike und Verwandtes: ein Beitrag zur Geschichte der Rechtsidee bei den Griechen*. Leipzig: S. Hirzel, 1907.

Hoenig, S. B. *The Great Sanhedrin: A study of the origin, development, composition and functions of the Bet Din ha-Gadol during the Second Jewish Commonwealth*. Philadelphia: Dropsie College, 1953.

Hölscher, G. "Josephus", *PWRE* 18 (1916), 1934-2000.

——. *Der Sadduzäismus: eine kritische Untersuchung zur späteren jüdischen Religionsgeschichte*. Leipzig: J. C. Hinrichs, 1906.

Holtzmann, O. *Neutestamentliche Zeitgeschichte*. "Grundriss der theologischen Wissenschaften", 2d. series, Bd. 2. Freiburg-Leipzig: J. C. B. Mohr, 1895.

——. "Der Prophet Malachi und der Ursprung der Pharisäismus", *Archiv für Religionswissenschaft* 29 (1931), 1-21.

Hooker, J. T. "Χάρις and Ἀρετή in Thucydides", *Hermes* 102 (1974), 164-169.

Howard, G. "Kaige Reading in Josephus", *Textus* 8 (1973), 45-54.

Hultgren, A. J. *Jesus and his Adversaries: The Form and Function of the Conflict Stories in the Synoptic Tradition*. Minneapolis: Ausburg, 1979.

Hummel, R. *Die Auseinandersetzung zwischen Kirche und Judentum im Matthäusevangelium*. "Beiträge zur evangelischen Theologie", 33. Munich: Kaiser, 1966.

Hussey, M. D. "Origin of the Name Pharisee", *JBL* 39 (1920), 66-69.

Isser, S. "The Conservative Essenes: A New Emendation of *Antiquities* XVIII.12", *JSJ* 7 (1976), 177-180.

Jacob, B. *Im Namen Gottes: eine sprachliche und religions-geschichtliche Untersuchung zum Alten und Neuen Testament*. Berlin: S. Calvary & Co., 1903.

Jaeger, W. *Aristotle: Fundamentals of the History of his Development*. Oxford: University Press 1948.

Janson, T. *Latin Prose Prefaces*: *Studies in Literary Conventions*. "Acta Universitatis Stockhol-
miensis: Studia Latina Stockholmiensia", 13. Stockholm-Gotborg-Uppsala: Alm-
qvist & Wiksell, 1964.
Jeremias, J. *Jerusalem zur Zeit Jesu*: *kulturgeschichtliche Untersuchung zur neutestamentlichen
Zeitgeschichte*, 2. Auflage. Göttingen: Vandenhoeck & Ruprecht, 1958.
Johnson, B. "Der Bedeutungsunterschied zwischen ṣadaq und ṣedaqa", *Annual of the
Swedish Theological Institute* 11 (1977/78), 31-39.
Kajanto, I. *God and Fate in Livy*. "Annales Universitatis Turkuensis", B. 64. Turku:
Turun Yliopiston Kustantama, 1957.
Kallai, Z. "The Biblical Geography of Flavius Josephus", *Fourth World Congress of Jewish
Studies (1965)*, IV (1967), 203-207.
Kieval, P. "The Talmudic View of the Hasmonean and early Herodian Periods in
Jewish History". Dissertation, Brandeis, 1970.
Klausner, J. *The Messianic Idea in Israel*: *From its Beginning to the Completion of the Mishnah*,
trans. W. F. Stinespring. London: George Allen and Unwin, 1956.
Klein, R. W. "Aspects of Intertestamental Messianism", *Concordia Theological Monthly*
43 (1972), 507-517.
Kleinknecht, H. and W. Gutbrod, "νόμος", *TDNT*, IV, 1023-1051.
Knight Jackson, W. F. *Elysion*: *on ancient Greek and Roman beliefs concerning a life after death*.
London: Rider & Co. 1970.
Knox, W. L. "Pharisaism and Hellenism", in *Judaism and Christianity*: *Three Volumes in
One*, edd. W. O. E. Oesterley, H. Loewe, and E. I. J. Rosenthal. New York: Ktav,
1969 [1937-38], 61-111.
Kohler, K. "Pharisees", *The Jewish Encyclopedia*. New York: Ktav, 1904, IX, 661-666.
Krenkel, M. *Josephus und Lukas*: *der schriftstellerische Einfluss des jüdischen Geschichtschreibers
auf den christlichen nachgewiesen*. Liepzig: H. Haessel, 1894.
Kümmel, W. G. "Die Weherufe über die Schriftgelehrten und Pharisäer (Matthäus 23,
13-36)", in *Antijudäismus im Neuen Testament? exegetische und systematische Beiträge*.
Munich: Kaiser, 1967.
Lachs, S. T. "The Pharisees and Sadducees on Angels: A Reexamination of Acts
XXIII.8", *Gratz College Annual of Jewish Studies* 6 (1977), 35-42.
Laqueur, R. *Der jüdische Historiker Flavius Josephus*: *ein biographischer Versuch auf neuer
quellenkritischer Grundlage*. Darmstadt: Wissenschaftliche Buchgesellschaft, 1970
[1920].
Laurin, R. B. "The Problem of Two Messiahs in the Qumran Scrolls", *Revue de Qumran*
4 (1963), 39-52.
Lauterbach, J. Z. "The Pharisees and their Teachings", *HUCA* 6 (1929)), 69-139.
——. "The Sadducees and Pharisees: a Study of their Respective Attitudes toward the
Law", in *Studies in Jewish Literature*: *issued in honor of Professor Kaufmann Kohler . . .
on the occasion of his seventieth Birthday*. . . . Berlin: Reimer, 1913, 176-198.
Leach, A. "Fate and Free Will in Greek Literature", in *The Greek Genius and its Influence*:
Select Essays and Extracts, ed. L. Cooper. New Haven: Yale University Press, 1917,
132-155.
Leipoldt, J. and W. Grundmann. *Umwelt des Urchristentums*, 3 vols. Berlin: Evangelische
Verlagsanstalt, 1965-66.
Le Moyne, J. *Les Sadducéens*. "Études bibliques". Paris: Lecoffre, 1972.
Leszynsky, R. "Pharisäer", in *Jüdisches Lexicon*: *ein enzyklopädisches Handbuch des jüdischen
Wissens in vier Bänden*, edd. G. Herlitz, B. Kirschner *et al*. Berlin: Jüdischer Verlag,
1930, 4:1, 894-896.
——. *Pharisäer und Sadduzäer*. "Volkschriften über die jüdische Religion", 1:2. Frankfurt
a. M.: J. Kaufmann, 1912.
Levi, I. "Les sources talmudiques de l'histoire juive. I: Alexandre Jannée, et Simon Ben
Schetah", *Revue d'Études Juives* 35 (1897), 213-283.
Levine, I. L. "On the Political Involvement of the Pharisees under Herod and the Pro-
curators", *Cathedra* 8 (1978), 12-28 [Hebrew].

Lévy, I. *La Légende de Pythagore de Grèce en Palestine*. "Bibliotheque de l'École des Hautes Études", 250. Paris: Libraire Ancienne Honoré Champion, 1927.

Lieberich, H. *Studien zu den Proömien in der griechischen und byzantinischen Geschichtsschreibung*, I: *Die griechischen Geschichtschreiber*. Munich: J. G. Weiss (J. Olbrich), 1899.

Lieberman, S. *Greek in Jewish Palestine: Studies in the Life and Manners of Jewish Palestine in the II-IV Centuries C.E.* New York: Jewish Theological Seminary of America, 1942.

——. *Hellenism in Jewish Palestine: Studies in the Literary Transmission, Beliefs and Manners of Palestine in the I Century B.C.E.- IV Century C.E.* "Texts and Studies of the Jewish Theological Seminary of America", 18. New York: Jewish Theological Seminary of America, 1950.

Lightley, J. W. *Jewish Sects and Parties in the Time of Christ*. London: Sharp, 1925.

Lindars, B. "Jesus and the Pharisees", in *Donum Gentilicum: New Testament Studies in Honour of David Daube*, ed. E. Bammel, C. K. Barrett, W. D. Davies. Oxford: Clarendon, 1978, 51-63.

Lindner, H. *Die Geschichtsauffassung des Flavius Josephus im Bellum Judaicum*. "Arbeiten zur Geschichte des antiken Judentums und des Urchristentums", 12. Leiden: E. J. Brill, 1972.

Liver, J. "The Doctrine of Two Messiahs in Sectarian Literature in the Time of the Second Commonwealth", *HTR* 52 (1959), 149-185.

Loewe, H. "The Ideas of Pharisaism", in *Judaism and Christianity: Three Volumes in One*, edd. W. O. E. Oesterley, H. Loewe, and E. I. J. Rosenthal. New York: Ktav, 1969 [1937-38], II, 3-58.

Loftus, F. "The Anti-Roman Revolts of the Jews and the Galileans", *JQR* 68 (1977), 78-98.

——. "A Note on σύνταγμα τῶν Γαλιλαίων: B.J. iv 558", *JQR* 65 (1975), 182-183.

Lohse, E. *Umwelt des Neuen Testaments*. "Grundrisse zum Neuen Testament", 1. Göttingen: Vandenhoeck & Ruprecht, 1971.

Long, A. A. *Hellenistic Philosophy: Stoics, Epicureans, Sceptics*. London: Duckworth, 1974.

Long, H. S. "Plato's Doctrine of Metempsychosis and Its Source", *Classical Weekly* 41 (1948), 149-155.

Longenecker, R. N. "The Melchizedek Argument of Hebrews", in *Unity and Diversity in New Testament Theology: Essays in Honour of George E. Ladd*, ed. R. Guelich. Grand Rapids: Eerdmans 1978, 161-185.

Lüdemann, G. *Paul, Apostle to the Gentiles: Studies in Chronology*, trans. S. F. Jones. Philadelphia: Fortress Press, 1984.

Luther, H. *Josephus und Justus von Tiberias: ein Beitrag zur Geschichte des jüdischen Aufstandes*. Halle: Wischan & Burkhardt, 1910.

Luz, U. "Jesus und die Pharisäer", *Judaica* 38 (1982), 229-246.

Maier, G. *Mensch und freier Wille: nach den jüdischen Religionsparteien zwischen Ben Sira und Paulus*. "Wissenschaftliche Untersuchungen zum Neuen Testament", 12. Tübingen: J. C. B. Mohr-P. Siebeck, 1981.

Mansfeld, J. "Providence and the Destruction of the Universe in Early Stoic Thought: with some remarks on the 'Mysteries of Philosophy'", in *Studies in Hellenistic Religions*, ed. M. J. Vermaseren. "Études Préliminaires aux Religions Orientales dans l'Empire Romain", 78. Leiden: E. J. Brill, 1979, 129-188.

Manson, T. W. "Sadducee and Pharisee: the Origin and Significance of their Names", *BJRL* 22 (1938), 144-159.

Mansoor, M. *The Dead Sea Scrolls: A College Textbook and a Study Guide*. Leiden: E. J. Brill, 1964.

Mantel, H. D. "The Sadducees and the Pharisees", in *The World History of the Jewish People. First series: Ancient Times*. vol. 8: *Society and Religion in the Second Temple Period*, edd. M. Avi-Yonah and Z. Baros. Jerusalem: Massada, 1977, 99-123.

——. *Studies in the History of the Sanhedrin*. Cambridge, Mass: Harvard University Press, 1965.

Marcus, R. "Pharisaism in the Light of Modern Scholarship", *The Journal of Religion* 32 (1952), 154-164.

———. "Pharisees, Essenes, and Gnostics", *JBL* 73 (1954), 157-161.

Martin, Luther H. "Josephus' Use of *Heimarmene* in the Jewish Antiquities XIII, 171-3", *Numen* 28 (1981), 127-137.

Mandell, C. W. *Tacitus: the Man and his Work*. New Haven: Yale University Press, 1957.

Merkel, H. "Jesus und die Pharisäer", *NTS* 14 (1968), 194-208.

Meyer, B. F. *The Aims of Jesus*. London: S.C.M., 1979.

Meyer, E. *Ursprung und Anfange des Christentums*, 3 vols. Stuttgart-Berlin: J. G. Cotta, 1921-23.

———. "Zur Theorie und Methodik der Geschichte", in his *Kleine Schriften: zur Geschichtstheorie und zur wirtschaftlichen und politischen Geschichte des Altertums*. Halle: Max Niemeyer, 1910.

Meyer, R. "Die Bedeutung des Pharisäismus für die Geschichte und Theologie des Judentums", *TLZ* 77 (1952), 677-684.

———. "Geschichtserfahrung und Schriftauslegung, zur Hermeneutik des frühen Judentums", in *Die hermeneutische Frage in der Theologie*, edd. O. Loretz and W. Strolz. Freiburg: Herder, 1968.

———. "Σαδδουχαῖος", *TDNT*, VII, 35-54.

———. *Tradition und Neuschöpfung im antiken Judentum: dargestellt an der Geschichte des Pharisäismus: mit einem Beitrag von H.-Fr. Weiss: der Pharisäismus im Lichte der Überlieferung des Neuen Testaments*. "Sitzungsberichte der sächsischen Akademie der Wissenschaften zu Leipzig, philologisch-historische Klasse", Bd. 110, Heft 2. Berlin: Akademie, 1965.

Meyer, R. and H.-F. Weiss. "Φαρισαῖος", *TDNT*, IX, 11-48.

Michel, O. "Ich Komme [Jos. Bell. III. 400]", *TLZ* 24 (1968).

———. "Studien zu Josephus: Simon bar Giora", *NTS* 14 (1968), 402-408.

———. "Zur Arbeit an den Textzeugen des Josephus", *ZAW* 83 (1971), 101-102.

Milik, J. T. *Ten Years of Discovery in The Wilderness of Judaea*, trans J. Strugnell. "Studies in Biblical Theology", 26. London: S.C.M. 1959.

Misch, G. *A History of Autobiography in Antiquity*, 2 vols, trans. E. W. Dickes. "International Library of Sociology and Social Reconstruction". London: Routledge and Kegan Paul, 1950.

Moehring, H. R. "The *Acta pro Judaeis* in the Antiquities of Flavius Josephus", in *Christianity, Judaism, and other Greco-Roman Cults: Studies for Morton Smith at Sixty*, 4 vols., ed. J. Neusner. "Studies in Judaism in Late Antiquity", 12. Leiden: E. J. Brill, 1975, III, 124-158.

———. "Josephus on the Marriage Customs of the Essenes, Jewish War II: 119-166 and Antiquities XVIII: 11-25", in *Early Christian Origins: Studies in honor of H.R. Willoughby*, ed. A. Wikgren. Chicago: Quadrangle Books, 1961, 120-127.

———. "Novelistic Elements in the Writings of Flavius Josephus". Dissertation, University of Chicago, August, 1957.

———. "Rationalization of Miracles in the Writings of Flavius Josephus", *Studia Evangelica* 6 (1973), 376-383.

Momigliano, A. "Ancient History and the Antiquarian", *Journal of the Warburg and Courtauld Institutes* 13 (1950), 285-315.

———. *Essays in Ancient and Modern Historiography*. Oxford: Basil Blackwell, 1977.

———. "Josephus as a Source for the History of Judaea", *Cambridge Ancient History*, X: *The Augustan Empire 44 B.C.-A.D. 70*, edd. S. A. Cook, F. E. Adcock, and M. P. Charlesworth. Cambridge: Cambridge University Press, 1966.

———. "Problems of Ancient Biography", in his *Quarto Contributo alla Storia degli Studi Classici e del Mondo Antico*. "Storia e Letteratura", 115. Rome: Edizioni di Storia e Letteratura, 1969, 77-94.

Montet, E. "Le premier conflit entre Pharisiens et Sadducées d'après trois documents orientaux", *Journal Asiatique* 9 (1887), 415-423.

Montgomery, J. A. "The Religion of Flavius Josephus", *JQR* 11 (1920-21), 277-305.

Moore, C. H. *Ancient Beliefs in the Immortality of the Soul: with some account of their influence on later views*. "Our Debt to Greece and Rome". New York: Cooper Square, 1963.

——. *Pagan Ideas of Immortality During the Roman Empire.* "The Ingersoll Lecture, 1918", Cambridge: Harvard University Press, 1918.

Moore, G. F. "Fate and Free Will in the Jewish Philosophies According to Josephus", *HTR* 22 (1929), 371-389.

——. *Judaism in the First Centuries of the Christian Era, the Age of the Tannaim,* 3 vols. Cambridge, Mass: Harvard University Press, 1927-1930.

——. "The Rise of Normative Judaism, I", *HTR* 17 (1924), 307-373.

Morel, W. "Eine Rede bei Josephus (Bell. Jud. VII 341 sqq.)", *Rheinisches Museum for Philologie* 75 (1926), 106-115.

Mosley, A. W. "Historical Reporting in the Ancient World", *NTS* 12 (1965-66), 10-26.

Neusner, J. "Josephus's Pharisees", in *Ex Orbe Religionum: Studia Geo Widengren,* I. Leiden: E. J. Brill, 1972, 224-253.

——. *From Politics to Piety: The Emergence of Pharisaic Judaism.* Englewood Cliffs, NJ: Prentice-Hall, 1973.

——. *A Life of Rabban Yohanan ben Zakkai (ca. 1-80 C.E.).* "Studia Post-Biblica", 6. Leiden: E. J. Brill, 1962.

——. "Pharisaic Law in New Testament Times", *Union Seminary Quarterly Review* 26 (1971), 331-340.

——. "Pharisaic-Rabbinic Judaism: A Clarification", *History of Religions* 12 (1973), 250-270.

——. "Pre-70 C.E. Pharisaism: the Record of the Rabbis", *CCARJ* 19 (1972), 53-70.

——. *The Rabbinic Traditions About the Pharisees Before 70,* 3 vols. Leiden: E. J. Brill, 1971.

——. "The Rabbinic Traditions about the Pharisees in Modern Historiography", *CCARJ* 19 (1972), 78-108.

Nicklesburg, G. W. *Resurrection, Immortality, and Eternal Life in Intertestamental Judaism* (Cambridge, Mass: Harvard University Press, 1972.

Nicolaus, M. *Des Doctrines Religieuses des Juifs pendant les Deux Siècles antérieurs à l'Ere Chrétienne,* 2d. edn. Paris: Michel Levy, 1867.

Niese, B. "Josephus", *ERE,* VII, 569-579.

——. "Der jüdische Historiker Josephus", *HZ,* n.F. 40 (1896), 193-237.

Nikolainen, A. T. *Der Auferstehungsglauben in der Bibel und ihrer Umwelt.* I: *Religionsgeschichtlicher Teil.* "Annales Acadamiae Scientiarum Fennicae", 59. Helsinki: A. G. der Finnischen Literaturgesellschaft, 1944.

Norden, E. *Die antike Kunstprosa,* 5th edn. Darmstadt: Wissenschaftliche Buchgesellschaft, 1958 [1898].

Nötscher, F., ed. *Vom Alten zum Neuen Testament: Gesammelte Aufsätze.* "Bonner Biblische Beiträge", 17. Bonn: Peter Hanstein, 1962.

Oesterley, W. O. E. *The Jews and Judaism during the Greek Period: The Background of Christianity.* London: S. P. C. K., 1941.

—— and G. H. Box. *The Religion and Worship of the Synagogue: An Introduction to the Study of Judaism from the New Testament Period.* London: Pitman, 1907.

Olitzki, M. *Flavius Josephus und die Halacha.* Berlin: H. Iskowski, 1885.

Palm, J. *Über Sprache und Stil des Diodoros von Sizilien: ein Beitrag zur Beleuchtung der hellenistischen Prosa.* Lund: C. W. K. Gleerup, 1955.

Paret, H. "Über den Pharisäismus des Josephus", *TSK* 29 (1856), 809-844.

Parkes, J. F. *The Foundations of Judaism and Christianity.* London: Vallentine-Mitchell, 1960.

Patterson, R. L. *Plato on Immortality.* University Park PA: Pennsylvania State University Press, 1965.

Pelletier, A. *Flavius Josephe, adapteur de la lettre d'Aristée.* "Études et commentaires", 45. Paris: Klincksieck, 1962.

Peter, H. *Wahrheit und Kunst: Geschichtsschreibung und Plagiat im Klassischen Altertum.* Leipzig-Berlin: B. G. Teubner, 1911.

Petersen, H. "Real and Alleged Literary Projects of Josephus", *American Journal of Philology* 79 (1958), 259-274.

Pfeiffer, R. H. *History of New Testament Times: with an Introduction to the Apocrypha*. London: Adam and Charles Black, 1949.

Pick, B. "A Study on Josephus with Special Reference to the Old Testament", *Lutheran Quarterly* 91 (1889), 325-346; 599-616.

Pines, S. "A Platonistic Model for Two of Josephus's Accounts of the Doctrine of the Pharisees Concerning Providence and Man's Freedom of Action", *Immanuel* 7 (1977), 38-43.

Polish, D. "Pharisaism and Political Sovereignty", *Judaism* 19 (1970), 415-422.

Posnanski, A. *Über die religionsphilosophischen Anschauungen des Flavius Josephus*. Breslau: T. Schatzky, 1887.

Preisker, H. *Neutestamentliche Theologie*. "Hilfsbücher zum theologischen Studium", 2d. series, 2 Bde. Berlin: A. Töpelmann, 1937.

Przybylski, B. *Righteousness in Matthew*. "SNTS Monograph Series", 41. Cambridge: University Press, 1980.

Rabin, C. "Alexander Jannaeus and the Pharisees", *JJS* 7 (1956), 3-11.

Rajak, T. *Josephus: the Historian and his Society*. "Classical Life and Letters", London: Duckworth, 1983.

———. "Justus of Tiberias", *CQ* 23 ë(1973), 345-368.

Rappaport, S. *Agada und Exegese bei Flavius Josephus*. "Veröffentlichungen der Oberrabbiner Dr. H.P. Chajes: Preisstiftung an der israelitisch-theologischen Lehranstalt in Wien", 3. Vienna: A. Kohut Memorial Foundation, 1930.

Rasp, H. "Flavius Josephus und die judischen Religionsparteien", *ZNW* 23 (1924), 27-47.

Reinach T. *Textes d'Autres Grecs et Romains relatifs au Judaisme*. Hildesheim: G. Olms, 1963 [1895].

Reesor, M. E. "Fate and Possibility in Early Stoic Philosophy", *Phoenix* 19 (1965), 285-297.

Reicke, B. *Neutestamentliche Zeitgeschichte: die biblische Welt 500 v. - 100 n. Chr.* Berlin: A. Töpelmann, 1965.

Reiling, J. "The Use of ψευδοπροφήτης in the Septuagint, Philo and Josephus", *NovT* 13 (1971), 147-156.

Revel, B. "Some Anti-Traditional Laws of Josephus", *JQR* n.s. 14 (1923-24), 293-301.

Richards, G. C. "The Composition of Josephus' *Antiquities*", *CQ* 33 (1939), 36-40.

—— and R. J. H. Shutt. "Critical Notes on Josephus's *Antiquities*", *CQ* 31 (1937), 170-177, and 33 (1939), 180-183.

Ringgren, H. "The Problem of Fatalism", in *Fatalistic Beliefs in Religion, Folklore, and Literature*, ed. H. Ringgren. Stockholm: Almqvist & Wiksell, 1967, 7-18.

Rist, J. M. *Stoic Philosophy*. Cambridge: University Press 1969.

Rist, M. "Apocalypticism", *IDB* I (1962), 157-161.

Rivkin, E. "Defining the Pharisees: the Tannaitic sources", *HUCA* 40 (1969) 205-249.

———. *A Hidden Revolution*: Nashville: Abingdon, 1978.

———. "Pharisaism and the Crisis of the Individual in the Greco-Roman World", *JQR* 61 (1970), 27-53.

———. "Pharisees", *IDBS*, 657-663.

———. "Prolegomenon", in *Judaism and Christianity: Three Volumes in One*, edd. W. O. E. Oesterley, H. Loewe, and E. I. J. Rosenthal. New York: Ktav, 1969 [1937-38], I, vii-lxx.

———. "Scribes, Pharisees, Lawyers, Hypocrites: A Study in Synonymity", *HUCA* 49 (1978), 135-142.

———. *The Shaping of Jewish History: A Radical New Interpretation*. New York: Charles Scribner's Sons, 1971.

———, H. Fischel *et al.* "A Symposium on the Pharisees", *CCARJ* 14 (1967), 32-47.

Ross, J. *The Jewish Conception of Immortality and the Life Hereafter: An Anthology*. Belfast: Belfast News-Letter, Ltd. 1948.

Roth, C. "The Constitution of the Jewish Republic of 66-70", *JJS* 9 (1964), 295-319.

———. "The Pharisees in the Jewish Revolution of 66-73", *Journal of Semitic Studies* 7 (1962), 63-80.

Rubenstein, R. L. "Scribes, Pharisees and Hypocrites: A Study in Rabbinic Psychology", *Judaism* 12 (1963), 456-468.

Russell, D. S. *The Jews from Alexander to Herod*. "New Clarendon Bible". Oxford: Oxford University Press, 1967.

———. *The Method and Message of Jewish Apocalyptic: 200 BC-AD 100*. Philadelphia: Westminister, 1964.

Safrai, S., M. Stern et al., edd. *The Jewish People in the First Century*, I. "Compendia Rerum Iudaicarum ad Novum Testamentum". Assen: van Gorcum & Co., 1974.

Salomon, M. *Der Begriff der Gerechtigkeit bei Aristotles: nebst einem Anhang über den Begriff des Tauschgeschäftes*. Leiden: A. W. Sijthoff, 1937.

Sandbach, F. H. *The Stoics*. "Ancient Culture and Society". London: Chatto & Windus, 1975.

Sanders, E. P. *Paul and Palestinian Judaism*. Philadelphia: Fortress, 1977.

Schalit, A. "Josephus und Justus", *Klio* 26 (1933), 67-95.

———, ed. *Zur Josephus-Forschung*. "Wege der Forschung", 84. Darmstadt: Wissenschaftliche Buchgesellschaft, 1973.

Schiffman, L. H. *The Halakhah at Qumran*. "Studies in Judaism in Late Antiquity", 16. Leiden: E. J. Brill, 1975.

Schlatter, A. *Der Bericht über das Ende Jerusalems: ein Dialog mit Wilhelm Weber*. "Beiträge zur Förderung christlicher Theologie", 28. Gütersloh: C. Bertelsmann 1923.

———. *Kleinere Schriften zu Flavius Josephus*, ed. K. H. Rengstorf. Darmstadt: Wissenschaftliche Buchgesellschaft, 1970.

———. *Die Theologie des Judentums nach dem Bericht des Josefus*. "Beiträge zur Förderung schriftlicher Theologie", 2:26. Gütersloh: C. Bertelsmann, 1932.

———. *Wie sprach Josephus von Gott?* Gütersloh: L. Bertelsmann, 1910.

Schmid, W. *Der Atticismus in seinen Hauptvertretern von Dionysius von Halicarnassus bis auf den zweiten Philostratus*, 5 vols. Stuttgart: W. Kohlhammer, 1887-1897.

Schreckenberg, H. *Rezeptionsgeschichtliche und Textkritische Untersuchungen zu Flavius Josephus*. "Arbeiten zur Literatur und Geschichte des hellenistischen Judentums", 10. Leiden: E. J. Brill, 1977.

Schubert, K. "Jewish Religious Parties and Sects", in *The Crucible of Christianity: Judaism, Hellenism and the Historical Background to The Christian Faith*, ed. A. Toynbee. London: Thames and Hudson, 1969.

———. *Die Religion des nachbiblischen Judentums*. Vienna-Freiburg: Herder, 1955.

Schuhl, P. M. *Le Dominateur et les Possibles*. "Bibliothèque de Philosophie Contemporaine, Histoire de la Philosophie et Philosophie Générale". Paris: Presses Universitaires de France, 1960.

Schürer, E. *Geschichte des jüdischen Volkes im Zeitalter Jesu Christi*, 3./4. Aufl., 3 vols, Leipzig: J. C. Hinrichs, 1801ff; ET, *The Jewish People in the Time of Jesus Christ*, 3 vols. Edinburgh: T. & T. Clark, 1890 (cf. also G. Vermes).

Schwark, J. "Matthäus der Schriftgelehrte und Josephus der Priester: ein Vergleich", *Theokratia* 2 (1970-72), 137-154.

Schwartz, D. R. "Josephus and Nicolaus on the Pharisees", *JSJ* 14 (1983), 157-171.

———. "KATA TOYTON TON KAIPON: Josephus' Source on Agrippa II", *JQR* 72 (1982), 241-268.

Segal, M. H. "Pharisees and Sadducees", *The Expositor* 8 (1917), 81-108.

Sherwin-White, A. N. *Roman Society and Roman Law in the New Testament*. Grand Rapids: Baker, 1963.

Seyrig, H. "Monnaies Hellénistiques", *Revue Numismatique*, 6th series, 6 (1964), 55-65.

Shutt, R. J. H. "The Concept of God in the Works of Flavius Josephus", *JJS* 31 (1980), 171-189.

———. *Studies in Josephus*. London: S.P.C.K., 1961.

Sieffert, F. "Pharisäer und Sadduzäer, in *Realenzyklopädie für protestantische Theologie and*

Kirche, 3. Auflage, ed. J. J. Herzog, rev. A. Hauck. Leipzig: J. C. Hinrichs, 1896-1913, XV, 264-292.

Siegfried, W. *Der Rechtsgedanke bei Aristoteles.* Zurich: Schulthess & Co., 1947.

——. *Studien zur geschichtlichen Anschauung des Polybios.* Leipzig: B. G. Teubner, 1928.

Simon, M. and A. Benoit. *Le Judaisme et le Christianisme antique d'Antiochus Epiphane à Constantin.* Paris: Presses universitaires de France, 1968.

Smallwood, E. M. "Domitian's Attitude toward the Jews and Judaism", *Classical Philology* 51 (1956), 1-13.

——. "High Priests and Politics in Roman Palestine", *JTS* 13 (1962), 14-34.

——. *The Jews under Roman Rule: From Pompey to Diocletian.* "Studies in Judaism in Late Antiquity", 20. Leiden: E.J. Brill, 1976.

Smith, M. "The Description of the Essenes in Josephus and the Philosophumena", *HUCA* 29 (1958), 273-313.

——. *Jesus the Magician.* London: Victor Gollancz, 1978.

——. "Palestinian Judaism in the First Century", in *Israel: Its Role in Civilization*, ed. M. Davis. New York: Jewish Theological Seminary of America/Harper & Brothers, 1956.

——. "What is Implied by the Variety of Messianic Figures?" *JBL* 88 (1959), 66-72.

Stern, M. *Greek and Latin Authors on Jews and Judaism*, 3 vols. Jerusalem: Israel Academy of Sciences and Humanities, 1980.

Stettner, W. *Die Seelenwanderung bei Griechen und Römern.* Stuttgart: W. Kohlhammer, 1933.

Steuernagel, C. "Pharisäer", *PWRE* 38 (1938), 1825-1935.

Stock, St. G. "Fate (Greek and Roman)", *ERE*, V, 786-790.

Suffrin, A. E. "Fate (Jewish)", *ERE*, V, 793-794.

Tcherikover, V. *Hellenistic Civilization and the Jews*, trans. S. Appelbaum. Philadelphia: Jewish Publication Society of America; Jerusalem: Magnes Press, 1959.

Thackeray, H. St. J. *Josephus: the Man and the Historian.* New York: Jewish Institute of Religion Press, 1929.

——. "On Josephus's Statement of the Pharisees' Doctrine of Fate (Antiq. xviii, 1, 3)", *HTR* 25 (1932), 93.

Theiler, W. "Tacitus und die antike Schlicksalslehre", in *Phyllobolia: für Peter von der Mühll*, edd. O. Grigon et al. Basel: Benno Schwabe & Co., 1946, 35-90.

Thoma, C. "Die Frömmigkeit im pharisäisch-rabbinischen Judentum", *Emuna* 7 (1972), 324-330.

——. "Der Pharisäismus", in *Literatur und Religion des Frühjüdentums: Eine Einführung*, edd. J. Maier and J. Schreiner. Würzburg: Echter Verlag; Gütersloh: Gerd Mohn, 1973.

——. "Die Weltanschauung des Josephus Flavius: dargestellt anhand seiner Schilderung des jüdischen Aufstandes gegen Rom (66-73 n. Chr.)", *Kairos* 11 (1969), 39-52.

Thompson, W. G. Review of J. Rohde, *Die redaktionsgeschichtliche Methode*, in *Biblica* 50 (1969), 136-139.

Toynbee, A. J. *Greek Historical Thought: from Homer to the Age of Heraclitus.* "A Mentor Book". New York: New American Library, 1952.

Torrey, C. C. "Apocalypse", in *The Jewish Encyclopedia.* New York: Ktav, 1901, I, 669-675.

Trude, P. *Der Begriff der Gerechtigkeit in der aristotelischen Rechts- und Staatsphilosophie.* "Neue Kölner Rechtswissenschaftliche Abhandlungen", 3. Berlin: W. de Gruyter, 1955.

Turner, C. H. "Note on 'Succession' Language in non-Christian Sources", in H. B. Swete (ed.), *Essays on the Early History of the Church and the Ministry.* London: Macmillan & Co., 1918, 197-199.

Tyson, J. B. "The Opposition to Jesus in the Gospel of Luke", *Perspectives in Religious Studies* 5 (1978), 144-150.

Urbach, E. E. *The Sages: Their Concepts and Beliefs*, trans. I. Abrahams, 2 vols., 2d. edn. Jerusalem: Magnes, 1975.

Usher, S. *The Historians of Greece and Rome.* New York: Toplinger, 1970.

van Tilborg, S. *The Jewish Leaders in Matthew.* Leiden: E. J. Brill, 1972.

van Unnik, W. C. *Flavius Josephus als historischer Schriftsteller.* Heidelberg: Lambert Schneider, 1978.

———. "Flavius Josephus and the Mysteries", in *Studies in Hellenistic Religions*, ed. M. J. Vermaseren. "Études Préliminaries aux Religions Orientales dans l'Empire Romain", 78. Leiden: E. J. Brill, 1979, 244-279.

Vermes, G. *The Dead Sea Scrolls: Qumran in Perspective.* London: Collins, 1977.

———, F. Millar, and M. Black, edd. *The History of the Jewish People in the Age of Jesus Christ*, by E. Schürer, 3 vols. Edinburgh: T. & T. Clark, 1979ff.

Wacholder, B. Z. *The Dawn of Qumran: the Sectarian Torah and the Teacher of Righteousness.* Cincinatti: Hebrew Union College Press, 1983.

———. *Nicolaus of Damascus.* "University of California Publications in History", 75. Berkeley-Los Angeles: University of California Press, 1962.

Wächter, L. "Die unterschiedliche Haltung der Pharisäer, Sadduzäer und Essener zur Heimarmene nach dem Bericht des Josephus", *ZRGG* 21 (1969), 97-114.

Weber, F. *Jüdische Theologie auf Grund des Talmud und verwandter Schriften*, 2. Auflage. Leipzig: Dorffling & Franke, 1897 [1880].

Weber, M. "Die Pharisäer", in *Gesammelte Aufsätze zur Religionssoziologie*, III: *Das antike Judentum*, 2. Auflage. Tübingen: J. C. B. Mohr-P. Siebeck, 1923, 401-442.

Weber, W. *Josephus und Vespasian: Untersuchungen zu dem jüdischen Krieg des Flavius Josephus.* Berlin-Stuttgart-Leipzig: W. Kohlhammer, 1921.

Weiss, H.-F. "Pharisäismus und Hellenismus: zur Darstellung des Judentums im Geschichtswerk des jüdischen Historikers Flavius Josephus", *Orientalistische Literarzeitung* 74 (1979), 421-433.

Wellhausen, J. *Die Pharisäer und die Sadducäer: eine Untersuchung zur inneren jüdischen Geschichte.* Greifswald: L. Bamberg, 1874.

Wells, G. L. and E. F. Loftus, ed. *Eyewitness Testimony: Psychological Perspectives.* Cambridge: University Press, 1984.

Wendland, P. *Die hellenistisch-römische Kultur.* Tübingen: J. C. B. Mohr, 1912.

Wenley, R. M. *Stoicism and its Influence.* "Our Debt to Greece and Rome", 7. Boston: Marshall Jones Co., 1924.

Westerholm, S. "Jesus, the Pharisees, and the Application of Divine Law", *Église et Théologie* 13 (1982), 191-210.

Whittaker, M. *Jews and Christians: Graeco-Roman Views.* "Cambridge Commentaries on Writings of the Jewish and Christian World, 200 BC to AD 200", 6. Cambridge: University Press, 1984.

Wild, R. A. "The Encounter Between Pharisaic and Christian Judaism: Some Early Gospel Evidence", *NovT* 27 (1985), 105-124.

Windelband, W. *A History of Philosophy: with especial reference to the formation and development of its problems and conceptions*, 2d. edn., trans. J. H. Tufts. New York: MacMillan, 1910.

Wittmann, M. "Aristoteles und die Willensfreiheit", *Philologische Wochenschrift* 34 (1921), 5-30.

Yavetz, Z. "Reflections on Titus and Josephus", *Greek, Roman, and Byzantine Studies* 16 (1975), 411-432.

Zeitlin, S. "The Origin of the Pharisees Reaffirmed", *JQR* 59 (1969), 255-267.

———. *The Rise and Fall of the Judaean State: A Political, Social and Religious History of the Second Commonwealth*, 3 vols. Philadelphia: Jewish Publication Society of America, 1962-1978.

———. "The Sicarii and Masada", *JQR* 57 (1967), 251-270.

———. "Spurious Interpretations of Rabbinic Sources in the Studies of the Pharisees and Pharisaism", *JQR* 65 (1974), 122-135.

———. "A Survey of Jewish Historiography; from the biblical books to the Sefer Ha-Kabbalah with special emphasis on Josephus", *JQR* 59 (1969), 37-68, 171-214.

——. "Who Were the Galileans? New light on Josephus' activities in Galilee", *JQR* 64 (1974), 189-203.

Ziesler, J. A. "Luke and the Pharisees", *NTS* 25 (1979), 146-157.

——. *The Meaning of Righteousness in Paul.* "SNTS Monograph Series", 20. Cambridge: University Press, 1972.

INDEX OF MODERN AUTHORS

INDEX OF GREEK WORDS

INDEX OF ANCIENT GROUPS AND PERSONALITIES

DATE DUE

HIGHSMITH   # 45220